MEMOIRS OF SIR JOHN RERESBY

The *Memoirs* of Sir John Reresby are a standard source for the social and political history of England in the later seventeenth century. As Justice of the Peace, Governor of York, and Member of Parliament for that city and the borough of Aldborough, he was a crucial point of contact between central and local government at a time of strain between the two. He tried to serve both the Crown and the established Church, but like others found this difficult enough in Charles II's reign, and impossible in James II's, when he became caught up in the Glorious Revolution in the north of England.

Professor Andrew Browning's edition of the *Memoirs*, published in 1936, is an established classic. It has been long out of print and hard to obtain, and this new edition will be welcomed by specialists in the period, particularly for the fresh material it contains. This comes largely from the substantial Mexborough archives in Leeds, which contain Reresby's own correspondence (over 2,500 letters). The editors have also used an earlier draft of the *Memoirs* covering the years of the Exclusion crisis.

The editors have supplied a new preface, and additional notes.

MARY GEITER obtained the degree of M.Phil. at Leeds University in 1989 with a dissertation on the political career of Sir John Reresby.

W. A. SPECK is Professor of Modern History at Leeds University.

MEMOIRS

OF

SIR JOHN RERESBY

THE COMPLETE TEXT AND A SELECTION
FROM HIS LETTERS

EDITED WITH AN INTRODUCTION
AND NOTES
BY

ANDREW BROWNING

SECOND EDITION
WITH A NEW PREFACE AND NOTES
BY

MARY K. GEITER AND W. A. SPECK

LONDON
OFFICES OF THE ROYAL HISTORICAL SOCIETY
UNIVERSITY COLLEGE LONDON, GOWER STREET
LONDON WCIE 6BT
1991

First published 1936
Second edition published 1991

Distributed for the Royal Historical Society
by Boydell & Brewer Ltd
PO Box 9   Woodbridge   Suffolk IP12 3DF
and Boydell & Brewer Inc.
PO Box 41026   Rochester   NY 14604   USA

ISBN 0 86193 128 9

British Library Cataloguing-in-Publication Data
Memoirs of Sir John Reresby: The complete text
and a selection from his letters. – 2nd ed.
I. Browning, Andrew   II. Geiter, Mary K.
942.06
ISBN 0–86193–128–9

The paper used in this publication meets the minimum requirements
of American National Standard for Information Sciences –
Permanence of Paper for Printed Library Materials, ANSI Z39.48–1984

Printed in Great Britain by
St Edmundsbury Press Ltd, Bury St Edmunds, Suffolk

CONTENTS

PREFACE TO THE SECOND EDITION

The late Professor Browning's edition of the *Memoirs of Sir John Reresby*, which ran to only a limited number of copies and has long been out of print, is now a rare item. It is fitting that the Royal Historical Society should seek to supply the deficiency with this reprint, since he was its benefactor, leaving it a generous legacy in his will. His edition superseded all previous versions and established a definitive text, which appears unaltered here. The opportunity has however been taken to add to his scholarly apparatus.

An examination of the manuscript version in the British Library established that Browning had closely observed the editorial conventions which he spelled out on page xvi. We discovered no discrepancy to match that of the missing ampersand on page 214 which we pointed out in our article 'The reliability of Sir John Reresby's 'Memoirs' and his account of the Oxford parliament of 1681', *Historical Research, 62* (1989), 105. Other than that, apart from some inconsistencies, e.g. in the retention or removal of brackets in the manuscript, which could well have been deliberate editorial decisions, the discrepancies were trivial.

Reresby deleted some passages of his manuscript. Some he had inked over so completely that they were indecipherable. Hence, presumably, their silent omission from the Browning edition. Those that can still be read, however, reveal an interesting pattern. Sir John had, apparently, systematically, removed references to his family, for example the births and deaths of his children. It is perhaps significant that he also eliminated details concerning his family when he came to write up this fair copy from the only surviving earlier version of the *Memoirs*, the 'French draft' preserved as Mexborough MS MX/242, which we also discuss in our article. Thus in the final version he mentions that on 11 July 1681 he and his wife 'had a falling out at our parting, which gave me some trouble'. The draft records, in Reresby's imperfect French, that 'quelque petite froideur fust arrive entre moy et la femme causé de ne l'avoir laissé aller avec moy a la campagne et augmenté par quelques lettres d'un style degoustant que j'eu receu de sa part pendant mon absence'. The letters from Frances to which Sir John refers do not appear to have been preserved.

This process of emendation suggests a sequence which Reresby followed in writing up his *Memoirs*. Initially, as Browning surmised, Sir John intended them for his descendants, as is shown by his 'French draft' and his *Family History*. As he commenced the final draft he edited out some details pertaining to his family, but retained others which could only interest his own posterity. Finally he decided systematically to delete all intimate references concerning his family, thus making his *Memoirs* more a commentary on his role in local and national politics. The fair copy was therefore almost certainly the final version, which Reresby completed shortly before he died. In its final form it was apparently intended for publication. Had he lived longer it might well have been published soon after the Revolution. Instead it was not until the general election of 1734 that the first edition appeared.

Professor Browning's footnotes exploited all the extant correspondence of Sir John known to scholars in 1936. Since then, Reresby's 'in' letters, numbering some 2,500, along with other personal papers, have been deposited by the Earl of Mexborough in the Record Office of the Leeds Archive Service at Sheepscar Central Library. We wish to thank him for his permission to cite, and to quote these papers. In the margins of the text we have added symbols which refer to documents in the Mexborough manuscripts, and to other papers, cited in the corresponding footnotes. The selection has been restricted to sources which amplify or document the information supplied in the text. Thus any letters mentioned by Reresby are documented wherever possible. Most of those written before 1688 have survived. Why none are extant after March that year can only be surmised. Reresby himself does not appear to have destroyed them, for he refers to correspondence received by him as late as 5 April 1689. The first 'in' letter he notes was one he received early in 1663, which has apparently not survived. He also notes the receipt of two from the Duke of Buckingham and Sir Henry Belasis in June 1666, which again do not appear to have survived. There is, however, a letter from John Beaumont of 1 July 1666 which refers to the raising of troops by Buckingham, the incident mentioned in the *Memoirs*. This is therefore used for the first cross reference from the text to the correspondence. Other letters are also cited which indirectly shed light on events chronicled by Reresby. The first direct reference to a letter in the text which is preserved among the Mexborough manuscripts is one from Lord Arlington dated 7 March 1666/7.

Besides Sir John's 'in' correspondence the Mexborough papers contain some materials in his own hand: e.g. a few copies of replies to letters; the diary of the Oxford Parliament of 1681; and the 'French draft' of the *Memoirs*. This draft covers the period 24 July 1680 to 12 December 1681, and is an earlier version of the passages in the *Memoirs* which occupy pages 197 to 240 of this edition. We have drawn attention in the footnotes to passages which differ significantly from the final version. The idiosyncratic French is Reresby's own rendition.

In addition to the Mexborough papers other sources have been used to illuminate passages in the *Memoirs*, among them the Copley MSS in the library of the Yorkshire Archaeological Society in Leeds, the Dartmouth MSS in Stafford Record Office, and the Hastings MSS in the Huntington Library, San Marino, California. We also consulted manuscript collections used by Browning which have migrated since his day: e.g. the Spencer Papers formerly at Althorp, and the Preston Papers previously available only in a report of the Historical Manuscripts Commission. Both collections are now in the British Library. A grant from the British Academy facilitated access to these repositories.

It becomes clear from this additional documentation that the *Memoirs* were far more than a compilation from original letters. Sir John Reresby obviously based his account on a carefully preserved collection of correspondence, as our citations indicate. But he integrated them much more meticulously into a narrative than has been previously assumed. Only now that his own papers are available to scholars can Sir John's achievement be fully appreciated. Certainly we came to value his accomplishment more by placing it in this documentary context, which we completed in two stages. The introduction was written by Speck and the notes were added by Geiter, who had completed a Master's thesis on Sir John and was therefore more fully acquainted with his papers. This division of labour broke down as each contributed something to both sections, so that the outcome is one for which they are jointly responsible.

Mary K. Geiter
W. A. Speck

Note on Additional Footnotes
Unless another location is given, all references are to the Mexborough MSS deposited in the West Yorkshire Archives Service, Sheepscar Library, Leeds. Correspondence is cited by the call number, minus the prefix MX/R, and the name of the correspondent. Unless otherwise indicated all letters were addressed to Sir John Reresby.

PREFACE TO THE FIRST EDITION

Of the many memoirs and diaries which constitute one of the distinctive features of English history in the later seventeenth century, the *Memoirs* of Sir John Reresby, the *Diary* of John Evelyn, and the *Diary* of Samuel Pepys have suffered a curiously similar fate. Published originally in abbreviated and inaccurate form, they have undergone much amplification and correction, and passed through many editions, without ever appearing in a shape sufficiently complete and exact to satisfy historians. For some time all three have been undergoing a further, and one may hope final, revision. As the *Memoirs* of Sir John Reresby anticipated by nearly a century the publication of both its rivals it may seem not unfitting that it should now be the first to be presented in a genuinely complete form. Sixty years ago the claim was made for one edition that the corrections and amplification it embodied were such as to make it 'a substantially new work.' That claim is made again, with equal if not greater justification.

In the preparation of this edition most generous assistance has been derived from many quarters. The late Duke of Leeds and the present Duke permitted the editor to make a thorough examination of the large collection of Leeds manuscripts fomerly preserved at Hornby Castle. The Earl of Lindsey similarly permitted an inspection of the Danby papers in his possession. Earl Spencer most courteously allowed full use to be made of the very valuable and interesting collection of letters and documents in Reresby's handwriting preserved at Althorp. Sir George Reresby Sitwell communicated some very useful information and suggestions. Mr David Ogg of New College and Mr E. S. de Beer read the entire proofs, and placed their intimate knowledge of the later Stuart period unreservedly at the editor's disposal. Mr J. E. Tyler of Sheffield University supplied an immense amount of information about local Yorkshire affairs. To the kindness of these and other helpers such merits as this book may possess are largely due, and to them all the editor offers his most sincere thanks.

UNIVERSITY OF GLASGOW
January 1936.

INTRODUCTION

I. THE MEMOIRS

THE original introduction of Sir John Reresby to the reading public was apparently due, at least in part, to political circumstances.[1] In the spring of 1733 Walpole's excise proposals had aroused intense excitement, and by providing all the discontented with a popular weapon of attack against the ministry had raised the hopes both of the opposition as a whole and of the Tories in particular. At York as elsewhere party passion ran high; and with a general election imminent, and the long-anticipated second volume of Burnet's *History of My Own Time* holding out an immediate promise of historical ammunition for the Whigs, it was presumably felt that the moment had come for the Tories also to furbish up any historical weapons they might possess. What was wanted was not a violent Tory pamphlet, calculated to alienate any Whig support available, but a moderate account of the part played by the Tories in previous reigns, which should commend their attitude to as large a circle as possible. This seems to have been found in the narrative left behind by Sir John Reresby for the instruction and edification of his own descendants,[2] and the result was the appearance in the following year of a Yorkshire royalist account of later Stuart history in a thin octavo volume entitled *The*

[1] The obvious suggestion, that the first edition of the *Memoirs* was intended to mark the hundredth anniversary of Reresby's birth, must be abandoned in view of the fact that in that edition the portion giving the date of his birth and dealing with his early life is deliberately omitted.

[2] That Sir John wrote with his descendants in mind is clear both from his own express statements (e.g. *infra*, p. 286) and from the general tenor of what he has to say.

ix

Memoirs of the Honourable Sir John Reresby, Bart., and last Governor of York, containing several Private and Remarkable Transactions from the Restoration to the Revolution Inclusively. Published from his Original Manuscript.[1]

So successful was the venture that a quarto edition of the *Memoirs* followed almost immediately, differing little from the octavo edition apart from the correction of a few errors and the introduction of some others;[2] while a year later the original edition was reissued with the addition of a short list of errata and a sixteen-page index.[3] Thereafter the political importance of the *Memoirs* presumably declined;

---

[1] London. Printed for Samuel Harding, Bookseller, on the pavement in St. Martin's Lane, 1734. Price 4s. 6d. bound. In the British Museum is a copy of this edition with some interesting notes scribbled on the fly-leaf and margins. These are not, as the British Museum catalogue conjectures, the work of Francis Wrangham, although the volume in which they appear bears the book-plate of his son, Digby Cayley Wrangham. They were written not long after the publication of the volume, possibly by an earlier member of the Wrangham family, certainly by a well-informed individual of moderate Whig views, who could remember his father's grief at the death of Charles II, and whose wife's uncle was actually in York at the time of the Revolution. Their evidence regarding the reasons for the publication of the *Memoirs* is suggestive. On the fly-leaf is written, " This was printed, I guess, on the occasion of the criticall county election this May at York, 1744." On page 147 is a further note, " the city [i.e. York] was very Toryish at the election 1734, when Sir John Kay was invited to their election against Sir William Milner, and Sir Miles Stapleton, of a small estate compared with Sir Rowland Wynn, was chosen against him by the high sheriff's return." The date " 1744 " in the first note is of course a slip for " 1734." There was no election for York County or York City in 1744. A fairly complete picture of the election of 1734 at York can be drawn from *The Wentworth Papers*, edited by J. J. Cartwright.

[2] *The Memoirs of the Honourable Sir John Reresby, Baronet, and last Governor of York, containing several Private and Remarkable Transactions from the Restoration to the Revolution Inclusively.* London. Printed in the Year 1734.

[3] *The Memoirs of the Honourable Sir John Reresby, Bart., and last Governor of York, containing several Private and Remarkable Transactions from the Restoration to the Revolution Inclusively. To which is added a Copious Index.* London. Printed for Samuel Harding, Bookseller, on the pavement in St. Martin's Lane, 1735.

but its historical value became more apparent, and for nearly a century it was accepted as giving the best picture available of English life during the reigns of Charles II and James II.

Towards the close of that period, however, dangerous rivals appeared in the diaries of John Evelyn [1] and Samuel Pepys,[2] and it is possibly in anticipation of the publication of one or other of these that a fresh edition of Reresby's *Memoirs* was prepared. During the interval a manuscript had come to light giving an account of Reresby's experiences on the Continent between 1654 and 1658. Of this a version was now prepared,[3] prefixed to the already published *Memoirs*, and the whole issued in 1813 as *The Travels and Memoirs of Sir John Reresby, Bart., the former (now first published) exhibiting a View of the Governments and Society in the Principal States and Courts of Europe during the Time of Cromwell's Usurpation; the latter containing Anecdotes and Secret History of the Courts of Charles II and James II. Illustrated with Forty Portraits and Views of the most remarkable Persons and Places mentioned.*[4] A companion edition, without illustrations, appeared at the same time,[5] and this was reissued, with some changes

---

[1] First published as part of *Memoirs illustrative of the life and writings of John Evelyn* in 18:8.

[2] First published as part of *Memoirs of Samuel Pepys* in 1825.

[3] That Reresby actually wrote an account of his travels on the Continent is conclusively shown in his *Memoirs* (*infra*, p. 7). That the published *Travels* is not an exact transcript of any such account is obvious to any one acquainted with Reresby's literary style.

[4] London. Printed for Edward Jeffery, Pall-Mall; Sherwood, Neely and Jones, Paternoster-Row; and J. Rodwell, New Bond-Street. By B. McMillan, Bow-Street, Covent-Garden. 1813. Price Four Guineas unbound. The illustrations are not of great value, having been prepared for and used in other publications.

[5] *The Memoirs and Travels of Sir John Reresby, Bart., the former containing Anecdotes and Secret History of the Courts of Charles II and James II ; the latter (now first published) exhibiting a View of the Governments and Society in the Principal States and Courts of Europe during the Time of*

in the title-page and index, in 1821 and 1831. Finally in 1904 the volume of 1813 was reprinted as *The Memoirs and Travels of Sir John Reresby, Bart.*, edited by Albert Ivatt with a few notes, and including for the *Memoirs* the index of the 1735 edition.

Meanwhile a version of the *Memoirs* in Sir John Reresby's own handwriting had come into the possession of the British Museum.[1] On this was based *The Memoirs of Sir John Reresby of Thrybergh, Bart., M.P. for York, &c., 1634-1689, written by himself*, edited by James J. Cartwright and published in 1875,[2] which claims, by implication at least, to be a complete and exact reproduction of the original, and has been accepted by historians as the standard text.

For more than half a century there have thus been available substantially two versions of the *Memoirs*, which may for purposes of convenience be termed the 1734 version and the 1875 version. So glaring are the discrepancies between these versions as to have given rise to the conjecture that they may be derived from different sources, the latter from the manuscript in the British Museum, the former from some earlier and slighter sketch, or possibly series of notes, drawn up by Reresby and now lost. For the truth of this conjecture, however, there is not a particle of genuine evidence. Both versions of the *Memoirs* are almost certainly based on the manuscript now in the British Museum, and the differences between them are in reality nothing more than a monument to the perverse ingenuity of their editors.

Of the 1734 version little need be said. In no genuine sense is it an edition of the *Memoirs* at all. It is rather a paraphrase or fairly elaborate summary, written, not in the language of Sir John Reresby, or even in that of the

Cromwell's Usurpation. London. Printed for Edward Jeffery, Pall Mall, and J. Rodwell, New Bond-Street. 1813. Although the title-page is thus altered the index to the omitted illustrations is retained.

[1] Purchased in June 1873 and catalogued as Add. MSS. 29440-1.

[2] London. Longmans, Green and Co.

seventeenth century, but in that of the time of Walpole. In broad outline its matter and arrangement are derived from the *Memoirs*; but in the process of rewriting the length of the narrative has been reduced, by condensation and omission, to about one-third of the original, while all exact correspondence has been destroyed. It cannot be too strongly emphasised that no reliance whatever can be placed on the 1734 version as regards details either of fact or of phraseology.

By comparison the 1875 version may claim to bear some real resemblance to what Reresby actually wrote. It is obviously based upon a genuine transcript of the manuscript in the British Museum, but a transcript in connection with which the transcriber or the editor has been guilty of practically every fault that could conceivably be committed.

Most serious are the faults of omission. Well over one hundred lengthy passages of the manuscript, as well as thousands of paragraphs, sentences, phrases and single words, have been, apparently deliberately, left out. In all, material amounting to about 40,000 words, or roughly one-fifth of the total, has been excised. The main reason appears to have been a desire for brevity, becoming more pressing as the work proceeded. It is significant that the great bulk of the omissions belong to the last seven years covered by the *Memoirs*, although towards the very end again, when enough space had presumably been saved, the omissions become comparatively slight.[1] But another powerful reason appears to have been the desire to maintain a standard of decorum quite out of keeping with the ideas of the seventeenth century. Hence the excision of one or two somewhat unsavoury stories at the very beginning of the narrative.[2] Hence also the

[1] For the years 1682-8 the 1875 version prints roughly 80,000 words, while the manuscript contains about 115,000 words.

[2] Unfortunately these stories, and other omitted material as well, appear in the 1734 version. Thus all who accepted the 1875 version as complete

constant omission, or alteration, of all words and phrases which might be deemed likely, even by the most censorious, to bring the blush of shame to the cheek of modesty.[1]

Scarcely less serious to the historian is the confusion introduced into Reresby's system of dating. The year for Reresby began on March 25[2], and the phrase "this year," which he frequently employs in his narrative, indicates a period of twelve months commencing on that day. But the 1875 version of the *Memoirs* is arbitrarily divided into chapters[3] based on a year beginning on January 1.[4] Moreover it includes in the text, sometimes in the body of paragraphs, but more generally as headings for them, the dates which in the original manuscript are placed in the margin opposite the events (not always easily identifiable) to which they are intended to refer. Such a transference of dates would have been difficult to accomplish satisfactorily even with a complete text. With an incomplete text it has proved quite impossible, and has

and accurate were forced to regard them as interpolations on the part of the first editor, and some very remarkable explanations were invented for their insertion (*The Edinburgh Review*, October 1875, p. 395 note).

[1] Typical examples are the deletion of the words " into his drawers " in the story of the unfortunate Dutchman who tried to enter Bologna (*infra*, pp. 15-6), and the omission of the phrases " my then mistriss " and " in her bed " from the account of Reresby's parting interview with Elizabeth Hamilton (*infra*, p. 32). The latter is the more inexcusable inasmuch as it was quite customary in the seventeenth century for great ladies to grant interviews when in their beds, and the word " mistress " had no sinister significance, implying in this case merely that Reresby was paying his court to her.

[2] The old or official practice, which was already passing out of use. In the following pages dates from January 1 to March 24 are referred to as intermediate between two years.

[3] Chapter 1, although ostensibly part of the *Memoirs*, is not actually so at all, but is an introductory compilation derived mainly from other writings by Reresby.

[4] This point is rather unfortunately emphasised by the fact that Reresby customarily treats the Christmas and New Year period, stretching across the limits of these artificial chapters, as one, and delights to give an account of the festivities with which he celebrated it.

scarcely even been seriously attempted. Dates the insertion of which has proved troublesome have been
simply ignored. Others have been included in what is
undoubtedly the wrong place. Where paragraphs have
been omitted the dates attached to them have not in-
frequently been assigned, if that appeared convenient, to
the following paragraphs. Occasionally dates for quite
a considerable stretch of the narrative have been rendered
inaccurate by an omission or misunderstanding at the
beginning.

From the literary standpoint also the 1875 version
must be completely condemned. Not merely does it
make no attempt to reproduce the spelling of the original,
but it utterly fails to retain the style. Although not re-
written to anything approaching the same extent as the
1734 version, it is quite definitely modernised in many
respects. Archaic words have been replaced by later
terms. The grammar has been constantly altered, with
the object, presumably, of making it better, and the effect,
only too frequently, of making it worse. Most inexcusable
of all, the northern provincialisms, so typical of Reresby,
and so characteristic of an age when men were not yet
ashamed of the district in which they were born, have been
swept away. The whole text, in fact, has been emas-
culated, and robbed of almost everything that would
suggest its author or the period of its composition.

Even when these major failings have been admitted,
many others of less importance remain to be indicated.
Mistranscriptions are deplorably common, and are often
of such a character as to alter completely the meaning of
the passage concerned.[1] Not merely sentences but entire

[1] To this category belongs the often-quoted statement that the Duke of
Monmouth lived with Lady Henrietta Wentworth " according to the rules
of his convenience." This appears both in the 1734 version and in the
1875 version. The word Reresby actually wrote, however, was not
" convenience " but " concience " (infra, p. 386), and the point he had in
mind was Monmouth's repeated declaration that he regarded Lady
Henrietta as his wife before God.

paragraphs have been transferred from one part of the narrative to another, for reasons which it is hard sometimes even to guess. Phrases which appear in the 1734 edition have been repeated, although there is no authority whatever for them in the manuscript. The text, in fact, is not only incomplete but thoroughly unreliable.

Where previous editors have erred so grievously it is the obvious duty of a new editor at least to give a clear and honest account of the principles which have guided his work. In the following pages the text of the *Memoirs* preserved in the British Museum has been reproduced as exactly as seemed at all practicable. No omissions whatever have been made, with the exception of one or two passages rendered illegible, apparently by Reresby himself; the original arrangement, wording and spelling have been scrupulously retained; marginal dates have been placed as precisely as possible where Reresby placed them. On the other hand, punctuation and the use of capitals have been modernised; contracted words have been expanded; marginal dates have been reproduced in a standardised form;[1] obvious omissions on Reresby's part have been supplied within square brackets;[2] and in a very few cases towards the end, where the manuscript has become worn, the elucidation of a word or phrase has been aided by reference to the older versions of the text.

No previous edition of the *Memoirs* has been provided with any notes worthy of the name; nor indeed does Reresby's plain and straightforward narrative call for any very elaborate annotation. It is, however, full of errors, both of fact and of date; it contains innumerable references to places, events and individuals whose identity is

---

[1] Considerations of expense alone would have made this necessary. Reresby writes his marginal dates in every conceivable form, from " 1 Jan." to " January the first." The size of margin required to accommodate the lengthiest of these would have been preposterous.

[2] This has been done most sparingly. Reresby makes many slips, but reflection frequently shows that apparent slips are not really slips at all.

not immediately apparent; and it is surprisingly meagre in its account even of some events with which Reresby was intimately associated. Correction, identification and elaboration have accordingly been made the principal objects of the notes to the text which follows. Corrections have as a rule been confined to serious errors, and even where minor mistakes have been indicated it is more with the intention of illustrating Reresby's failings than with any hope of correcting his narrative on every point. Identifications have been made as brief as possible. Additional material has been drawn almost entirely from Reresby's own writings, and especially from such letters of his as have survived. Unless already published in some easily accessible source of information these letters have as a rule been printed verbatim, and should prove of value both in themselves and as enabling a comparison to be made between what Reresby wrote to his contemporaries and what he wrote for the benefit of posterity.

II. THE VALUE OF THE MEMOIRS

In assessing the historical value of the *Memoirs* it is essential to remember that although written almost in diary form the narrative is not in actual fact a diary, or contemporary account of events compiled more or less day by day. As the title chosen by its author implies, it is a collection of reminiscences, gathered together towards the close of that author's life. Apparently about the year 1679 Sir John Reresby became inspired with the idea of assembling everything he could relating to himself and his family, and arranging it in such a form as would make it of service for the edification of his descendants. Possibly his first effort in this direction was the so-called " letter-book " preserved in the Bodleian Library.[1] Possibly his second

[1] Rawlinson MSS. D. 204.

effort was the genealogical account of the Reresby family usually referred to as his *Family History*.[1] Almost certainly his last effort was the *Memoirs*.

That the " letter-book " is not a genuine letter-book, in the sense of a register of letters of some particular category or categories, is obvious at a first glance. The letters it contains are a selection assembled for some definite purpose, possibly that of illustrating Reresby's wide connections, more probably that of providing examples of various styles of letter-writing for the use of his family. Ten of them, labelled " Love Letters " and addressed in several cases " To Cœlia," are quite plainly letters to Frances Brown, written eight before and two after Reresby's marriage with her, and represent, no doubt, a vast mass of similar correspondence. The remainder are classed as " Letters of Businesse," and are addressed to a great variety of prominent men, only a few of whom figure more than once in the collection. Interspersed with the letters are what charity might call " verses " on various subjects, usually connected with " Cœlia," the whole constituting apparently the cream of Reresby's literary output up to 1679.

The *Family History* is a work of more industry and merit. Based partly on deeds and charters, partly on ancient pedigrees, and partly on information collected by Reresby from his contemporaries and immediate predecessors, it is a praiseworthy attempt to trace the fortunes of the family of Reresby from its foundation to 1679, the year in which at least the greater part of the account was written.[2]

---

[1] British Museum Add. MSS. 29442-3.

[2] The date is specifically given more than once in the *Family History* itself. In the preliminary dedication the purpose of the compilation is clearly set forth:

1. To instruct posterity as well as the living how long it hath pleased Providence to continue us in the same name and place, and to incite them therby soe to demeane themselvs according to the rules of concience and honour as to obteane a longer continuance of the same mercy.

2. To save such the labour of turning over a great many obscure papers

Whether as part of the originâl plan or not, it concludes with a brief and completely unsatisfactory sketch of Reresby's own career up to the time of Monmouth's rebellion.[1]

In dissatisfaction with this sketch is almost certainly to be found the origin of the *Memoirs*. During the closing years of the reign of Charles II Reresby had risen to a position of very real eminence in public life, and must have felt that the part he was playing could not fittingly be commemorated by a few paragraphs added to a genealogical account of his family.[2] Shortly before or shortly after the death of Charles II, accordingly, he appears to have embarked on an elaborate account of his own life,[3]

as are curious to know what hath passed in their familie, and that please themselves (as I have done) with *olim memenisse*.

3. To preserve memorials of some things of use as well as of curiosity, which age as well as want of care to preserve hath near already consumed.

4. To restoor such to their deserved places in the pedigree as have been omitted, either by neglect, or bycause yonger children, their memory it should seeme formerly seldome surviving their poor annuitys.

5. To show who have been the true patrons and foster-fathers of their families, that their memories may be honoured and exemples followed (Add. MSS. 29442, f. 1).

[1] The sheets containing the greater part of this sketch have been much damaged ; but it seems clear that it was begun on a very moderate scale, which was drastically reduced until the narrative petered out altogether.

[2] That Reresby had a fairly clear idea of the provinces appropriate to his *Family History* and his *Memoirs* is indicated by the fact that the births of his children, originally recorded in the latter, were ultimately transferred, as genealogical material, to the former.

[3] Any conclusion regarding the date of compilation of the *Memoirs* must be based primarily on the *Family History*, which could hardly have ended as it does if the *Memoirs* had then been written, and on the internal evidence of the *Memoirs* itself. The former suggests a date certainly after 1679 and probably as late as 1685. The latter, while in general confirming this estimate, is of little assistance towards making it either more exact or more certain, partly because there is no evidence that the manuscript in the British Museum is not a revision of an earlier draft, partly because of the serious unreliability of Reresby in matters of detail. The fact that Reresby does not mention an event or refer to an individual by a particular title is no proof or even strong suggestion that at the time he wrote the event had not happened or the title been conferred. A courtier who could mistake

which he continued until, warned perhaps of his approaching end, he brought it almost absolutely up to date just before his death.[1]

Thus it is impossible to regard the first half of the *Memoirs* as a contemporary narrative, and it is doubtful whether the bulk even of the remainder may be considered more than semi-contemporary. The very moderation of Reresby's language and opinions suggests that he habitually wrote some time after the event; and the same conclusion is indicated by many individual entries, which contain references to occurrences of later date.[2] On the other hand, Reresby undoubtedly had a great amount of good contemporary material in his hands on which to base his narrative. He had his *Family History*; his account of his early travels; presumably all his letters to his wife; notes of proceedings in the Parliaments of which he was a

the day and hour of Charles II's death (*infra*, p. 351) and confuse the titles of his own chief patron (*infra*, p. 217) was capable of any slip. Nor is the converse type of evidence much more conclusive, principally because it consists almost entirely of short phrases, which could with the greatest ease have been inserted in a later revision of a first draft. Many references (to Rochester as Treasurer, *infra*, p. 67; to Charles Ingleby as serjeant, p. 197; to the dismissal of Halifax, p. 204) suggest the reign of James II as the period of composition even of the early part of the narrative. On the other hand some phrases ("our King," *infra*, p. 13; "his Majesty," p. 27; "his now Queen," p. 40) amount almost to proof that Charles II was still alive when Reresby first began to write.

[1] The last entry in the *Memoirs* is dated May 5, 1689. Reresby died on May 12. The inscription on the monument which his widow erected to his memory at Thrybergh is printed in Joseph Hunter, *South Yorkshire*, ii. 44.

[2] Even as late as October 17, 1688, Reresby was writing a month or more behind time (*infra*, pp. 521-2). On the other hand, as early as 1686 he appears to be writing fairly near the event. Under date March 29 he records a robbery committed upon him in London by some person or persons unknown (*infra*, p. 418). Under date May 19 of the same year he records the conviction and punishment of the culprit, whom he mentions by name (*infra*, p. 426). The conclusion would seem to be that the entry under the former date was written before the latter date; but one hesitates to build on so slender a foundation in the case of Reresby.

member ;[1] letters, proclamations and other official documents sent to him as justice of the peace, deputy lieutenant, sheriff, and Governor of York; probably notes of his conversations with Halifax and other great men; together with an enormous mass of private correspondence both received and sent.[2]

It is in large measure the nature of this material which is responsible for the principal characteristics of the *Memoirs*, and particularly for that serious lack of balance which is its outstanding feature. Specially prominent is the almost complete gap in the narrative from the close of 1667 to the beginning of 1675.[3] During practically the whole of that period Reresby was without active official duties of any kind,[4] and so had no official correspondence. As he spent practically all his time with his wife and young family, he had no need of domestic correspondence.[5] Thus when he came to write his *Memoirs* he can have found very little material for these years, and seems to have relied largely on notices in newspapers and on household accounts.

For the last ten or twelve years of his life, on the other

---

[1] These notes are specifically mentioned only once (*infra*, p. 98); but there is no reason to suppose that Reresby's practice of note-taking was confined to one session. The serious inaccuracy of his notices of Parliamentary affairs, in fact, rather suggests that he was relying on private, and not on official, sources of information.

[2] The constant references to and even quotations from letters received, which appear in the *Memoirs*, show that these letters were regularly preserved ; and at least in the later years of his life it appears to have been Reresby's practice to arrange them methodically in bundles (*infra*, p. 455). That copies of letters sent were retained with similar regularity is not so clear ; but several references, as well as the mere existence of the " letterbook," make it plain that the retention of copies was at least common.

[3] For these seven or eight years the narrative contains only about 5,000 words.

[4] He ceased to be sheriff of Yorkshire in November 1667, and was not even sworn a justice of the peace until three years later (*infra*, p. 79).

[5] The last surviving letter from Reresby to his wife is dated March 21, 1665/6.

hand, his material appears to have been almost over-whelming, and roughly three-quarters of his entire narrative is accordingly devoted to that period. Had he only possessed more skill (or possibly patience) in dealing with this material, the result might have been of the very greatest historical value. The task of piecing together his documents, however, and basing his personal remin-iscences upon them has clearly proved beyond his capacity. The reminiscences are prevented from flowing smoothly by the constant effort to provide them with a foundation of documentary evidence. Yet the reliance on documents is neither sufficiently extensive nor sufficiently methodical to change what is essentially a collection of reminiscences into anything worthy to be called a history. Confusion is everywhere apparent. Accounts of the same event are given in different places under different dates.[1] Vague entries are made about matters of which Reresby obviously has no genuine recollection.[2] An uneasy suspicion is repeatedly aroused that what is being presented is really no more than a poor resumé of badly arranged letters.[3]

Nevertheless in its own rather scrappy fashion Reresby's narrative is of very considerable value indeed. It gives an account, plain at times almost to the verge of baldness, of the life of a typical member of the class which in the seventeenth century formed the backbone of English society. In spite of many omissions it paints a true, if rough, picture of the era in which its author lived. The average Englishman of the later seventeenth century was neither a Pepys nor an Evelyn; but large numbers had much in common with Reresby.

[1] *Infra*, pp. 208-9, 242.

[2] *Infra*, p. 87, the Stop of the Exchequer.

[3] Had Reresby relied solely on his memory he would have been much more sparing of his dates. As it is, he seems to derive the majority of his dates from letters, with only the dates of the letters to guide him, and the result is constant small inaccuracies.

On this fact more than on any other, perhaps, the value of the *Memoirs* depends.   Without the charm of Pepys's *Diary*, it is no less convincingly real, and to that *Diary* it constitutes a singularly effective counterpart.   The aspects of the national life with which Reresby was best acquainted are just those with which Pepys was comparatively unfamiliar—life in the country as distinct from life in the town, the army as distinct from the navy, local as distinct from central administration.   Even at Whitehall Reresby, unquestionably a gentleman by birth, was thoroughly at home in circles where Pepys was always more or less an intruder.   His outlook is much more restricted than that of Pepys, his perceptions not so keen, his frankness, though at times sufficiently great, not quite so overwhelming. But he has this in common with the great diarist, that it was his object to give an unvarnished account of his experience through life, and on his own rather lower level he has been not unsuccessful in doing so.

III. THE AUTHOR OF THE MEMOIRS

Sir John Reresby has received distinctly hard measure at the hands of posterity.   By some regarded as a mere rough country squire, he has by the majority been depicted in the somewhat contradictory character of a supple-minded and self-seeking courtier.   For both these conceptions of him there is a measure of justification, but neither can be accepted as embodying anything like the whole truth.

Undoubtedly Reresby was quarrelsome, addicted to the use of violence, and none too refined in his ideas and manners;[1] but the lack of refinement was of the age

[1] When it is remembered that the *Memoirs* was written for the instruction and edification of posterity one can only marvel at some of the incidents (e.g. *infra*, pp. 14-5, 34-5) which the author has seen fit to include.

rather than of the man, while the quarrelsomeness evinced in his many " affairs of honour " appears from his own statements to have been less a natural quality than a weapon deliberately assumed to enable him to hold his own in all company in spite of his small stature and slight lameness. Equally undoubtedly Reresby was first and foremost a Yorkshireman, whose interests centred mainly in local and country affairs; yet he was almost as thoroughly at home in the wider world of society and politics which found a focus in London and Westminster, and was better acquainted with Western Europe than all but a small number of the Englishmen of his day. His travels on the Continent had been extensive and prolonged,[1] and his interest in affairs outside England never declined.[2] It is significant that he was at different times seriously considered as a possible envoy to the Emperor, and to the courts of France, Spain, Denmark and Sweden.[3]

For this one may surmise that he was largely indebted to his command of languages other than his own. Not merely had he a schoolboy's acquaintance with Greek and the familiarity with Latin still expected of an educated man of affairs,[4] but he could speak French sufficiently well to be mistaken for a Frenchman,[5] was almost equally

[1] He left England in April 1654, and did not permanently return until August 1660.

[2] It is unfortunate that the 1875 edition of the *Memoirs* omits, as unimportant, practically all Reresby's references to foreign affairs. In themselves these references are almost valueless, being based largely on the *London Gazette*; but they help to show where Reresby's interests lay.

[3] *Infra*, pp. 173, 234, 242, 292, 301.

[4] Although trained in both classical languages (*infra*, p. 2), Reresby appears to have neglected Greek after reaching manhood. His continued acquaintance with Latin, however, is attested by frequent Latin tags and quotations, as well as by his ready use of mediaeval charters in his *Family History*.

[5] The progress of his studies in the French language is recorded *infra*, pp. 2, 7-8, 19, 28.

well acquainted with Italian,[1] and had probably a slight knowledge of German and Dutch.

Like so many of his contemporaries, also, he was a musician of some ability. From the age of eight he had been able to play upon the violin any tune that he heard, and he had in addition received instruction both on the guitar and on the lute.[2] His interest in music persisted through life,[3] though as he grew older it seems to have found a rival in gardening and architecture.

Strangely enough it was as a writer that Reresby inclined to fail. His prose, both in his letters and in his more formal works, is clear, terse and vigorous, but not that of a highly cultured man. His verse, if it is to be taken seriously at all, can only be described as deplorable. Like most would-be versifiers, Reresby can generally manage with some success the first two or four lines of any composition; but thereafter both sense and rhythm rapidly deteriorate. Among the sets of verses which he considered worthy of preservation in his " letter-book " there is not one of any real merit whatever.[4]

---

[1] Even before he left France he had made himself fairly proficient in the Italian language, and his stay in Italy greatly increased his proficiency (*infra*, pp. 11, 13, 76).

[2] *Infra*, pp. 2, 7-8, 11.   [3] *Infra*, p. 58.

[4] Of his political effusions the most imposing is " The Relation of a Plott (discovered in the year 1664) in mock-verse to my honoured uncle Sir Thamworth Reresby," which begins :

> Knowing your love to th' state and the politicks
> Although my knotty muse has gott the rickitts,
> I'le tell you of a suttle plott in verse
> Newly discovered, breif as Doctor Pierce.
>   (Rawlinson MSS. D. 204, f. 104.)

Amatory verses are much more numerous, a characteristic " Epigramme," written " On Cœlia's petting when I was to goe a journey," reading :

> As executioners can mercy showe
> By giving warning 'fore they give the blowe,
> That soe the soule before shee's disposes'd
> May be prepar'd to quit it's wonted rest,

Nevertheless it is easier to defend Reresby against the charge of lack of culture than to meet that of self-seeking. Public life under Charles II and James II was full of difficulties for any conscientious politician, and although Reresby might conceivably have been prepared to sacrifice himself for the sake of his principles, he certainly was not prepared to sacrifice his family. Hence much in his conduct which was not inspired by the highest motives, and which those whose principles have never been subjected to any particular strain may feel in consequence that they are entitled to condemn.

It should, however, be emphasised that the particular incident on which stress is most commonly laid, Reresby's alleged desertion of the opposition for the Court party in 1677,[1] will not bear the interpretation which is generally placed upon it. Like many others among the Yorkshire nobility and gentry Reresby first entered public life as one of the group of young Cavaliers who followed the Duke of Buckingham, and in that capacity held a number of local offices as a supporter of the government. In 1666, however, he alienated Buckingham by casting doubt on his personal courage,[2] and the breach thus occasioned was made permanent by his action a few months later in publishing, as sheriff of Yorkshire, a

> Soe Cœlia, that I might less trouble finde
> To leave her, in compassion seem'd unkinde.
> *(ibid.,* f. 96.)

Equally typical is " A Sonnet " dealing with the somewhat unpromising theme " On Cœlia's telling me of my faults." It begins:

> Love like a chimist can extract
> Vertue from every word and act,
> Alter the gross into refinde,
> Excuse what's done by what's designd.
> *(ibid.,* f. 97.)

[1] *Infra,* pp. 110-3.

[2] Reresby admits that he was in the wrong to criticise his own superior officer; but the criticism was made in private conversation with a friend, who betrayed him *(infra,* pp. 60-1).

proclamation which had been issued for the Duke's arrest.[1]

The result, as far as he was concerned, was his identification with the rival faction in Yorkshire which acknowledged the Earl of Burlington as its chief, and, as a natural consequence, his dismissal from all his offices as soon as Buckingham recovered favour. Thus there is nothing surprising in the fact that when a number of Yorkshire constituencies fell vacant in 1673 he was induced to come forward as a candidate for Parliament in opposition to his former patron.[2] No betrayal of his principles was involved, for Buckingham had long abandoned the Cavalier aspect of his very composite policy, and had associated himself with the attitude of toleration to Catholics and Dissenters, and friendship with France, embodied in the Declaration of Indulgence and the attack on the Dutch.

A very different situation arose, however, with the fall of Buckingham from power and the rise to high office of the Earl of Danby. As soon as he could contrive to consolidate his position Danby repudiated Buckingham's policy, and strove by every means at his command to rally round the throne the Cavalier element which his predecessor had alienated. That Reresby, a friend and neighbour of the new minister, was won over is not in the least to his discredit. The charge of political inconsistency based upon his apparent change of attitude should be laid, not at his door, but at the door of the government. It is significant that in spite of the very troublous times which followed 1677 nothing in Reresby's conduct after that date provides any foundation for a charge of real lack of principle. Never an opponent of the government, he yet never lent any countenance to what he considered its excesses under James II. His attitude was not a very lofty one, but it was fundamentally honest, and based on a good deal of

[1] *Infra*, p. 64.   [2] *Infra*, pp. 88-91.

sound common sense.[1] His implicit claim, that if others had adopted the same attitude, the Revolution would have been unnecessary,[2] has perhaps more justification than is at first sight apparent.

IV. THE AUTHOR'S ANCESTRY

In the *Family History*, which he dedicates " to his honoured uncle, Sir Tamworth Reresby, Knight," Sir John Reresby tentatively finds the origin of his line in a certain Adamus de Reresby and Guido his son, who lived in the time of Edward the Confessor; but he considers that he is on unquestionably firm ground in placing at the head of his pedigree Sir Adam de Reresby, who married Anne, daughter of Sir Andrew Beak, and had five children, of whom the solitary son, Alexander, continued the line. For Alexander he produces evidence in the shape of deeds,[3] and from him he traces the descent of the family, supporting his statements at each step by similar evidence, down to his own day.

[1] He makes no secret whatever of his general outlook, an outlook which it is difficult perhaps to admire, but impossible to condemn (*infra*, pp. 174-5, 362, 401).

[2] e.g. *infra*, p. 533.

[3] His reasons for including Sir Adam as well might not entirely commend themselves to genealogists.   " I confess I finde noe deeds concerning him, but conceive that it is a sufficient proofe that he was father to Alexander, bycaus it doth soe appear by an antient pedigree which hath ever been receivd and allowed in the familie, and that since he must have had some father it is as probable he might have been of that name as of another " (*Family History*, i. f. 5).   The whole problem of the origin of the Reresbys is discussed by Sir George Reresby Sitwell in *The Barons of Pulford*. Adamus, Guido and Sir Adam are rejected as mythical, and the pedigree of Alexander is traced back to Hugh Fitzosbern, lord of Pulford in Cheshire, who had also been settled at Ormesby in Lincolnshire since shortly after the Conquest.

The original Adamus and Guido, however, were supposed to be connected with Lincolnshire, and it is with that county that Alexander was also principally associated, owing to his marriage with Juliana de Reresby, near Lincoln. The connection of the Reresbys with Derbyshire and the West Riding of Yorkshire began with Isorius de Reresby, son of Alexander, who flourished during the earlier part of the thirteenth century, and married Amicia, eldest daughter of John Deincourt and coheiress of her mother's father, Serlo, lord of Plesley and Ashover in the county of Derby. The son of this marriage, Ralph de Reresby, inherited Plesley, which he later exchanged for the manor of Ashover,[1] and also came into possession of the manor-house called the Ickles in the lordship of Brinsford;[2] but his greatest acquisitions for his family were due to his marriage with Margaret, daughter of Ralph de Normanville, and sister and heiress of Adam de Normanville. In right of his mother, Adam de Reresby, the offspring of this union, eventually came into possession[3] of the manor of Thrybergh and the advowson of the church there, together with the lordships of Brinsford, Great Dalton, Little Dalton and Bolton, all in the West Riding of Yorkshire.

Thrybergh had long been the principal seat of the Normanvilles, and it soon came to be so regarded by the Reresbys also.[4] Manor, township and parish combined,

[1] Alienating his original estate in Lincolnshire to the Abbey of Barlings.

[2] Always written thus by Sir John. The modern form of the name is Brinsworth.

[3] Probably in 1316 (Hunter, *South Yorkshire*, ii. 38).

[4] It is perhaps an indirect proof of this that St. Leonard, the tutelar saint of Thrybergh, was supposed to have been a member of their house. " Tradition will have him " declares Sir John, " to have been one of the familie of Reresby, and conveys to us a long story concerning him, the substance of which is this—that one Leonard de Reresby, serving his prince in the holy warr, was taken prisner by the Saracens, and ther deteaned captive near seven years ; that his wife, according to the lawe of the land, was towards being married to another ; that being apprehensive

situated about three miles from Rotherham and nine from
Doncaster, it formed a singularly compact and convenient
estate, and for some time the chief object of the Reresbys
appears to have been the extension of their possessions
in its neighbourhood.   Under either Adam de Reresby
or his son Ralph the Ickles had apparently been alienated;
but this loss was made good by Ralph's son, Thomas de
Reresby, who served in the Hundred Years' War against
France and received the honour of knighthood from
Edward III himself.   Sir Thomas married Cecilia, sister
and coheiress of John de Gotham, and by this means
gained for his family complete possession of Brinsford,
including the manor of Ickles.   This Sir Thomas was
succeeded by a second Sir Thomas, who purchased lands
adjoining Thrybergh, and he in turn by a third Sir Thomas,
married to Maud, daughter of Sir John Bosvile of Cheviot,
and remarkable principally for his seven sons and eleven
daughters depicted along with their parents in the north
window of Thrybergh church.

Already by this time three younger members of the
family of Reresby had held the living of Thrybergh; but
at the beginning of the fifteenth century an unusual step
was taken when William, eldest son of the third Sir

of this accident, by the power of prayer hee was miraculously delivered,
and insensibly conveyed with shackles and gives or fetters upon his limms,
and laid upon the East Hill in Thriberge Field as the bells touled for his
wife her second marriage, which her first husband's return prevented,
though he presently died soe soon as brought into the church, wher he
desired to pay his first visitt.   I shall not undertake either to comment or
extenuate upon this story either to make it more or less probable.   Only
this I must say, that superstition gave that credit either to this or the like
story, that an antient cross remains till this day upon the same East Hill,
though defaced in the late time, called St. Leonards Cross ; the church
of Thriberge and the great bell are dedicated to St. Leonard ; his picture
in chains and fetters was in the church window till of late broaken down ;
and as some will have it, his festivall observed in the familie on White
Sunday, and his fetters preserved in the house till my great-granfather
Sir Thomas Reresby his time, that in his absence they were converted into
plowe shares by his wifes order " (*Family History*, i. f. 17).

Thomas, was presented to the rectory, with the result that after the death of Sir Thomas in 1439 it was the second son Ralph who eventually inherited the estate. Rather more than a century later a similar interruption took place in the regular line of descent, Thomas, the grandson of Ralph,[1] being succeeded, not by his eldest son, who died before coming of age, but by his second son Lionel. Otherwise, however, the descent was perfectly regular, from father to eldest son in each generation, until the time of Sir John Reresby himself.[2]

Lionel Reresby, who married Anne, daughter of Robert Swift, a wealthy merchant of Rotherham, was remarkable chiefly for his excellent management, which enabled him not merely to marry his eight daughters to husbands " of good fortune and quality," but at the same time to consolidate and increase the family estate. From Roger Vavasour, who had married his sister Ellen, he purchased the manor of Denby, and at his death shortly before the accession of Queen Elizabeth his possessions in Yorkshire included the manors of Thrybergh, Brinsford, Ickles and Denby, as well as extensive lands in Haworth, Masborough and Rotherham.[3] Meanwhile, however, the Derbyshire estates of the family had not been neglected. Thomas, the son and heir of Lionel, married Margaret, daughter of Thomas Babington of Dethick [4] in the county of Derby, and Sir Thomas, the eldest son of this marriage,

---

[1] Ralph died in 1463 ; his successor, another Ralph, who lived to more than eighty years of age, in 1530 ; and Thomas about 1543.

[2] Sir John was very proud of this feature of his ancestry—" nineteen descents, nine of which have been knights or baronets, in all which the estate never went out of the direct line or to a second brother but twice, once by the eldest brother's entring into religious orders, another time by the death of the elder brother the estate devolved to the secound " (*Family History*, i. f. 5).

[3] The list is given in greater detail in Hunter, *South Yorkshire*, ii. 40.

[4] The grandfather of Anthony Babington, leader of the Catholic conspiracy against Elizabeth, who was executed in 1586.

increased the paternal possessions in Ashover by the purchase of Babington's Manor there. Under this Sir Thomas, indeed, the material prosperity of the Reresbys reached perhaps its highest level;[1] but before his death in 1619 a complete change had taken place. Much of the family estate was sold, the Derbyshire lands were mortgaged,[2] and the remaining lands were left heavily encumbered.

It is about this point that the *Family History* ceases to be a mere genealogical collection, and becomes based to a large extent on personal reminiscences passed on to Sir John by men who were still alive in his day. Much of it is still genealogical in character, or concerned exclusively with the Reresby estates, and much of it is in substance reproduced in the *Memoirs*; but the remainder is sufficiently of the nature of a prologue to that work to merit being printed verbatim. Sir John has naturally much to say about Sir Thomas Reresby, for one of his own main tasks in life was to restore the family fortunes, and repair the devastation which that unfortunate man had wrought:

The reasons given for Sir Thomas his great expences and debts were his following the Court without any other recompence then empty knighthood (though very rare and consequently of great honor in thos days); an expensive wife;[3] his accompanying my Lord Zouch, sent anno 1593 embassador into Scotland;[4] an humor to live high at the first, which he did not abate as his fortune decreased; his quarrell with Sir William Wentworth, and his giveing him a box on the ear at Rotherham sessions upon the

[1] " The greatest and freest estate both reall and personal of any heir of the familie to that day " (*Family History*, i. f. 44).

[2] *Infra*, pp. 82-3.

[3] Mary, daughter of Sir John Monson of South Carlton, Lincolnshire, whom he married on June 3, 1588.

[4] Edward la Zouche, eleventh Baron Zouche of Harringworth. The object of his mission to Scotland was to concert measures with James VI against Spain.

bench ; and his buildings [1] ... [He] was sherif of Darbyshire, which office he is reported to have performed at too prodigall a rate, in the year 1613. I find amongst old papers a bill of fair for provisions the Lent assizes, with this superscription upon it with Sir Thomas his own hand—The stuarts appointment for Lent assizes att Derby when I was sherif for that county—wherin I find 15 severall sorts of foule, amongst others yong swanns, knots, herns, bitters, &c., three venaison pastys appointed for every meale, 13 severall sorts of sea fish, 14 severall sorts of fresh-water fish, each appointed to be ordered a different way, &c. Another great occasion of his expences was his great charge of children and great attendance, seldome going to church or from home without a great many followers in blew coats and badges, and beyond the usuall nomber for men of his quality and fortune.

His ill management sett aside, he was certainly a fine gentleman, both as to person and parts. He was very tall, well shaped, his face was hansome and manly, and was well behaved. His conversation was pleasant and witty, and his company very acceptable to persons of the best quality of his nighbourhood, especially George, the great Earle of Shrewsbury,[2] then most commonly resident either at Sheffield or Worsop manors. I had the greatest part of this character of him not only from thos that knew him and had lived with him as his servants, but from the late old Duke of Newcastle, who was educated with the said Earle of Shrewsbury [3] and remembred Sir Thomas Reresby as acquainted with him in that familie very perticularly. . . .[4]

He was certainly a man of great courage, though he expressed it not seasonably in gieveing Sir William Wentworth (father to the first Earl of Straford) a box on the ear upon the bench at the generall sessions held at Rotherham, the 8 of October, anno 41° Elizabeth. The whole narrative of this matter came lately to my hands as it was represented by Sir William Wentworth his freinds

[1] Details of the buildings follow.

[2] The sixth earl, whose second wife was the famous Bess of Hardwick. From 1569 to 1584 he was entrusted with the custody of Mary Queen of Scots.

[3] William Cavendish, later Duke of Newcastle, was brought up in the household of Gilbert, seventh Earl of Shrewsbury, who was his father's half-brother.

[4] A letter follows, written by Sir Thomas Reresby from Edinburgh in 1593 to the seventh Earl of Shrewsbury.

to the then Earl of Shrewsbury, and since found amongst the said
earls papers, the short of which is as follows: That in the year of
the Queen 39, a dispute hapning between them as to some propriety
of lands in Hoton Roberts, Sir Thomas Reresby sent his uncle
Leonard Reresby [1] to the said Mr. Wentworth to lett him know
that he was informed that the said Mr. Wentworth had challenged
him, and which if true, he, the said Mr. Wentworth, was a lyer
and a coward, and further that on Thursday after he might find
Sir Thomas in a close of his own in Hoton aforesaid, with one
servant with him, if he had ought to say to him. To whom Mr.
Wentworth answered that such snares could not catch him, and
advised Mr. Leonard Reresby to advise Sir Thomas to live at home
in peace like a gentleman, but sent two gentlemen the day appointed
to the place, wher they found Sir Thomas, to acquaint him that
the said Sir William Wentworth had noe malice nor quarrell to
him.

Two years after, on the 8 of October the 41 Elizabeth, they both
meeting on the bench at Rotherham sessions, ther hapned a dispute
concerning the return of jurys and concerning the escape of a person
out of the stocks, whether negligent or volontary, between the two
knights, which at the last flew soe high that Sir Thomas tould Sir
William, A turd in your teeth, thou art a rascall, a villain, and
darrest not draw a sword ; I sent you a challenge before this which
thou durst not accept. To which Sir William replying that he
said untruly herein, Sir Thomas smote him on the face with his
hand, and after pulled him soe hard by the ears that he made them
bleed ; the servants after, espousing their masters quarrell, drew
their daggers, insoemuch that the rest of the justices had much
adoe to keep the peace in the court, and to hinder Sir Thomas
following Sir William when he went to his inn. However, Sir
Thomas waylaid him in a street wher he used to pass homewards,
but Sir William not going that way Sir Thomas returned to the
bench. For this Sir Thomas was fyned 1,000 l. in the Star
Chamber, but not haveing paid it all till King Jams came into

---

[1] Leonard, fourth son of Lionel Reresby, " who marryed [Catherine],
the daughter of Thomas Hardwick of Petterneuton near Leeds, Com.
Ebor., and had issue an only daughter called Editha, whom Francis Tindal
of Brotherton, Esquire, marryed without her father's consent, and had by
her 500 l. per annum land of inheritance and several children. The heir
of the familie continues ther at this day [c. 1679]. This Leonard dyed at
the parsonage in Barnbrough [1613], which he then had in farme "
(*Family History*, i. f. 40).

England, he obteaned the Kings generall pardon under the great seale, which released the remainder. For this he was also putt out of commission of the peace, as I soppose, for I find noe mention of his name in the clerke of the peace his roules after that time ; but he continued deputy lieutenant and capitain of 200 private men, as appears by a roule of their names and respective abodes within Strafford and Tickill proportioned by my Lord Darcy,[1] Sir Thomas Reresby, and Robert Swift, Esquire, then deputy lieutenants, the VI of August, anno 1602,[2] primo Jacobi.

Some say that being a man of a high sperit, and his lady (who had changed her religion to papist) not soe observant of him as she ought to be, disagreeing with him concerning their daughter, my Lady Campall,[3] gave him soe great a discontent that he fell sick upon it, during which sickness she never would visit him (as one of her woemen tould me) till he was past recoverie, and then persuaded him to goe to a hous he had at Newarke for change of aire, wher he dyed in May, anno 1619.[4] . . .

The Lady Reresby, widow, kept possession of Thriberge Hall for some time, till Sir George her son, coming from Ickles to make her a visit and finding her abroad, shutt the doors and kept the possession till he dyed, which his mother to return, being then at Deneby and hearing Sir George was sick, sent her gentlewoman, Mrs. Skinner (who tould me the story), under pretence of enquiring after his health, to get him arrested, which was performd by two bailifs which attended on Mrs. Skinner as servants as Sir George laid sick in bed. This lady lived afterwards at Chesterfield and last at London, wher she marryed again, one Sir Simion Stuard, but

[1] John Darcy, third Lord Darcy of Aston.

[2] Presumably a mistake for 1603.

[3] Their second daughter, " Elizabeth, baptized the 18 October 1601, married to Sir John Cambell of Scotland " (*Family History*, ii. f. 2).

[4] " When he was about fifty-five years of age, and was buried the first of June 1619." An elaborate account is given of the provisions of his will, and a statement of the tenure of the lands still in his possession—" The mannors of Thriberge, Great Dolton, Little Dolton, held of the Lord Scroop of his mannor of Boulton in free socage ; the mannors of Deneby and Mexbrough of the King of his honor of Tickill, being part of the duchy, by knights service and the yearly rent of 16s., and his lands in Hoton Roberts, held of the King of his mannor of Tickill in soccage, &c. The mannor of Brinsford was then the possession of Sir George Reresby, who was twenty-nine years of age at the death of Sir Thomas."

disowned him afterwards, nor was he able to proove the marriage.[1]
Then she last married one Mr. Ballard, who had a competent
estate, which he spent whilst her husband, and then dyed ; but she
lived till above eighty years of age, and lies buried in the chappell
of Sommerset Hous in the Strand.   She was a woeman of wit, but
of a masculin sperit, a too great lover of sack as she grew into years,
and unfortunate both to her husband, her son, and the familie. . . . [2]

Sir George Reresby, Knight, eldest son and heir of Sir Thomas,[3]
marryed Elizabeth, second daughter of John Tamworth, Esquire,
squire of the body to Queen Elizebeth, which John Tamworth
married Dorothy, daughter and heiress of Sir Thomas Coleby,
Knight, sergient-at-law to the Queen.   They had issue (besides
John, who dyed yong) Bridget, married to William Molins of the
county of Oxford, Esquire ;   Catherin, married to Sir George
Dalston of Dalston, Com. Comberland, Knight.   Thes three
sisters were coheiresses of a great estate, viz., the mannors of
Louden and Gonthorp, Com. Nottingham ;   Holstead, worth
1,000 l. per annum, Com. Lechester ;   the mannors of Langton,
Kingston and Kripton, Com. Dorset ;   the mannor of Blackpatch
Hall in Radnorshire in Wales, all to above the value of 3,600 l. per
annum.   Sir George was marryed about the age of 18 years,[4] and
knighted 12 Jacobi.   His father gave him private education and

---

[1] Her third daughter, Mary, married Robert, the eldest son of Sir
Simeon Steward (*Family History*, ii. f. 2).

[2] An account follows of Sir Thomas's seven sons and four daughters,
of whom only one besides the heir merits attention, the second son, Gilbert,
" brought up with Isabel, Infanta of Spain, then Governess of the Low
Countrys, wher afterwards being out of page he commanded a company,
and after a regiment of foot ther for many years, till following Count
Mansfelt in his revolt from the Infanta (being sopposed to be in leage with
the Counts wife) he lost his command and fled to Paris, wher he dyed many
years after in good esteem, as I have heard ther from persons that knew
him.   He had issue Eugenius, who did patrizare as to his courage (he
served long in the civill wars at home, then went into France, and was
killed in a duell by a Frenchman near Saumur) ; and Mary, a fyne woeman
both as to beauty and parts, who married Sir Edward Fortescue, Knight,
yonger brother to Sir John Fortescu, Com. Bucks., to whom she bore issue
male."

[3] " Christned by George, [sixth] Earl of Shrewsbury " (*Family History*
ii. f. 1).

[4] In the margin is added, " Anno Domini 1606, October the 7th.   Ex
registro."

not much learning, though he could not but be very capable of it, haveing (as appears by the character of those that knew him, as also by the management of his concerns) a good naturall witt and judgement.

Being marryed, Brinsford and Ickles were setled upon him and his lady for their present maintenance and for jointure to her in case of survivorship,[1] his lady's estate being most of it in reversion, her mother being then liveing, who had it in jointure. Soe that Sir George lived at the Ickles for the most part that his father lived, and it is said that ther was not that warmth of affection between the father and son that ought to have been, for I have heard that Sir Thomas was jealous that Sir George desired his death, and that he expressed it by takeing my father, then very yong, in his arms and saying he might possibly live to revenge his quarrell, which was construed to wish the same to Sir George.

After the death of Sir Thomas Reresby, Sir George came to make his mother a visit at Thriberge, wher finding that shee was gone out of the hous he shutt to the doors and kept her out of possession all the time of his life, as is before related. However, after a long and chargeable suit he had been ejected by due cours of law had he lived but one terme longer. By his death, Sir John Reresby, his son, compounding with his granmother to pay soe much yearly for her life out of the whole estate as her jointure, this unfortunate suit dyed also. Nor could Sir George have been able to defend it soe long had not Sir Simion Stuard of the Isle of Ely (who pretended to be married to the said Lady Reresby, relict of Sir Thomas) released all the title, claime, &c., that he or his lady had in the said lands to Sir George, by deed bearing date the 20 September 1620, which was so ill ressented by the lady (amongst other things) that she denyed her marriage with Sir Symion, which was, it seems, soe privately performed by a priest (if at all) that it could never be prooved.

Sir George was remarkable for being expensive in cloaths and in his journeys, but a great manager at home. He was thought to have mony by him when he dyed, but he sould more then he bought to the familie. . . . [2] Sir George as to his person was very tall and hansome (as appears by his picture at length), brown hair and a red beard. He never took any publique imployment upon him in his

[1] In the margin is added, "The jointure was dated, as appears by Sir George his office, 10 September 8° Jacobi."

[2] An account follows of his purchases and sales, and of the burdens with which he encumbered his estates.

country, as being discouraged from it by being noe schollar and his wife being a papist, who had changed her religion after her marriage, though I have heard it from thos that were servants in the familie that Sir George did both live and die a firm Protestant. His not being concerned in the country business gave him the more leisure to attend that of his estate, as to which I find he was very exact by a book of accounts of his time, though he left the familie affairs and much of the husbandry to the care of his lady.

In the said booke I find an abbrigement of all the Brinsford leases, notes of the brass, peuter, linnin, and other goods and furniture belonging to the hous, and a perticular of sheep and other goods, with memorandums of mony lent and laid out, in which he was soe perticular that I find this amongst others written with his own hand, viz., Item, lent my wife at Lenten fair, 4s. 9d.

His diversion was sometimes haukes, but his chiefest was his breed of horses, in which he was very exact ; but his breed was not in that reputation to gett any profit therby, and the keeping of much ground in his handes both at Thriberge and Ickles for the running of his horses, which he might have lett at good rates, made it the more expensive.

Sir George died of a consumption in the room over the north porch about the age of forty-three, and was buried in Thriberge Church the 4th of February 1628. He outlived his father but ten years. He left his eldest son, and my father, but eighteen years of age, and then at Cambrige. His wardship was begged by some courtier, which his mother bought off for a small thing, though she made him pay 2,000 l. for monys pretended that she had disbursed upon that account when he recieved his wives portion. After the marriage of my father my granmother remooved to the Ickles, which was her jointure, wher she continued many years. Towards the latter end of the wars shee went to London, and continued ther till she died. She was a very comly woeman for her age, tall and straight, of quick apprehension and of a good judgement, but much led and persuaded by her confessor and preists. At my going to travell she recommended to me the Roman religion, desiring me to consider it well, for that ther I should see it in its splendor, wheras it was under a cloud in England. And truly I doe believe it was the greatest reason that she disposed of her own land away from me that I could not be prevailed upon to change my religion, for I ever carried myselfe with great respect towards her, and found her very kind to me in all things but in that most materiall circumstance.

This Lady Reresby dyed in London about the 10th of Aprill 1665, aged above seventy years, and disposed by will of the greatest part of her estate to Sir Tamworth Reresby, her eldest son then liveing, viz., her lands in Hamshire, Nottinghamshire, &c.; but charged that and some other lands formerly disposed of with 120 l. per annum to her yongest son Leonard, soe that the familie had this advantage however by that match of Reresby with Tamworth that though the widow enjoyed a great jointure for many years out of her husbands estate, and left nothing to the eldest sonne, yet she maintained and provided for the yonger children out of her own estate of inheritance. The occasion of her death was a sore which she had long endured in her leg, which gangrend, though she had something of a lethargie also. She lies buried in [1]   Church in London, wher ther is a vault belonging to the Tamworths. . . . [2]

Sir George Reresby had issue :

1. Sir John Reresby, Baronet, christned by my Lord John Darcy the 11 day of Aprill, anno Domini 1611.

2. George Reresby, who prooved very wild, but a man of great courage and conduct in the late civil warr. He might have had very good commands in the Kings army, but contented himselfe with his first, of lieutenant to Sir Thomas Glemham to his troop of hors under Sir Marmaduke Langdale, whom he accompanied in that famous raising of Pontefract siege, and gott in it perticular honor. After the war was ended he came to Thriberge and ther dyed. He was buried in that church the 6 of July, anno Domini 1646.

3. Sir Tamworth Reresby, lieutenant-colonel for the King in my Lord of Newcastles army under Colonel Aire of Hastop in his regiment of foot, afterwards major to his regiment of hors, wher he continued till Adderton More fight. Ther the Kings party being routed he escaped, and continued in the garrison of Basyn Hous till it was taken, and himselfe also, wounded in his head and severall parts of his body, and sent prisner to Ely Hous in London. He continued ther four months, till by the favour of a woeman whos hous joined to the chamber wher he lay he broak a passage into her hous and escaped in woeman's apparell, fled to the King at Oxford, wher he continued to the end of the warr.

[1] A space is left in the text.

[2] A pedigree of the Tamworths follows, which traces the descent of that family from Sir Nicholas Tamworth, Knight, Lord of Tamworth in the time of King John, and his son Sir Giles, who accompanied Richard I to the siege of Acre.

He married Mrs. Mary Preston, widow of William Molins of Sherfield Court in Hamshire, Esquire, who had a good jointure and the management of her son's estate till of age. After the Kings return hee was knighted, and my granmother at her death setled all the lands of inheritance then in her power upon him, excepting what she gave to her yongest son Leonard, as is before mentioned. His lady died about fourteen years agoe, and the knight is yett a healthfull, hansome man. He continues a widdower, lives constantly in London, and follows the diversions of a much yonger man. At this time, being the year 1679, he is above sixty years of age.

4. Jarvase Reresby, who dyed yong. ⎫ Being twins, both born the
5. Charles Reresby, who dyed yong. ⎬ 25 of August, anno Do-
                                        ⎭ mini 1619.

6. Ralph Reresby, baptized the 16 of November 1623.

7. Francis Reresby, who was buried the 11 of February 1628.

8. Leonard Reresby, baptized the 4 August 1628, now liveing in the year 1679. He was never married.

Sir George his daughters were thes :

1. Mary Reresby, a fine person of a woeman by relation. She dyed the first Christmas after my father was married, found herselfe ill as she was danceing, went presently to her chamber, and dyed suddenly, which I the rather mention to showe the uncertainty of this life.

2. Jane, who lived to about fifty years of age but never married.

3. Elizebeth, a hansome, proper woeman of great witt and conduct. . . .

4. Caterin, who died yong.

5. Diana, who behaved herselfe disobediently to her mother, which was a great affliction to her. She married one Keeble, son to [the] great lawyer in the late times, and as I take [it] a judge ;[1] but shee approved soe little of her husband the next day that she would never own him for her husband. When she dyed she had near three thousand pounds, for which few of her relations were the better.

6. Caterin (her sister of that name being dead), who was deformed as to her person and cast away herselfe by marrying one much inferior to her, after which her mother would never see her.

[1] Joseph Keble, son of Richard, who was one of the commissioners entrusted with the custody of the great seal after the execution of Charles I, was a barrister and reporter of legal cases, not a judge.

7. Dorathy, who dyed unmarried and was buried in Thriberge Church in February, anno Domini 1648.

Sir John Reresby, son and heir of Sir George, was created baronet upon the 16 day of May 1642, married Frances, daughter of Edmond Yarburgh of Snaith Hall in the county of Yorke, Esquire. He was born in Aprill 1611. Sir George Reresby, finding the defect of schollership in himselfe, repaired it as to the education of his eldest son, whome he brought up at school, and sent him to Cambrige, wher he had continued near three years fellow commoner in Jesus College, when he was forced to return home upon the death of his father, being then near eighteen years of age. His condition as to his present fortune was narrow at the time of his marriage, and for some years after, so that his exceeding the limits of his fortune, and his saile both of lands and wood, may seem the more excusable.

The whole estate at that time was the mannor of Thriberge, lett at or about that time, as appears by rentall, bysides the

Demain lands and milns for	299	0 10	per annum.
(The old parke being computed in this at 50 l. per annum)			
Deneby Lordship lett then for	249	12 0	per annum.
Mexbrough then lett for	120	0 0	per annum.
Hoton lett at the same time for	70	17 0	per annum.
Woodlaiths then lett for	60	0 0	per annum.
Ickles and Brinsford lett for	429	8 4	per annum.
Totum	1228	18 2	

[1] He was a lover of hawkes for some time, but he left that off soon after and kept beagles, and was weary of them after a short tryall, but was ever constant to his garden. When as the Scotch warr broak out my father was major to the militia regiment within the weapontack of Strafford and Tickill and the other hundreds adjoining, the collonell of it at that time being Sir George Wentworth ; and in the year 1639 he marched to Yorke, wher the regiment was appointed to rendevous in order to their going to fight the Scotts, but the peace being concluded he went noe further. This voyage, however, was very unfortunate to him both upon the account of the expence and an ill accident that befell him, which was this :

He being in company with Mr. Rooksby (afterwards Sir William),

[1] A complete page has been torn out of the manuscript at this point.

a captain in the same regiment, and one other gentleman in a tavern in Yorke, a gentleman unknown to any in the company (being something in drinke) would force himselfe into the room, and ther behaved himselfe soe abusevely that my father thought himselfe concerned to putt him down the stairs. The gentleman makeing resistance fell down and broak his skull, and dying not long after, my father was tryed as guilty of his death, but was acquitted by the jury, the chirurgian that had him in cure deposing upon oath at the tryall that he dyed of the pox, which he had excessively upon him, and not of the wound in his head.

In the year 1642, when that that unhappy war began between the King and Parlament, though his own principles lead him to be loyall, most of the gentlemen of the nighbourhood takeing up arms for the Parlament, he considered for some time how to declare himselfe, but at the last was active in the commission of array to raise men for the King, was with my Lord Newcastle in his army, was in severall of the Kings guarisons, as Yorke, Newark, &c.; yet he never would accept of any command. However he was as much exposed in his estate, and sometimes in his person, as thos whos titles of command made them seem more active, till his being taken prisner secured him in some measure from the danger of the latter, though not of the first.

The manner of his being taken was in Bramley, as he was travelling in the night from Newarke to his own hous to see my mother, wher a partie of hors comming to quarter mett him, and one of them clapping a pistoll to his brest bid him stand and declare who he was, which he refuseing to doe, and putting spurrs to his hors, the souldier had shott him, but that by providence the pistoll only fired in the pan, but did not discharge. However being persued by the whole party he was stopt at a gate, and forced to surrender himselfe prisner. Being taken, he was conveyed to the Lord Fairfax (then generall of the Parlament forces), who committed him for some time, but at the last by the intercession of friends was prevailed with to make his own house his prison, to which he was strictly confined and under very severe penalties. This was in the year [1644].

He continued at his hous at Thriberge according to his engagement till the begining of March 1645/46, that the Kings affairs being in a desperate condition, his armys being routed, and most of his guarisons surrendered into the Parlaments hands, he obteaned leave to goe to London to compound for his estate, which was under sequestration. But finding when he came ther that he could not effect itt without takeing certain oaths which his concience would not allowe of (the Covenant being one), he returned *re infectâ*, and calling by the way at my Lord Allenton's [1] in Cambrigeshire, whom he called brother (they being dear friends, as appears by the kind letters that passed between them), he ther gott a surfitt of oisters, which with his journey putt him into a feaver, of which he dyed a fortnight after his return home, upon the [21] of Aprill, anno Domini 1646. I remember (though I was then but twelve years old) that hee desired my mother not to trouble herselfe that he had not succeeded in his business, since he was returnd with this comfort both to her and himselfe of bringing with him a safe concience.

His will bore date the 10th day of June 1643, by which he gave severall legacies, and made provisions of 60 pounds per annum as annuities to each of his yongest sonns (the yongest excepted, who was then unborn), and of 1,000 pounds to my sister Elizabeth, out of the lordship of Brinsford and Ickles, which by the strictness of law he had noe power to doe, the said mannor of Brinsford and Ickles not being only out of his present possession, but the reversion being out of him likewise, he haveing granted the said mannor to Mr. Gouldsmith and Mr. Adams, in collatarall security for my confirming their purchasses of Mexbrough and Woodlaiths, whenas I came of age, which being entailed lands he had noe power to make saile of without my concurrance. The reason that he made soe good provision for his yonger sons was the expectation, his mother being then possessed of a great part of her own estate of inheritance, that she would have left a considerable share of itt to his eldest ; but notwithstanding my disappointment as to that, and the doubt of his own capacity in law to charge the said estate, I thought myselfe obliged to perform his will in that perticular, and have constantly done it without the least scruple.

As to his person he was certainly one of the hansomest men of his time, tall, straight and well proportioned, his face very good but manlike, his hair brown and thick, his mine gentile but haughty, insoemuch that many that knew him adjudged him proud at the first sight, but found him very obligeing when once acquainted with him. He was extream active, danced in perfection, leaped further then most men, as King Charles the First did acknowlege when he leaped with him at Doncaster, going then into Scotland. He seldome used his stirrop to mount his hors, but vaulted upon him, and would frequently leap into the third saddle.

[1] William Alington of Horseheath Hall, Cambridgeshire, who had been created Baron Alington of Killard in the peerage of Ireland.

He was not less happy as to his inside then his out, haveing an extraordinary intellect, a solid judgement, a facetious witt, a hansome confidence, but a little subject to stammer or rather speake his words thick if in passion, to which he was something prompt, tho it was presently past, for he was of an extraordinary good nature. Great lamentation was made for him at his death by the country, foreseeing how much he must be wanted in severall respects, especially as to the office of justice of the peace, as to which he was both diligent and knowing, as may be seen by some charges left behind him which he gave at the sessions.

He was learned both in the Greek and Lattin tong, read and writt much, as may appear by severall things of his composure and written by his own hand now in my custodie, especially some letters, a book of characters, which are very ingenious, some verses, &c. But he is chiefly to be read in his excellent book of essays or off advice to his children, especially to me his eldest son. . . . [1]

My mother, as I have said before, was daughter of Edmond Yarburgh of Snaith Hall in the West Riding of the county of Yorke, Esquire, who married one of the daughters and coheiresses [2] of [Thomas Wormley] [3] of Bawnhall, by whom he had also issue Sir Nicholas Yarburgh ; Thomas Yarburgh, Esquire, of Campsall, barrester-at-law, a gentleman of great knowlege in the statute and civill laws, and of considerable use and assistance both to his friends and country, especially in the due and diligent execution of the office of justice of the peace ; John Yarburgh, who dyed yong ; Edmond Yarburgh, Doctor of Phisick. This branch was descended from the familie of Yarburgh of Yarburgh in Lincolnshire, the first line whereoff being now extinct, it is since become the inheritance of Sir Thomas Yarburgh, son and heir of Sir Nicholas aforesaid.

My mother brought a portion of between three and four thousand pounds to this familie, was a woeman extraordinarily hansome, endowed with a great share both of witt and judgement, was an affectionate wife, a tender mother to her children, and understood that difficult mean in her expences of doing everything with a good appearance and yet with good management, which was manifest by her paying 500 l. of my fathers debts in five years time of her widowhood and liveing plentifully at Thriberg all the time

---

[1] The dedication of the book follows, together with some description of it.

[2] Sarah, the younger daughter.

[3] Sir John leaves a blank space here.

out of noe great estate. Ther was but one thing to be objected in her perticular, which was her second mariage, haveing soe many children at the same time ; and yet she was the more excusable in this that she married a gentleman of a competent estate, one that proovd kind and just to herself and children, as also that she was but a yong widow when she changed her condition. She married James Moyser of Beaverley, Esquire, to whom she had issue four sons and one daughter, John Moyser, the yongest, only surviveing at this day.

From this point onwards the *Family History* covers practically the same ground as the *Memoirs*, and ceases to be worthy of separate notice. Sir John Reresby had seven sons, John (the author of the *Memoirs*), Tamworth, Edmund, George, Gervase, Francis and Yarburgh; and two daughters, Bridget and Elizabeth. Of these Tamworth,[1] George,[2] Francis[3] and Bridget all died young; the others are noticed in sufficient detail in the *Memoirs*. The account of his own career given by Sir John in the *Family History* is very unsatisfactory, and such portions of it as possess independent value find their appropriate place in footnotes to his larger work. Its nature is best explained by the author's own apologetic introduction:

Here possibly it may be expected that I should be more exact and perticular in the account I am now to give of myselfe then in that given of my predecessors ; to which I answer that it is easier to a painter (especially an ill one) to draw another mans picture then his own. *Seipsum noscere (multo magis representare) est difficilimum, et non est cujusvis.* A man that paints himselfe stands in his own light, soe that he is forced to take his figure from his shadow, and the glass that gives it may either flatter him or be suspected to doe soe. As to which matter that I may avoid censure by reason of mistakes which a man in this case is subject to committ in his own favour, I shall only draw the gross lines of my own little story, without any other gloss or embellishment then that of thruth, which shall be an ornament to the narrative, whatever it proove to the person.

[1] Born in April 1635 (*Family History*, ii. f. 9).

[2] " Born at Snaith. He lived to be a hansome youth and died yong " (*ibid.*, f. 10).

[3] " Born the 12th of February 1641 " (*ibid.*).

MEMOIRS OF SIR JOHN RERESBY

I was born April the 14th, Anno Domini 1634, between 1634 seven and eight in the morning,[1] in the great chamber of Thriberge Hall, in the West Rideing of the county of Yorke, the first son of Sir John Reresby, Baronet, by Frances his wife, daughter of Edmond Yarburgh of Snaith Hall, Esquire. By a fall from the window I disjointed my left knee at two years ould, which being concealed and neglected at the first could never after be reduced,[2] but being active, by exercize (as I grew up), it became near as usefull to me as the other in danceing, fenceing, or any other action performed with moderation.

My father died at the age of thirty-five years, Anno 1646 Domini 1646, haveing been taken prisner two years before by the Parlament's party and confined to his own hous, leaveing me, then twelve years of age, with four sons more and one daughter, to the care of an affectionate mother. He died endebted 1,200 l. (besides the saile of between two or three hundred pounds per annum), not thorow ill husbandry, but by reason of the warr and the narrowness of his then present fortune, ther being two great jointures out of his estate till about three years before he dyed. This put him likewise upon the saile

---

[1] " Christned by the same Lord John Darcy that was godfather to my father, Sir Francis Foljambe, and my granmother Yarburge upon the 29 day of April 1634 " (*Family History*, ii. f. 9).

[2] " Being three years of age I disjointed my left knee by the neglect of a maid, who lett me fall from a window, the cure wheroff prooveing difficult by haveing an ill bone-setter at the first, my [? time] for some years was devided between home, Lincolnshire, Sommersitshire, London, wher the fame of knowing chirurgiens or bone-setters persuaded my carefull parents to send me to seek remedie " (*ibid.*, f. 11).

of a large wood, all of it great timber, that stood in the parke.

As the late unfortunate King Charles the First passed by Rotherham,[1] brought back by the Parlament forces when sould by the treacherous Scotts, my mother sent me to wait upon him, who said I was the son of an honest man.

I lived in the country, and was instructed at home by a 1649 tutor that lived in the hous, till near the age of fifteen. By this time my mother had paid my father's debt, and then went to live at London, takeing me, my second brother, and sister[2] along with her (being then about thirty-four years of age and very hansome, soe that her greater then usuall expence in her way of liveing and her second marriage few years after was the more excusable).

Not long before my comming up to London I had broaken my left thigh in two places, which was perfectly recovered at that time.   I was soe great a lover of musique that from eight years of age I plaid all the tunes I could sing upon the violin without being taught, and soon learnt any tune that I heard.'   At London my brother Edmond and myselfe were putt to school in Whitefryers, wher I soon found the disadvantage of learning at home, many boys much yonger then myselfe being much better schollars.   We continued ther six months, and then went to a school in Endfield Chace, wher we were instructed in Latin, French, writing, and danceing.[3]   I continued ther two years, which time I endeavered to employ as well as twas possible to repair that which I had lost before, wherby I came to a very passable proficiency in Latin, Greek, rhetorick, &c.   The only defect of the school was scarcity of diet, which was none to me, my master's

---

[1] In February 1646/7.   [2] Edmund and Elizabeth.

[3] " The Blew Hous, a then famous school for gentlemen's sonns, wher Latin, French, writing and danceing were severally taught in soe good a method that they seemed noe hindrance one to another " (*Family History*, ii. f. 11).

sister (that took a perticular kindness to me) repairing
that want by suffering me to eat when I pleased.   It had
been wondered at by some, I being above seventeen years
of age at my comming from school, and fitt for the university some months before, that I was persuaded to
abide ther soe long ; but my mother's aversness to
remoove me sooner (remarried at that time to James
Moyser, Esquire, a very hansome gentlemen, but of an
indifferent fortune) made me willingly comply with her
plesure, and for this reason of my own besides, to be as
perfect as the school could make mee.

I first went from school to Thriberge, wher I continued *Sept.* 2
with my mother four months, and soon after was admitted 1651
of Trinity College in Cambrige under Doctor Duport,
my tutor ;[1] but the College not being willing to allowe
me the ranke and privilege of nobleman, by reason of an
Act of Parlament then lately made (or rather an ordinance), wherby all persons upon whom the King had conferred any honour after his leaveing the Parlament and
his going to Oxford were to be degraded,[2] my mother
rather advised me to goe to London, ther to be admitted
of Grays Inn, which I did accordingly.   Though I was
of Grays Inn I was lodeged in the Temple, to be near my
oncle Yarburgh, second brother to my mother, a then
student of that society.   It was then that my mother

[1] James Duport, one of the most famous of seventeenth-century scholars,
created D.D. of Cambridge University by royal mandate in 1660, appointed Master of Magdalene College in 1668 and Vice-Chancellor of
the University of Cambridge a year later.   In 1651 he was Fellow and
Tutor of Trinity College, and Regius Professor of Greek in the university.

[2] In November 1643 Parliament had declared void all honours conferred
by the King since May 22, 1642, on those in opposition to it.   This just
failed to include the Reresby baronetcy, which had been granted six days
earlier, and it was no doubt relying on the terms of this enactment that
Sir John prepared to go into residence at Cambridge early in 1652.   In
February of that year, however, Parliament further disallowed all honours
granted by the King since January 4, 1641/2, and Sir John, finding his
own title thus denied recognition, decided to abandon his proposed
university career altogether.

allowed me a servant, and gave me forty poundes, which
I managed soe well that it served all my expences for
1652 five months.   Here I had the small-pox, but very
favourably.   My second brother was bound apprentice
to a woollen drapier about this time.[1]

Being lett loos thus into the world I made acquintance
with severall persons, more perticularly with one Mr.
Amstrother, a relation, a gentleman lately possessed of a
good estate by the death of his mother, and then married,
but very extravagant.   A great many yonger brothers
that had noe fortunes, and reformed officers[2] of the Kings
army depended of him for their meat and drinke, he usually
paying the reckning for the whole company whilst he had
any mony, for which he had no other consideration then
flattery and a formall respect soe long as he was able to
purchass it at the rate of his estate.   My circumstances
would not allowe me to be with him and such company
ofton, nor indeed my genius, swearing, gameing, and all
manner of debeauchery being too much their passtime,
though I cannot pretend to have been at that age the most
stanche man in the world.   However, I never missed to
imploy a considerable part of the day to some sort of
study, and the exercizes of musicke and danceing, which
I then chiefly followed.

1653   In the month of August I returned to Thriberge, wher
I was used by my mother (a woeman of a great sperit)
like a minor (though wardships were then not in use);[3]
but my father in law[4] treated me with all civility and respect.

---

[1] As Edmund was born on March 28, 1636 (*Family History*, ii. f. 10),
this would be about the natural time for him to embark upon his apprentice-
ship.   The repetition of the statement concerning him under date 1658
(*infra*, p. 22) may therefore be disregarded.

[2] Officers left without commands owing to the reforming or disbanding
of their companies.

[3] Having been abolished by order of the two Houses of Parliament,
together with tenures by homage and knight service, in February 1646.

[4] Regularly used by Reresby in the sense of " step-father."

Besides my mother's jointure she claimed Poclinton leas
in Thriberge as executrix to my father, which was of
certain lands belonging to that school [1] soe intermixed with
others that it was hard to distinguish what were thos or
my own, soe that my mother gave me for my subsistance
as she pleased.

In October she consented to my return to London,
and gave me seventy poundes for my expences.   This
winter I followed my study and exercizes pritty close,
findeing going into company not soe fitt for me as others,
being naturally very jealous, especially of thos I did not
well know, and too apt to take notice of any carriage or
word that looked like a disrespect, which temper engaged
me in some quarrels very early.   One of the first was with
one Mr. Spencer, who seeming to take it ill that I drew
my sword to show it a gentleman, one Sir Thomas
Spencer, who desired to see it, we first fell to wordes, and
from that to fighting in the room, till three falling upon
me (being all the company but myselfe), my sword was
broaken and taken from me that night.   The next day
I sent him a challenge by Sir William Poultney,[2] who
accepted it at the first, but upon better thoughts sent a
gentleman with the offer of any other satisfaction rather
then fighting, which I was prevailed with by Mr.
Anstrother to accept, on condition that he made publique
submission before the same company and such others as
I should appoint to be ther, wher the whole company was
to be entertained at his charge, which he willingly
accepted and performed accordingly.

Though I loved reading, and kept what I had learnt,

[1] Pocklington Grammar School, founded in 1514.   Pocklington is in
the East Riding, sixteen miles south-east of York.   The lands belonging
to the school were first brought to the Reresby family by the Sir Thomas
who mortgaged their Derbyshire estates.   " He tooke the leas of Poclinton
School lands in Thriberge, which hath been of good use to the familie, at
the rent of 24 l. a year and 20 l. fyne " (*Family History*, i. f. 45).

[2] Possibly the grandfather of the famous statesman of the eighteenth
century.   This Sir William, however, was not knighted until 1660.

yet I found but very little progress in my studies for want
of some able person to direct me in that perticular.
Besides, I found ther was little means of improovement
for a gentleman as to other respects in England, the
nobility and gentlemen of the best ranke and estates
liveing retired in the country, to avoid the jealousies of
the then suspicious goverment of every act or word that
could be construed in favour of the royall familie, wherby
to draw them into the dangers and forfitures of delin-
quencie.   And such as lived in town were either such
zealots in the rebellious, scismaticall superstitions of thos
times, or soe very debauched on the other hand, that it was
very hard for a yong man to avoid infection on one side
or the other.

Thes considerations wrought not only upon me to
aske, but upon my mother to allowe me leave to goe to
1654 travell.   I sett forward for France in Aprill[1] 1654, being
then twenty years of age, Cromwell haveing the year
before declared his ambition in the dismission of the late
Parlament,[2] the calling of another,[3] in the subdueing of
Ireland, and makeing the army entirely at his devotion,
by which he did as he pleased in the three kingdoms.
My friends recommended to me for gouvernor or con-
ductour in this voyage one Mr. Leech, a devine, a late
fellowe of a college in Cambrige,[4] a very good man and a
great schollar, to whos care and instruction I confess I
owe the few improvements I attained to in point of learning and morals.

[1] On April 15 (*Family History*, ii. f. 11).

[2] The Long Parliament, the expulsion of which by Cromwell on
April 20, 1653, meant the destruction of the last vestige of lawful authority
in England.

[3] The Little Parliament or Barebone's Parliament, which first met on
July 4, 1653.

[4] William Leeche, matriculated sizar from Magdalene College, Michaelmas 1621; B.A., 1625-6; M.A., 1629; B.D., 1636; Fellow till 1644,
when he was ejected (J. and J. A. Venn, *Alumni Cantabrigienses*, iii. 68).

I have writt a small treatess of my travels formerly,[1]
and therfore shall only briefly touch upon such things as
most nearly related to me abroad, or were therin wholly
omitted.   We passed by the way of Rie and Diepe, and
thence to Paris by Rhoan.   At Paris I see the King, the
Duke of Yorke, and Prince Robert [2] playing at billiards
in the Palais Royal, but was incognito, it being crime
sufficient the waiting upon his Majesty to have caused
the sequestration of my estate, had it been known to
Cromwell.   I stayed noe longer in Paris then to gett my
cloaths and to recieve my bils of exchange, and soe went
to live in pension or boarding hous at Bloys.   The Duke
of Orlians,[3] the only brother of the late King Louis the
13th, lived at Bloys at the same time, wher his whole diversion was his garden, furnished with the greatest variety
of plantes and flowers of any place of Europe.   One
Maurison, a Scotchman, was his herbalist.   I imployed
my time here in learning the language, the ghittar, and
danceing, till July ; and then, ther haveing been some *July*
likelyhood of a quarrell between me and a Duch gentleman in the same hous, my governor prevailed with me
to goe live at Saumure [4] with one Mr. Lech (afterwards
Sir Robert Lech), a relation to my governor that had
followed us from England to travell in our company.
At Saumurs, of addition to the exercizes I learnt at

[1] Presumably the treatise printed in 1813 in *The Memoirs and Travels
of Sir John Reresby, Bart.* The original manuscript of the *Travels*
cannot now be traced.

[2] Since the close of the civil wars Prince Rupert, in command of a
royalist fleet, had been preying on English commerce, but he spent more
than a year in France between March 1653 and June 1654 before settling
for the remainder of the Commonwealth period in Germany.

[3] Gaston, Duke of Orleans, a prominent figure in the Fronde, which had
come to an end less than two years before Reresby met him.   He was the
father of a famous daughter, Anne Marie Louise de Montpensier, *la
Grande Mademoiselle.*

[4] Chosen probably as one of the two towns where the French Protestants
were allowed to have a university.

Bloys, I learnt to fence and to play of the lute. Besides that, I studyed philosophy and the mathematiques with my gouvernor, who read lectures of each to me every other day.

1655   After eight months stay I had gott soe much of the language to be able to converse with some ladys in the town, especially the daughters of Monsieur du Plessis. One of them, called Madmoiselle de Boragan, sent for me one night to wait on her to a ball, wher a gentleman, being her servant, grew soe jealous of her comming with me, and of the civilities I performed towards her, that he challenged me that night to fight him the next day.   I came accordingly to the place and at the time appointed, but he was hindered by some of his own friends, who suspected the thing, and afterwards wee were made friends, but the lady would see him noe more.

April   In that month I began to make the little tour or circuit of France, and returned to Saumurs after some six weeks absence.

July   I went (desirous to avoid much English company then resident at Saumurs) to Mans, the capitall town of Mayenne, with the two Mr. Leche's and one Mr. Butler. We lodged and were in pension at the parson's or minister's hous ; ther were then noe strangers. Ther was severall persons of quality (French) that lived ther at that time, as the Marquis de Cognè his widow, the Marquis de Verdun, and severall others, who made us partakers of the pastimes and diversions of the place. All that winter few weeks did pass that ther were not balls three times at the least, and we had the freer accesse by reason that the woemen were more numerous then the men.

1656   I stayed ther till Aprill 1656, and then returned to Saumur with my governor alone. My two companions went to Paris. Severall persons of quality of the country comming to Saumur's fair, I fell ther acquainted with Madam du Terra, wife to a gentleman of 4,000 livers a year, a yong lady well accomplisht as to singing and playing of the chittar, but especially danceing. I had then an English boy that plaid perfectly well of the bag-pipe, that I carried after with me through all my travels (a sort of musicke more to be liked for the extraordinari-ness of it abroad then the exactness), whom shee took great pleasure to hear. After that acquaintance soe begun she came ofton to Saumur, and I was ofton invited to their hous in the country, wher the husband recieved me with all kindness.

One day, goeing to wait upon her to the walkes in the medows beyond Saumur Bridge (the rendevous of persons of quality in sommer evenings), noe person in company with her but Madmoyselle de la Jeauniere, her sister, a gentleman of the town (a Frenchman), being in drinke, lett fall some words which reflected upon her, speakeing them soe audebly that I see she heard them as well as myselfe ; but neither of us took notice of them to each other. The next morning I sent him a challenge by one Mr. Harwood, an English gentleman, which he refused to answer. The day following I took my friend and a servant with me, and meeting him as he came from mass gave him severall blows with a cudgell, which he went his way with without drawing his sword.

The night after, three or four of us being together in the street when it began to be dark (going to give a serenade to some of our acquaintance), the said gentleman with ten or twelve more sett upon us with their swords drawn, which obliged us to defend ourselves as well as we could, but retreating all the while, till we gott into a hous without much harm, and then they fled. The day following I had notice that my adversary had taken the law to his secound, that he had taken out processe or an arrest against me, and that if he seizd me he would lay me in prison and make me pay considerable dammages for the batteries before I could be released. This hapned very unhappily to one that expected monys from England, and had none to remoove with, or any conveniencie, which obliged me to repair to Monsieur de Cominge, then governor of the castle, who infinitely disapprooved of the Frenchman's carriage and gave me sanctuary ther for some days.

June   My mony not being yet come, and not thinkeing it safe to stay longer ther, I went to Thoars, the seat and residence of the Duke de la Tremoulle (then Governor of Britaigne), seven leags from Saumure, wher I lived in a private hous some six weeks, ofton waiting on the Duke. He was soe civill to me that he tould me noe arrest should be ther executed upon me, invited me to dinner, took me ofton abroad with him on horsback to take the air ; but the Duchess, being a rigid Protestant, and suspecting that ther was a greater kindness between Madam du Terra and me then ther really was (for she was a near nighbour to that place), seemed more reserved towards me.

July   My letters of exchange came to hand the latter end of July, and then I resolved to see Italie, and at the same time to turn off my governour, Mr. Lech (my allowance not being sufficient to defray the charges of soe many in that voyage),[1] though I parted with him unwillingly, and shall ever own the blessing of being soe long under the conduct of soe learned and soe pious a man.   I went first to Saumurs, and soe cross the country without guide or company, only my footman, first to Tours, then to Bourge, Bourbon (the famous spaw or bath), Moulins (famous for the manufacture of scissars and other edge tools), and soe to Lyons, hireing hackney horses from town to town.

I stayed at Lyons three months, wher I mett Sir Charles Shelley, my cozen,[2] Sir William Wiseman,[3] and Sir Edward

---

[1] " My allowance abroad being but two hundred pounds a year, and my governor his sallary and maintenance amounting to a moytie of it " (*Family History*, ii. f. 12).

[2] The second baronet, of Michelgrove, Sussex.   His grandmother was Jane, eldest sister of Sir George Reresby.

[3] Of Canfield Hall, the second baronet.

Maunsell of Wales,[1] and severall other English, who intended for Italie as well as myselfe.   I made a perticular acquaintance with a nun of the Carmelite Convent, a woeman of witt and beauty, which helped to pass away the time whilst I stayed ther.   I learnt of the famous du Rut of the lute all that time.   The Duke de Guise[2] was sent in September to recieve the Queen of Swede[3] *September* from the French King, who had quitted her religion and kingdome not long before, and now came from Italie to see France.

The news came as we were ready to sett forward for Italy that the plague (which twas hoped would abate towards winter) did very much spred, and was now violent in Rome, which discouraged all the gentlemen from makeing that journey but only one, Mr. Berry of Canterbury, two Italians, and myselfe, for I resolved to trust to Providence rather then not see soe fine a place, haveing but that opportunity for it, and understanding that language already pritty well.   I had had a quarrell with this Mr. Berry formerly at Saumure.   We fell out at play, and I gave him a box on the ear, for which he challenged me, and as we were going to fight the gover-nour, hearing of it, sent and prevented us and made us friends.

We sett forward the 18 of October, and agreed with *Oct. 18* a messenger or *procaccio* to conduct us with horses and all other nescessarys for our journey from Lyons to Padua, which was the worst way, but we were forced to goe it, ther being noe other passage opon by reason of the

---

[1] Probably Sir Edward Mansel, fourth baronet, of Margam, Glamorgan-shire, who represented Glamorgan in Parliament under Charles II and James II.

[2] Louis Joseph, great-grandson of that Henry, Duke of Guise, who played a prominent part in the Massacre of St. Bartholomew, and was assassinated in 1588.

[3] Christina, daughter of Gustavus Adolphus, who ascended the Swedish throne on his death in 1632, and in 1654 abdicated in favour of her cousin Charles X.

plague.   From Lyons we first went to Geneva (soe famous
for the residence and preaching of Calvin, one of the first
authors of the Reformation), from thence to Zurich and
severall other considerable towns in Switserland, soe
thorow the three cantons of Rhaetia (or the country of the
Grysons), soe to Valtalina, wher we entered the state of
Venice and passed thorow Bressa, Bergamo, Verona, all
fine cittys, the last though the most famous for its amphi-
theater, one of the most entire and magnificent Roman
structures of that kind in all Italie.   The Alpes are the
worst to pass this way of any other, and the danger the
greatest for the banditti ; but by good fortune many of
them had been kild the day before we passed near Bergamo,
in a combate between them and severall of the country that
had risen on purpose to disperse them, soe that we passed
safe without injurie either to our persons or purses, which
few had done that way for some time before.

Nov. 13   We arrived at Padua the 13th, but with great difficulty
upon another account, for all places being very fearfull of
infection in a time of the plague, we were stopped at
every town and village till we produced our letters of
health (or passes from one place to another), which we
were forced to take from the officers of every town to
show what way we had passed.   And none was suffered
to enter without thes, but he must make quarantain, or
abide in the pest hous forty days, to show he was free from
the plague.

At Padua we learnt that the infection rather encreased
then otherways at Rome, Naples, Genua, &c., soe that
the passes and commerce continuing shutt up it would
be impossible to look that way for this winter.   Ther
were some English gentlemen in that University then,
some students of the civill law, others of phisique.[1]   Of

---

[1] The influx of English students to the University of Padua had begun
as early as the sixteenth century. Sir Francis Walsingham had studied
law there, and William Harvey, the discoverer of the circulation of the
blood, had studied medicine.

these were Mr. John Finch, brother to the since Earl of
Nottingham and Lord Chancellor, and himselfe since
embassador at Constantinople to our King.[1] He was
Syndique ther in that year, an office like that of vice-
chancellor in our universitys.[2] Mr. Berry putt ourselves
into the way of liveing for strangers in that place, which
was takeing lodgeings in a hous with some other English,
wher everyone contributed soe much weekly, and performed the part of stuard and bought provisions in their
turns, which is easily performed ther by strangers, noe
man demandeing more then the settled price by the
magistrates for his commodity.

I passed this winter ther and at Venice (where I went
often) very pleasantly. The exercize I followed was
chiefly musique. My studys were the language and the
mathematicks, for which science ther was an admirable
master, especially for fortification.[3] I followed also
fenceing and danceing, but in a quite different method
to that of France.

We had scarse been ther one month when my comrade
Mr. Berry fell in love with a curtisan, daughter to the
landlady of the hous, that came accidentally to visit her
mother from Venice, wher she was kept by a Dutch
marchant. But the terms Mr. Berry offered her were
soe much better then thos of her former lover that she
accepted the latter, and lived privately in the hous as his

[1] John Finch and his elder brother Heneage, who was created Earl of
Nottingham in 1681, were sons of Sir Heneage Finch, Speaker of the
House of Commons in the first Parliament of Charles I. John took the
degree of M.D. at Padua, was knighted in 1661, appointed ambassador at
Constantinople in 1672, and died in November 1682, a few weeks before
his brother.

[2] Padua, however, like its parent university, Bologna, was a student
university, and the syndics, of whom there were two, one chosen from the
faculty of law and the other from that of medicine, were elected by the
students.

[3] " I was matriculated (or admitted) of that university, wher I studyed
the mathematicks, especially fortification " (*Family History*, ii. f. 12).

mistriss, her father and mother consenting to the happy disposall of their daughter. The quean was hansome and subtile, and gained soe entirely upon him that in a short time she managed him and his as she pleased. In the time of carnaval we went to Venice, wher he took a hous for his misse, and furnished it from the Jews at soe much weekly according to the custome.

One day, going to the Piatza of St. Marke (wher all people mett after dinner in mascarade, and that person thinkes himselfe happyest that findes himselfe most followed for being the most extravagant in dresse, &c.), I putt my boy that plaid of the bagpipes into two peticoats, one over his shoulders, the other about his wast, that playing as he went nothing could be percieved of that instrument save the sound, which did soe much surprize (that country not affording any of that musick) that I had the whole croud after me that day, and the boy had like to have been pulled in pieces to find out the thing, though generally they doe offer noe violence to persons in disguise.

Mar. 26 We returned to Padua. I endeavoured then all I
1657 could to persuade my comrade to quitt his mistrisse, that we might travel into some other part of the country ; and the better to gain him I privately made love to her, intending if I gained her to tell him of her inconstancy as an argument to persuade him to leave her, and in case she proov'd cruell and tould of me then to persuade him that I only attempted it as a proofe of her for his service. The whoor being subtile seemed to consent to meet me at such a time and place, but begd of me a bended jacobus which I used to wear about my arme well known to Mr. Berry, but as soon as he came in tould him the whole story, which I being jealous of overheard, harkning behind the wainscot, their chamber joining upon mine. She aggravated the story with all the ill circumstances immaginable, tould him I had spoaken ill of him and lessened him in severall perticulars to magnifie myselfe, and

that according to the use and custome of that country
noebody could pardon such an attempt and soe managed,
and that it deserved noe less a revenge then the loss of
my life, for it was her business to make a breach and
seperation between us that she might keep him to herselfe.

Seing the thing carryed to this height I sent for
Mr. Berry early the next morning, and without takeing
notice of what I had heard tould him that after findeing
noe argument could prevaile with him to leave that
woeman I had the day before endeavoured to persuade
her to be faulse to him, not with intention to lie with her,
but to use it as a persuasion not to loos his time any
longer in staying with soe perfidious a slutt ; and to show
that all this was true she had promissed to comply with
me such a day and in such a place, which I was sure she
could not deny.   At this he tooke me in his armes, telling
me she had tould him the story, but he was satisfyed now
that it was with noe ill intention towards him, and it
should make noe difference between us.   This made
him, however, something cooler towards his woeman,
not knowing but she might have tould least I should tell
first.   And she grew soe angry at me that she gave me
something lying in her mother's hous which had like to
have killed me, being sick severall days of a disease that
had the symtomes of poison.

The passage being now opon to Florance by the way   *April* 16
of Bologna and Ferrara, I persuaded him at the last to
goe thither with me.   We found it very difficult to travell
by reason of the plague, every town wher we came
refuseing us entrance, least we should have come from
some infected place, till we produced our bills of health,
which we had at all places as we past ; for if anybody
wanted them they were either put into the pest hous for
forty days or sent back from whence he came ; and sometimes they were shott by the sentrys, as a Duchman had
been not long before at Bologna, entering at the gate
without produceing his bill of health, thinkeing that he

had left it ; but after he was kild it was found slipt
thorow a hole in his pockit into his drawers. In few
days we got to Florence, of whos advantages as to its
palaces, greatness, and scituation I have made large mention in the book of my travels.

Ferdinand the 2nd was then the Great Duke,[1] a man of
great sence, but not personable, who had then parted beds
from his Duchesse,[2] a beautifull woeman, being jealous one
of another. He was very civill to strangers, especially
the English. He had a great correspondency with the
Protector, fearing his power at sea. I had ofton accesse
to him. Amongst other times, as he was playing at pell
mell, he red a letter to me of news which he had not long
before recieved from England ;[3] and another time,
going to see his country hous called Poggio Achaiano,
he sent me and my company with two dishes of fish and
twelve bottles of rare wine.

May 10 One day as I was practiceing on the lute Mr. Berry
came to me, and saying something that displeased me,
I gave him a sharp answer, which put him into that heat
that he tould me he had not forgott the old affront which
I once did him to give him a box on the ear ; besides I
had robbed him of his greatest satisfaction in this world
in persuadeing him to leave his mistrisse at Padua ; and
that he expected I should give him immediate satisfaction
with my sword in my hand. Findeing that it was not
to be avoided, I went with him out of one of the gates,
wher as we were going to draw our swords one Mr. Kent,
one that laid in the same hous, that had overheard our
dispute and apprehending the consequence, came with
two more gentlemen and parted us, and that evening made
us good friends.

[1] Ferdinand II, Grand Duke of Tuscany 1621-70, the patron of science.

[2] Victoria, Princess of Urbino.

[3] " Finding that I had learnt the language passably well [he] did ofton
discours me as to our home affairs, which were then the miracle, as Cromwell the terrour, of the whole world " (*Family History*, ii. f. 12).

We stayed a fortnight togather after this, and then went severall ways, he to renew his old amour at Venise, and I to see such other parts of Italy as ther was any accesse to by reason of the plague, as Pisa, Pistoya, Lygorne, wher I recieved great civilities from English marchants. After some short stay ther I returned to Florence, wher, dispaireing to see more of Italy, the sickness encreaseing at Rome, Genua, Naples, &c., with the heats, I went by sea to Venise,[1] wher I arrived in July, and parted from *July 28* thence and Italy (wher I had constantly followed the exercises of danceing, musique, fenceing, and the study of mathematiques) the 6 day of August for Germany, to *August 6* see the election of the new Emperor, the old one being dead not two months before,[2] in company of two French gentlemen, a high German of the town of Elbin, and my own boy.

From Venice we went to Mestra, soe to Trent (famous for the Generall Councill held ther), soe to Inspruck, the capitall citty of Tyrole, wher the Archduchesse then dwelt, and her fair daughter, since marryed to the Emperor.[3] I had the curiosity, and the company from thence, to goe out of our way to see Munkn in Bavaria, wher that Elector[4] keeps his court in the finest palace of that part of the world. Osbourg was the next citty of note that we passed thorow, an imperiall or hans town, famous for its fortifications, buildings, and the preaching of Luther ther. In four days we gott from thence to Francfurt, the place destined for the election of the Emperor. Severall times we were much straitned for

[1] By Bologna and Ferrara, and then down the Po to Chioggia, where he took ship (*Memoirs and Travels*, pp. 99-100).

[2] The old Emperor was Ferdinand III, who had died on March 23/ April 2, 1657.

[3] Anne, daughter of Cosimo II, Grand Duke of Tuscany, was the wife of the Archduke Ferdinand Charles, Count of Tyrol. Her daughter Claudia Felicitas, suggested as a second wife for James Duke of York in 1673, married the Emperor Leopold I.

[4] Ferdinand Maria, Elector of Bavaria 1651-79.

lodgeing and diet thes last days journey, the country lying much ruined and uninhabited since the last warrs in thos parts.[1]

I passed the time that I stayed here divertingly enough, the embassadours of France and Spain, thos of severall electours and other princes of the Empire haveing made very splendid entrys, each of them contending to outdoe one another in gallantry and entertainments ; but Monsieur le Duc de Grammond and Monsieur de Lyone,[2] both joined in commission from the French King, much exceeded the rest.   The want of the language and the too great plenty of liquor (which is too much imposed upon strangers in that country) was the most troublesome.

Oct. 10 I stayd ther till October the 10th, when findeing that a great many difficultys relating to the interests of different princes must be first reconciled before the election could be,[3] I began my journey for Holland down the river Rhyne, wher passing by Mentz, Coln, Wesele, Schenkenscans, Neiumegn, and many more considerable places, I arrived safe with some Duch gentlemen of my
20 company at Rotterdame, October 20th.   Here I left the great boats and my company, and went with my boy in a passage boat to Delph, and soe for the Hague.

That night I went to a French play, putting on a good suit of cloaths which I had gott made by the French embassador's tailer at Francfurt, wher were the Princess Royall,[4] the Queen of Bohemia,[5] &c.   I kissed the

[1] The Thirty Years' War, which had come to an end nine years before this.

[2] Antoine, Duc de Gramont, and Hugues de Lionne, best known as Minister for Foreign Affairs to Louis XIV from 1663 to 1671.

[3] The election did not actually take place till nearly a year later, Leopold, the son of Ferdinand III, being unanimously chosen Emperor on July 8/18, 1658.

[4] Mary, eldest daughter of Charles I of England and widow of William II of Orange.

[5] Elizabeth, daughter of James I of England and widow of Frederick V, Elector Palatine, the " Winter King " of Bohemia.

Princesse of Orang her hand that night by another name,
whom I had the honour to entertain in French (which I
spoke very readily) for some time, but did not own myselfe
to be an Englishman, for fear I might have paid dear at
home for that compliment should it have been known to
the Protector.   The fear of being discovered made me
leave that agreable place the next day, to goe for Anster-
dam by the way of Harlam by boat.

Haveing spent about ten days to see the most considerable parts of Holland, I went to visit Flanders by
the way of Anwarpe by boat.   Ther rose soe great a
storm after we had passed Dort that the mast was broaken,
and we were driven soe farr out to sea that we gott not to
harbour of five days.   Besides, we had laid but in provision for four days, soe that we had near been starved
had we not mett with a boat of mussles, which, without
either bread or drinke, I thought the best meat I ever eat.
The old Duke of Newcastle (though then but Marquisse) [1]
lived at Antwarpe at that time of his banishment, but I
durst not visit him for fear of being discovered.

I stayed ther two days, then went for Brussels in the
boat of common passage.   I met therin with Mr.
Howard, brother to the Duke of Norfolke, since Cardinal
Howard,[2] who takeing me for a Frenchman would needs
tell me all the story of our English civill warrs, his own
and families sufferings therby, which I knew as well as
himselfe.   I putt myselfe in pention at Brussels, wher
I passed for a Frenchman ; only I ran the hazard of being
found out ofton by my footman, who could never learn
any language well but his own.   Don John of Austria,

---

[1] William Cavendish, governor of Charles II when Prince of Wales, and
chief representative of the royalist cause in the north during the Civil War.
He was created Duke of Newcastle in 1665 and died in 1676.

[2] Philip Thomas Howard, third son of Henry Frederick, third Earl of
Arundel.   His elder brothers, Thomas and Henry, were successively
fifth and sixth Duke of Norfolk.   He was raised to the cardinalate in
1675.

then Governor of the Netherlands,[1] lived ther, and the Prince of Conde,[2] who lived in some splendour. But the King of England could not live up to their height, being banished also then out of France at the instance of Cromwell ; and the pention formerly allowed him from that Crown was withdrawn, soe that his Majesty then subsisted ther at the charge chiefly of the King of Spain.[3]

Nov. 24
[16]57

I embarked for Llussing, wher I was forced to abide till the first of January, and then found an opportunity of passage for St. Valery in France, with three Frenchmen and my boy ; but by very bad weather I was driven to a little village in Normandie called Calleuz. We hired a cart ther that carryed us ten miles to Diepe, and from

Jan. 6
1657[/8]

thence we gott to Paris in three days upon the 6 of January. I putt myselfe ther into a pension (wher ther were none but Frenchmen, most of them officers of the army) in the Isle of the Palace. I passed the winter very well, and gott a great many French acquaintance, and went sometimes to the French Court, and as ofton to the Queen Mother of England[4] as I durst. I followed here the exercizes of musick, fenceing, danceing, and mathematiques as before.

One day, walkeing over Pontneuf, and haveing a belt with large sylver buckles, a man well dressed, as he

[1] Don John of Austria, natural son of Philip IV of Spain by Maria Calderon, an actress, was Governor of the Spanish Netherlands from 1656 to 1659.

[2] Louis II of Bourbon, " the Great Condé," victor of Rocroi and Lens, and one of the most famous of French commanders. During the troubles of the Fronde he had formed an alliance with Spain, and he remained faithful to his country's enemies until the conclusion of the Peace of the Pyrenees in 1659.

[3] Charles II had left France in the summer of 1654, when the growing friendship between Cromwell and Mazarin made it clear that his expulsion was imminent, and after two years spent mainly at Köln had settled first at Bruges and then at Brussels. His alliance with Spain was formed in the spring of 1656.

[4] Henrietta Maria, sister of Louis XIII of France and widow of Charles I of England.

came after me, rubbed a little upon me as he passed by, and soe persued his way, but I thought a little faster then ordinary.   Another following after (but not of his company) tould me my belt was cutt behind, and the buckle was gone with the part which was cutt.   This gave me presently suspicion that it was the man gone just before, though his appearance and dress (for he had a sword and a good cloake) spoake him noe man to doe such an action. However, I thought the best way to succeed was to be bould, soe overtakeing him I drew my sword and bid him restoor my buccle which he had cutt off, which without any denyall he produced and restoored, begging that I would not expose him to publique shame, but lett him goe.   After some few stripes with the flatt of my sword I lett the rascall run his way, and the rabble shouting after him.   I tooke two French footmen to wait on me, and turned my English boy into page, and lived as hansomly as I could till I went for England, a man's respect ther being only suitable to his equipage and way of liveing.

I returned for England by the way of Diepe, being not *May* 10 very well.[1] My mother was then at London, and was 1658 very pressing with me to marry, offering me some fortunes, more perticularly Mrs. Hotham,[2] worth as it was believed 3,000 l., and who had more kindness for me then I desired, haveing not the same for her, insomuch that some years after she being suspected to have a bastard, I was thought to be the father, though very undeservedly.   She after married the hier of the family of Cooper, of Nottinghamshire.[3]

The citizens and common people of London had then

[1] " Soon after my arrivall I fell ill of a could and an ague, which continued long with me and reduced me to great weakness " (*Family History*, ii. f. 12).

[2] Sarah, daughter of Sir John Hotham, the first baronet and Parliamentary leader, executed in 1645 for intriguing with the King.

[3] Cecil Cooper of Thurgarton.

soe far imbibed the custome and manners of a Commonwealth that they could scarce endure the sight of a
gentleman, soe that the common salutation to a man well
dressed was " French dog," or the like.   Walkeing one
day in the street with my valet de chambre, who did wear
a feather in his hatt, some workemen that were mending
the street abused him and threw sand upon his cloaths, at
which he drew his sword, thinkeing to follow the custome
of France in the like cases.   This made the rabble fall
upon him and me, that had drawn too in his defence, till
we gott shelter in a hous, not without injury to our bravery
and some blowes to ourselves.

Ther was little satisfaction in that town in thos days.
Ther was noe court made to Oliver but by his own party,
and then only in case of business or by the officers of the
army.   Ther were noe comodys or other diversions
(which were forbidden not only as ungodly, but for fear
of drawing company or nombers togather), and ther was
noe business for any man that loved monarchy or the
family of Stuard ; soe that the nobility and gentry lived
most in the country.   Nor were thos of the royall party
more secure ther then in the citty, ther being spies in all
places upon their words and actions.

August 6   I went for Yorkshire and wintered with my father in
law, who had left Thriberge and then lived in Yorke.   I
was very ill all that winter.   My second brother Edmond
was bound prentice about this time to a woollen draper,
my third brother Jarvage[1] to a Spanish marchant.

Sept. 3   Died the Protector, Oliver Cromwell, one of the
greatest and bravest men (had his caus been good) that
the world ever produced.   For his actions, I leave them
to be enquired after in history.   For his person, haveing
never seen him very near but once (at the audience of an

---

[1] " Born the 6 of November 1640, little but well proportioned, one of
an active and ingenious speritt. . . .   He and I did soe much ressemble
each other that we have sometimes been taken one for another " (*Family
History*, ii. f. 10).

embassador in Whitehall),[1] I can only give this discription of him, that his figure did noe ways promisse what he performed.   He was personable, but not hansome, nor did he look great nor bould.   He was plain in his apparell, and rather affected a negligence then a gentile garbe. He had tears at his will, and was certainly the greatest dissembler upon earth.

His son Richard, who was a gentleman that lived altogather in the country and was not acquainted with such politiques, was proclaimed Protector in his room. He was confirmed by a Parlament which he called, wher the Scotch representatives sate as well as the English ; but this Parlament not pleasing his Highnesse was soon dissolved,[2] and himselfe did not long survive them, the officers of the army, the chiefe of which were Lambert,[3] Okey,[4] and Desbrough,[5] &c., causeing the remainder of the old Parlament of 1640 to be called again,[6] which for the small nomber was called the Rump.   His Highness was content to lay down his dignity,[7] and all affairs were next governed by a council of state, consisting of the officers of the army and some select members of Parlament or the Rump.

[1] " Publique audience to the Spanish embassadour, whom he received with as much distance and ceremony as if he had been the greatest of kings " (*Family History*, ii. f. 13).

[2] The Parliament met on January 27, 1659.   It proved favourable to Richard, but quarrelled with the army, under pressure from which it was dissolved on April 22.

[3] John Lambert had been deprived of all his commands in 1657, but his reputation with the army was so great that in April 1659 his commissions had to be restored, and he played a prominent part in subsequent events.

[4] John Okey had been cashiered for opposing the settlement effected by the Instrument of Government, and was not reinstated until after the recall of the Long Parliament.

[5] John Desborough, who had married Oliver Cromwell's sister Jane.

[6] It reassembled on May 7, 1659.

[7] His submission was communicated to Parliament on May 25.

The Duke of Buckingham,[1] who had been with the King the greatest part of his banishment, had disobliged and left his Majesty in Flanders some time before, and was now in England endeavouring to marry the daughter and heiresse of Thomas Lord Fairfax, formerly generall of the Parlaments army, to whom was given the greatest part of the said Duke's estate, in consideration of his service to the State.[2]   He was the finest gentleman of person and witt I thinke I ever see, but could not be long serious or mind business.   He behaved himselfe with some insolency towards his Majesty, which was the caus of their quarrell.   I was first acquainted with him at this time.   He expressed a kindness towards me from the first time I see him.

August 1   This year ther was a generall plott or conspiracy to
1659   rise in arms in the northern parts of England amongst the loyall party, and to declare for a free Parlament, hopeing such a Parlament might restoor the King.   Sir George Both[3] was the chiefe in this business ; but the design was discovered before it took the right effect, and severall of the principall persons were seized and putt into the Tower.   I was very ill at that time.

My fathers third sister, Elizebeth, first married to Sir Francis Foljambe of Aldwarke[4] (by whom she had noe issue),

---

[1] George Villiers, second Duke of Buckingham.

[2] Thomas, third Baron Fairfax of Cameron, appointed Parliamentary commander-in-chief in 1645 by the ordinance for new modelling the army, had resigned in 1650 rather than take part in the invasion of Scotland, and spent the remaining twenty years of his life in retirement at Nun Appleton in Yorkshire.   His only child, Mary, married Buckingham on September 15, 1657, and the Duke thus eventually united the estates and territorial influence enjoyed in Yorkshire by Fairfax and by his own father, the favourite of James I.

[3] Sir George Booth, created first Baron Delamere in 1660.   Reresby speaks of the conspiracy as though it were confined to the north, but it was intended to be a general movement.   August 1 was the day fixed for the rising.

[4] The first baronet, then a widower.   He died in 1640.

then to Mr. Horner,[1] yonger son to Sir John Horner of Somersetshire (to whom she bore one only daughter that survived,[2] married to Sir Roger Martin of Suffolk), then to my Lord Monson,[3] one of this Rump Parlament, was a very notable woeman, only she was a little too masculine. By means of this marriage our family enjoyed a passable indulgence, the wife haveing power to doe what she pleased with her husband, and his lordship haveing power to prevaile with his brother members and the governors of that time for his friends as they desired. But soe soon as that power did abate, this lady, my ant (haveing born one daughter [4] to my Lord Monson, since married to Sir Phillip Hungate of Yorkshire, and haveing sufficiently enriched herselfe by severall jewels and a great part of his personall estate), did seperate herselfe from him ; and he, running himselfe into a great debt, turned himselfe over into the King's Bench, wher he was found at the Kings restoration, and was tryed and condemned as a traitor by Act of Parlament for being one of the Kings judges in the High Court of Justice. But his sentence did not extend to execution, only to be carried upon a hurdle with a rope about his neck to the place of execution, and to imprisonment for life and forfiture of estate. He lived till the year 1673. After his death the King was pleasd, at my intercession, and in consideration that my family had been ever loyall, to restoor my ant to her honour of Vicecountesse Monson of Ireland, her husband haveing forfited his title and degree of Vicecount Monson of Castlemain of that kingdome by his attainder. This lady at sixty years of age married Adam Felton, Esquire, for her fourth husband, son of Sir Henry Felton, Baronet,

---

[1] Edward Horner, of Mells, Somerset.   [2] Tamworth.

[3] Sir William Monson, created Viscount Monson of Castlemaine in 1628. Although nominated one of the judges at the trial of Charles I, he refused to take part in the final proceedings, and later declared that his object in serving at all was to save the King. Elizabeth Reresby was his third wife.

[4] Elizabeth.

of Suffolke,[1] of some twenty-four years of age, an action noe way suitable to the former conduct of her life.

This year I entered to the only estate I had, which was Thriberge, then letten for three hundred fifty five pounds a year, or therabouts (the rest being then in jointure to my mother and granmother); and the lease of Poclinton landes in Thriberge falling to my mother as executrix, I was forced to purchass at the price of all arrears due to me from my mother as guardian to me during my minority, which I knew was not an equall consideration for it, the arrears upon an exact account being 2,000 l. at the least, and the leas being of much less value. But I ever had a reverence for my mother, was unwilling to be at difference with her and my father in law, a very civill gentleman, one that never medled with his wives fortune, and thos lands were soe very nescessary to me that I could not well improove or make advantage of the rest of my landes in Thriberge without them.

My annuall expences in relation to my estate were thes:

	£	S	D
The charge of keeping the gardens -	25	0	0
That of my parke - - - -	10	0	0
My bailifs wages - -- - -	10	0	0
The rent of Poclinton - - -	24	0	0
A rent charge out of Thriberge to one Constable - - - -	32	0	0
Besides repairs of the hous, assesments and other dues and accidentall charges, which might well be computed at - -	30	0	0
Totum disbursement -	131	0	0
Totum estate - - -	355	0	0
Soe that the clear estate for subsistance was only - - -	224	0	0

[1] Adam succeeded his father as third baronet in 1690.

I was at London some part of this sommer, wher by *Aug.* 12 the disputes between our new governours, the ambition of some and jealosies of others, the dislike of the Parlaments proceeding on one hand and the haughty and insolent demeanour of the officers of the army on the other, it was easy to decern that a door was oponing for the Kings return into England. And yet to showe the effect of fear, for all the Rump and the army were even detested by the generallity of the nation as well as all Christendome, yet were they congratulated in their new power from all forraign princes and from all counties and corporations of England ; and I was present at a dinner given to Lambert and other officers of the army at the charge of the citty of London, which was more costly and splendid then any one of thos many which I have since seen given by that citty to his Majesty, soe much more is awe prevelent then love.

Not continuing well as to my health and the late disappointment to the King's friends by the discovery of Sir George Booth's plott inclined me to return again into France, wher I went, haveing obteaned leave of the Council of State, about the end of October, with Sir Thomas *Oct.* 20 Yarburgh, my cozen jermain, a yong gentleman that had a mind to travell. We arrived at Paris by the way of Calais in November, stilo novo, wher I continued very ill a great part of the winter ; but after, by Gods great mercy to me, I perfectly recovered.

Soe soon as I had putt myselfe into some equipage I endeavoured to be acquainted at the Queen Mother of England's Court, which she then kept at the Palais Royal, which I did without any great notice taken of it in England, the King and Dukes being then banished into Flanders, and none of her children with her Majesty but the Princesse Henrietta Maria.[1] Few Englishmen

---

[1] Henrietta or Henrietta Anne, youngest daughter of Charles I and favourite sister of Charles II. In 1661 she married Philip Duke of Orleans, brother of Louis XIV, and thereafter played a considerable part in maintaining friendly relations between the rulers of England and France.

makeing ther their court made me the better recieved.
Besides, speakeing the language of that country and
danceing passably well, the yong Princesse, then aged
about fifteen years, used me with all the civill freedome
that might be, made me dance with her, played on the
harpsicals to me in her Highnesses chamber, suffered
me to attend upon her as she walked in the guarden
with the rest of her retenue, and sometimes to toss her in
a swing made of a cable which she satt upon, tyed between
two trees, and in fine suffered me to be present at most of
her innocent diversions.

The Queen commanded me to be ther as often as I
conveniently could.   Her Majesty had a great affection
for England,[1] notwithstanding the severe usage that she
and hers had recieved from it.   Her discours was much
with the great men and ladys of France in praises of the
people and of the country ; of their courage, generosity,
good nature ; and would excuse all their miscarriages in
relation to unfortunate effects of the late warr as if it
were a convulsion of some desperate and infatuated
persons, rather then from the genius or temper of the
kingdome. And as a little remarke of her Majestys
kindness to the English, carrying an English gentleman with me one day to Court, he, thinkeing to make
himselfe extraordinary fine, had a guarniture of rich
rubin to his suit, in which was a mixture of red and
yallow, which the Queen observeing called to me, and
bid me advise my friend to mend his fancy as to his
rubins, thos two colours togather being ridiculous in
France, and might give occasion to the French to laugh
at him.

Severall English and Irish familys, either from choice
or banishment, lived ther at this time, amongst others my
Lady Hambleton, wife to Sir George Hambleton and

---

[1] " She was generally kind to [the] English, but was pleased to recieve
me as one of her familie, and called me *un des nostres*, or one of us " (*Family
History*, ii. f. 13).

sister to the Duke of Ormond,[1] whom I liked soe well [2] that after she came with her mother into England, as she did soon after, I had probably married her, had not my friends strongly opposed it, she being a papist, and her fortune not very great at present. She married afterwards the Count de Grammont,[3] brother to the duke of that name in France.

I had three cozens of the family of Moulins then in the English Convent sur le Fosse at Paris, one of them an antient lady and since abbesse of it.[4] The Queen used to goe thither very ofton, and to retire for some days. She would tell me that my Lord Germain (since Saint Albans) [5] had the Queen in the greatest awe that could be. Indeed it was sufficiently discoverable that he had a great interest with her, for he was master of her horse, disposed of most of the concerns of her family, but that he was married or had children by her, which some have reported, I did not believe then, though it was certainly soe. I had the advantage of Doctor Cozen's company ofton, then chaplyn to the Queen, and since the Kings restoration Bishop of Durham,[6] who preached to some English every Sunday (which we requited with some contribution for him).

[1] Mary, third daughter of Thomas Butler, Viscount Thurles, and sister of James, Marquis and later Duke of Ormonde, had married Sir George Hamilton, fourth son of James, first Earl of Abercorn.

[2] This should be " whose daughter Elizabeth I liked so well."

[3] Philibert, Comte de Gramont, the hero of the famous *Mémoires de Grammont* written by her brother Anthony Hamilton.

[4] Bridget and Dorothy Mollyns were admitted to the Convent of the Canonesses of St. Augustin in the Rue des Fosses-Saint-Victor two years after its foundation in 1633. Anne was admitted in 1644. All three were daughters of William Mollyns and Bridget Tamworth, whose sister Elizabeth was the wife of Sir George Reresby. Dorothy, the second daughter, became abbess in 1674, resigned in 1678, and died in 1689 at the age of eighty-four (F. M. Th. Cédoz, *Un Couvent de religieuses anglaises à Paris*).

[5] Henry Jermyn, created Earl of St. Albans in 1660.

[6] John Cosin, one of the strongest supporters of Protestantism at the exiled Court, consecrated Bishop of Durham in 1660.

He took great pains to confirm me in the Protestant religion, which was not very nescessary, haveing never as yet heard or seen anything amongst thos of the popish persuasion to invite me to change my religion.

Feb. 15   Being not well in health, I retired to a private lodgeing [1659/60] (my mony too being short), pretending to be gone into the country.   Ther were very few besides my servant that knew of my retirement, but one Mr. Urkart, a Scotchman that had been long a captain in the Regiment of the Crown.   My bill of exchange came for 60 l. at this time, and I entrusted him to recieve it, which he did, but the next day, falling to play in a gentleman's hous as he was bringing it to me, lost it every farding.   However, within few days he found credit enough to borrow 40 pistols, which he very welcomly brought me, and he paid me the rest before I left Paris.

The Court of France was very splendid this winter. A great maske was danced at the Louvre, wher the King and the Princesse Henrietta of England danced to admiration.   But ther was a greater resort to the Palais Royall then to the French Court, the good humour and witt of the Queen Mother of England and the beauty of the Princesse her daughter giveing greater invitation then the more perticular humour of the French Queen, being a Spaniard.[1]

The only affront by a stroake that I ever recievd in my life was at this time, after I came abroad, that striveing to gett into the playhous thorow a great croud, a page, tall and well clad, thrusting upon me, and I rebukeing him for it, gave me a box on the ear, and as soon as he had done gott out of the playhous.   I followed him, and did what I could to learn who he was or his master, but all to noe purpus, for he gott out of my reach.

About this time came the welcome newes that General Monk[2] was comming to London, and would declare for a

---

[1] Anne of Austria, elder daughter of Philip III of Spain.
[2] George Monck, created Duke of Albemarle in 1660.

free Parlament, which happily came to pass the Aprill *April* after, 1660. This Parlament voted the return of the 1660 King from his long, severe banishment, who accordingly arrived in England with his brothers, the Dukes of Yorke and Glocester,[1] from Flanders with a generall consent, a thing never read of in story, that when monarchy was laid aside at the expence of soe much blood it should return again without the shedding of one drop. He came to Dover the 25th of Aprill.[2]   *April 25*

The Queen Mother recieved the news of his Majestys happy restoration and arrivall with all the markes of joy immaginable, and amongst others gave a splendid ball at her Court, wher all the persons of the greatest quality of France were invited, and all the English gentlemen then at Paris had admittance. Haveing not been very well (as I said before), I would have excused myselfe from danceing, but the Queen commanded me to take out the Cardinal's niece, since the wife of the Duke of Mazerine,[3] which I obayed.

I stayed at Paris till August, wher I recieved more honours from the Queen and the Princesse her daughter then I deserved, and which I endeavoured to acknowlege by all the constant duty and attendance I was able to performe. The 2nd[4] of that month I sett forward for *August 2* England, but before I went desired to know of her Majesty what service she would please to command me to the King, who tould me she would write by me, and ordered me to attend her the next morning for her letter.

---

1 Henry, Duke of Gloucester, youngest son of Charles I.

2 Possibly Reresby is thinking of the Parliament or Convention, which met on April 25. Charles landed at Dover on May 25, and entered London four days later, on his birthday.

3 Hortense Mancini, the fourth and most renowned of the five nieces of Cardinal Mazarin. In 1661 she married Charles Armand de la Porte, Marquis de la Meilleraye, who was shortly afterwards created Duc Mazarin.

4 In the text " 2nd " has been altered to " 20th," but without any corresponding change in the date in the margin.

Haveing recieved it and taken my leave I desired to know
if it required hast.   Her Majesty said noe, for it pour-
ported little besides a perticular recommendation of me
to her son the King.   After this I went to take leave of
Mrs. Hambleton, my then mistriss, and the next morning,
being that which I came away, I had the satisfaction to
see her in bed, and I thought her the finest woeman in the
world.   My Lady Hambleton writt to her brother, my
Lord of Ormond, by me, to introduce me to the King.

   I sett forward for England as aforesaid in the company
of my Lord Clifford, son to the Earle of Burlinton,[1] and
of his brother, since kild at sea,[2] by the way of Diepe, wher
a man of warr that was sent on purpas stayed for them,
but falling sick at Roan was left behind for the present,
and following to Diepe found them gone (the wind serveing) two days before, and with them severall other passengers that had waited ther some time for soe good an
opportunity.   Being thus left alone, out of hopes of any
company to contribute to the charge of a better boat, and
my mony being very low, I accepted of a seaman's offer to
carry me to Rie in his single shaloupe,[3] man'd with only
himselfe and his boy, the passengers being only me and
mine (a Moor that then waited on me), all the cabin to the
boat being a hole at the poupe-head which would not
recieve halfe of my body.   In this manner I committed
myselfe to God and the sea, and being happily becalmed
all the time arrived at Rie by rowing all the way some
twenty-four hours after the man-of-warr, and overtook
my Lord Clifford rideing post before he reached London.
At London I mett my mother and most of my relations,

---

[1] Charles Boyle, whose father Richard, second Earl of Cork, was then
Baron Clifford of Lanesborough in the English peerage, and was not
created Earl of Burlington till 1664.

[2] Richard, killed in the battle off Lowestoft on June 3, 1665.

[3] " Which not being much bigger then a large pair of owers was one of
the first boats of that kind by report that had adventured upon soe long a
passage " (*Family History*, ii. f. 13).

comd up as they were from all parts of England to see the King.

I was presented by the Duke of Ormond (then but *Aug.* 27 Marquis) to the King in the privy gallary at Whitehall, and gave him the Queens letter, who asked me severall questions concerning her and my voyage. Some few weeks after I came acquainted with Mrs. Brown, daughter to William Brown, Esquire, barrister at law, of the familie of Sir Wolston Brown, sent by King Henry the Eight with the Lord Darcy with forces to assist the King of Arrogan against the Moors, wher he was knighted by that King, and had a Canton of Granada added by him to his arms, which the family bears to this day.[1] Haveing more inclination for this gentlewoman then any I had seen before, I forgott Mrs. Hambleton, and had noe disposition to make application to others, though I was pressed to doe it by my mother and relations, bycaus their fortunes were more considerable then hers.

I came into Yorkshire, and after some short stay at my *Sept.* 10 own hous at Thriberge went for Yorke by the way of Selby, wher a quarrell hapning between my company and some others about first going into the boat, I was struck over the head with a cudgill, which provouked me to wound one or two with my sword. This gave soe great an alarme to the country people ther met togather upon the occasion of the markit that I was encompassed, and two gentlemen with me and our servants, and after a long defence pulled off my hors, and had certainly been knocked on the head had I not been rescued by my

---

[1] Reresby's information on this point, as is made plain in the *Family History*, is derived from Sir Richard Baker's *Chronicle of the Kings of England* (cf. ed. 1684, p. 255). William Brown, who died on April 6, 1654, had married Frances, daughter of Sir Henry Frankland of Aldwark, and sister of Henry, who succeeded to the Aldwark estate. Of the children of the marriage one son died early; but the other son, William, and the daughters, Frances and Honora, the former of whom had attracted Reresby's attention, are all frequently noticed in the *Memoirs*. Henry Frankland married Dorothy, daughter of Thomas Holcroft, and his children are also frequently mentioned.

Moor, who gott hould of the man's arm that had me down, as he was going to give the blowe. Being gott up again, I defended myselfe till I gott into the hous of an honest man, that gave us protection till the rabble was appeased.

From Yorke I went to Mauton, a famous fair for horses, wher with other gentlemen I was invited to dinner at Sir Thomas Norclifs, who had severall hansome daughters,[1] especially one who was to be speedily married to a yong gentleman with whom I had a quarrell about his mistriss which had near spoiled the match. We should have fought the next day, but considering better of it he submitted (though it was he that had recieved the affront, for I threw a glass of wine in his face), and soe we were reconcild.

Oct. 10   I returned for Thriberge, and soon after to London in the stage coach. In this journey ther hapned an adventure which I cannot but relate. We had for company in the coach a parson, his wife, Mr. Francis Moyser (a hansome yong gentleman), and a yong gentile woeman (and very hansome), servant to a lady of quality that was going up to London in another coach. Mr. Moyser had been long enamoured of this yong woeman, but was much concerned to see her pay me soe much respect as she did the first day ; soe that fearing she had more kindness for me then he desired, he watched us soe narrowly at the inns that I had noe opportunity to be with her alone, till the third day, the coach breakeing three miles short of our inn, I took my mans hors, and prevailed with her to ride behind me whilst the rest of the company, that had noe horses, were forced to march afoot. By this means I had her above an hour to myselfe before they arrived, and had gained such interest in her that I had her consent to doe what I pleased, which however I managed with discretion. She tould me that

---

[1] Sir Thomas Northcliffe, whose seat at Langton was three or four miles south of Malton, had six daughters, four of whom eventually married.

Moyser had never obteaned any favour from her, and that she could not affect him.

My granmother Reresby at my return to London gave me mony to buy coach and horses. I stayed ther all the winter, and was much at the Kings Court, and ofton at the Queen Mothers, who was arrived from Paris in November, and lived at Sommerset Hous in the Strand.

At this time the Court at Whitehall (the Duke of Yorke and the Duke of Glocester haveing theirs distinct from the Kings) was very splendid. The kingdom at this time was very rich, and all people well satisfyed with the King's return ; or such as were not durst not oppose the current by seeming otherwise. Not but it was likely that a considerable nomber could have wished it otherwise— such as had lost commands in the army, which was now disbanded, or estates which they had quietly enjoyed in the late time out of the Crown lands, the bishops, or the dean and champter's, or the delinquents ; dissenters in religion ; and thos of Commonwealth principles.

The King at this time did not soe much trouble him-selfe with business. All things went on easily and calmly. He had a Parlament faithfully inclined to the Crown and Church, ready to doe what he could reasonably desire for the service of either, as may be easily seen by the Acts made by them for setling the legislative power, the militia of the kingdome, and the revenue for his Majestys raign.[1] The businesse was much left to the management of the Earl of Clarendon, then Lord Chancellor ;[2] and the King, as he was of an age and vigour for it, followed his pleasures. And if amongst thos love prevailed with him more then others, he was thus farr excuseable, besides that his complexion led to it, the woemen seemd to be the aggres-sours, and I have since heard the King say did sometimes

[1] The reference seems to be, not to the Convention of 1660, but to the Cavalier Parliament which met in 1661.

[2] Edward Hyde, Lord Chancellor at the exiled Court since 1658, created Earl of Clarendon in April 1661.

offer themselves to his imbraces. The two dukes, his brothers, were noe less lovers of the sex then himselfe.

This winter the King's ant came (or soon after) from the Hague to live here, the Queen of Bohemia, who had tasted a great deale of misery in her time ; and the

Sept. 23 Princesse of Orange, his sister, was then also com'd into England ; who both dyed soon after, as also the Duke of Glocester.[1]

The Queen Mother did ofton aske me if the King had done anything for me, and what I desired, that she might speake on my behalfe. The thruth is, I did not persue my own advantage at that time as I might have done. I went to Court more to converse and look about me then to be soe assidious or diligent near thos princes as I ought to have been. I relyed much on the Queen's kindness to me and power with the King, but was disappointed by the

Jan. 2 Queens leaveing England soon after the death of her
[1660/1] children, and her returning for Paris with her daughter the Princess Henrietta unexpectedly.

6   In this month of January some discontented scismaticks raised a small rebellion in London, and were headed by one Venner,[2] their captain, but were dispersed before they came to any considerable head by a party of the guards.

7 The same night they went out of the town, and rallyed again in Cane Wood, near Highgate, wher a party of hors of the guards, commanded by Sir Thomas Sands,[3] persued them. Being desirous to see a little action, I took one of my coach horses and sett my man upon the other, and joined Sir Thomas Sands (for I had noe saddle horses then in town). After seekeing in the wood till

---

[1] The sequence of events is here somewhat confused. The date in the margin, which refers to the year 1660, is that of the arrival in England of Mary, Princess of Orange. Elizabeth, Queen of Bohemia, did not reach England till the close of May 1661. The Duke of Gloucester died on September 13, 1660 ; Mary on December 24 of the same year ; and Elizabeth on February 13, 1662.

[2] Thomas Venner, a wine cooper and leader of fifth-monarchy men.

[3] Sir Thomas Sandys was then a lieutenant in the King's troop of guards.

midnight by moonshine we came to a little hous, wher the people tould us they had been desireing victuals some time before, and that they could not be farr off. About one hour after wee found some of them in the thick part of the wood, who discharged upon us with their muskits, but by reason of the moons setting gott from us and marched into London again before break of day, wher they were defeated by some of the train-bands and the hors guards, their captain taken prisner with about twenty more, and were all hanged, drawn, and quartered. They dyed resolutely, and unrepenting of their crime. Some twenty of the rebels had been kild before in the severall skermishes, and as many of the Kings men, one of which was shott with a muskit bullet not far from me in Cane Wood.

This winter came Mrs. Hambleton with her father and mother for England, and severall endeavours were used to renew the friendship between us, but after the sight of Mrs. Brown I could not return to that application. This lost me some interest at Court with the family of the Duke of Ormond, her eldest brother James being of the bedchamber to the King ; [1] and her second brother George had a great command in the French Kings army, in which service he was kild ; [2] and his other brother had the same fate at sea in the secound Duch warr.[3] Mrs. Hambleton

[1] James Hamilton enjoyed great favour with Charles II and was employed on many missions, especially to France. He was later appointed groom of the bedchamber, and was fatally wounded in the fight off Schonvelt on May 28, 1673.

[2] George Hamilton had been page to Charles II during his exile, and after the Restoration entered the English army. In 1667 he was deprived of his commission in the King's troop of guards because as a Catholic he refused to take the oath of supremacy, and shortly afterwards he entered the French service, where he eventually rose to be Maréchal du Camp or Major-General. A few months later, on May 22/June 1, 1676, he was killed at Saverne while commanding the rear-guard in Luxemburg's army.

[3] The words " his other brother " refer to James, not to any of the four remaining Hamilton brothers.

married afterwards the Count of Grammont of France, brother to the Duke of that name.

1661

April 23 Charles the 2nd., our gracious soveraign, was crowned at Westminster the 23 Aprill with all the splendour and magnificence that such a ceremony could be performed with.   He dined with all the nobility that day in Westminster Hall at severall tables, the King proceeding the day before from the Tower to Westminster in order to this ceremony.   The triomphall arches, pagiants, musick, made to recieve and entertain him and the whole Court and other attendants as he passed, were finer and richer then was ever known upon the like occasions in England, of all which I was an eye witness ; but as to perticulars it is more the business of an historian then mine to relate them.

May 8 The Parlament, newly called, assembled at Westminster, wher the Hous of Lords was restoored to its just right.   And the Commons were generally chosen of loyall families, but yong men for the most part, which being tould the King he replyed that was noe great fault, for he would keep them till they got beards.[1]

One evening, makeing my court at the Queen of Bohemia's, Mrs. Hambleton came in, and whilst I was enterteaning of her my Lord Canarvan [2] (who was a weak man), seeing a hansome woeman, came up to us and began to talke to her.   Another gentleman and myselfe, knowing the Queen loved mirth, resolved to divert her.   I came

[1] Yet nearly a hundred members of the Long Parliament which had first met in 1640 were returned to the House of Commons, fully half of the Convention again took their seats, and vacancies due to death were so numerous that in seven years 129 new members had to be elected (W. C. Abbott, " The Long Parliament of Charles II," in *English Historical Review*, xxi. 21 et seq.).

[2] Charles Dormer, second Earl of Carnarvon.

to my Lord, and asked him if he had any relation to that lady.   At the same time I sent the other gentleman to whisper him in the ear that I was a collonel lately arrived from France, and that lady was my mistris, and that he feared I ressented his discoursing with her.   This made him presently come aske my pardon before the Queen, protested he knew nothing of her being my mistriss, which I seeming something avers to be satisfyed with, he made such submissions as diverted the circle for some time.   This Queen dyed some months after.

I mett one Mr. Calverley, of the hous of Calverley of *July* 4 Calverley,[1] at Mrs. Browns lodgeing, wher he giveing me very rude words, and denying to give me satisfaction for them, I cudgelled him in Holborn.[2]

[1] Edmund Calverley of Calverley in Yorkshire, who died in 1658, had six sons, who all seem to have been alive at this time.

[2] Immediately after this incident Reresby would seem to have left London for the north, for the earliest extant among his letters " To Cœlia " are dated from York in the weeks following :

July 8th, 1661, from York.—Not to give you the recitall of a journey wheroff the repetition must afflict me, since undertaken without you, I must tell you that I have performed it as poore penitents doe a pilgrimage enjoyned them as a pennence for some great offence.   Had I been my own coachman I should have turnd back severall times, and never have thought any the right way but what led towards your dear selfe.   But mine like an unhumain roague, notwithstanding my ofton crying out, Not soe fast, drove with as little pitty as the executioner doth his office upon criminells condemd to be torn in pieces with four horses.   Since my being here all things have answered the expec[ta]tion I had of them before I came.   How time may alter them I know not, for I can yet bringe my-selfe to have a charity for nothing, scarce for my meat and drinke further then I thinke it needfull to continue me in a capacity to expresse myselfe, Yours, J. R.   (Rawlinson MSS. D. 204, f. 82.)

Yorke, August 2nd, 1661.—Last night, coming late from the Spaw, I received yours, and am glad to hear of your recoverie.   If you have suffered in any respect since my coming downe you have not done it alone, for I have had my share, and wish I had had yours too for both our satis-factions.   As to my promesse of the picture I shall endeavour to perform it, though you must expect it ill done ; nor were I in another place could I undertake to send you a good copie of soe bad an originall.   I confesse the adventure of the ensigne is remarkable.   Adieu.   (*Ibid.*, f. 80.)

This summer was the first time that the Duke of Yorke took perticular notice of me. Being in discours with some Frenchmen and the French embassador,[1] the Duke joined in discours with us in the presence at Whitehall, being a great lover of that language and kind to thos that spoake it. The next night he talked to me a long while as he supped with the King.

October The Duke of Buckingham, being Lord Lieutenant for the West Riding of Yorkshire, gave me a commission for deputy lieutenant, and another for cornet to his volontier troop, consisting of soe many gentlemen listed under him that were willing to serve the King at their own charge. Sir Jourdin Crosland, Governor of Scarbrough Castle,[2] was lieutenant to the troop.

[1661/2] I was a good part of the spring with my mother in Yorkshire, and returned in Aprill to London.

[1662]

May 19 In May following the King went to recieve the Infanta of Portugal,[3] his now Queen, at Portsmouth, and the greatest Court that I ever see attend him in any progresse. I followed the Duke of Buckingham thether, who gave me all the accommodation I could desire, in a hous he had taken on purpas, all the time the Court remained ther, which was very near one month.[4] The Queen arrived the 14th, and after his Majestys arrivall and the consummation of the marriage, performed by the Bishop of

[1] Godefroy, Comte d'Estrades, who arrived in London on July 7, 1661.

[2] Sir Jordan Crossland of Helmsley, Yorkshire, appointed Governor of Scarborough Castle and captain of the garrison company stationed there in 1661.

[3] Catherine of Braganza. The date in the margin is that on which Charles left London.

[4] Scarcely so long. Charles and Catherine left Portsmouth on May 27 and the honeymoon was spent at Hampton Court.

London,[1] the rest of the time of their stay was passed in feastings, balls, and all sorts of diversions.

All this time it was very decernable that the King was not much enamoured of his bride. She was very little, not hansome (though her face was indifferent), and her education soe different from his, being most of her time brought up in a monastery, that she had nothing visible about her capable to make the King forgett his inclinations to the Countesse of Castlemain (since Duchesse of Cleveland),[2] by whom the King had had a child[3] and had afterwards many more, and who was then the finest woeman of her age. It was suspected that my Lord Chancellor Hide, afterwards Lord Clarendon, the great minister of state at that time, that made the match, was noe stranger to the Queen's defects, and to one more, which was that she had a constant flux upon her that made her unlikely (if not incapable) to have issue ; and that he did it the rather for this, that soe in probability the crown might descend to the Duke of Yorke, who was contracted (if not then marryed) to his daughter.[4]

This sommer I came into Yorkshire, and was at *June 2* Thriberge, wher my mother and her husband, Mr. Moyser, as yet did continue, till July, that I went to Scarbrough Spawe. Ther was many persons of quality that went that sommer for their health or their diversion. There was amongst others a lord that had a fine woeman to his wife (a relation of mine). The lord after a short stay was for going away with his lady, that tould me she

---

[1] After a secret Catholic ceremony on May 21 the marriage was celebrated according to the rites of the Church of England by Gilbert Sheldon, Bishop of London, later on the same day.

[2] Barbara Villiers, married in 1659 to Roger Palmer, who was created Earl of Castlemaine in December 1661. Barbara herself was created Duchess of Cleveland in 1670.

[3] Anne, born February 25, 1661, claimed by Roger Palmer as his own child but afterwards acknowledged by the King.

[4] Anne Hyde, privately married to the Duke of York on September 3, 1660, and acknowledged by him as his wife before the close of the year.

had a mind to stay a little longer. I endeavoured to persuade his lordship to it, but could not prevaile ; but finding he had a friend with him who had much power to persuade him, I went and tould him that except my lord stayed some few days longer I should look upon him as the reason of his going, and should expect reparation from him for that neglect putt upon by my lords refuseing to doe what I desired. Hee seemed very much inconcerned at what I said, and declared he would give me what satisfaction I would desire the next morning (it being then late). I answered I would not trust him except he laid with me all night, which he did ; but the next morning he was of another mind, and went and prevaled with my lord and his company to stay some time longer, which putt an end to the dispute.

My mother was ther at the same time, and Mrs. Brown. That lord's lady and I went from Scarbrough to be gossops to a child of Sir Thomas Heblethwaits;[1] but I returned again to Mrs. Brown, who had been at Aldwarke with her uncle Francland some time before, and left London to avoid the importunity of some friends (her mother amongst others) who had been very pressing with her to marry a gentleman of a considerable fortune, which she pretended to refuse upon my account.[2] My granmother Yarburgh died this year, a very pious woeman and an excellent mother, but did leave my mother not

---

[1] Sir Thomas Heblethwayt of Norton had five sons and four daughters. The reference is probably to Montague, the fourth son.

[2] Reresby himself was being subjected to very similar pressure, and another of his letters " To Cœlia " was intended to assure her that he would not give way :

August 23, [16]62, Thriberg.—I have received yours, and wish you would not longer harber thos jealousies I discover by it you entertain. The place you suspect is soe strongly fortified with your forces that twill certainly bide a long seige, nor need you fear it being undermined soe long as it hath soe expert a counterminer as yourselfe. One smile from you can doe more then all the caresses in the world from others, and your eyes persuade more then the tonges of your whole sex. Such is the influence you have upon yours, J. R. (Rawlinson MSS. D. 204, f. 79.)

what she expected, being never perfectly reconciled to her for marrying her second husband.

In October the Duke of Buckyngham, haveing recieved a new commission for Lord Lieutenant of the West Rideing, sent me two commissions, one for deputy lieutenant, the other for cornet to his volontier troop, which consisted of gentlemen of the West Rideing that listed themselves and appeared in his Grace his troop at their own charge. The lieutenant to it was Sir Jordin Crosland, a fine gentleman and a good souldier, then Governor of Scarbrough Castle.

Near this time, it being feared that the seeds of the late *November* insurrection had sown themselves in this part of the king-dome, the deputy lieutenants recieved orders to make a generall search for arms, and to enquire into peoples principles, and how they stood affected to the Goverment. The citty of Yorke and the Ansty were allotted to Sir Thomas Slingsby [1] and me as our province in this matter. *January*
[1662/3]

Ther had been severall meetings in different divisions of the deputy lieutenants for the taxeing all mens estates towards the militia, according to the new Act of Parlament for that purpass,[2] and after ther was a generall meeting at Yorke, which compleated that business.

Mrs. Hotham, falling very sick at that time, sent me her will by her maid, being then in Yorke, by which she left me the greatest part of what she had, but recovered to dispose of it and her person togather.

My poor mother continued extreamly afflicted with the gout all this winter at Thriberge, wher I stayed with her for the most part, and was very pressing that she would consent to my marrying Mrs. Frances Brown ; but she, believing that I might forgett her in time and choos somebody of a greater family and fortune, denyed me ; and I, resolveing not to marry without her consent, was

---

[1] Of Scriven, the second baronet. He had been Sheriff of Yorkshire in the previous year, and in 1670 was to be elected M.P. for the county.

[2] The Militia Act of 1662, 13 & 14 Car. II, cap. 3.

content to stay, but found my kindness was soe great for her that it was not easy to alter it.[1]

It was this year that I lett leases of my lands in Thriberge, and improoved my rents near one hundred pounds per annum, besides a years rent for a fyne for the most part. It was then likewise that I planted a close of six acres, called the Infield, on the north side of Thriberge Hall.

Anno Domini 1663

I went for London in March. Whilst I was in the country I recieved a letter from one that had been a souldier in Cromwels army, who pretended he was able to discover to me a place in Templebrough (part of my estate near Ickles) wher some considerable sum of mony had been hidden in the late warrs, which letter was dated from the Sign of the Cross near Moorfields in London. In April I took Mr. Tindall, my relation,[2] with me, and went to see if I could find out this place in London, and the man. After enquiry for him in severall houses, as we came out of one we met a gentile kind of a man in an alley, who tould me I came from a baudy hous. Not likeing the salutation I tould him he lied, for we knew it not to be such ; but he makeing a froward reply, I gave him a

---

[1] From another of his " love letters," however, it is clear that Reresby felt it his duty about this time to free Frances Brown from her engagement to him :

Thriberge, 1663.—Had I not considered your last as a double letter, both in respect of its own value and of what it inclosed, I should scarce have been soe ready to have made answer to your first, since you confesse yours but an answer to my secound. Though I gave you your libertie I gave you none to be silent, and for that of disposing of yourselfe I know not why it should displease you, if you mistrust not yourselfe that having it in your own power you might incline to make use of it. But 'cause you fear you cannot continue kinde to me without being forcd to it, I resume again the power you once gave mee of confining of you to myselfe for the object of your value. Adieu. (Rawlinson MSS. D. 204, f. 71.)

[2] William, second son of Henry Tindall of Brotherton, whose father Francis had married Edith, grand-daughter of Lionel Reresby.

box on the ear. It should seem he had been shooting
in a great cross-bow, which he had under his cloak, with
which he struck at me before I could gett out my sword,
but missed me. By this time my cozen Tindall comes
up to him, whom he also struck at, and hitting on the
head knockt him down. By this time I came up, and
makeing a pass he wounded me with the end of the bow-
last in my sword hand, that I had much to doe to hould
my sword, till, recovering myselfe a little, I ran in upon
him and wounded him in the belly. By this time the
rabble came about us, and seized of us and carried us
before a justice of the peace, who bailed us upon Citty
security for 2,000 l. The man was in danger of death
for six weekes, which caused us to abscond till we com-
pounded the matter for 50 l., and then we appeared again,
the man also recovering soon after.

This sommer the Duke took a fancy (and sometimes *June*
the King) to buckhunt in Enfield Chace and the Forest,
wher, haveing an excellent hors, I had the honour to
attend them sometimes. One day my Lord Ogle his
hors (since the Duke of Newcastle)[1] tireing, I lent him
mine, and took my man's. The King dined that day at
Sir Edward Wroth[2] his lodge with the Duke his brother,
the Duke of Buckingham, and made us all sitt down that
hunted with him, wher he was in good humour and dranke
very hard. Ten days after, attending the Duke again at
the same sport, ther being noebody in at the death of the
buck but the Duke, one of his querries, and myselfe, my
hors by a sudden turn, rideing before his Highness, gave
me a fall. The Duke was soe kind to ride after my hors
to take him, till some of the company came in to doe it.

[1] Henry Cavendish, Earl of Ogle, sole surviving son of William, Duke
of Newcastle, whom he succeeded in 1676.

[2] A mistake, apparently, for Sir Henry Wroth, of Durants, Enfield,
captain in the royal regiment of horse guards commanded by Aubrey de
Vere, twentieth Earl of Oxford (cf. p. 48 *infra*, where the same mistake is
repeated).

Another time, the King being in the field and I following close behind him, a dog roused a buck out of a bush, that leapt over my hors head, and very near the Kings crupper, and was near touching me with his head.

July 12   Sir Henry Bellasis [1] sent to invite me to dinner to the Bear at the bridge foot, wher on Mack de Mar, an Irish gentleman, was to give him a venison pasty.   After dinner he provoaked me to give him some language, which he soe farr resented that he demanded satisfaction, either by my denying that I meant any injury to him by the saying of the words, and asking his pardon, or by fighting with him.   I denyed the first, and soe being challenged was obliged to fight him that afternoon in Hide Parke, which I did, an Irish gentleman that he met by the way being his secound, and Sir Henry Belasis mine.   At the first pass I hurt him slightly on the sword hand, and at the same time he closeing with me we both fell to the ground (he haveing hould of my sword and I of his).   Sir Henry and his man were fighting at the same time close by, and Sir Henry had gott the better, wounded the other in the belly and disarmed him, and was comming in to us as we were both risen and I had gott his sword out of his hand, which I took home with me, but sent it to him the next day. The secound to Mac de Mar was in danger of death by his wound for some weeks, which made us abscond.   I was with the Duke of Buckingham the best part of this time at Wallinford Hous.[2]   But at last it pleased God he recovered.

August 2   I sett forward for Yorkshire, and was soon after followed by the Duke of Buckingham, who by order from the King was sent to his lieutenancy of the West Rideing, and ther raised the militia to oppose a rebellion which, as the Court had intelligence, was ready to breake out in thos parts.

---

[1] Sir Henry Belasyse, eldest son of John, first Baron Belasyse, one of the five Catholic lords impeached in 1678.

[2] The London residence of the Dukes of Buckingham, purchased by the first Duke from Lord Wallingford in 1622.

The partys concern'd in the carrying on of this design were some officers of the late Parlament army, and some dissatisfyed persons upon account of looseing their Crown and Church lands by the Kings return, and dissenters in point of religion. The chiefe of them were Mr. Rimer [1] and Mr. Oates,[2] men of three or four hundred pounds per annum. Divers others, and some of eminencie, as Sir John Hotham and Mr. Stocdale of Knaisbrough,[3] were examined and committed to Yorke upon this suspicion. The discovery came from one Collonel Smithson and Collonel Greathead,[4] who had been in service against the King and were sollicited to engage with thes rebels, who pretended they would and mett to consult with them for carrying on the plott, but discovered it from the first to Sir Thomas Gower,[5] who advised them still to dissemble till they had drawn in all the friends they could to joine with them, and then to give evidence against them, which some condemned in Sir Thomas, bycaus upon their severall examinations (in the takeing of which I was concerned as a deputy lieutenant) ther seemd some to be engaged not soe much from inclination as persuasion of thos that evidenced against them.[6]

The rendezvous of the militia was appointed near

[1] Ralph Rymer of Brafferton, father of Thomas, the editor of the *Fœdera*.

[2] Thomas Oats of Morley, formerly a captain in the Parliamentary army, described by Bishop Parker as " the leader of the conspirators " (*History of his own Time*, ed. 1727, p. 78).

[3] William Stockdale, who had been returned to Parliament by Knaresborough both in 1660 and in 1661.

[4] Joshua Greathead, the principal witness against the conspirators, rewarded in December with a gift of £100 and a promise of a collectorship of the excise in Yorkshire (*Cal. S.P. Dom.*, 1663-4, pp. 383, 387).

[5] Of Stittenham, the second baronet. He was then Sheriff of Yorkshire.

[6] " Their general complaint was that those that witnessed against them were the persons that drew them in to do what they did " (Carte MSS. 81, f. 220).

Pontefract, Sir George Savils regiment of foot,[1] the Dukes own volontier troop, and Sir Edward Wroth his standing troop of my Lord Oxford's regiment to quarter within the town, and the rest of the forces in the towns and villages adjacent.[2] The night it was expected the rebels would rise I was scarce gott to bed at the Dukes quarters when Mr. Fairfax (since Lord Fairfax)[3] came with intelligence that they were mett in a wood called Farnley Wood near the town, and were marching towards it to surprize it. The alarme was presently given, and all went to their arms ; but it prouved a false alarme in part, for it was true that they had mett in the wood, but finding their nomber not suitable to what they expected, and that we were prepared for them, they dispersed themselves and went home about breake of day. However, about one and twenty of them were discovered not only to have been in thes councils, but at this riseing, and were all found guilty of high treason by a speciall Commission of Oyer and Terminer brought down to Yorke for their tryall in January following, and fifteen of them were executed, of which Rimer and Oates were the chiefe, their quarters sett up in severall parts of the county, and their estates begd by Sir Thomas Osburn,

[1] Sir George Savile, who was to become famous as Marquis of Halifax, and to be Reresby's own chief patron, was then colonel of one of the West Riding regiments of foot.

[2] Sir John himself, having been hurriedly summoned to York, was dispatched to Leeds, and wrote to Frances Brown before his departure :

Yorke, October 14th, [16]63.—I was yesterday sent for in all hast by the Duke of Buckingam, and am this morning upon a march with the rest of the gentlemen of this lieutenancy and the militia of the same towards Leeds, wher for certain a considerable nomber of the discontented partie are up in armes. But I have greater ennemies yet then thes to encounter, *scilicet* my ill fortune, which is still offering some new occasion or other to keepe me from you, and ever such as are irresistable, for nothing in the world but a care of my honour could have longer deteined me from kissing thos dear hands. Adieu. (Rawlinson MSS. D. 204, f. 72.)

[3] Henry, son of the Rev. Henry Fairfax of Bolton Percy. He succeeded to the title in 1671 on the death of his cousin, the Parliamentary general.

since Lord of Danby,[1] and Sir Jurdin Crosland, my lieutenant.

The Duke went from hence to Yorke, wher he stayed some weeks takeing the examinations of the prisners, and diverting himselfe at nights with his deputy lieutenants and officers, or danceing with the ladys, wher hapned many adventures.

I went for London, upon a quarrell between Mrs. *Sept.* 6 Brown and me, and the opposition I found amongst my friends to consent to my marriage. I gott leave to goe for France, and a pass from the Generall the Duke of Albemarle to carry with me some English horses, which I provided accordingly ; but my mothers importunity stopt my journey, who was com'd up to London for her health, and continued ther that winter.

Anno Domini 1664

Sir Henry Bellasis haveing made some wast in his *May* 2 estate, his father, my Lord Bellasis, advised him of thinkeing to repair it by getting a rich wife, he haveing now continued a yong widdower three years. This councill and his circumstances made him marry a yong lady, daughter to my Lady Ermin, his mother in law, worth 1,000 l. per annum.[2] But his inclinations were soe extreamly sett on another lady, Mrs. Garterod Pierpoint,[3] that he could never remoove them from thence all the time that he lived (though he marryed the other),

[1] Sir Thomas Osborne, successively Viscount Latimer, Earl of Danby, Marquis of Carmarthen and Duke of Leeds.

[2] Sir Henry Belasyse married Susan, younger daughter of Sir William Armine, the second baronet, of Osgodby, Lincolnshire, who died in 1658. His father, Lord Belasyse, had previously married Sir William's widow, Anne, daughter of Robert Crane of Chilton, Suffolk. Anne, however, died on August 11, 1662, and Susan's marriage did not take place till October 20 of the same year.

[3] Gertrude Pierrepoint, third daughter of William, the second son of Robert, first Earl of Kingston.

and used to say that since he could not marry her noebody else should, for he could not endure to thinke of any man's enjoying of her but himselfe. The yong lady all this time gave him noe encouragement in the least, but was exactly vertuous, which made this humour of his the more extravagant. At this time a report ran that ther was a treaty of marriage depending between this lady and Mr. William Russell, second son [of] the Earl of Bedford, but since Lord Russell, by the death of his elder brother; [1] and Sir Henry, to persue what he had declared, sends me with a challenge to Mr. Russell for haveing (as he pretended) heard that he should have reflected upon him and some friends of his by words, wheras the thruth was he was angry for his pretending to Mrs. Pierpoint. When I came to Mr. Russell, he seemed concerned more at the reason of the challenge then at the challenge itselfe, haveing (as he said, and I did believe) never spoaken ill of Sir Henry nor his friend, and not knowing the true caus, and therefore denying the words. Sir Henry at my instance proceeded noe further, especially for that he heard the treaty was broaken off. The lady long after (and after Sir Henry's death) was marryed to the Marquis of Halifax,[2] and the Lord Russell was he that was after convicted and executed for high treason, 1683.

The warr now broake out between us and the Dutch. The Parlament being called voted that they would stand by his Majesty in this warr with their lives and fortunes,[3] *August* 20 and then the Parlament was prorougued till the 20th of August, and afterwards by proclamation till November

[1] Francis Russell, eldest surviving son of William, fifth Earl and later first Duke of Bedford, died in 1678, leaving his younger brother William, " the patriot," heir to the title.

[2] In November 1672, when Sir George Savile was only Viscount Halifax. She was his second wife.

[3] The reference is to the address of both Houses presented to the King on April 27, 1664, some months before the outbreak of war, in which the Dutch were denounced as enemies of English trade, and support was promised against them.

the 24. The Parlament then meeting voted a supply to the King, for the carrying on of this warr, of 2,500,000 l., and his Royall Highness, then High Admirall, sett to sea the 9th.   I was now resolved to goe volontier in this *Nov. 9* service, and was not without hopes to be aboard the Duke his own ship.[1]   In order to this I bought a bed, cloaths, and all nescessaries for sea ; on the 15 went to aske leave *Nov. 15* of the King, and to recieve his commands to the Duke, intending to part the next day.   The King tould me that he consented to my going, but had letters to write to the Duke which he would send by me, and bid me stay for them from day to day (expecting, I found afterwards, first to hear from the Duke), till, on the 2nd of December, *Dec. 2* his Majesty tould me he should not now write, nor did I need to goe, for that the Duke would be speedily on shoar (not being, it seems, able to oblige the Dutch to

---

[1] Reresby appears to have spent the summer in the north, and to have gone to London early in November with the object of offering his services at sea.   Two of his letters to Frances Brown belong to this period :

Thriberge, October 11th, [16]64.—You tell me in yours that my picture was welcome to you.   I am sure the newes that it was is soe to mee ; but as to my being in an ill humour when it was drawne, you have reason to think it if you judge of the humour by the face, though I was in a worse for fear it would not be well accepted.   That jealousie being over, I am now seized by a worse, that you have shewed soe much favour to the coppy that you have none left for the originall.   If you have any, reserve it till I see you, for I could be jealous of my own picture in that perticuler, that am wholly yours.   Adieu.   (Rawlinson MSS. D. 204, f. 73.)

Thriber, November, [16]64.—As some thinges are best disscribed by telling of you what they are not, then what they are, and great goods are best understood by comparing them with their contrary ills, I never knew what it was to have you till I found what it was to want you.   And when I seeke remedie for the trouble of your absence thes few dayes past by considering how happy I was in your company some monthes, it avails me noe more then a cordiall long since taken for a new distemper, which having had its operation only now serves to make me impatient till I have it againe. I foresaw my disquiet before you went, but was resolved not to presse you to stay or to anythinge else that your freinds shall looke upon as inconvenient for you, and shall beleive everythinge mine (save one) that is your benefitt.   Adieu.   (*Ibid.*, f. 75.)

engage) ; and soe both the Duke and the fleet returned till the next spring.

This winter my mother consented to my marriing Mrs. Brown, thinkeing it might be a means to fix me at home, which was performed at St. Dunstans Church upon the 9th of March, 1664.[1] My wife her fortune was not 1,200 l., and my estate, in present possession, only Thriberge, which was soon after encreased by the death of my granmother Reresby.   She gave all her own land to Sir Tamworth Reresby, my oncle, and to her daughters, and part also to her yongest son, called Leonard.   Some parts of it she had disposed of in her lifetime to them and others. Soe that nothing came to me but what she could not hinder me of, which was Ickles and Brinsford (her jointure), and yet I never knew of any quarrell she had to me, but my being a Protestant.   However, thos guifts seldome prosper out of their right cours, for I have since lived to see Sir Thamworth and Leonard sell all their land, and to hide themselves for fear of arrests.   The first had 400 l. a year, besides a great sum of mony left him by his mother, and the latter had 120 l. per annum ; but the whole estate which my granmother had and disposed of from the familie was 1,200 l. per annum, as Sir William Dalston [2] assured me, who enjoyed as much then in right of his mother, sister and equall co-heiresse with my

---

[1] The marriage must have been arranged somewhat hastily, for the last surviving " love letter " from Reresby as an unmarried man shows that six days before the event both he and Frances Brown were in the north :

March the 3rd, [16]64[/5], Thriberge.—Notwithstanding it was but five in the afternoon when you writt your last, you might well be going to bed, for I finde you wanted sleep, or else I hope you had not writt after the manner you did.   For keeping of Lent, it needs not as to my perticuler ; tis pennence sufficient to me that you keep it.   Therfore pray you give it over, and send me word when we shall both fall to flesh togather.   Let me hear from you ere I sett out for London, which will be very speedily, as you value his satisfaction that is yours. Adieu. (Rawlinson MSS. D. 204, f. 74.)

[2] The first baronet, son of Sir George Dalston and Catherine, the youngest daughter of John Tamworth.

granmother.   All the benefit we recieved by her was that she provided for the yonger children.

The provision for my brothers and sister by my fathers will was out of Brinsford and Ickles, but that bequest was void, he haveing convayed that estate in collaterall security for some lands he had sould, which were entailed upon me before he had charged them by will.   However, I gave my sister security for the 1,000 l. left her by my father, and paid my brothers their annuities, as well obliged to it by affection as my father's intention, as if I had been soe by lawe.

I carryed my wife to Statfird to her ant Francland's *March* 18 hous, wher we continued some months, though myselfe was most in town, especially on the days.

[1665]

I came with my family to Thriberge,[1] wher I found my *June* 12 hous in a ruinous condition, and all the furniture remoovd to Beaverley (wher my father in law had built a hous, and lived with my mother) except four beds, six dishes, six pair of sheets, some furniture for the kitchin, six silver spoons, a large silver sault (given me by Sir Francis Foljambe, my godfather) and some ould heirlooms, some eight old pictures and as many bookes, with very little more ; and with this stock I began the world.

My wife her portion was soon gone in paying my debts, which were about 600 l., and provideing stock and nescessaries for my hous and grounds.   The rentall of Brinsford and Ickles did then amount to 429 l. 2 s. 4 d. per annum, and I paid annually out of it to my brothers and sister 220 l.[2]   My yongest brother I placed at St.

---

[1] " That summer, finding that nothing came from Court, and that attendance ther was chargeable, I betook myselfe to the country " (*Family History*, ii. f. 13).

[2] " I paid 60 l. anuity to my brother Edmond, 60 l. to Jarvase, and 60 l. per annum interest for 1,000 l., my sister Reresby's portion " (*ibid.*).

John's College in Cambrige, wher he soon after obteaned
a schollarship, and some time after that a fellowship.[1] My
second brother Edmond had been bound apprentice to a
woollen draper, but had left his trade. I found him in
the country when I came down ; but he stayed ther not
long, but went to traile a pike in the Kings regiment of
Guards, was afterwards volontier in the three engagements
between us and the Duch at sea in the second warr, and
was recompenced with a collours at his return to land,
some time after with a partisan in the same regiment,
which he after sould, and his annuity to me of 60 l. per
annum, and with that mony was allowed by the King to
buy a company, of which he is now captain. My third
brother Jarvase went marchant into Spain about this time,
wher he continues as yet. My sister and my wife's sister
lived with me and my wife. Her only brother was at
St. Omer at school.

A great plague began this sommer at London, of which
ther dyed 97,306 persons.[2] It was soe violent that people
would usually fall down dead in the streets as they went
about their occasions ; which puts me in mind of a true
story of a bagpiper that, being dead drunke, fell on sleep
in the street, wher betimes in the morning he was taken
up and thrown into the cart amongst the bodys found dead
of the sicknesse, that were carrying out of town to be
buried. It being but then about daybreak and the

[1] Yarburgh, " born the 28 of August, 1645," after his father's will was
drawn up, was presumably receiving the remaining £40 which Sir John
was paying to his brothers and sister. He was educated at Sedbergh,
admitted a pensioner at St. John's on June 7, 1665, became " first schollar
of the hous," and in 1669, after graduating B.A., was appointed to a
fellowship, which he held for nearly twenty years (*Family History*, ii. f. 10;
Venn, *Alumni Cantabrigienses*, iii. 442).

[2] This is the total figure given by the Bills of Mortality for the year; the
deaths admitted to have been due to the Plague number only 68,596. It
is almost certain, however, that both figures are serious underestimates.
Many deaths went altogether unrecorded, and cases of plague were by no
means always recognised (W. G. Bell, *The Great Plague in London in* 1665,
p. 325).

morning dusky, the piper wakened as the cart was going, and takes out his pipes, raiseth himselfe, and begins to play. Thos that drove the cart, seing the motion but imperfectly and hearing a strange noise, ran straight away very much frighted, and reported they had taken up the divel in the forme of a dead man.

My marriage spoiled my going to sea this sommer, *June 3* wher his Highness had been ever since Aprill, and in June had gott a glorious victory over the Dutch.[1] The King went to Salisbury some part of this sommer.

His Royall Highness and his Duchesse came to Yorke, *August 5* wher they stayed till September 23, that the Duke went for Oxford, wher the King was to meet the Parlament. The Duchesse went not till some time after. Most of the gentry attended at York whilst their Highnesses were ther. The Duke passed his time in shooting, flying, and other exercizes, the Duchesse in recieveing the ladys, which she did very obligeingly. One evening haveing a little snake (which I kept in bran in a box) in my hand as I was in the presence, one of the maids of honor seing of it was frighted. The Duchesse, hearing the noise and what was the occasion, desired to see the snake, and took it into her hand without any fear. This Duchesse was Chancellor Hide his daughter. She was a very hansome woeman, had a great deale of witt ; therefore it was not without reason that Mr. Sydney, the hansomest youth of his time, then of the Duke's bedchamber,[2] was soe much in love with her, as appeared to us all, and the Duchesse not unkind to him, but very innocently. He was afterwards banished the Court for another reason, as was reported.

The Duchesse in her return laid at Welbeck,[3] the old

---

[1] The battle off Lowestoft, which might have proved a real disaster for the Dutch had it been properly followed up.

[2] Henry Sidney, appointed Groom of the Bedchamber to the Duke of York and Master of the Horse to the Duchess in 1665. He was created Earl of Romney by William III in 1694.

[3] The Nottinghamshire seat of the Duke of Newcastle.

Duke of Newcastle being alive, wher she was splendedly entertained, the Duke of Yorke haveing directed that the same respect should be paid her wherever she passed as if he was present. The Duke of Buckingham and my Lord Ogle had a quarell ther.

October 5   I went to Oxford, to putt the King in mind of his promisse to make me high sheriff for the county of Yorke the ensuing year, but heard Sir Francis Cob (who had been sheriff this very year, and had been at some extra-ordinary charge in attending upon and recieveing the Duke and the Court at Yorke) had obteaned the Kings promess to continue it for another year, and at his Highness his intercession. To be further informed, I went to the Duke and informed him of my pretentions, and desired his assistance, who confirmed what I had heard before, but tould me if I had spoake to him sooner he would have done the same thing for me, adviseing me still, if I had the King's promisse before, to persue it. However, I thanked him for the liberty which he gave me, but said I would rather expect a little longer then appear in anything wher his Highness was concerned for another. The Duke took this very kindly, went with me to the King, and presented me to him for the next year after, who gave me his hand to kiss, and his word once more for it.

The Parlament gave the King 1,250,000 l.[1]

Dec. 2   I returned to Thriberge, and kept my first Christmas, wher Sir Henry Belasis came stayed a great part of it with me.[2]

---

[1] Voted on October 11 for the war with the Dutch.

[2] The date in the margin may be that of Sir Henry's arrival. Reresby, in any case, appears to have returned to Thrybergh by the middle of October, as he wrote then to his wife, who was still in the south :

Thriber, October 13, 1665.—I have received two letters, which I have kissed as ofton as they have lines, and should have devoured them ere this had I not feared they would have infected me with hypocrasie. If they be as reall as obliging, I am too happy ; if not, I am abused. I hear his High-nesse intends to goe in person to sea against the Dutch. If soe, pray give me an account by the first that I may come up to attend him. I am glad

The French King declared warr against England, and *Jan.* 1
the King returned to London with the Court not long [1665/6]
after.

[1666]

This spring I mended a great part of my hous, which
was very ruinous to the south, the timber being decayed
as well as the outside, which was only laths and lime or
ruff cast, with which it was covered.[1]

I recieved a letter from the Duke of Buckingham that *June* 20
the King had given him commission to raise a troop of
horse, had chosen me for his cornet, and therfore desired *
me to raise some fit men for that service, and to meet him
with them at Yorke with all hast. At the same time I
had a letter from my friend, Sir Henry Belasis, telling me
how he had endeavoured to be lieutenant to the Duke,

to hear of your family accomodation, and beg you will not misse one post,
since the greatest satisfaction this solitude affords is to hear from you. The
best company I have is the box in my pockett. Adieu. (Rawlinson MSS.
D. 204, f. 77.)

[1] To this spring belongs the last surviving letter " To Cœlia." The fact
that it is dated from Reading suggests that Sir John and Lady Reresby were
temporarily in London :

Redding, March 21, 1665[/6].—I durst not disobay you in giving you
an account of my yesterdayes journey thus far, which was certainly the most
pleasant one I ever performed. You must know the coach was gone long
before I left you, and I made soe much hast to overtake it (by reason of the
excessive raine) that I thinke my horse had run over it had not a very ill face
in the boot and the yelling of a childe made him boggle. Upon further
search who was in the coach, I found the rest soe sorted to her in the boot
that I vow I thinke the comlyest person amongst them was my More.
Ther was a butcher's wife for one, with her bratt not six months ould, who,
poore woeman, having taken solomne leave of her freinds in aile, rendered
it most freely when she came to that unusuall motion of the coach, whilst
the childe straining itselfe with crying restored it as fast upon the mother
backward. Thes two ingredients composed such a perfume that you may
be sure I rather chose to be wett to the skinn then come amongst them.
Though this account be not cleanly I am sure it is perticular, and soe far
according to your order, which I hope will procure your pardon. If ther
be any fault I hope you will lay it upon your own curiosity, not my obedience. I shall thinke it years til next week. Adieu. (*Ibid.*, f. 78.)

* 2/6: J. Beaumont, 1 July 1666.

but that he came too late, Sir Jurden Crosland being
resolved upon before ; but that he had soe great a mind
to be in the same troop with me that if Sir Jurden would
relinquish his claim for 100 l., he impowred me to offer
it to him, not doubting but that the Duke would be well
pleased with it. (At this time Sir Jurden Crosland was
also Governor of Scarbrough Castle.) The Duke soon
after sent me my commission from the King for cornet,
July 6   dated the 6 July.

The whole troop was raised before the end of July, all
of them gentlemen (being in nomber fourscoor) or ould
souldiers, besides officers ; and the servants that belonged
to the troop were as many as their masters. We soe
ordered the matter that Sir Henry Belasis was soon after
admitted lieutenant instead of Sir Jurden Crosland.[1]
All the officers loved musick soe well that the Duke had
a sett of violins, Sir Henry had another, and I also had
three that played very well, one of the violin, one of the
theorbo, and one of the base viall.

We continued in quarters at Yorke two months,
during which time the Duke exercized the troop himselfe
three times a week. During this time my Lord Cardagan [2]
came into the north to see some relations he had ther, with
his lady,[3] the Earl of Shrewsbury [4] and his lady,[5] and a
great retenue. The Duke begining then that fatall amour
with my Lady Shrewsbury (which after cost her husband
his life) prevailed with that company to make some stay
in Yorke, wher he entertained all the company at a vast

---

[1] All the commissions were signed as early as June 30 (Dalton, *English
Army Lists*, i. 59), but by July 28 only Sir Henry's had been received, and
Reresby wrote that day to Joseph Williamson, then secretary to Lord
Arlington, asking him to expedite the rest (*Cal. S.P. Dom.*, 1665-6,
p. 587).

[2] Robert Brudenell, second Earl of Cardigan.

[3] His second wife, Anne, daughter of Thomas, Viscount Savage.

[4] Francis Talbot, eleventh Earl of Shrewsbury.

[5] His second wife, Anna Maria, elder daughter of the Earl of Cardigan.

expence in my Lord Erwins [1] hous for a whole month.
The days were spent in visits and play and all sorts of
diversions that place could afford, and the nights in
danceing sometimes till day the next morning. Only
the two earls, not being men for thos sports, went to bed
something early.

I sent at this time for my wife to wait on the Duchesse
of Buckingham, who, good woman, percieved nothing
at that time of the intrigue that was carrying on between
her husband and the Countesse of Shrewsbury ; but her
stay ther was but short, it being noe good school for a
yong wife. This design, or rather practice, was not
however concealed to all people, for my Lord Brudenall,[2]
brother to the Countesse, tould me one day over a bottle
of wine that comming hastily thorow the dineing room
the evening before he see two tall persons in a kind posture, and he thought they looked like the Duke and his
sister, but he would not be too inquisitive for fear it should
proove soe. And one night my Lord Brudnall was sent
for from the tavern very late to his sisters chamber to
[make] her and my Lord Shrewsbury friends, they haveing
had a great quarrell of jealousie concerning the Duke ;
and yet the Countesse had soe great a power with her lord
that he stayed some time after that.

Soon after this company was gone my Lord Falconbrige [3] came to dine with the Duke, wher a great deale of
company was present (and Sir George Savile amongst
others, since my Lord Halifax, who had also a troop of
hors), when a quarrell hapned between the Duke and his
lordship upon some words spoaken by the Duke, which
his lordship ressented, and returned such to his Grace
that Sir George Savile was imployed to carry his lordship

[1] Henry Ingram, created Viscount Irvine and Lord Ingram in the
peerage of Scotland in 1661.

[2] Francis, Lord Brudenell, eldest son of the Earl of Cardigan.

[3] Thomas Belasyse, second Viscount Fauconberg, created Earl Fauconberg in 1689. He was a son-in-law of Oliver Cromwell.

a challenge.   I, suspecting something of the matter by
what I had heard at dinner, went and offered the Duke my
service for secound ; but he tould me he knew not whether
it would come to fighting or not, if it did he had made
choice already of Sir George Savile.   Soon after, as I was
in the Minster, Sir George came by and desired me to
provide him a longer sword (his being too short), by which
I found the challenge was accepted, and, watching the
Dukes motion, followed him and the rest at a distance to
the field, soe as I was not percieved, and by the benefit of
a hedge was soe near wher they stood to fight that I
heard and see all that passed.   Sir William Francland [1]
was secound to my Lord Falconbrige.   Three of the
four drew their swords, but the Duke I found had more
mind to parley then to fight, and kept his in the scabard,
till takeing some verball and superficiall satisfaction of
my Lord Falconbrige, the dispute went noe further.

I was sorry to see my captain come of soe calmly in
this matter, and telling Sir Henry Belasis of it in friendship,
he tould it to another when he was drunke, who tould it
the Duke.   Some days after this the troop marched to
quarter in Doncaster, wher, finding the Duke to frown
upon me, I understood from a friend the caus of it,
went presently to Sir Henry, who said he believed he
had said something of it when he was drunke, but would
deny it that he heard it from me, if the Duke asked him
of it, but from his cozen, my Lord Falconbrige [2] (for he
had heard him say something to the same purpas).   I
tould him it became me soe ill, being the Dukes officer,
to reflect on my captain, that if he laid it to me it must
occasion a quarrell between him and me, and that Sir
Henry Belasis was the last man that I desired to have a
difference with.   He promessed me to disown the whole
thing as to me, confessing his fault to reveale anything

----

[1] Fauconberg's son-in-law, the first baronet, of Thirkleby.   He was only
a very distant relation of the Franklands of Aldwark.

[2] Sir Henry and Lord Fauconberg were first cousins.

that was tould him in confidence.   Soon after the Duke
sent for him and me, wher he owned he had said what he
heard, but not from me, nor could he well recollect from
whom, but he thought from my Lord Falconbrige.   This
made the Duke appear reconciled to me, though I found
he never was perfectly, but suspected me still.

The Duke left the troop, laid that night from Doncaster   *August 2*
at Thriberge, wher I entertained him at supper with all
the nighbouring gentry as well as I could.   He appeared
extreamly pleased with his reception, and the next day
went towards London.

Some eight days after, Leeds being looked upon as the
most disaffected place of that country, we had orders to
goe and quarter at Leeds, wher the lieutenant, Sir Henry
Belasis, marched the troop, and I followed soon after from
Thriberge.   We continued ther untill the 29 of September
following, when, everything being quiet at home, that
troop, as well as all the rest new levyed, were reduced.
In this troop severall yonger brothers of good families
were private troopers, as Major Gower, Sir John Keys
brother,[1] Mr. Audbrough, Leonard Reresby,[2] and
Edmond Reresby my brother, since captain of the
guards, with many others.

A happy victory was obteaned by his Majesty's fleet
under the command of Prince Rupert against the Dutch.
The Duke of Albemarle was also one of the admirals in
this engagement, who maintained the fight with fifty of his
Majesty's ships against eighty great ones of the ennemy.[3]
This was soon after secounded with another victory,[4] soe

---

[1] Robert, brother of Sir John Kaye of Woodsome, the second baronet.

[2] Youngest son of Sir George.

[3] The engagement referred to is the Four Days' battle of June 1-4, which
was, if anything, a victory for the Dutch.   Owing to the division of the
English fleet Albemarle had to maintain the contest unaided until Rupert
came up on the third day.

[4] The battle off the North Foreland of July 25, in which the Dutch were
decisively defeated.

that the Duch were forced in September to retire into
their harbours towards the latter end of August.[1]

Sept. 2 A great and dismall fire began in Pudding Lane within
the citty of London, which, notwithstanding all the
endeavours that could be used, burnt to asshes the greatest
part of that great and splendid citty in the space of four
days. It did not stopp till it came to Temple Barr.
Many were the conjectures of the caus of this fire ; some
said it was done by the French, others by the papists ;
but it was certainly meer accident. But, however it
hapned, the dreadfull effects of it were not soe strange as
the rebuilding was of this great citty, which, by reason
of the Kings and Parlaments care (then sitting),[2] and
the great wealth and opolency of the citty itselfe, was
rebuilded most stately with brick (the greatest part being
before nothing but lath and lime) in four or five years
time.

October 2 I went for London to putt the King and Duke in mind
of their promess to make me high sheriff of the county,
wher I noe sooner appeared before the Duke of Yorke
but he tould me, I remember'd you for all you was not
here, and your business is done for you. And at that time,
to speake the thruth, noe prince was observed to be more
punctuall to his promess. I found what the Duke had
tould me to be true. The King did graciously confirm
it, and named me high sheriff for the county of Yorke the
year ensuing, for all I was not of the three in the list
presented to him by the judges.

Soe soon as my commission was sealed I went for my
own hous in Yorkshire, and from thence in few days for
York, wher great application was made to me for offices ;
but I made choice of one Mr. Thomas Fairfax for my

---

[1] The meaning of this is by no means clear. The Dutch put to sea twice
after their defeat, but were forced on both occasions to retire, and opera-
tions came to an end towards the close of September.

[2] Parliament was not actually sitting at the time of the Fire, but reassembled on September 21.

under-sheriff, and one Kays for my seale keeper.   The
geoler then gave me 160 l. to have the custody of the gaol.
I had the same sume presented me for the county court,
and I made of the bayliwicks about 145 l.—in all about
465 l., besides the profits of the seale, which made it in
the whole near 12,000 l.[1] But the charges of both
assizes, sallaries to officers, liveries and equipage, took
off soe much that I cannot say I saved clear 200 l., all
charges considered.

Whilst I was at London I gott the broad seale passed
in favour of one Mr. Tooker to have the sole makeing of   *
steele for fourteen years, according to the statute for new
inventions,[2] who covenanted to give me 100 l. yearly out
of it for the fourteen years.   But by denying another
part of the profit, who knew the secret as well as hee, the
patent was reversed, and we lost all.

I recieved by warrant under the Privy Signet three [1666/7]
prisners, whos names were Johns, Jobson, and Atkison,
from London, supposed to have been in the late plott, to
be tryed the next assizes.   Sir Thomas Gower was to
draw up the charge against them.   My Lord Arlinton,
Principal Secretary of State, writt to me at the same   †
time, recommending the care of that affair to me.   The
letter and warrant were both dated the 7 of March,
1666/7.[3]

My Lord Tresurer Southampton[4] and my Lord *March 7*
Ashley[5] writt to me at the same time recommending the   †
                                                            ‡

---

[1] Obviously a mistake for 1,200 l.

[2] Tooker was the manufacturer.   The grant of sole making, dated
November 1666, was in favour of Sir John Reresby and Sir Thomas
Strickland (*Cal. S.P. Dom.*, 1666-7, p. 304).

[3] The warrant is calendared *ibid.*, p. 551.   The names of the prisoners
were Roger Jones, Robert Joplin, and John Atkinson.

[4] Thomas Wriothesley, fourth Earl of Southampton, Lord High
Treasurer since 1660.

[5] Anthony Ashley Cooper, better known by his later title of Earl of
Shaftesbury.   He was at this time Chancellor of the Exchequer.

---

* 2/11: William Morice, 16 February 1666/7, refers to a petition lodged against
the patent; 2/15: Joseph Williamson, 19 (March or April) 1666/7.

† 2/9, 10: letters from Secretary of State, Lord Arlington, 7 March 1666/7;
2/15.

‡ Cf. 2/3. This letter from Southampton and Ashley, 5 March 1666/7, confirms
that Reresby was not, as Browning states, wrong in his dates; see also Mary K.
Geiter and W. A. Speck, 'The Reliability of Sir John Reresby's *Memoirs* and
his account of the Oxford Parliament of 1681', *Historical Research*, 62 (1989),
106.

speedy collection of the poule in that county lately given to the King by Act of Parlament.[1]

The Duke of Buckingham, haveing been some time in disgrace at Court, absented himselfe, and was suspected of some ill practices against the King, insoemuch as a proclamation was issued out to apprehend him,[2] and dispersed into severall parts of England to be published, and amongst others to me as high sheriff of the county. I confess I was at some loss to know how to act in this matter, between the obligation of my place and that which I had formerly had to that Duke. But the judges comeing down to the assizes at Yorke advised me to proclaime it, which for ever after lessened me in the esteem of that lord. His Grace by this means lost all his imployments, and my Lord Burlinton succeeded him in that of the lieutenancy of the West Rideing.

March 16 By letter dated the 16 of March my Lord Burlinton desired my assistance to provide him deputy lieutenants and officers for the militia, severall gentlemen laying down their commands that had held them under the Duke of

---

[1] The poll-tax granted for the Dutch War, estimated to bring in £500,000. It seems probable that Reresby has misdated Southampton's letter by a month, as what appears to be his reply runs as follows :

February 20th, [16]66[/7], Yorke.—My Lord, That of your Lordships dated the 6t of the instant came to my hands the 10th, in observance to which at a generall meeting of the Comissioners for the Poll of the whole county at Yorke we devided ourselves into the severall weapontacks of the three ridinges, and have agreed to proceed with all the care and diligence for the just and speedy raising of such monyes as fall to be levied within our severall devisions, as very sensible of what consequence it is in this conjuncture soe to doe ; and as to any perticuler promotion it may any way receive from me, your Lordship may be assured of it from, My Lord, Your most faithfull and most humble servant, J. R. (Rawlinson MSS. D. 204, f. 29.)

[2] The proclamation for Buckingham's apprehension was issued on March 8. Reresby was so doubtful what to do with it that he wrote to Williamson for advice (*Cal. S.P. Dom.*, 1666-7, pp. 553, 559).

Buckingham,[1] as Sir George Savile (since Marquiss of Halifax), who was collonel of foot and deputy lieutenant ; Sir Thomas Osburn (since Earle of Danby), another collonel of foot and deputy lieutenant, and almost all their officers.   However I soe ordered the matter with the assistance of some others that his lordship (though himselfe not much acquainted in the West Rideing) was supplyed with new officers.   My Lord was very pressing that I would accept of the command of Sir Thomas Osburn's regiment, which laid round about me, and to which my father was major in the Scotch warr ; but I had some reasons to refuse it, and only accepted of a commission for deputy lieutenant, but found him Sir John Lewis for collonell of that regiment, and Sir Jervase Cutler for lieutenant-collonell, and they found their own officers.[2]

We had warr with Denmarke at this time.

The Parlament that had sate from the 18 of September was upon the 8th of February proroagued to the 10th of October next.

Anno 1667

The assizes were appointed this year in March.   I took a hous in the Minster Yeard, wher I entertained all

---

[1] Reresby's reply hardly suggests that Burlington went quite so far at this early stage :

Yorke, March 27th, 1667.—My Lord, I have received the honour of your Lordships, and by it an assurance of your being our lord lieutenant, which we had but the rumour of before.   As to the gentlemen under your Lordships command, I presume you will finde their usuall alacrity and endeavours for the Kinges service, since it is that which is the first motive of kindenesse in all honest men to thos his Majestie shall please to sett over us, and which can continue noe longer then they persue the same.   For my own part, I have not only publick but private obligations to serve your Lordship in any capacity your Lordship shall doe me the honour to imploy me in, with all the integrity and affection that bycomes, My Lord, Your most obliged and most humble servant, J. R.   (Rawlinson MSS. D. 204, f. 33.)

[2] Not without difficulty.   The regiment still lacked officers as late as June 15 (Cal. S.P. Dom., 1667, p. 191).

* 2/20: Burlington, 16 March 1666/7; see also 3/15: Burlington, 26 March 1666/7, in which Burlington expresses the hope that he will see Reresby and the gentlemen whom the king will appoint as Deputy Lieutenants. The letter which Browning quotes from Rawlinson MSS. D. 204 fol. 33 is in answer to this one. See also Althorp MSS. B6: Burlington to 'My Ld', no date: 'Sir John Reresby, our high Sheriff has very handsomely carried himselfe having prudently suppdest the seeds of some discontents which upon the first newes of the change of the lieutenancy were sowed at York'.

commers for ten days togather. My friends sent me twixt two and three hundred liveries. I kept two coaches, one for myselfe, another for my under-sheriff, had my own violins ther all the assizes, gave a ball and entertainment to all the ladys of the town. This assizes cost me 300 l. and od pounds.

The Duke of Buckingham his disgrace being now blown over, he was restoored to his lieutenancie of the West Rideing ; but he gave noe commissions of lieutenancy, &c., to thos that had taken them under my Lord Burlinton.[1] My Lord Burlinton was telling the Duke of York one day that he had omitted me in the list of his deputy lieutenants. His lordship tould me that his Highness replyed that his Grace would never pardon me for relateing his behaviour in his quarrell with my Lord Falconbrige to Sir Henry Belasis. The thruth is his temper was soe suitable to the Kings he had much to doe to be angry with him long, which made him dispence with many insolences. For example, after the battle of Worchester, the Duke of Buckingham saveing himselfe by flight in Holland, he reported that the King had ill behaved himselfe in that conflict, and that he laid now hidden in some gentleman's hous, wher he laid with his wife, and was happier in his own opinion then if he was upon his throne;[2] which being tould to the Princess of Orange, she forbid him to come to Court. I myselfe have heard him in his mirth make too bould with his Majesty and his brother.

During his disgrace the Duke layd concealed in Sir Henry Belasis hous, and ran a great hazard in this and some other perticulars for his sake ; and when he was restoored, Sir Henry had soe ill returns for what he did

---

[1] This belongs to the autumn rather than the spring of 1667, and is repeated in its proper place (*infra*, p. 72).

[2] Charles II was defeated by Cromwell at Worcester on September 3, 1651, and wandered about England for nearly six weeks, in constant danger of capture, before he was able to take ship at Brighton for France.

(as he tould me himselfe) that for some slight jealousie
he had of him for the Countess of Shrewsbury (altogather
undeserved) he never came nor sent to see him all the while
he laid ill of the wound given him by Mr. Porter, which
put a period to his dear life.[1]

I had orders from Court to give notice to the lords *May 25*
lieutenants or their deputies to draw some of the militia
to the seaside towards Burlinton, it being fear'd the Dutch
would make a descent upon that coast ; but my Lord
Belasis, then lord lieutenant of the East Rideing, thought
it not needfull soe soon, Sir Jeromy Smith being com'd
with his squadron to secure that coast.[2] About this time
I recieved a letter from my Lord Burlinton, who was then   *
a great friend of my Lord Chancellor Clarendon's (an
alliance being now concluded between them, Mr.
Laurance Hide, since Lord Rochester, Lord High
Tresurer of England, second son to the Lord Chancellor,
haveing marryed my Lord Burlinton's daughter),[3] wherby
he acquainted me that he had made my Lord Chancellor
and my Lord Arlinton sensible of my services to the
Goverment, and of the obligations I had laid upon him
in perticular.[4]

[1] Thomas Porter, the dramatist, was one of Sir Henry's most intimate
friends, and the duel, which took place on July 28, 1667, caused somewhat
of a sensation by the silliness of the quarrel between them. Both of the
combatants were wounded, but while Porter recovered, Sir Henry died
ten days later (Pepys's *Diary*, July 29, August 8, 1667).

[2] The squadron in the North Sea commanded by Sir Jeremy Smith was
scarcely strong enough to be of much practical service, consisting as it did
of 4 fourth-rates, 7 fifth-rates, a yacht and 3 ketches (*Cal. S.P. Dom.*, 1667,
p. 77).

[3] Laurence Hyde married Lady Harrietta, daughter of the Earl of
Burlington, in 1665. He was created Earl of Rochester in November
1681, and Lord High Treasurer in February 1685.

[4] Reresby was no less complimentary, writing to the Lord Chancellor
to assure him of Burlington's success in his new office :
Yorke, May the 1st, [16]67.—My Lord, Ther hath soe little of consequence passed in thes parts since I had the honour to be sheriff (for which I
owne myselfe much obliged to your Lordship), that I durst not presume to

* 3/18: Burlington, 9 May 1667.

June 4   I had a letter from Secretary Maurice,[1] wherby he
 *   ordered me to send up one Levens,[2] a prisner of state then
in my geole, which I observed.   But I found afterwards
it was not regular, for I ought not to have parted with him
without a habias corpus.   About this time I had notice
 †   to write to my Lord Belasis that some foot and a troop
of hors should be sent to reinforce his lordship in the
East Rideing from the deputy lieutenants of the West
Rideing, if he soe desired, which was done accordingly.

29   A peace was concluded with France, Denmark, and
the States Generall ; but before it was sufficiently known
the Dutch sent a part of their fleet up the river Thams
as high as Chatham,[3] wher they burnt severall of his
Majestys ships, and putt the whole citty of London into
such a fear that they were ready to leave their houses and
estates to the mercy of the ennemy, whom they believed
already at their backs.   The militia of the City and severall

trouble your Lordship till the arrivall here of our lord lieutenant gave me
this just subject of a letter.   His lordship arrived on Thursday last,
attended by much gentry out of all the three ridings (especially the West),
amongst which were the deputy lieutenants and field officers of the West
Riding.   Not to trouble your Lordship with a long relation, the appearance
was soe universall that it plainly shewed a great affection to his Majesties
service, as well as a perticular respect for my Lord of Burlinton and the
memory of the family of the Cliffords, formerly of great interest in this
country.   My Lord was pleased to improove thes by his great civilities to
the gentry, and his kindenesse to thos who were formerly in office by confirming of them in the same, soe that I darr assure your Lordship they
parted very well satisfied one with another.   My Lord, Your most
obedient humble servant, J. R.   (Rawlinson MSS. D. 204, f. 42.)

[1] Sir William Morice, Secretary of State from 1660 to 1668, mainly
through the influence of his relative and patron, General Monck.

[2] Captain William Leving, one of the malcontents who was about to turn
informer.

[3] The Treaty of Breda, which put an end to the war between England
and the United Provinces, was signed on July 21/31.   Negotiations had
been proceeding for some time without much success, and the attack on the
Thames, which culminated in the breaking of the chain across the Medway
and the bombardment of Chatham on June 12, was intended to force
matters to a conclusion.

* 3/30: William Morice, 8 June 1667; 3/4: certificate from William Morice.
He has received from William Bellwood the body of William Levins a captain,
sent from York to London by Reresby, 21 June 1667.

† 3/1: J. Belasyse, 25 May 1667.

of the guards were drawn down to oppose them, wher a great many were killed before they could repulse them.

The Parlament was prorougued near this time till October, which had then given his Majesty a tax upon land.[1] The King, wanting mony by advance, sent to borrow it in severall parts of the kingdome, and in Yorkshire amongst others, offering to give security out of the said tax to repay it. A meeting of the deputy lieutenants was held at York to this purpass, my Lord Burlinton being again lord lieutenant of the West Rideing by another disgrace that the Duke of Buckingham laid under;[2] but no mony could be gotten, they and others excuseing themselves to my Lord Burlinton, and soe to the King, by reason of the povertie of the country.

One Mason, a prisner of state, sent down guarded by some ten troopers of the guard to be tryed at Yorke, was rescued by five men at Ferrybrig and taken from them. One Scott that commanded the guard was killed, and some of the party ill wounded. I passed ther about a quarter of an hour before the fact was done. Hue and cry, with

---

[1] Parliament, which already stood prorogued to October, was hastily summoned to meet on July 25, adjourned on that day to July 29, and then prorogued to October 10. The tax to which Reresby refers is the eleven months' assessment granted at the close of 1666 and calculated to produce £1,256,000.

[2] Buckingham had not suffered a second disgrace, nor had Burlington received a second appointment. Possibly Reresby's repeated confusion on this point is due to the fact that during the summer Burlington was away from his post, and in his absence Sir John felt it expedient to write for advice on this matter of the loan to Lord Fauconberg, Lord Lieutenant of the North Riding :

June 15th, [16]67.—My Lord, The deputy lieutenants of this West Riding having lately received a letter from his Majestie to endeavour the advance of mony by way of loane within the same, to which purpas I conceive your Lordship hath also another, I desire that in the absence of our lord lieutenant your Lordship would acquent us with the method you intend to observe in this affaire, which will be of direction to us at our meeting within this lieutenancie ; but whether a generall meeting of the three ridinges might not be more for this service I leave it to your Lordship to consider. J. R. (Rawlinson MSS. D. 204, f. 50.)

---

* 3/19, 20: These letters from Burlington dated 28 and 15 July respectively, show that Reresby was not confused since his Lordship wrote from Londesborough acting as Lord Lieutenant, asking Sir John and the Deputy Lieutenant for a written explanation of their failure to find the money which he could put before the King.

all other endeavours, were used to take the rescuers, but all ineffectually. I gave my Lord Arlinton a speedy account of the whole matter.[1] We since understood that one Mr. Blood[2] (the same that took my Lord of Ormond prisner out of his coach in London streets, stole the regall crown, and did severall desperate actions afterwards) was the chiefe of the party. And yet the King, haveing taken him, though fitt to pardon him for all thes crimes.

July 30
*

I found by a letter dated that day from my Lord Arlinton that the said rescue was thought the most insolent act against the King and the Goverment that had hapned of a long time ; as also that the late project of the loan for the King had produced a small effect all over England.

August

The sommer assizes were held at Yorke, which lasted ten days and cost me 300 l. The troubles and fears of people were soe great at this time that ther was but little business of law, which made my profit proportionable. Mr. Justice Turner and Mr. Justice Rainsford[3] were the two judges that came that circuit. Ten were condemned and executed that assizes for murder, hors stealing, and other felonies.

My Lord Southamton, Lord High Tresurer of England, being lately dead, the said office was first putt into the hands of four commissioners,[4] viz., the Duke of Albemarle;

[1] The letter giving the account, wrongly dated August 22, 1666, is printed in Hunter, *South Yorkshire*, ii. 41. Captain John Mason was rescued on July 25, 1667, near Darrington. Scott was not the commander of the guard, but a citizen of York travelling in the company of the soldiers (*Cal. S.P. Dom.*, 1667, pp. 326, 331, 337).

[2] Colonel Thomas Blood, the most notorious ruffian of the Restoration period.

[3] Sir Christopher Turner and Sir Richard Rainsford were both Barons of the Exchequer. In February 1669 Rainsford was transferred to the King's Bench, and in April 1676 he was appointed Lord Chief Justice.

[4] Southampton died on May 16, 1667. The commissioners appointed to succeed him were five in number, including, in addition to those mentioned in the text, Sir Thomas Clifford, later Lord Clifford of Chudleigh, who was himself for a short time to be Lord High Treasurer.

* 3/29: Arlington, 30 July 1667.

my Lord Ashley, afterwards Earl of Shaftsbury ; Sir
William Coventry,[1] who was secretary to the Duke of
York;   and   Sir   John   Duncombe.[2]   The   Parlament
haveing sit from the 29 of July by prorogation,[3] amongst
other thinges fell upon the then great favourite, the Earl
of Clarandon, Lord Chancellor of England and father in
lawe to the Duke of York.   And as an impeachment was
prepareing against him, the King took from him the great
seale and gave it to Sir Orlando Brigeman as Lord
Keeper.[4]   Some months after my Lord Clarendon, fearing
the persuit of his adversaries in and out of Parlament,
thought fit to retire secretly into France, wher he dyed
some years after.[5]

The greatest ennemy that this earl had in the Hous of
Lords was the Duke of Buckingham, and Sir Thomas
Osburn (since Earl of Danby) in the Hous of Commons,
which was the first step to Sir Thomas his future rise, by
the helpe of the Duke of Buckingham, who was now
perfectly restoored to the Kings favour and acted as
principal minister of state.   The King consulted him
chiefly in all matters of moment, the forraign ministers
applyd themselves to him before they were admitted to
have audience of the King, &c. ; but he was soe unfit for
this charactere, by reason of his giveing himselfe up to
his plesures, that (turning the night into day and the day
into night) he neglected both his attendance upon the

[1] Fourth son of Thomas, first Baron Coventry, Lord Keeper in the reign
of Charles I.

[2] On the resignation of Lord Ashley in 1672 Duncombe became Chancellor of the Exchequer.

[3] The meaning of this is not clear.   Parliament met on October 10, the
day to which it had been prorogued on July 29.

[4] The dismissal of Clarendon and the appointment of Bridgeman both
took place on August 30, before Parliament met, and were designed to
avert the fury roused by the mismanagement of the war during the two
previous summers.

[5] Clarendon left England on November 29, 1667, and died at Rouen on
December 9/19, 1674.

King, the recieveing of ministers and other persons that waited to speake to him, and indeed all sort of business, soe that he lasted not long.

The lieutenancy being now in the Dukes hands and taken from my Lord Burlinton, I was one of thos in the West Rideing with many more that his Grace was angry with. My Lord Burlinton speakeing to the King of this, and of the services I did him in that country, the King spoake more kindly of me then I deserved, and said he would make peace between us. But whether his Majesty attempted it or not I never enquired, or applyed myselfe to his Grace, for haveing gaind his displesure for nothing but the prefering the Kings service to his friendship, I was not sorry that he frowned upon me for doing my duty. And this the King understood very well.

August 9   My Lord Arlinton writ to me to have an account of the goale and what prisners of state were ther.[1]

My second brother began then to traile a pike in the Kings regiment of guards under Collonel Russell.[2]

[1] Arlington's letter, dated September 9, and Reresby's reply, dated September 20, 1667, are summarised in *Cal. S.P. Dom.*, 1667, pp. 451, 474.

[2] John Russell, third son of Francis, fourth Earl of Bedford, who commanded the King's regiment of foot-guards from 1660 to 1681. That Edmund Reresby, whose service hitherto had been that of a volunteer, enlisted in the ranks only after Sir John had made every effort to secure him a commission, is shown by the following letter from the latter to George Saunderson, fifth Viscount Castleton in the peerage of Ireland, at that time M.P. for Lincolnshire :

October the 27, [16]67.—My Lord, Though I know it is in a manner robbing of the publick to engage your Lordship in any privat concern during the session of Parlament, yet I must beg one favour of you, which is this. His Highnesse was pleasd a year since to recommend my brother for ensigne in the guardes to Collonel Russell, who promessed the Duke he should have the third vacancie that fell, the two former being pre-engaged. Since this ther have many falne, which I suppose my brother missed of by his not being ther. Now that he is comd up to town I only beg you will please to let him wait on your Lordship to the Collonel and to reminde him of his promesse, that it may be done without my troubling the Duke any more concerning it. My Lord, I am Your humble servant, J. R. (Rawlinson MSS. D. 204, f. 45.)

* 3/10: Halifax, 21 September 1667, mentions that he will see Buckingham on Reresby's behalf; 3/24: Burlington to Reresby, 24 October 1667. Burlington recommended Reresby to the king and to Arlington who was a very good friend of Buckingham. A further letter from Burlington, 3/21, 3 December 1667, informs Reresby that he has persuaded Arlington to speak to Buckingham on Sir John's behalf.

† 3/28: Arlington, 9 September 1667.

‡ 3/5: Russell, 24 September 1667. This letter, which precedes the one from Reresby to Castleton, confirms Edmund did miss out by not being in town.

I went to London to pass my account of sheriff in the *Oct.* 20
Exchequer, and it haveing prooved noe beneficiall year
I beg'd two hundred pounds of fynes and estraits which
I had in my hands of the King, which he granted me ;
but Sir William Couventry, then one of the four Commissioners of the Treasury, persuading me rather to stay
for something more considerable, made me loose it.[1]   By   *
the best computation I could make I gott not clear by
being high sheriff above 300 l.

My poor mother, that continued to have her health
very ill at Beaverley, came this year early to Thriberge,
wher I recieved her with that respect and kindness due
to soe descreet and carefull a parent as she had been in all
things but her second marriage.

1668.   †

It was this year that I began to build that side of the *March*
hous towards the church at Thriberge with stone, which
was only before latts and ruff cast, and to lay the garden
walls in lime and sand, and to make them higher, my
father haveing before encompassed the same ground with
a lowe dry wall : not but that Sir John Reresby, my
father, was exactly curious in his garden, and was one of
the first that acquented that part of England (soe far
north) with the exactness and nicety of thos things, not
only as to the form or contriveance of the ground, but as
to excellency and variety of fruits, flowers, greens, in
which he was rather extravagant then curious, for he
placed his pleasure not only innocently but principally
in it.

All this was of little advantage to me, for though I was
at charge of keeping servants to prevent it in my absence
and minority, much of this went to ruin and decay, and the

---

[1] Reresby also endeavoured to secure a second year of office as sheriff, but
without success.   His letter to Williamson on the subject, dated Thrybergh, September 28, 1667, is summarised in *Cal. S.P. Dom.*, 1667, p. 489.

Russell went on to write: 'let mee reminde you of what you did promise me,
which was that your brother should come to the towne and traile a pike in the
regiment, of whome I have not heard any thinge to that purpose, and to deal
ingeniously with you I had rather have men first souldiers then officers'.

* Reresby erased an entry for December here: 'I returned to Thriberge and kept
open Christmas. My daughter Mary was born between five and six on Xmas
day'.

† Letters in the Mexborough correspondence suggest that Reresby left London
shortly after his visit to the exchequer and arrived back at Thrybergh sometime

forme of gardning was soe different to what was used at this day that it was almost as chargeable to me to putt the ground into that method and forme, as also to replant it, as if it had never been enclosed.   I made this sommer the *jett d'eau*, or the fountain, in the middle of the parterre, and the grotto in the sommerhous, and brought the water in lead pipes.   I then built the north side of the hous also with stone, which was ruff cast before.

September   In Michaelmas Terme I sued out my *quietus est* out of the Exchequer for being high sheriff of the county.[1]

About that time dyed my poor mother at Beaverley,[2] a woeman of incomparable witt, judgement, beauty, and of great piety and conduct ; only her second marriage was thought not altogather to her advantage.   She left liveing four sons and one daughter by my own father, and two sons by Mr. Moyser ; the eldest dyed soon after. She lies buried as she desired at Thriberge, near the asshes of my father, wher I have dedicated a small monument to their memories.   God prepare me to followe them to that last home.   That year I kept opon Christmas at Thriberge.

[1] The settlement of his accounts proved to be a matter of some difficulty. The Treasury officials refused to be satisfied (*Calendar of Treasury Books,* ii. 595) until Reresby had complained to the House of Commons of the way in which he was being treated and made the following appeal to Lord Ashley :

May 9th, [16]68.—My Lord, Upon my address to my Lord Cheife Baron and your Lordship by order of the House of Commons, representing the illegall proceedings and demands of some officers of the Exchequer in the passing of my sherifs accounts, your Lordship was pleased to promess me all legal releife, which having a second time been denied by Baron Spilman, I thought it my duty rather to apply myselfe to your Lordship then againe trouble the House in a perticular which I am confident is both in your Lordships power and principalls to rectifie for, My Lord, Your most humble servant, J. R.   (Rawlinson MSS. D. 204, f. 51.)

[2] " My dear mother died in August 1668.   Her jointure, which was Deneby and Hoton, and lett at 450 l. per annum, then returned to me " (*Family History*, ii. f. 14).   The inscription on her tomb at Thrybergh, however, gives the date as September 7, 1668 (Hunter, *South Yorkshire,* ii. 44).

---

before 5 November 1667. From February 1667/8 until April 1670 there is no correspondence listed in the Mexborough papers.

. . .[1] the Duke of Newcastle, late generall of the Kings [1668/9] army in our civil warrs. He was then near eighty years of age, but very ingenious and present to himselfe. He used to say that he hoped to see five generations of my family, that he knew Sir Thomas Reresby very well,[2] and desired to be godfather to my son, if he lived till one was born to the family. My Lord Castleton and my Lady Vicecountesse Monson, my ant, were the Duke his partners at the font.

The Parlament had sate this year, but done little of importance, as also the year before some few bils past. I went to London in the spring with my family, wher the Court and town were in great joy and galentry, peace being now concluded with France, Denmarke, and the States Generall, and also with Spain.[3] Embassadours extraordinary were sent and reciev'd with great splendor to confirm the same between the said princes.

[1] A portion of the text deleted at this point refers to the birth of Reresby's eldest son on January 7, 1668/9, between five and six in the morning (*Family History*, ii. f. 17). Newcastle had already promised to be godfather, and Reresby immediately wrote reminding him of this, and desiring that the child should be called William :

January 9th, [16]68[/9].—May it please your Grace, To say that I know not whether I am prouder of having a sonne, or of the honour your Grace promessed me of being his godfather, is not to flatter your Grace but myselfe. My Lord, I reed that the Romans, when they did *manumittere* or enfranchize their sclaves, would sometimes in token of libertie give them their own names. I desire that my sonn and family may have that badge or cognoisance of being your Grace his servants. For though your Grace hath lived to create a great many admirors, I may say we are not only soe made, but born, of our family, which I hope the due respects paid to your Grace for soe many succeeding generations may testifie, and which shall ever continue to be performed by Your Graces most humble servant, J. R. (Rawlinson MSS. D. 204, f. 52.)

[2] Newcastle was actually twenty-seven years of age when Sir Thomas died, and had he been born only a few years earlier might have seen Sir John's great-great-grandfather, Thomas Reresby.

[3] The Peace of Aix-la-Chapelle, concluded on April 22/May 2, 1668.

1669

April   The Prince of Tuscany [1] came to London with a retenue
and equipage suitable to his quality.   The King entertained him magnificently.   After some time he kept hous
at his own charge, wher he had all the portable raraties
for food and drinke Italy could afford.   I dined twice with
him.   He was very kind to me, as he was to all thos that
had travelled in Italy and spoake the language.   The Prince
of Denmarke was ther also this spring, who some years after
[married] the Princess Ann of England.[2]   All thes jollities
were turned into mourning by the death of the Queen
Mother of England, who dyed near this time at Paris.[3]
She was a great princess, and my very good mistresse.

The Earl of Straffords butler, one that had got eight
or nine hundred pounds in service, dyed at Brinsford, a
lordship of mine.   I then being at London when I had
notice of it, I begged it of the King, who was pleased to
give me that estate.   My Lord of Strafford afterwards
petitioned the King for it, pretending that he was at the
time of his death actually in his service, and that the
said estate was acquired in his service, and noe caviat
haveing been put into the office obteaned a secound grant
of it.   This pretention on both sides bred some cooleness
*   between his lordship and me, and severall letters passed
between us.   At last it was agreed that what part of the
estate laid within my lordship should be mine, and what
was in other places should goe to him.[4]

[1] Cosimo de' Medici, who became Cosimo III, Grand Duke of Tuscany,
on the death of his father Ferdinand II in 1670.   An account of his travels
in England was published in London in 1821.   He arrived in the capital
on April 5.

[2] George, second son of Frederick III of Denmark, married Anne,
second daughter of the Duke of York, on July 28, 1683.

[3] Henrietta Maria died at Colombes on August 21/31, 1669.

[4] The origin of the controversy was the suicide of one Bromley, butler
to William Wentworth, second Earl of Strafford.   Bromley's estate was
thereby forfeited, and Reresby obtained a grant of it along with Edward

* The letters to which Reresby refers are not extant.

I took down an old dovecoat which had been antiently *May* placed just before the gates on the north side at the

Progers, groom of the bedchamber, to whose influence his success was probably due (*Cal. S.P. Dom.*, 1670, p. 572). The difficulty which Sir John found in making the grant effective is shown by the following letter which he wrote to Progers :

Thribergh, February the 15th, Anno Domini 1670[/1].—Sir, I received a letter from my brother the last post importing that you had met with new difficulties in our businesse, and that my Lord Secretary Arlinton had been earnest with you that we would resigne our claime to my Lord of Strafford, who entitles himselfe to the estate in dispute, promessing for soe doing to obteane me something from the King of a greater value. Sir, I am very unwilling therto for thes reasons : First, bycause when I was assured of the thing (as I beleived) by the Kings promesse to us both, and yours to mee, I endeavoured myselfe as much as I could to find out wher the estate was lodged, which I could not doe without entitleing myselfe therto, and if now it be disposed of to others, I must needs be reputed either unjust or indiscreet, in being soe inquisitive after what did not appertain to me ; and to excuse it by saying it was once given, but afterwards retaken, is rather to improove then abate the reflexion. Secondly, though the losse be not valuable to you, it is to me ; and as for promesses of repairing it to be otherwais, I dar not confide in them, for when I was sheriff of this county, which the King gave me as an intended benefitt, it proov'd a losse by reason of the Dutch War hapning that year, wherupon I petitioned the King, and was in a faire way to be reimbursed out of the Kings rents in this county, had not Sir William Couventry, then Comissioner of the Treasurie, prevailed upon me by the like promesses to desist till the Kings coffers were fuller, since which time I have never obteaned anything in consideration of this and other losses sustained in the Kings service, till this hapning within my own mannor, fortune joined with the Kings favour to bestow it upon me, in which if I be disappointed I have little reason to hope for anything hereafter.

I could give other reasons why I would not release my claime in this perticular could it be avoided, as cheifly that some of my Lord Straffords relations might be disappointed, who from former differences bytwixt us as to *meum* and *tuum* have used, I soppose, their interest with my Lord to be the more active to defeat me in this perticular. But however, rather then displease the King, I shall submitt to what you judge fittest to be done. Only this I desire from you, that if ther be a nescessity to satisfie my Lord of Strafford (though it is impossible this should—my Lord hath too vast pretentions from Court to take up with such trifles—such drops fill not the sea), quitt not till I know it, and come up that I may ascertaine something to myselfe in lieu of it, for I would not willingly let goe a bird and hould nothing but the fethers, that am Your most humble servant, J.R. (Rawlinson MSS. D. 204, f. 55.)

comeing into the hous, built with wood and lime, and built another of stone north-west to the hous, as it now stands.

The same summer I took down an ould piece of building called the Newwork, a wood building and low, which stood west to the hous, conteaning four or five rooms, and was irregular to the rest of the building. And instead therof I built the tower in the same place suitable to that at the east end built by Sir Thomas Reresby, which made the hous with some other alterations very regular.

Oct. 19   The Parlament met at Westminster according to the prorogation.

November   The Parlament was proroagued by commission [1] till the 14 of February ensuing, at which time it reassembled.

The Parlament of Scotland then in being enacted severall lawes.[2]

January   That great and faithfull subject, Collonel Monk, Duke [1669/70] of Albemarle, generall of all his Majestys forces, dyed at his apartment at the Cockpit at Whitehall.[3] The King, in commemoration of his services, conferred the lieu-tenancy of Devon, and the office of gentleman of the bedchamber, on his only son,[4] and gave him his fathers garter. This family owns a relation to mine by the Yarburghs. His body was buryed in April following [5] at the Kings charge in Westminster Abbay with great solemnity.

February   The Parlament met at Westminster according to the prorogation.

[1] On December 11.

[2] The second Scottish Parliament of the reign of Charles II met on October 19 and was adjourned on December 23, 1669.

[3] On January 3.

[4] Christopher Monck, second Duke of Albemarle, the elder and only surviving son.

[5] April 30. The long delay was due to the elaborate official prepar-ations.

Anno Domini 1670

This year I was confined to Thriberge to finish the inside of the tower of which the case was built the year before, and to make new seeleing or limework to most of the rooms throughout the whole hous, which was much decayed, and to new wainscot severall of the rooms, and to paint the whole hous. I was the first in thes parts that began to rebuild or repair my hous according to the mode of that time, which others have since followed with more advantage ; but I was confined to the model, the height and proportion of rooms, and, which was worst, to a narrow purs. But yet I may say that I made it as convenient a hous as any of theirs.

My father haveing sould a great deel of fine timber in the old parke, and reduced his parke to soe narrow a compas just before the hous that the deer did not live or encrease to any nomber, I added some field land to it, which I exchanged with the tenents for other land with a brow, or cliff of wood, belonging to the common, all *June* lying to the south, and encompassed it with a stone wall.

Mr. Stricland, houskeeper of the mannour of York to *August* the King, and his reciever of the duty of hearth mony,[1] dyed. I desired my Lord Burlinton to speake to the Duke of Yorke to beg the succession of both thos places for me. The Duke tould his lordship that if he had but mentioned it two hours sooner it had been done, for his Majesty had granted to another but so long before.   *

I had been for some time in commission of the peace for the West Rideing, and had refused to be sworn, to avoid the trouble as well as to gain time to study the statute lawe. At last, findeing it of some use as well to ones selfe as others, and being much importuned by friends to take it upon me, I was this year sworn, and have since

[1] Walter Strickland, receiver of hearthmoney for the city of York and the West Riding, and receiver-general of aids for Yorkshire.

* Reresby here erased an entry recording the birth of his son Tamworth in September.

endeavoured to acquitt myselfe of that office according to my duty.

It was this sommer that the Princess of Orlians, the Kings sister, came over to Dover,[1] wher the King, the Duke of York, and the whole Court, went to meet her. It was here that she confirmed his Highness the Duke in the popish religion, of which he had not as yet been suspected, and it was said to be one of the greatest arguments that his mother the Queen had commanded him upon her last blessing to profess that religion. Before that he was thought rather inclineing to favour the Presbuterians ; for not long before, a nonconformist minister being prossecuted at Pomfret sessions for preaching in convinticle upon the statute, it was reported that both his Highness and the Duke of Buckingham (then principal minister of state) had writ in his favour to the justices. But the Duke, as I was attending upon him in St. James his Parke, called me to him, and discourseing that thinge with me, said it was a mistake, that he had not concerned himselfe in it, although he was soe much the friend of that sort of people that he wished the law had not been put in execution against him (or to that effect) ; but that he did not write.

He bad me at the same time represent him, upon occasion, as noe ennemy to such. I tould his Highness ther was one Mr. Vincent, my kinsman, in town, a leading man of that party.[2] He bad me bring him to Court, which I did the next day, and his Highness took him aside and discoursed him a great while. Most believed that this was done by the Duke out of politie at this time, for ther was some that discoursed of an intrigue then on foot to

---

[1] Her visit was part of the intrigue which led to the signing of the secret treaty of Dover on May 22.

[2] William Vincent, citizen of London, whose elder brother, Thomas Vincent of Baronborough, married Susan Wormley, elder sister of Reresby's grandmother, may perhaps be identified with the William Vincent whose house at Hounslow was licensed as a place of Presbyterian worship in 1672 (*Cal. S.P. Dom.*, 1672, pp. 476, 577).

devorce the King from the Queen, which he endeavoured,
by thus courting of all partys, to prevent.

The Duke of Orlians had been jealous for some time
before of the Count de Guiche,[1] and, if storys be true, not
without ground.   It was said, too, that she was in love
with the Duke of Monmoth[2] whilst at Dover.   However,
things had been soe represented to the Duke her husband
that she dyed suddenly after her return to Paris,[3] and not
without notorious suspicion of being poysoned.

The Prince of Orange came to London to visit the *October*
King.[4]

The Parlament mett that month according to the prorogation,[5] and sat till March.   During this session Sir
John Couventry[6] reflected upon the King's wenching in
some speech he made in the Hous, which being tould the
Duke of Monmoth, he sett Sir Thomas Sands (an officer
of the guards) and three or four more to waylay him as
he went late home to his lodgeing, who, takeing him out
of his coach, slitt his nose.[7]   This being complaind of in
the Hous did soe inflame the Hous that it occasioned the
frameing of that Act against malicious maimeing and
wounding.[8]

I was stopped in one way leading from the Dun Miln
towards Naumarsh Common by one Mr. Hatfield, owner

[1] Armand de Gramont, nephew of the hero of the *Mémoires*.

[2] James Scott, natural son of Charles II by Lucy Walters, created Duke
of Monmouth in 1663.

[3] June 20/30, 1670.

[4] William of Orange, then barely twenty years of age, landed at Margate
on October 29, reached London on November 2, and remained in England
more than three months.

[5] On October 24, the day to which it had adjourned.   It sat until
April 22.

[6] M.P. for Weymouth; son of John, elder brother of Sir William
Coventry.

[7] December 21.

[8] The Coventry or Maiming Act (22 & 23 Car. II, cap. 1), which
declared such an offence to be felony without benefit of clergy.

of Kilnhurst, and I was again stopped by Mr. Hurst, owner
of some lands leading to Aldwarke Wear. I brought my
action against them both, and rather then dispute it both
granted me free passage.

Jan. 20   I went for London. It was about this time that I
[1670/1] bought some land of John Farburn which cost me 160 l.
within the lordship of Mexbrough, but none of thos
sould by my father nor of thos belonging to the Abbay
of Munckburton.

Anno Domini 1671

The Prince of Orange being at this time com'd into
England, to pretend to the Lady Mary, eldest daughter
of his Highness the Duke of Yorke, the King recieved him
(both upon the account of his relation and merit, being a
very personable and hopefull prince) with great splender.
Amongst other of his entertainments the King made him
drinke very hard one night at a supper given by the Duke
of Buckingham. The Prince did not naturally love it,
but being once entered was more frolick and merry then
the rest of the company. Amongst other expressions of
it he broake the windowes of the maids of honour their
chambers, and had gott into some of their apartments,
had they not been timely rescued.[1] I soppose his mistris
did not less approove of him for that vigour.

It was this year that I endeavoured to retrive that great
and antient estate lately belonging to my family, called
Asshover in Derbyshire. It consisted of three mannours
*   called Reresby's Mannour, Babinton's Mannour, and
Peschal's Mannour. The two first belonged to Sir
Thomas Reresby, my great-grandfather, the one by
descent, the other by purchass, valued at this day at
800 l. per annum. Sir Thomas did mortgage thes two

---

[1] This incident cannot be correctly dated, as the Prince took his departure from England on February 15, more than a month before the official
year 1671 began.

---

* The will of Sir Thomas Reresby is located in B.L. Add. MSS. 6669, fol. 62.
The correspondence in bundle 4 of the Reresby letters also relates to this matter.
This correspondence covers most of 1671 and the spring of 1672. 11/139: draft
answer from 'Your Ld' to Mr. Webster, no date, concerning the dispute. There
are a few letters dated as late as March 1672/3 (see 5/1, 3, 5, 10, 13, 14, 15,
15a). The claim is recorded in Cambridge University Library Additional MS
3913.

mannours to Sir Samuel Tryan for 800 l., and charged
them besides with 3,000 l. for portions to two of his
daughters, and soon after dyed. Sir George Reresby,
that had the equity of redemption in him, neglected to
look after it till the creditours and thos that marryed the
two daughters gott a decree in Chancery to sell the estate,
soe that it was aliened and never reguarded in his time.
Sir George, dying, left my father Sir John under age and
ward to his mother, who had more care of her own land
(for she was an heiresse) then of that of the family. Soon
after my said father was marryed he began to look into
the state of the saile, and commenced suit against the
purchassours. But the contest being likely to be tedious
and chargeable, and he being very narrow in his fortune,
and the civil warrs comming on, he closed with some
offers of small sums of mony for accommodation, and
confirmed the purchassours estates.

When I came to look into this affair, I found it in this
desperate condition. However, I first preferred a bill in
Chancery against the purchassours, which they gott dismissed ; and then I petitioned the Hous of Lords, wher
they fearing my interest (more then the equity of their
caus, which was backed with a possession of fifty years),
they offered me some composition for agreement. The
thruth is I found by severall of the lords that ther was
little hopes to succeed in that Hous after soe antient a
possession and a decree of that standing, and most, the
confirmation of my father, from whom I claimed, soe that
I accepted 500 l. which the purchassours gave me, being
more then my father had gott to confirm their estates
thirty years before. This was a great loss to the family
(for which Sir George was the most to blame), for besides
that it was our most antient estate, and that the revenue
was now actually worth 800 l. per annum (as I said before),
ther hath been lead gott out of that land since the saile of
it worth four-scoor thousand pounds, besides what lies
ungotten at this day.

April 31   An, Duchesse of Yorke, dyed, and declared herselfe
a papist at the time of her death.[1]

It was at this time that [I] had commenced suit against
the Countesse Douagere Strafford [2] (who lived then at
Hoton Roberts) for planting a warren and oponing a
quarry upon the common, which I opposed as a freehoulder within Hoton and lord of Deneby.   But it
went noe farther, my lord of Strafford and her ladyship
both consenting that the warran should be destroyed and
the quarry filled up.

This year I took in that part of the parke with a wall
that lies beyond the ponds to the south.   It was this
summer also that I paved the courts and built the long
stable to the hous at Thriberge.

December   I kept opon Christmas this year at Thriberge as
formerly.

The Parlament had sate this year and enacted severall
bils.

March 17   Warr was declared against the States Generall.

[1671/2]   The citty of London had recovered its selfe in a great
measure out of its asshes, and was soe far rebuilt this year
that the King was invited into it on my Lord Maiors Day
to dinner, which he accepted of.

March 15   The King did issue out his proclamation for indulgence
to tender conciencys.   This made a great noise not only
in the succeeding Parlaments (wher at last it was reversed) [3]
but throughout the kingdome, and was the greatest blowe
that ever was given, since the Kings restoration, to the
Church of England, all sectarys by this means repairing
publiquely to their meetings or conventicles, insoemuch
that all the lawes and care of their execution against thes

---

[1] Her death took place at St. James's on March 31, 1671.   She had
been received into the Catholic Church some months earlier.

[2] Elizabeth, daughter of Sir Godfrey Rodes, who had been the third
wife of the great Earl of Strafford.

[3] It was cancelled by the King on March 7, 1672/3, and Parliament was
informed of the cancellation on the following day.

sepretists afterwards could never bring them back to due conformaty.

[1672]

This sommer the French joined with us at sea against the Dutch, and betrayed us at the same time, for in the sea fight upon the 18 of May [1] the French squadrons stood *May* 28 off and left us and the Dutch to dispute the day, wheras if they had com'd up and assisted the Duke of Yorke, who then commanded the whole as High Admiral, we had gott a most signall victory.   And yet we had soe much the better that after a fight of eight hours the Duch fleet   * retreated.   In this fight dyed Edward Mountaigue, Earl of Sandwitch, vice-admirall.[2]

My brother went to sea volontier (I mean the captain, Edmond Reresby), and was in all this engagement, wher he behaved himselfe soe well that he was soon after pre-ferred from ensign to lieutenant in the Kings own regiment of guards.[3]

I went to London with my family, and stayed ther all *Sept.* 28 winter.

[1] The battle of Southwold Bay, fought on May 28.   The date in the margin, originally May 18, has been altered to May 28, but that in the text has been left untouched.

[2] The early patron of Samuel Pepys.

[3] His commission as ensign is dated November 19, 1670; as lieutenant, September 18, 1673; as captain, September 1, 1680 (Dalton, *English Army Lists*, i. 113, 159, 276).   On his promotion to the rank of lieutenant Sir John wrote the following letter of thanks to his colonel, John Russell :

October the 2nd, 1673.—Sir, As the honour you have done my bro'her in preferring him is not only to him but his relations, tis fitt they should acknowlege it as well as himselfe.   To see him advanced after soe generous a manner must needs be of satisfaction to us all, but to him the most that hath receivd it as an effect of your favour.   Sir, however he deserves it, I wish he may live to requite it by performing his duty in serving the King and (next to him) yourselfe, which certainly by your kindenesse to him you have obliged a great many others to endeavour both upon a publique and a private account, as to the latter especially, Sir, Yours, J. R.   (Rawlinson MSS. D. 204, f. 59.)

* 5/4, 7, 9: letters from Reresby's brother, Edmund n.d. + 1 June 1672 provided Sir John with this information.

My Lord Halifax came this year first into business, and was sworn of the privy councill.[1]   He was soon after sent in commission with the Duke of Buckingham and my Lord Arlinton as imbassadors into Holland, but to noe purpas, for the warr continued.[2]

My ant Monson, wife of the Lord Monson, my fathers third sister, first marryed to Sir Francis Foljambe, then to Captain Hornor, then to this unfortunate lord (one of the late King's judges, condemd to perpetuall confinement and degraded by Act of Parlament), being desirous to be restoored to the dignity of Vicecountess Castlemain of the kingdome of Ireland, desired me to make what interest I could with his Majesty to obtean it.   I gott severall friends to moove the King in that perticular, chiefly my Lord Ogle (then of the bedchamber, since Duke of Newcastle) and my Lord Arlinton.   In fyne the King, out of consideration of the loyalty of her own family, was pleased to remoove the stain that was upon her from the treason of her husband, and to restoor her by a perticular grant to her said honour,[3] for the obteaning of which she presented me with one hundred pounds.

Dec. 12   I was informed that the King intended to make a fort at Burlinton,[4] and to furnish it with stoores and canon for the security of collier ships and other traders and marchantmen that passed by that bay, which were ofton trapt by the Dutch.   I immediately applyed myselfe to the Duke of Yorke to intercede for me to his Majesty that, in case that

---

[1] April 17, 1672.

[2] The commission was not originally a joint one.   Buckingham and Arlington set out on June 22 with instructions, dated the previous day, to seek some accommodation between the belligerent powers.   Halifax had left a week earlier on a mission of congratulation to the French King on the birth of a son.

[3] The warrant for the grant is dated April 11, 1673 (*Cal. S.P. Dom.*, 1673, p. 134).

[4] There already was a fort at Burlington or Bridlington, with three guns, but it was in a very decayed condition (*Cal. S.P. Dom.*, 1671-2, pp. 263, 580).

design went on, I might have the command of that place. His Royall Highness did speake to the King for me, who promessed the fort should be raised, and that I should be governor of it, and appointed the Master of the Ordinance [1] to send down an ingeneer to take a plattform or modell of the fortification.   But whilst this was in hand the Duke refused to take the oaths which were tendered to him as Admirall of England,[2] and therby declared himselfe a Roman Catholique, and laid down all his imployments, soe that nothing more was done in my affair for that time.

This year I built the barn and oxhous of stone which stands north-west of the hous, instead of one of latts and lime which stood in the very front of it.   *

The King haveing borrowed the greatest part of the *December* ready coin of the nation of the gouldsmiths (at that time called bankeers) shutt up the Exchequer, which caused the most considerable of them to breake, and an infinite of people, whos mony thos bankers had borrowed at interest, to be undone.[3]

The Parlament assembled at Westminster according *Feb.* 4 to the prorogation, at which time Mr. Seamure was first [1672/3] chosen Speaker of the Hous of Commons.[4]

[1] Sir Thomas Chicheley, M.P. for Cambridgeshire, and stepfather of Lord Halifax.   He was appointed Master of the Ordnance on May 18, 1670.

[2] June 15, 1673.

[3] The Stop of the Exchequer is misdated by a year.   A preliminary suspension of payments was ordered on December 18, 1671, and the order suspending payments for a period of twelve months followed on January 2, 1671/2.   Possibly Reresby was thinking of the extension of this suspension for a further period of four months, which was authorised on December 11, 1672.

[4] When the Commons assembled on February 4 Sir Job Charlton was chosen Speaker, but within a fortnight he complained of indisposition and desired leave to resign.   On February 18, accordingly, Edward Seymour, eldest son of Sir Edward Seymour of Berry Pomeroy, was chosen in his place, and remained Speaker, with one short interval, until the dissolution of Parliament in January 1678/9.

* Reresby here erased an entry recording the birth on 9 January of his third daughter.

Anno Domini 1673

I continued this year to build the parke wall as I
enlarged it, and liveing the most part at Thriberge applyed
myself to the study and exercize of the office of justice of
the peace, and had soe much business that my clerk confessed that he made above 40 l. that year of his place.

My nighbour Sir Thomas Osburn rose this year to the
great office of Lord High Treasurer of England, my Lord
* Clifford laying down the staff and confessing himselfe a
papist.[1] The Duke of Buckingham was the main instrument to effect this for Sir Thomas, by makeing a bargain
between my Lord Clifford and him, which was that Sir
Thomas should officiate the place and give Clifford halfe
the salary, and then prevailed with the King to give the
staff to Sir Thomas, then created Vicecount Dunblain,[2]
though afterwards he was made Earl of Danby, and had
a patent passing for marquiss just as he fell into disgrace.

The warr continued this year with the Dutch. Prince
Rupurt was admiral for us, and the Count d'Estrees [3] for
the French King. We had two victorys over them.
† In one wee lost that great seaman Sir Edward Spragg.[4]
My brother Edmond was at sea again this year and in
both thes engagements, but came off very safe.

The Parlament had mett in the spring, and was adjourned till October. Sir Francis Gooderick being dead,
one of the burgesses for Audbrough, I was persuaded by

---

[1] Clifford resigned and Osborne was appointed on June 19.

[2] Sir Thomas had been created Viscount Osborne of Dumblane as
early as February 2, 1672/3, but his Scottish title secured little recognition
in England. After his elevation to the post of Treasurer he was raised to
the English peerage, as Baron Osborne of Kiveton and Viscount Latimer,
on July 23, 1673.

[3] Jean, Comte d'Estrées, Vice-Admiral of France.

[4] Three important engagements took place, on May 28, June 4 and
August 11, all of which proved indecisive. Sir Edward Spragge, then
admiral of the blue, lost his life in the last of them.

* 7/12: Halifax, 19 June 1673.

† 6/13: Edmund Reresby, 15 August 1673.

Sir Henry Goodrick [1] (who had some interest ther, and stood also for burgess of Bouroughbrig, a nighbouring town, wher ther was also a vacancy by the death of Sir Robert Long) [2] to stand for Parlament man. My doing business at Yorke and in severall other parts of the county, and being most commonly at the generall sessions, and frequently giveing the charge, made me known to that side of the county, though soe remote from my own hous. I was also well acquainted with some gentlemen (besides Sir Henry Gooderick), nighbours to that place, who gave me their interest ; but my greatest obligation was to Sir Henry. This Sir Henry Goodrick was a gentleman of fine parts naturally, and thos improoved by great reading and travell, one that being fixt at his excellent seat at Ribston, near Knaisbrough, pleased himselfe ther, and had noe thoughts (noe more then myselfe) to be in any publique business that might call us out of the country, till thes vacancys falling out tempted us to it. He was, after his being known in Parlament, sent by King Charles the 2nd his embassador into Spain, [3] and we always continued soe kind friends that we called brothers.

The state of that Parlament was this at that time, that all things had been carried on from the time of its being called (which was soon after the Kings restoration) with great calm and success for the advantage of the Crown. They had given the King a very great revenue upon tunnage and poundage, the excize on severall sorts of liquours, hearth mony, besides temporary taxes, ariseing to above three times more per annum then any other king of England had before. [4] This began to weigh heavy upon

[1] Eldest son of Sir John Goodricke, the first baronet, whom he succeeded in November 1670. Sir Francis was his uncle.

[2] Auditor of the Exchequer. He died on July 13, 1673.

[3] In November 1678.

[4] Reresby is speaking of the figure which the revenue was calculated to reach. In reality the regular revenue since the beginning of the reign had amounted only to about two-thirds of its estimated value, and fell far short of the perfectly legitimate expenditure of the Government.

* Bundles 6 and 7 of the Reresby Correspondence give details of the election. The earliest letter from N. Hayes, dated 23 August 1673, assures Reresby of Halifax's support in the election. 1/124: H. Goodricke, 30 October 1673. Cf. Mary K. Geiter, 'The Political Career of Sir John Reresby 1673–1689' (unpublished M.Phil., Leeds University, 1989; hereafter cited as Geiter, 'Reresby'), pp. 1–24.

the country, and to make them repine, which stirred up
some gentlemen in both Houses to oppose this currant
(which was called the Country party, in opposition to thos
others whom they called the Court party). The first of
thes pretended to protect the country from being over-
burdened in their estates, in their privileges and libertys
as Englishmen, and to stand by the religion and goverment as established by law. The other declared for that
too, but at the same time for the King to have a sufficient
revenue and power for the exercize of his regall authority,
without too much depending upon the people, since it
had prooved of soe ill consequence in the exemple of his
father.

This difference made gentlemen more active to come
into Parlament as oppertunity offered, as their inclinations lead them to one side or the other, which was the
caus of great competitions in elections, and of great
charges to thos that stood, insoemuch as it did cost some
persons from one or two hundred pounds to two thousand.
This was not all the reason of some mens soe eager
endeavours to be Parlament men neither. Such as were
in debt found protection by it (this Parlament haveing sitt
soe long, and meeting soe ofton), and others had gotten
great places and presents from Court to stand by that
interest. Soe that it was noe wonder, when I offered
myselfe to stand at Audbrough, if I had noe fewer then
five competitours, which were Sir Jerome Smithson,[1] Mr.
Richard Audbrough, Sir John Hewley,[2] and Mr. Long.
Ther were none of thes that I apprehended soe much as
Mr. Benson,[3] the most notable and formidable man for
business of his time, one of noe birth, and that had raised
himselfe from being clerk to a country atturney to be
clerke of the peace at the Old Bailiff, to clerk of assize of

*

[1] Of Stanwick, the second baronet.

[2] Of York, knighted in June 1663.

[3] Robert Benson, of Red Hall, Wrenthorpe. His son Robert was
created Lord Bingley of Bingley in 1713.

* 4/1: Progers, 25 February 1670/1. A reference in this letter to Benson's suit
against Monckton, over some property, shows that he was aware of Benson's
influence. Benson was also a favourite of Danby who at this point was in the
ascendant.

the northern circuit, and to an estate of 2,500 l. per annum, but not without suspicion of great frauds and oppressions. Besides, he was the great favourite of my Lord Dunblain, then Lord High Tresurer of England.

The way that had been used time out of mind in that borough for chooseing Parlament men was only by nine electours, the owners of nine bourgage houses.   But Mr. Wentworth, lord of the mannour,[1] pretended that long since ther were twenty-four houses that had right to elect, which being at this time in his own possession, he had given (and his predicessours) but one voat for them all, and therfore pretended to alien and sell them now to create soe many more voats.   Thes Mr. Wentworth gave to Mr. Benson.   Mr. Long stood by the popularity, or the househoulders at large that paid scot and lott.   I stood by the only known way of electing, which was the nine (of which I had the majority), and all the rest desisted before the time of election ; soe that the sheriff made a double return of Mr. Benson and me, but did not return Mr. Long.

Being at London I sollicited the Hous of Commons that a day might be appointed to determin the merit of the return between Mr. Benson and me, which he also desired.[2]   But before the day of hearing came the Parlament was prorougued till the 10th of November next, soe that I was at the charge of bringing up witnesses to London to noe purpas.

Jan. 7 [1673/4]

Feb. 24

The Houses being risen, I was informed by some of the members of the Lower Hous that Benson had thrown some reflexions upon me in his discours, as if I was a friend to the Court interest, and it was doubted how I

[1] John Wentworth, younger brother of Sir George Wentworth of Woolley, to whose estates he succeeded in 1660.   In 1653 he had married Elizabeth, daughter of Arthur Aldburgh of Aldborough, and had purchased the whole of the manor from Arthur and William Aldburgh.

[2] James Long also petitioned the Commons on January 7 (*Journals of the House of Commons*, ix. 290).   Benson's case as against both Reresby and Long is summarised in *Cal. S.P. Dom.*, 1675-6, p. 69.

stood inclined to the Church.   Upon this I writt to him,
and sent the letter by my brother the lieutenant, that I was
not against useing all fitt and lawfull means for his success
of his caus in Parlament ; but if he went about to make it
appear better by makeing me or mine appear wors then
we deserved, and by unjust reflexions upon either me or
it, he should give me satisfaction for it.   He sent me word
that thos that had tould me soe did him wrong, that he
never had said anything to my prejudice, nor never would,
and gave it me under his hand.

I returned to Thriberge soon after, wher I passed the
summer.   I laid out that year near 500 l. in land in
Mexbrough and elsewher.

1674

This spring I sett that walke with asshes and sicomores
that leads down to the ponds, and soe to the parke wall
towards Rotherham.   And though I might have planted
trees of better kindes, yet I found that thes agreed best
with the soile, and were of the speediest grouth.   I then
made also the two lowest fish ponds in the park, and
stoored them with tench and carpe.

September   The Duke of Albemarle came down to visit the Duke
of Newcastle and my Lord Ogle, who then lived at Worsop
Mannour.   His lordship sent for me to wait on the Duke,
with whom I then made soe great an acquentance that his
Grace kept me ther eight days.   He tould me I was
related to him by the Yarburghs, and ever after called me
cozen.

His Highness the Duke of Yorke declared his marriage
with Mary, daughter to the Duke of Modena, who had
arrived here not long before with the Duchess her mother.[1]

[1] Mary Beatrice d'Este was the only daughter of Alfonso IV of Modena,
who died in 1662, and his wife Laura, of the house of Martinozzi.   She
married the Duke of York by proxy at Modena on September 20/30,
1673, and on November 21 at Dover the marriage was confirmed by
Bishop Crew of Oxford.

* 6/15: J. Moyser, 14 November 1673. Reresby must be referring to this letter
in which Moyser, his stepfather, urges Sir John to return to London before
Parliament meets.

The nation was much troubled at the match, she being a strict papist, and the match carryed on by the interest of the French King.

The Duke of Buckingham fell again into the Kings *November* ill opinion, by the means of the Duchess of Portsmouth,[1] a French lady, and then the Kings mistris that had the best interest with him, a very fine woeman, and as most thought sent over on purpas to ensnare the King, who was easily taken with that sort of trap. His Grace endeavoured by the means of my Lord Treasurer to be restoored, but could not effect it. The thruth is my Lord Tresurer was not soe zealous to bring it to pas as he ought to have been, considering that he was chiefly obliged to the Duke of Buckingham for his white staff, for which he was accused of ingratitude by others as well as the Duke himselfe.

One thing that the King took ill of him at this time was that being sommoned before the Hous of Commons to give some account of certain matters which they looked upon as miscarriages of goverment whilst he was chiefe minister, he did not only appear, which he needed not to have done, being a peer, and without the Kings leave, but to excuse himself reflected upon others, and behaved himselfe in that assembly in too submissive and mean a manner.[2] However that did not excuse him, for the Commons made an address that it would [please] the King to lay him aside as to all his imployments of trust and profit, and he was called to answer at the barr of the Hous of Lords for his scandalous liveing as man and wife with my Lady Shrewsbury (haveing one of his own), and having kild my Lord of Shrewsbury after he had debauched his wife.

[1] Louise Renée de Kéroualle, whose influence over the King dated from 1671 or earlier, and who was created Duchess of Portsmouth in August 1673.

[2] He was heard in his defence by the Commons on January 13 and 14, 1673/4.

The lieutenancie of the West Rideing was given to my Lord of Danby, Lord Tresurer, who immediately sent me a commission for deputy lieutenant.[1]

In November the King prorougued the Parlament untill the 13 of April.

*   This year I began to build the two little towers at the east and west ends of the hous for closits, and continued

---

[1] The Treasurer, who was not created Earl of Danby till the following June, was given Buckingham's place at the head of the West Riding in February 1673/4. A few weeks later Reresby wrote to him regarding the affairs of that district :

Thriberge, April 17, 1674.—My Lord, I thought myselfe obliged to acquent you that the day after my arrivall in thes parts the counstables of Sheffield came to me to complaine of a great ryot ther committed the 24 of the last month by the apprentices and rabble of that place, who to about the number of 100 entered the Corn Market and severall shops in the town, tooke away from the owners all such pecks and halfe pecks as they found gaged according to the standard, and brooke them, saying they would have the large measures formerly used before the late Act. Severall of them clapt in the stocks by the counstable were rescued by their fellowes, till after having continued togather near two houres they repaired to their respective homes. They further complained that the 30th of the same month towards evening ther mett againe of the same sort of people to about the number of 300 in the street, making proclamation for all apprentices to be ready the next day to breake the new measures, which they accordingly did to a great nomber till dispersed by the officers with halbardeers. The cheife of the town, fearing the like mischeife might happen the next markett day, being the 7th of the instant, having threatned noe less by severall writings sett upon the Maypoule and the church doores, Mr. Edmonds and myselfe went with our servants to Sheffield, wher by binding some of the known leaders to their good behaviour and securing of others wee discouraged the rest from any further attempt for that day. On the 15th the ryot was enquired of by the jurie returned by the sheriff according to our precept, and fifteen persons found guilty, five wherof we apprehended and imprisoned till they paid their fines. The rest absconde for the present, but a capias is issued out against them, by which soe soon as they are taken we shall proceed to fine and imprison them according to the statute. My Lord, though it be my opinion that soe considerable a thing of this kinde could scarcely be attemted by such a sort a people without some incouragement from others, yet I rather beleive it from the mean then better sort of the inhabitants, who truly seemd both active and diligent for the discovery and punishment of the ryoters. I am Your Lordships humble servant, J. R. (Rawlinson MSS. D. 204, f. 60.)

---

* Reresby here erased an entry recording the birth of his daughter Margaret.

to make walls to the additionall part of the parke in winter.

I kept Christmas at Thriberge, wher I entertained severall friends that came to visit me from Audbrough and that side. I bought then a hous in Audbrough and the fee farm rent of Ickles from the Crown.

1675

The time for the meeting of the Parlament approaching, *April 6* I with my wife and family went for London, wher we came safe. The Houses being mett I petitioned the committeè of privileges and elections that the merits of my return and of the caus might be tryed togather, which was voted (Mr. Longs friends in the committè being for this as well as mine). Mr. Benson, surprized with this, thinkeing he had the better of the return by a trick he had played, $*$ petition'd the whole Hous [1] that the merit of the return might be first tryed, which the Hous remits back to be considered of again by the committè. Sir Thomas Meers,[2] then chairman of the committè, tould me that the committè was disposed to confirm what they had done, but were soe angry at the same time with Benson for petitioning the Hous against their voat, that he rather advised me to lett the return be first tryed, not doubting but that I might gett into the Hous. I consented to this, and the 13 day of Aprill [3] was the day named for hearing.

The day before I was advised that the return had been altered by some artifice since it came out of the sherifs hands, and before it was returned into the Crown Office, in favour of Mr. Benson. The words of a double return are thes: *Executio istius brevis patet in quibusdam indenturis huic brevi annexis*; and Benson had caused it

[1] On April 17 (*Journals of the House of Commons*, ix. 318).

[2] Sir Thomas Meres, M.P. for Lincoln, one of the more conservative among the opponents of the Court.

[3] An obvious mistake, as April 13 was the first day of the session.

$*$ *Calendar of State Papers Domestic 1675–1676*, p. 69: 'Mr. Benson's case with Sir John Reresby and Mr. Longe.'

to be altered thus: *Executio istius brevis patet in quadam indentura huic brevi annexa*, as if his indenture was only returned, and mine fixed to the writt to noe purpas. When it came to be heard I prooved soe plainly by Sir Henry Gooderick, who was then of the Hous, that the return was altered since it came from the sheriff, that Benson lost the caus by the very art wherby he hoped to have gott it, and I was voted the sitting member. The next day upon the report of the voat of the committè it was confirm'd by the Hous; and being sworn I was conducted into the Hous by my Lord Russell, eldest son to the Earl of Bedford, and the Lord Cavendish, eldest son to the *April* 14 Lord Devonshire,[1] and ther took my place upon the 14 of Aprill, being my birthday.[2] Thus it pleased God to make the weake to overcome the strong.

Being thus recieved into the Hous of Commons, I found the two factions extream warm one against the other. The Court part was very pressing to gett mony to supply the Kings occasions, the other for gieving noe more without some new lawes for the better securing the Protestant religion and property. Most part of the time being spent in debates *pro* and *con.*, little was effected, for the two partys were soe near equall that neither of

---

[1] William Cavendish, eldest son of William, third Earl of Devonshire, was then M.P. for Derbyshire and a prominent member of the Country party. Before coming up to London Reresby had written to him asking for his assistance at the trial of his election :

March the 19th, [16]74[/5].—My Lord, Some extraordinary occasions confining me for some time to this place, I hope your Lordship will excuse me if I renew my request to you at this distance for your assistance as to my disputed election. My Lord, I know your interest to be soe great in that House that your kindeness is deservedly followed by the major and discreet part of it, and I should be sorry not to gaine it, if any endeavour of mine can merit it either from your Lordship or them ; soe that what you shall thinke fitt to promess for me to your freinds shall be performed to the power of Your humble servant, J. R. (Rawlinson MSS. D. 204, f. 19.)

[2] The report of the committee was made to the House, and Reresby was voted the sitting member, on April 24 (*Journals of the House of Commons*, ix. 323).

* Public Record Office, Indentures C 219/50, 53.

them durst put it to a question. In June Doctor Sherley [1] prefers a petition to the Hous of Lords against Sir John Fagg, a member of the Lower Hous, to appear and answer a caus which he had brought into the Lords Hous, and a sommons was sent to Sir John accordingly. This the Commons considered as a breach of privilege, and were in soe great a heat upon it that severall bould voats passed in either Hous, the one against the other,[2] upon that occasion, which caused the King to adjourn the Parlament.[3]

During this short time of sitting in the Hous I confess I thought the country party had great reason in their debates ; but I was carefull how I voted, the merit of my caus being yet behind.

My Lord Treasurer was faln upon in the Hous of Commons, but came of very well for that time.[4]

I returned for Yorkshire, and continued to build and enlarge the parke towards the old parke, dividing it into two by a wall. Of one moytie I made a farm or two, the other I added to the parke. *June 24*

My Lord Darcy of Aston was at this time at great difference with his brother in law Sir Henry Marwood,[5] high sherif of the county, and both of them complaining to me I endeavoured to make them friends, and effected it. This sommer I bought of one Sturdy one moytie of

[1] Thomas Sherley, M.D., physician in ordinary to Charles II.

[2] Sir John Fagg, M.P. for Steyning, was in possession of the estate of Wiston, which had been sold by Sherley's grandfather. Sherley attempted to recover the estate, and on the case being decided against him in Chancery, appealed to the House of Lords. The quarrel between the two Houses, due to the refusal of the Commons to allow Fagg to answer while Parliament was sitting, continued throughout May.

[3] On June 9 Parliament was prorogued to October 13.

[4] Articles of impeachment were introduced against him on April 26, but the charges were unconvincing in character and poorly supported, and were all dismissed by May 3.

[5] Henry Marwood, who did not succeed his father as second baronet until February 1679/80, had married Margaret, sister of Conyers Darcy, son and heir of Conyers, Lord Darcy and Conyers, created Earl of Holderness in 1682.

a rent charge issuing out of my estate, 36 l. per annum, contracted by Sir George Reresby.   It cost me 225 l.

The Parlament being to meet speedily, I went for *Sept.* 28 London the 28th of September.

The committè of elections had noe sooner sate but my two competitors, Benson and Long, petitioned against me that a day might be named for the hearing the merit of the caus or election between them and me.   It was their business to gett a speedy day, but mine (since I was in possession) to gett as long a day as I could, and by the interest of my friends gott it putt of for six weeks, or indeed for that session, for the other business of the Hous was soe great that the Parlament was proroagued before the election came to be heard.

I took a perticular or journall with my own hand of what was debated and passed this session (too long to be inserted here), but the chiefe matters were thes:

The King in his speech had tould us that he was four millions in debt, besides what he owed to the gouldsmiths or bankeers of a vast summ more (for the which he then paid neither principle nor interest, to the ruine of many families).[1]   It being put to the voat whether mony should be given or not, twas carryed in the negative by four voices only, when ther was near 400 members present.[2] But it appearing that both the Dutch and French did exceed us both in the proportion and nomber of our ships, 300,000 l. was voted to be given the King for the building of 20 ships, viz., 1 of the first rate, 5 of the second rate, and 14 of the third.

Severall ways were debated for the raising this summe.

[1] Charles was not quite so plain about his financial position as Reresby makes out, nor were the bankers being quite so badly treated.   Compound interest at the rate of 6 per cent. calculated half-yearly was being regularly added to the sums due to them.

[2] On October 19.   The question was whether the Commons would take off the anticipations on the royal revenue, which were believed to amount to £1,000,000, and the decisive vote was 172 to 165 against the Government (Grey's *Debates*, iii. 311).

Some were for the way of land tax, others by subsidy, some for raising it upon the Jewes, others by poull, others upon French commodities, others upon consumption of our own and upon marchandize. At last it was agreed to be laid upon land, to be paid in eighteen months, to be lodged apart in the Exchequer and appropriated to that use, with very severe penalties upon the officers which should apply it to any other uses. The proportion of the sum, the time of its being raised, and thes other circumstances, did noe ways satisfie the Court. Voated further, That the customes haveing been formerly given to the King for the maintenance of the fleet, that such a claus to confirm it should be inserted in this bill, or a perticular bill prepared for it. Mr. Waller the poet,[1] an ould Parlament man, said this was the most nescessary thing that could be, for the riches and strength of all countries is proportionable to their trade, therfore trade must both inrich the country and mentain itselfe, therfore the customes must defray the fleet, for if it be done by land as much goes out of the kingdome that way as trade brings in, and soe the nation would soon be ruined.

The condition of the fleet at that time, as it was given in by the officers of the navy to the Hous, were 8 first rates, 9 secound rates, 43 third rates. The French had at that time 26 more of thes rates then we, and the Dutch had 14 more.

Severall grivences were complained of in the Hous this session, which were reduced to three heads:

1. As to religion, as simony, plurality of liveings, suffering conventicles, debauchery.

2. In trade.

3. In civill goverment.

It was voated that athisme, debauchery, and impiety practiced in this age be inserted as one grievence. It being notoriously suspected that some members of that

---

[1] Edmund Waller, then M.P. for Hastings. His speech, delivered on November 8, is given in Grey's *Debates*, iii. 428.

Hous did recieve rewards from Court to give their voats as was desired on that side, it was voted that a committeè should be appointed to form a kind of oath or test, to discover what sums of mony or offices had been given to Parlament men to gain their voats.

The French trade was then complained of as out-ballancing ours 1,300,000 *l.* per annum.

It appeared, upon debate of the mony to be given to the King, that every 1,000 l. a year had paid 100 l. since the Restoration in taxes to the Crown.

It was voted another grievance that the justices of the peace should be sommoned to appear before the Councill, ther to give an account for what they did juditially.

Nov. 14   The business of Luzance [1] took up some time in the Hous. This Luzance was a French Jesuist, lately con-verted to the Church of England, and made his recanta-tion sermon in the French Protestant Church in the Savoy, wher he very much laid opon the falacies of the Roman Church and reflected upon them. The whole party being very angry at him for it, one Doctor Burnet,[2] a Jesuist and confessor to the Duchesse of Yorke, finding him alone in his chamber (with three more that stood at the door), threatned to kill him, except he would promess to return to the Church of Rome, and presently recant his sermon preached at the Savoy under his hand, and goe speedily for France.

Finding himself in this pinche he engaged to doe all this, till he gott his liberty; and then presently went and revealed it to Doctor Breval,[3] a converted Jesuist, who the next day acquainted me with it, and I tould it the Hous.[4]

---

[1] Hippolyte, son of François Chastelet, who had taken the name " de Luzancy."

[2] Father St. Germain, otherwise known as Dr. Burnet.

[3] Francis Durand de Bréval, created D.D. of Cambridge University and prebendary of Westminster in the autumn of 1675.

[4] Other authorities do not assign to Reresby quite as prominent a part in this as he claims. The House was informed of the matter on November 8

* 10/14: Vicur, 2 March 1675/6; 10/15: G. Breval, 3 February 1675/6; 10/20: H. Marwood, 4 January 1675/6; 10/77: G. Breval, 17 February 1675/6. Reres-by's account is not necessarily contradictory of his claim that he 'tould it the Hous'. A probable scenario was that Reresby saw Russell and Goodricke in the hall and reported to them. Russell then related this version to the House. Cf. Geiter, 'Reresby', pp. 53–57.

The Commons tooke the matter with great warmth, appointed a committè to examin the matter, and me to bring Luzance before it the next day, wher he appeared and testifyed the whole thing to be true.   This was the first time that I presumed to speake in that great assembly or in any committè, wher the next day I was obliged to doe it ofton in this matter.

Upon the report from the comitteè to the Hous my Lord Cavendish called me up to give an account to the Hous of some other things which Luzance had acquainted me with.[1]   One was that two French Protestants had been threatned (being merchants of good ability and credit) by some papists, that except they were less severe against Romanists they should shortly see the Protestant blood flowe in London streets.   The Hous, upon this information by me, appointed a committè to enquire into the thruth of it, to which Luzance, being sommoned to appear, testified the thruth, and gave the words under his own hands to the committè.   The party that tould him them, being sent for, also appeared, and justifyed thos threats had been used to them from some French papists, but (whether gained by that party or in fear of them) gave in only such names as were of persons either absent or of small repute, soe that little light appeared by it.   But this and other such informations concerning the height and bouldness of the papists did soe exasperate the Hous that many motions were made to reduce them.   Some were for a speedy confinement of them to the country, others for banishment, others for disarming them, &c.

Hearing of a quarrell between my Lord Cavendish and Collonel Thomas Howard (the first a member of our Hous, the other brother to the Earl of Carlisle, a

by William Russell and Sir Henry Goodricke, and Reresby was not even a member of the committee appointed to investigate it (Grey's *Debates*, iii. 419 *et seq.* ; *Journals of the House of Commons*, ix. 370).

[1] The report was made on November 13.   Reresby's speech is recorded in Grey's *Debates*, iv. 8.

papist),[1] and that the collonel had spred abroad a letter or libel reflecting upon his lordship and Sir Thomas Meers, another member of that Hous, I acquainted the Hous with it, and mooved that care might be taken to prevent the further consequence of this quarrell. The Hous took care of my Lord Cavendish (who was very brave) in this matter, but not of Sir Thomas Meers, not fearing that his courage would draw him into much danger. I mooved upon this that the same engagement might be taken from Sir Thomas that was from my Lord nott to stirr further therin ; which Sir Thomas took soe kindly, he being chairman of the comittè of elections, that I made him my friend by it ever after.[2]

Soon after, the matter of Doctor Sherley's petitioning the Lords against Sir John Fag was again renewed, which had broake up the Parlament the last time. Some thought the King had consented to it, not likeing the warm proceedings of both Houses; others that some lords of the country interest had persuaded Sherley to it, wherby soe to blowe up the difference concerning privilege between the two Houses, that the King should be obliged either to proroague, adjourn, or dessolve them, they fearing that if this Parlament should sitt much longer the greater part might be soe gained by mony or places as to doe whatever the Court desired of them ; and my Lord Halifax (then in the interest of my Lord Shaftsbury, his oncle,[3] who was faln out with the Court, being noe longer Lord Chancellor) tould me [this] was his opinion.

[1] Thomas Howard, brother of Charles, first Earl of Carlisle, had been lieutenant-colonel of the regiment of foot raised under his brother's command in 1673 and disbanded in 1674 (Dalton, *English Army Lists*, i. 135). The paper which he dispersed is printed in Newdigate-Newdegate, *Cavalier and Puritan*, pp. 74-5.

[2] This story hardly agrees with Reresby's statement that his first speech in the Commons was in connection with the Luzancy affair, for the paper circulated by Howard was brought before the House on October 13, the first day of the session.

[3] Shaftesbury's first wife was Margaret, daughter of Thomas, Lord Coventry, and sister of Anne, Halifax's mother.

Whatever the caus was, the effect was that the Commons denying that their member should plead at the barr of the Lords during a time of privilege, it was voted that *Nov.* 18 the Lords, by recieveing any appeale from any court either of law or equity against a member of the Lower Hous during a session of Parlament, were therby infringers of the privileges of the Commons of England; and that such lawers as did attend as council to plead in any such caus at the Lords barr should be deemed betrayers of the rights of the Commons of England, and proceeded against accordingly; and that the said voat should be affixed on the door of the Hous of Commons, of Westminster Hall, and of the Inns of Court, which was done accordingly. The same day it was voted by the Lords that the said voat was illegal and unparlamentary, and tending to the dissolution of the Goverment; and further, that they would never recede from their right of judicature by appeales from courts of equity.

It was then putt to the question if the King should not be petitioned to to dessolve this Parlament. This was carryed in the negative by two voices only. This proceeding of both Houses did extreamly dissatisfie the King. The Lords who had given their voats for dissolveing this Parlament protested against the negative voat, and did, enter their reasons for soe doing in the journals. Things going thus, the only expedient was [to] dismiss the Parlament, which the King did by proroageing it to the 10th day of February next.[1]

Before I left London, at the interposition of my Lord Ogle, I went with his lordship to see the Duke of Buckingham, knowing before that he would recieve me kindly.

I sett out for Thriberge, wher I found my family well. *Dec.* 1 I kept a great Christmas that year. Ther dined with me on New Years Day 300 people at the least.   *

[1] Parliament was prorogued on November 22, not to February 10 following, but to February 15, 1676/7.

* Reresby here erased an entry which apparently related to the birth of another child.

1676

At the Lent assizes at Yorke I communicated a letter, which my Lord High Tresurer had directed to me to that intent, to the justices of the peace of the West Rideing.[1]   The occasion of it was this:

Hallamshire, a corner of the West Rideing of five miles distance round from Sheffield, is a corporation of cutlers by Act of Parlament, wher the manufacture of makeing edge tooles is carryed on by severall furnices or blowing houses, wher the iron and steele is heated and prepared for the makeing of knives and sissers, &c.   The recievers of hearth mony had levyed this duty upon the poor smiths for thes furnices or forges, and the corporation of cutlers had spent near 200 l. in law with the King to try the right of this matter, concieveing they were not liable to pay by Act of Parlament, without bringing it to any certain issue. They then came and complained to me as the next justice of the peace of this oppression, and desired my opinion of it.   Upon weighing the matter I tould them that I concieved that thos furnices or forges came within the quality of blowing houses, which were litterally exempted by the statutes of hearth mony, and were therfore not liable to pay; and did further (the officers being com'd to make distresses) grant my order for redelivery of such distresses, and persuaded some nighbouring justices to joine with me in it.   Till this time the justices of the peace had refused to appear in this matter, which had obliged the corporation to spend soe much mony at common law. The collectors obayed our order, but complained above of me for obstructing his Majestys revenue, and of Sir

*
†

Godfrey Copley.[2]   Upon this account it was that my Lord Tresurer had written the said letter, purporting that upon

[1] The letter, dated February 24, 1675/6, is summarised in *Calendar of Treasury Books*, v. 137.

[2] Of Sprotborough ;   created a baronet on June 17, 1661.   He was first cousin of the Lord Treasurer.

* 9/13: Copley, 13 November 1675. This letter shows that it was difficult to define what constituted a hearth. In Sheffield cutlers used hearths for both domestic and commercial activities. Copley and Reresby were charged with obstructing the revenue.

† 9/2: William Frankland, 9 January 1675/6; 9/10: Robert Ethrington, 12 February 1675/6; 10/76: William Hickman, 11 May 1676. These letters illustrate the complexity of the Hearth Tax. Cf. Geiter, 'Reresby', pp. 59–66.

good advice with the Kings Council the said hearths appeared liable to pay the said duty, that the order granted for the redelivery of the distresses was illegall, with advice not to be too forward or busy in obstructing the Kings revenue.

This letter being communicated to the justices of the peace of the county at the assizes (wher we were about forty togather), it was unanimously agreed upon (considering the said Acts) that such sort of forges ought not to pay, and that the order granted by me &c. was legal, and subscribed a letter to his lordship under all their hands to the same purpass.[1] My Lord Tresurer answered that letter soon after, directing his answer to my Lord Fairfax,[2] who communicated it at another meeting to the justices at Yorke. But that letter had also the same effect, and the justices persisted in the same opinion as before,[3] notwithstanding that my Lord Chiefe Justice North[4] and Baron Bertue,[5] who came down judges that assize, endeavoured to desuade us from it. I did not please at Court by this proceeding, but whatever I lost ther I gained in my country.

Some three years before, being sued by the Duke of Norfolke[6] for my carriers comming into Rotherham to

*

---

[1] This letter, dated March 7, 1675/6, is summarised in *Calendar of Treasury Books*, v. 417. There are thirty signatures.

[2] Dated March 18, 1675/6 (*ibid.*, p. 159).

[3] Their reply, dated May 2, 1676, is *ibid.*, p. 417.

[4] Francis North, created Chief Justice of the Common Pleas in January 1675. At the close of 1682 he was appointed Lord Keeper, an office which he retained, with the title of Baron Guilford, until his death early in the reign of James II.

[5] Vere Bertie, fourth son of the second Earl of Lindsey and brother-in-law of the Lord Treasurer.

[6] Thomas Howard, restored to the dukedom of Norfolk in December 1660. The Duke, however, was confined as a lunatic in Italy, and Reresby's reference seems to be to his brother, Henry, Earl of Norwich and Earl Marshal, who succeeded him as sixth Duke of Norfolk in December 1677.

---

* 11/8: Halifax, 13 June 1676, alludes to a proposal of Reresby's to solve the Hearth Tax dilemma (apparently a clause to exempt forges under certain conditions). Halifax cautioned him to wait because 'at this time I do not think it seasonable'. That the idea was not dropped altogether is shown by a letter from the cutlers of Hallamshire, dated 6 May 1679, requesting that Reresby introduce such a clause. 14/154.

July

fetch groyst to Ickles miln, I had a verdict at Yorke ; the year after, his Grace brought it about again, and gott a verdict against me; and this sommer, it being tryed the third time, the verdict was this, that such persons as were tenents to the Duke or the mannour ought to grind at the lords miln; that such inhabitants as were not (as severall of them were) had right to grind wher they pleased.   My Lord Chiefe Justice North seemed very partiall to the Duke in the hearing of this caus.   However, he could not gain the point contended for, which was to have Rotherham an entire soke, wher noe carriers ought to come in to fetch corn but the lords.

July

My competitor Mr. Benson, who had greatly ingratiated himselfe with my Lord High Treasurer under pretence to find out extraordinary ways (by concealements, fyns, and forfitures, &c.) to gett the King mony (and none more able then himselfe, being very arch and notable, and understanding the pleas of the Crown), had obteaned a promess of a patent, to pass under the great seale, to be an assistant to my Lord Tresurer, by way of discovery, &c., for the improovement of his Majestys revenue, as also to be made a judge.   But one day, as he was returning from his lordships to his own chamber in Grays Inn, it pleased God to dispose of him otherwise, for as he was going up the stairs to the passage at the end of

*

the hall he was seized with a fitt of apoplexy, and soe dyed without speakeing one word.

September

I bought a close and some land in Bradmarsh of John Chadwick of the value of 5 l. 12 s. 6 d. per annum.

October

I bought six pounds per annum in a hous and lands in Mexbrough of one Wortley, which had been given to Leonard Reresby, a yonger son of Sir Thomas Reresby, and sould by him to Wortley.

And bycaus the way of liveing and conversation amongst ones nighbours at this time may something divert thos that come after to be informed of it, take here a perticular of such gentlemen as came and stay'd at my hous this

* 10/4, 38: both letters, dated 11 July 1676, tell of Benson's death, but the former by Reresby's brother Edmund is the more informative. In describing Benson's actions on the day of his death Edmund related that 'he went well in ye morning to my Lord treasurers (where he never faild once a day to make his court, through whose intrest if he had lived had suddenly been maid a judge) & whilst he was there findeing himselfe not well, tooke cooch [*sic*: coach] & when he came to Grays inn gate lighted to goe to his chamber but before he reacht ye hall fell downe on his face wch he broke with the fall & never spook word, but after 2 or 3 grones dyed immediately'.

summer, some two or three nights, some four or five—
Sir Scroop Howe and his brother;[1] my oncle Yarburgh and
his wife;[2] my oncle Yarburgh of Doncaster, his wife[3] and
children; my ant Vicecountess Monson, her husband
(being marryed the fourth time to Adam Felton, Esquire),
with her daughter by Monson, came from Suffolke and
stayed here a month; my second brother, lieutenant in
the guards, and my third brother, marchant, lately
arrived in England, stayed here a month; Mr. Moyser,
my father in lawe, once alone; a second time he came and
stayed with my Lord Clifford; Sir Thomas Yarburgh and
his lady;[4] my Lady Downs, wife to my Lord Downs;[5]
Mr. Blythman and his wife; Mr. Edmonds, both justices
of the peace;[6] my Lord Darcy (not long before marryed
to the Countess of Southampton) and his lady;[7] Anthony
Francland of Aldworke,[8] Esquire, cozen german to
my wife; my Lord Ogle, since Duke of Newcastle, and
Mr. Fane of Raby Castle,[9] but they only dined; the

[1] Sir Scrope Howe had entered Parliament as member for Nottinghamshire only a short time before Reresby himself was returned, and had joined
the opposition. He had three brothers, to any one of whom Sir John may
be referring.

[2] Thomas Yarburgh of Campsal and his first wife, Ann, daughter of
Thomas Ellis of Nothill, Bedfordshire.

[3] Edmund Yarburgh and Anne, daughter of Thomas Stanhope of Stotfold.

[4] Sir Thomas, the head of the family and Reresby's first cousin, had
married Henrietta Maria, eldest daughter and co-heiress of Colonel Thomas
Blagge of Hollinger, Suffolk.

[5] Dorothy, daughter of William Johnson of Wickham, Lincolnshire, the
second wife of Sir John Dawnay, created first Viscount Downe in the
peerage of Ireland in 1680.

[6] Jasper Blythman of Newlathes, who married Catherine, daughter of
Richard Mountney of Rotherham; and Henry Edmunds of Worsborough.

[7] Conyers Lord Darcy married as his third wife Frances, daughter of
William Seymour, second Duke of Somerset, and widow of Lord Treasurer
Southampton.

[8] Eldest son of Lady Reresby's uncle Henry.

[9] Christopher Vane, son of Sir Henry Vane the younger, created Baron
Barnard of Barnard Castle in 1699.

high sheriff and his lady,[1] with more too tedious to mention.

The inhabitants within the liberty of Hallamshire came then to complain of a great exaction upon them by the clerk of the markit within that liberty, who had farmed that office of the Duke of Norfolk, for makeing every man pay fourpence for sealing a peck (or other measure) or a yeard, wheras the statute allowes but one penny, and for setting great fynes upon the lands of such as refused to pay the said rates. I convened the offender, and bound him over to the sessions, wher he was soe handled that he ran away out of the country. However, to be revenged of thos that had complained of him, he returnd severall fyns into the Exchequer, and gott them estroyted; but I stopped the estroyts in the sherifs hands till the assizes, then acquainted the judges with the whole practice, who provented the issues above and soe saved that part of the country near 200 l.

*

I had a fine More about sixteen years of age (given me by a gentleman, one Mr. Drax, who had brought him out of the Barbadoes), that had lived with me some years, and dyed about this time of an imposthume in his head. I
Oct. 20 recieved an account in October (six weeks after he was buried) from London, that it was credibly reported ther
† that I had caused him to be gelt, and that it had occasioned his death. I laughed at it at the first, knowing it to be false, as a ridiculous story, till I was further informed that this came from the Duke of Norfolke and his family, with whom, as I have said before, I had had some suits and differences, and that he had waited upon the King to beg my estate in case it prooved forfited by this felony. I then thought it convenient to send for the coroner to vew the body by a jury before the body was too much decayed, least a decay by rotteness in that part might be imputed to an insision. The coroner sommons a jury, and doth

---

[1] Sir Edmund Jennings of Ripon, and Margaret, daughter of Sir Edward Barkham.

* Reresby here erased an entry referring to his wife.

† Bundle 10 in the Mexborough MSS. contains details of the incident and shows the strong support which Reresby received from his peers. Cf. Bodleian Library, Rawlinson MSS. D. 204, fols. 22, 23, 24; Geiter, 'Reresby', pp. 67–70.

his office.   But when they came to uncover the breast,
it was soe putrifyed they would goe noe further, but upon
the examination of eleven witnesses (some that laid him
out, the rest that saw him naked, severall bycaus of his
colour haveing the curiosity to see him after he was dead)
gave in their verdict that he dyed *ex visitatione Dei* (or by
the hand of God).

This would not serve, for within few days after ther
came one Bright, a lawyer, one Chappell, an atturney
(both concerned in the Dukes affairs), and one Buck, a
chirurgien, of Sheffield (whom I had caused to be prossecuted not long before for haveing two wives), with some
others, with my Lord Chiefe Justice warrant directed to
the coroner to take up the body, who refused to execute it,
saying he had done his office already.   However thes
embassadours took up the body, and Buck, under pretence to vew the cod better, would have lifted it up with
a penknife, which was not suffered, least by that instrument he should have given the part the wound he sought
for.   But that which was not only a mercy but a miracle,
when the cod came to be fairly vewed, notwithstanding his
being buried near two months, and the rest of his body
much putrified, it was as sound and firm as when he was
born; soe that they went away with as much confusion and
shame as they deserved.

This was a black and yet a ridiculous malice, for had
the thing prooved to have been done all their art could
never have fixed it soe as to have brought either me or my
estate into danger.   My Lord Chiefe Justice Rainsford
granted this warrant illegally, the information of the fact
being not given upon oath.   He confessed to me afterwards he was misled in the thinge, and that the Dukes
sollicitour was very urgent with him to grant that warrant.
The Duke of Yorke tould my brother Edmond that he
wondered to hear soe much discours of the thruth of a
thing which he always did believe to [be] false.   My Lord   *
Ogle tould me (and soe did my Lord Treasurer afterwards

* 10/27: E. Reresby, 28 October 1676; 11/5: Lord Ogle, 1 October 1676;
10/94: Godfrey Copley, 14 November 1676.

himselfe) that he (meaning my Lord Treasurer) had taken great pains to prevent the begging of my estate with the King, and I believed it to be true; but I fear it was with design, had it prooved a forfiture, to have beg'd it himselfe, for some tould me soe afterwards. However, I endeavoured to find out the bottome of this matter, and to be repaired in some measure, as you will read hereafter.

November

*

The decree in the Exchequer this term confirmed the verdict at the assizes upon the tryall twixt my Lord Marshall and me about our milns, and that court ordered my Lord to pay me 20 l. costs.

December   I kept Christmas at Thriberge.

February   I went to London with my wife, who, poor woeman, had
[1676/7]   not been well for some time.   I went well guarded for fear of some of my back friends and highwaymen, haveing caused one of the chiefe of them to be taken not long before.

I noe sooner arrived at London but my Lord Treasurer sent to speake to me.   I went to his lordship, and found [him] very free in his discours upon severall subjects, but most lamenting that his countrymen would not give him opportunity to serve them near the King; made severall protestations that all the jealousies of such as called themselves of the country party were groundless; that the King to his knowlege had noe design but to preserve the religion and goverment as established by lawe; and wished that neither himselfe nor posterity might prosper if he did not speake his beliefe; that if ther was any danger to the goverment, it was more from thos that pretended to be zealous for it, who, under that colour, were straining matters to soe high a pitch on that side (by pinching the Crown in supplys and in the prerogative) as to create discontents betwixt the King and his people, that confusion might be the issue; and therfore desired me to be carefull not to imbarke with that sort of people.   I replyed that I hoped I was not one to suffer myselfe to be misled; I should have noe other guide in that Hous but my reason and concience, and therfore could not followe any faction

* 10/43: Edmund Reresby, 18 November 1676.

or party; that as much as I yet understood of the duty of a member ther at this time, it was to be moderate and healing between the two extreams, and to have a due reguard to the King's prerogative as well as the liberty of the subject.

It is very true that till that time (that my Lord Treasurer used soe many asseverations of the Kings intention of continuing to govern by law, and made it pritty clear to me that some of the chiefe of the country faction were driveing on their perticular interest under colour of the publique good) I had much more beliefe of their thruth and sincerity.

I arrived at London. The Parlament mett the 15th. *Feb.* 10 That which the King did chiefely desire of us this session was a convenient sum for the building and rigging the ships. The country party obstructed all they could the giveing above 400,000 l.; the Court party were for a million, or 800,000 l. at the least; the moderate men were for 600,000 l., which sum was granted, and for which sum I gave my voat, for the building of thirty men of warr of severall rates.[1]

My Lord Treasurer took this soe well, that I went not to the height with thos men that did all they could to weaken the Crown, that he would needs carry me to kiss his Majestys hand, which ceremony I had not then performd since my arrivall in town. He presented me to him in the lobby of the Hous of Lords, next to the Prince his lodgeings, ther being noebody present but the King, his lordship, and myselfe. My Lord tould the King a great many good things of me more then I deserved, but last that as my family had been loyall he knew my disposition was to follow the steps of it, and the best way to be confirmed in that was to understand how little thruth ther was in the pretences now sett on foot to withdraw gentlemen from their duty in that perticular.

The King said he had known me long, and hoped I

---

[1] The vote for £600,000 passed on February 21.

knew him soe well that I should not believe thos reports of him. I know, says he, it is said that I intend the sub-version of the religion and goverment, that I intend to govern by an army and by arbitrary power, to lay aside Parlaments, and to raise mony by other ways. But every man, nay thos that say it the most, know it is false. There is noe subject that lives under me whos safety and well doing I desire less then my own, and should be as sorry to invade his property and liberty as that another should invade mine. Thos members of Parlament, said the King, that pretend this great zeale for the publique good, are of two kindes, either such as would subvert the goverment them-selves and bring it to a commonwealth again, or such as seem to joine with that party and talke loud against the Court, hopeing to have their mouths stopped by places or preferments. Indeed my Lord Treasurer had named some of the heads of that party to me, that had desired such and such things of the King, and would have com'd over upon thos terms.

I replyed that it was true that the pretences were many and plausible (I believed to some) that thos people made to oppose that which others understood to be his Majesty's interest, but it had gained little upon me, that had the honour of being soe long known to his Majesty, and had been soe lately confirmed in my beliefe by thos assurances recieved from my Lord Treasurer; that I should never to the best of my knowlege doe anything but what became a true and faithfull subject, and what should be consistant with the prosperity of his Majestys royall person and goverment. The King tould me that he was very well pleased that he had seen me, commanded me to wait upon him sometimes, and said I should have access to him when and wherever I desired it.

This condescention in the King to give soe mean a person this satisfaction did much convince me of the reality of what he said, joined with the temper and constitution too of the prince, who was not stirring nor ambitious, but easy, loved pleasures, and seemed chiefly to desire quiet and security for his own time.

A great difference being at that time between the Lord Martial of England, Lord Henry Howard (though comonly called the Duke of Norfolke), and his yonger brothers about an,[1] the brothers came and petitioned the Hous of Commons, setting forth the injustice done them by my Lord Martiall, and not only to them, but to their eldest brother, the Duke of Norfolke, whom the said Lord Martial kept up at Padua as a madman, though very well in his senses, and therfore desired that the Hous would please to move the King that the Lord Martiall might be obliged to send for him into England.[2]   Upon this ther began a debate in the Hous of the condition of the said Duke, and many did argue as they did believe that he was in a good condition of health, and was only kept ther by his brother to enjoy his estate.   Whereupon the gentlemen of the Hous that had been abroad in that part were desired to declare their opinions in what condition they had seen him; and myselfe amongst others did say what I knew of him at that time that I see him ther, which was that to the best of my observation he had all the markes imaginable of lunacy and distraction upon him.   This it seems being tould my Lord Martial, who knew very well that I had noe obligation from him to say anything that might turn soe much to his advantage as this did, sent a gentleman to me, one Mr. Anslowe, the next day, to thanke me for acting soe generously in the concern of a person that had not appeared my friend soe much as he ought to have done, and yet he had not appeared against me in many perticulars wher I was jealous of him, and perticularly in that of the blackamore; and that he intended to wait upon me to satisfie me further of it.

[1] A word or phrase has been omitted here.

[2] The petition was presented to the Commons on February 19, and referred to a committee, to which Reresby was added on the following day (*Journals of the House of Commons*, ix. 385).

I answered that I was surprized with this compliment from a gentleman to whom I intended none, what I said being only in reguard to thruth; however I was not sorry that it had soe hapned that I had obliged my Lord by it, and since he declared he was not concerned in that black affair of the More, I should prevent his lordship, and wait upon him. Within two or three days I went to see him. He recieved me with all the expressions of kindness imaginable, and wished that neither himselfe nor posterity might prosper if he was any way consenting or assisting against me in that matter. I tould his lordship that I was obliged to believe him bycaus he said soe, but if he was not I was sure his servants was, desired his leave that I might use my endeavours to find it out. He said with all his heart he did not only agree to it, but would helpe me in it; and soe we parted in great friendship. His lordship came to see me soon after. I was not sorry for this unexpected effect of this thing, for though a man must not doe mean things to make great men their friends (bycaus they have a great deale of power), yet it is a follie to omitt such an opportunity of being reconciled to them. It is not wise to have a poor man one's ennemy, if it can be helped, much more a rich.

The Hous of Commons, however, mooved his Majesty by the privy councillors who were members of that Hous to send for the Duke of Norfolk, but he took noe notice of the petition.

I very ofton visited and dined with my Lord Tresurer, and ofton waited upon the King, and when he see me would aske what past.

March 18   I entertained him a great while in the Duchess of Yorks bedchamber upon the transactions of that day in the Hous of Commons.[1]

The business of this session had gone on pritty coolly in both Houses, and my Lord Tresurer did soe order the matter that the Kings party encreased rather then the

[1] The Commons did not meet on March 18, which was a Sunday.

other; but it was much feared that some voats were gained more by purchass then affection.

1677

The Commons voted a second address to be made to *March* 29 the King, that he would please to make alliances for the preservation of Flanders in the possession of King of Spain, but with this limitation, that the King should not be obliged to return any answer to the Hous upon that addresse; and yet a great many that would have drawn the King into inconveniences would have had the King urged to declare his intent therin, which must have been either to disoblige the nation on one hand, or to declare a warr with France on the other, before he was prepared to make it.

The same time I had a great deale of discours privately with my Lord Tresurer in his own chamber. He ther shewed me severall letters (with their answers) which he had written to Mr. Wentworth and others not to disturb me in my election, which was yet endeavoured on the behalfe of the town, though Benson was dead.[1]

A box upon the ear was given that day in the Hous of Commons; but the occasion being accidentall, after some debate it was thus ended, that both the gentlemen engaged themselves to the Speaker that nothing more should be done in it.[2]

I entertained the King in the Duchess of Portsmoths 30 chamber with the Marquis of Worchester.[3]

[1] A petition presented to the Commons on February 19 had to be withdrawn because it was not properly supported ; but on February 26 another * petition was presented, and referred to the committee of elections and privileges (*Journals of the House of Commons*, ix. 385, 389).

[2] The origin of this affair was no more than a friendly scuffle between Andrew Marvell, the poet, who represented Hull, and Sir Philip Harcourt, M.P. for Boston.   Some members wished to magnify the incident, and the House as a whole thought it necessary to intervene in the interests of decency and order (Grey's *Debates*, iv. 328-31).

[3] Henry Somerset, third Marquis of Worcester, created first Duke of Beaufort in 1682.

* 10/96: G. Copley, 24 March 1676/7.

April 12   The King and the Duke had both of them interested themselves soe far in the matter of my election, that it being to be tryed very soon (being at the Kings riseing that day) the King gave order to his servants that were members to attend the committè, and to assist me when it came on.   The same day the Duke of Albemarle came down to engage his friends to be for me.   The Duke of Yorke concern'd himselfe very earnestly for me.

April 12   Being alone with my Lord Tresurer in his coach going to Westminster, I tould him that some of the discontented party did resolve to hasten the mony bill as fast as they could, that soe the Parlament might rise before Easter, and the publique bills that were prepareing might be left unpassed, hopeing by this to dissatisfie the nation, and to afford caus of complaint against the King, as if the Parlament met for nothing but to give mony.   His lordship said that the King was aware of that, and had prevented it by a message intended that day to be delivered by Secretary Coventry[1] to the Hous, to this effect, that if anything remained to be done which that Hous did judge nescessary for the good of the nation, that the King would give them time to finish it after Easter, and when they were ready he would pas their bils; which was said according y.[2]

My Lord Tresurer sent for me among others that evening, and desired us to assist what we could to reconcile a difference likely to happen between the two Houses about frameing the bill for the 600,000 l. to be given the King, which might endanger the loss of the bill.

The thing was this.   The Commons had made a claus in the bill that the officers of the Exchequer should give an account to that Hous of the laying out of that mony to the uses to which it was given.   The Lords had added

---

[1] Henry Coventry, elder brother of Sir William, had been appointed Secretary of State in 1672.

[2] The message was delivered to the Commons on April 11 by Coventry's colleague, Sir Joseph Williamson, who had succeeded Arlington as Secretary in 1674.

another to that, which was that thos officers should be accountable to both Houses. The Commons would not allowe of this, saying the Lords could neither add nor deminish in bils for mony; as it was peculiar to the Commons to give mony, soe it was only proper to them to have an account of its laying forth. The Lords replyed that to deny them to call the officers of the Exchequer to an account was to deny them their privilege of judicature which they had as the supreme court; and were possessed of it in the very like case, for when mony was given by the Convention for disbanding the army, an account of laying it out was ther enacted to be given to their Hous as well as the other. In fyne, both adhearing to their point, the King prevailed with the Lords to rase their claus out of the bill, and the other continuing it passed after in that method; soe the Commons gott the better.

My Lord High Tresurer and the Duke of Newcastle *April* 19 went to Windser to be enstalled Knights of the Garter. I waited upon them, supped that night with the Duke, and dined the day after with the Countess of Danby,[1] my Lord's own [table] being filled with the Knights assisting to that ceremony, amongst which were Duke Lotherdale,[2] the Duke of Albemarle, the Earls of Oxford and Mougrave,[3] &c. This ceremony was more solomn and splended then usuall by reason of the great nomber of coaches that attended my Lord Tresurer, being forty-six with six horses apiece.

The King of France had not long before this gott a victory over the Prince of Orange,[4] and in his return by

[1] Bridget, second daughter of Montague Bertie, second Earl of Lindsey.

[2] John Maitland, Duke of Lauderdale in the Scottish peerage, Secretary for Scottish affairs and virtual ruler of Scotland.

[3] John Sheffield, third Earl of Mulgrave, who rose high in the favour of James II and became Lord Lieutenant of the East Riding of Yorkshire in 1687. He was created Marquis of Normanby in 1694, and Duke of Buckingham and Normanby in 1703.

[4] At Cassel on April 1/11.

Calais sent over the Duke of Crequy [1] and the Archbishop of Resms [2] to compliment our King, who returned it by sending over my Lord Sunderland [3] to the French King. This gave just caus to thinke that ther would be noe warr between the two kings, as the Parlament had advised. I see a copie of the letter from the French King brought by the Duke de Crequy to ours, [4] which began with this stile or tytle:

Tres haut, tres excellent, et tres puissant Prince, tres cher, tres aimé bon frere, cosin, et allié.

The thruth is the King of England's newtrality, or looking on, very well deserved thes or greater compliments from France at that time.

May 6   The postmaster of Doncaster haveing disobliged me (one Hunt), I endeavered to put him out; but finding greater opposition then I expected from the Bishop of Durhim, [5] Duke Lotherdale, and severall other persons of quality that used to lie at his hous, I could not effect it, till, speakeing twice myselfe to the Duke of Yorke, he granted my request, and gave it to my quarter-master of a militia troop that kept an inn ther. [6]

---

[1] Charles de Blanchefort, Duc de Créqui, elder brother of the Maréchal de Créqui.

[2] Charles-Maurice le Tellier, who became coadjutor to François Barberini, Archbishop of Reims, in 1668, and succeeded him in 1671. His father was Louis XIV's famous minister, Michel le Tellier, and his elder brother was the still more famous François-Michel, Marquis de Louvois.

[3] Robert Spencer, second Earl of Sunderland, Secretary of State under Charles II, President of the Council under James II, and Lord Chamberlain under William III. He was accompanied on this mission by Louis, Lord Duras, who had married Mary, daughter of Sir George Sondes, Earl of Feversham, and was shortly going to succeed to his father-in-law's title (*Cal. S.P. Dom.*, 1677-8, pp. 94-8).

[4] The letter, dated April 13/23, 1677, is printed in Mignet, *Négotiations relatives à la succession d'Espagne*, iv. 446-7. Crequi's mission in England lasted from April 17 to May 5 (*Recueil des instructions, Angleterre*, ii. 216).

[5] Nathaniel Crew, who had been translated from Oxford in 1674.

[6] Thomas Madox, who was killed in a quarrel in 1681.

The poor smiths of Halamshire sent me up a letter and *May* 8
petition, setting forth that the officers for collecting that   *
duty had made new distresses upon them for smiths forges.
I went and soe represented the poverty of that sort of
people to my Lord Tresurer, the illegality of it according to the intention of the statute, and the certain difference it would create between the Kings officers and
the justices of the peace, that he ordered his secretary to
write to the collectors not to proceed to distrain for such
hearths till the explanatory bill did pass (ther being a bill
before the Commons at the riseing of the Parlament for
the explaneing of that and some other obscure parts of
the Chimney Acts); but noe such bill did ever pass, soe
that all the said clauses have since been interpreted in
favour of the Kings revenue.

My Lord of Ormond and my Lord Tresurer had not
been very good friends.   The King, however, had peiced
them upon condition they should not impeach each other
without acquainting one another first with the matter.
My Lord of Ormond first broake his word, and informed
the King that my Lord Tresurer had cheated him in the
excize.   My Lord Ormond said the Tresurer had first
complained of him to hinder his going for Ireland (wher
he was Lord Lieutenant before).   This came to a great
heat at Court; but the King, that loved quiet though he
paid for it, believed neither of their complaints, and made
them again friends; soe my Lord was sent into Ireland
with his former dignity.[1]

I was in private with my Lord Tresurer in his chamber 11
till after one a clock at night, wher he tould me severall
matters.   I obteaned some favours of him at that time.
One was a further security to the smiths of Hallamshire
not to be troubled as formerly; a pardon for a highwayman condemd to be executed, upon promess to discover
his accomplices, but being saved he soon fell to his ould
kind of life and was afterwards hanged; another was a

[1] He set out for Ireland at the beginning of August 1677.

* 1/130: Jo. Cressett, no date, ?7 May 1677.

promess of 10 l. to any person that such [1] catch a robber
on the highway, which was after published by proclamation.   I complained to him of the injustice done me in
that foolish story that was raised concerning the blacka-
moor, and of the Kings being soe ready to grant my
estate.   He said he did not believe the King had given it,
for that he had desired the King not to be too hasty in that
perticular, believeing it was a lie; but was of opinion
with me that it was a fitt occasion to aske something of the
King by way of reparation, and that he would assist me
therin.

His lordship was then soe free with me as to tell me
that though [the King] denyed almost nothing to the
Duke, his brother, yet he did not really love him.

He tould me then that the King had noe mind to fall
out with France; but if the Parlament would engage him
in that warr, their best way would be to give him a good
sum to make preparations for it, which could not be less
then 600,000 l.   By this means, if the King took it, he
would be obliged to goe on in the war.   If the Parlament
refused to trust him, he had a good reason not to imbarke
himselfe in it, for then the King might argue, How may
I confide in my Parlament to give me mony to carry me
through the warr, that will not sufficiently supply me to
make preparations for it ?   But I easily discovered that
thes were artifices to gett mony.

He said further that the King in honour ought not to
joine with the Confederates against France; that in all
the treatyss of peace the King of England was nam'd as
the principal in that warr; that he did actually joine with
France in the beginning, and went off contrary to his
promesse, and now to turn his arms against France would
not look well nor just to the world.   His lordship tould
me that this was the King's own argument upon their
discourseing of the warr between themselves, and that
he had made the King this answer, that his Majesty

[1] ? 'should.'

should not reguard that soe much, for the French King plaid him the same trick when Chancellor Hide was chiefe minister.   The King answered that was bycaus he had a prejudice to the Chancellour.   The Lord Tresurer replyed, whatever was the caus the thing was done.

He was soe free as to tell me further that the Duke was the chiefe carrier on of the French interest; that he now made it his business to court the sectarys and phenaticks, hopeing therby to strenthen the popish interest; that his Highness was soe bigoted in that religion that when the Archbishop of Reims was here, went into our churches and kneeled during the time of divine service, the Duke would not be persuaded soe much as to come into the door.   He said the Duke was unhappy in servants that had not much sence, but that his confessour [1] was a notable man, and had great interest with him; but that he as well as his master were against a French warr.   But his lord-ship declared himselfe for it.

I went to visit the Duke and Duchesse of Lotherdale [2] at their fine hous at Ham.   After dinner the Duchesse in her chamber entertained me with a long discours of matters of state.   She had been a beutiful woeman and the sopposed mistris of Oliver Crumwell, and was then a woeman of great parts.   She and her Duke (that was much governed by her) were entirely in my Lord Tresurer's interest.[3]   She chiefly complained of the Duke's adhering to papists and fenaticks, and of his putting the King upon

May 12

---

[1] Father Thomas Bedingfield.

[2] Elizabeth, eldest daughter of William Murray, Earl of Dysart.   She was Lauderdale's second wife.

[3] The malcontents in Scotland were in close communication with the opposition in England, and an alliance between the King's ministers in both countries was a natural result.   Among the Leeds MSS. are a number of letters from the Duchess of Lauderdale to the Countess of Danby in which this community of interests is emphasised.   In one the Duchess writes : " Both my Lord and myself are as much obliged to my Lord Trea-surer and your Ladyship as is possible.   Our principalls are the same, our intrest is the same, and our difficultyes not much unlike."

the change of lord deputys of Ireland soe ofton to promote the popish interest, and gave me severall instances to proove it that I had not heard before.   She gave me also the whole scheme of the state of Scotland at that day, which, her husband being Lord Commissioner, she had good reason to understand.   But the Scots being a mercinary people, when the Duke was sent afterwards into that kingdome, whatever they were before they then changed into another thing.

The day after, I went and asked Mr. Secretary Williamson if ther was any entry made in his office concerning the begging of my estate.   He tould me he durst only own it to me in private, but it was true that upon some rumour of a forfiture of it by some act of mine, Mr. Felton of the bed chamber [1] (yonger brother to him that had marryed my ant Monson) had begged it of the King, and entered a caviat therof at his office.

May 19   I obteaned of my Lord Tresurer to carry me to the King, wher I begged two thinges of him.   One was that he would please to order Mr. Secretary Williamson to raize out a caviat which had been entered with him, upon his Majestys granting my estate to Mr. Felton, reputed to be forfited upon the rumour of the death of the Moor; and secondly that he would please to lay his commands upon my Lord Chiefe Justice Rainsford to discover to me at whos sollicitation and upon what suggestion it was that his lordship granted out the warrant to the coroner to take up the body six weeks after it was buried.

As to the first, the King said he did not remember the giveing my estate to any person, but if any such caviat was entered he should have order to putt it out.   For the second, he directed my Lord Treasurer to send one with me to my Lord Rainsford from him to doe what I desired, which he did the day after by his secretary.   And when we came to my Lord Chiefe Justice, he tould me the whole matter, and begged my excuse for haveing been soe very

[1] Thomas Felton.

forward in that matter, as indeed he had reason, haveing done more then he could justifie, for he had given his warrant upon a bare suggestion of the Moor's dying by such an act, and without takeing any information either in writing or upon oath.

The Parlament met at Westminster the 21 according *May* 21 to the adjournment. The King, speakeing to both Houses,[1] acquainted them that he could not make such alliances as they desired without they would first give him mony to make preparations for warr. The Commons, upon the debate concerning the Kings speech, would not consent to give mony, but voted the contrary, till his Majesty had first entered into alliances; and at the same time that an addresse should be humbly made to him to enter into a league offensive and defensive with Holland and the rest of the United Provinces, for the safety of thes kingdomes, for the recovery of Flanders, and to abate the power of the French King.

The said addresse being presented to the King,[2] he 28 returnd this answer to it, that we had exceeded the methods of Parlament in that addresse; that we had entrenched upon his prerogative by not only directing him to make alliances, but by pointing out to him what thos alliances should be, and with whom they should be made; that the power of makeing peace or warr only belonged to himselfe, and if that was taken from him he should only have the name of a King, and then what states or princes would treat with him; for which reason, as well as want of mony, he should not comply with their address. However, he should doe that which became him for the good of his kingdomes, and ordered the Parlament to be adjourned till the 16 of July following.

The Speaker (which was Mr. Seamure) returning to the Hous did adjourn the Hous, but without putting the question, and by the Kings order or command. This

[1] On May 23.
[2] On May 26. The King returned his answer on the 28th.

(as was mooved) being without president did soe dis-
compose the Hous that some were offering to hold the
Speaker in the chair; but he leaped from it very nimbly,
for he was in fear that many being dissatisfyed with his
Majestys speech would have made some mutinous speeches
before he could adjourn, and with good reason.   I was
of thos that thought the Commons outwent their due
limits in wording their address, in nameing the countrys
with which he was to make his alliances and the manner of
them (viz., offensive and defensive); for besides the
undecencys of it, the Secretarys of State then of the Hous
tould us the thing would be granted if we did not loos it
in the manner of asking it.   Indeed the nation did then
very much desire a war with France, and the King, its
thought, might have been gained to it if the Duke had not
been soe avers to it.

June 1   Following the Duke down the gallary to his closit in
Whitehall, I went up to him to thanke his Highness for a
favour he had granted me.   He said that he was lately
informed that I should say in company that as for my
Lord Tresurer I knew that he was for makeing alliances
with Holland and the Netherlands for the warr against
France, but the Duke did much oppose it.   I replyed
whoever informed his Highness soe had not spoaken the
thruth; that I might possibly say in discours upon that
subject that my Lord Tresurer was for a warr with France;
but that I should undertake to say that his Highness was
either for it or against it was a presumption I could never
be guilty of; if I knew not my duty, good manners would
make me carefull of nameing him in any concern of soe
high a nature, and humbly desired that he would please to
tell me who was his informer.   By this time his Highness
was arrived to his closit door, wher he stopped and said,
Doe not trouble yourselfe, for I never believed it, but must
not tell you my authour.   However, it is sometimes fit to
tell men what we hear that the thruth may the better be
discovered.

Being with my Lord Tresurer, he tould me the excize *June 2*
would be lett to farm, and if I thought it would be any
advantage to me I might be concerned in it.   I thanked
his lordship, and said I would consider of it.   But the
thruth was, though great estates had been gotten by
farming that and other branches of the Kings revenue, yet
I never intended to interest myselfe in it, for noe man was
beloved in his country that did; and being a justice of the
peace, and haveing ofton punished thos concerned in the
collecting of that duty for transgressing the law in the
method of it, I thought I should be censured if I should
then make myselfe of that nomber.

About this time I had fresh complaints from the smiths
of Hallamshire of new demands of hearth mony for their
forges.   Upon my representing it again to my Lord
Tresurer, and laying the small profit it would bring in to
the King, and the great poverty of thos smiths, he confirmed his order to the farmers and officers not to disturb
thos people any more in that perticular, by which means
they were at quiet a long while after, though thos sort of
smiths payed for their forges in all other parts of England,
and my Lord Maior of Yorke [1] and two justices of the peace
of Nottingham were sent for up before the King and
Councill for mentaining that such forges ought not to
pay, wher his lordship receved pardon recanting his
opinion, but the two justices were putt out of commission.[2]   *

I heard that my Lord Yarmouth [3] was one of thos that
had begd my estate upon the story of the Moor, and that
he was com'd to town.   I presently went to find him at
his own hous, wher I had some difficulty to be admitted

[1] Francis Elcock.

[2] The two Nottinghamshire justices, Gregory and Pierrepoint, were put
out of commission in July.   In November two justices of the North Riding
of Yorkshire, Sir Henry Calverley and John Gibson, were dismissed for
the same reason (Hist. MSS. Com., *Finch MSS.*, ii. 45, 46).

[3] Sir Robert Paston, created Viscount Yarmouth in 1673 and Earl of
Yarmouth in 1679.

* 10/97: Robert Pierrepont to Ralph Eaton, 3 July 1676, requesting a copy of
the Yorkshire petition from Reresby so that it can be used as a model for the
one to be drawn up at the Nottingham assize.

(for I had never seen him), and asked him the question if it was true, saying that I had reason to believe that thos that were soe forward to beg my estate had been as busy to make the story. He foreswore very bitterly that he had ever asked it of the King, or knew anything of it further then that one Wright, sollicitor to the Lord Henry Howard,[1] did come and tell him that ther was likely to be such a forfiture, and advised him to use his interest with the King for it, but that he did absolutely deny to harken to it, saying that he would not be richer for the misfortune of others; that it was, he believed, malice against me, and that he would serve me all he could to find out the authours of it. I made him give it under his hand that he was noe party to the begging of my estate, or otherways interesting himselfe in that matter.

The same day I found out Mr. Wright, and threatned to bring my action of scandall against him upon the information I had from my Lord Yarmouth, except he would tell me the whole intrigue of it. He did then ingeniously confess that both Bright and Chappell before mentioned had given him an account of the Mores death by that means, with all assurance of the thruth of it; and that he telling my Lord Henry Howard, his lordship sent him to my Lord Yarmouth to aske of the King my estate, which he had begged accordingly.[2] I was very much surprized to hear two noblemen make their honour soe cheap as to deny with oaths and asseverations what was

---

[1] Son and heir of Henry, sixth Duke of Norfolk.

[2] Among the Leeds MSS. is a letter from J. Wright to Lord Yarmouth, dated October 28, 1676, which shows that the latter was more deeply involved in this affair from the very beginning than he cared to admit. The most significant part of it reads: " I have not had any intimations in that busines of Sir John Reresby since I had the honour of waiting upon you, nor doe I expect to have any till they are able to give me an account of the successe of that warrant which I sent downe yesterday was seven-night. I doe not doubt but those that have the management of it there will doe it with all prudence and care, and your Lordship shall not faile of imediate notice of all occurrents as fast as they come to my knowledge."

true; but I considered that stirring further in it would but make more noise of soe foolish a story in the world, and that it ought to be sufficient to me that, as a signe of their shame and repentance, they had both of them given themselves the lie.

Haveing taken leave of the King and Duke, I returned *June* 13 to Thriberge. As soon as I arrived the corporation of cutlers sent their Master and officers to thanke me for the good offices I had done them at London with my Lord Tresurer, and would have made me a hansome present, but I refused to accept of it.

The begining of July my Lord Duke of Newcastle (the old Duke being dead) sent to desire me to accompany him into Staffordshire, wher he was to see his estate, which I promessed some days after.

I attended the sessions at Rotherham,[1] and went soon *July* 10 after to meet some other deputy lieutenants to settle the militia at Yorke.

The Earl of Burlinton, Lord Lieutenant of the West *Aug.* 13 Rideing,[2] came and laid at Thriberge one night.

I went to dine at Sheffield at the Cutlers' Feast, being 25 invited by the corporation, wher I was recieved by the Master and his assistants in the street with loud musick, the shouts of the rabble, and with ringing of bels; and being after conducted into the Town Hall, was entertained with a very good dinner and great plenty of wine.

I met the Duke of Newcastle at Chesterfield, and 27 accompanyed him as farr as the High Peake in Darbyshire, wher talkeing to the Duke, and the way being very strait, my hors was forced to goe upon a slippery stone, soe that all his legs flying at one from under him, he fell

---

[1] Part of the business of the justices at this meeting, and also at their autumn meeting at Barnsley, was to consider the unauthorised emigration of dissenters from the West Riding to America. Reresby's letters dealing with the matter are printed in *American Historical Review*, ii. 472-3.

[2] Burlington had ceased to be Lord Lieutenant of the West Riding in the autumn of 1667, and did not hold that post again until 1679.

flat upon my right leg and put my knee out of joint.   The Duke leaped from his hors, and helped to carry me into a little alehous hard by, wher I prevailed with him to leave me with my servants and two of his gentlemen, who all went severall ways to find a bone-setter.   At the last they found four that pretended to be versed in that art, but soe little understood it that they put me to a great deale of pain to noe purpas, for they set my knee wrong, as it prooved afterwards.

After three days lying in much pain, I ventered home in the Earl of Rutland's[1] hors-litter which I borrowed, and at Thriberge I sent for another bone-setter, who put me to as much pain as the former, with as little successe. Yet soon after I found one Middleton, who by God's mercy did reduce it indifferently well, though not perfectly, the cap of the knee being broaken.   This was a great affliction to me, the other knee haveing been disjointed when very yong and never well reduced; but it was the will of heaven, and I deserved it for my sins. However by God's mercy I had very good use of both after all this.

I laid seven weeks by this accident, during which time I was visited and enquired after by all my nighbours, especially the Duke of Newcastle, who came with my Lord Ogle[2] to see me three days after my return.

Oct. 19   I was soe well that I went on horsback to Barnsley sessions, and soon after to Leeds, wher my Lord Fairfax, Sir Henry Gooderick, Sir John Kay, and myselfe setled the militia of that devision.   I was ther perticularly invited by the maior and his brethren, for some services done that corporation a little before with the judges, concerning their being excused to serve upon jurys at assizes or sessions out of their own limits.

At this time was the marriage agreed on between the

---

[1] John Manners, eighth Earl of Rutland.

[2] Henry Cavendish, only son of the new Duke of Newcastle.   He died in his father's lifetime on November 1, 1680.

Prince of Orange and the Lady Mary, first daughter of
his Royall Highness,[1] which gave great content in the
nation and abated the fears of popery that she was marryed
to a Protestant prince. My Lord of Danby, Lord
Tresurer, believed to be an adviser of this match, got a
reputation by it.

Much company came to my hous, amongst others my Oct. 25
Lord Clifford and my Lord Castleton.

The Parlament that was to meet the 3rd of December 26
was declared by proclamation intended to be prorougued
to the 4th of April.

Notwithstanding the said proclamation, the business Jan. 4
of the nation soe requireing it, the Parlament was ap- [1677/8]
pointed to meet the 10th of January, soe that I sett
forward for London the 4th, before I had ended Christmas,
which I had kept with entertaining my nighbours and
tenents, as I had done other years.

I arrived ther in company with Sir Henry Gooderick, 10
in whos coach I went up. The day after, the Parlament
being adjourned for fifteen days,[2] I informed myselfe of
affairs.

I dined with my Lord Tresurer, who recieved me 12
kindly. The next day I kissed the Kings hand and the
Dukes. His Highness tould me amongst other things
that the reason of this short adjournment was bycaus the
King could not soe fully acquaint both Houses with the
caus of calling them at this time till he had a more perfect
account of a treaty which was now frameing with Spain;
and after some other discours of publique concern I gave
him some assurances of my duty and respect, desireing
him not to harber any thought of what he had formerly

---

[1] The marriage was arranged on October 21, formally announced to the
Privy Council on the following day, and solemnized on November 4.

[2] Reresby is guilty of some confusion at this point. On December 3
Parliament was adjourned to January 15. There was no meeting on
January 10, and no further adjournment until that to January 28, which
is mentioned below.

said he had been tould I should discours concerning him and my Lord Tresurer.

Jan. 15   The Houses met, and were further adjourned to the 28th.

Sir Solomon Swayle,[1] my fellow burgess of Audbrough, being likely to be put out of the Hous of Commons for suspicion of being a papist, I gave my interest ther to Sir Thomas Mauliverer[2] to succeed him, he being recommended to me by my Lord Tresurer and others.

28   The Parlament met, and the King, in his speech to both Houses, said that he was entered into a strict alliance with the Prince of Orange and with the United Provinces to oppose the grouth of the French King and the progress of his arms in Flanders, &c., and desired mony to carry it on.

The Commons voted thankes to the King,[3] to be presented to him by way of an address, for the care he had expressed of the Protestant religion in marrying his niece to the Prince of Orange; but that they could not give him any supply for that warr except his Majesty and his allies would engage not to lay down that warr till the Treaty of Perenea[4] was performed, and til that king was reduced to the condition as he then stood, for without this neither this kingdome nor the rest of Christendome was safe.

30   The Commons voted the sum of 70,000 l. to be given for the royall enterment of King Charles the Marter, and for makeing a monument for him.

Supping that niht with my Lord Tresurer, he said he fully intended to solicite the King to doe something for me, but had not yet found anything that was proper for me.   But if he had really meant it I knew he might have done it before then.

---

[1] Of Swale Hall in South Stainley, created a baronet in 1660.

[2] Of Allerton Mauleverer, the third baronet.   [3] January 29.

[4] The Treaty of the Pyrenees between France and Spain, signed on November 7/17, 1659.

We had an answer from the King to our address, *Feb.* 4 wherby he pressed the giveing of mony to carry on the warr, and to invite us the more to it, made the Hous acquainted what alliances he had made. This soe wrought upon the Hous that, it being put to the question, it was carryed by 42 voats to assist his Majesty in that warr, and to consider of the way to doe it. But it being late, the debate was put of til morning.

Waiting on the Duke of Yorke that morning, he spoake 5 a good while to me concerning this matter; and being the night before with my Lord Treasurer, the schesm was laid how to proceed the next day.

There had hapned many warm debates as to this affair, and the reason of the great opposition it found was a desire in some to oppose the Crown, though in the very thing they wished for themselves (for this nation is always desirous of a war with France), and a jealousie in others that the King intended to raise an army but never designd to goe on with the warr; and truly some of the King's party were not sure of the contrary. Soon after, it was voted by the Commons to give mony for the raiseing of 26 regiments of foot, 4 of hors, and 2 of dragoons, with a navy of 90 men of warr for a warr against France.[1]

Upon this occasion of warr, haveing notice that it might be possible to repair the fort at Burlinton, I applyed myselfe to my Lord Treasurer to gett me the command of it, if it should be done; but he tould me that would not be thought nescessary, that coast lying more to Holland then France. Soon after I applyed myselfe to the Duke therin, who tould me it might be of use, and that he would promote it for me all he could. Haveing tould my Lord Treasurer what the Duke had promessed, 14 he also assured to speake for me to his Highness and to assist to it.

The 23 of March was appointed by the Hous for the

[1] The vote for the navy passed on February 6, and for the army on February 8.

hearing the caus of my election before the committeè of privileges, and my Lord Tresurer promessed to speake to Sir William Wentworth[1] for me in that concern, which he did in the lobby of the Lords Hous in my hearing, wher, like himselfe, he promessed my Lord very fair, but did nothing.

The same day I tould the King and Duke some things which had passed in the Hous of Commons, and the doubts that some had expressed ther whether the ratification of the peace twixt us and Holand was yet passed. The King said that the league offensive and defensive was signed by the States, soe that they could not goe back; but the ratification was not yet sealed, the severall provinces haveing not yet confirmed the act of their deputys, and of the council of eight who had recieved it.

Feb. 15   I dined with my Lord Treasurer, who said that he had a long discours with the King and Duke of my affair of Burlinton, and that he hoped it would succeed.

18   The business of giveing an aid to the King came in debate in the Hous of Commons, wher it was controverted, and many difficulties and mistrusts of the King started. Amongst others, I spoake and shewed the nescessity of a trust in this perticular, and how impossible it was (tho ther might some ground appear for it) to recede at this time of the day.

*   I had the newes the same day of the death of Sir Godfrey Copley, Baronet, of Sprodbrough, high sheriff then of this county of Yorke, a fine gentleman of good credit in his country, and of excellent naturall parts, and a good justice of the peace. His son[2] writt to me by an expresse to speake to my Lord Tresurer (who was his relation) to be continued in that office for the remaining part of the year. I was in the Hous when I recievd the letter, but went presently to Wallinford Hous and found

[1] Of Northgate Head, Wakefield, son of Sir William, younger brother of the first Earl of Strafford.

[2] Another Sir Godfrey.

* 12/158: T. Vincent, 18 February 1677/8; 1/94: F. Reresby to Sir John, [18 February] 1677/8.

his lordship was gone to Wimbleton.[1]   I was forced to stay to watch his return till ten at night, and prevailed with his lordship to goe that night to the King, least others should gett in before us.   We found the King at the end of the long gallary at the Duchess of Portsmouth's, and the King presently granted our request.   And the next day the patent for the high sheriff was gott out for the son before it was known that the father was dead, for which trouble I had afterwards but very indifferent returns, as the sequall will manifest.

The same day the Commons voted the grant of one million to the King, to enable him to make warr with the French King for the preservation of Flanders.

The Duke of Yorke tould me that as to the goverment *Feb.* 19 of Burlinton I might depend upon it to be granted. Severall gentlemen had regiments given them, as Sir Henry Gooderick (whom I called brother from an entire friendship that was between us) and Sir Thomas Slingsby, both of this country.[2]   But I was every whit as well content with my goverment, the King by the Dukes means grant-   * ing me a sallary of 200 l. per annum, and an independent company of one hundred men to reside in the guarrison.

Came newes that the French had taken Ghent and 27 Bruges, and that Oastend was beseiged, wherupon the King caused sixteen hundred men to be presently drawn out of the guards and his other forces here, and to send them immediately to Oastend, under the command of the Duke of Monmoth,[3] amongst whom my brother

---

[1] Wimbledon House, purchased by Danby from the Earl of Bristol in 1677.

[2] Goodricke and Slingsby were both given regiments of foot, the commissions for which were dated respectively February 26 and February 27, 1677/8 (Dalton, *English Army Lists*, pp. 219, 220).

[3] The news, which was false, arrived on February 26. A body of 1,600 men under Thomas, Lord Howard of Escrick, was immediately dispatched to Ostend, and a day later the Duke of Monmouth followed with 100 men of the horse guards on foot (Williamson's Diary in B.M. Add. MSS. 28040, f. 49).

---

* 13/7: Newcastle, 25 March 1678. Newcastle wrote that Reresby's commission was 'worth three regiments'.

Edmond, captain in the Guards, was one. This news of the French success gave a great alarm to Flanders, England, and Holland.

The same day the Commons upon this newes grew very warm, and began to reflect on the King's ill councils, that had not advised him to this warr sooner. They named noe man then, but it was plane that they pointed at the Duke of Yorke and my Lord Tresorer.

Feb. 28   Attending at the King's levy, the King tould me (and some other Parlament men then present) that except the mony voted to be given to make levys was dispatched, it would come after the French King had done his worke. His Highness said to me that morning, too, that his friends would have a hard taske upon them that day, for he was informed that some in the Hous resolved to renew the debate concerning ill councellors. I said it was not very likely, for I was tould the day before by a leader of the anti-Court party that it was not now a time to raise differences at home when we were in war abroad; and it prooved as I said.

March 2   The newes came that Gant and Bruges were not taken, as had been reported, and that Monsieur de Ruvigny [1] was comming, on the part of the French King, with offers of peace to our King. The Parlament grew jealous that they would be accepted. However our forces went forward on their march to Oastend.

The same day, waiting upon the King at the Duchess of Portmouth's (the Duke and my Lord Treasurer being in consultation with his Majesty ther about giveing out of commissions, that affair being over), his Highness, before I could aske him if he had pleasd to remember my business, informd me that order would be given for the drawing of my commission. My Lord Treasuror assured me of it at the same time.

[1] Henri de Massue de Ruvigny, who succeeded his father as second Marquis de Ruvigny in 1689 and, having entered the service of William III, was created Earl of Galway in 1697.

The bill for raiseing mony by the way of poule was *March* 4 perfected,[1] and the King and his Royall Highness discoursed very much of the war; but twas suspected that they thought more of a peace.

Being near the Duke in Whitehall, as he and my Lord 6 Treasurer were whispering togather, the Treasurer, looking upon me, spoake again to the Duke, wherupon his Highness came to me, and asked me if I had my commission. I answered noe. But, said he, I will give order concerning it to the Secretary. And accordingly as I stood behind him the next day, as he dined with the King, he spoake to the Secretary (pointing to me at the same time), which the Secretary tould me was concerning my commission, which was sealed some days after. This was a commission for raiseing an independent or unregimented company of foot, to consist of 100 men, 1 lieutenant, 1 enseign, 3 sergiants, 3 corporals, and 2 drummers. The King and Duke were soe kind as to lett me name my own officers, soe I chose one Mr. Adams of Woodlaiths for my lieutenant, and my wifes only brother for my enseign [2] (who, poor gentleman, dyed after at Burlinton).

I desired his Highness to remember the commission 10 which he had promessed to get for me for governor of Burlinton. His Highness discoursed many things with me at the same time concerning the guarrison to be form'd ther. He tould me further that he was inform'd of a dessein in the Hous of Commons to fall upon him and my Lord Tresurer, and desired [me] to oppose it. My Lord Tresurer assured me of the same thing, and to be done that day; that amongst other things they laid to his charge a treaty between the King and the Prince of Orange, which was printed, as being the adviser of it; but that it was a forgerie, for ther was really noe such treaty,

---

[1] The Poll Bill was not passed by the Commons until March 8.

[2] William Adams and William Brown. Their commissions, and Reresby's own commission as captain, are dated March 10 (Dalton, *English Army Lists*, i. 231).

or if ther were did he thinke it at all to the disadvantage of England; another of his crimes would be for adviseing the King to make peace, which he never did, though it was not impossible but such a thing might be, and if it were, it was from nothing but the Kings own judgement, who was very much inclined that way (if it were lawfull to say soe).

March 13   I had my commission of captain.

14   Severall speeches were made, of jealousies and fears, and perticularly of the army which was now raiseing, as if it were rather intended to sett up absolute monarchy then to make warr with France. Complaints were made of the councils, and of the chiefe ministers that gave them, but noebody was named. This long debate ended in voating an address to be made to the King, to desire his Majesty, before that they proceeded to give any more mony, he would please to declare warr against France, and withcall his embassador from the French Court. It was very stiffly debated that it should have been added to the address that his Majesty would please to put away thos evell councellours from about him, that had given him the advice to adjourn the Parlament in May last, and had hindred a warr with France all this time. At last it was put to the question whether it should be part of the address or not, and it was carryed in the negative by five voats only.[1]

The same night, being with the Duke, he asked me severall questions of things that passed in the Lower Hous. He spoake kind things of me to the Duke of Monmoth, and I kissed his hand for my commission received the day before. I was with the King at the French play that night, wher he talked to me a great while.

16   By the Commons it was resolved that a day should be named to take the state of the kingdome into consideration in relation to popery.

19   My Lord Treasurer, haveing sent for severall members

[1] The voting was 135 to 130 (Grey's *Debates*, v. 247).

of that Hous (and me amongst others) to the Treasury
Chamber, tould us that it became all good subjects to
withstand such motions and proceedings as much as
might be, which were only offered to perplex and disturb
the publique peace, and to give jealousie of the goverment.   The Duke tould me that amongst other things
it would be mooved that all popish recusants should be
disarmed (as a ridiculous thing).

This day in the afternoon I had a quarrell at the King's
playhous upon this occasion.   As I sate in the pit a
gentleman whos name I afterwards heard to be Mr.
Symons came and placed himself next to me, and not
content to rest ther, after a while desired me to give him
my seat, or to exchange with him (pretending he was to
speake to one of his acquentance on the other side).   I
had noe mind to quitt my seat, which was better to see
then his.   Besides, he haveing been drinking, his manner
of askeing was not altogather soe gratefull, insomuch as
I denyed it.   Hereupon he said I was uncivil, and I tould
him he was a rascall; upon which words we were both
prepared to strike one another, had not a gentleman that
sate near us (one Sir Jonathan Trelany)[1] put his hand
between us to prevent it.

After a while (when I saw noebody observed us) I
whispered him in the ear to followe me out, telling him
I would stay for him at the out door.   But before I gott
thether, one (that observed my speakeing to him and
going out upon it) acquainted the captain of the guard,
who was accidentally at the play, with what had passed,
and that we should certainly fight if not prevented, who
sent one after me and another to him to secure us by a
guard, till being the next day brought before the Duke of
Monmoth (who acted as Generall), he made us friends,
who had not been long ennemies, for I had never seen the
gentleman to my knowlege before in my life, nor scarce
after but once in the street that he desired to give me a

---

[1] Sir Jonathan Trelawny, M.P. for Cornwall, the second baronet.

bottle of wine, and tould me he was very sorry that he had the misfortune to have a dispute with one of whom he heard soe good a character.

ANNO DOMINI 1678

March 25   I found that Sir William Wentworth plaid a deceitful game with me as to my election in Parlament.[1]   I complained to the Duke of him, who, according to his promesse, spoake to him to deale more fair in the matter.   But, said the Duke, I did not well understand his answer, and the thruth is his sence was not always soe clear as to be well apprehended.   His Highness then asked me if I was sure to come in Sir Solomon Swale's place in case he quitted his session in Parlament (for being a papist he only stayed till he should be put out of the Hous, or recieve the Duke's commands to make his exit).   I replyed I hoped that I was.   Then, said he, I will send to him upon your account that he come noe more into the Hous.

Sir Solomon went out of town soon after, and I obteand of his Highness to speake to Sir Allan Apsley, his paymaster of the houshould, father in law to Sir William Wentworth,[2] to speake to his son, that I might now have noe more trouble.   The Duke did it, and tould me Sir Allan answered that it was the interest of Mr. Wentworth's family that the election should be made after their usuall manner, and if that were done they had noe mind to put me out of the Hous.   He bad me speake to Sir Allan myselfe.

*
[*Apr.*] 10   [3] Haveing some private intimation that one Belamy,[4] a
†

[1] Cf. Reresby's letter to John Wentworth, dated March 7, 1677/8, and Wentworth's reply, dated March 18, in Hist. MSS. Com., *Various Collections*, ii. 386-7.

[2] Sir William had married Sir Allen's daughter Isabella.

[3] A line referring to the birth of Reresby's fourth son George is struck out at this point, and with it the date April in the margin.

[4] William Bellamy, wine merchant.   He was heavily indebted to the Crown (*Calendar of Treasury Books*, v. 959 and *passim*).

* Reresby here erased an entry recording the birth of his son George.

† 1/88a: Reresby to Belamy, ?10 April 1678, (copy). Reresby asked Belamy to pay his brother Gervase; 12/25: Edmund Reresby, 6 July 1678; 12/27: Gervase Reresby, 10 May 1678; 12/161: Gervase Reresby, 23 May 1678; 12/189: Gervase Reresby, 7 November 1678. Gervase asked his brother to order the sale of the oils which Reresby was holding.

Spanish marchant in London, was in danger to breake, that had some effects of my brother's in Spain in his hands of great value, I found him out after two days search, and upon condition that I could obtean of my Lord Treasurer to release a debt which he owed the King obteaned an assignment of oiles of him for my brother's use worth 2,000 l. My Lord Tresurer prevailed with his Majesty to release part of his debt to Belamy. The next day he broake for fifty thousand pounds, and my brother lost 3,000 l. besides what I saved for him, which put him much back both in his credit and trade.

The Parlament met, ther haveing been a short adjurnment to that day.[1] The Speaker not being very wel, and my Lord Tresurer and he not very kind, he gott another soon chosen into the chair. The Houses were further adjourned to the 28 of April.[2]

My Lord Treasurer had obteaned of the King for me to be governor of Burlinton, and my commission was signd,[3] and I had a privy seale granted for a sallary of 200 l. per annum out of the Exchequer.[4]

A great part of my time was now taken up to sollicit my friends that were members of the Lower Hous to be present when my caus came on at the comitteè.

I tould the Duke that I now dispaired (since his Highness his intercession could not prevaile to prevent the Wentworth endeavours to throw me out of the Hous) of any composure of that matter; it must come to tryall; and desired he would command his servants that were of the Hous to assist me therin. He called for Sir John Worden,[5]

April 11

12

14

---

[1] From March 27.

[2] Edward Seymour's indisposition was intimated to the Commons on April 11, and Sir Robert Sawyer, who was later to be attorney-general, was chosen in his place. On April 15 the new Speaker was approved by the King, and the same day both Houses adjourned to April 29.

[3] Dated April 8, 1678 (*Cal. S.P. Dom.*, 1678, p. 103).

[4] Dated April 30, 1678 (*Calendar of Treasury Books*, v. 981).

[5] M.P. for Reigate. He had been created a baronet in 1672.

* 1/69: Frances Reresby to Sir John, 5 May 1678.

† 12/13: William Adams, 3 May 1678. Adams informed Reresby that his cousin Dobson was able to obtain the promises of several parliament men to help Reresby's cause.

his then secretary, and bad him with the rest of his servants to attend the comitteè, for he would not loos me, right nor wrong.   Notwithstanding this order from the Duke, and one to the same purpas from the King, many of the Court did not appear, and Sir William Wentworth underhand, under colour of a family right, managed the thing to his utmost against me.   It was a great fault in our princes, that though upon request made to them they would grant and give orders for the thinge desired, but took little care how they were obayed therin, which prooved of ill effect to them, sometimes in things of greater moment.

April 16   The Master of the Ordinance had orders to lay out a hundred pounds to repair Burlinton Fort at the key.

21   At the Dukes levy I desired him to order his people once more to attend the comitteè that afternoon (it being the day of my election).   The Duke of Monmoth, to whom I had made noe application, tould me he had already ordered all the officers that were Parlament men to be ther, for he then was declared Generall.   The King was soe zealous for me that he had charged some of his servants, with some threats, to attend the tryall, as I was tould, not being by, and himselfe confirmed it to me as he came out of his bedchamber.   My Lord Tresurer tould me the same, and carryed me with him in his coach that day to the Hous, ordering two of his gentlemen to be at the lobby door to speake to Parlament men as they came in.   In the afternoon the caus came on, and after a long debate, and the question put, I lost it by two voats only, ther being upon a division of the comittè 94 to 96. This was absolutely lost by the remisness of the Court party that did not attend, for the caus was the clearest for me that could be.   But that would not prevaile with the advers party, who, as they were more diligent, soe they were also more violent against thos they opposed then the other.

The next day my Lord Tresurer complaind with some

bitterness of severall that the King himselfe had spoaken to that were absent; that all the Kings business was like to be lost the same way, and that he never see his Majesty more concerned in a thing then he was in this; but concluded that care should be taken to mend the matter, if possible, when the report was to be made to the Hous.

The King that afternoon came to me as soon as he saw me at my Lady Portsmoths, and exprest his concern for my disappointment, and said with an oath that he would lay aside such servants as had disobayed him in this matter. I humbly beg'd that noebody might suffer for me, but if he pleased to make some exemples upon a more deserveing occasion it might proove of use to his service. He bid me not be discouraged; it was not for my own sake, but his, that I met with soe many adversarys in that Hous, for he heard that my caus was the justest in the world.

The Duke comming in soon after tould me perticularly what he had said to severall to persuade them to be for me, who had promissed, who had failed, who had attended, who had not; and knew all perticulars of the tryall as if he had been upon the place. I replyed that his Highness did engage all the world to his service by that great industry which he used wher he was pleased to concern himselfe, but that my adversarys had made me more considerable then I deserved to be, not only by the great opposition they made against me, but by giveing a hallowe in the Hous by way of triomph when they found I had lost it. Well, said the Duke, be not discouraged; if you goe out of the Hous we must make use of you in some other station more considerable. I heard that the King, when he was acquented by somebody that the opposite party should give a kind of hallowe (or noise of joy) when I had lost it, should say, Thos that would halow him out of that Hous would hallowe me out of the kingdome.

The King had condescended soe far as to acquaint the Commons with the heads of the treaty he was then to make with the Confederates to have their advice upon it.[1] But the anti-Court party smelt the design, and would have evaded medling in the matter, knowing that would engage them to give mony to carry on the war, which they would not believe the King designd in earnest. Instead of that ther was many warm speeches against evel counsellors and ministers, nameing noe perticular men, but they were well understood.

May 4   However, it was carried in the Hous that a speedy address should be made to his Majesty to enter into a league offensive and defensive with the Confederates for abateing the power of France.

6   My Lord of Danby writt to the Speaker[2] to give me what assistance he could in the report to be made of my caus from the comitteè to the Hous the next day. He also took a list of such as had been absent before, and sent to them personally to attend the Hous at the time of the report.

7   I had the gout seized of me, but moderately, and by good fortune my caus was not reported by reason of some heats in voating occasioned by the news then arrived that we and Holand were concludeing a peace with France. One voat was that an address be made to his Majesty to lay aside thos councellers that did advise him to give thos answers to the two Houses upon their late addresses to his Majesty for a warr against France. The thruth is, this gave some credit to the other party, severall wel-meaning men beginning to fear that the army now raised was rather intended to awe our own kingdome then to war against France (as was at first suggested by them).

8   It being put to the question whether an address should be made to the King for the laying aside Duke Loderdale of the kingdome of Scotland from all imployment, it was carried in the negative by one voat only.[3]

---

[1] When Parliament reassembled on April 29.

[2] Edward Seymour, re-elected that day in place of Sir Robert Sawyer.

[3] On May 7 the Commons resolved, by 137 votes to 92, that an address should be presented to the King desiring him to remove Lauderdale from

The question was again put and carryed, that such May 10 councellors as had advised the King to make such answers to the late addresses from his Parlament, being betrayers of the King and kingdome (or to that effect), an addresse should be humbly presented to his Majesty to lay them aside from his councils and their other imployments. This address was presented,[1] and his Majesty's answer this—that the said addresse was soe extravagant he was not willing to give such an answer to it as it deserved. Lotherdale was perticularly named in that addresse. The same day it was carryed (and but by one voat in a full Hous) that the King's message lately sent them to consider of some means for a supply to his Majesty for the paying off his fleet should not be observed.[2]

The King, being advised of their high proceedings, May 13 proroagued the Parlament to the 23 of that instant May, which cutt off all their voats and proceedings upon all bils, and what had been voated in the committeè as to my election, the report not haveing been made to the Hous.

Now it was generally believed that the peace was concluded between us, the Confederates, and the King of France. We blamed the States for being soe ready to goe into it; they the Spaniard, that was ready to make offers of warr, but had neither men, arms, nor mony in Flanders to defend it; and both blamed the Parlament of England that, when it should be giveing mony and makeing other provisions for warr, employed their time to quarrell at home with the Goverment and with one another.

---

his councils and presence. The division mentioned by Reresby, in which the voting was 152 to 151, took place on May 8 on the first paragraph of the address, and marked the Commons' disapproval of the form in which it had been drawn up. But the original resolution was not affected, and was eventually added to the more important address of May 10 (*Journals of the House of Commons*, ix. 477-80).

[1] May 11.

[2] The division was on the previous question for adjourning the debate concerning supply, and the voting was 178 to 177 against putting the question.

May 23   The Parlament met, and the King speake to them more briskely then usually, tould them the peace was very near concluded between France and the Confederates, which displeased extreamly.

The Duke tould me that day, though the army should be disbanded, my goverment of Burlinton should stand. My adversarys in my election preferred a petition against me to the Hous the same day. It was brought in by Mr. Herbert,[1] which provoakd me to declare to several persons (and some of the best quality) that it was out of private prejudice as wel as publique, he not haveing forgot since I threw a glass of wine in his face at Padua.

24   The Duke sent for Sir William Wentworth to the Princes lodgeings at the Lords Hous, and commanded him again to desist in his prossecution against me; and my Lord Tresurer tould me he had soe threatned the knight that he had promessed to desist, provided Sir Solomon Swaile would leave the Hous and make room for his friend,[2] which the Duke said he should. The Duke tould me as much myselfe the next day at his levy.

This peace with France, when ther was like to be soe strong an union to reduce that proud and potent King to better manners, was very displeaseing to England. The King, to throw the caus of it upon the Commons, tould us in his speech it was their voating that noe mony should be given till they had some security as to religion, that they would not direct nor advise him concerning the warr, nor assist him, till he had changed his councillors, and

---

[1] William Harbord, M.P. for Clifton, Dartmouth and Hardness, one of the most active critics of the policy of the Court. The petition he presented was on behalf of the burghers of Aldborough ; but owing to some exceptions taken to it he had to consent to its being withdrawn (*Journals of the House of Commons*, ix. 482).

[2] His cousin, Ruisshe Wentworth, son of Sir George, brother of the first Earl of Strafford, and Frances Ruisshe. Sir William had put Ruisshe forward as a candidate for Aldborough at least as early as the autumn of 1677 (Hist. MSS. Com., *Various Collections*, ii. 386, 388).

consequently the little hopes the Confederates could have of helpe from him (joined with the bad condition of Spain), that made them hearken to a peace. To this the sluggish motion of the Germains, the hard and tedious getting them togather (their princes consisting of soe many different interests), and the poverty of the States Generall, contributed not a little.

Our King was chiefly condemn'd in this affair for deferring soe long to enter into this alliance, which had he sooner done the French King would never have darr'd to proceed in the warr, or at least have made soe great a progress in Flanders, and have made soe good an end for himselfe as he did by this peace. To this our King said he could not have believed that the French King was able to weather out a war soe well as he did against all Europe in a manner (himself and the King of Sweden only excepted, that sate newters); and in case the many ennemys he had had humbled him, England had reason to be content to look on, to enjoye the whole trade itselfe in the meantime, and to reap the benefit of other men's victorys in the issue as well as themselves.

My Lord Tresurer made me a compliment about my *May 27* speaking in the Hous of Commons, and tould me I should command his services for myselfe or relations, which made me desire a bon from him on the behalfe of Sir Thamworth Reresby. He promessed to speake to the King for him. That day, attending the King as he walked in St. James his Parke, he tould me he had accommodated the difference with Sir William Wentworth about my election, and that now I might be at rest. I most humbly thanked his Majesty for the honour he did me for interesting himselfe soe farr for one soe little able to serve him, but I would make it my business to deserve it as much as I was capable, &c.

Notwithstanding all thes engagements to the King 30 and Duke, he had the impudence (I mean Sir William Wentworth) to prefer another petition against me as to

my election.[1] I tould the King and Duke of it both in
the parke, who said he had acquainted them with some
nescessity to lodge a petition to preserve the right of the
family's claime, but not with the least design to give me
any further disturbance. The thruth is he managed this
matter soe very foolishly, both with the King and Parlament, that he became the contempt of both; and his
father, Sir Allan Apsley, and some other relations, were
noe less angry with him then others, one that marryed his
sister [2] saying oponly one day that though the King should
pardon him he was lost for ever to the world. I was
tould the day after the Duke had writ to Sir Solomon
Swaile to quitt.

That day a voat passed in the Lower Hous for disbanding the army.

June 2　Speakeing to Sir Allan of his son Sir William Wentworth's proceeding, he desired me not to disquiet him
with it, that he was a foole, and that if my case came to
be tryed he would himselfe voat against him in the
committeè. The same day I was served with an order
to try the caus the 15 instant. The King and Duke were

3 tould by my Lord Tresurer in the Hous of Lords. The
latter sent for us both into the lobby, tould Sir William,
You abuse both the King and me by giveing this gentleman all this trouble contrary to your engagement; but
let him be quiet or look me in the face, nor wil the King
ever forget it. Sir William would have said something
in excuse of himselfe. The Duke would not hear him,
but parting from him in angre tould him he was governed
by a company of knaves, and was himselfe a fool.

I had paid noe kind of civility to Sir William for a

---

[1] Exception was taken to this petition also, on the ground that there was
an affidavit upon the same paper ; but on the question being put whether
the petition should be read, the voting was 139 to 115 in favour of accepting it. The tellers for the majority were Sir William Wentworth and
William Harbord (*Journals of the House of Commons*, ix. 485).

[2] Edward Skinner, of Thornton College, Lincolnshire, who married
Anne Wentworth.

considerable time, he had acted soe ill towards me; and
yet durst not quarrel too far with him, the King and Duke
being soe far possessed with the matter. But standing
by when he was thus ruffled by his Highness, he comes
up to me, and instead of being angry that I was the caus
of this ill usage to him, supplicates me to assist him to gett
out of this business, promessing if I would intercede for
him to the King and Duke he wold doe all that in him laid
that I should have noe more disturbance as to my election.
I replyed that it was now more the Kings busines then
mine, since he had done me the honour to interest himselfe soe far in my election, and most his own; and therfore he might act in this concern as he pleased for himselfe,
and that would be best for me; but I should not trouble
the King or the Duke till I see some effects of his endeavours. I tould him, moreover, that I heard he had
reflected upon Sir Edmond Jennings,[1] a member of
Parlament, for something he had said in the committeè
in favour of me and my caus; that he had reason rather
to take at me in that case, for I was ready to justifie whatever my friends either said or did upon my account. He
tould me he was very well satisfyed in all that Sir Edmond
Jennings had said or done.

The Commons voted 200,000 l. to be given to the *June* 4
King for disbanding of the army, but under great restrictions, least the King should take the mony and imploy it
to other uses. It was therfore under such penalties to
the officers of the Exchequer, and such others thorow
whos hands it came, that they durst not imploy it but to
the right purpass. When it was soe secured the mony
was very willingly given, the nation (and its representatives) dreading nothing soe much as a standing army.

Sir Solomon Swaile, who was now convicted of popery,
was fàln upon in the Hous of Commons,[2] being absent,

[1] Jennings had been one of the tellers for the minority in the division of
May 30.
[2] June 5.

and was ordered to attend the Hous by letter from the Speaker on Monday following, and that a copie of his conviction should be produced at the same time.

June 8   Sir William Wentworth asked leave of the King to goe post into Yorkshire to his cozen Wentworth of Woolley, to see if he could bring him to reason in my concern. That day, being with Sir Henry Gooderick, whom I called brother, and his lady (the finest woeman, one of them, in that age),[1] he seemed to take something ill from her and me as we were discourseing very innocently togather; but it was too groundless to continue.

13   One Mr. Benit,[2] a member of the Hous, reflected upon my Lord Latimor[3] and his family, speakeing in the Hous. My Lord stayed til the Hous rose, and then takeing Benit by the sholder (I being with his lordship) challenged him to fight him the next day. I offered my Lord my service in that matter, but Benit was more valient in words then deeds, and desired pardon.

20   Sir Sollomon Swaile was expelled the Hous for being a papist,[4] and a voat passed at the same time that the Hous would not concern itselfe in matter of elections any more during this session.

21   Sir William Wentworth returned, pretending he could
*   not persuade his cozen Wentworth to desist. A new writ was obteaned for the chooseing a new member at Audbrough in the stead of Sir Sollomon Swaile. My Lord Tresurer prevailed with my Lord Chancellor to
22   bring it with him to the Charterhous[5] the 22, wher I dined

---

[1] Mary, sister of George Legge, who was raised to the peerage as first Baron Dartmouth in 1682, and given command of the English fleet at the time of the Revolution.

[2] Thomas Bennett, M.P. for Shaftesbury.

[3] Edward Osborne, Viscount Latimer, eldest son of the Earl of Danby, was M.P. for Corfe Castle.

[4] June 19.

[5] Finch and Danby had both been appointed Governors of the Charterhouse in 1674.

* 1/92: Reresby to J. Wentworth, 7 July 1678 referring to his discussion with Sir Alan Apsley, William Wentworth's father.

with their lordships, and it was given to the under-sheriff of Yorkshire, with this order from the Lord Tresurer, to execute it, and to make the return as I directed, and he would justifie him in it.

I desired his lordship to beg the Kings leave to goe down, both by reason of that business and my own, haveing been soe long absent from my wife and family. He desired me to stay one week longer, pretending it nescessary for the Kings service, and that he was desirous to doe me some service otherways before I went.

Ther was fresh discours of a war with France, that King and ours differing about the interest of the King of Sweeden,[1] which the French would have adjusted before they would deliver up the towns they had taken in Flanders; but I thought it impossible by what I heard, and seing the King, Duke, and French embassadour[2] soe ofton very merry and intimate at the Duchesse of Portsmouth's lodgeings, laughing at thos that believed it in earnest.

Sir William Wentworth and the under-sheriff both *June* 30 came to me and put me in hopes that old Wentworth * would now desist.   My Lord Tresurer the next day gave me two letters, written with his own hand, the one to Mr. Wentworth, the other to the high sheriff.   The first conteaned reasons and entreatys to lett me be noe more disturbed, the second to desire the sheriff to execute the writt in favour of Sir Thomas Mauliverer, to be elected † the same way that I was, in Sir Soloman's stead, except Mr. Wentworth would acquiesce, for his great design was to have the elections soe made as to preserve, or rather create, the power of makeing them in his own family and as he pleased.

I returned safe to Thriberge the beginning of July.

---

[1] Charles XI. The Swedes, who had intervened in the European struggle on the French side, had been heavily defeated at Fehrbellin, and Louis XIV was insisting that all they had lost must be restored to them.

[2] Paul de Barrillon, Marquis de Branges, whose long embassy in England continued from the close of 1677 to the Revolution.

* 1/64: John Shales, no date [January – June 1678], stating that he has the support of the Duke and Danby and hoping that Reresby will also support him.

† 12/47: Nathaniel Hayes 25 June 1678; 12/53: H. Edmunds, 16 June 1678.

Soon after I was at Audbrough, wher I had Mr. Wentworth's promess to rest undisturbed as to my own
election, and wher Sir Thomas Mauliverer was chosen
instead of Sir Solomon Swaile.[1]

July 15 The assizes were held at Yorke, wher I had a tryall
with Mr. Bright, the knave that had been the great agent
in contriveing and manageing that invention of the Moor.
I heard that he had said that I had caused the boy to be
guelt, which occasioned his death, for which words I
brought my action, and recovered of him 100 markes,
and, more then that, my credit, all the world being convinced of the malice and falsehood of the inventer.

From Yorke I went to my goverment at Burlinton,
wher I found a very good company of 100 men,[2] and the

*

[1] The negotiations which preceded the election are illustrated by the
correspondence printed in Hist. MSS. Com., *Various Collections*, ii. 388-91.
On July 12 Ruisshe Wentworth was returned, and the same evening
Reresby wrote to the Duke of York and to the Earl of Danby explaining what
had occurred. His letter to the former runs as follows :

I have soe deep a sence of your Highness his grace and bounty towards
me expressed upon numerous occasions (especially in being graciously
pleased to interest yourselfe as to my election in Parlament), that I doe
presume by this to return your Highness my most humble thankes and
this account of its success at the same time. Upon the execution of the
writt for choosing a member in the place of Sir Solloman Swaile, Mr.
Wentworth offered, in case I would weaken the nomber of the 9 by persuading them to withdraw their voats, wherby his freind might more
clearly be chosen by the 24, that he would give me noe disturbance as to
my own election. But finding I could not honestly consent to that (for
then I should have injured the interest by which I was elected) I prevailed
at the last with Mr. Wentworth (provided that I would stand neuter at
the election and noe ways interest myselfe as to the sherif's return) to pass
his promess as to my own quiet ; soe that the day of election ended in the
choice of Sir Thomas Maliverer by the major nomber of the 9, and of
Mr. Wentworth by the majority of the 24, who was also solely returned.
Sir, according to my duty in many respects I pray for your Highness his
health and prosperity, and beg leave to subscribe myselfe Your Highnesses
most obedient &c., J. R.—Audbrough, July the 12 (Rawlinson MSS.
D. 204, f. 78).

[2] "Very good men and excellently well disciplined." Reresby was
expected at Bridlington on July 22 (*Cal. S.P. Dom.*, 1678, p. 307).

* Cf 12/19: Godfrey Copley, 8 July 1678. After informing Sir John Wentworth
of the day of the election, Copley immediately passed on the information to
Reresby.

inhabitants very kind to me. Only some of the nighbouring gentlemen tooke it not soe wel that a gentleman
of another rideing was preferred to that command before
them.

The fort was well repaired to the sea, and the plattform
with twelve gunns mounted upon it in good order, and
the governor's hous, wher the gunner lived, newly fitted
with a place for the stoors.[1]　I stayed here but five days,
and returned to Thriberge, wher I gave the Duke an
account how I found the guarrison.

My wife's only sister, that had lived with me since my
marriage, left my hous upon some discontent to live in
another place, and roved from one relation to another,
till at last going to London she renewed her acquaintance
with a gentleman that never designed to marry her
(though he had formerly pretended to her), was rob'd
by him of the greatest part of her fortune, and at last dyed
miserably.

The sessions for the West Rideing were held at *August* 6
Rotherham, wher I gave the charge. Most of the
justices laid at my hous.

Came the newes that the peace was concluded between 16
the French and the Dutch,[2] wherupon the King proroaged
the Parlament till October the first.[3]

I returned, and carryed my family to Burlinton, wher 22
I stayed near three weeks. At my return to Yorke I met
the commissioners for the tax given the King to disband
the army, wher we did execute it for the West Rideing.
The Parlament was again further proroagued till the 21 of
October by proclamation, till the Houses mett and were
accordingly proroagued.

---

[1] This happy result had not been achieved without some disputes
between Reresby and his storekeeper, Thomas Aslaby, who was super-
intending the alterations (*Cal. S. P. Dom.*, 1678, pp. 163, 175, 599-600).

[2] At Nymegen, July 31/August 10, 1678.

[3] Parliament had been prorogued for a fortnight on July 15, and was
being held in abeyance by short prorogations.

*

* The details of repairing and supplying the fort are laid out in the letters in
bundle 12, particularly 12/16: Robert Banks, 15 September 1678; 12/21: T.
Aislaby, 2 August 1678.

October   The beginning of this month I was taken with an unaccountable disorder in my head, that I could not thinke nor doe anything with satisfaction; nor could I give any reason for it, noebody, I thanke God, either being, or haveing reason to be, more satisfyed in their low condition then myselfe (and ther were many in a much higher that had less caus to thinke themselves happy then myselfe); but I presume it proceeded from the spleen. It was some time ere I could recover myselfe, but I thanke my mercyful God I was never soe troubled before nor since.

10   Now came the first newes of the Popish Plott, or a design of the papists to kill the King, and of its discovery. It is not possible to imagin what a ferment the artifice of some, and the reall beliefe and fear of others concerning this plott, putt the two Houses of Parlament and the greatest part of the nation into.

Oct. 20   I got to London with my wife and family.

21   The Parlament assembled, at the opoming of which the King tould us in his speech that he had kept the army longer on foot then by the Act for disbanding of it was allowed, but he had done it to preserve the rest of Flanders, which was very chargeable to him; that he was in a great deale of debt; that his revenue would not defray the charge of the goverment; that he would informe them of it, by laying the whole scheme of his income before them, and then doubted not but they would give him an increase to it; that ther had been a design to take away his life by the Jesuists and their party, but he would not enter into perticulars of that, least some should thinke that he said too little, and others that he said too much; but he would leave the whole thing to their enquiry.

The two Houses (especially the Commons) took fire presently at it, and voted an address to be presented to the King that all papists should be immediately sent ten miles from London. Sir Edmondbury Godfrey, a justice of peace of Middlesex, who had taken some examinations

privately brought to him of this plott, after haveing been
missing three or four days from his hous, was found dead
in some fields near the town,[1] sopposed to be kild by some
papists, which increased the suspicion.

The first discovery of this was by one Doctor Oats,[2]
who haveing, as he pretended, some jealousie of such a
design, dissembled himselfe to be a papist, went and
admitted himselfe of the Jesuist College at St. Omers,
wher he discovered the whole matter, discovered it to one
Doctor Tong, an English devine,[3] who tould it to my Lord
Tresuror, and he to the King privately,[4] but soe that ther
was noe light nor discours of it for a month after or
therabout.

I being with the King at the Duchess of Portmouths *Oct.* 23
lodgeings (my Lord Tresurer present), the King tould
me he did thinke it some artifice, and did not believe one
word of the plott.

Mr. Coleman, secretary to the Duchess of Yorke,[5] a 25
rigid papist and an ambitious man, being comitted and
his papers seized some days before, the King tould me
and some others then waiting upon him that they conteaned planely a design to introduce popery; that ther
were amongst them severall letters to and from Father

---

[1] Sir Edmund Berry Godfrey had earned his knighthood and a great
reputation by staying in London throughout the Plague year and endeavouring to relieve distress. His body was found on October 17 in a
ditch on the south side of Primrose Hill, but the manner in which he met
his end has never been satisfactorily determined.

[2] Titus Oates, the notorious informer. The degree of D.D., which he
claimed to have received from the University of Salamanca, was one of
the jests of his opponents.

[3] Israel Tonge, one of the most fanatically anti-Catholic of the London
clergy.

[4] The first intimation of the conspiracy was given on August 13 to the
King himself through a further intermediary, Christopher Kirkby, who
held an appointment in the royal laboratory. Charles, who entirely dis-
believed the story, entrusted the investigation of it to the Lord Treasurer.

[5] Edward Coleman, whose presence in the Duke of York's household
had already led to considerable trouble.

La Shase,[1] the King of France his confessor, and the Popes nuntio at Paris,[2] to breake the present Parlament as too firm to the Church of England, to gett mony from France to carry on the design, and some reflexions on the King; that he ofton made use of his Royall Highness his name, as not altogather a stranger to the designe, &c.; but his Majesty did not believe ther was any design upon his life.

The Duke of Yorke seemed concerned at this impudence of Coleman's, declared his ignorance of his correspondence ther, or of anything that it treated of in his letters, and desired his friends of both Houses to declare it for him. The Commons were very warm against my Lord Treasurer for not makeing the plott sooner publique, since the King might have been killed in the meantime. I was the first that tould my Lord this newes before the King, who said my Lord was not in fault as to that, for he had commanded him to keep it secret to discover the thruth of it the better.

To give a perticular account of this plott is not the business of this worke. The severall naratives of the witnesses to it before the Houses of Lords and Commons, the courts of justice, upon the tryalls of thos that were accused to be concerned in it, will show that sufficiently. Only in generall, Doctor Oats, Mr. Bedloe,[3] Dugdale,[4] and many others, did endeavour to proove a design to settle popery in this kingdom by killing the King and the Duke of Monmoth, that soe the Crown might without competition devolve upon the Duke of Yorke. The King was to be killed by poisning by Sir George Wakeman, his phisition, who was tryed for it;[5] the Queen privy to it;

---

[1] François de la Chaise.

[2] Presumably Cardinal Albani, internuncio at Brussels, is intended.

[3] William Bedloe, a disreputable adventurer, who claimed that Oates had anticipated revelations he was on the point of making himself.

[4] Stephen Dugdale, one of the minor witnesses to the plot.

[5] Wakeman was physician in ordinary to the Queen. His acquittal in July 1679 was the first serious blow to the credit of the plot.

then by stabbing; severall dealt with to doe it, and Bedloe amongst others, who swore he attempted it at Windser upon the servant of Mr. Killigrew, a bedchamber man,[1] waiting for the Kings going to bed, and did actually kill him, believeing it was the King. The thruth is, such a person was stabd upon a bed, wher the King had thrown himselfe a little before, comming from a debauch, but believed by another accident. The blow being given, an army of 50,000 papists was imediately to rise, headed by severall persons of the popish religion of the first quality, who had all their severall places of generall, admiral, tresurer, chancellor, and other offices of the army and of the Crown assured to them by commissions from the Pope; much of which appeared very improbable, but such was the torrent then that noe doubt was to be made of what was said.

I desired the Duke of Monmoth to grant an allowance *Oct. 28* for fire and candle for my company at Burlinton, which he granted.

Contrary to Mr. Wentworth's engagement another petition was presented to the committè of elections to disturb my sitting and choice as a member of Parlament.[2] I writt to him and the sheriff, which last was, I feard, a conspiritor with him, for all I had obteaned him that office by the means of the Lord Tresurer, as I have declared before, upon the death of Sir Godfrey Copley, his father. My Lord Tresurer, who was his cozen, bid me write one for him also to the sheriff, to discourage the   * design against me, which I did, and his lordship caused it to be transcribed, and signed it without altering one word.[3]

[1] Thomas Killigrew, groom of the bedchamber in 1660 and master of the revels in 1673 ; author of several plays and founder of Drury Lane Theatre.

[2] The petition, in the name of the burghers of Aldborough, was presented on October 26 (*Journals of the House of Commons*, ix. 522).

[3] On November 9 this letter reached Copley, who replied two days later   † with an account of his having " discoursed the businesse with Mr. Wentworth and urged his promise and engagement," but without any very satisfactory result (Leeds MSS.).

* 1/69a: copy of a letter, in Reresby's hand, from Danby to Mr. Wentworth striking a deal whereby there would be no further harassment of Reresby in his election.

† The letter which Reresby sent is in the Yorkshire Archaeological Society Library, Copley Correspondence, Copley I 1662–77, BRA 133, fol. 27, 7 November 1678; 12/79: G. Copley, 9 November 1679, appears to be the reply.

Nov. 1 All the begining of this month was taken up in the Hous of Commons in hearing severall witnesses as to the plott, who came in plentifully, the King, at the request of the Commons, giveing indemnity to such as could discover anything concerning it, however deeply ingaged in it themselves, and allowing maintenance to them besides. After a little time it came to this voat in the Lower Hous, that the Hous was of opinion, from the evidence that appeared by Coleman's letters, the informations of Oats and others, that ther was a hellish and damnable design to assassinate and murder the King, and to subvert the religion and goverment as established by law.

4 The Hous of Lords haveing requested his Royall Highness to withdraw himselfe from the Kings councils, he consented. The Hous of Commons was higher, and were for remooveing him from the Kings person; but some argued that to be dangerous, least he might be persuaded to putt himselfe at the head of the popish party. Some mooved that he should be sent out of England. The King and Duke himselfe spoake to all their friends to oppose that, which was done effectually, for noe resolution being taken that day the debate was adjurned to the 8th of November. However, though it was not voted, most of the Hous seemed to be of opinion that the Duke's being of that persuasion was the main encouragement to the papists in thes attempts.

5 Came forth the proclamation for the banishment of papists ten miles from London.

6 *and* 7 Severall of Coleman's letters which he had receved from severall Jesuists in France, Flanders, Ireland, some directed to him, others to the Dukes confessor, were read publiquely in the Hous (thos that were in French being before translated into English by a comitteè appointed for that purpas, of which I was, and translated six for my share).[1] By severall of the said letters the design did

*   [1] Only one of these can now be identified (Hist. MSS. Com., *Fitzherbert MSS.*, p. 98).

* 26/8 is another letter translated by Reresby: 'PLC' [Père la chaise] to [Coleman], Paris, 23 October 1675.

plainly appear to introduce popery, and by means pernicious to the King and goverment, but not soe far as was pretended. The 7th, being with my Lord Treasurer (as I had been three times before that week with others) to consider what would be fittest to be complyed with to fram an Act to lessen the popish interest in this kingdome, his lordship tould us the King would be content that something were enacted to pare the nailes (to use his own phrase) of a popish successor; but that he would not suffer his brother to be taken away from him, nor the right line of the succession of the Crown interrupted. The King spoake to the two Houses to the same effect the next day.[1]   *Nov.* 8

Being Sunday, the Commons sat till four in the afternoon to examine Bedloe, who gave an account of the killing of Sir Edmond Bury Godfrey by two of my Lord Belasis servants and two priests in Sommersit Hous,[2] accused that lord of being privy to the design of killing the King, and confirmed many other perticulars of Oats his evidence. This Bedloe was the son of a cobler in Wales, but had cheated a great many marchants abroad and gentlemen at home, by personating my Lord Gerrard[3] and other men of quality, and by divers other cheats; and when he was taxed with it he made it an argument to be more credited in this matter, saying noebody but a rougue could be imployed in such designs.   10

I found something in one of Colemans letters which I had to translate, which seemed to justifie the Duke in something that he was suspected to be an abetter of as to this plott. I presently showed it to my Lord Treasurer, and then to his Highness, who made good use of it.   12

A jealousie now appeared to arise between the Duke and my Lord Tresurer. The Duke thought my Lord promoted secretly the councils for his leaveing the Court,

---

[1] Actually on November 9.   [2] The residence of the Queen.

[3] Charles Gerard, created Baron Gerard of Brandon in 1645, and Earl of Macclesfield in 1679.

that he might have the King more absolutely in his own power; and my Lord (that I believe endeavoured to serve the Duke all he could, though noe friend to his religion) ressented the Dukes suspicion.

Severall addresses were now presented to the King from the Hous of Commons, one for a commission to the justices of the peace to offer the oaths of allegiance and supremacy to such persons as they suspected within ten miles of London, to try if they were papists; another (which was twice offered) that all persons that lodged at Whitehall (whether servants or not to the Court) should be offered the oaths, and be dismist in case they refused to take them.

Nov. 13 That great bill passed in the Hous of Lords to incapacitate the popish lords to sit ther if they refused the oath of allegiance and supremacy,[1] though my Lord High Treasurer said in my hearing the night before that he was sure that bil would never pass in that Hous. Bedloe the same day desired the Commons to intercede to the King for his pardon, he haveing further matter to discover concerning a great man at Court, but would not reveale it till he had his pardon, which the King granted.

The Duke of Holsten's resident[2] haveing, it seems, reported that my Lord Treasurer was a pentioner of France, or at least his lordship being soe informed, sent for the said resident, and me to be present when he examined him about it, who did absolutely deny it.

18 I acquented his lordship that Monsieur du Croc (the said resident) had assured me the day before that the Commons would certainly fall upon him, and that it was in his power to take of the edge of one most violent against

[1] The second or Parliamentary Test Act. Introduced in the Commons on October 23, it passed the Lords with some amendments on November 20.

[2] An adventurer named Du Cros, who claimed to be in the service of Christian Albert, Duke of Holstein-Gottorp, but was suspected to be in the pay of France.

him.[1]   I tould him more that I heard from others, that
my cozen Ralph Mountaigue, since Lord Mountaigue
(lately recalled from being embassadour in France and
now member of our Hous),[2] would accuse him ther.   My
Lord rejected both, saying the latter durst not impeach
him, for he had letters to show from him, whilst embassador, that made out how endeavouring he was to persuade
him to accept the French Kings mony, but he absolutely
refused it.

The Duke tould me the same day that he expected to
be attacked by the Commons, and hoped his friends would
stand firm to him.   Sir Joseph Williamson, Secretary of
State, was then committed by the Hous to the Tower for
passing the musters of some popish officers without
offering them the oaths, though he had his Majestys order
for it.

Bedloe, being further examined before my Lord Chiefe
Justice,[3] accused my Lord Carenton[4] and my Lord Brudnall
to be privy to the plott.   The former was therupon committed.   He said further that 10,000 Spaniards were to
land at Burlinton, and to be commanded by Sir Henry
Tichburn[5] as general and Sir Francis Ratcliff[6] as lieutenant-
general; which was very improbable, Spain not haveing
men at this time to supply and defend their teritories,

[1] Notes in Danby's handwriting of information supplied by Du Cros,
dated November 19, 20 and 24, 1678, are B.M. Add. MSS. 28043, ff. 1-2.

[2] Ralph Montagu succeeded his father as third Lord Montagu of
Boughton in January 1684, was created Earl of Montagu in 1689, and
Duke of Montagu in 1705.   In 1678, while ambassador in France, he
became involved in an unseemly quarrel with the Duchess of Cleveland,
and in an effort to defend himself against her accusations, hurried home
without leave, only to be dismissed from all his posts.   On October 31 he
was elected M.P. for Northampton, and prepared to attack Danby, on
whom he laid the blame for his dismissal.

[3] Sir William Scroggs, appointed Chief Justice of the King's Bench in
May 1678.

[4] Francis Smith, Viscount Carrington.

[5] Sir Henry Tichborne, the third baronet.

[6] Sir Francis Radclyffe, created Earl of Derwentwater in 1688.

either at home or abrode, which gave France soe great advantage against it.

Nov. 21   His Majesty tould me that Bedleau was a roague, and that he was satisfyed he had given some false evidence concerning the death of Sir Edmondbury Godfrey.

In prepareing the bill for purgeing the Hous of Lords of such as refused to take the oaths it was putt to the voat whether his Royall Highness should be excused from takeing the said test. It was carryed in the affermative by two voats only.[1] If this had been carryed against him he would also have been voated from the King's presence. I spoake for the Duke in this debate, and had his Highness his thankes when I waited upon him.

My brother, Sir Henry Gooderick, haveing then a regiment of foot in the army, one of his captains threw up his commission upon some disgust and challenged his collonel. He accepted the challenge and came to seek me to be his secound; but not finding me at home he took Sir Thomas Mauliverer, who ran his adversary thorow the body, and Sir Henry wounded and disarmed his.

26   Doctor Oats, being further examined of the plott, accused the Queen to be privy and consenting to the King's being to be kild by poyson, when he had some days before taken his oath at the barr of the Hous of Lords that he had discovered all that he knew of the plott, and of any person of quality concerned in it.

The same day it was voated in the Lower Hous that the army should be speedily disbanded.

Mr. Bedloe did give evidence that there was a consultation at Somersit Hous, wher the Queen, my Lord Belasis, my Lord Powis,[2] and four French abbots being

---

[1] A proviso exempting the Duke of York from the test to be taken by members of both Houses had been attached by the Lords to the bill. This was accepted by 158 votes to 156.

[2] William Herbert, who succeeded his father as third Baron Powis in 1667, was created Earl of Powis in 1674 and Marquis of Powis in 1687. He was one of the five Catholic lords accused by Oates and committed to the Tower on October 25.

present, it was agreed that the King should be poysoned; that the Queen wept, but at last did consent to it; but this he had only from Mr. Coleman.

Were imployed in takeing the oaths and the test by the *Nov.* two Houses of Parlament. All the popish lords were 30, 31 banished that Hous by it save three that swore. The Commons did generally take the oaths, &c.

My wife and familie came up to me to London.

It was voated by the Commons that an address be made *Dec.* 1 to the King from that Hous, representing to him the ill state of the nation, and the danger it was in by his Majestys rather following private councils then thos of his two Houses of Parlament. My Lord Treasurer was struck at, and some others of the Cabinet Council, by this addresse. This voat was carryed by twenty-two voats,[1] and some of the Courts friends were for it, which made some jealous that the Duke, being noe longer in councils, was fearfull my Lord Treasurer should have too much power with the King, and was therfore consenting that he should be thus remooved. It was said, too, that some had persuaded the Duke (but unjustly) that my Lord did persuade the King that ther was something of probability in the accusation of the Queen, that he might harken to a devource, and marry another more likely to bring children to the Crown.

The bils for the disbanding the army and raiseing mony for that service, and for the better conviction of popish recusants, took up the time of both Houses, wherin hapned many warm debates too long here to be named, the Commons not suffering the Lords to alter a mony bill.

Being at supper with some ladys, one Mr. Adams, that 12 had ressented something from me not long before, seing my footman at the door, said something that reflected

---

[1] It was intended to form part of an address to the King on the state and dangers of the nation, and was carried on December 2 by 138 votes to 114 (*Journals of the House of Commons*, ix. 551).

upon me and the company. I sought for him the next day, but could not find him. However he hearing that I had been at his lodgeing was easily induced to aske pardon, which he did afterwards before the Earl of Alesbury.[1]

Dec. 16   The King, haveing caused Mr. Mountaigu's papers to be seized, gave this account of it to the Lower Hous,[2] that he, haveing been his embassador at the French Court, had ther treated with the Pope's nontio, without commission from him; and that he had done this to find out the subject of that treaty. Mountaigue, on the other hand, declared in the Hous that it was my Lord Treasurer had wrought upon the King to doe this, knowing that he had letters under his lordship's own hand sufficient to ruine him, which he had used this artifice to gett from him; and that notwithstanding most of his letters had been seized, yet he had secured the most material. One of them produced in the Hous, bearing date March the 25, [16]78, was to this purpas—that he was to acquaint that Court with the great difficultys he mett withall here to conclude a peace between us and them, for fear the Parlament should find it out; however he had order from the King to bid him treat with them for a peace, as well between them and the Confederates as ourselves, upon condition the French King would give ours 600,000 livers[3] per annum for three years togather after the peace was concluded, our King, disgusting his Parlament by that means, not being to expect any mony from them of soe long; that when he writt back to the Secretary here of this transaction he should not mention anything of the mony, &c.—signed, Danby.

This putt the Hous into a flame, and it was presently mooved that he ought to be impeached of high treason, for this was endeavouring to devide the King from his

---

[1] Robert Bruce, only son of the first Earl of Elgin, created Earl of Ailesbury in 1664.

[2] December 19.   [3] Really 6,000,000 livres.

Parlament, and to make it of noe use.   This seemed to
carry on the same design with Coleman in his letters, to
gett mony from France.   One Mr. Powell [1] said further
that it was to take upon him to usurp a power to the
exclusion of other councillers, who had right to advise the
King as well as himselfe, the very treason which was laid
to the charge of the Spencers and the Duke of Ireland in
Richard the Secound's reigne.

To this was answered that this was not soe great an
offence to write this by the King's own order, which was
expressed in the letter itselfe, and would be owned (as
sopposed) by the King at this time; that the King had
power to advise with which of his councellers he pleased,
and if his Majesty saw that the Confederates would make
a peace (which we must followe), wher was the harm to
make what advantage we could to ourselves by it, and to
spare at the same time the purses of his subjects.

The secound letter purported an assurance that ther
was inclinations of a very fair understanding between us
and his Majesty of France, with advice to hasten the peace,
bycaus the Duke seemed every day more and more averse
to it, with mention of some towns as cautionary to be
delivered up by the French to the Confederates upon concludeing this peace.   Mr. Mountaigue declared in the
Hous that the French King was willing to deliver up two
towns more then he did in the former treaty, but that my
Lord Treasurer was soe earnest and pressing for mony
that he made the terms much wors for the Confederates;
but could not averr that he knew of any mony paid actually
either to him or to our King.

Other things were then laid to the Lord Treasurer's
charge, amongst others the male-administration of his
office and the lowness of the Exchequer.   To this it was
answered by his lordship's friends that 600,000 l. debt

---

[1] Henry Powle, M.P. for Cirencester, one of the more moderate members of the opposition and Speaker of the Convention in 1689. His speech
on this occasion is printed in Grey's *Debates*, vi. 351-2.

had been paid since his lordship came into office, and noe mony was given all that time to the King but what was appropriated to the uses to which it was designed.

He was further accused (his letter bearing date 2 5 of March, [16]78, and the Act by which mony was given the King to enter into a warr against France being passed the 20th) with deludeing the nation, first to advise the King to take mony to raise an army for warr, and at the same time to treat for mony from France to make a peace, which looked as if a standing army was designed to enslave us at home, not to make warr abroad. Voated upon the whole that an impeachment be drawn up against my Lord Treasurer, and a committeè was accordingly appointed to doe it.

Mr. Mountaigue was very justly censured in this matter for discloseing thes things which passed thorow his handes when a publique minister without the King's leave.

I spoake for my Lord Treasurer in this debate.

Jan. 7 My Lord Treasurer endeavoured to take away the credit of his accuser by writing to the Speaker and sending him two of Mr. Mountaigue's letters, written from France, which were read in the Hous.[1] In one he gave this account, that Monsieur de Ruvigny was sent into England by the French King, hopeing by his relation to my Lord Russel's lady [2] to make an interest in that lord and the other anti-Court partys in our Hous, wherby to make the King jealous and to possess him with a wors opinion of this Parlament. The secound said that Ruvigny had commission to complain of my Lord Treasurer to the King for reguarding more to make himselfe popular with the Parlament then to persue his master's

---

[1] December 20. It is difficult to see what is the significance of the date in the margin.

[2] William Russell had married Rachel Wriothesley, daughter of the fourth Earl of Southampton by Rachel de Ruvigny, sister of the first Marquis de Ruvigny.

interest, for he advised the King to war with France to
please them, when he knew it was to the King's prejudice.
It advised further that if Ruvigny was but disappointed
in gaining upon the malecontents of the Hous, the King
might certainly gett mony from France, and therfore it
was his Majesty's interest to send him back with all
speed, which would certainly raise the markit for a
peace.

By thes letters Mountaigue appeared guilty and active
in the same offences of which he accused the Treasurer;
but my Lord had soe many ennemys that the whole
reflexion and violence was only against himselfe.   In
fyne, the tide was not to be stemd, and thes six articles were
read, debated, and passed against his lordship of high
treason:

1. That his lordship had traiterously usurped the
royall power by treating with forraign ministers without
the privacie of other privy councellours concerning a
peace with France, contrary to an Act of Parlament.

2. That he had traiterously endeavoured to subvert
the antient goverment of this kingdome by adviseing the
raising of an army under pretence of a war against
France, and by keepeing it on foot contrary to an Act of
Parlament, wherby to create jealousies of the goverment
in the mindes of the people.

3. That he had traiterously endeavoured to alien the
hearts of his Majesty from his people and Parlament by
treating with the French King to supply his Majesty with
a great sum of mony.

4. That he was popishly affected, that he had concealed the plott to the hazard of the King's life, and discouraged the King's evidence in the discovery of it.

5. That he had traiterously mispent the revenue of the
Crown in passing privy seales for 190,602 l.[1] for pensions
and private services in two years time, and in deverting
one entire branch of the revenue to private uses.

[1] The sum stated was £231,602.

6. That he had obteaned severall guifts of the King of his antient Crown lands, contrary to two Acts of Parlament.

Ther was much debate whether any of thes (were they true) would amount to high treason, none of them being within the statute of Edward the Third. It was answered that that Act of Parlament limits only the construction of treason in other courts, not in Parlaments to make other things treason, either declaratory or by bill. This was denyed as to makeing declaratory treason, for if a Parlament had that power, then what need was ther of a bill for the attainder of the Earl of Strafford.

It was further argued for my Lord Treasurer that if the King had the power of makeing peace and warr, he had it also to command his ministers to treat of it, and noe Act of Parlament could take away that fondamentall right of the Crown; that twas dangerous to extend the construction of treason too farr; the more treasons the more snares to us and our posteritys. I spoake twice in this debate this day. At last, the question being putt whether an impeachment of high treason upon thes articles against his lordship should be carried up to the Hous of Lords, the Hous devided. The ayes were 179, the noes 130.[1]

[Dec.] 23   The impeachment was carried up to the Lords barr, wher it was presently debated whether his lordship should withdraw. It was carried in the negative by 20 voats. Both Houses adjourned for Christmas Eve and Christmas Day only.

26   The Houses mett. The Commons heard some evidence concerning the death of Sir Edmondbury Godfrey, and quarelled with the Lords concerning the amendment they had made in the mony bill for disbanding the army.

---

[1] The reference seems to be to the first of five divisions taken in connection with the impeachment. Danby's friends proposed that the articles should be recommitted, and their motion was rejected by 179 votes to 135 (*Journals of the House of Commons*, ix. 562).

I spoake that day both with the King and Duke, who both declared that they would adhear to my Lord Treasurer.

The Lords voated that his lordship should not be com- Dec. 27 mitted. The same day the dispute between the two Hous[es] concerning the mony bill was decided by a conference, and the bill passed both Houses.[1] The King, observeing that the Earl of Strafford was violent against my Lord of Danby in the Hous (which indeed was from a personall peake he had to him for obstructing a pension which he had from the Crown),[2] tould me he wondered at it, since his father came to that unfortunate end by the same method of proceeding.

When it was least expected the King proroagued the 30 Parlament to the 4th of February, some said in favour of the papists, others of the Lord Treasurer, others in defence of his prerogative, which was more then one way invaded by the proceeding of the Commons. But he declared at the same time that he intended to disband the army and to persue the plott.

It was reported that Mr. Mountaigue was withdrawn, Jan. 1 and true, for he was soon after discovered in a disguise [1678/9] at Dover, going for France.[3]

The same day both the Duke and my Lord Treasurer said the King designed to keep my company standing if possible; however, if the Parlament should disband that with the rest of the army, he would give me some other imployment of as considerable value. Some murmurs were frequent in this interval of Parlament that the army

---

[1] The point at issue was whether the money for disbanding the army should be placed in the hands of the Chamber of London or lodged in the Exchequer. Conferences were held on December 26 and 28, but agreement was not reached, and the bill did not pass.

[2] There are letters on this subject from Strafford to Danby, dated June 9 and 20, July 14, 1675, and June 17, 1676, among the Leeds MSS.

[3] He was arrested at Dover on January 19 (Cal. S.P. Dom., 1679-80, pp. 42-3, 46).

was not disbanded, and that three prisners condemd for the plott were respited from execution.[1]

Jan. 6   Being at a play wher I sate near Collonel Macarty,[2] who was shortsighted, a gentleman in drinke quarelled with him, and drawing his sword passed at him before Macarty was ready, or indeed saw it, and had certainly wounded him, had not I putt by the sword with mine that was drawn whilst he recovered himselfe; but they were then parted without harm. Macarty was to fight him the next day, but I tould the King of it, who caused them to be both secured and made friends.

21   The Duke of Norfock made me a visit.

24   My Lord Treasurer sent for me, and tould me the King had declared that he would desolve that Parlament, and advised me to make an interest as soon as I could in order to a new election, for another Parlament would be speedily called. This Parlament was very loyall and firm for the most part both to the King and Church, which made that part which was otherwise desirous to gett it dissolved; and the way they found out for it (as was credibly reported) was to persuade the Treasurer to obteane it of the King, promessing him if it succeeded ther should be noe further prossecution against him in the next Parlament. But they deceived him, as appeared afterwards.

31   Both the King and the Duke advised me to stand for the next Parlament, and both of them assured me of the continuance of my gouverment at Burlinton, and of their assistance in case it came to a contraverted election.

---

[1] William Ireland, John Grove and Thomas Pickering. They had all been convicted and sentenced on December 17, and the delay in arranging for their execution had caused trouble in Parliament even before the prorogation. Ireland and Grove were eventually executed on January 24, and Pickering suffered the same fate on May 9, 1679.

[2] Justin MacCarthy, third son of Donogh, first Earl of Clancarty, at that time colonel of a regiment of foot. He later became lieutenant-general in Ireland under Tyrconnel, and was created Viscount Mountcashel by James II in 1689.

The proclamation being then com'd out for chooseing *Feb.* 4
a new Parlament, I took my leave of the King and the
Duke. My Lord Treasurer carryed me to his Majesty,
and thanked him for his promess to me to preserve my
goverment. The King replyed that I had served him
faithfully, and that he intended to be kind to me. My
Lord Treasurer writt by me at the same time to the high
sheriff of Yorkeshire[1] to be kind to me in the return. I
then also took leave of the Duke of Monmoth.

I took room in a hackney coach to Yorke, leaveing my 5
wife and family in town.

I arrived at Yorke the 11, at Audbrough the next day, 11
wher the five antient burgesses of the nine offered to elect
me and my partner, whom I named (Mr. Ardinton),[2] with
little expence. My adversarys, who stood upon another *
interest, which was that of Mr. Wentworth, were Sir
Godfrey Copley (who was sheriff the year before by my
means, as I have mentioned) and one Mr. Wentworth.[3]
By my interest with the then sheriff I gott the day of
election putt off till the 28, in which time I went and †
disposed of my affairs, and saw my four yongest children
at Thriberge.

Ther was great dispute as to elections over all England
at this time, as men stood affected to the goverment and
to the then ministers, and as men believed them well
intentioned or otherways.

I then mett with the ill newes of the death of my
brother Brown, my wife her only brother, ensign to my
company at Burlinton, a hansome ingenious yong man.
He was bred to the law, but an airiness of spirit, an
excellent voice, which usually makes men lovers of company, took him off from his studys, and drew him into
some prodigallity. However, he left me a hous at Yorke
worth 25 l. per annum, and to his godson, my son

[1] Richard Shuttleworth.

[2] Henry, son of William Arthington of Arthington.

[3] Ruisshe Wentworth.

* 14/62: John Tempest, 13 February 1678/9, confirms this. His son-in-law,
Sheriff Shuttleworth, sends his assurance that the election will be by the nine.

† 1/75: E. Morris, 'Thurs. night' [1679]. Morris's predictions that Reresby
would be returned without difficulty could not have been more inaccurate.

John,[1] with all the land he had in England; 500 l. legacy to my wife; 500 l. to his other sister, Mrs. Honora Brown; and made me his sole executor, which was worth 200 l. more.

I percieved by my nighbours that came to visit me in the country that it was very much poysoned with an ill conciet of my Lord Treasurer, as concerned in the design to bring in popery.

Feb. 26   I returned to Audbrough, wher I understood that Mr. Ardinton (Mr. Wentworth, who was to be brother burgesse with Sir Godfrey Copley, being elected in another place)[2] was also elected upon the interest and foundation wher Sir Godfrey Copley was to be elected (which was by old Mr. Wentworth's way of chooseing),

28   soe that he was at the day chosen both ways, both by the majority of the nine and by the freehoulders at large, soe that my indenture and Mr. Ardintons was signed by 5, Sir Godfrey's and his by 48.   Mr. Shuttleworth was then high sheriff, a timerous man, and much inclined to return the indenture which had most names to it rather then mine.   Sir Godfrey had three lawyers at the place of election to plead the legality of it, and the danger of it to the sheriff if he refused to return it.   I had noebody to plead my caus but myselfe, noe lawyer nor assistant, Mr. Ardenton being sure both ways.   But I soe ordered the matter, that after a debate of almost two hours the sheriff and his officers were convinced by my reasons to return my indenture singly, which was a providence, and gained me some repute of parts in the opinion of three hundred persons then present, gentlemen and others.   Most of the gentry dined with me that day.   The charge of this election cost me about 40 l.   It cost Sir Godfrey Copley above 200 l.

March 1   I returned to Thriberge.

3   I sett forward for London, and arrived the sixt.   The

---

[1] Sir John's third son, " born the tenth of February, three quarters of an hour after ten in the morning, Anno Domini 1675 " (*Family History,* ii. f. 17).

[2] Liverpool.

Parlament mett that day, and a differance hapned in the March 6
Hous of Commons, who would have chosen one [Speaker],[1]
and the King did recommend another,[2] soe that they refused
to doe business, and adjurned the Hous to the 7th, from
that day to the 8th, and soe to the 10th.

I mett the King in his royall robes and his crown upon 7
his head as he went out of the Hous of Lords, who stopped
to aske me if I was elected.   I answered, yes.   He said
he was glad of it.

I found to the surprize of all men at my return that the
King had commanded the Duke to goe into Flanders.
Some said this my Lord Treasurer had obteaned to gett
the King to himself.   Others said it was to avoid the
violence of both Houses against the Duke, from the
suspicion of some that he was of the plott.   But it was,
I presume, chiefly to remoove all jealousie from the
Parlament that his Majesty was not at all influenced by
popish councils, noe, not his brothers.

The Commons began to be angry again at the Treasurer for the Speaker that they had a mind to being
refused by the King, saying he was the occasion of it,
bycaus he was not his lordship's friend.   The dispute
continued between the King and the Commons till at last
they addressed to the King, beseeching him not to invade
their undoubted privilege to choos their Speaker.   The
King still insisted upon it as his to allowe their choice,
without which he was noe Speaker.   It was the opinion
of all the mederate men in the Hous that such punctillios
did not deserve to occasion delays when ther laid business
of such importance before them, but the angry party
would not submitt, soe that by way of expedient the King
did proroague the Parlament the 11th to the 15th instant,
and then Sergiant Gregory was chosen Speaker,[3] which
all sides agreed to.

[1] Edward Seymour.   [2] Sir Thomas Meres.

[3] William Gregory had had little of the Parliamentary experience desir-
able in a Speaker, having been returned as member for Weobley on

And now the storm began to fall soe heavy upon my Lord Treasurer that he was persuaded to incline to deliver up his staff, and with it his office, hopeing to appease both Houses by it. I was against it, I confess, soe long as he found the King stick to him, and said it would rather be a means to make his ennemys more fierce; the Lords would fear him less when he was out of power, and the Commons not love [him] the better. Now severall persons gott into good imployments, not by my Lord's kindness soe much as by giveing mony to his Lady, who had driven a secrett trade of takeing bribes for good offices (and not without my Lord's knowlege). I knew it, but had neither the face nor the desire to come in at that door, which made me postponed to some that, as I thought, deserved as little as myselfe. But thos that were soe admitted stayed not long in their places after his lordship's exit.

March 17 The comitteè appointed to examin the plott heard Oats and Bedloes evedence, wher the latter accused the Treasurer for tampering with him to fly in this intervall of Parlament.

* 19 The 11 of Aprill was appointed by the comittè of privileges for the trying the election at the petition of Sir Godfrey Copley, and it was ordered that the high sheriff should be sent for up to answer his makeing a single return; soe severly did all things goe with my Lord Treasurer's friends.

20 A message was sent to the Lords to desire that my Lord Treasurer might be committed, the Lords haveing voted before the same day that his lordship should have eight days to bring in his defence.

22 The Commons repeated the former message to the Lords.

23 The King came to the Hous of Lords in his roabes and with his crown upon his head, tould both Houses that it

March 7, 1677/8. His tenure of the Speakership, although quite successful, was of short duration, as in April 1679 he was appointed a Baron of the Exchequer, being knighted at the same time.

* 16/14: Simon Warner, 7 March 1678/9, indicates Reresby's anticipation of problems; 14/130: Order of the Committee of Elections and Privileges of the House of Commons setting the date for Reresby's hearing on 11 April, dated 19 March 1678/9.

was by his perticular order that my Lord Treasurer had
written thos two letters to Mountaigue, and that it was not
my Lord Treasurer that concealed the plott, since it was
himselfe that tould it to his lordship from time to time as
he thought fitt. His Majesty declared further that he
had given my Lord Treasurer his full pardon, and he
would, if need required, give it him again ten times over;
however, he intended to lay him aside from his imployments, and to forbid him comming to Court.[1]

Some would have persuaded him to have fled, and the
two Houses would have been content with it, for the
Lords had a conference with the Commons about makeing
a bill to banish him, but the Commons desired some days
to consider of it, hopeing he would withdraw in that time.

I see my Lord at midnight as he came out of his closit *March* 24
from adviseing what to doe with his friends. He gave
me a great many thankes and good words, tould me he had
recommended me to the King as a fitt person to goe invoye
to France, and tould me wher I was to apply myselfe in
his absence if I wanted anything with the King.

[1679]

The Commons fell into a great heat, dynyed to comply 25
with the Lords in their bill of banishment as too moderate
a punishment, but sent to demand justice of their lordships against the Treasurer, declareing that he ought not
only to be punished in his own person, but in his posterity,
to be an exemple to others to behave themselves better in
that place. Before this message came to the Lords they
had changed their minds and sent the Black Rod for my
Lord Treasurer,[2] but he had absented [himself], and it was
then doubted the King began to cool towards him.

---

[1] This speech was delivered on March 22, and was the cause of the
Commons repeating their message to the Lords. March 23 was a Sunday,
and the Houses did not sit.

[2] Reresby's dates seem to be a day wrong about this point. These are
the events of March 24.

It is very unhappy for a servant to serve an unconstant or unsteady prince, which was a little the fault of our master. It is certain if the Treasurer would but have used the best means he could for himselfe he might have come off better; but he ressolved rather to suffer then to say what might have reflected either on the King or others near him, as he since said himselfe. This great change, I confess, made me seriously reflect upon the uncertainty of greatness. It was not many months that few things considerable passed or were granted at Court but with the knowlege or consent of this great man. The King's brother and favourite mistriss were glad to be fair with him, and the generall address of all men of business was to him, that was not only Treasurer but chiefe minister, that did not only keep the purse but was the first and greatest confident in business. Now he became neglected of all, was forced to abscond, in danger to loos all he had gotten and his life with it; and his family, raised from private gentleman to marquis (for a patent was then passing for that honour),[1] was now upon the brinke of falling to less then yeoman, insoemuch as the meanest subject would scarce now have changed conditions with him, whome the greatest envyed soe lately before.

This confirmed me in the opinion that a middle estate was ever the best, not soe low as to be trodden upon nor soe high as to be in danger to be shaken with the blast of envie, not soe lazie as not to endeavour to be distinguished in some measure from men of the same ranke by ones own industry nor soe ambitious as to sacrafice the ease of this life, and the hopes of happiness in the next, to clime over the heads of others to a greatness of uncertain continuance. And I take this to be the fitt and just care of a father of children, and of the chief of a family, soe to endeavour to provide for the one and improove the other as not to

---

[1] A warrant for the title of Marquis of Danby had been given him on March 16 at a meeting of the Cabinet Council as part compensation for the loss of his offices. The grant was never carried any further.

endanger the ruine of both.   It was my kindness to this, I confess, as much as anything in my own temper, which made me lance into the world at elder years, when I had passed my yonger (and was fitter for business) more retiredly, as what I have given an account of heretofore will demonstrate.   But when I had children, as I had at this time, I resolved to make use of thos few parts which God had given me to try if by any just and safe means I could acquire something to mend their condition, which by God's mercy to me I in some measure succeeded in.

I writt to his Royall Highness and gave him an account *March 25* how affairs passed here.

Severall disputes hapned between the two Houses in the case of this lord, the Lords adhearing to their bill of banishment, the Commons to their bill of attainder, till at last it came to a free conference.   This business and that of the plott took up the time of both Houses for a long time.   It was suspected this while that my Lord of Danby laid concealed in Whitehall.

The King seemd not concerned at his parting thus with his brother and his Treasurer,[1] nor what use the Parlament would make of it, which it was suspected would be to gett their own friends into offices, and obteane some snip of the prerogative in consideration of the mony they gave to his Majesty.   Such elections as were tryed went against thos that had any friendship for the Treasurer, lett their caus be never soe just.   Sir Edmond Jenings, Sir Francis Lawly,[2] Sir Charles Wheeler,[3] all put into good

---

[1] " What will become of the Earl of Danby I know not ; . . . this I shall only assure you, that the King is no more concerned for him than for a puppy dog, nor for what becomes of the Duke of York neither " (Viscount Conway to Sir George Rawdon, May 3, 1679, in *Hastings MSS.*, ii. 388).

[2] The second baronet, of Spoonhill ; M.P. for Shropshire in the previous Parliament ; described by Andrew Marvell as " a pensioner, one of the horses in Madam Fontelet's coach " (*Seasonable Argument*).

[3] Of Birdingbury, Warwickshire ; M.P. for Cambridge University in the previous Parliament ; " a foot captain, who once promised himself to be Master of the Rolls, now Governor of Nevis " (*ibid.*).

places at Court by the means of his lordship, were all displaced, and severall others.

April 17   My Lord of Danby, haveing surrendered himselfe, was committed to the Tower, wher I went to visit him.[1] He appeared not much concerned.

18   I was a good while with the King, who promessed to assist me by commanding his servants and friends that were of the Hous to attend the committè when my caus came on.

19   The Privy Council, consisting of fifty lords, was discharg'd, and another called or chosen of thirty of thos lords and commoners that had chiefly opposed the Kings interest (as lately managed) in both Houses, as my Lord Russell, my Lord Halifax, my Lord Cavendish, &c. The Admiralty was put into commission, and soe was the Treasury. The Duke of Monmouth was believed to be at the bothom of thes councils, and twas certainly here that he began to sett up for himselfe.

23   The time comming on for my election to be tryed, I sollicited the Duke of Monmoth (the man then in power) to assist me by his friends in the tryall of my election.

*   He promessed to doe it, and the Duke secounded me to him, telling him he would oblige him by it, it being for his cozen. The latter invited me to dinner with severall Parlament men, and recommended me with earnestness to their assistance (I mean the Duke of Albemarle).

25   My Lord Danby returned his answer to his impeachment to the Upper Hous, pleading the Kings pardon. It was sent down to the Lower, wher it was referred to a committè to be considered of; the result of which was that his Majesty had noe power to grant a pardon in this case. The same day both Houses began to reflect on the Duchesse of Portsmouth.

26   The Commons resolved to sitt the next day, being

---

[1] Danby surrendered himself to Black Rod on April 15, and was committed by the Lords to the Tower on the following day. April 17 is presumably the date of Reresby's visit.

* 14/95: Edward Morris, 1 April 1679; 14/107: James Moyser, April 1679. Reresby had been trying to gather support from the Aldborough voters in his contested election. While Moyser's letter gave him no hope of Lord Clifford's support, Morris advised Reresby of the best witnesses, but transportation would be needed for their journey to London.

Sunday, to consider of the means for the preservation of his Majesty's person; and it was then voted that the best *April* 27 way was to prevent the succession's falling into the hands of a papist, and that the Duke of Yorke being such was the reason of the late conspiracy against the King's person and goverment, and the religion as by law established.

My Lord Vicount Halifax, being now of the Council and entring into business, though a great ennemy to the Earl of Danby, professed a kindness to me, and said he would befriend me as to my election, noe man haveing more interest with the Commons then he had; but whether it was fear to disoblige his party, &c., I found he was not very warm in the matter.[1]   Most of the other lords and

[1] Hitherto Reresby had looked to Danby as his patron, and so long as he continued to do so he could scarcely hope for genuine support from Halifax. By the end of June, however, all probability of Danby's restoration to favour had vanished, and the promotion of Halifax to the rank of earl in July was seized by Reresby as an excuse for offering his congratulations and services, and soliciting support in the new Parliament which had meanwhile been summoned. The portion of his letter printed within square brackets has been struck out, but the remainder is interesting both as illustrating his views and marking his change of allegiance :

Thriberge, August 15, 1679.—My Lord, I have had late encouragement from my bourough to hope that I may be ther elected in this Parlament ; and I confess I have made some steps towards it already, but shall proceed noe further till I have your Lordships allowance, haveing experienced the difference between your Lordships assistance and neutrality when thos causes come to be tryed before the committeè of privilege. I confess, my Lord, I have been very modest in makeing applications wher I feared they might be misconstrued, or that anything did stick to make them not well received, as mine might seem to deserve from your Lordship under my late circumstances. But I shall not suffer in your Lordships opinion, I hope, when I assure your Lordship that I was noe confident to that great lord of thos ills sopposed to be contrived against you on the one hand, noe more then I was privy to that advantage which you then only intended, but which you will now certainly effect to the goverment by your wise and disinterested councils on the other.

My Lord, I must confess myselfe a true servant to the goverment [soe long as I find it doth not intrench upon the libertie of the people], and if I did anyways err in the method of that service, at a time when your Lordship was not concern'd but was only pleased to look on, I know not how better to convince your Lordship of that reall respect I have for your Lordship,

gentlemen of the Privy Council, though very great patriots before in the esteem of both Houses, began to loose their credit with them in some measure; soe true it is that the Court and country liverey can never be worn togather.

Some lords that had been committed to the Tower, and my Lord of Danby (the former for the plott and all for high treason) desired that council might be assigned them, which was denied by both Houses, for it was resolved that council might be assigned in cases of felony or treason in a perticular fact, but not for a generall defence.

May 7   My caus came on to be heard before the comittè of elections, wher all the advers party did muster strongly against me, and yet I only lost it by two voats, which I looked upon as halfe a victory at that time of the day.

11   Was appointed to consider of his Majesty's speech, as to that part wher he tould us that he was willing to concur with his Parlament in passing a bill for limitting a popish successor, soe that he should not be able to alter the goverment and religion as now by law established, but he would not suffer the succession itselfe to be touched. Against this day a committè was appointed to examin Coleman's letters, and to make a report to the Hous of whatever related therin to the Duke of York. The committè reported that they found in the said letters that the Duke had written thrice to the Pope; that his first letter miscarryed, the secound gave soe great satisfaction to his Holiness that the ould man wept for joy, the third was to excuse his consenting to marry his eldest daughter to the Prince of Orange, the nescessity of affairs requiring it in that conjuncture (or to that effect); that in the treatys which Coleman managd with the French King's confessor

and of the defference I have ever had for your judgement, then to offer myselfe yet to persue the same good ends by your Lordships advice, which I shall ever observe and perform as being, My Lord, Your faithfull humble servant, J. R.   I congratulate your Lordships late promotion to your additionall honour. (Rawlinson MSS. D. 204, f. 74.)

(Le Shase) he used the Duke's name and authority for promoting the Catholique caus, and for setling that religion in England; but ther was nothing mentioned of the Dukes being concerned in any other part of the plott, or in the design of attempting upon the King's life.

A debate then began what method to follow, whether the Hous should proceed to frame a bil after the method offered by the King, or of exclusion from the Crown. Thos that were for the bill of limitation said that the goverment and religion might be as safely preserved that way as the other, for by that a small revenue might be setled upon a popish successour whilst he continued of that religion; the militia might be setled out of his power; a Parlament should be impowred to be called or to assemble whenever the present King dyed, and to sitt six weekes to settle the kingdome, to appoint Protestant officers, military and civill, to choos bishops, which the successor, if a papist, should have noe power to nominate.

To this was answered, this was to alter the very frame of the goverment and of monarchy, to make it a republique; nor would it proove of any use, for the King was king by the fondementall law of this land, the head of the three estates, insoemuch that such a Parlament when soe called could doe nothing without him; that whilst he had the title of King, he would exercize the power of a king; that this was therfore not soe safe a way to proceed as by utter exclusion. It was argued that this was wors then the other, for this was takeing away absolutely his birthright, which the Duke had as much to the Crown, should the King die without issue, as any man ther had to his fathers estate; that it was not likely that a prince of that spirit would be easily soe disinherited; that whenever it had been formerly attempted in case of the Crown in this kingdome it never succeeded, but right prevailed at the last; that civill warrs had formerly cost England dear upon thes occasions; that success would revers all attainders, and should the Duke arrive that way to the Crown both the overthrow of religion and the goverment would be more to be feared then whilst ther was yet a probability of comming to it peaceably.

May 12   I tould the King my fate in the committè. He said he was sorry for it, but they should not stay long behind except they used himselfe and his brother better. His Majesty promessed me the continuance of the command of Burlinton with the salary of 200 l. till a company fell, which I should have in lieu of mine now to be disbanded with the rest of the army.

14   The King sent a message to the Commons to thinke of raising mony for setting out a fleet, and for navall stoors, which were wanting in all the magazines in England. Upon taking the said message into consideration, it seem'd to be the opinion of the Hous that noe mony should be given for any use whatsoever till the succession was changed, religion secured, and all officers whom they disliked removed all over the kingdome. The debate ran to this effect, but noe voat did pass, only that the further consideration of this matter should be adjourned for eight days.

The lords in the Tower for the plott and my Lord of Danby being shortly to have their tryals, a question rose in the Lords Hous whether the bishops ought to be present in cases of blood. The Commons, thinkeing thes spirituall lords would be too favourable, took the consideration of it into their Hous, and were of opinion they ought not to be present. The Lords ressented this from the Commons, saying this was a branch of their judicature wher the Commons had nothing to doe to intermeddle. At last the dispute grew very warme on both sides.

May 15   The report being made from the comittè of privileges
*   by the chairman to the Hous of the voidance of my election, it was confirmed by the Hous,[1] and I lost my

---

[1] The Commons also resolved that the right of voting at Aldborough lay with the inhabitants paying scot and lot (*Journals of the House of Commons,* ix. 622).

---

* Cf. Historical Manuscripts Commission, *Various Collection,* II, 395: Sir Godfrey Copley to Mr. Thos. Wheateley, 8 May 1679. This letter confirms that Reresby's date is out by one week. Reresby exaggerated the length of time that he spoke. Copley states that the 'whole house echoed with the word withdraw, and when the counsel were gone, it was supposed Sir John Reresby should have said somthing, but he withdrew and did not'.

session in Parlament.   I spoake near halfe an hour before
I went out, showing the unreasonableness of my adversarys
plea, the justice of my own, and the integrity of my principles both as to religion and the goverment.   The Duke
of Albemarle carryed me that afternoon to a play, which I
had not had leisure to take the diversion of for some time.

At this time the state of the kingdome and goverment
looked very melancholy.   The King was poor, the officers
of [the] Crown and of the Houshould clamorous for
their salarys and wages, which had not been paid for some
time.   Sir Robert Howard, one of the chiefe officers of
the Exchequer,[1] said in the Hous of Commons that ther
was not mony sufficient for bread for the Kings family.
There was noe stoors in the magazins, neither for sea or
land forces; the guarrisons all out of repair, the platforms
decayed, the canon unmounted; the army devided, some
for the Duke of Yorke, others against him, and the officers
of state the same thing; the Parlament or the major part in
a ferment, glad of thes publique devisions that they might
the better clip the prerogative, lessen monarchy, and carry
on their private designs; the King and his brother
devided, and soe followed by the advers party (that promessed if he would grant to comply with them, and dis-
inherit the Duke, they would sett him at ease in all other
perticulars) that he scarce knew how to resolve.

The Duke of Monmoth, whom the King personally
loved very well, was manifestly in the councils against
his oncle the Duke, for all his creatures in the Hous voted
against him, and noe men more in his esteem then the
Earls of Shaftsbury, Essex,[2] and other heads of that

---

[1] Auditor of the Exchequer.   He is best known as a mediocre dramatist
and as brother-in-law of Dryden.

[2] Arthur Capel, created Earl of Essex in 1661, Lord Lieutenant of
Ireland from 1672 to 1677.   A strong opponent of arbitrary power, he
allowed himself to become implicated in the Rye House conspiracy, and
after arrest committed suicide in the Tower.   For the statement constantly
made by the opponents of the Court, that he was murdered, there is no real
foundation.

caball. The reason of this was that though the Duke of
Monmoth was very hansome and accomplished as to his
outside his parts were not suitable, and Shaftsbury had
persuaded him that was the Duke once disinherited he
had the fairest claime to the Crown, either by the King's
declareing that he was marryed to his mother, or by his
being made legitimate by Act of Parlament.   To obviate
this, the Duke of Yorke had obteaned of the King to
declare oponly in Council that the Duke of Monmoth was
his naturall son, and that he was never marryed to his
mother.[1]   And yet ther were many that did undertake to
defend that witness was to be produced that was present
at that wedding, and that ther was a record of it kept in a
black box in the custody of some of the Duke of Monmoth's friends.

May 21   The Lords voted that the bishops might be present at
the tryall of the Lords, and the Commons did committ the
bill of exclusion.   Upon the question putt for the said
commitment, ther was 240 affirmative, 128 negative.[2]
My successour in the Hous, Sir Godfrey Copley, voted
for the bill.

23   I was at the King's coucheè.   I wondered to see him
soe chearfull amongst soe many troubles; but it was not his
nature to thinke much, or to perplex himselfe.   I had the
fortune to say something then that pleased the King.   My
Lord Duke of Newcastle, one of the bedchamber, being
in waiting, his Grace tooke this opportunity to say kind
things of me to his Majesty.   The King came to me,
reassured me of my command, and tould me he would
stick to his old friends.

29   The Lords haveing voted that they did persist in their
opinion that the spirituall lords should be present at the
tryall of the prisners, especially of the Earl of Danby, as

[1] On March 3, 1678/9, just before the Duke left for Flanders. The
declaration was made at the instance of Danby with the object of reconciling
the Duke to his temporary exile.

[2] The voting was 207 to 128.

to the validity of his pardon (which was his plea), and the
Commons haveing voted that the said lords should not be
present, and that they would only proceed against that
earle, and not the rest of the prisners, though the time
appointed was com'd for the tryall of them all, the heats
grew soe great between the two Houses that his Majesty
came and tould them that he found not how they could
anyways be reconcil'd, and therfore he proroagued them [1]
untill the 14 of August.   The citty of London, wher the
anti-Court party had a great interest, seemed soe angry
at this prorogation that some thought they would have
risen; but all, with much adoe, kept quiet.

I fell ill that day of the gout in both feet, which I never
had soe generally before.   It held me till the 12 of June.

The news came of a riseing in Scotland, to the nomber
of 7,000 men; [2] that they had burnt severall Acts of
Parlament, as the Acts of Uniformaty and Episcopacy,
and that which took away and condemd the Covenant.
They sett forth a declaration which was for Jesus Christ,
the Kirke, and the Covenant.   Some troops being ordered
to march against them were routed. [3]   Some more troops
were ordered to march against the rebels, amongst others
two regiments of the Duke of Monmoth; and he was
ordered to goe post into Scotland to head the forces,
which he did, and arrived at Edenbrough the 20 of
June.   *June* 20

The 22 the King tould me that he had an account that 22
the two armys were but ten miles from each other, that
his army did not consist of above 1,200 men.   The
rebels were above 6,000 strong.

I took leave of the King the same day to goe into

---

[1] On May 27.

[2] Following the murder of Archbishop Sharp on May 3, a rising began
on May 29, the anniversary of the Restoration, at Rutherglen, which
rapidly involved the whole south-west of Scotland.

[3] At Drumclog on June 1.   The defeated troopers were under the
command of John Graham of Claverhouse.

Yorkeshire. His Majesty gave me repeated assurances to keep his promesse of continuing the goverment to me, and of haveing the next independent company that fell, saying that he knew my fidelity and loyalty, not by my words but my services.

June 23   Came the newes that the rebels were defeated in Scotland by the Duke of Monmoth,[1] and that they made a very poor defence.

24   I sett forward for the north with my wife and nine servants. By the way I had a relaps of the gout, and my wife a little fitt of the stone. However we reached to

30   Thriberge the 30.

July 1   I recieved a letter from my Lord Burlinton, who succeeded my Lord of Danby in the lieutenancy of the West Rideing of Yorkeshire,[2] wher he invited me to Yorke with the rest of the gentlemen of that Rideing whom he designed to make deputy lieutenants. He had not been formerly soe kind to me as the former services in that office (as I thought) deserved. However I waited upon him, and was prevailed upon to recieve a commission for that, as also for a troop of hors which I had commanded under the Earl of Danby. He complimented me very much as to the benefit he pretended to have by my assistance in that business, and all I found by it was the trouble of penning the orders, and to be called the best versed in business of that kind.

9   Hearing the Duke was to be at Doncaster, post out of Scotland, I went to meet him, and sent halfe a buck and some extraordinary sorts of wine to entertain him ther. He came not in till midnight, when we expected him noe more that night. I was gott into the bed designd for his Grace. Before I could gett on my cloaths, the Duke came with Sir Thomas Armstrong,[3] who were glad to find

[1] At Bothwell Bridge on June 22.

[2] The warrant for his commission is dated April 30, 1679 (*Cal. S.P. Dom.*, 1679-80, p. 133).

[3] Formerly a royalist and an active supporter of the Restoration, for his

something ready to eat. The Duke sate up but a short time, and would not have the sheets changd, but went into the same bed. The next morning he borrowed my coach (that which he designd to get haveing but four horses) to Bautry. Sir Thomas tould me that the King had heard some lies of the Duke, and had sent for him out of Scotland in hast. It was found afterwards that after the victory he was laying the foundation for the succession in that kingdome, and makeing himselfe popular by the industry of his agents and friends.

At my return from Doncaster my son William fell sick of the smallpox, and escaped the danger of them very narrowly; but God restoored him.

Severall gentlemen of the country came to boull with *July* 11 me, amongst others Mr. Edmonds and Mr. Batty, the lieutenant and cornet to my troop, that came to offer their continuance in their former commands.

I heard the present Parlament was dessolved. I writ 12 presently to Audbrough, to give my friends notice that I 	* intended to stand as their burgesse for the succeeding Parlament.

The sessions being held at Rotherham, I gave the 22 charge. One Mandevile was indicted for speaking treasonable words of the King. He was a known adversary of mine. I was less severe towards him for it in that place.

There came twenty-two gentlemen to boull with me. 24

The assizes held at Yorke, wher I attended. Ther 28 was great factions for chooseing knights of the shire. The competitors were the Lord Clifford, Lord Fairfax, and Sir John Kay. The two first had been for the county in the former Parlament. I inclined to the first and last.

I went from Yorke to Audbrough. I called the 30 burgers togather. It cost me 20 l. to entertain them, and they gave me hopes to choos me, saying it was a just

services towards which he was knighted. At this time he was the chief adviser of the Duke of Monmouth.

* 14/78: Nathaniel Bladen, 10 July 1679.

return for being the authour of this popular way of electing.

[*Aug.*] 7   [1] The Master of the Cutlers of Hallamshire came and invited me to their feast.   They promessed me faithfully at the same time to give their voats for knights of the shire as I should direct them, but abused me in it, which I afterwards justly ressented.

8   I recieved commissions for myselfe and officers of my militia troop.

15   I mett the deputy lieutenants at Doncaster to settle the militia of thos parts.

20   I went to Audbrough, the writt being arrived and the day of election being appointed by the sheriff the 25 of August, wher I found severall of my pretended friends had receded from their promesses.   Indeed, in most of thes little burroughs, which consisted of mean and mercinary people, one had noe man sure longer then you was with him, and he that made him drunke or obliged him last was his first friend.   However, of 66 electors or voaters for members of Parlament, ther continued 37 firm to me; but the precept being gott into Sir Godfrey Copleys possession and Sir Bryan Stappleton's,[2] who joined togather against me, I found the return would be made in favour of them, and they would be the sitting members.   I therfore contented myselfe with putting a publique affront upon Sir Godfrey Copley, who had done unhansomly with me in the management of this matter (which he putt up very patiently), and turned my back of further pretending to stand for burgess for that Parlament.

26   I bought a farm in Rotherham of six poundes a year.

Thos that stood for knights of the shire in this Parlament were my Lord Fairfax, my Lord Clifford, and Sir

---

[1] A paragraph has been deleted at this point, together with the accompanying date in the margin.

[2] Sir Bryan Stapleton of Myton, Yorkshire, had just succeeded his father as second baronet.

John Kaye. The sectarys and phenaticks stood for the two lords, amongst which my friends at Sheffield (who had been soe much obliged to me upon account of their chimny money and other things) did assist, and in opposition to Sir John Kay, whom I had recommended as my friend; soe much at this day did faction prevaile above friendship. After this I concerned myselfe very little for the Sheffieldians. This was the second time that town had prooved treacherous to this family. The first was in the begining of the late civil warrs, that my father, being the next justice of the peace and very kind and useful to them (before the breakeing out of the warr), was the first afterwards whos hous they plundered; and we recieved more injury from that quarter in the warr time then from all the rest of the Parlament's army.

At this time the Duke, who had been sent abroad, came home unexpectedly to see the King, who had not been very wel, as was pretended. The Duke of Monmoth (who thought he had the King then entirely) knew nothing of it till his Highness came to Windser;[1] and ther was not above four people knew of it till he arrived, soe close could the King be wher he concieved it nescessary. My Lord Feathersham, who was the chiefe instrument in the Duke of Yorkes being recalled, tould me afterwards the whole story.

I went to Welbeck, wher the Duke of Newcastle kept *Sept.* 4 me with him four days, though I intended but a short visit. One day we went and dined with the good Earle of Devonshire at Hardwick, wher he entertained us before and after dinner with excellent buck hunting in his park. My Lord Cavendish was there, and some other persons of quality, who were all of opinion that this Parlament (consisting most of the exclusianists that were of the former Parlaments) would not last long.

I went for Yorke to choose knights of the shire, and 14 had ordered my friends that went from this side, and would

[1] Early on the morning of September 2.

* 1/65: Sir John Kaye, 1679, writes of the unkindness of Sheffield and Doncaster.

voat for Sir John Kay, to meet me at Tadcaster. Ther
appeared about 500 freehoulders; but the whole nomber

* from severall parts that accompanyed him into Yorke
that day were believed near 6,000. Finding the next
day that the pouling of soe many persons as appeared on
all sides would proove very tedious, and most chargeable
to Sir John Kay, who stood single against the two lords
who joined purses and interests togather, I proposed that
they should all return home, and the poule to be adjourned
to the next market towns that laid most convenient for
them, nameing four for the West Rideing, two for the
North, and two for the East, with certain days when to
appear to be pouled; all which was well accepted as well
by the gentlemen as freehoulders, whos respective
occasions made them glad to be at their own houses, and
to do their busines nearer.

Sept. 22   Was the day named to poule at Pontefract. My
†   friends that went in with me stayed for me at Rigstone
Hill a little longer then ordinary.[1]

---

[1] The circumstances of the election are very fully described in a letter
which Reresby wrote at this time to the Earl of Danby :

Thriberge, September the 27, [1679]—My Lord, I thought fitt to
acquaint your Lordship with this short account of our country concerns,
that notwithstanding the Lords Fairfax and Clifford doe vigourously joine
against Sir John Kay, assisted with most of our Yorkshire members of
Parlament (who have experience of their merit) and the entire dissenting
party in matter of religion, it is believed that the last, by the helpe of the
gentry and their interest (of which he hath far the greater part), will be
fairly chosen belowe, if he find equall measure above. At Yorke Sir John
had much a greater appearance, but fearing that a poule would proove too
chargeable to him in that place, I mooved the adjurnment of the poule into
severall parts of the county, which was accepted on all hands. The first
place was Pontefract on Monday, Teusday and Weddensday last, wher
Sir John had the advantage at my leaving the town, and expected a great
many more friends at Wakefield yesterday and to-day then either or both
of his competitors.

To give your Lordship an account how this corner of the county is
divided, ther is neither deputy lieutenant nor justice of the peace in the
three next weapontacks for the lords, except Mr. Darcy, Sir Ralph Knight
and Sir George Cook, soe that I am not singular in opposing the son of our

* 18/4: Reresby to Sir John Kaye, 22 September 1679 (copy), assuring Kaye
of his support in the election for knight of the shire.

† 14/17: Thomas Belton, 20 September 1679, acknowledges Reresby's instruction to gather his supporters from the surrouding area and to meet him in
Pontefract at Ringston Hill.

That day Sir John Jackson of Hickleton (the last of his family, and the fourth heir from its first being raised)[1] came to me at Pontefract (ther haveing been some coolness between us before) and tould me I had affronted him in bringing in his tenents with me to voat for Sir John Kay, when he designed to bring them in himselfe. I answered that I writt to all (or sent to them) that I thought qualified to voat to come in, without reguarding who was their landlords, but if he took that ill in his own perticular I was a man to give him what satisfaction he required. But I found him not much inclined to fight, for after severall words he tould me that he neither desired to court my friendship nor enmity. Then I tould him we were very equall in that perticular, for I thought his friendship was very little to be valued or enmity to be feared; and soe we parted.

I came home to Thriberge, wher I mett a present of *Sept.* 23 wild sort of sheep (which I turnd into my parke) sent me from the Duke of Newcastle, a great rarity at that time.

The Duke of Newcastle sent to me to bear him company 27 to Nottingham to see his castle ther, which was almost finished, but chiefely to recieve a treaty of marriage which

Lord Lieutenant. I suppose your Lordship may have heard that I made some interest in Audbrough to be chosen of this Parlament, and had good reason to be assured of the majority of votes ; but finding that the sheriff had putt the precept in the hands of Mr. Wentworth's bailiff (who was resolved to return Sir Godfrey Copley and Sir Brian Stapleton, right or wrong), I thought it best to desist, knowing too well what favour I was to expect from a committee of privileges. My Lord, I shall be glad to hear of your health from some of your servants, and that your Lordship may be happyly and speedily rid of your restraint is the hearty prayer, My Lord, of your most faithfull and most humble servant, J. Reresby. I should be glad to be serviceable here to your Lordship, for I thinke not of leaveing thes parts this winter. On Monday I goe to Nottingham with the Duke of Newcastle, who is much your Lordships servant. (B.M. Add. MSS. 28053, f. 228.)

[1] Sir John, the second baronet, ruined his family by his extravagance, and died unmarried at the age of 27. He was not, however, the last of his line, as he was succeeded by his half-brother, Bradwardine Jackson.

was offered by Sir William Clifton [1] with one of his Grace his daughters. The next day the Duke and I dined at Clifton at Sir William his invitation, and all seemed to be agreed; but the match broake off afterwards, and Sir William went into France some years after and dyed unmarried. Returning with the Duke to Welbeck the day after, we had the newes that the King had taken away the Duke of Monmoth's commission of generall,[2] and that he was gone for Holland,[3] and that the Duke of Yorke was gone for Flanders;[4] soe that noe man scarce understood how the King resolved to behave himselfe between his brother and his son.

Oct. 14   I was at the generall quarter-sessions held at Barnsley, wher I understood that Sir John Kay had desisted from standeing for knight of the shire, and that the two lords would now be chosen without competition.

     At this time the Duke of Yorke, being only gone to fetch his Duchesse, that he had left ther, returned with his whole court to London from Flanders, and desireing the King that he might rather remain (if he must be absent) in some of his Majestys dominions, was sent into Scotland.

20   The Parlament was proroagued to the 27 of January.[5]

27   Their Royall Highnesses came in their way northwards, and laid at the Duke of Newcastles, wher I waited upon them, and staid ther at his Grace his request to entertain the lords that supped at the secound table till midnight, and then went home to recieve the Duke with other gentlemen the next day upon his entrance into the county of Yorke, which I did with at least fifty gentlemen of the nighbourhood. The Earl of Strafford and my Lord Castleton mett him also, but very poorly attended.[6]

---

[1] Of Clifton Hall, Nottinghamshire, the third baronet.

[2] September 10.   [3] September 24.   [4] September 25.

[5] Parliament was prorogued on October 17 to January 26, 1679/80.

[6] All Reresby's dates, in this account of the Duke of York's progress, appear to be about a week too early. The Duke left London on October

* 14/126: J. Peables, 28 September 1679; 14/ 172c: Sir John Kaye, 14 October 1679. Kaye topped the poll at Wakefield but feared defeat at Skipton and Knaresborough so gave us the contest.

My Lord Shaftsbury was turned out of all councils,[1] and the exclusianists began to dispond.

The Duke and Duchesse lay at Pontefract.   *Oct.* 28

They went to Yorke, wher they stayed some days. 29 Ther all the loyall gentry waited upon them, and paid them their respects.   Thos of another party were distinguished by not doing it, and the citty of Yorke itselfe recieved his Royall Highness and the Duchesse but very coldly, which hee never forgott afterwards.[2]   And one Mr. Thomson,[3] who had taken the fittest hous in town to lodge their Royall Highnesses, was hardly persuaded to quitt his hous, or to lend it them for soe long, and when he did he took away all his furniture.

I tooke leave of him at Yorke; and my wife of the Duchesse, at their going away, wher they both thanked us for our respects towards them.   Indeed, I had presented his Highness with venaison and wines, and entertained some of his favourites at my hous in Yorke; but it was not worthy of his notice.   His Highness further assured me that at his return he would show me some markes of his friendship.[4]

27, and reached Welbeck, where Reresby waited upon him, on Monday, November 3.   His entrance into Yorkshire was on November 4, when he reached Doncaster ; and he lay at Pontefract on the night of November 5. He arrived at York on Thursday, November 6 (Hist. MSS. Com., *Ormonde MSS.*, New Series, v. 231, 234-5).   *

[1] October 15.

[2] The King's reprimand to the city is summarised in *Cal. S.P. Dom.*, 1679-80, p. 278.

[3] Edward Thompson, Lord Mayor of York in 1683.

[4] It was partly, no doubt, to strengthen the good impression he had made that Reresby wrote shortly afterwards to John Churchill, later Duke of Marlborough, then gentleman of the bedchamber to the Duke :

December 12, 1679.—I confess, Sir, it is the first time that ever my curiosity made me inquisitive as far as Scotland ; nor had I been soe at this time if their Highnesses, by changeing the scene from north to south, had not made me (as well as many others that wish their happyness) as impatient of hearing from Edenbrough as London.   Thus you see how Courts can alter places in some respects, tho not in all, for I doubt you find the climate

* 14/4: J. Peables, 3 November 1679, states that the duke was due 'tomorrow night'.

Nov. 5   Being the night before the Duke left Yorke, he made a supper, and made all thos gentlemen that had attended upon him in his journey, and lords of his own retenue, to sit down with him at the table, and was very merry.

I was tould that day by a gentleman who had been in company with Sir John Jackson the day before, that I was to prepare myselfe to expect a challenge from that knight, for he had laid a wager with this gentleman of a guinney that he would send me one that day before three a clock. This person laid that he durst not doe it; but I presume the gentleman won, for I heard nothing of him till some weeks after, that I was tould he was dead.

Soon after the Duke of Monmouth returned out of Flanders,[1] wher he was sent by the King, without his Majestys leave, which extreamly displeased the King, insoemuch as he devested him of all his imployments.

Dec. 20   About this time the Parlament was proroagued to the 11 of November next following.[2]

I kept Christmas at Thriberge with the usual solemnity.

March   I recieved orders from the Lord Lieutenant to meet the [1679/80] rest of the deputy lieutenents at Pontefract, wher we took some care to have the militia put into some order, to be in more then usuall readyness.

Soon after I heard the Duke and Duchesse were com'd

as could as it was before, and the temper of the people much the same. But, Sir, I doe not presume to make scrutenys of this nature further then I should be glad to hear of the Dukes good reception and satisfaction in all places. I only desire that by two lines you would doe me the favour to informe me of the health of their Royall Highnesses, your own, and the rest of your friends ; and that when you are tired with such troubles as thes from hence, and such others as I soppose you may meet with wher you are, and leave Scotland, that you will rest yourself by the way with your J.R. (Rawlinson MSS. D. 204, f. 1.)

[1] November 28.

[2] This statement is quite inaccurate. Parliament was kept in abeyance by repeated short prorogations, the last of these being to October 21, 1680, when it was at length allowed to meet.

to Londone, sent for from Scotland by the King;[1] that the two brothers met very kindly, and that the King should say that noebody should separate them hereafter.

I went to Welbek, wher the Duke of Newcastle gave *March* 10 me a letter to the Duke of Albemarle in a matter of concern. I went from thence to Rufford, wher my Lord Halifax was comed from Court, and angry with the measures then taken.

I was at the Yorke assizes.   15

I had a little fitt of the gout in my knee, which lasted 19 three days.

Anno Domini 1680

I went for London. My chiefe business was to gett *April* 1 the 300 l. arrears due to me for mine and my companys pay ever since we were disbanded, and to gett my goverment continued; but the Duke haveing now the applications of all men, being fair with the King, and the Duke of Monmoth removed, made him find less leisure to hear or to assist his friends. Nor indeed was it then to be hoped to obtean the latter, the King being every day rather retrenching then encreaseing his charge, that he might have less occasion for his Parlament, that he dispaired then to find in good humour if it should be called.

Ther were great meetings of persons dissatisfyed with the Court, wher they laid their heads togather to oppose that interest wherever the King's occasions required assistance, were it in Parlament or elsewher. Thes were called cabails. The Duke of Monmoth, my Lord Shaftsbury, my Lord Russell, my Lord Cavendish amongst others were the principal that assisted in thes meetings, which changed from hous to hous for more privatie every night, the publique outcry and pretence of fears being popery and the Kings safety.

The King and Duke, being at Windser, came once a 21

---

[1] Reresby was unable to wait upon them because they went by sea, reaching London on February 24.

week only to London to Council. I gott some friends to speake to the King for me, but it had noe successe.

April 26 I went to Sir Thomas Player[1] and Sir Gilbert Gerrard,[2] two of the commissioners for disbanding the late army. They tould me they had paid all the mony, and had none left in their hands to satisfie my arrear; but I soe ordered the matter with them, partly by fair means and partly by threats, that they paid me sixty pounds, and, as they pretended, out of their own purses.

May 8 I went to Windser, wher I tould the Duke a piece of newes of a design laid by some persons to proove the Kings marriage with the Duke of Monmoth's mother, and the way to obviate it; for which he thanked me, and tould me, without askeing it, that he had spoake to the Master of the Ordenance in my business.

The King ther showed me a great deale of what he had done to the hous, which was very fine, and what he intended to doe more, for it was then that he was finishing that excellent structure. The King lived ther very privately at this time. Ther was little resort to him, and he passed his day in fishing or walking in the parke, which indeed he naturally loved more then to be in a croud or in business.

9 I gave his Highness a copie of the deposition which one had made concerning the business of the Kings marriage with the Duke of Monmoth's mother, and by mistake I gave him in the same a bil of exchang for 148 l. The next day (when I thought I had lost it) he returned it to me laughing, and said I had trusted him with that sum. I answered that I was glad it was faln into soe good hands. He spoake at the same time to my Lord Sunderland, Secretary of State, for me; but that lord was not soe kind

[1] Chamberlain of London, in succession to his father, another Sir Thomas. He was M.P. for the city and a determined opponent of the Duke of York.

[2] Of Fiskerton, Lincolnshire, created a baronet in 1666. He was M.P. for Northallerton from 1661 to 1681.

to me as I hoped our old acquentance deserved. Him and the Duchess of Portsmouth had at that time great power with the King, but the Duke the most of any.

I came back to London. The Duke of Holstein's *May* 10 envoyè returned with me in my coach. I ther understood that Mrs. Honora Brown (my wife her only sister) was ill of a dropsey, and that some bad acquaintance, who had gott into her good opinion and estrang'd her from her relations, had not only wasted a great part of her fortune, but had persuaded her to settle the remainder of it by will upon them.

I returned to Windser, and understood that my Lord 15 Sunderland had spoke to the King, and that his Majesty had referred the matter of continuing the goverment of Burlinton, and paying the arrear of my sallary of 200 l. per annum, to the Lords of the Treasury. I thanked the Duke and his lordship for this favour, but found the thing was likely to be soe teadious, and my business was soe pressing at home, that I ressolved to leave it to a fitter opportunity, and soe desired his Highness to give me his comands for the country. He thanked me for my respects, and bid me continue my kindeness to him, assuring me he would befriend me wher it laid in his power. I gave him my assurances of all service and duty; and then tould him I was desirous to be obliged to noebody but himselfe, and therfore begged that when he had an opportunity he would speake to the King to send me envoyè extraordinary to some Prince or Court, which his Majesty had formerly promessed to doe for me, provided his Highness thought me fitt for an imployment. He replyed that he believed I was qualified for it, and that he would certainly remind the King of it.

I tooke leave of the King, who had some fits of an 17 ague, but was recovered. He laid his hand upon my shoulder, said that he was very sensible of my services, and they should be recompensed. I putt him in mind of his promess to send me abroad, and tould him my Lord

of Bath [1] was present when he was pleasd to make it.   The
King tould me he remembred it perticularly, and would
perform it upon the first occasion.   I still persued,
however, the continuance of my goverment at Burlinton,
but not successfully; the business of Tangers, viz., the
sending over of men to defend it against the Mores, and
the charge of the Mole, took up all the mony and the
statesmen's thoughts at this time.[2]   However I continued
my commission, but no mony.

June 2   I tooke leave of my Lord of Danby in the Tower, wher
meeting my Lord of Bath, my Lord of Danby's brother-
in-law,[3] he ingaged him to sollecit thes concerns for me to
the King.

The same day, being sent for by my wife her sister, I
went to visit her, found very weake in bed.   She did not
*   tell me how she had setled her portion, only desired me
to lend her mony, which I presumed would never be
restoored; but, however, I did accommodate her with
some guinnies.

3   I began my journey for Yorkshire in my own coach,
but before I writt this letter to his Royall Highness,
†   which was delivered by a friend:

May it please your Highness,
Being prevented of waiting upon your Highness
by my sudden departure to give you an account of the
establishments as to gunners in other guarrisons, I presume to doe it this way, and to acquaint your Royall
Highnesse that all goverments (Burlinton only excepted)
have at the least two gunners each.   This, Sir, makes me
the more confident to desire that I may not meet with a
perticular discouragement by being denyed the same

[1] John Grenville, Earl of Bath, Groom of the Stole to Charles II.

[2] Tangier had come to Charles as part of the dowry of Catherine of
Braganza, and a final effort was being made to provide it with a safe
anchorage and render the English hold over it secure.

[3] Danby's daughter Martha had married Charles, Lord Lansdowne, the
Earl of Bath's eldest son.

* 15/65: C. Darwent, 26 June 1680, informs Reresby that his sister-in-law had
ten days at the most to live. But what really concerned Reresby was the contents
of the will which, Darwent warned him, was to be executed by a false friend.

† 18/67: Edmund Reresby, 15 June 1680. The friend turned out to be Reresby's
brother.

establishment for that place, bycaus the refusall of it may lessen the credit which I am ambitious to preserve in the world for his Majestys and your Highness his service, and of being yet thought worthy of continuing in that little command that am,

May it please your Highness,
Yours, J. R.

I gott home to Thriberge the 8th.   I found all things *June* 8 ther in good order, by the conduct of a discreet wife.

We held a private sessions at Rotherham, and that *July* 5 day I had newes that my wife her sister was dead, that thos that had prayd upon her whilst she lived had gott as much as they could of her estate that remained after her death, and had obliged her to make a wil, and to dispose   * of it to them.   But with much trouble and suit afterwards I gott some 300 l. clear, besides charges.

The generall sessions was held at Rotherham, wher I 20 gave the charge.

I mustered my troop, and exercized it at Rotherham. 23 It quartered ther three days.

The assizes were held at Yorke, wher ther was a very 24 great appearance of gentry and others, some for business, but more for curiosity, severall persons of quality being ther to be tryed for high treason for being of the Popish Plott.   Many had been tryed in London and found guilty upon the evidence of Oats, Bedloe, and others, &c.; and the persons to be tryed here, being of the county and the place wher it was said they conspired, were the Lady Tempest, daughter of Sir Thomas Gascoin,[1] Mr. Ingleby, a lawyer (since made sergiant),[2] Mrs. Presset, and one Mr. Twing, a priest.[3]   Sir Miles Stappleton of

[1] Sir Thomas Gascoigne of Barnbow, Yorkshire, the second baronet, then in his eighty-fifth year.   His eldest daughter Anne had married Sir Stephen Tempest of Broughton, Yorkshire.

[2] Charles Ingleby, sworn serjeant-at-law, April 28, 1687.

[3] Mary Pressicks and Thomas Thwing.

* 15/81: C. Darwent, 1 July 1680; 15/2: C. Darwent, 3 July 1680; 15/82: J. Frankland, 3 July 1680. Frankland informed Reresby that a Mr. Butler was the executor.

Carleton[1] was to have been tryed also, but was not then *pro defectu juratorum*.

The evidence against thes were one Boldron and Mawbray.[2]   The one was taken a poor boy out of charity by Sir Thomas Gascoin, brought up in his hous, then made overseer of his collery, and runing in debt to his master intended (for he had been evidence also against him) to pay him and his family this way what he owed to him (an ill piece of gratitude). Though some had been found guilty in London upon this or the like evidence, yet it found soe little credit in this county that three of the four were acquitted, as also one Pickering,[3] who was indicted for being a priest upon the same evidence; soe that Twing was only found guilty of high treason, a priest being more his guilt then the plot.

One Mr. Tankard being of the jury and appearing active to clear the prisner, the judge reflected upon him in court, which, being a man of sperit, he was not able to bear, and complaining to me, I advised him to get some gentlemen of the country, his friends, togather, and offered myselfe to attend them to the judge, to represent him another sort of man then he took him to be.   Ther met upon this occasion above twenty gentlemen, amongst which were my Lord Fairfax and many others of the first ranke, who all agreed that I should speake for them to the judge.   We went all in a body, and I delivered their sence to the judge in such manner concerning the gentlemans worth and reputation that the judge was willing to aske him pardon oponly in court the next day, which he took for sufficient reparation.

A petition was offered this assizes to the grand jurys from some of the anti-Court party for the sitting of the Parlament, in the name of the whole county.   One Mr.

---

[1] Created a baronet in 1662.   He was a nephew of Sir Thomas Gascoigne.

[2] Robert Bolron and Lawrence Mowbray or Maybury.

[3] William Pickering of Stanton Lacy.

Darcy, being of the grand jury, instead of recieveing the petition tore it in pieces; and the next day ther mett at least fifty gentlemen, who desired me to draw up something to expresse an abhorrance of such proceedings (the King being the only fitt judge when Parlaments ought to sit). I drew it, and all the gentlemen subscribed it; and the judge was sent to, and made acquainted with it by the high sherif, and desired to make it known to his Majesty, which he did accordingly. The King took it well, but we were complained of for it in the Hous of Commons the next session of Parlament, and got of very hardly.

I returned to Thriberge, and the same day I putt the *Aug.* 1 deer at large into the additional parke.

I was at Doncaster by the direction of the Queens 9 council to take an examination of some persons that had reflected on her Majesty. I recieved a letter the same day from Sir John Worden, secretary to the Duke, of his Highness his thankes for the account I had given of the proceedings at the assizes at York.

In my return from Buxton, wher I went the eleventh 11 for my wifes health, I returned by Chatsworth, wher the good Lord Devonshire recieved me with great kindness. I sent my wife the direct way, and met her at Sheffield, wher the Corporation of Cutlers and some principal men   * of the town, hearing I was to pas that way, came to me at my inn, and with great importunity prevailed with me, notwithstanding their late ingratitude (for in a nighbourhood wher Providence hath placed one to live, and their family to abide, as one that hath power must sometimes ressent ill things, soe they must sometimes forgive), to recieve a treat they had prepared for me then, as also to dine with them at their feast a week after, &c., or therabouts.

I went with my wife and family to the Cutlers feast at 28 Sheffield with some nighbours I took with me to the nomber of near thirty hors. The Master and wardens, attended by an infinite croud, mett me at the entrance

---

* Cf. Mexborough MSS MX/242 (hereafter cited as French draft), p. 3, where Reresby refers to his problems forgiving the cutlers for failing to oblige him 'dans l'affaire de l'election des chevaliers pour le parlement *comme est avant dit.*' (our italic). This indicates that the draft is a fragment of a longer account now lost. Cf. *supra* p. 187 for the election of knights of the shire in August 1679, at which the cutlers let Sir John down by not supporting Sir John Kaye. They apologised for this when Reresby dined with them. French draft, p. 5. The draft has entries for 16, 17, 20, 24 and 25 August. The entry for the 25th, p. 4, records that 'le maitre de la Compagnie des cutlers me vint prier encore d'aller a leur festin le 26'.

into the town with musique and hoboys. I light from my coach, and went afoot with the Master to the hall, wher we had an extraordinary dinner; but this was at the charge of the Corporation of Cutlers. In the afternoon the burgesses of the town invited me and all my company to a treat of wine at a tavern, wher we were very well entertained, soe that all things seemed indifferently well over at this time.

Aug. 30   I went and dined with the Duke of Newcastle at Welbeck, who met me upon the staires in the court. He recieved me with great kindness, and oponed himselfe very freely to me in severall concerns of his own and the publique. I laid that night at Rufford with my Lord Halifax. I found his lordship more favourable then heretofore in relation to Court matters, but not thorowly reconciled, and very implacable to my Lord of Danby, whos friend he knew me to be. But I sufficiently satis-fyed him by some discours I then had with him that I was never soe much that lord's friend as to be less his.

Sept. 2   I had the newes that one Bedloe, a principal evidence in the Popish Plott, was dead.[1]

3   The Duke and Duchess of Newcastle came and dined at Thriberge. I entertained them the best I could, and his Grace liked my wine and drunke freely of it.

6   I went as far as Booth ferry, intending a visit to the Earl of Burlinton at Lawnsbrough; and haveing passed the ferry, as I was going out of the boat, a hors turning suddenly in the boat threw me down, soe that I fell out of the boat with my elbow upon the shoar, and putt my shoulder out of joint. Ther hapned a bone-setter to live at Houden, who presently came and reduced it. I laid at Houden that night, and returned homewards the next day. It was halfe a year before it was perfectly well. Noe man had scarce more misfortunes then I of this kind, yet it pleased God to restoor me after them all.

The last of September I went for London by Cambrige,

[1] He died on August 20.

* Cf. French draft, p. 6. 'En fin je trouvay qu'il [Halifax] estoit mal avec Shaftsbury et quelques autres de cette partie et que en cas qu'il fut bien traitté qu'il seroit bientost dans les Interest de la Cour.'

to see my brother Yarburgh Reresby, fellow of St. Johns.
I passed also at Newmarket, wher the King then was.
I went from thence to Berry,[1] to visit my ant Monson, soe
that it was the 14th before I gott to London. $\qquad$ *Oct.* 14

It was again discoursed that the Duke of Yorke was to 16
depart before the meeting of the Parlament, some said to
obay the King, others to avoid the violence of both
Houses; for it was plain that the papists were very bould,
being supported by the Duke's interest with the King, who
was at this time the chiefe manager and directer of affairs.

The Duke and Duchesse took their leaves of the King, 21
and began their voyage by sea for Scotland. The night
before their departure I kissed his Highness his hand,
tould him I was sorry some small pretentions which I had
troubled him with had succeeded noe better, but I did
not blame his Highness in the least, &c. He tould me
I had noe reason, for he had done all he could doe for me,
and would stil doe soe.

The Parlament mett.[2] The King, amongst other 22
perticulars of his speech, tould them that they should doe
what they could devise for the security of the Protestant
religion, provided they did not offer to devert the direct
line of the succession.

My Lord Ogle, only son to the Duke of Newcastle, 28
dyed,[3] who, had he lived, would have been the greatest
subject for estate of the kingdome, being married to the
only daughter and heiresse of the Earle of Northumberland, since remarried to the Duke of Sommerset.[4]

This month and the next the Commons proceeded to
frame a bill to exclude the Duke from the succession,
notwithstanding his Majestys direction against it. And
thos gentlemen of Yorkshire and others, which had

---

[1] Bury St. Edmunds. [2] October 21. [3] November 1.

[4] Elizabeth Percy, sole heiress of Josceline, eleventh Earl of Northumberland, married Charles Seymour, sixth Duke of Somerset, in May 1682,
after the murder of Thomas Thynne, her second husband (*infra*, pp.243,
249).

counter-petitioned or declared their abhorrance to the late tumultuary petitioning for the Parlament's sitting, were voted betrayers of the libertys of the people and abbettors of arbitrary power. A comitteè was also appointed to inquire in that matter, and after, the persons that were concerned in it, and two members of that Hous that signed that abhorrance were conven'd before the committè (both of Yorkshire);[1] but I had penned it soe carefully that noe great exceptions could be taken at it, and soe they gott off.

*

I now took a hous in Lecester Fields by the year.

Nov. 5   The Parlament persued the Duke soe violently, and the King was in soe great want of mony, that some believed he would abandon his brother.

6   I went to Mr. Leg (since Lord Dartsmoth), who tould me he began to dispond himselfe, but he hoped now again. He was then master of the hors to his Highnesse.

7   Attending at the King's supper, I tould him I was threatned by some of the Hous of Commons to be called to an account for writing the abhorrance, and signing of it with the rest of the Yorkshire gentlemen. He answered me thus, Doe not trouble yourselfe; I wil stick by you and my old friends, for if I doe not I shall have noebody to stick to me. Yet a great many feared he would not, for the want of mony was soe pressing, and the offers of Parlament men soe fair, if he would relinquish his brother, that noebody seemed secure which way he would bend. That which made people the more jealous was that severall that were wel in the Kings esteem appeared for the Bill of Exclusion, and the Duchesse of Portsmouth was known to incline to it, whether coningly to gain the good opinion of that party (that were before her greatest ennemys), or to comply with the French, whos tool she was (for they were for anything that would disturb us in England), is uncertain.

---

[1] The committee was appointed on October 27 ; the two Yorkshire Members of Parliament summoned before it were Sir Thomas Mauleverer and Sir Bryan Stapleton (*Journals of the House of Commons*, ix. 640, 644).

* Cf. French draft, p. 8: 'Je pris une maison par Annee pour 2 Ans'.

Being at the Duchesse of Portsmouths with the King, *Nov.* 12
he was very free in his discours concerning the witnesses
of the Popish Plott, making it clearly appear that severall
things which they gave in evidence were not only improbable but impossible.

Was one of the greatest days that was ever known in 14
the Hous of Lords.   As the matter was extraordinary,
viz., cutting of the liniall descent of the Crown (for the
bill haveing passed the Commons they had sent it up to
the Lords), soe was also the debate.[1]   Ther was a great
party in that Hous for the passing of that bill, and great
speakers, of which the chiefe was the Earl of Shaftsbury.
The chiefe manager against it was the Earl of Halifax,
which was a great surprize to many, he haveing gone along
with my Lord Shaftsbury and that interest for some years.
But this not being agreable to his judgement he opposed
it vigorously, and haveing a great deale of witt, and both
judgement and eloquence with it, he made soe fine and
soe powerfull a defence that he only (for soe all confessed)
persuaded the whole Hous against [it], soe that after the
debate had lasted ten hours, the question being putt
whether the bill should pass that Hous, it was carryed in
the negative.

The King was soe wel pleased with this days worke
that he soon after took this great lord (for indeed, considering all, he was the greatest in parts I ever knew) into
business.   And the Commons at the same time were soe
angry at him that though they could not regularly take
notice of what any man said in the other Hous they voated
and sent an address to the King to desire that he might be
laid aside, or remooved from his councils and presence.
They made his haveing advised the dissolution of the last
Parlament the caus of this addresse, but the true reason
was known.   The answer his Majesty gave to this was

---

[1] The Exclusion Bill was passed by the Commons on November 11, but
was not carried up to the Lords until the 15th, and it is the events of that
day that Reresby describes.

that if the Lord Halifax had done anything contrary to law, lett him be prossecuted and punished accordingly; but he was not satisfyed he had, and therfore would not part with him, or to that purpas. One would thinke that soe signal a piece of service as this could never have been forgot by the Duke. Yet when he came to be King he remooved him from Lord Privy Seale, wher he found him when he came to the Crown, to Lord President of the Council, to make room for another, and afterwards laid him quite aside.

Nov. 22 I was in discours a long while with his Majesty. I tould him amongst other things that I doubted much whether I should be taken notice of in the list which the Lords had voted to be given in to them of all military officers, ther being at present neither company nor gunner at Burlinton to make it appear a guarrison; if I was, I presumed I should be putt into the nomber of such as that Hous intended to petition his Majesty to lay aside from their imployments. He answered, let them doe what they would, but he would never part with any officer at the request of either Hous, for his father had lost his head by that complyance, but as for him, he would die another way.

24 My Lord Halifax tould me that he had noe ways deserved this heat of the Commons against him. I said he ought not to be concerned, for he had gott more friends by it then he had lost that would stick by him. He said that he would venter his life with thos friends.

Ther was some tampering, but privately, to make a devource by Act of Parlament between the King and the Queen; but I dar say without the King's approbation, though he seldome or never made use of her as his wife, she haveing a continuall flux of blood in her secret parts, and was known to have soe before their marriage, which made my Lord Chancellor Hide persue it the more, his own daughter being marryed to the heir of the Crown.

25 A gentleman told me (one Rombal, that had been

consul in Spain)[1] that he could be a good witness in Parlament to null the marriage, should that matter come on, for he could proove not only from reputation, but more notorious evidence, that her condition of health would not allowe her to have children when she was married to the King, &c. I persuaded him to give it in writing, which he did; and I confess I gave it to my Lord Clarendon (the Queens gentleman of her hors),[2] that such practices might be prevented, and such authours of them discouraged.

    I went to wait on my Lord Halifax, who, after the *Nov.* 28 great service he had lately done the Crown in casting out the Bill of Exclusion of the Hous of Lords, was looked upon as the riseing man and first favourit. He carryed me with him in his coach to Whitehall. The next day he invited me to dinner with him in private. He tould me that it was to be feared that some unhappy differences might arise in the nation from thes disputes about the succession, and in case it should come to a warr it might be convenient to form something of a party in one's thoughts. He tould me that he knew very well ther was but one other and myselfe that had any considerable interest in my nighbourhood, asked me my opinion how their inclinations stood. I tould him I had an account in writing of all men of note therabouts, and would wait of him the next day with their names and characters. I did soe, and he did agree with me that the loyall interest was not only much more numerous, but consisted of more wealthy and active men, and that thos that were soe busy in Parlament against the Court were men of little power or esteem in their country.

    Began the tryall of my Lord Stafford[3] by his peres in *Nov.* 30 Westminster Hall, which was the most solemn thing I

---

[1] Henry, younger brother of William Rumbold of Burbage, Leicestershire.

[2] Henry Hyde, the second earl, eldest son of Lord Chancellor Clarendon. He had entered the service of the Queen as early as 1662.

[3] William Howard, Viscount Stafford.

---

* Cf. French draft, p. 13: 'J'espray par la advancer mon affaire particuliere que je traittay alors avec ce Seigneur'.

† Cf. *ibid*, where Reresby agrees to draw up a list of the men of note 'par un livre que j'avois en ville de toute le Noblesse etc'.

ever saw; and great was the expectation of its issue, it
being doubtfull at that time whether ther were more that
believed ther was a plott to take away the Kings life by
the papists, or not.   The tryall was by way of impeachment by the Commons, and they chose this lord to try
first, believeing him weaker then the other lords then in
the Tower for that crime, and soe less able to make his
defence.   However, he pleaded for himselfe to a miracle.
The three chiefe witnesses against him were Doctor Oats,
Dugdale, and Turbervile.[1]   The first swore he had brought
him a comission, signed by the Pope, to be paymaster of
the army to be raisd against the King; the second, that
his lordship offered him 500 l. to kill the King; the third,
that he had offered him a reward for the same thing, but
at another time.   They seemed soe positive in this and
other dangerous evidence that myselfe (that sate and heard
most of the tryall) knew not what to believe, had the
evidence been men of any credit; but ther were such
incoherences, and indeed contradictions in my judgement,
appeared towards the latter end of the tryall (joined with
the ill reputation of the witnesses), that for my own part
I was satisfyed at last of its unthruth.   However the
party was soe strong that persued the caus against him
more then the man, that he was voated guilty, ther being
54 lords affermative and 32 for negative or not guilty.[2]
He heard his accusers and defended himselfe with great
resolution, and recieved his sentence with noe less courage, which stayed by him till he laid his head on the
block, protesting his innocency to the very last.   My
Lord Halifax was one of the thirty-two lords, and the King,
that heard all the tryall, seemed extreamly concerned at
his hard and undeserved fate.

---

[1] Edward Turberville had been in the service of the Earl of Powis and
had attended the English College at Douai. After assisting in the prosecution of Lord Stafford he went over to the other side, denounced Oates,
and gave evidence against Shaftesbury.

[2] The actual figures were 55 and 31.

The two Houses were now very busy, that of the Lords
to form a Bill of Comprehension for all Protestant dissenters, or to bring them within the privilege of the law
by indulgence to tender conciences; the Commons to
frame an Act of Security greater then what the law yet
provided against papists.

Being at my Lord Halifax his hous, I saw the French [*Dec.*] 18
embassadour come in privately, which was some surprize
(it being then unknown that he sett up for chiefe minister),
for he came for busines.

The same day it was asked of the Comons what they
would doe for the King after soe long sitting to noe effect
in the matters the King required of them.[1] It was
answered, and by a voat of that Hous, that they would
putt his Majesty into a condition to defend Tangers,
would pay all his debts, putt the fleet into good condition,
make him able to assist his allies, provided he would grant
their petitions in relinquishing the Duke his brother, pass
an Act for the more frequent meeting of Parlaments, and
change such officers about him as that Hous should
nominate. Some believed that the King would be
tempted to comply; but the next day my Lord Halifax
tould me that ther was noe probability of it, for it was like
offering a man mony to cut of his nose, which a man would
suffer for a greater sum.

The same day my Lord Stafford came to the Hous of
Lords, and was admitted under the hope that he had
something to discover or confess of the Popish Plott;
but instead of that he protested his innocency, and accused
my Lord Shaftsbury for keeping correspondence with the
papists, and for sending him to the Duke of Yorke to
desire him to use his interest with the King to dissolve
the long Parlament, as the best thing to be done for the
popish interest.   *

---

[1] The question was raised by a speech delivered by the King to both
Houses on December 15; it was debated by the Commons on the 18th; and
the answer of the House was embodied in an address adopted on the 20th.

---

* French draft, p. 15, has an entry for 20 December 'les 3 messieurs du parlmt
dinant chez moy me disent peut estre que Halifax ne avoit pas qu'il sera
prosecute d'avantage et qu'on n'a point de matiere contre luy mais si le Roy
accepte l'addresse dessiné il le voyra. Je luy dis ce qu'ils disent. Il repondit
qu'il sen soucia pas et qu'il les desfia et qu'il n'y soumettroit jamais'.

*

The Duke of Newcastle spoake for me to the Duke of Albemarle in a concern which had noe effect. I dined the same day with Sir Patience Ward,[1] Lord Mayor of London.

24   I was at the Kings going to bed. Ther was but four present; and his Majesty, being in good humour, spent some time upon the subject of showing the cheat of such as pretended to be more holy and devout then others, and said they were generally the greatest knaves. He gave us severall exemples of them, and named some eminent men of the present age, and some mitered heads, which he prooved not the best for passing for the most devout or pious; but thes were some of them men that the King had noe reason to love upon a politique account. He was that night two hours putting of his cloaths, and it was halfe an hour past one before he went to bed. He seemed extream free from trouble or care at a time one would have thought he was under a great deale, for everybody guessed that he must either dismiss the Parlament in few days or give himselfe up to what they desired.

25   The Duke of Newcastle came to visit me. We had a long discours of present affairs, and noebody could tell which way things would goe.

26   I recieved the sacrament at the hands and in the chappel of that excellent man, Doctor Gunning, Bishop of Ely.[2] Ther came and recieved with us Doctor Oats, the famous evidence of the Popish Plott. We dined togather afterwards at the Bishops table, wher the Doctor, blown up with the hopes of running down the Duke, spoake of him and his family after a manner which showed himselfe both

[1] A strong supporter of the opposition to the Court, who had to go into exile in 1683 and was not restored to favour until after the Revolution. In the three Exclusion Parliaments he represented Pontefract, to which his family belonged, but in the Convention of 1689 he sat as Member for London.

[2] Peter Gunning, famous as a preacher on the Royalist side during the Civil War. After the Restoration he became Regius Professor of Divinity at Cambridge, and Bishop first of Chichester, then of Ely.

* French draft, p. 16. The matter of concern was Reresby's request for an independent company.

a foole and a knave. He reflected not only upon him personally, but upon the Queen his mother, and her present Majesty, till, noebody darring to contradict him (for fear of being made a party to the Plott), I at last did undertake to doe it, and in such a manner that he left the room in some heat. The Bishop tould me this was his usuall discours, and that he had checked him formerly for takeing soe indecent a liberty, but he found it was to noe purpas.

The Lord Stafford was beheaded on Tower Hill, wher *Dec.* 29 he absolutely denyed the crimes for which he suffered, and after soe convinceing a manner that all that saw him believed it.

I dined the same day with my Lord Halifax. He said to me, Well, if it come to a warr, you and I must goe togather. I tould his lordship that I was one that was ready to followe him, whatever hapned, but that if the King expected his friends to be hearty and steddy to him he ought to encourage them a little more; acquainted him with some of my disappontments at Court after several promesses, and tould him I should be glad that his Majesty would send me envoye to some part of the world. He reply'd, We must have you in business; we have need of such men as you nearer home.

The King returned an answer to the Hous of Commons, *Jan.* 4 that he still persisted in the same resolution, not to consent [1680/1] to disherison of the Crown, but would have it continue in the same line. This angered them soe much that it caused them to pass some violent voats[1] against such as they tooke to [be] the chiefe advisers of the King in this matter, as the Earls of Halifax, Clarendon, Feathersham, the Marquis of Worcester, and Mr. Hide, since Lord   * Rochester. The Parlament was proroagued upon this from the 10th to the 20 of January. Some thought it 10 was in order to dissolve them; others laid wagers the King would lett them sit at the time and pass the bill.

[1] January 7.

---

* Cf. French draft, p. 18. This acknowledges Lord Rochester only as 'Mr. Hide', a description which dates this draft earlier than the *Memoirs*.

The same day, waiting on the Lord Halifax, he complained of the unjust severity of [the] Commons against him in their voat, which was that he was a promoter of popery and betrayer of the libertys of the people. He said that were a man never so innocent, it comming from the representatives of the people, it was too heavy for any single person to bear; therfore he had thoughts to retire from Court; but that he would goe his own pace, and not just be kiked out when they pleased; and in case the King should at any time have occasion to use him in what was just, he would be ready to serve him; that as to my perticular, if I would trust him, he would tell me when it was time to appear for the Kings service; that I should run the same fortune with him, for I was one that the Goverment ought to be glad to have in busines (with other kind expressions more then I deserved). At the same time he complaind of unsteadyness of the Kings temper, that whilst he seemd to approove the council you gave him he harkned to other councels at a back door, which made him wavering and slowe to ressolve. He promessed, however, to obtean of the King to gett a gunner established at Burlinton fort.

Jan. 11   I waited on my Lord of Danby in the Tower. He complained to me of the incertainty of the Kings humour. He said that though the Duke had but little power with him as to himselfe, yet any minister should find he had the most interest as to any other person or concern; and that he defyed any minister about him to find out when the Parlament would sitt, or what he would doe when it mett, though they should know what he said. The Duke of Newcastle tould me that day that he was to wait on the King the next day, and that he believed his Majesty would wish him to take some imployment upon him;[1] but he said the King did not offer it at a better time, and he

---

[1] Possibly the post of Secretary of State, from which Sunderland, who had supported the Exclusion Bill, was shortly to be dismissed (Foxcroft, *Halifax*, i. 278).

would not accept it in soe dangerous a one as this was.
This confirmed to me what my Lord Halifax said some
days before, that the Kings changeableness and silence
in affairs at that time made people in fear to serve him.

The citty of London petitioned the King by their *Jan.* 13
Common Council for the sitting of the Parlament at the
appointed time.   The Kings answer was, that was not
their busines.

The Duke of Newcastle tould me that the King had 15
spoaken to him to the same purpas he imagined, and that
he said he would speak further to him when Halifax and
he were togather.   His Grace tould me further that he
had been discourseing my Lord Halifax concerning me,
and that he had tould his lordship that he loved me better
then he did.

I dined with the Earl of Burlinton, who tould me this 18
Parlament would be dissolved, and a new one called to sit
at Oxford the 15th of March.   My Lord Halifax seemed
avers to this dissolution in his discours; but it was but a
grimmas, for he had noe reason to wish that Parlament   *
long lived that had used him with such freedome.   He was
jealous also that my Lord of Danby would come out of the
Tower, and be receivd again into councils.   If that
hapned, he resolved to retire, and advised me not press
to be in imployment till things were upon another
foot.

My Lord Duke of Newcastle acquainted me with the
intended dissolution, which he had from my Lord of
Danby, which made him believe that he was yet in councils.   His Grace took it ill from my Lord Halifax that he
had said nothing of this matter to him, saying it was not
useing him like a brother.   The thruth was my Lord
Halifax did soe overtop the other in all qualifications of
mind that he did not make him much his confident in
anything, or that his sence deserved it.   When this dissolution hapned, it was believed my Lord Danby would be
released upon the King's pardon.

* Cf. French draft, p. 21, which states that Halifax told Reresby that the
dissolution was 'contre son gré et qu'il y eust d'apparence que les conseils
papists prevaloyent'.

Jan. 20   I tould my Lord Halifax, and tould him I had considered of his advice not to enter at present into publique imployment as things stood, and that I had great deference for his opinion in all things, but I thought it might be convenient as to my own private concern as soon as could be, and not of prejudice to me in relation to the publique; for as to my own interest I was under an obligation to be much in town, and had already taken a hous ther for the advantage of my children in their education, and the profit as well as credit of an imployment ther would be of double use to me at that time. As to the objections that men of estates ran some hazard to take business upon them at this time, I answered that danger did not appear at present, and it was time enough to retire when it did; and then there was some credit to quitt a good office from principle of honour or concience, and to showe the world at the same time that a man was thought worthy to be imployed and trusted in his generation. His lordship answered that he was satisfyed with my reasons, and would doe me all the favour he could to obtean it.

21   I went and dined with him that day. He tould me he thought to retire, but was not at all dissatisfyed with the King, but feared the Dukes prevalency with the King would carry councels too farr.

For himselfe he seemed to hould his resolution to retire, but said Mr. Hide (since Lord Rochester), Chiefe Comissioner of the Treasury and his perticular friend, should be ready to serve me when any vacancy of value hapned.

22   His lordship went the next day for the country. I waited upon him as farr as Hatfield.

23   I waited upon my Lord Hide (for he was made soe about that time),[1] who said my Lord Halifax had recommended me to him in soe perticular a manner that he would serve me in what he could. I returned him my thankes, and owned the obligations I had to my Lord

[1] Created Viscount Hyde of Kenilworth on April 23, 1681.

Halifax for doing me soe great an honour.   I assured him
that if it was my good fortune to be recieved into his
Majesty's service by his kindness (or otherwise), I would
performe it with all the faithfulness that could be ; but
that this would cost him a double trouble, first to find the
imployment, and then to gain it for me.   He promessed
to use his endeavours for both.

I heard one Maddox, whom I made postmaster of   *Jan.* 24
Doncaster some time before, was then murdered by my
Lord Eglinton, a Scotch lord,[1] that had run him thorow   *
the body upon a quarrel at play as he was sitting in a
chair.   I went and desired my Lord Feathersham to
beg his estate of the King for him and me, if it
prooved forfited, which his Majesty readily granted ;
but he afterwards obteaned his pardon both for life and
estate.[2]

I obteaned the postmaster's place for Jack Madox,   25   †
his yonger brother, who was quartermaster to my
militia troop.

As I went with the Duke of Newcastle to visit the Duke 26
of Albemarle he said that he thought my Lord Halifax
had done wisely to withdraw himselfe, for this would
abate the odium concieved against him by Lord Shaftsbury and his party when they saw the same measures
persued when he was not in councils, and that he had
given him advice to doe soe.   I confessed I had advised
him to stay, for if he went off not dissatisfyed, but returned
again to Court, the world would say that his councels were
followd though he was absent, and soe he might bear the
blame for councels that were not his own.

The discours being now warm for a new Parlament,
I asked the King if he would have me to stand to be a
member of it.   I showed his Majesty a letter at the same

---

[1] Alexander Montgomerie, eighth Earl of Eglinton.

[2] His petition for pardon, claiming that he acted in self-defence, is
summarised, along with evidence on his behalf, in *Cal. S.P. Dom.*, 1680-1,
p. 155.

* 15/109: T. Yarburgh, 15 March 1680/1.

† 16/10: John Maddox, 22 January 1680/1, requesting his brother's place.

time from Mr. Tankard,[1] wherby he promessed his assistance at Audbrough in that service. The King pressed
me to goe down to stand, but I tould his Majesty the other
gentleman would stand if I did not, who was an honest
gentleman and much disposed to his service. Then he
left it to my own choice. His Majesty then promessed
me a good liveing for my yongest brother, and a fellowship at Manchester [2] when void, but neither succeeded.

Jan. 30   The King began to remoove from Court some few
officers that were in with the Exclusianists ; but that lasted
not long, for though he loved neither them nor their
proceedings it was not in his nature to doe harsh things
long, though my Lord Alesbury, the Chancellor of the
Exchequer,[3] assured me it would goe on.

Feb. 4   I had a letter from Mr. Tankard that he had noe mind
to stand for Parlament man this time, therfore desired
me pressingly to come down and accept of his interest,
which at last I accepted.

5   I took leave of Mr. Hide, who promessed me all the
good offices he could as to what he had promessed my
Lord Halifax upon my account.

The same day the Duke of Newcastle spoake very
kindly to the King of me.

7   I took the opportunity of going down to the country
with his Grace, who desired my company, and gave me
room in his first coach with himselfe and Duchess, and
treated me and my servants all the way. He travelled
indeed like a great prince, with three coaches, and about
forty attendants on horsback. He was too obligeing to

[1] Christopher Tancred of Whixley, who was Sheriff of Yorkshire in
1685 and 1686, and was returned M.P. for Aldborough in 1685, 1689
and 1690.

[2] Manchester parish church had been made collegiate in 1422. On the
establishment of the bishopric of Manchester in 1847 the warden and fellows
became the dean and canons, and the parish church became the cathedral.

[3] The Chancellor of the Exchequer at this time was Sir John Ernley.
Ailesbury never held that position.

* 1/101: C. Tancred, 24 January 1680/1.

† 1/72: C. Tancred, 12 February 1680/1.

** French draft, p. 25, states that the living promised to Reresby's brother was
one in Dorset, and that it was rumoured to be about to become vacant by the
preferment of a dean to a bishopric.

‡ There is in fact an ampersand between 'Lord Alesbury' and 'the Chancellor'
in the text. (B.L. Add. MSS 29441 fol. 105v). cf. French draft, p.26: 'my Ld
Alsbury et le Chancellʳ de l'Exchequʳ'.

me in that journey in forceing me to accept the second chamber wherever we lodged, before his own daughters. The hous being narrow the third night wher we laid (for we were five days going betwixt London and Newarke), I stole out of the hous and went to another inn; but his Grace came himselfe for me and brought me back, and sent out his own people. He unbosomed himselfe to me in this journey. Tho he was a true servant to the Crown he liked not the measures then on foot, and thought the times but slippery.

At Newarke I took leave of his Grace, wher I had *Feb.* 12 appointed a charriot to meet me from Thriberge, though I had brought a led hors with me all the way. I went by the way of Rufford, and stayed with my Lord Halifax till the next day. His lordship tould me the King would 13 not call a Parlament soe speedily as was believed; that the King was slowe to ressolve wher any difficulty arose; that he intended to goe to Parlament whenever it assembled, but that afterward he would leave the Court and business, except his Majesty would be advised to doe such things as were for the publique good, change some officers about him, and take such in their rooms as would act according to the present councels ; for it would ruin all if his Majesty continued to advise with thos of one interest this day, and harken to thos of another to-morrow, nor could his ministers be safe under such uncertaintys; and if he would be advised, it was in the Kings power to make all his opponants tremble. In fyne, he tould me a great part of his thoughts, and made me many professions of friendship.

My Lord, though he was brother-in-law by marriage to the Duke of Newcastle,[1] yet thought it fitter to treat with him by a third hand in the affair of marrying his eldest son, my Lord Eland,[2] to my Lady Catherin, the

[1] Frances, Duchess of Newcastle, was the eldest sister of Gertrude Pierrepoint, Halifax's second wife.

[2] Henry Savile, Lord Eland, who was still a year short of his majority.

Dukes third daughter,[1] and therfore desired me to recommend it to his Grace. I did soe upon the terms my Lord Halifax desired, which was to have 15,000 l. portion with the lady. The Duke was not avers to the match, but to the conditions. He would not part with ready mony, but was content that his estate should be devided amongst his daughters at his death. But that pleased not the Earl of Halifax, soe that nothing was agreed on at that time.

Feb. 15   I went for Audbrough, and in my way thether at Ferrybrig I mett an express sent by the bourough to invite me to come over, with a promess to choos me for one of their burgesses in Parlament. I stayed ther that night, being stopt by the waters ; and the next day I was at Pontefract, wher Sir John Dawney,[2] Sir Patience Ward, and Sir John Kay being candidates for Parlament men ther, and that the day of election, the two first were chosen, and the last was outvoted.

17   I came to Audbrough, wher I found Sir Godfrey Copley, who stood by Mr. Wentworths interest. He had been very pressing to obtean the possession of the precept, that they might goe to election, fearing I should set up some other to defeat him ; but the sheriff would not part with it til I came. Sir Richard Graham[3] was then high sheriff of the county, my perticular friend, one that I had been intimate with both in France and Italy.

20   The election was made of Sir Godfrey and me for burgesses in the ensuing Parlament without any com-

---

[1] His fourth daughter. The negotiations for the marriage of Newcastle's five daughters, who all in the end contracted brilliant alliances, form quite a part of the social history of the period. After the death of their brother, Lord Ogle, they were destined to share among them one of the greatest inheritances in the country.

[2] By this time Viscount Downe.

[3] Of Norton Conyers, the first baronet. He was appointed sheriff again at the close of James II's reign.

* 15/48: Sir John Kaye, 17 February 1680/1. Kaye describes the treachery of The burgesses and 'a fool and a knave'; 39/26: Christopher Tancred, 28 February 1680/1, wrote saying 'the day the Lords [Clifford and Fairfax] were elected a greater sham was put on the country than the petishan which was offered to the Grand Jury'. It was also at this time that the copy of Sowry's speech which was read to the newly elected members was sent to Reresby. This paper was virtually a party manifesto by the Whigs.

† 15/36: R. Grahme, 16 February 1680/1; 15/50: E. Morris, 13 February 1680/1. Bundle 15 contains more letters concerning the election; see also Geiter, 'Reresby', chapters 2 and 3.

petition.[1]   The charge of it, in treating the electors and several gentlemen that came to see me, cost me 43 l.

The next day being Sunday,[2] I went and laid at the high *Feb.* 21 sherifs, that lived not far from Audbrough.

I returned to Thriberge, wher I found my five fine 23 boyes in good health.   Two indeed were at Rotherham school, the three others at home.   Some days passed in looking into my business and takeing my accounts (which I always endeavoured to doe exactly), in makeing and receiveing visits from my nighbours.   One day ten gentlemen came and dined with me at once.   That day we made a debauche.

I recieved congratulations by letters from the Duke of 25 Newcastle and the Marquis of Halifax upon the subject of my election (my Lord, I thinke, was then made marquis).[3]   *

I went towards London, takeing Welbeck in my way. *March* 5 I found myselfe ill three days before of a could, which did end in a pain in my right side like a stitch.   I apprehended a pluracie, for which I lett blood, and was better after it. The Duke entertained me with telling me all his concerns, and by some part of his discours I discovered that he was jealous of my Lord Marquis of Halifax, in the perticulars of getting a better interest in the country then himselfe, and of haveing a better at Court also, for he had lately obteaned of the King to make Sir John Dawney a Scotch

---

[1] February 19. Shortly afterwards Reresby wrote to the Earl of Danby announcing his success :

March the 3rd [1681], Thriberge.—My Lord, Soe soon as I returned out of the north I thought it my duty to give your Lordship notice that you have a servant elected bourgess for the bourough of Audbrough to serve in the next Parlament, and I wish that every man that sits ther may have the same wishes and inclinations to serve you that he hath that is, My Lord, Your Lordships most faithfull and most humble servant, J. Reresby. To my knowlege some of the hearts of the Lords doe melt towards you. I wish thos of the Commons may doe the same. (Leeds MSS.)

[2] February 20.

[3] His promotion to that rank did not take place till August of the following year.

---

* The letters from the duke and earl are lost, but the entry in the French draft, p. 30, on 23 February 1680/1, refers to letters from the two gentlemen.

vicount, when his Grace had been labouring to obtean that honour for his brother Chenay[1] without success. He showed me a letter at the same time from my Lord Sunderland, wherin he complaind in divers respects of my Lord Halifax (for though the latter marryed the sister of the other[2] they were at variance), and perticularly for cheating (as he called it) of 25,000 l., that Sir John Dawney (then Lord Down) had promessed him to get him his patent, by the hand of my Lord Halifax, which he obteaned to pass by another interest, and kept the mony to himselfe ; but my Lord Halifax gave a different account of it. When I took leave the Duke desired to know if I wanted anything by his means to the King, that he would interest himselfe ther for me the best he could.

As to the business of giveing his daughter the Lady Catherin to my Lord Eland, I found him infinitely avers to it, upon the subject of paying ready mony for a portion. He tould me his Duchesse was more against it then himselfe. I spoake to her of it myselfe, and found it very true. However at the last he tould me the thing might not be impossible in a little time, if my Lord Halifax would take 9,000 l. of his mony, and an assignment of 6,000 l. due to him from the King; but he would first see my Lord Eland, for he heard he was very debauched.

March 6   I went that day to Rufford, wher I acquainted the Marquis with what had passed, only in general that he might know how to govern himselfe better with such a man. But he tould me that the Duke was of soe changeable and jealous an humer that it was not possible to keep friendly with him. I tould me Lord nothing of what my Lord of Danby[3] had written to his Grace concerning my Lord Downs, for that would rather have improoved their

---

[1] Charles Cheney of Chesham, who had married Newcastle's eldest sister Jane. He was created Viscount Newhaven in the peerage of Scotland on May 17 following.

[2] Lady Dorothy Spencer, Halifax's first wife.

[3] Lord Sunderland is presumably intended.

*

* French draft, p. 32, makes it clear that Reresby is referring here to a letter from Danby to Newcastle informing him of the growing animosity between Sunderland and Halifax.

emnity then their friendship. My Lord tould me some began to question whether or noe the King would continue constant to his brother, or take part with the Duke of Monmoth, who was now treating to make his peace.   *

I went to Nottingham towards London, wher I took *March* 7 the stage-coach for myselfe. My servants rid on horsback.

I reached London, wher I found all well under the care 11 and management of a prudent wife.

Haveing setled some affairs ther, I went to Oxford.   21

I kissed the Kings hand, who recieved me kindly. I 22 acquainted him that I had directions from severall gentlemen of the county that they had noe interest or part in the petition offered to the knights of the shire of Yorkeshire at their election, to prossecute the Bil of Exclusion against the Duke of Yorke; and that it was only six or seven factious persons that had managed that business, though it passed for a more generall thing. His Majesty answered that he had recieved some short account already to the same purpas, and bid me return his thankes to thos that did not interest themselves in that concern.

The Parlament mett.[1] The Court was at Christ 23 Church. The Commons sate in the Schools,[2] but were much straitned for room, ther being a very great appearance of Parlament men. His Majestys speech to both   †
Houses was very gracious, endeavering to heall all differences and to remoove all jealouses as to religion, &c., and offering al ways or means to secure the Protestant religion except that which former Parlaments had soe much driven at, viz., the utter exclusion of his brother from the name and power of a king. The first thing that was debated was whether or noe (notwithstanding what the King had said to them) a Bill of Exclusion should be

[1] March 21.

[2] The Lords sat in the Geometry School, the Commons in the Convocation House.

* French draft, p. 34, has an entry for 7 March indicating that Sir John Kaye attended Reresby to Rufford where they discussed the affairs of Yorkshire with Halifax: 'et nous jugeames en general que le roy y eust la plus grande partie de la Noblesse de beaucoup et que nous y aurions bon interest pour le servir et nous resolusme d'y travailler et pour engager nos anys pour soutenir le gouvernemt sur le mesme pie quant au prince et au peuple et la religion protestante'.

† 17/27a/b: abstract of Saturday's debate; see Mary K. Geiter and W. A. Speck, 'The Reliability of Sir John Reresby's *Memoirs* and his account of the Oxford parliament of 1681', *Historical Research*, 62 (1989), 107–112.

framed and brought in.   It was voted that the security of his Majestys person and of the Protestant [religion] should be taken into consideration the 26 instant.

In the meantime ther was not much passed of moment; only an impeachment was ordered to be prepared against Mr. Fitzharris.[1]   The occasion of it was not to hang him, but to preserve him, and the reason of it this: This Mr. Fitzharris had been a witness for the Popish Plot, but before that had been taken frameing a very scandalous libel against the King and the Goverment,[2] set on, as was reported at Court, by some of the Duke of Monmoth's party, for the which he was committed in order to his tryall.   But the zealous part of the Commons, pretending or suspecting it was an artifice of the Court to prevent his further evidence in the Plott, impeached him only to keep of his tryall at the common law in case that a dissolution or prorogation should happen, for when the supream court is possessed of a caus, civil or criminal, it superseds all proceedings of inferiour ones in that perticular.

The chiefe arguments used for bringing in the Bil of Exclusion in that debate were thes—that nothing could effectually secure us against popery but that.   Now for the better understanding the rest of the reasons it is nescessary to know that it was universally agreed by the whole Hous that popery was to be kept out; the difference was only in the means.   The King had offered, as I said before, at the opining of this session, that he would agree to anything wherby to quiet the minds of his people in that perticular, except excludeing his brother.   It was mooved, therfore, by Sir Thomas Littleton [3] (one that had

---

[1] March 25.   Edward Fitzharris was an Irish Catholic whom both the Court and the Parliament hoped to use to serve their own ends.

[2] " The True Englishman speaking plain English in a Letter from a Friend to a Friend," printed in *Parliamentary History*, iv. App., No. xiii.

[3] The second baronet, M.P. at that time for Yarmouth in the Isle of Wight.   He died shortly afterwards and was succeeded by his son, another Sir Thomas, with whom he has sometimes been confused.

been a fierce man of that party, but now gained by the
Court) that a Bill of Seurity for the Protestant religion
should be brought in, and to consist of thes heads, without
absolute exclusion of the Duke—that the Duke should
have only the name, and the Princesse of Orange the
regency or the power; that if a Parlament were in being
when the present King dyed, it should be impowred to
sitt (the judges and all other officers of the Crown to
continue till religion and property were secured); and if
ther was noe Parlament, then that one should assemble of
cours for that purpass, and to prevent the Dukes tampering to hinder this, that by the same Act he should be
banished 500 miles from England, not to return soe long
as this King lived.

To this it was answered, the name and power of King
could not be seperated in England; that the father would
soon find a way to devest his daughter of that power; that
regency was never known but in case of lunacy or minority; and the Duke was not of a temper to be soe easily
governed.   It was replyed again as to that, that regencys
had been allowed, and some were at this day, in case of
other incapacitys besides lunacys, as formerly in France,
and now in Portugal; that princes were seldome soe
complimentall to one another as to give up or resign
kingdomes, though to a father; and as to the authority
of a Parlament to doe this, noe question but the same
power that could alter the goverment could also modifie
it.   But exclusion was the word.   Some seven or eight
disobliged lawyers and able speakers in the Hous, with
severall others that had been soe active in this matter that
they thought, should the Duke ever come to the Crown,
he would never forgive them, prevailed soe far that it was
voted a bill to be brought to disenable James, Duke of
Yorke, to succeed to the imperiall crown of this relme.
Some made soe bould with the Duke in this debate that
they reflected on his courage and honesty, and spoke very
unsuitably to his merit.

The Lords refused to recieve the impeachment carryed up by the Commons against Fitzharris, saying that he being already indicted at common law, and in a way of tryall by his peers, as Magna Charta did direct, they see not how their Hous could take cognisance of his offence. The Commons were very angry with the Lords, and voted that this proceeding of the Lords was a stop to justice, a breach of privilege of Parlament, and a hinderance to the further discovery of the Popish Plott; and that for any inferiour court to proceed therin was a high breach of the privileges of Parlament whilst an impeachment was depending.   The heats grew very great in both Houses upon this account and that of the Bill of Exclusion, and the Commons did really believe that the King would have yielded to it, he haveing yielded soe far to them already and being in great want of mony.   Besides many that were near the King that desired it gave them hopes to *March* 28 press him stil to it.   But upon the day when the King had appointed the Theater [1] to be made ready for the Commons to sit in (they haveing complained of the straitness of the Schooles to recieve them) the Black Rod came and commanded the Commons to attend at the barr of the Hous of Lords, wher being com'd, the King being in his roabes tould both Houses that he found ther was a difference [between] them, which might probably increase if they sat any longer, and therfore it was his plesure to dissolve that Parlament.   This blow was soe little expected that some were of opinion ther would have been some stirrs or riseings in London upon it.

It was observed that many of the discontented members of both Houses came armed and more then usually attented, and that ther was a design to have seized the King and restrained him til he had granted their petitions. But if any such design was, they either wanted courage or time to execute it, for the King went in all speed away for

[1] The Sheldonian Theatre, built at the expense of Archbishop Sheldon, which had been opened only twelve years earlier.

London the same day, my Lord Halifax for the north, and I for London.

His Majesty was very kind in takeing several opportunities to speake to me whilst I stayed at Oxford. I was also ther very much obliged to the Duke of Newcastle, and my Lord Halifax tould me his thoughts with great freedome. His lordship was, I found, as much in councels as before, but he would not be known to be soe. When he took leave of the King he recomended me to his Majesty, speakeing more of my capacity and rediness to serve him then I deserved. The King laid both his hands upon me, thanked me for my constancy to his interest, and bid me [be] assured of his affection.

When the Duke of Newcastle waited the same day on the King to take his leave, I was present. His Grace spoake very favourably of me to him, and said that he had nothing to aske his Majesty but that he would please to be kind to me, which he should consider as done to himselfe. Both the Duke of Newcastle and my Lord Halifax presented me the same day to my Lord Hide, the greatest favourit in appearance of the Kings at that day.

It was plane by this dissolution, as wel as what I had from my Lord Halifax and others, that the King would not relinquish his brother, and did not thinke of calling another Parlament of a long time. The thruth was that the question was not now whether the Duke should succeed or not, but rather whether it should be a monarchie or a commonwealth. Some of the party had blab'd it in the Hous that this was not only the material bil that they intended should pass this session to secure the people of England from falling under popery and absolute goverment; that it was nescessary that both the military and civil power should be put into other hands, and that the present officers of both ought to be examined and changed; insoemuch as the King was tould that if he quitted the Duke, it was but to be a step both to quitt all his friends and servants afterwards, and to fall entirely into the hands of people that he had reason to thinke were not soe wel affected to his person and goverment.

Before my Lord Halifax went, he writt to my Lord Hide, or rather Mr. Hide, for he had not that honour conferred upon him, I remember, til afterwards, and by this token, that he sate with us in the Hous of Commons, and cryed in a speech which he made ther in defence of the Duke and of his religion (I mean his own), somebody haveing reflected upon him for being popishly inclined. The contents of that letter was to desire Mr. Hide to be mindful of me, and to obtean some place for me. I gave him the letter when I came to London, but I found noe great warmth in his way of recieveing it. I gave my Lord Halifax an account of it, who writ to me from Rufford that I should visit him and press him in it, and that I had free leave to make use of his name wher I see occasion, for he did not desire I should be fed with vane hopes.

ANNO DOMINI 1681 [1]

April 13   My wife miscarryed, but the child was soe yong it was not known whether it was boy or guerle.

20   I was at the Kings going to bed (as I was three times in one week). His discours was generally of the impossibility of such a thing as the Popish Plott, and the contradictions of which it was framed; that he intended that Fitzharris should come immediately to his tryall, but in all thes affairs the lawes should have their cours, and whatever his own private opinion was, he would govern himselfe according to them. Indeed it was a great happiness to his people to live under soe just and soe gracious a prince.

26   I heard of some dangerous words, amounting, as I thought, to high treason, spoaken by a person of noe

*   mean quality. His examinations had been taken by a

---

[1] The official year had begun before the dissolution of Parliament, but Reresby presumably did not wish to introduce a cross-heading in the middle of his account of the session.

---

† French draft, p. 41, describes the person as a 'phanatique'; 18/12: James Blythman, 17 April 1681, further identifies the accused as one Hinchlife of Peniston.

justice of the peace in the country, who sent them up to
me.　I showed them to the King and the Secratary.　The
King gave order that the party should be prossecuted the
next assizes.

I begged at the same time the estate of my wife her
sister, which, as I said before, she had bequeathed to one
Mr. Hambleton;[1] but he being a papist, and since convicted by my endeavours, he was not capable to be an
executor, nor any other in trust for him.　His Majesty
gave it me very freely when I tould him the perticulars,
but the difficulty of it was how to find a great part of it,
which Hableton had gotten and concealed.

The King and the whole Court parted for Windser.　His *April* 28
Majesty had, since the dissolution of the last Parlament,
put forth a declaration full of fair promesses to his people,
assuring them of his intentions to govern according to
law, &c.　This gave a great satisfaction, and he recieved
the thankes of the citty of London by the Lord Maior,
and of severall other countys and corporations in England,
soe that all things began again to look fair and calme.

Mr. Fitzharris came to be arraigned at the Kings *May* 4
Bench barr, wher by his councel he refused to plead,
saying that he was impeached in Parlament for the same
crimes for the which he stood ther to be indicted, but
mentioned noe perticular treasons, which the indictment
did.　The councel for the King replyed that his plea was
evasive, bycaus it [did] not mention what thos treasons
were, and therfore it appeared not whether they were the
same or not.　And soe both sides demurred.

It was argued at the bar, but the case being soe 7
extraordinary by reason both of its own weight and the
severe voat of the Commons at Oxford, the judges took

---

[1] From two documents preserved among the Spencer MSS. at Althorp,
in which Reresby sets forth his pretensions, this can be identified as
Anthony Hamilton, possibly the author of the *Mémoires de Grammont*.
The estate was left in trust to Sir James Butler, a prominent lawyer and
justice of the peace for Middlesex.

May 11 time to consider of it, and upon the 11 day they passed judgement for the King.

15   It pleased God to visit me with a rhumatisme, which first began like the gout in my foot, and after seized of one part of me after another, that I had scarce any part of me free.   I kept my bed for one month, and was soe weake that I was not able to turn myselfe without helpe, soe that I dispaired of recovering, all means and care of me by my wife and the best phisitions affording noe reliefe, till by takeing asses milke first, and cowes milke afterwards, I recovered to a miracle.   Though I paid dear for the experience, I must own a great deal to Providence for the discovery of this medicin milke, which agreed soe perfectly wel with my body (being purgative) that I must own a more perfect health then I used to have for many years since to it only, by drinkeing a pint of it every morning new from the cow, which was both my breakefast and phisick.

My Lord Halifax came to town about this time, and visited me thrice in that weake condition.   The last time that he came he tould me that he had desired of his Majesty to promesse me the reversion of the goverment of Yorke, my Lord Fretwell[1] being then governor but of great years and infirm, which the King had promessed his lordship to give me in case he dyed, with a company of foot.   This was, I confess, an imployment that both for the honour and conveniency of it (being in my own country) I had reason to be very pleased with, as I was, had it been in present.   But ther was two hazards in it. One was the uncertainty of its fall, and of the sallary his Majesty would give with it, it not being reasonable for me to hope for the same with my Lord Fretwel, who had suffered very much in his estate for the Crown in the late warrs, and had more to support the honour of a pere of England, which his Majesty had lately conferred upon him.

[1] John Frescheville, created Baron Frescheville of Staveley in 1664.

In this time Fitzharris had sentence of high treason passed upon him, and was executed accordingly. My Lord Shaftsbury and Lord Howard were clapt into the Tower, and my Lord Halifax tould me ther would be enough produced against them to hange them both.

My eldest daughter [1] fel ill of the small-pox, which I *June* 12 feared would not only ruin a fyne face, but her life also, which troubled me to that degree that I relapsed into my former distemper for some days. But it pleased God to restoor her, without prejudice to her features or complexion.

I was presented to the King at Hamton Court in his *July* 7 closit by my Lord Halifax (who was become the entire favourit), to take my leave of him, being to goe speedily for Yorkshire. My Lord spoake very kindly of me to his Majesty in many respects, and of my capacity to serve him, and of my diligence in business; and desired him to confirm to me the promess he had made to him, that I should succeed my Lord Fretwel in the goverment of Yorke. His Majesty did it very cleverly without the least hesitation, and gave me his hand to kiss upon it, saying at the same time that he knew how well I deserved of him.

I sett forward for Yorkshire, leaveing my wife and 11 family at London. She had behaved herselfe with care * of me in my sickness; but we had a falling out at our parting, which gave me some trouble.

At Grantham ther was a great entertainment given by the Earl of Lyndsey,[2] Lord Lieutenant of Lincolnshire, to the deputy lieutenants, justices of the peace, and other gentlemen of that county. I went to wait on his lordship only to see him in passant (being very wel known to him), but he kept me soe long to be a witness of his feast that I

---

[1] Frances, " born about a quarter of an hour after one a clock in the morning upon the 8t day of January, anno 1665 " (*Family History*, ii. f. 17). She was Sir John's eldest child.

[2] Robert Bertie, third Earl of Lindsey.

* See page ii for fuller explanation.

suffered by it in my health some days after.[1] My journey was some addition to my ilness, which encreased soe fast

July 17 that the day I gott home I fel again into my rhumatisme, kept my bed fifteen days, and took noe nourrishment but milke for a whole month, which restoored me perfectly.

August   I was at the generall sessions at Rotherham, wher ther

*   appeared nine justices of the peace.   Some of them (two of which were Sir Thomas Yarburgh, my cozen germain, and my oncle Thomas Yarburgh of Campsal) came and laid at my hous.

A Parlament was held in Scotland at this time, wher the Duke of Yorke was High Commissioner.[2] A great many gentlemen went from the north of England to wait upon him, which I excused to him that I did not (by Mr. Darcy and others) by reason of my sicknesse.

15   I had a letter from the Lord Halifax, wherby I under-

---

[1] The nature of the entertainment, which took place on July 14, is described in a letter written by Reresby to the Earl of Danby, Lindsey's brother-in-law :

July the 18 [1681], Thriberg.—My Lord, I should not have given your Lordship this trouble at this time had I not mett with the occasion of it by meeting some of your Lordships relations in my journey, who commanded me to give your Lordship an account of their welfare. It was my Lord of Linsey, who mett a numerous gentry of his lieutenancie at Grantam on Thursday last in order to the signing an addresse of thankes to the King. His lordship made me dine with him, and at the same time a witness of one of the greatest entertainments I ever see given. There were eight chines of beef, as many venison pastys, as many hanches boiled, with all other varieties of gross meats and foule at our table. Ther was another table in the same room, two rooms more below, and two other houses in the town taken up, and provision made at my Lords charge for all thos that came upon that occasion ; soe that if good meat and drinke will make men loyall (which used to be a good argument with Englishmen) my Lord spares noe cost to effect it in his lieutenancie. I hope you will please to excuse the manner of this, being forced to write it in bed being relapsed since my journey. I am, my Lord, Your Lordships most faithfull and most humble servant, J. Reresby. (Lindsey MSS.)

[2] The Duke opened this Parliament, the first which had met in Scotland for nine years, on July 28.

---

* 17/44, 45, 46: C. Tancred, 27, 15, 14 June 1681, describe the debate over the signing of an address to the king about the dissolution of the Oxford Parliament. 18/117: Richard Grahme, 20 July 1681.

stood I was in his thoughts, and that he was concernd for my ilness.

I waited on the Duke of Newcastle at Belsover. As soon *Aug.* 18 as he see me upon the terasse wher he was walking, he ran down stairs to meet me, and was very kind and opon to me. But I could not gain upon him to give 15,000l. to his daughter Catherin with my Lord Eland in present; but he said he might possibly doe it in a year's or two's time, if he could gett mony; but if he would have her upon the possibility of her share of his estate when he dyed, or soe much mony as he should leave her then, he was content. I gave my Lord Halifax his answer,[1] but it did not please him to marry his son ther upon thos terms.

I returned home. My Lord Duke would needs come 19 with me four miles in my coach on my way, and gave my coachman ten shillings, and five shillings to the postilion. He also presented me with a book of the Antiquities of Nottinghamshire, written by Doctor Thoreton,[2] wher he ofton takes notice of my family.

I went to Yorke, wher I caused a monument to be 22 erected for my wife her father in Cony Street Church,[3] an eminent man of the law in his time, and ever reputed a very honest lawyer, which is not very usual, and to gett an estate too, being but a yonger brother, which he did. I made some visits during my stay ther to my Lord Burlinton at his hous in the country, and to Mr. Moyser, my father-in-law, to see my brother, his only son by my mother, whom I had not seen since he was a child. He

---

[1] Reresby's letter to Halifax, thanking him for his enquiries about his health, and giving an account of his visit to the Duke of Newcastle, is preserved among the Spencer MSS. at Althorp. It is dated Thrybergh, August 20, 1681.

[2] The *Antiquities of Nottinghamshire* by Robert Thoroton, published in 1677. Thoroton himself died in 1678.

[3] The parish church of St. Martin the Bishop in Coney Street. The inscription on the monument, dedicated by Lady Reresby on July 22, 1681, is printed in Drake's *Eboracum*, p. 328.

was then twenty-one years of age and a hopeful yong man. They lived then at Beaverley.

Aug. 29   The Earl of Devenshire sent to me to desire me to come and see him at Chatsworth, which I could not obay him in, designing soon for London.

Sept. 1   I was invited to the Cutler's Feast at Sheffield, wher my Lord Darcy and severall other gentlemen of the country appeared. The King haveing put forth a very gracious declaration to all his subjects, for the which most countys and corporations of England had returned their thankes to his Majesty by way of address, I advised them of Sheffield to doe the same. They desired time to consider of it.

2   The Duke of Newcastle sent me two pied deer and a wild tup for my parke.

5   My troop mustered at Doncaster, wher I entertained my officers and the company at dinner. I returned the same day.

* 9   The Master, wardens, and town-clerke of the Corporation of Cutlers in Halamshire came to my hous, tould me they did thinke it convenient to present an address to the King as I had advised them, and brought me one signed by 550 hands, desireing me to carry it and offer it humbly to his Majesty when I went up, which I accepted.

13   I went towards Newmarket, wher the King then was. I carryed my two eldest sons with me, intending to put them to school in the south, finding they improoved but little in the country. The face of things began much to alter in England at that time. The Duke, that was in Scotland, was extreamly courted by that kingdome. The Parlament called ther confirmed the succession and uniformity of religion, in opposition to popery and phenaticisme, which were two extraordinary acts at such a time,[1]

---

[1] One of the Acts declared that no difference in religion could alter the right of succession to the crown ; the other imposed on officials a test so self-contradictory in its terms that nobody could take it with real sincerity.

* 18/51: Newcastle, 23 September 1681. Newcastle compliments Reresby on the 'miracle' of convincing the cutlers to make an address to the king on his declaration.

and had a great influence upon England, and much discouraged the anti-Court party. My Lord Halifax was
chiefe favourit and minister at this time.

I laid at Cambrige in St. John's College at my brothers *Sept.* 15
chamber. He entertained me and my sons ther three
days. I see Sturbige Fair, which was held ther at the same
time.

I went from Cambrige to Newmarkit, wher I first 19
waited upon my Lord Hide, desireing him to introduce
me to the King to present him with an addresse. About
twelve that day he appointed me to attend in such a room,
wher the King came, ordered me to read it, and afterwards
takeing it of me gave me his hand to kiss. Afterwards I
waited of the King into the room, wher he asked me many
questions of the cituation and extent of Hallamshire. I
tould him it was a body of hardware men, or makers of
edge tooles, incorporated by Act of Parlament, and it
extended five miles round in compas from Sheffield, being
a very populous place. My Lord Hide took me that day
to dine with him at my Lord Conways, then Secretary of
State.[1]

I went a hawkeing with the King, wher I had oppor- 20
tunity to speake to him a good while, and to tell him some
things relateing to his service. I complained to him of a
nighbouring justice of the peace, who refused to sign the   *
addresse, though he lived within the compas of Hallam-
shire, and to discourage others from doing it. The King
tould me he should not stay long in commission, but I
had some reasons that prevailed with me not to persue the
businesse soe farr.

That afternoon I went to Berry, to see my Lady Monson, my ant.

I returned to Newmarkit, went to hawke with the King 22
in the morning, and in the afternoon set forward for
London, wher I arrived safe the next day with my sons.

[1] Edward, second Viscount and first Earl of Conway, who succeeded
Sunderland as Secretary of State on February 2, 1681.

* French draft, p. 49, shows that the justice of the peace to whom Reresby
referred was Francis Jessop. Reresby did not pursue Jessop's removal because
he was apprehensive that it would also alienate the town which was loyal to the
justice.

I found my wife and family wel at London.

   25   I went to wait on the Earle of Halifax (for he was soe created at that time),[1] who desired me to write by the first post to the Duke of Newcastle that his lordship did now thinke noe more of the proposed marriage between his son and the Dukes daughter.   I had recieved a letter from his Grace the day before upon that subject, which I showed my Lord Halifax, which gave ground for it.   The same day his lordship tould me the King resolved to make some new levies of dragoons, and that I should have a troop if I desired one, which I said might doe wel to entitle me the better to the reversion of the goverment of Yorke.

I dined with the Lord Maior of London, one of the faction,[2] wher some reflection being cast upon the Court I answerd it the best I could.   One cannot immagin how every little fellowe undertook to censure the King and his proceedings at that time.

   The same day I heard that the Earl of Halifax was censured for accepting (with three more) of a commission from the King to dispose of all ecclesiastical liveings (as vicars-generall) in the Kings guift.[3]   It was called a kind of takeing a branch of the royall authority to themselves, or a skreening of Majesty, that ought to transfer its own bounty to the subject.   Ther was noe colour for this complaint, ther being presidents in the case, and perticularly when King Henry the Eighth did vest the same authority (with much greater extent) in the single person of my Lord Cromwel.   When I tould my Lord of it, he laughed at their malice.

   [1] He had been made an earl two years earlier.   Reresby presumably is thinking of his elevation to the rank of marquis.

   [2] Sir Patience Ward.   His successor had already been chosen but had not been sworn.

   [3] This commission to manage the ecclesiastical patronage of the Crown, the most important members of which were the Archbishop of Canterbury and the Bishop of London, was unpopular because it seemed to foreshadow a revival of the Ecclesiastical Commission.

The King returned to London from Newmarkit.   *Oct.* 12

My Lord tould me that my Lord Shaftsbury had writt 13 to the King that if he would please to release him out of prison, he would engage to goe to Carolina (a remote plantation) [1] and never more to return into England; that the King had refused him, and was resolved to leave him to the law. He further tould me that if it were not for the King of France his interest here he did not question but to put England into a very happy state and condition in a short time; but ther was now noe hopes of a Parlament, except that King should make some new attempt upon Flanders, and an emergency of that kind would venter as it might be handled to reconcile all things.

This occasion hapned soon after, that news came that the French King had taken Strasbourg,[2] wherby the command of the Ryne would fall into his hands, which would soe cutt off the commerce and trade of the Low Countrys with Germany that it must engage them to submit to France, except we entered into a leage with the Low Countrys to defend them against France. This they did very earnestly sollicit; but our King could afford them noe helpe without a Parlament to supply him with mony, which it was feared the present jealousies would either prevent, or, if they gave him mony, would not trust him with the disposal of it. The King of France knew this and made an advantage of it, soe that the good my Lord Halifax expected from this occasion did not appear very probable as yet.

One Rous, a servant to Sir Thomas Player, chamber- 19 lain of London (a great phenatick and opposer of the Court), being indicted at Guildhall for high treason, the sherifs of London packed a jury that acquitted him; for all ther was plane evidence by six witnesses to proove the

---

[1] Shaftesbury was one of the group of proprietors who had planted Carolina at the beginning of the reign. He and his adviser, John Locke, had taken a very real interest in its development.

[2] September 20/30.

bil of indictment, yet the said grand jury found it *igno-ramus*.[1] This was looked upon as the more irregular, bycaus a grand jury ought to find the bils upon probable evidence, since that opons but the way to tryall by the second jury that is to find the prisner guilty or to acquitt him, according as matter of fact shall be prooved against him. But soe great was the anti-Court interest then in the Citty that the jurys would seldome find for the King.

The same day my Lord Halifax going in my coach to Whitehall, I desired him to speake to the King that I might be putt into commission of the peace for Middlesex and Westminster. I thought it might give me an opportunity to serve the King, and to make myselfe known to him in a province which I had diligently studyed a great part of my life. His lordship at the same time said that he should be glad to see me in more considerable business then that, and believed that ere long an envoye or embassador would be sent to the Emperour, and that he would use his interest with the King to choose me for that service, but not except I desired it, and believed the goverment of Yorke would not fall very soon. I replyed that my Lord Fretzwel was of great years, and not likely to recover to live very long; however I left myselfe entirely to his lordship's disposal, and was willing to serve the King in such a station as he thought the fittest for me.

The King talked to me a great while that evening, walkeing in St. James his Parke, and at the Duchesse of Portmoths. The subject was most of the late unjust verdicts and proceeding of the jurys in London and Middlesex, as to which he used this expression, It is a hard case that I am the last man to have law and justice in the whole nation.

Oct. 20   His Majesty went to see a new ship lanced at Dedford

[1] The trial was at the Old Bailey on October 18 (*Cal. S. P. Dom.*, 1680-1, p. 521). John Rous did not escape for long, as he was executed on July 20, 1683, for complicity in the Rye House Plot.

in his barge. I waited upon him to the water side, wher
he seeing me called me into the barge. He that was
named to be captain gave the King a great dinner, wher
his Majesty commanded all the gentlemen to sit down at
the same table. He was very serious that day, and seemd
more concerned that[1] the greatest business did usually
make him.

I dined with the Earl of Feathersham, where we made *Oct.* 23
a more then usuall debauch.

That evening I met the King going to councel, and
desired him that a notorious robber, one Nevison,[2]   *
haveing broaken the goale at Yorke and escaped, he would
be pleased to grant a reward of 20 l. to thos that would
apprehend him, and to make it known by issuing out a
proclamation to that purpas. The thruth was, he had
committed severall notorious robberies, and it was with
great endeavours and trouble that I had gott him apprehended at the first ; and since his escape he had threatned
the death of severall justices of the peace, wherever he
mett them, though I never heard that I was of the
nomber. The King's answer (my Lord Halifax being
present) was this, that a proclamation would cost him
100 l., but he would order 20 l. to be paid by the sheriff
of that county to him that took him, wherever it was;
and that it should be published by the *Gazette*, which was
the same thing. The roague was taken not long after,
and hanged at Yorke.[3]

I had begd of the King some mony that I had discovered in the hands of a convicted papist, which belonged
to my wife her sister. My Lord Halifax spoake to my
Lord Hide, first Lord Commissioner of the Treasury,
that dined ther that day, to befriend me in the getting of
it, which he promessed me, for it might first be forfited to
the King before I could pretend to it, and then only of the
King's guift.

[1] ? " than." [2] John Nevison, the famous highwayman.
[3] Early in 1685.

---

* 18/30: W. Simpson, 25 October 1681. Nevison had been convicted of horse
stealing at York in 1676 and reprieved following the intercession of Sir Godfrey
Copley. After his escape he had murdered one fletcher.

Oct. 29   A new Lord Maior of London was chosen.[1] The King
*   being invited did him the honour to dine with him at
Guildhall.   The showe and dinner were very great and
splended.   I dined that day at the table of my Lord
Maior.

Nov. 4   I was to see my Lord of Danby in the Tower.   He
was not in charity with the then ministers, as appeared by
his discours, seeming to reflect upon them as inclineing
too favourably to the Earl of Shaftsbury, and in other
perticulars.

5   I tould the King the story of Sir Henry Goodrick, then
embassador in Spain, whom I called brother, of whom I
had recieved a late account, that going to shoot some
miles from Madrid, in his return home he light upon
some thieves that had sett upon a coach full of ladys
with an intent to rob them, but before they could effect it
Sir Henry and his followers attacked them, wounded
some and dispersed the rest, and rescued the ladys.

6   I acquainted my Lord Halifax with what was the
remarke of my Lord of Danby and others, viz., that the
ministers seemed more moderate in the case of my Lord
of Shaftsbury then heretofore, and that they treated with
him to let him goe at large.   His answer was that people
were too ready to pass their judgement, but if it were soe,
what could the King doe better; he had as good be set at
liberty upon terms as by a jury, which would be sure to
acquitt him should he be brought to tryall, though never
soe guilty; nor could he doe the King that harm if he
were out as such an act of mercy and legality would doe
him good.   The same day one of the under-secretarys
tould me that the King would prossecute him to the
utmost, and that ther was sufficient matter against him.

My Lord Halifax had spoaken to my Lord Chancellor
to put me into commission of the peace for Middlesex;

---

[1] Sir John Moore, a supporter of the Court. The election was on September 29, the formal admission to office and dinner at the Guildhall on
October 29.

* 18/23: Sir John Kaye, 28 October 1681. Kaye asserted that, according to Dr.
Johnson, the new mayor was a kinsman of Sir Patience Ward, former MP for
Pontefract. This is significant in view of Kaye's last defeat at Pontefract.

but he answered (as his lordship tould me that day) that he could not admit me bycaus I was noe freehoulder in that county. I answered that was noe reason, bycaus I could name severall that had noe more freehould then me and yet were in commission. Then, said my Lord Halifax, I wil speake to him again, that it is fitt either thos should be put out or you accepted. His lordship did soe, and my Lord Chancellor then thought it reason- *Nov.* 12 able to name me to the King, and to putt me into commis- sion for Middlesex and Westminster.

I was sworn of the commissions accordingly. 18

My Lord Halifax, that was noe ways inclineing to the French interest, was noe favourit to the Duchesse of Portsmouth. The King was troubled at it, his business meeting with some rubs by this difference. However the King made them friends that day outwardly, but not 20 thorowly, for that was impossible, they going upon two soe different interests.

The King resolved that my Lord Shaftsbury should 23 be brought to tryall, to which purpas a commission of Oir and Terminer was issued out of purpass.[1] The most capitall things against him being committed in London, the jury was returned ther for the finding of the bill, and though ther were eight witnesses that swore to the bil, and a paper was produced conteaning matter of high treason which was sworn to have been found amongst his papers in his closit by a Secretary of State,[2] yet the grand jury brought it in *ignoramus.*

He was enlarged upon his habias corpus; and bycaus 28 the rabble in the Citty had made bonefires the day of the bill against him being found *ignoramus,* the justices of the peace in London and Middlesex had orders to prevent

[1] The commission was opened at the Old Bailey on November 24.

[2] A project for an association to defend the Protestant religion and exclude the Duke of York from the throne, identified by Sir Leoline Jenkins, who had succeeded Henry Coventry as Secretary in 1679. It was unsigned, and not in Shaftesbury's handwriting.

the like disorders that day, by sending the constables and beadles to disperse such meetings. A great many were jealous, considering my Lord Halifax his relation to him, that he was not sorry that he was com'd out of prison; and that which made me doubt it the more was that, waiting upon that lord a little early, I found one of my Lord Shaftsbury's gentlemen with his lordship. However my Lord Halifax dinyed it to me very seriously, and said he would speedily convince the world of the contrary by his demeaner in his perticular.

*

Nov. 29   It being the King's custome as he returnd from his walke before dinner from St. James his Parke to discours the forraign ministers, who usually attended to meet him in the ante-chamber, he did it that day upon the subject of the hard measure done him by my Lord Shaftsbury's jury, and it fell to my share to explain severall things in French before his Majesty relating to that matter.

Dec. 1   A perticular private sessions was appointed to be sate at Westminster to take a return made by order of the King and Councel of the number of all papists (forraigners and others) resideing within that liberty; but the return was soe defective that upon my motion the constables were sent back and ordered to make another a week after, and to give it in upon oath. Matters ran very high at this time against that interest.

4   Was the sessions held at Hicks his Hall for the county of Middlesex, wher I assisted. The same day the King declared his displeasure against the Duke of Monmouth in several perticulars, but especially for his offering to be baile for my Lord Shaftsbury. The next day he disposed of the Master of the Hors place to the Duke of Richmond, his son by the Duchess of Portsmouth [1] (formerly the Duke of Monmouths), and gave the command of

---

[1] Charles Lennox, first Duke of Richmond, was then only nine years old. His formal appointment as Master of the Horse was made early in 1682.

* 18/94: Newcastle, 26 November 1681, claiming that the court designed to save Shaftesbury.

one of his regiments of foot guards to the Duke of
Grafton, his second natural son by the Duchesse of
Cleveland.[1]

The King, to comply with the times (for everybody *Dec. 7*
suspected it was not his inclinations), sent for the justices
of the peace of Middlesex to appear before him in Council,
wher he gave them a severe repremand for soe remisly
enquiring after the nomber of papists and the prossecution of them.   He spoake not himselfe, but did it by my
Lord Chancellor, and directed that strict care should be
had and taken about it for the time to come.

The same day, comming from visiting the Duchesse
of Portsmouth, my Lord Halifax tooke me home with
him from Whitehall.   I acquainted him in the way that
the general report was that he opposed the Duke of
Yorke's interest with the King, and his return into
England from Scotland, which the Duke pressed extreamly.   He replyed that it was wel if the Dukes being
too hasty in that matter did not turn to his injurie; that
he had a sort of hungry servants about him that were still
pressing his return, and would never let him alone til, out
of interest to themselves, they put him upon that which
would turn to the prejudice of their master by the ill
timeing of it.   The thruth was, whilst the Duke was near
the King everybody believed him led most by his advice,
and consequently that popish councils were most prevalent; and he did a great deale of good in Scotland by
his influence and watchfulness in that mutinous kingdome.   However other causes were found out by the
papists and the Dukes creatures for his stay ther, viz.,
that it was to give better opportunity for his ennemies to
worke him out his brother's good opinion, and that the

---

[1] Henry Fitzroy, first Duke of Grafton, was generally regarded as the
ablest of the King's natural sons.   His commission as colonel of the first
regiment of foot guards, the command of which had been resigned by John
Russell on account of increasing age, is dated December 14 (Dalton,
English Army Lists, i. 289).

ministers might have the King to themselves and guide him by their own influence.

My Lord Halifax said at the same time that ther was great partiality in the judgement of men as to his perticular, for in justice they should as wel take notice of things done to the advantage of the Duke as what appeared to be otherwise; but noebody commended the ministers for getting in the Duke of Richmond to be Master of the Hors to the prejudice of the Duke of Monmouth, which would proove a great barr to his return near the King; and the greatest service one could doe his Highness was to prevent the Duke of Monmoth's coming to Court.

Dec. 10   I sent one Mr. St. Johns to the goale for wounding another gentleman whom he drew upon, being drunke in the street. The poor gentleman that was wounded dyed the same day.

12   My Lord Halifax said he had spoake to the King of
*   me, and that he now hoped I should be sent abroad speedily with a very honourable commission.

16   The justices of the peace of Midlesex at Hicks his Hall resolved, in obedience to the laws and his Majestys commands in Councill, to put the laws in execution against Protestant dissenters and conventicles.

18   Haveing writt to my Lord Halifax to thanke him for his late assurance that I was in his thoughts, he tould me that day that ther was some stopp as to my being sent abroad, but that he would slip noe opportunity to doe me a kindness either in that or some other thing, and that he found the King had a good opinion of me, and was sufficiently disposed to show me his favour. He tould me further that had ther been any considerable sallary with it, he intended to have made me one of the commissioners of the Master of the Horses place for the Duke of Richmond, who was too yong to execute it in person and therfore did it by deputys.

†   19   Came the news of the Earle of Argiles condemnation

---

* 18/8: Newcastle, 9 December 1681.

† 18/5: Newcastle 10 January 1681/2. The commission abroad which Reresby hoped for, that of envoy to France, went to Lord Preston.

in Scotland,[1] which much discouraged the Presbiterian interest both ther and in England.

Seven justices of the peace attended the Bishop of *Dec.* 20 London [2] to treat with him by order of sessions concerning accommodating some French Protestants [3] with lodgeing in their great workehous at Clarkenwell till they could be setled elsewher, amongst whom I was appointed to manage that treaty with the said bishop as prolocutor.

My Lord Halifax, meeting me at the Secretarys, 24 carried me to dinner, and tould me by the way that he did believe the difficultie which had been started as to my being sent abroad seemd now to be remooved in some measure, and that the King (who had spoaken kindly of me lately upon that occasion) would send me in the quality of envoye extraordinairy to the Court of Denmarke, from whence my Lord Bodnam [4] was not long before recalled. This week noe less then ten severall duels were fought in London.

Came news of the Earle of Arguiles escape out of 25 prison,[5] at which the King seemd concerned, and of the King of France his laying claime to the country of Liege. I recieved some days before some assurance of being elected burgess of Audbrough, in case of a new Parlament, but my Lord Halifax advised to make noe answer to them till he see more as to the sopposed voyage.   I that day,

[1] Archibald Campbell, the ninth earl. He had refused to take without qualification the test imposed by the Scottish Parliament, and was sentenced to death for treason and leasing making.

[2] Henry Compton, generally known as the Protestant bishop, who later took an active part in the Revolution.

[3] The persecution which was to culminate four years later in the revocation of the Edict of Nantes was already driving many Huguenots to seek refuge in England.

[4] Robert Robartes, Viscount Bodmin, eldest son of John, first Earl of Radnor. He had been recalled in April, 1681 (Luttrell, *Brief Relation*, i. 75).

[5] Through the devotion of his stepdaughter, Sophia Lindsay, who visited him accompanied by a page, with whom he changed clothes.

being Christmas Day, recieved the sacrament at the Bishop of Ely's chappell, wher I dined the same time with his lordship with Doctor Oates, whom I took up for speakeing reflectingly on the chastity of the late Queen Mother.[1]

Dec. 28 My Lord Halifax directed me to be at Whitehall at the riseing of the Cabinet Council, saying the King might possibly thinke fitt to speake to me concerning going to Denmarke; but he said nothing to me either then or before at the Duchesse of Portsmouth's, wher his Majesty discoursed with me upon other matters. Afterwards my Lord tould me the King first intended to name me in Councill for that embassy the Sunday following, but that I might depend upon the thing.

31 The Earle of Huntinton,[2] my Lord Ealand, and some others dined with me, wher we ended the year in a more then ordinary debeauch, which God forgive me, it neither being my custome or inclination much to doe soe.

Jan. 1 At evening I mett my Lord Halifax at his return from
1681[/2] the Cabinet Councill, who tould me ther was some stop as to the time of my going for Denmarke, but not as to the thing, and [if] I stood in the Kings way he might possibly speake to me of it himselfe. Soon after the King came into the withdrawing room, wher the Queen was at cards, and seing me ther tould me in my ear that he expected some further account from the King of Denmarke before he intended to send to that prince; but whenever he sent he had pitched upon me for that service. I replyed that his Majesty reposed a great trust in me, and one very honourable; I wished my capacity might answer my desires and endeavours to serve him, and then I doubted not but I should be able to effect it.

---

[1] This appears to be a repetition of the incident mentioned on p. 208 above. The earlier date is probably the correct one.

[2] Theophilus Hastings, seventh Earl of Huntingdon, a supporter of Shaftesbury and Monmouth. At this time, however, he was turning towards the Court.

The King was pleasd to answer that he made noe doubt of that.

My wife and eldest daughter being that night at Court, the guerle was taken notice of for hansome.

I was to attend the French embassador to give him an *Jan.* 2 answer to a quœre he putt to me the day before, how a French footman that had robbed his master at Paris might be taken and punished here, wher he had refuged himselfe.

I dined that day with my Lord Halifax at my Lord Conways, Principall Secretary of State. I acquented the King and my Lord Halifax at the same time with an affidavit made before me as a justice of the peace the same day, concerning a pre-contract between Mr. Thyn[1] and Mrs. Trever[2] before his marriage with my Lady Northumberland, for ther were endeavours to null the said marriage, it not haveing been consummated and my Lady Northumberland haveing fled from Mr. Thyn into Holland;[3] at all which the Court was not dissatisfyed, the husband being one that had opposed its interest and engaged himselfe in that of the Duke of Monmoth.

I gave the King a copie of the affidavit, which he had 3 commanded me to prepare the day before. I was a long time that evening in discours with the Duchess of Portsmouth, who was ill of the pain of her stomach, a distemper which she had long suffered under by fits, and declared that night she would get leave of the King to goe for cure of to the waters of Buxton.

I carried a gentleman, one Mr. Grant, a great man of 4 the phenatick party, to wait upon my Lord Halifax, who

[1] Thomas Thynne of Longleat, known from his great wealth as " Tom of Ten Thousand."

[2] Only daughter of Sir John Trevor, who had been Secretary of State from 1668 to his death in 1672. Thynne was believed to have seduced her, and had in consequence been involved in a duel in the spring of 1678 (Hist. MSS. Com., *Rutland MSS.*, ii. 49-50).

[3] When this marriage took place, in the summer of 1681, Elizabeth Percy, although already a widow, was only fourteen years of age.

acquainted him with severall treacherys committed by some great men and in great imployment at Court against his lordship, and that had been instrumentall in exasperating the Hous of Commons against him in the late Parlaments; which my Lord tooke as a service done him, since at the least he knew therby how to avoid and beware of them for the future. The same time I brought a gentleman to my Lord to aske him pardon for some things that he had been reported to have said of his lordship; and the thruth is, not only from policie (which teacheth that we ought to let noe man be our ennemy when we can helpe it), but from his disposition, I never see any man more ready to forgive then himselfe. I remember his expression to him was this, Sir, if you have not said the words, I am very glad of it; if you have, I am soe too that you find caus to be of another mind. In some private discours the same time his lordship tould me that thos which belonged to the Duke of York made him madd, for that ther were few amongst them that had common sence. He then spoake that a Parlament was not farr off.

My poor wife had at this time a fitt of the gout, tho an extream temporate woeman.

Jan. 5   I went to see my Lord of Danby at the Tower, wher he tould me severall perticulars of my Lord Sunderland's railing against my Lord Halifax, though his brother-in-law. I found he spoake this with some satisfaction, being himselfe noe friend to that earle; but I presumed to tell his lordship that as I was a friend to them both I wished that he, as a prisner, would forget all things of animosity against one in power, as my Lord Halifax was, for when a Parlament came his lordship might need the assistance of him and his friends.

That evening I was invited to a club of aldermen of the Citty and some men of quality at Court, that mett to consult for the Kings service, and ther found that dayly the Kings interest improoved within the limits of London.

My Lord Halifax tould me that Sir Thomas Yarburgh *Jan.* 8
had writt to him a letter to beg the Mannor of Yorke of
the King, wher the Gouvernor did frequently live,[1] and
showed me his letter, but promessed me to prevent the
grant of it either to him or any other person.　Going the
same day to wait upon Mr. Leg, Master of the Ordinance,
he promessed to give me a gunner to take care of the
cannon and ammunition at Burlinton Fort, which I most
desired, that by such an establishment I might better
pretend to the gouverment and sallary of 200 l., for which
I had yet my privy seale.

Began the sessions of the peace for Westminster, for 9
which I had taken forty-seven recognisances in less then six
weeks time, and few of the other justices had above six
or eight, one excepted that had thirty.

The sessions of the peace ended at Westminster, wher 12
I had attended all the four days.　Upon the 11th the
Morocco embassader had his audience, who was recieved
with a more then ordinary ceremony, the King believeing
that a commerce between that Emperour and this kingdome might proove of great advantage to us, we haveing
soe fitt a place for a staple or stoorhous of our own commodities upon their contenent as Tangers.　That embassadours present to the King was two lyons and thirty
ostriges,[2] which his Majesty laughed at, saying he knew
nothing fitter to return for them then a flock of gheese.[3]

This day I was at the Old Baily, wher the sessions 17
began (that for Hicks his Hall haveing begun the Fryday
before); severall persons were ther found guilty of murder

[1] The King's Manor, or royal palace at York, was built by Henry VIII
from the ruins of St. Mary's Abbey and enlarged by James I.　In the
seventeenth century it was largely used as a residence by the King's representatives, the Presidents of the Council in the north and the Governors of
York.

[2] The lions were put into the Tower and the ostriches sent to St. James's
Park (Luttrell, *Brief Relation*, i. 156).

[3] His present eventually took the form of three hundred firelocks (Newdigate-Newdegate, *Cavalier and Puritan*, p. 171).

and felonys committed by me. The sheriffs of London had some days before been blamed by the King in Council for not obaying his Majestys order for the transporting of six condemn'd popish priests, which they had excused themselves in as not haveing his Majestys publique direction or order before, and pretending some defect in the warrant they had recieved, but did then promess to obay it. However this day they made new scruples what to doe in that matter, telling all the judges then present in sessions that they durst not deliver up the said priests, being condemd persons, without either haveing a pardon from them, a habias corpus, or the order of that court, and desireing the judges opinion at the same time. But their lordships refused to give them directions therin, of *Jan.* 17 which matter I gave the King and my Lord Halifax an account that night.

The same day I moved the justices of the peace for Middlesex, at the adjournment of the sessions at noon, to this purpas, that the first address of thankes to the King for his gracious declaration had been offered by them, and since followed from all parts of England; but that the justices of the peace for the countys of Dorset and Sommersit had now been before them in another address to his Majesty, wherby they did express their detestation of an association lately produced upon the tryall of my Lord Shaftsbury, and said to be found in his closit, conteaning absolute rebellion and subversion of the goverment; but that I hoped they would follow at least the exemple of the said countys by the like application to his Majesty, which they unanimously consented to, and ordered Sir William Smith,[1] the then chairman, to draw up an address accordingly.

That night I waited upon the King in the bedchamber, wher I tould him what I had done, desireing to know his pleasure if he approved it, to the end I might further advise the justices to proceed as they had resolved or to

---

[1] Of Reddiff, Buckinghamshire; created a baronet in May 1661.

desist, the day following being the end of our sessions. His Majesty replyed that when the late addresses did first begin he was not much satisfyed with them, but when they began to encrease he was glad to find them soe numerous, and that he was of the same opinion in this perticular, and should be pleased that this intended abhorrancie of the association might proove as generall as the former addresses. His Majesty amongst severall other expressions to me at the same time said thes words, that he thanked me for my endeavours in this and other perticulars of his service, that whenever I had a mind that I should freely have accesse to him, for he had a kindenesse for me and a good opinion of my judgement.

The intended address being drawn up and communi- *Jan.* 18 cated to the justices for their approbation by the chairman, Sir William Smith, I made some objections against the form, it being too severe and reflexive upon the jury that had acquitted my Lord Shaftsbury and upon his lordship, it not being our business to arraigne persons over again, or to censure men, but the thing of the association; wherupon it was referred to Mr. Brigeman and me to alter, which we did to the satisfaction of all the gentlemen, and went that night to present it to his Majesty, who recieved it graciously, assureing us that he would ever govern according to the known lawes.

I dined with my Lord Lomley[1] at my Lord Feather- 22 sham's, wher my Lord Lomley declared his speedy intentions to quitt his place of Master of the Hors to the Queen, which he had thus long enjoyed as independent of Master of the Hors to the King; but the Duchesse of Portsmoth had prevailed with the King to alter his patent, and to make him an officer under the Duke of Richmond,

---

[1] Richard Lumley, Viscount Lumley of Waterford in the peerage of Ireland and Baron Lumley of Lumley Castle in the peerage of England. Although brought up a Catholic, he became a Protestant during the reign of Charles II, played an active part in the Revolution, and in 1690 was created Earl of Scarborough.

contrary to his promess. And indeed the Duchesse was sometimes to blame in things of this nature, for she, to show her power with the King (which was very great) and her friendship to some, would ofton make the King breake his engagement to others, which was not to his honour. And yet his Majesty was not at this time charmed with her bed, for it was generally believed that he had not laid with her since he was at Newmarket at least four months before.

I found this day that one of the three ministers was reconcileing himselfe to a great man that was noe friend to my Lord Halifax, which I acquainted my Lord with, least it might proove to his disadvantage, which he tould me would be of good use to him. That night I discoursed the King a great while at my Lady Portsmouth's.

Jan. 28 Came news from Flanders of vast dammage done to Ostend, Antwarpe, and other parts of that country by the greatest inundation that ever was known. Holland also suffered soe vastly by thos floods that the greatest part of Zealand was laid under water, severall towns and villages, with their inhabitants, were drowned, insomuch as it was believed that to repair the losses would cost ten millions sterling. The levels in Yorkshire and Lincolnshire were by the same fate laid under water. The continuall rains of this winter had occasioned thos floods, which were almost without intermission, nor was ther any frost longer then for one night, or any snowe all that time till the beginning of February.

February Now was the great expectation whether a Parlament would be called or not, the ministers of state not agreing in the thing. My Lord Halifax argued for it for thes reasons, that all Christendome desired it, France only excepted, and that nothing ought to discourage it at home but the fear that they might fly upon high points, which if they did, the King might dismiss or dissolve it when he pleased, and show the world that it was their fault, not his, that he endeavoured to give satisfaction to his people

*

* 20/21: H. Marwood, 23 February 1681/2, shows Reresby beginning to make interest again in case of an election.

by frequent Parlaments; but if the King and they agreed, his Majesty would then gain the great point to be united at home and formidable abroad. Seamure and Hide, that were more in the Dukes interest, were against it, fearing that not only the succession but themselves might be attaqued in the next Parlament.

I recievd the sacrament in order to the takeing the *Feb.* 4 oathes as a justice of the peace, which I performed at the King's Bench barr on the 5th. 5

Ther hapned the most barbarous murder that had 12 hapned in England for some time.[1] Mr. Thyn, a gentleman of 9,000 l. a year (lately marryed to my Lady Ogle, who repenting of the match had fled from him into Holland before they were bedded) was sett upon by three ruffyans, and shot to death as he was coming along the street in his coach. He being one deeply engaged in the Duke of Monmoth's interest, it was much feared what construction might be made of it by that party, the authors escapeing and not known. I was at Court that evening when the King, hearing the newes, seemd much concerned at it, not only for the horrour of the action itselfe, to which his good nature was very averse, but also apprehending the ill constructions that the anti-Court party might make of it.

At eleven a clock the same night, as I was going into bed, Mr. Thyn's gentleman came to me to grant a hue and cry, and soon after the Duke of Monmoth's page, to desire me to come to him at Mr. Thyn's lodgeing, sending his coach to fetch me, which I made use of to goe to him. I found him surrounded with severall gentlemen and lords, friends to Mr. Thyn, and Mr. Thyn mortally wounded by five bullets, which had entered his belly and side, shott from a blunderbush. I granted immediately severall warrants of search for severall persons suspected to be privy to the design and that might

---

[1] About 7 p.m. at the corner of Pall Mall and St. Alban's Street near Charing Cross.

give some intelligence of the partys that had acted that murder. At the last, by intelligence from a chairman that had the same afternoon conveyed one of the ruffyans from his lodgeing in Westminster to take hors at the Black Bull, and by a whoor that used to visit that gentleman, the constables found out both his lodgeing in Westminster, and ther took his man, a Swed by his nation, who, being brought before me, at last confessed that he served a gentleman, a German captain, that had tould him that he had a quarrell with Mr. Thyn, and had ofton appointed him to watch his coach as he passed by; and that perticularly that day, soe soon as the captain did know that the coach was gone by, he had booted himselfe, and with two others, a Swedish lieutenant and a Polander, gone, as he sopposed, in quest of Mr. Thyn on horsback.

Feb. 13   By this servant I further understood wher possibly the captain and his two friends might be found, and after searched severall houses with the Duke of Monmoth, Lord Mordent,[1] &c., as he directed us, till at six a clock in the morning, haveing been in chace almost the whole night, I personally took the captain at the hous of a Swedish doctor in Lecester Fields, going first into the room, followed by my Lord Mordent, wher I found him in bed and his sword at some distance from him upon the table, which I first seized and afterwards his person, committing him to two constables. I wondered to see him yield up himselfe soe tamely, being certainly a man of great courage, for he appeared inconcerned from the begining, notwithstanding he was very certain to be found the chiefe actor in the tragedie. This gentleman had not long before commanded the forelorn hope at the siege of Mons,[2] wher only two men besides himselfe of fifty under his command came off with life, for which the Prince of Orange made him a lieutenant in his guards,

---

[1] Charles, Lord Mordaunt, better known as Earl of Peterborough, a title which he inherited on the death of his uncle, the second earl, in 1697.

[2] Besieged by the French in the summer of 1678.

and the King of Sweden gave him afterwards a troop of hors.

Severall persons suspected for accessarys and the two accomplices, viz., the Swedish lieutenant and the Polander, whos names were Stern and Borosky (and the captain's name was Fratz),[1] were soon after taken by constables with my warrant and brought to my hous, wher before I could finish all the examinations, the King sent for me to attend him in Councill, which was called on purpas for that occasion, with the papers and prisners. His Majesty ordered me to inform him of my proceedings in that matter, both as to the way of the prisners apprehending and their examinations, and then examined them himselfe, giveing me order at the riseing of the Councill to putt what had been said ther into writing and form in order to the tryall. This took me up a great part of the day, though I desired Mr. Brigeman,[2] one of the clerks of the Council and a justice of the peace, to assist me in that matter both for the dispatch and my security, the nicity of the thing requireing it, as will hereafter appear.

The Councill meeting again, amongst other things to *Feb.* 15 examin the governer to yong Count Conismarke[3] (a yong gentleman resident in Monsieur Fauberts acadamy in London),[4] sopposed to be privy to the murther, the King sent for me to attend the Councill, wher he confessing that the eldest Count Conismarke[5] (who had been in England some months before, and had made addresses to my Lady Ogle before she had marryed Mr. Thyn)

[1] John Stern, George Borosky, and Christopher Vratz. The last was a veteran Dutch adventurer, who had seen service all over Europe.

[2] William, nephew of Sir Orlando Bridgeman.

[3] Philipp-Christoph von Königsmarck, a boy of fifteen. His governor was a certain Frederick Hanson.

[4] A fashionable school for riding, fencing, and similar accomplishments.

[5] Karl-Johann, elder brother of Philipp-Christoph, the representative of a well-known Brandenburg family, who, although only twenty-four years of age, had had experience of warfare and intrigue in many lands. His sister was the mother of Marshal Saxe.

had ten days before the murther com'd *incognito* into England, and laid disguised till it was committed, gave great caus of suspicion that the said Count was in the bottom of it.   Wherupon his Majesty commanded me to goe search his lodgeing, which I performed with two constables, but found he was gone the day after the deed was done bytimes in the morning, of which I presently returnd to give the King an account.

I severall times after this attended the King, both privately and in Councill, to inform him from time to time as new matter did occurr, and as I gathered new light from the further examination either of the same prisners or of others suspected to be concerned.   Upon the whole matter we discovered, partly by the confession of the ruffians and the information of others, that Captain Fratz had been eight years a companion and a perticular friend to Count Conismarke (one of the greatest men in the kingdome of Sweden, his oncle[1] being at that time governor of Pomerania, and near being marryed to that Kings ant); that whilst he was here in England some months before, and had made addresses to the Lady Ogle (the only daughter and heiresse to the Earle of Northumberland, marryed after to the now murdered Mr. Thyn), the said Count had ressented something as done towards him as an affront from the said Mr. Thyn; and that the said captain, out of friendship to the Count (but as he then pretended not with his privitie), was resolved to be revenged of him, to which intent he, with the assistance of the said Stern and Borasky, had committed this soe barbarous act, by obligeing the last to discharge a blunderbush upon him in his coach, the other being present.

I was glad to find in this whole affair that noe English person nor interest was concerned, the phenaticks haveing buzzed it already abroad that the design was chiefly against the Duke of Monmoth; and I had the

[1] Otto-Wilhelm, his father's brother.

Kings thankes oftener then once, my Lord Halifax his,
and severall other's, for my diligent discovery of the true
caus and occasion as well as the authors of this matter.
The thruth is the Duke of Monmoth was gone out of the
coach from Mr. Thyn an hour before; but I found, by
the confession both of Stern and Borasky, that they were
ordered not to shoot in case the Duke were with him in
the coach.

It was much suspected all this while that Count
Conismarke was not gott over sea, and on the 20th [1] he was *Feb.* 20
found by the Duke of Monmoth's servant disguised at
Gravesend alone, comming out of a sculler, intending the
next day to goe aboard a Swedish shipp. The King,
haveing notice, called an extraordinary Councill to
examin him that afternoon, at which I was present. He
appeared before the King with all the assurance immaginable, was a fine gentleman of his person, his hair was the
longest for a mans I ever see, for it came below his wast,
and his parts were very quick. His examination before
the King and Council was very superficiall, but he was
after that appointed the same day to be examined, by
order of the King in Councill, by the Lord Chiefe
Justice,[2] Mr. Brigeman, the Atturney General, and myselfe, which was accordingly done; but he confessed
nothing as to his being either privy or concerned in the
murder, laying his lying here concealed upon the occasion
of his takeing phisick for a clapp, and therfore was
unwilling to discover himselfe till he was cured; and his
going away in a disguise after the fact was done upon the
advice of some friends, who tould him that it would
reflect upon him were it known he was in England, when
a person that was his friend was under soe notorious a
suspicion for committing soe black a crime, and therfore
did endeaver to gett away, not knowing how far the laws

---

[1] Really on Sunday, February 19. His examination, however, took place
on the 20th.

[2] Sir Francis Pemberton, who had succeeded Scroggs in April 1681.

of this land for that very reason might make him a party.

This night I was with the King at his going to bed, wher, discoursing as to this matter, I found he was willing Count Conismarke might come off.

Sir Thomas Thyn[1] telling my Lord Halifax that I had taken a great deale of pains in this matter, his lordship bestowed a greater compliment upon me (being then present) than I deserved, saying, He doth not only behave himselfe well in this, but in all other things which he undertakes.

25   The King being to goe speedily to Newmarket, and it being reported that the Duke of Yorke was to come from Scotland to make a visit to his Majesty ther, I pressed my Lord Halifax to fix the goverment of Yorke, which the King had promessed me, least it might likewise be desired by his Highness for Sir Thomas Slingsby, who was well in the Dukes favour, and who, haveing some time before purchased the Lord Fretwels troop of hors,[2] was very desirous to succeed him in that goverment also, either by purchass or favour.

26   A gentleman that kept the French acadamy in London, one Monsieur Faubert, came and desired me to direct him (if ther was any method to be followed) for the saveing of Count Conismarkes life, insinuating at the same time that as he was a gentleman of a vast estate he was sensible he could not lay it out to greater advantage then to support his innocencie, and to secure him against the danger of the law in a strange country. I tould him that if he was innocent the law would acquitt him, though he was a forraigner, as well as if he were a native; but that he ought to be carefull how he made any offers of that kind,

---

[1] Sir Thomas Thynne of Kempsford had succeeded his father as second baronet in 1681. He was first cousin of the murdered man, whose property he inherited, and at the close of the year was raised to the peerage as Viscount Weymouth.

[2] In the royal regiment of horse guards commanded by Lord Oxford.

it being rather the way to make a man of honour his ennemy then to gain him for his friend. This was one of the first bribes of value that ever was offered me, which I might safely have gotten without discovery and without doing much for itt; but I always believed that mony soe gotten was noe addition to what we possess, but rather the caus of its wast (*male parta male delabuntur*), and therfore I denyed it, as I ever did and I hope shall be able to resist temptations of that nature.

The bils against the three murderers of Mr. Thyn *Feb.* 27 had been found against them as principals, and against the Count as accessary at the sessions at Hicks his Hall, wher the sessions had begun the 20th of February and ended the 28, all the rest of the persons apprehended or bound over for that offence being reserved as witnesses till the tryall. On the 28 they were tryed at the Old 28 Bailiff, wher, after a tryall that lasted from nine in the morning till five in the afternoon, and a very strict prossecution by the relations of Mr. Thyn, the three were brought in principals of the said murder, and recieved sentence of death accordingly; and the Count was acquitted as not accessary by the same jury, it being *per medietatem linguæ*, according to the privilege of strangers. I carryed the King the news the first of this matter, who was not displeasd to hear that it had passed in this manner. The party of the Duke of Monmoth, who all appeared to countenance the prossecution, were extreamly concerned that the Count did escape.

I tould my Lord Hallifax that the better to secure the *March* 2 goverment of York I was willing to purchass the present possession of the goverment, if my Lord Fretzwell would quitt it for a reasonable rate, which it was not unlikely he would doe, considering his age and infirmitys. His lordship tould me he thought it not soe prudent to venter to give mony upon it, considering my Lord Fretzwel's age; but if I desired it he would speak to the King and obtean leave to treat with him about it. The

same night his lordship carryed me to his Majesty in the
bedchamber, ther being noe person present but we three.
His Majesty tould me I had leave to buy the present
possession of that command, if Fretzwell and I could
agree of the price; but he advised me against it, saying
it was impossible his lordship could live two months,
being burnt down to the sockit (as his Majesty termd it)
or quite wasted; but that he left it to my own choice,
assuring me of this, that if [I] survived him I should certainly succeed him in that command; that neither Sir
Thomas Slingsby nor others should deprive me of it,
though the Duke himselfe should intercede for them;
and that I should have the first independent company
that fell, though such a vacancie should fall out before the
goverment.   My Lord Hallifax tould the King that he
should be glad to see me actually in some place of credit
in his service, for that noebody deserved it more, or was
better able to serve his Majesty then myselfe.   The King
replyed that he knew that.   All I said was, that though
I could not pretend to merit the character his lordship
had given of mee, yet I should ever make it my business
to be as faithfull and diligent in any post wher his Majesty
should pleas to place me as another; desired time to consider what I should doe as to the purchass, and that his
Majesty would pleas, however, to continue me governor
of Burlinton, and the sallary belonging to it of 200 l. a
year (which the Commissioners of the Treasury were
endeavouring to retrench), which his Majesty did perfectly promesse me.

March 3   I thought it was better to try the continuance of my
Lord Frezwels health a while longer then to purchass,
especially hearing that he was not likely to live very long;
and the thruth is, I rather did this to fix the thinge by
getting a reassurance of the King's promess in that perticular then out of any design to buy, from the begining.
My Lord Hallifax this 3rd day of March obteaned from
the King for me that I might putt in caviats in the office of

both secretarys to prevent the obteaning of the next independent company that fell by any other person. And the King, at my own request, was pleased to promess me that when a vacancie did happen of his pages of honour, that he would take my secound son Tamworth[1] into that place, of which I was glad of, believeing that he might proove very fitt, by reason of his quickness and apprehension, for a court. Ther was nothing to be said against soe considerable a preferment for a yonger son but the vices of the place (to which youth is more apt to incline then riper age); but God's grace is sufficient to steer and direct men in all places.

This afternoon I went in the barge of the Duke of Albemarle, with his Grace and the embassador of Morocco, to the bear garden, to see the bateing of bulls and bears for the diversion of his Excellencie.

The King and Queen went to Newmarkit. The *March* 4 Duchesse of Portsmouth went the day before for France.

The captain and other two that were guilty of Mr. 10 Thyns murder were hanged in the same street wher it was committed. The captain dyed without any expression of fear, or laying any guilt upon Count Conismarke. Seing me in my coach as he passed by in the cart to execution, he bowed to me with a steady look, as he did to thos he knew amongst the spectatours before he was turned off. In fine his whole carriage, from his first being apprehended till the last, relished more of gallantry then religion.

The part I had in the discovery and prossecution of this murder had made me generally known in the new employment of justice of the peace for Middlesex and Westminster; and ther hapned another thing that assisted to it in some measure, which was the setting up of a manufacture of woole for the maintenance of the poor within St. Martins parish, which was very much oppressed

---

[1] " Born the 17 of September, between the hours of four and five in the afternoon, Anno Domini 1670 " (*Family History*, ii. f. 17).

with them before, and to which my endeavours did much contribute.

March 12   His Highness the Duke of Yorke arrived at Newmarket from Scotland,[1] which he had long endeavoured to get leave to doe, some adviseing the King against it.

16   My Lord Hallifax tould me I must goe with him the next day in his own coach to Newmarket, which I accepted of as a great honour done to me.   He complained to me the same day of some hardships he laid under in the administration of publique concerns from the great indiscretions of some near the King, whom notwithstanding the King very well knew and laughed at in private, yet entrusted in great affairs.

17   Ther being noebody in the coach with his lordship except myselfe, he discoursed with me concerning his son, severall other private matters and some publique, expressing in all he said the wonted goodness, honour and discretion with which he allways both spoake and acted, for certainly ther never lived a man in the world of more witt and judgement then himselfe.   Amongst other things he was saying how free he had been with the Duke of Yorke in the point of changeing his religion, for he had writt to him that except he became a Protestant his friends would be obliged to leave him, like a guarison that one could noe longer defend, and that his Highness answer was that then his case was more desperate then he understood it to be before, for that he could not alter his principals; however, he doubted not but his Highnesse would recieve him with kindness (as he did, and in thruth had great reason to doe, for it was his lordship's industry and arguments in the Hous of Lords chiefly that stem'd the tide as to the Bill of Exclusion in that assembly).

18   We arrived before noon at Newmarket.   That day I was presented to the Duke by my Lord Halifax, who was very kind to me in his expressions.   I recieved an account

---

[1] He came by sea to Yarmouth, where he landed on the 10th, and reached Newmarket on the evening of the 11th.

ther of my Lord Fretzwels being desperately ill, and my
Lord thought fitt to putt the King again in mind of his
promess to me of the goverment of Yorke, least Sir
Thomas Slingsby, who had a design to gett that reversion
(haveing bought my Lord Fretzwels troop of hors some
months before with that intent), should stepp in before
me, he haveing just at that time brought up an address to
his Majesty from the grand jurys and the gentry at the
assizes at Yorke, in abhorrencie of the association found
in the Earl of Shaftsbury's closit.   My Lord stayed ther
till the 26.   I laid in the same lodgeings with his lordship, *March 26*
and was presented to his Royall Highnesse by my Lord,
who, after great outward expressions of respect and kindness to his lordship, and a long private audience given
him, recieved me also very obligeingly.

The King was soe much pleased in the country, and soe
great a lover of the diversions which that place did afford,
that he lett himselfe down from Majesty to the very degree
of a country gentleman.   He mixed himselfe amongst
the croud, allowed every man to speak to him that pleased,
went a-hawkeing in mornings, to cock matches in after-
noons (if ther were noe hors races), and to plays in the
evenings, acted in a barn and by very ordinary Bartlemew-
fair commedians.   My Lord Halifax was not only
pleased to make me the companion of his journey, but to
own me in all companys and take me with him to all
places.   We commonly dined during his lordship's stay
ther either at my Lord Conways, the French embassadors,
or the Duke of Albemarles.   The croud was soe great
here by reasons of the Dukes first arrivall ther and every-
bodys coming to wait upon him, and of severall abhor-
rencies brought up and presented to the King from all
parts of England, that ther was not beds for the company.
My Lord Halifax renewed his request for me to the King
concerning the goverment of Yorke, least others might
have it.   His Majesty said he might rely upon his word
in it.

* 18/39: Thomas Fairfax, 18 March 1681/2; 20/15: H. Marwood, 23 March
1681/2. Both letters describe Slingsby's rush to the king which, according to
Marwood, was to the displeasure of the Whigs.

[1682]

March 27   At our return to London I found his lordship Fretzwell could not live many days, and being dead the 2nd
of Aprill, returnd to Newmarkit with my Lord Hallifax
letter to the King.

April 4   His lordship shewed me the letter before it was sealed,
and ther was in it thes kind expressions, that he did
recommend me to his Majesty for the employment he
had promessed me (my Lord Fretzwell being dead),
which he did the rather bycaus he had heard him express
his good opinion of me soe ofton, and that he knew I was
able to serve his Majesty in that or a greater employment,
for his own private friendship should never prevaile with
him to offer any person to his service that was not in his
judgement qualified for it, &c.

His Majesty, haveing read the letter, tould me that my
Lord Hallifax needed not have writt soe much in my
commendations, for that he did very well remember his
promesse, and was as ready to perform it from his own
disposition to be kind to me as from his lordship's recommending of me.

At my leaveing London I had endeavoured by my
Lord Hallifax interest with my Lord Hide (who was
Chiefe Commissioner of the Treasury) to obtean his
consent that I might petition the King for the same
allowance as governor as my Lord Fretzwell, which was
five hundred pounds per annum. But his lordship
pleaded the Kings poverty, and would not consent to it.
However, I presumd to aske it of his Majesty, who did
graciously bestow not only that upon me, but all the privileges and advantages that his lordship formerly enjoyed

*   as governor, as the use and benefit of the King's hous,
ther called the Mannor, &c.; for upon the first promesse
I only expected 300 l. yearly sallary.[1]   And here I have

---

[1] His commission as governor is dated April 10, 1682 (Dalton, *English
Army Lists*, i. 294).

* The bulk of the letters in bundle 20 deal with Reresby's receipt of his
commission as Governor of York.

reason to praise Almighty God that, considering I had noe great relations or friends to assist or helpe me but thos God had raised up to me by my own industry, noe extraordinary parts, and a very mean figure or person, that he was pleased to give me soe honourable and profitable an imployment, when men much exceeding me both in quality, merit, and in service to the Crown, were ready to starve for bread. I had considerable rivals in this pretention, the Earls of Huntinton, of Scarsdale,[1] and of Burlinton, who being Lord Lieutenant of the West Rideing opposed me in it, lookeing upon it as an encroachment upon his command. My Lord Conniers was another that expected it, Sir Thomas Slingsby and others; but the King stood by me against all pretenders.

I after acquented the Duke with it, who tould me that the King never expressed himselfe kind towards me, that he was not very well pleasd with it, and that he was glad it was in soe good hands.[2]

I had for some days much trouble in this businesse, and chiefly by the means of my Lord Burlinton, who, hearing that the command of the militia within the citty of York was given to me by my commission (he being the lord lieutenant of that place), opposed my haveing that power. But the King ordered it that when they were ther as part of the garison they should be commanded by me, or in case of tumults, insurrections, or other occasion wher I should have need of them for his Majesty's service.

His Highness had a splendid entertainment by the *April* 20 Artilary Company of the citty of London, of which I was that day made free by his Highness the Duke of York's command.

I had the generall congratulations of my acquaintance, 23 which was very great amongst all sorts of people by reason

[1] Robert Leake, the third earl, who had succeeded to the title the previous year.

[2] It is almost certain that Reresby has made some slip in this sentence, but it is not quite clear what he intended to say.

of my being soe long known at Court and my late acting as a justice of peace in Middlesex, wher I had behaved myselfe in some remarkable concerns with all the diligence and integrity I was able to expresse.

This day his Majesty and the Duke, with the Queen, went to continue at Windser.

April 24   My Lord Halifax tould me some of my adversarys, or rather competitors as to my late imployment, had endeavoured to represent me as not haveing any considerable interest in my country, which his lordship knew, he said, to be malicious.

25   His lordship desired me to goe with him and my Lord Hide to dine with my Lord Maior, wher their lordships were recieved with great respect. After dinner we dranke more healths then was usuall.

28   I went to Windser (severall more justices of the peace for Westminster following the day after) to present an address to the King from the grand jury for that libertie and themselves, which the King (and especially the Duke of Yorke) recieved very kindly, ther being some expressions therin of thankes to the King for his love and care of his brother; and his Highness tould me in perticular that he ever expected my assistance in that kind wher it came before me that himselfe should be concerned.

Ther hapned an accident here that I was concerned [in], for my boy knocking at the door of a gentleman wher his lodger was sick in bed, the gentleman's servant that was sick came out and offered some affront by language for the boys knocking soe hard. Another gentleman's man came out upon the alarm, and after that a third, giveing me very ill language, and fetching each of them a stick threatned to strike if I would not depart, and upon my takeing hould of one of them was as good as their word. At the last I was forced to retire, and soon after returning with my friend to learn the names of their masters, to make them give me satisfaction, they prooved to be two

of her Majestys priests. The next day the priests sent
their servants to be dealt with as I should appoint, which
was all the reparation to be expected from persons of their
function.

I returned for London.   *April* 30

The Duke of Yorke returned for Scotland by sea, and *May* 3
I went with my Lord Faukland,[1] my Lord Lexinton[2] and
others in my Lord's barge down with the Duke, till he
went abord his yatt. He then proposed to return and
bring the Duchesse with him (then with child) in a month's
time.

I found at this time that my only sister, who was then
about forty years of age and had lived with the reputation
of a discreet woeman, findeing that noe better fortune did
offer itselfe (for she was not hansome), was very near being
married to an Irishman, who had raised himselfe from a
common souldier to the degree of a lieutenant in the
French army, but had little or noe estate but the pay of a
reformd officer. I did all I could to prevent a misfortune
of this kind both to herselfe and her family, and by threats
of what I would do to her, and by disparagements of her
gallant, I thought I had prevaild with her to thinke of
him noe more, when the next day I found (by his sending
a gentleman to enquire of me and my brother the captain,
who it was that had informd us of such reports to his
prejudice) she held a correspondencie yet with him, and
tould him what we had said of him. We tould him we 4
were not to name authors, but should be able to proove
both his meanesse of estate and his once haveing been a
common souldier, and that I would never consent to her
marriage with him; and the same day I so far prevaild
with her as to leave her lodgeings and to come and protect
herselfe in my hous. After this I hourly expected to
hear further from him, for the man was brave, and had

---

[1] Anthony Cary, fifth Viscount Falkland, grandson of the more famous
Lucius, second Viscount, who fell at Newbury.

[2] Robert Sutton, second Baron Lexington.

kild a gentleman in a duel in France, one Hudson. At the last he writt severall letters to her, in one of which, that came to my hand, he said he knew how to ressent it from thos that should hinder his seeing her. However, he never took that cours, and I prevailed with her to goe with me into Yorkshire.

May 9   I had a long discours with my Lord Halifax as to severall concerns. I found he was very steddy for a Parlament, and thought the Duke had gott noe advantage in the King's good opinion by his journey into England. Nor indeed were the Kings own friends much pleased with it; but his servants, that gained by his being here, put him upon it.

10   Came the news that his Highnesse had like to have been cast away in his journey to Scotland. The ship was lost by running upon the sands in Yarmouth Road, and severall of the passengers lost; but this was soon after contradicted.

That day I took the oaths as governor of Yorke and justice of the peace within the liberty of St. Peters in Yorke. I was in all thes commissions at that time, viz., as governor of Yorke, governor of Burlinton, captain of a troop of hors in the West Riding of the county of Yorke, justice of the peace for that rideing, for Middlesex, for Westminster, and the liberty of St. Peters within the citty of Yorke, as also deputy lieutenant for the said West Rideing.

The same day, going to dine with the Earl of Ailsbury (my wife and eldest daughter being in the coach), the pearch broake, and two footmen behind it fell under the coach and were in danger of being killed, but by Gods mercy sustained noe great harm.

12   Came the account that the ship called the *Glocester* (a third rate in which the Duke went for Scotland) was cast away on Yarmouth sandes,[1] and all the passengers, save the Duke and about 160 persons. Among thos that

[1] May 6.

were lost was my Lord O'Brian,[1] Lord Roxbrough,[2] Mr.
Hide,[3] my Lord Clarendon's brother; all which prooved
too true.

The envy of my being preferred to the goverment of
Yorke showed itselfe by severall little insinuations of thos
that apprehended themselves fitter for it, which my Lord
Halifax tould me he had recieved from third handes;
but (which was as great an obligation as his first endeavours to obtean it) he said he must ever make a difference
of men by his own tryall, and not by the opinions they had
of themselves.

Waiting upon my Lord Halifax, he tould me that the *May 22*
day before, being Sunday, the Duke of Monmoth came
to him after prayers, and asked him if the report was true
that his lordship had advised his Majesty in Councill that
a proclamation should be issued out forbidding all people
to keep him company; that his lordship replyed he was
not obliged to tell him whether he did or not; to which
the Duke said that ther needed noe proclamation to
prohibit his keeping his lordship company, and that if it
were in another place he would have said more to him;
and soe they parted. The Duke behaved himselfe very
foolishly in this, both as to the wise and the gallant part,
for it must needs disoblige the King to question a privy
councillor for the advice that he gives him in Council, and
if he intended a quarrell he should have chosen another
place to have spoaken in, and have said more or nothing
at all. And soe I tould his lordship, offering to serve
him with my life if any more hapned upon it; but his
lordship replyed, if that were he would make use of somebody that he esteemed lesse then he did me, but did not

---

[1] Donatus, Lord O'Brien, grandson of Henry O'Brien, seventh Earl of
Thomond.

[2] Robert Ker, third Earl of Roxburgh.

[3] James Hyde. What must be almost his last letter, written from the
Downs on May 3 to Lord Hyde, is printed in Singer, *Clarendon Correspondence*, i. 67.

concieve himselfe obliged to fight upon that account, though he should be ready to defend himselfe, for he carryed a sword by his side.

May 23 Ther was a Councill held at Hamton Court, wher my Lord Halifax tould me (as soon as the Councel rise) that an order had ther passed to this effect, that forasmuch as the Duke of Monmoth had used some threatning speeches to a member of that board, in relation to something said in Council to his Majesty, his Majesty did consider it as an unmannerly insolence against himselfe, and did therfore charge all his servants, and such as had any dependency upon him, not [to] keep company with or frequent the said Duke of Monmoth for the future.

26 Since the takeing of my sister into my hous to prevent her undoing by her marrying the Irish lieutenant I had heard nothing from him, but suspected she did yet keep a secret correspondencie with him contrary to her ofton repeated assurances to the contrary, and which confirmed me the more was that upon this day at evening he was seen to come very drunke before my door, and to stand gazeing at the windows for a sight of his mistriss; but some person in the room shutting the window, he pulled down some white railes that stood on one side of the door, and soe departed.

At my return home I found my wife and family in disorder, fearing the due ressentment I ought to have of such an action, for this foolish behaviour of his was not only publique to the family but the whole street, and therfore sent my brother to him to tell him that what he had done to my hous I considered as done to myselfe, and therfore expected from him the satisfaction of a gentleman, which was to meet me with his sword and his friend behind Southamton Hous that day at two in the afternoon, for he haveing changed his lodgeing, my brother could not

27 find him till near ten a clock upon the 27th. When my brother came to him he would not own the fact, but said if I would have him to fight he would meet me at the time

and place; but before we could meet his carriage was soe publique that somebody gave notice of it to my Lord Martiall, who sent a sergiant-at-arms and secured him in his lodgeing, and after some time found me at my brother's and secured me also.

The next day he denyed that it was he that did the thing (for he was asshamed of it, such things, wher a man hath a quarrell, not being fitt to be done to houses, but persons, not oponly, but privately), or if he did it he said he was drunk, not knowing what he did, and asked pardon; upon which I owned I had sufficient satisfaction, and my Lord took both our engagements to stirr noe more in that matter. I made all the improovements I could of this soe ill carriage of the lieutenants to my sister towards not only myselfe but her, to lessen her kindness to him, which she then seemd to ressent.

My Lord Halifax sent for me to goe in the coach with *May* 28 him and my Lord Hide to Windser, but being under restraint (as before declared) I could not goe then.

Which was the Kings birthday, I followed after; but 29 the joy usually expressed on that day was much dampt by the Kings being not well, of which he recovered in two days to the joy of the nation.

I took my leave of the King, intending speedily for *June* 1 Yorkshire, who was very kind to me in his expressions. I came from Windser in coach with my Lord Halifax and Mr. Seamure.

I took leave of the Duke and Duchesse, then arrived 2 from Scotland. The Duke tould me that he confided in me as much as any of the King's subjects, and doubted not of my respects towards him. The day after they went to Windser.

I had a long discours with my Lord Halifax, wher I 3 offered him my advice that I feared he was too frank with some joined with him in business and in the Kings favour, that did betray him; and that he should keep himselfe under more reserve if possible. He answered he knew it, but could not well avoid that freedom in businesse, but hoped his integrity would support him.   I had severall directions from him at the same time how to comport myselfe in the north, not soe fitt to be here inserted.

Some days were spent to prepare for my journey, till *June* 12 the 12th of June I went with my wife, sister, and my family to Thriberge, wher by Gods mercy I arrived safely, 16 being met by some friends by the way upon the 16, wher I found my affairs in pritty good condition, and my nighbours for the most part well pleased with the honour his Majesty had done me in giveing me the command of 26 Yorke.   I stayed ther to settle my affairs till the 26, that I went to take possession of my goverment at Yorke.

Some gentlemen in the nighbourhood, as well as thos more remote, had sent to know if their accompanying me to Yorke would be acceptable, which as I refused from noe gentlemen soe I desired from none, but was much surprized when I found myselfe mett upon the road by the high sheriff of the county[1] and severall gentlemen, all the bourough men of Audbrough, and citizens of Yorke to the nomber of near 400.   At Yorke ther was then but one company of foot, which was drawn out of the town; and the canon of Clifford's Tower was discharged to recieve me.   That night I treated a great part of the company at supper, haveing sent some venason and made preparation before in two houses.

27   I went to Cliffords Tower to take possession of it, with the high sheriff, Sir Michael Wharton,[2] Sir Henry Marwood and severall other gentlemen, which I found in pritty good condition as to repairs and stoors (pouder only excepted and canon).   I went afterwards to wait on my Lord Maior[3] and to show him my commission.   I tould him I understood that in my Lord Frezwels time the civill power had something entrenched upon the military,

1 William Lowther of Swillington.
2 Of Beverley, Yorkshire ; knighted on June 30, 1666.
3 John Wood.

which I should not suffer for the time to come; that if the souldiers committed capitall crimes, as treason or felony, I was willing (notice being first given to me) to deliver them up to justice; but for lesse crimes, as batteries, quarrels, or smaller misdemeaners, I expected complaint to be made to me, and to have the punishment of them myselfe; which his lordship confessed to be reasonable, though not long before he had bound the officer that was deputy governour to the peace. I tould his lordship further that I heard severall things were frequently said and acted to the prejudice of his Majestys service, which I desired he would take care to prevent for the future, otherwise I should be bound to represent it to the King; and that I thought this the best method of dealing frankely with his lordship, and of telling him what I designed to doe to keep a good understanding with him, with much more to the same effect.

His lordship took all very well, tould me he was obliged to me for my open and ingennious proceeding, said he did take notice of my authority and would pay all due respect to it, that what I seemed to insist upon appeared but reasonable, and that citty was much obliged to the King for giveing them a governor of their own country, &c. The thruth is that York was at that time one of the most factious towns of the kingdome, and began to fear (should the *quo warranto* succeed against the charter of London)[1] that their own was not a little in danger.

I stayed at the Mannour (wher I made all the preparation soe ruinous a place was capable of to recieve my family, which I designed to bring with me the next time) till July the 3rd. All thos days I returnd the visits of *July 3* thos that came to see me or to meet me at my comming

---

[1] The attack upon municipal self-government in England, which was to be one of the features of the closing years of Charles's reign, had been begun in the previous December with the issue of a writ of *quo warranto* requiring the city of London to justify the liberties it exercised.

to town, and kept a table for all thos that did me the favour to dine with me during my stay ther.

Before my going to York the smiths of Hallamshire came to desire my assistance as to the excuseing them from payment of the hearth duty for their smyths forges, which the King's officers began again to demand of them. They said that in my absence they had applyed themselves to other justices without successe, and were very pressing that I would relieve them as I had formerly done. The thruth is, tho other gentlemen had declined them, I was satisfyed that the law was for them; but for me to be active against the King's officers in the matter of his revenue, when others had desisted, I feared might sett me ill with the Lords of the Treasury, who might represent it ill to the King. However, thinkeing it just to helpe them, I writt to my Lord Hallifax, setting forth the justice of their caus, and desireing that as the King's officers had for some years forborn collecting the duty upon smiths forges within that precinct, partly bycaus the law was not very clear in the point, and partly out of consideration of their poverty, his lordship would pleas to intercede to his Majesty that they might still be excused. I used severall other reasons to enforce this, as the reputation it would be to his lordship amongst his contrimen to doe noe less then my Lord Danby had done before upon the same occasion; that it was better they should have the obligation of it to the King then to the justices of the peace, who perhaps might at the last be brought to relieve them; that it was but some 60 l. yearly loss to the King, and the payment of it might ruin some hundreds of persons.

July 4   I recieved an answer from my Lord Halifax, which gave me some hopes that some stop would be putt to the collecting of this duty upon them.[1]

12   I made a visit to the Duke of Newcastle, who enter-

[1] Reresby received Halifax's letter on his return to Thrybergh on July 4. His reply acknowledging it, dated Thrybergh, July 5, 1682, is preserved among the Spencer MSS.

tained me with great kindness for two days. I had some
affairs to discours with him from my Lord Halifax, in
which I recieved all satisfaction. He gave me a mair and
foale at our parting of his own breed.

His Grace came with me to Rotherham, wher we made *July* 15
also a visit to the Duke of Norfolke, lately comd into the
country with intention to build at the college ther,[1] it
being his Duchesse her jointure.

Was our sessions at Rotherham, wher I gave the charge 18
to the jury. The same day the Duke of Norfolke invited
me and all the rest of the justices to dinner. We were
eight ther in nomber, viz., Sir Henry Marwood, Sir
Michael Wentworth of Woolley,[2] Sir Raufe Knight,[3] Mr.
Edmonds, Mr. Blythman, Mr. Ramsden,[4] Mr. Gysop,[5]
and myselfe. The laws haveing been put more vigorously
in execution against nonconformists of late than hereto-   *
fore, Mr. Gysop (a known favourer of dissenters) made
some scruple to joine with us in that proceeding. After a
long debate in a private room to satisfie his doubts in that
point, he cast some reflexions on the proceedings of the
justices in their former sessions, as well as on thos ther
present, declareing that all their proceedings and warrants
were illegall; to which I replyed that it was something
saucy to arraign soe many gentlemen of quality concerned
in the commission of the peace for his single opinion.[6]

[1] Jesus College, founded in 1483 by Thomas Scot, otherwise known as
Thomas Rotherham, Archbishop of York.

[2] Son of John Wentworth of Woolley.

[3] Sir Ralph Knight of Langold, Yorkshire.

[4] John Ramsden, Sheriff of Yorkshire in 1673.

[5] Francis Jessop of Broomhall, Yorkshire.

[6] A more intelligible account of the preliminaries leading to this dispute
is contained in a letter from Reresby to Halifax, dated " July the 19,
Thriberge," preserved among the Spencer MSS. :
 . . . Most of our business of sessions was to take the returns of constables
in persuance to warrants granted by all the justices of the peace of this
rideing (except Mr. Gysop and some few more that absented themselves
on purpas) in three former sessions what conventicles were kept within

* Cf. J. Hunter, *The life of Oliver Heywood One of the Founders of the
Presbyterian Congregation in the County of York 1630–1702* (1842), p. 293.
This account, which likewise loses nothing in the telling, differs slightly in its
ending. 'Sir John Reresby having given Mr. Jessop a wound on the cheek by a
leadstandish, which he threw at him, and was only prevented from attacking
him with his rapier by Mr. Jessop's son, then a stripling of fifteen.'

He stood up and retorted with great insolency, You are very impudent. At which words I took up a leaden standish (he sitting behind a table and at some distance from me) and threw it at his face, wher the edge lighting upon his cheek cutt it quite thorow. We after this drew our swords and I went into the middle of the chamber, but the company prevented his following of me and afterwards reconciled us.[1]

I was sorry for this accident, it hapning at a sessions of the peace, but the provocation could not be passed over. At the same place I acquainted the cutlers with my Lord

their respective precincts, and the names of the teachers and persons resorting to them. . . . Mr. Gysop hath ever had a ressentment of my gaining an address from Sheffield and Hallamshire (that being his own nest), when he publiquely refused to sign it himselfe, saying he would not intermeddle in any disputes twixt his father and mother (meaning the King and Parlament), and endeavoured to prevent it in others. Now the constables of Sheffield (wher ther are severall conventicles) neglected to make a return of the aforesaid warrants ; and Mr. Gysop had refused to bind them over to answer that omission at this sessions, although he was impowred by a bench warrant soe to doe, and upon the debate of this proceeding did justifie himselfe and his godly party in what either he or they had done in opposition to seven justices of the peace then present.

When we could not fairly persuade him to be of our opinion I tould him he would doe well to write his own down, and we would have it consulted above whether he or we were in the right. He replyed in great heat he understood very well wher and how I consulted above. I confess I was not satisfyed with his reply, thinking it reflected further then upon myselfe, however only answered that I as well understood how he consulted underneath. Soon after some further debate as to the warrant and matter before us he plainly tould us that all the proceedings against the nonconformists and the warrants granted on that occasion were illegall. I said I was not here when anything was done in that concern, but it looked something saucy to arraign all the justices of the peace and all the proceedings of soe many sessions upon his own single opinion.

[1] " He confessing the justices of the peace were in the right, then drinkeing to me, saying he was sorry for his passion, and I declaring that then I was sorry for mine." Reresby concludes his letter : " My Lord, I only acquaint your Lordship with this that you may not be preposest by any false story, for thus I have it agreed to by all the justices then present under their hands ; and I beg that noe use may be made of it to his prejudice either by his being turnd out of commission of the peace or otherwise."

Halifax his directions, which were to informe them that he had in some measure prevailed that they should be excused from paying the duty of hearth-mony for their smiths forges, and that he would doe them what kindness laid in his power, either in that or any other concern.

I remooved with my family to Yorke, wher I continued *July* 21 some weeks. The assizes began the 26, wher ther was 26 nothing very memorable that passed more then the usuall affairs of that time. I kept a table. The high sheriff and most of the gentlemen of quality in town dined with me.

The judges went out of town upon Fryday the 4th.   *Aug.* 4

The guarison was much out of order by reason he that was captain of the foot company ther was a man of plesure, and remiss in either doing duty himselfe or seing it done by others. I went often upon the guard myselfe, caused a list of thos that mounted the main guard, or that of Cliffords Tower, to be dayly brought to me. I took exact care in the locking of the citty and castle gates, and brought matters to an indifferent good pass in a short time, both as to the repairs and furnishing of the Mannour as well as the other, though the latter was of great charge to me.

I heard at this time that my Lord Sunderland and Halifax were reconciled, which much surprized me, noe two men haveing been more bitter the one against the other, the relation between them (for my Lord Hallifax married the sister of my Lord Sunderland and had issue by her) softning, it seems, thos hard opinions they had one of another. At this time I recieved the good news that my Lord Halifax, my good and excellent lord, was made Marquisse Halifax.[1]

Ther hapned a great dispute between the high sheriff and me; the occasion of it was this. The place called 18 * Cliffords Tower, wher the stoors and magazins are, being named as part of the guarison of Yorke in my commission, I understood that ther was noe way to it but thorow the

---

[1] The patent is dated August 17.

* See Mary Geiter, 'Sir John Reresby and the Revolution of 1688', *Northern History* (1989), xxv.

Castle of Yorke, or Castle garth, within which compass
the geole for the county was then kept, and the keys of
the Castle yeard were in the custody of the sheriff or his
geoler.   I was empoured by my commission to take the
keys of the guarison and to keep them upon the guard in
the night, and had all thos of the citty; but the sheriff
claimd a prescription for the keeping of thes for the
security of his geole (my predecessor my Lord Fretzwell
haveing been soe remisse as not to assert his right in this
perticular).   But findeing I had a right to them, not only
by my commission but from the reason of the thing (noe
man haveing a command but he must have a way to it),
I demanded the keys.   The sheriff denys them.   I putt
other locks upon the gates.   The sheriff orders them to
be taken off.   I order sentinels to be sett at the doors to
secure the passage.   The sheriff complains of it to the
county, and writes a letter calling all the gentlemen
togather by a generall summons to meet him at Yorke
upon the 29 of August to advise him what to doe in this
case, pretending it an invasion by me upon the right of
the country.

Now this was very ill advised, for it appeared a kind of
appeling from the King (by whos commission I acted)
to the country, when noebody ought properly to determin it but the King from whom both the sheriff and myselfe derived our power.   And truly soe the country
seemed to believe, for partly I soppose for that reason,
and partly from the good opinion that the gentlemen had
of me in not being one to pretend to more then what was
my due in this or any other kind, instead of some hundreds
of gentlemen that the sheriff expected ther came not
twenty, and most of them at my request.   When they
were mett I, being invited to dinner by the sheriff, went
to them, tould them I came not as the governor of Yorke
but as a gentleman of the country, nor to appeale to them
as judges in the case, for noebody could be that but his
Majesty, but that by way of discours I would inform them

what I had done and my reasons for soe doing.   After a narrative of near an hour I gave them soe full satisfaction for my claim that they either all confessed that it was *coram non judice* and not their business, or that I had done but my duty, which putt the sheriff soe far out of his measures that we came to this agreement, that the keys of the great gate should be delivered up to me, and another also in dispute walled up till the Kings pleasure was fully known, and a third likewise in question should continue in the power of the sheriff till then.

I gave my Lord Halifax an account of this proceeding all along, as the sheriff did also, but he had soe possessed his lordship with it that he seemed to wish I had not begun it.   However [he] writt me word that if I did judge it soe immediately nescessary for the Kings service and the safety of the place, that he would assist me in my claim all he could.   At the same time he sent me another letter enclosed to the high sherif unsealed (to be sent to him when I had seen the contents as if it had comd another way), in which ther were thes words, that he did confess the calling of the gentlemen of the county togather upon this occasion to him seemed something extraordinary, which he hoped would make him the more carefull that noe ill effect might come of it, either in relation to his Majesty's service or the respect which was due to Sir John Reresby in the station wher he was under the King. I had after this another letter from his lordship, wherin he sayd that he would stand by me if I was in the right of this dispute, and bring me off fairly if I was in the wrong.

I sent up the copies of severall letters to his lordship *Sept. 2* written to me by gentlemen of the country, wherby they seemd to condemn the sheriff in his way of proceeding of calling the country togather in that manner.   I sent him five affidavits sworn to before a Master of Chancery by persons of credit, purporting that it had been the custome for the keys of the three doors in dispute to be delivered up to the Tower every night in the time of such as were governors of Yorke before my Lord Frezwell and in the begining of his time also.

Sept. 6 The only answer I recieved soon after was that I haveing had soe much the advantage in this dispute (with which his lordship was wel satisfyed, and with my whole proceeding in that affair), that he thought best not to trouble the King with any further determination of it at present, especially since the sherif found himselfe sufficiently disappointed in his claim and in the country's adhearing to him therin.

7 The Cutlers held their annual feast at Sheffield, to which (by the industry of Mr. Gysop) I was not invited. This he did not only out of private revenge, but for a publique end, that he might have a better opportunity to persuade them that they had the obligation rather to my Lord Clifford for their late deliverence from paying hearthmony for their forges then to me, my Lord Clifford being ther present, and being brother to my Lord Hide, the chiefe Lord Commissioner of the Tresury. By this art he hoped to engage them to voat for my Lord Clifford and my Lord Fairfax should a Parlament be called, in opposition to Sir John Kay, who was my friend. Upon this I gave over being soe industrious to helpe so ungratefull a sort of people, and soon after came a letter that the said forges were to pay the duty as well as other hearths (only the poorest sort of cutlers were to be excused), which did not pleas them, they haveing been generally excused heretofore by my intercession.

I returned to Thriberge from Yorke the 12th.

14 I mustered and exercized my troop at Rotherham, wher severall gentlemen mett me and dined with me that day.

25 I went to take leave of the Duke of Norfolke at Rotherham, who was then going for London, who parted with me very kindely, calling me his nearest and best nighbour. He tould me some news of confidence from above which I had heard before, though I seemed not to know it.[1]

---

[1] Possibly a reference to the appointment of Halifax as Lord Privy Seal, which followed on October 25.

My Lord Halifax haveing writt to me to sound my Lord *Sept.* 28
Duke of Newcastle if he was willing the former treaty
between my Lord Eland, his son, and my Lady Catharin
should be renewed, I went to wait on his Grace (carrying
my wife to doe her duty to the Duchesse), wher I stayed
till October the 1st. I found the Duke had a mind to *Oct.* 1
the thing, but thought it fitt it should begin without his
declareing himselfe one way or other, least it might seem
to be desired on the lady's side.

The Duke gave me the best mair and foall of his whole
breed, which he had promessed me before. His Grace
went September the 30 to Nottingham, being lord lieutenant of the county, to appease the disorders ther, two
maiors being sworn upon the grant of a new charter from
the King (the old one being delivered up), one by the
factious party pretending the old charter was yet in force,
the other by the loyall one.

October the first I recieved the sad news of an honest,
worthy, and brave gentleman's death, my lieutenant to
my militia troop of hors and my perticular friend. He had
only this fault, that he was too subject to the bottle; and
haveing been drinkeing with my Lord Castleton (ther
being some former falling out between them), the provocation was soe great from the lord that Mr. Batty (for
soe was his name) challenged him into my Lord's own
garden, wher they went and fought, and wher this poor
gentleman was killed.

I went to the sessions at Wakefield, wher we were ten 5
justices of the peace, and I gave the charge. Mr.
Peebles (whom I had before recommended to my Lord
Halifax to be made a justice of the peace) accepted of
being lieutenant to my troop instead of Mr. Batty, killed
the week before by my Lord Castleton.

In my return from Wakefield by Gods mercy I escaped 7
a great danger, my hors falling with me upon the edge of
a precipice; but I, throwing myselfe from my hors the
other way, gott noe great harm, and gave my hors the

opportunity to recover himselfe, though his hinder legs were already of the side of the banke.

Oct. 8　I was godfather to Mr. Turner's first son, chiefe stuard to the Marquiss of Halifax, who lived at Wakefield. The child's name was John.

10　I recieved a letter of thankes from the Marquiss of Halifax as to the management of the treaty aforesaid with the Duke of Newcastle, though I could not effect the setting on it on foot. However I sounded the Dukes thoughts and inclinations in the thinge as from myselfe, and in that manner that he did not in the least believe that I did it by any commission from the Marquisse, soe that upon the whole matter I found the Duke would give nothing with his daghter in present, but declared she should be worth 60,000 l. at his death or secound marriage, in case he survived his Duchesse and married again. But this did not satisfie the Marquisse, and yet he was pleased to find the utmost of what would be done without being seen to aske it, as appears by his lordship's letter to me *in hæc verba*:—I am to give you such thankes as are due to one that acteth not only as a kind friend but a wise one, in everything that is recommended to you. The part you lately undertook was of such a nature, both soe nice in itselfe and in respect of thos you had to deale with, that I know very few besides yourselfe that are capable of handling it in such a manner. But after this I must tell you that, let the thing in its selfe be never soe adviseable, the means of attaining it are soe uncertain, the partys concerned (to use noe harsher term) soe wonderfull, the incomparable mixture of hott and could, kind and jealous, soe very extraordinary, and to me soe extreamly discourageing, [that] I (who seldome have thought anything an equall price for a difficulty) cannot allowe myselfe to persue it any further, &c.

I now began to be sensible that though ther were few in the West Rideing that applyed themselves to the doing of the busines of the country, either as deputy lieutenant or justice of the peace, with more diligence then myselfe, it was hard for one to give the same satisfaction, now that I had soe great a marke of the Kings favour as the goverment of Yorke, as heretofore, &c. My superiours were secretly displeased that I had got that which they thought they deserved before me, my equals were soe too that I had gott before them by haveing the honour of that command, and both were jealous that whatever business was done wher I was present would be rather attributed to my conduct then theirs; and my inferiours (especially thos that were not friends to the Court) were jealous, though I acted with the same integrity between the King and the country, that I too much inclined to that interest. At the same time I had intimation from a privy councellor above that the Court was jealous that I too much adheared to the interest of the country in some matters of the Kings revenue which were judicially brought before me, and I was chidden softly by my Lord Hallifax in a letter for the same thing; soe that, finding it very difficult to steer an even cours amongst soe many severall and different persons and interests, I resolved first to keep the honour of my employment and the good opinion of my master and friends above (both for my own advantage and that of others that sought to me) as long as I justly and honestly could; and at the same time to doe country business, but only defensively and as it was brought to me, according to my conscience; declineing, however, to seek for it, or to rival thos in their ambition who had noe greater then to be esteemed leading men at a country sessions.

Being at Doncaster with two other deputy lieutenants *Oct.* 17 to settle some matters and to hear complaints relateing to the militia, I recieved a letter from Colonel Leg, Master of the Ordinance, intimating that Sir Christofer Musgrave, Lieutenant of the Ordinance,[1] was ordered to

[1] Third son of Sir Philip Musgrave of Edenhall, Westmoreland. He was made Lieutenant of the Ordnance in 1681, and succeeded his elder brother as fourth baronet in 1687.

come down to Yorke by the King to take a vewe of the condition of that guarison, which occasioned my speedy journey to that place. I gott thether early the next day, and waiting upon the lieutenant, he tooke the dimension and scituation of the Tower and Castle by the helpe of a survayer brought with him to that purpas, took an account of the stoors and ammunition in Cliffords Tower, and tould me the King intended we should be better supplyed, and that his Majesty would be at the charge to repair the defects of the Tower (especially the parapet which was too weake), and to bring the river about it.

Oct. 19   I returned home to Thriberge.

Captain Bristow, captain-lieutenant to my Lord Mougraves (the colonell of the regiments) own company,[1] haveing contracted a friendship with Mr. Butler,[2] the then geoler, had rather seemed to adhear to him then me in the late contraversie concerning the keys (which I ressented, hee being under my command), and to gratifie his friend had casheerd one Boldock, the gunner of Cliffords Tower, out of his company for in thruth haveing been faithfull for me in that business, though he pretended other causes. Ther was also one Newman, a servant of Butlers, who, for giveing me some information as to the custome of keeping the keys which was against his master, was put out of his service. Upon notice hereoff, being obliged to prevent any man's suffering if possible that had endeavoured to doe me service, I sent and writt to the captain to restoor the former to his place, and to list the secound in his company also, ther being a vacancy, which he evaded as modestly as he could.

Nov. 20   I returned to Yorke, wher I pressed the thing home, and not without some heat caused him to submitt to it, but findeing him of a troublesome temper desired above that his company might be exchanged for another, which

---

[1] John Bristow, lieutenant in charge of the company of which the colonel was nominally captain.

[2] Marmaduke Butler.

* Reresby recorded that the lord lieutenant took the dimensions the next day, i.e. 18 October, whereas in fact he did so on the 19th. Stafford R.O. Dartmouth MSS. D (W) 1778/V/III/0/2.

was granted, for I soon after recieved the King's orders for recieveing Captain Collenwoods[1] company from Hull, and the sending of that to that guarison.

My Lord Mougrave was now disgraced at Court for makeing some applications to my Lady Ann Steward, the Duke of Yorkes daughter, and suspicion of ad-hearing to the Duke of Monmoths interest. He had great employments at Court, which were disposed of after this manner: his bedchamber's place to the Earl of Feathersham, his goverment of Hull to my Lord Windser, Earl of Plymoth,[2] his lieutenancy of the East Riding to the Duke of Sommerset, and his regiment of foot to my Lord Chesterfield,[3] &c.

The sheriffs of Yorke being then chosen, I was invited to their feast with my Lord Maior, the aldermen and their wives, with a great deal of other company. My Lord and I sate at the upper end of the table, and the ladys below us. I did indeavour upon this occasion to deport myselfe with all the good humour and civility to the cittizens that was possible, the former animositys between the town and the guarison before my time, as well as a difference in principles, haveing made them strange the one towards the other; in which I soe well succeeded that I did not only obtean great expressions of kindness from them that day but some effects of it afterwards. Indeed the conjuncture of affairs at that time did in some measure helpe towards it, the Kings interest encreaseing every day both in London and the country. A loyall Lord Maior was this year chosen for the citty of London,[4] and two very good sheriffs.[5] My Lord Shaftsbury stole over sea into

[1] Francis Collingwood, captain in the Holland Regiment.

[2] Thomas Windsor, seventh Baron Windsor of Stanwell, was created Earl of Plymouth a few weeks after his appointment as Governor of Hull.

[3] Philip Stanhope, second Earl of Chesterfield.

[4] Sir William Pritchard. His election, which was carried only after a scrutiny, was regarded as a great triumph for the Court.

[5] Dudley North and Peter Rich.

Holland, and the charter of London was likely to stoop to the *quo warranto* brought against it.

Some few days after, my Lord Maior invited me to dinner, and my officers, with what company I would bring with me, and gave us a great entertainment. Severall aldermen and the Recorder did also invite me.

Nov. 28   I invited the sheriff of the citty, some aldermen, and the militia officers ther to dine with me, wher I gave them a good dinner and plenty of wine at the Manour, with musick, which was very excellent in that town at that time.

At my first being governor of Yorke the officers of five companys of foot within that place, of Sir Thomas Slingsby's regiment, were soe angry that Sir Thomas was not made governor that some of them said, when they heard that I had the command of the militia (which they were) within Yorke as well as of the standing force, that they would rather lay down their commissions than be commanded by me. At this time, being better acquainted, they changed their note, professing oponly that they did desire nothing more then an opportunity to venter their lives under me. And I heard after, that when they mett at their club, which they did once every week, they always drank my health before their colonels, and were kind to me in their discourse.

Dec. 2   Captain Bristow's company mutined upon the main guard, upon the occasion of some arrears due to them from the captain, as to which I must confess the captain was not to blame, the said arrears not being in his handes, but in his that commanded that company before. Complaint being made to me that one of them had drawn his sword upon the sargiant for endeavouring to quell them, I sent for the souldier, who denyed to obay orders, and the corporall (that commanded the guard) to seize him (all the rest of the company takeing their parts and saying if one suffered they would all fare alike). Haveing notice of this, I rose from dinner and went immediately with the inseign and my own servants to the guard, wher findeing them togather I seized the mutineer by the throat, took away his arms (with the corporall and two more of the ringleaders), committed them all four to the dungion for that night and the next day, and then cassheered the chiefe of them. The rest (submitting themselves and begging pardon by petition, I was willing to pardon) return'd to their duty. In such cases the remedie must be speedy and resolute.

Mr. Pudsey,[1] being appointed high sheriff of the county of Yorke for the ensuing year, came down then. The first thing he did was to quarrell with Mr. Butler, the former geoler, upon the subject of price, another offering 200 l. more to be soe this year then he was willing to give. I confesse I did not endeavour to reconcile this difference, knowing Butler to be of a turbulant and saucy temper. Besides, my Lord Duke of Newcastle had writt to the sheriff at my instance not to give too much credit to such officers of the late sheriff as had endeavoured to make a difference between him and me. In fine, all this with some other circumstances wrought soe well togather that Butler was putt out from being geoler, and the sherif was soe kind and reasonable that he delivered up to me the keys of the third gate of the Castle, that being the only thing remaining in dispute between the King and the county, or between the late sheriff and me. *Dec. 2*

The citty of Yorke had been more remarkable then most in England for height of faction; but finding that some of the leaders were willing to come off, I had upon the 4 of December some private discours with Alderman Ramsden, one of the most witt of the whole fraternity. I sett the danger soe well before him (except they made some speedy signs of repentance for their former carriage) that he confessed he was sensible of their errour as to many perticulars, viz., in choosing soe ofton the same representatives in Parlament when they knew how ungratefull it was to the King, in their unhansome reception *4*

[1] Ambrose Pudsey.

of the Duke of York when he passed thorow their citty, in petitioning for a Parlament but in neither addressing nor abhorring; but when that was done, feared their offence was too great for pardon, except they obteaned it at the price of their charter, which they were not willing to surrender. I asked him what he thought the citty might be persuaded to doe less then that. He said three things, if they would be accepted:

1. To lay aside Alderman Edward Tomson from being Lord Maior, to whom it came in cours for the next year (a peevish antimonarchicall fellow), provided his Majesty would command it by letter.

2. To choos a new high stuard, and to offer it to his Royall Highnes, in the place of their old one, the Duke of Buckingham (whom they would putt out), or to his lordship, should his Highness not accept it.

3. To elect better members of Parlament for that citty when ther should be occasion.

Thes things, he tould me, were fesible would they be recieved, which I presently writt to my Marquis of Halifax concerning.[1]

Dec. 7   I returned from Yorke (a place then full of company, my Lord Carlisle and many other families being comd to winter ther) to keep Christmas at Thriberge.

13   Hearing the sad news that the Duchesse of Albemarl was gone distracted (eldest daughter to the Duke of Newcastle), I went to condole with him at Welbeck, wher I found him very sensibly afflicted for soe great a misfortune.

20   I recieved a letter from the Marquiss of Halifax, wherin he gave me his thoughts that though he approoved the laying Alderman Tompson aside from being Lord Maior (as had been proposed), yet he thought it not safe to venture the King's letter upon it to the corporation except the successe was absolutely certain, and the rather

[1] An undated account of the situation at York, sent by Reresby to Halifax about this time, is printed *infra*, p. 579.

bycaus affairs went soe well above (especially that of the
quo warranto against the City charter) that all other
corporations would truckle, and should the Kings letter
not be considered it would rebound in the face of the
Court, and be an encouragement to that party; as to the
second, which was the choosing his Highness for their
high stuard, he did judge it unfitt for him upon severall
accounts, but for himselfe (if it were soe done as that it
should not seem to be desired by his lordship and that it
appeared, should the thing miscarry, that he had a considerable nomber of friends for him therin) he was content
to attempt it, and would putt himselfe and the management of it to me, useing this compliment, that he knew
himselfe to be in very good hands as to this affair if I
undertook it.

I returned him this answer, that I would not undertake
it but under such cautions as his lordship directed.

I recieved his Majestys order to admitt of the Majors[1] *Dec.* 21
company of my Lord Chesterfields regiment instead of
Captain Collinwoods (formerly designed) into the guarison of Yorke, and a very kind letter from the Earl of
Chesterfield as to my care in quelling the mutinie of his
own company.

I kept Christmas at Thriberge, which it was formerly 24
the custome to observe with great mirth and ceremony,
but was much lessened, few keeping up the custome of it
in thos parts at that time but myselfe when I was at
Thriberge. The manner of it for this year was thus:

Sunday, being Christmas Eve, I invited all the poorer
sort of my tenents of Deneby and Hoton, being nineteen
in nomber; on Christmas Day the poorer sort of Thriberge,
Brinsford and Mexbrough, being twenty-six; on St.
Stephens Day all the farmers and better sort of tenents of
Thriberge, Brinsford and Rotherham, being in all fifty-
four; on St. John's Day all the chiefe tenents of Deneby,
Hoton, and Mexbrough, being in nomber forty-five.

[1] James Sterling.

Dec. 30   On the 30 of December ther were invited to dine with me eighteen gentlemen and their wives from severall [1682/3] parts of the nighbourhood.

Jan. 1   Ther were sixteen more invited of gentlemen.

3   January the 3rd, twenty others.

4   Twelve of the nighbouring clergie.

6   Seven gentlemen and tradesmen of Rotherham and other places.

There laid at my hous of thes severall days, Sir Jarvase Cutler;[1] Anthony Francland, Esq.; Jasper Blythman, Esq., justice of the peace; John Peeples, Esq., a justice of the peace; Mr. Turner; Captain King, an officer from Yorke; Mr. Rigden, marchant of Yorke, and his wife, a hansome woeman; Mrs. Blythman and her daughter; Mr. Belton, an ingenious clergieman, butt too much a good fellow; the cornet and quarter-master to my troop, with others. For musick I had two violins and a base from Doncaster that wore my livery, that plaid well for the country; two bagpipes for the common people; a trompeter and drummer. The expence of liquor, both of wine and others, was considerable, as well as of other provisions, and my guests appeared well satisfyed. I dined two days from home this Christmas, one day at Sir Jarvase Cutlers, another at my Lord Straffords. Though such remarkes as thes may seem frivolous to others, yet to posterity of one's own family (for whom this worke is chiefly designed) they may appear otherwise, that sort of curiosity being as well pleased with enquiry into less things sometimes as greater.

10   I recieved the unwelcome news that the Kings councils were for his regulating or rather reducing of such guarisons as were thought least nescessary, and for that mony being employed in fortifying thos to the sea, as more usefull and nescessary, and that Yorke would be one of thos to be reduced. I writt presently to my Lord Privy

[1] Sir Gervase Cutler of Stainborough, Yorkshire, who had married Lady Reresby's cousin, Dorothy Frankland.

Seal concerning this matter, who writt me an answer
wherin he made use of thes terms, viz., that twas true he *Jan.* 18
was not unacquainted with some discourses of this kind,
which he did not acquaint me with since they would but
disquiet me; however he was not wanting in his care,
and used such caution in my concern that he hoped either
the thing would not be, or if it were a due consideration
would be had of me in the manner of doing it, &c.; that
thos who were the most eager to have it done did propose
that my sallary should be continued till some imployment
might be found out for me, but that he had and would
insist that nothing should be done of this kind except
care was taken to secure my credit as well as my profit;
that he had that very morning spoaken to the King, who
allowed him to tell me that the company should not be
remooved (as was reported to be intended forthwith), soe
that he hoped by some kind things the King said of me
he hoped it would not be in any man's power to persuade
him to doe a thing to my deminution. He further in the
same letter advised me to come up to London, ther being
severall things fitter for him to tell nearer hand then for
me to know from him at this distance; that I might depend
upon his utmost assistance, which he hoped might bring
this thing with my presence ther to such a determination
one way or other as should proove to my entire satisfaction. A letter more kind and condescending then
could possibly have been writt from any but the humblest
of men and the best and most generous of friends.

I went to Yorke, wher the report being gone before I 20
was glad to find that a great many that could have wished
it were noe guarison seemed concerned at the remooveall
of me from being governor. I stayed eight days, being
again entertained by my Lord Maior and others. As to
the business before mentioned of chooseing my Lord
Privy Seal high stuard for the citty of Yorke, I left it in
soe probable a way that it could not in reasonably
miscarry.

Feb. 9   I sett forward for London, as my Lord Hallifax had
14   directed, in the hackney coach, and on the 14th I arrived
ther.

15   Waiting on my Lord, he said thes things to me in return
of my thankes for his extraordinary kindness to me, that
soe long as he had power to serve any man, I might be
sure he would not decline the serveing of me.   He tould
me the steps and progress of his late dispute with my Lord
Hide, now made Erle of Rochester, the First Lord
Commissioner of the Treasory, occasioned by his lordship's telling the King of 40,000 l., which as part of his
revenue of hearth-mony was converted to some private
use of which the Lord Rochester could not but knowe,
and was grossly suspected to have a part; besides some
other miscarriages in the management of the revenue,
which noe man had the courage to informe his Majesty
of but my Lord Privy Seale.   He tould me they had first
a dispute about me, which he could not forgett, Lord
Rochester being angry at my being made governor of
Yorke when he endeavoured it for my Lord Burlinton,
and which his lordship tould me was the root of their
endeavours to throwe me out ever since; that he had
lately brought in my Lord Sunderland to be Secretary,[1]
by engageing the Duke of Yorke for him, who now
seemd kinder to that lord (who had done all he could
against him in the late Parlaments) then to his lordship,
who did all he could to serve him and had most considerably opposed the passing of the Bill of Exclusion (with
some other disappointments of the same kind from that
quarter); for all this he was very well with the King, and
it was not in their power to remoove him, though all the
other interest engaged against him.

As to my concern, I pressed all I could that I might be
continued in the same station and the goverment might be
upheld, and endeavoured to confute the reasons which my
Lord Halifax then tould were made use of for its reduction;

[1] January 31, 1682/3, in place of Lord Conway.

* 17/8: Reresby to Halifax, no date, ?Jan 1682/3 (copy), asking for assistance
in keeping his position as governor; 21/19: Reresby to Halifax, 14 January
1682/3 (copy), also asking for assistance to strengthen the garrison.

which he soe well approoved of that the next day,
carrying me alone to the King, he repeated them all to
him, and spoake soe kindly to him of me that I should
appear vane to repeat them, makeing himselfe a kind of
party as his friend in the narrative, and saying that this
was mearly contrived under pretence of service to the King
to gratifie Sir Thomas Slingsby, who expected the same
command and who was not capable to have served the
King in that post, or at the instance of the Earl of Burlinton and his friends, who had the same pretentions to that
command when I gott it; and he hoped his Majesty would
consider whether it was not better trusted in my handes
then his lordships.   His Majesty replyed that as to that
he needed not consider, for he was very well satisfyed it
was much more safe in mine (his Majesty, as I heard the
day before, not haveing much assurance of that lords
integrity).   He further said he would not doe nothing more
in that affair till he further thought of it, and tould me that
whatever had been done I might be sure it should noe
ways have been to my disadvantage, for I should loos
nothing by it.   I replyed that my Lord Halifax had taken
the pains to sett the whole matter soe fully before him that
I needed not to repeat anything of it, only beseeched his
Majesty, since I was in that command and had laid out
much mony to fitt myselfe for itt, if consistant with his
Majesty's service, that I might be continued in it; which
he said he would thinke of, and gave allowance to my Lord
to goe to my Lord Dartsmouth, late Colonell Legg, the
Master of the Ordinance, who was the great stickler in
it, and to discours my reasons with him in that matter.
The same day my Lord Hallifax made me dine with him.

My Lord Hallifax tould me some hard usage he had   *Feb.* 16
recieved from my Lord Rochester, contrary to their
mutuall engagments of confidence and frendship one
towards another when he first entered into business at
Court; and that when he had a promess to be Lord
President or Lord Privy Seal (which should first happen,

which the Privy Seal did), the Lord Rochester underhand did endeavour to obtean it for Mr. Seamure rather then his lordship; that the King gave him then the honour of marquiss, which he never desired, hopeing that it should satisfy him instead of Privy Seal, but that his lordship would not decline the other also, and soe gott both, which occasioned Mr. Seamur's leaveing the Court as dissatis-fyed; that however (the King commanding it) he would live fairly with him, but that he must give him some assur-ances of his being more his lordship's friend then my Lord Sunderlands ere he could much confide in him; that he would keep in his corner and hear what was offered for the Kings service, and not be affraid to declare what he heard to his Majesty's disadvantage, whoever was con-cerned in it; and whenever he had power he would distinguish between his friends and thos that were not soe.

Feb. 18   I mett my Lord Dartsmouth in the ante-chamber at Whitehall, who tould me he was sorry he could not come down himselfe to take a vewe of the condition of Yorke, but sent down the next to himselfe, which was Sir Christofer Musgrave, who had made a state of it, and soe represented it that it could not be putt into a con-dition defensible for soe great a place under the charge of 30,000 l.; that the King had therfore resolved to reduce it, but was soe kind to me as not to doe it till he had found out something else for me as considerable. I tould him I hoped the King would well advise before he left the first citty next to London (and not very well affected to the goverment) without a guarison; that though it might require a great summ to make the citty, the Castle and Cliffords Tower very strong, yet the Tower, which com-manded the whole citty, might be made very defensible for a small charge, and be able to prevent any sudden insurrection within the town, with one company of foot and 500 men of the militia now in the citty. He said ther would be still a face of a guarison, for the lord lieutenant,

---

* Dartmouth MSS. (W) 1778/V/III/0/2.

or he that commanded the militia regiment of the citty, might keep Cliffords Tower. I answered that whatever form of a guarison remained, I hoped the King would not committ the care of it to any person but myselfe.

And as we were thus discoursing this matter, came by the King and my Lord Halifax. The latter, seing us togather, called my Lord Dartsmouth, and, as he tould me afterwards, asked his lordship why he soe publiquely declared that the goverment of Yorke was to be sunke (for I had tould my Lord Hallifax the day before that one had acquainted me that my Lord Dartsmouth had said it oponly at his table the day before). Dartsmouth replyed that it could be noe secrett, when it came under publique consideration; but that he was ready, though order was given for the speedy sending away the company from Yorke to Barwick, to stop its march, when his lordship had desired it. My Lord tould him that the company should not have marched, though he had not countermanded the first order. A great deal more passed to the same effect, and perticularly I said that it was not a single calamity, for all the inland guarrisons and some seaport towns would also be slighted, and that he had advised the King, of one hundred and od guarrisons then in England not to leave above nine or ten, and to make them very strong and considerable; all which I related to my Lord Halifax. His lordship tould me he would speake noe more to my Lord Dartsmouth, but only to the King, and gett his resolution therin. But by this I found the business was concerted, and began to dispond of carrying my pretention in that perticular.

The fraud concerning the 40,000 l., lost to the King *Feb.* 19 in letting of the duty of hearth-mony by my Lord Rochester and the other Lords Commissioners of the Treasury, came to be argued by councell on both sides before the King, wher it did appear that the King did actually loose soe much of what he might have had from others. Yet soe great was my Lord Rochester's interest (being supported by the Duke of Yorke, my Lady Portsmouth, and my Lord Sunderland), that little notice was taken of it for that time; only wheras some of that lord's friends did reflect upon my Lord Halifax as too busy in makeing that discovery, the King justified him soe far as to say oponly that day in Court, upon the tryall, that his lordship had done nothing in that affair but by his order and approbation.

Feb. 20   My Lord Hallifax tould me I had formerly mentioned some desire to goe envoye extraordinary, and if I had the same inclinations now he durst undertake to gett leave for me to be sent in that quality to the King of Sweden.   I tould him I heard embassadours were but ill paid by the King, and that being now in another station I had noe mind to take an imployment of that kind.

I kissed the Duke of Yorkes hand that day, who seemed very civill, but his smiles were not always reall, though I never did anything to deserve them otherways.

21   My Lord Hallifax tould me this was not the only matter that would appear as to the ill management of the Kings revenue, and that the anti-Court party courted him at soe great a rate he feared it might occasion a jealousie elsewher.

24   The sessions of Middlesex at Hicks his Hall, which had lasted five days, ended the 24th of February, wher the most considerable business was in punishing such as resorted to conventicles.

The town's discours was generally concerning the difference of the two lords, wher my Lord Hallifax, that had discovered the cheat, had the generall applause. That day my Lord tould me that the Duke made it his business to clear himselfe that he was not concerned in the least on either side, and that he should come to him before his lordship would apply himselfe to his Highness

26 in that affair; that his lordship had been the day before with the King, and was two hours in private with him, wher he took notice that the report was that my Lord

Rochester was to have the white staff given him of Lord High Treasurer, but his lordship hoped it was not intended, bycaus at this time it would look ill in respect of the difference between the two lords, and seem to throw the right on that side wher his Majesty bestowed soe great a sign of his favour; that the King should say that he should not be Lord Treasurer the sooner for what had lately been done by my Lord Rochester in that concern, and was angry with my Lord Hallifax that he gave credit to any such rumour; that he had spoaken to the King in my concern also, and that his Majesty had assured him nothing should be further done as to the reduceing of the gouverment of Yorke for the present, nor hereafter but his lordship should know of it; therfore he advised me to goe down, and to gett the confirmation of this promess before I went, and that he would look after it in my absence; and that I might be assured in case he had any power it should never fall but I should be first rewarded with something most considerable.

I was betrayed at this time by one Mr. Blythman, my *Feb.* 27 nighbour in Yorkshire, who, being privy to part of an estate of my wives sisters for which I was in suit, went and discovered it to Sir James Butler, when at that time noe nescessity required it. The gentleman was one I had soe much obliged that I durst have trusted him in my greatest concerns. Lett men be therfore aware in confideing in any person, though never soe near in friendship or relation.

My Lord Hallifax tould me the Duke had assured him 28 that he was not concerned in the least in the difference between him and my Lord Rochester. My Lord replyed he was sure his Highnesse would never doe an ill thing towards him, and if he did, that his lordship would never doe anything to oppose him, but he could not serve him with the same zeale, and he might at some time repent that he had lost his service to the degree he desired to use it for him; that he had done in all this noe more then he was commanded to doe by the King, and who was ther soe great in the kingdome to be displeased with men's acting according to the King's command; that he found they had a mind (meaning Rochester) to be rid of him, and would possibly endeavour to make his station uneasy, but they should not remoove him, first, bycaus he would stay to serve the King, and secondly, to disappoint thos that endeavoured to contrive his absence; that all his lordship had attempted to doe in this matter was to save the King mony, and could ther be a greater service to his Highness in future then that; that the King had made him a bigger man then he deserved to be, but he was a gentleman, and that his Highness ought to consider thos that had escutions as well as thos that had none (three of the Dukes chiefe favourits, viz., Legg, Churchill and Hide, being scarce gentlemen); for his part, that he would never say anything but thruth to his Highness, and though it might look a little plain, yet nothing could carry more respect in the bothom then thruth, with much more to the same effect. To which the Duke replyed that whatever he said did seem very reasonable; that he was sensible of great obligations hee had to his lordship, and would never forgett them, but would serve him in what laid in his power, and his lordship should find it.

The same day his lordship said he had spoaken to my Lady Duchesse of Portsmouth, and tould [her], upon some discours, that he found in case of need of his Majestys favour he was not to expect many friends from that side of Whitehall; that she replyed that some that had been much his friends came thyther sometimes (meaning Lord Rochester), and she hoped they would be soe again. His lordship replyed that he doubted much, however, of her intercession in such a strait, and hoped, however, he should avoid comming into the danger of makeing use of it; at which she blushed, and seemed to be in some confusion. He said further that was he as yong as he had been hee could be as well with her as others. I replyed he must have two p's then, viz., the purs as well as the other, for soe my Lord of Danby was thought to keep in soe long with her.

The Court and the whole town seemed infinitely divided upon this matter.   Thos that had any dependency upon payments out of the Exechequer durst not but seem to side with Lord Rochester.   Thos that were thinkeing, serious men, that were independent and wished well to the goverment, commended the zeale and courage of my Lord Privy Seal, that would not see 40,000 l. of the Kings mony misimployed, and that durst complain of it wher soe great a man with his dependencies were made ennemys by it.   The Whiggs (as they then called them) or the anti-courtiers commended Lord Privy Seal, not only for the thing but as hopeing to gain him by this quarrel to more moderation.

I tould the King as he was going to bed that my Lord *March* 1 Privy Seale had given me some ground to believe from his Majesty that he would not sinke the garrison of Yorke without better adviseing upon it, and that when he thought it fitt to be done he would putt me into some better capacity of serveing him.   I tould him severall arguments used for the selling of the Mannor and for the disgarrisoning of Yorke, and my own reasons in answer to thos arguments, which his Majesty seemed to approove well of, and assured me that he would not doe it hastily, and if he did it he would be very kind to me in some other respect.

I judged it nescessary to say something to the Duke 2 of my concern (though I found most of his creatures concerned in it), and consulting my Lord Privy Seale, he advised me not to enter into the merits of it, but to touch lightly the thing.   Soe haveing admittance to him, I 3 tould him I was sensible that I was in a station of competition, and wher a man had that and was soe farr from Court as I was he laid under great disadvantages; but that since I had the honour of that command I had done nothing but what had been for his Majestys service and for his Highnesses in perticular, nor ever would, and if any one had represented me otherways it should appear as I said when it came to the test.   The Duke replyed that I had acted nothing otherways that he heard of, and did really confide in me that he had endeavoured to serve me, *March* 4 and would continue to doe soe.   The next day the King and he went for Newmarket.

At this time all Christendome seemed to be in danger of a warr, the rebels of Hungary haveing called in the Turks to assist them against the Emperour, and (one or two excepted) all the princes of the Empire, the Kings of Spain and of Sweden, joining in defence of the Empire against the Turke on one side and the French King (likely to fall upon Flanders or some of the princes of Germany) on the other, whilst we enjoyed a happy peace at home; and which was the more likely to make it last was the death of that soe busy and factious Lord Shaftsbury,[1] who was ded not long before into Holland.

5   I dined with severall wealthy citizens in London, as I had done twice before since my comming to town, and found it the most generall opinion ther that the Exchequer was not managed to the Kings advantage as it ought to be by the Commissioners, and that my Lord Privy Seale had done a great service to the Crown to reveal the late fraud, wondering that the King took noe more notice of it.   I tould my Lord this, with some other circumstances to the same purpas, who said it was nescessary for him to estrange himselfe from my Lord Rochester, least he might be thought to be privy, if not a party, to some things of which the other was suspected, &c.

The Kings revenue came now to about 110,000 l.[2] per annum, and ther was a project on foot to farm it, and offers were made of it accordingly at 140,000 l.[2] per annum by sufficient persons, and 500,000 l. was offered to be paid beforehand as a security, and not to be deducted till

---

[1] January 21, 1682/3.

[2] These figures should obviously be multiplied by ten.

the last half-year, this farm to continue for three years.
My Lord Privy Seal was believed to be the chiefe promoter of this, which my Lord Rochester as much underhand discouraged, insomuch as he sent to some of the
richest cittyzens, desireing them not to concern their
estates in this project. This one Hornby, a banker,
worth 80,000 l. by reputation,[1] confessed to me. It was
much admired that any one durst withstand soe great an
advance to the Crown for his private interest. My Lord
Privy Seale thanked me for this discovery.

One Green, a principal of hors in my troop,[2] had by the *March* 10
instigation of some of my country adversarys complained
to my Lord Burlinton of some hardships he had suffered
from me as to his contribution in that service, but
unjustly; which my Lord takeing notice of to me was
satisfyed with my defence. But ressenting that his
lordship should be soe easy to give ear to complaint against
me, I desired him he would not be of soe easy a faith as to
my perticular; that I had nothing but the honour of
serveing him for my reward, which I should ever be
desirous to preserve entire; and if I had noe respect for
his lordship yet I had soe much for myselfe as not to doe
anything either in that or any trust but what I should be
able to justifie myselfe in, with much more to the same
effect. Soe we parted seemingly good friends.

I was troubled at this time with the suit in Chancery
concerning my wives sisters estate, which was as vexatious
as it was unjust against me. I was forced to prepare my
answer before to the bill against me before I left the town,
and to sett out all the estate which I was privy to of hers,
Mr. Blythman haveing done it before.

My Lord Privy Seale and I went to Hide Parke in his 20
coach. He tould me he hoped I did not repent of my

1 Joseph Hornby, to whom the Government was indebted more than
£22,000 as a result of the Stop of the Exchequer.

2 A person on whom lay the obligation of providing one or more horse
soldiers for the troop.

comming up at his request, since I could not have been soe
well satisfyed how affairs went, both publique and private,
without being ther; that he knew not how long he should
keep his station (being driven at soe fiercely by some),
but he did thinke he had the King his friend, and could
not believe that he would part with him for haveing committed noe fault, except it were one to obay his commandes,
assureing me that he would ever use his interest soe long
as it continued to serve me, and in that perticular especially
of the goverment of Yorke. But, said he, times may
come, if the Court should fall into French councils, that
some other station may be fitter for you then that, and if
that come to pass I must quitt mine also, for I have greater
endeavours against me from the other side of the water
then from home.

I tould his lordship that either he must continue or be
laid aside. If the first, he must rise higher to some greater
post, and if he should arrive to any wher ther was any
room for me under him I would quitt any other imployment to serve him. If he went out, I cared not for
staying in; and if I did, he might be sure it should not be
longer then I could act upon safe and sure principals.

When I came into the country he bad me turn the
report of his disgrace into raillery, till he gave me notice
of his retreat, which he would doe early if he found it was
not to be avoided. I was to goe for the country the 23.
He desired to see me again before I went.

March 22 I went to see my Lord of Danby in the Tower. I
found him speak much more obligeingly concerning my
Lord Privy Seale then before; and amongst other things
he said his lordship had taken a prudent cours to declare
himselfe for a Parlament, and he was glad of it upon a
private account, for he dispaired of comming from thence
till ther was one. He said that Rochester and his party
might support themselves for a time, but the interest he
went upon could not last long, &c.

23 Seing my Lord Privy Seale and telling him what had

been said by my Lord Danby, I found my Lord much abated as to his enmity with that lord. He tould me he had ennemys enough besides, and that his displeasure against him was now ceased; but he would not make more ennemys by being his friend, as he had formerly done by being his ennemy. Soe that I found my Lord Privy Seale makeing up his interest on one side, as my Lord Rochester was endeavouring on the other, for he had also sent for Mr. Seamure to return to Court, and had promessed to be his friend. My Lord Privy Seale tould me that Seamure had made some proposals to close with him, and that a reconciliation was endeavoured by Rochester's friends between the two lords. I tould his lordship that in my poor opinion he had better stand upon his own interest then joine with either, for he had now gotten a nationall interest by what he had done in opposition to Rochester, &c., and in case he closed ther again he might loos that; and if he could support himselfe seperate he might keep both, or in case he fell the King would find the want of him soe much he could not be long spared from Court.

He said it would be hard for him to continue ther with thes men, for it was their interest to remoove him; they would be apt to play tricks for their own advantage, and knew, soe long as he was in a station to be informed of such carriages, he should ever reveale them to his Majesty. He said further that if they should gett the King to themselves they could not long keep him, for he had one quality that would preserve him from being very long in ill handes, which was he would hear all persons, and admitt of informations by the back door, when thos that seemed favourits little dreamt of it. He lamented the interest that the Duchesse of Portsmoth had with the King, she betraying him to France not only as to his councils but his bed, she certainly lying with the Grand Prieur,[1] a man

---

[1] Philippe de Vendôme, Grand Prior of France, younger son of the second Duc de Vendôme and Laura Mancini, the eldest of Cardinal Mazarin's five nieces.

of quality of France who ofton came over and made use of his love as the means for his better information and intelligence to his master the French King. He said the King was too passive in thes things, and that it was his greatest fault that he would not be persuaded to ressent some things, which he clearly saw, as he ought, and keep up that height which belonged to his dignity. As to my perticular, he tould me I had envyers as well as himselfe, and that when I came into the country I might endeavour to demean myselfe soe as to gain as much as it was possible. I said it would be hard to gain people in the post I was in, their envy being more, I hoped, against my preferment then against my person; but I would followe his advice in that as well as in all things else that I could possibly. I took leave of his lordship that night, and sett

March 23 forward for Yorkeshire the 23rd day of March.

Upon the whole matter I percievd my Lord Privy Seale had the better (and the most approovd) caus, and my Lord Rochester the better interest. The first weighed more in parts, in his family, estate, and his reputation in the nation; the other weighed more (though undeservedly) with the Duke of Yorke, the Duchesse of Portsmoth, my Lord of Ormond, and most of thos at Court, who depend upon the Kings purs, of which his lordship was the chiefe despencer. And the fear was that the diligence of thes soe near the King might worke upon him soe as to relinquish my Lord Privy Seale, that depended upon noe other person nor interest but his own, and thos services that he not only had performed but was best able to render the Crown.

[1683]

March 26 I arrived happyly at Thriberge, comming that day from Stamford, wher I found my wife and family well, *grace a Dieu*.

April 7 The Duke of Norfolke, being then comd to Rotherham to build at the College, came to visit me.

My Lady Duchesse came to see my wife.   *April* 9

I went to wait on his Grace the Duke of Newcastle at 10 Welbeck, wher he seemed soe concerned at the report of the goverment of Yorke's reduction that he offered to write to my Lord Rochester and the other minesters above how nescessary he thought it to be continued, and that he would doe the utmost he could to effect it. He asked me if I was to goe embassador for Spain, for he had heard from the Duke of Norfock (and others) that it had been offered to me. I tould him it had been proposed to me to goe abroad in that quality, but not for Spain; however, it was not improbable but if I had desired that station or province (the last envoye, Sir Henry Gooderick, being returned), I might have attained to it as well as others; but that now I was grown too ould to think of leaveing my own country, though for soe honourable an imployment.

He tould me a secret relateing to his family, that his daughter, the Duchesse of Albemarle, had recieved and concealed a love letter, which her lord knew of, which had made her dissemble herselfe distracted; but that she was not disordered, as she pretended; and that both the one and other were great misfortunes to him, yet he had rather she were guilty of the letter then the distraction, bycaus it was an imputation upon the rest of his children. He tould me severall other concerns of his familie, too tedious and not very pertenent in this place, and showed me severall letters from some great men, and one from my Lord Rochester wherin were severall professions of kindnesse from himselfe and assurances of the like from the Duke of Yorke towards his Grace.

I heard the citty of Yorke had made choice of the Duke 11 of Richmond for their high steward, which I was not sorry for as the affairs of that citty then stood, and the interest the Duchesse of Portsmoth then had with the King, my Lord Privy Seal haveing declined it out of respect to the Duke of Buckingham, who was to be putt out before any other could be admitted. The Duchesse took this very kindly, and upon reciet of the patent for that office, which the citty presented the yong duke with in a gould box, her Grace sent my Lord Maior a letter of thankes, wherin she said the King was well pleasd that the second citty of England had made choice of her son into that office, and assured him and the corporation of her utmost services. The Duke of Buckingham took it as ill on the other hand to be putt out, and writt a letter wherby they might easily know he did soe.

The Duke of Buckingham was at then very well with my Lord Privy Seal, soe that I was at some loss to know how to behave myselfe between thos two interests in this matter. However, I thought it fitt to write a letter to Colonel Oglethorpe,[1] chiefe commissioner of the Master of the Horses place under the Duke of Richmond, wherin I desired him to acquaint the Duke and the Duchesse of Portsmoth that I was glad that the place wher I had the honour of being concernd in that quality had exprest their loyaltie by makeing soe good a choice of a lord high steward, though they recieved much a greater by it then what they conferred; and that every person that had any concern in that citty would, I hoped, for the future endeavour to show their zeale for the King's service in the first place and next for his Grace his, which was well ressented.

April 17   The generall sessions was held at Pontefract for the whol West Rideing, wher appeard seventeen justices of the peace; but the business was chiefly managed by my Lord Downs, Sir John Bointon (the Kings sergiant-at-law),[2] Sir Jonathan Gennings [3] and myselfe.

---

[1] Theophilus Oglethorpe, father of the founder of Georgia. He was a favourite of the Duke of York, and played a prominent part in the suppression of Monmouth's rebellion.

[2] Sir John Boynton of Rowcliff, Yorkshire, made King's Serjeant in 1682.

[3] Younger brother of Sir Edmund Jennings of Ripon.

The day I returned from thence I fell ill of the gout *April* 20 in my foot. I had it but some few days with trouble, but I was concerned to see it revert, hopeing I had been cured of it by constantly drinking of milke every morning, which agreed very well with me, purged me like phisick.

I continued ill three weeks, and went for York with my *May* 23 familie soon after. I laid by the way at the hous of Sir Philip Hungate, who had lately married my cozen germain, Mrs. Monson, daughter to the Lord Monson, one of the unfortunate judges of the late King.

The 29 of May, being the Kings birthday, the sheriff of 29 the citty, three aldermen, and Mr. Chancellor of the Court of Yorke and severall other gentlemen dined with me, wher they were entertained with what provisions the place afforded, and with musick, the great gunns from the Tower; and at night the common people had wine and aile at a bonefire which was made before the Mannour gate. During my stay ther I was entertained at dinner by severall of the citizens with my wife and familie, and recieved great civilities from them. Only my Lord Maior (brother to Sir Henry Thomson, who died at that time, both very antimonarchicall persons) I had noe commerce with. At that time that citty began to be very fearfull that a *quo warranto* would issue fourth against their charter, the judges haveing about the 12th of June given their opinions unanimously that the charter and liberties of the citty of London were forfitted to the King.

I recieved about this time a letter of assurance from my Lord Privy Seale that he continued in the same degree of favour with his Majesty, notwithstanding many flying reports to the contrary, and bycaus it was noised abroad that he was not adviseing to the match then transacting between Prince George, third brother to the King of Denmarke, and my Lady Ann, second daughter to the Duke of Yorke.

I returned back to my own hous at Thriberge without *June* 16 any accident. God be praised.

June 26   Came the report of a dangerous conspiracie against the life of our souveraign lord the King,[1] laid by the anti-Court party, composed of such as had been disappointed of preferments at Court, and of Protestant dissenters. It was also against the Duke of Yorke, and intended to have shott the King and the Duke comming from Newmarket in his coach (the certain day of his return being known) by forty men well armd, who after the blowe given was to fly to London and to report that the papists had done it, wher ther was a body of men ready to rise, to make themselves masters of the City and Tower and consequently of the whole kingdome, the Prince of Orange being in Holland (the next right heir to the Crown), and the Duke of Monmoth being ready to head the rebeles.

This was most miraculously prevented by a fire hapning at Newmarket, which burning down a great part of the town caused the King's departure from thence ten days sooner. It was afterwards designed against the King and the Duke as they came from Hamton Court, which was after also disappointed by the Dukes not comming with the King, their design being either to kill both or neither. Thes and the like disappointments putt it into the head of one of the malincholy conspiratours that God (to use his own phrase) was against them in this design, which disposed him to goe and reveal it, which he did accordingly.[2] Upon this severall of the contrivers fled, as the Duke of Monmoth. My Lord Gray[3] made his escape after being taken. Sir Thomas Armstrong and many of them were taken and committed to the Tower, as the Earl of Essex, Lord Howard of Eskrick, Lord Russell, and many others. At the same time I recieved directions from Sir Lionell

[1] The Rye House Plot.

[2] The first informer was Josiah Keeling, an oilman.

[3] Forde Grey, third Baron Grey of Werk, a prominent Exclusionist and opponent of the Court. He took part in Monmouth's rebellion and the Revolution, and was created Earl of Tankerville by William III.

Jenkins, Secretary of State, to caus strict search to be made for one Mr. Goodenough and Mr. Nelthorpe,[1] two sopposed to be fled northwards upon the said account, which I first performed in the country by sending warrants of search and of hue and cry to severall places.

I went to Yorke, wher I used the same diligence, and *June* 28 gott my Lord Maior of Yorke to assist me therin by his civil power, he granting me a warrant directed to all constables to assist my souldiers in the said search, and was very ready to give me what assistance he could for the King's service in that perticular.

I had severall expresses to stop all suspected persons, 30 and to examin and committ such as I suspected dangerous, from the Secretary, my Lord Privy Seal, and Lord Lieutenant. I used what diligence I could in this affair, and gave an account above every post of my proceedings.[2]

My Lord Burlinton acquainted me that he had *July* 3

---

[1] Richard Goodenough and Richard Nelthorpe. They escaped at this time to the Netherlands, but returned with Monmouth.

[2] Several of Reresby's letters to Secretary Jenkins at this time are preserved among the State Papers. The earliest of them is as follows :

Yorke, June the 30, 1683.—Sir, In obedience to his Majesty's commands (recieved by the honour of yours dated the 26 instant) I, being then near Doncaster, caused the two next market towns, tho something distant from the road (viz., Rotherham and Sheffield), to be strictly searched, and going myselfe to Doncaster engaged the Maior ther to doe the same, and to make enquiry from time to time of all passengers that travell that way. I further caused the hue and cry (of which I have enclosed a copie) to be sent immediately northwards, and shall doe all I can in this place to promote the discovery of such villains. But really, Sir, the nomber of souldiers is soe small here, the gates soe many that ought to be watched, and the magistrats soe little to be trusted, that without some addition off force I fear I shall not be able in such a conjuncture to serve my royall master (whome I pray God preserve) soe effectually as I would, tho I will serve him all I can whilst I live that am, Sir, Your most humble and most faithfull servant, J. Reresby. I have lately recieved notice from my Lord Burlinton of my Lord Grays escape and the Duke of Monmouth absconding, and have given order that the centrys at each gate bring all passengers to me to be examined that come northwards and look suspicious. (S.P. Dom., Charles II, 425, No. 148.)

* 25/25: copy of search warrant, 1 August 1683.

appointed the deputy lieutenants to meet him at Yorke, and desired me to be ther. It was ther resolved that such as we sopposed to be disaffected and dangerous to the Goverment should be disarmed.[1]

The guarison at Yorke being but then weak, I desired my Lord Burlinton to assist me with the four companys of the militia only for eight or ten days till the danger might be over in some measure, which his lordship consented to, with this claus in the order, that whilst they continued in arms they should obay such orders as they should recieve from me as governor from time to time. Some of the deputy lieutenants tould my Lord before he signed the order that since he was lord lieutenant of the

---

[1] An account of this meeting and of the progress of his search was immediately sent by Reresby to Jenkins :

July 4th, [16]83, from Yorke.—Sir, By the messenger sent to search the hous of Nelthorp at Seacroft I have only learnt thus much, that the said Richard Nelthorp was seen at Leeds on Sunday last ; that Alderman Headley of the same comming into the coffyhous ther on Fryday last see a man booted in a by room, thought he had seen him, but could not recollect who he was till findeing the name of Goodenough the day after in the proclamation remembered it was hee. This was tould the messenger by Mr. Halton that keeps the coffyhous. The granfather of Nelthorp lives at Brigtown, and his oncle (or some of his near relations of the same name) lives in Barton in Lincolnshire near the sea, both disaffected persons to the gouverment. They are supposed to be fled that way.

The Kings arms were very lately pulled down and defaced at Heighlay, a town within one mile of Leeds.

My Lord Burlinton mett here yesterday his deputy lieutenants, wher it was ordered that the deputy lieutenants should meet in their respective divisions within this rideing, and consider of such persons to be disarmed according to law as may be justly suspected dangerous to the goverment. I continue to stop all suspicious travellers this way, but we shall not be long able to doe it, many of our souldiers being sick with continuall duty.

I believe the six Scotchmen who were directed, Sir, by your letter to be stopped by some justices of the peace if they passed this way are apprehended and secured at Ferrybrigg. One of them that denyed himselfe to be a parson at the first hath since confessed that he is one ; but I suppose you will have a more perticular account of this from the place wher they were taken. I am, Sir, Your most faithfull and most humble servant, J. Reresby. (S.P. Dom., Charles II, 427.)

* 24/25: copy of Orders to the Deputy Lieutenants of the West Riding sent to Reresby at York, 3 July 1683.

citty as well as of the county it might proove an ill president to direct the militia to be commanded by any person
but himselfe or two deputy lieutenants according to the
Act, which made him take time to consider further of it;
but I refuseing to admitt of any force into that citty that
was not commanded by myselfe only (as I ought by my
commission), and his lordship fearing to stand upon
niceties at such a time of danger, sent me the order as I
had desired it the next day, and the militia, being called
togather, obayed my order for eight days till dismissed.

My Lord Burlinton was under thes circumstances at
that time, that he was looked upon above as a cautious
man, that had noe mind to venter too far for fear of his
great estate, and soe seemed to carry fair with all partys.
This made him now more free then usuall, that he might
not be suspected to incline in the least to that faction,
wherfore he courted me at a great rate, writt to me every
day, advised with me, sometimes by letter sometimes by
meeting me in the middle way between Lawnsbrough
and Yorke, in all directions which he recieved from
above; desired me to joine with him in the forming and
signing a congratulatory address to the King for his
escape from this danger; and desired me to frame a letter
for him to the deputy lieutenants, ther being more present
that understood the method of thos things better then
myselfe, though he passed this compliment upon me
before them all, that noe man was better in that sort of
composure.

I was invited to dinner to my Lord Maior, who gave *July* 6
me a very hansome entertainment and declared his great
desire to keep a fair correspondencie with me, owning
how much the citty had been obliged to me, but shewed
the Kings command for it from the Secretary at the same
time.

Six Scotchmen being stopt at Ferrybrig by directions
from the Secretary, comming from London towards
Scotland, and being but slightly examined by the justice

of the peace, I caused them to confess much more to me, which I transmitted to the Secretary,[1] as also the examination of another of that nation, who was sent to Yorke Castle and prooved a very dangerous roague. Thes seven were sent for up by habias corpus to the King and Councill, and gave evidence above, as other Scotchmen did upon their examination, that the conspiracie was generall in both kingdomes amongst the discontented and phenatique party, and that severall, being or pretending to be Scotch pedlers, were emissarys from thence to keep correspondence with that party here. Upon this I writt up above to offer if it might not be seasonable to caus a strict search to be made for all Scotch pety chapmen or pedlers, and to caus such as were found dangerous upon their examinations before the next justice of peace to be secured, the rest to be whipt and passed according to

[1] Reresby's letter accompanying his additional information runs as follows :

Yorke, July the 7, 1683.—Sir, Though I yet continue to take a strict account of passengers this way (which I am the more enabled to doe by some assistance from the militia, who are now under arms for eight days by my Lord Burlintons direction in this guarrison), I find noebody that gives any just ground of suspicion. One Mr. Drake, Mr. Andrew Jailer, Mr. Ralph Ward of this citty haveing of late absented themselves (but as their friends pretend only upon the account of writts *de excommunicato capiendo* out against them for not comming to church), I have caused their houses to be searched for arms (another deputy lieutenant joining with me), but found very few. Upon intimation also that Sir John Brooks and Alderman Waller of this citty (to Sir Thomas Mauleverer) had arms in their houses they were searched. In the first gentlemans were found four backs, brests, and head pieces, five blunderbushes and muscates, and four muskets in the latter ; but thos are found to belong to the militia. We have searched for more arms, but find very few. One person who was found hideing himselfe upon this search (and prooves to be a nonconformist person or schoolmaster) I have bound over to the sessions.

The six Scotchmen, being sent to the goale here from Ferrybrigg, I have though fitt to re-examin, and to transmitt to you what they say, that compareing it with the former examination (sent up, I suppose, by the justice of the peace) you might pleas to see if it vary from it. I am, Honoured Sir, Your most faithfull and most humble servant, J. Reresby. (S.P. Dom., Charles II, 427.)

* 27/40: copy of examinations taken before Reresby, 6 July 1683.

the statute.[1]   This was very well approved, and at our next sessions at Leeds and Rotherham many were taken and examined, amongst which some of them prooved

[1] This letter, written to Secretary Jenkins, has also been preserved :

Yorke, July 11, [16]83.—Sir, Could ther be a greater reward for doing a mans duty in the concern of the Kings service then the act itselfe, I am sure I should recieve it by the great honour you doe me to approve my endeavours therin thus far.   Sir, since my last another Scotchman (taken by my first enquiry about Doncaster and convayed before Sir Michael Wentworth, the next justice of peace) was brought lately to the goale here. He seems to be a dangerous fellow, as you will find by his enclosed examination, and confessed, as he tels me, little of what you will see ther before the justice by whom he stands committed.   When he and the six Scotchmen (who parted from hence this day in obedience to the Kings writt) first mett in the goale they seemed to be acquainted, but denyed to be soe afterwards. I have since re-examined them, but find noe other matter but what I transmitted, Sir, to you in my last ; only I omitted one circumstance, that one of them (as I remember twas John Cook) was under a great disorder as he was examined, and fell down in a sound, but pretended (returning presently to himselfe) that it was only an effect of wind.

Sir, if I may presume to tell you my thoughts, I fear that such emissarys as thes from Scotland did not come to contrive and carry intelligence as to the plott, but to be active therin when it broak out.   We have observed in some parts of this county that greater nombers of Scotch pedlers then usuall (within ten or twelve months last past) have flocked to us, and especially to the most remarkable places for faction, and have sould godly bukes, as they called them, and pamflets from Scotland, which occasioned our order of sessions at Doncaster (at request) six months agoe, and since at Pomfret three months after, that they should be whipt and passed for vagrancy to their own country, according to the statute of the Queen.

Haveing yesterday advised with my Lord Burlinton I have thoughts of going to our sessions that hould this and the next week, to promote some things for his Majestys service, and amongst others to advise a generall search to be made for roagues and vagrants (amongst which pedlers and petty chapmen are comprized, by that statute, of all nations), such as are taken to be carryed before the next justice of the peace to be examined, and if found dangerous as to act or principle to be secured, the rest punished and passed according to lawe.   My lord lieutenant hath ordered his deputies to caus a more strict search to be made for arms, which will speedily be putt in execution through this rideing.   If, Sir, you have any commands for me by the next post after you recieve this, I desire you would pleas to direct your letter to me to be left with the postmaster of Doncaster. Your letters the post after will find me here, that am, Sir, Your most humble and most faithfull servant, J. Reresby. (S.P. Dom., Charles II, 428.)

dangerous and declared it their opinion that in some cases it was lawfull to take up arms against the King, especially in that of concience.

July 12   My Lord Burlinton desired me to goe to Leeds to promote this search after Scotchmen and the disarming of the disaffected, which I did with the approbation of all the deputy lieutenants and justices of the peace, ther being some fiveteen in nomber.

13   I came to Thriberge, wher I found my third son John very ill of a bloody flux.

17   The Teusday after I went to Rotherham sessions, wher I persued the same worke, and caused strict watch and ward to be continued in that division.

19   I designed to return to Yorke the next day, but was prevented by the unhappy death of my poor boy, a very hopefull and witty youth. His flux (being oponed) appeared to be caused from an obstruction in his gutts. This was a very sensible griefe to me and his mother.

In this time I had recieved six letters from Mr. Secretary, in one of which ther was this expression: I see how diligent and zealous you have been in his Majestys service and in the faithfull discharge of your duty in all things relateing therunto, &c.; I would encourage you to goe on in his Majestys service as you have constantly done, which hath justly gained you my esteem.

And four letters had come to me since the discovery of the plott from my Lord Privy Seal, in some of which were thes words, viz.: The accounts you give from Yorke are well recieved here, and I am sure when anything is to be done for the King's service or the security of the Goverment you will recommend yourselfe soe as to be distinguished from thos who are less capable of doing it. In another letter was this: I have given the King an account of what you did at Leeds, which is very well approoved of. I am not to detract from others, but I must thinke that it is very well for the Kings service that Sir John Reresby hath soe great a part in promoteing it, haveing skill as well as zeale, things that are not always joined in the same person. You need noe other directions then to continue to doe well, in which you can as little faile as I can of being, Dear Sir, Your faithfull humble servant, Halifax (soe good and soe much too kind was the greatest of men to one of the least deserveing).

Severall of the conspirators were now tryed and executed, and by the most plain evidence that ere was made out against men in soe capitall a crime, viz., Captain Walcop,[1] my Lord Russell, eldest son and heir to the Earl of Bedford, Mr. Rous and Mr. Hone,[2] &c., as to whos perticular charges of crime, and of others that died after them, I leave it to history.

Began the assizes at Yorke. The same day I arrived *July* 23 ther and gave a habias corpus for Gibson[3] to the sheriff, inclosed from the Secretary of State to me, wherby he was soon after sent to London.

My Lord Burlinton appointed me to meet him at 24 dinner at the high sherifs, which I excused myselfe from for many reasons. In the afternoon he came to my hous, wher severall of the deputy lieutenants mett him, and we advised togather as to some things before omitted for the disarming of persons, his lordship haveing recieved some check from above for not being soe strict as he ought to have been, wherupon he tould me that he wished he had followed my advice in that perticular. The high sheriff came to see mee the same day, and most of the gentlemen in town being with me, we ther resolved to draw up an addresse to the King to congratulate his late happy delivery from the conspiracie, which was left to Sir Jonathan Gennings, Mr. Tindall[4] and myselfe to compose,

---

[1] Thomas Walcot, " an Irish gentleman that had been of Cromwell's army " (Burnet, *History of My Own Time*, i. 543).

[2] William Hone, a joiner.

[3] James Gibson, *alias* James Johnson, one of the men arrested in the north. Depositions against him are in S.P. Dom., Charles II, 428.

[4] Bradwardine Tindall of Brotherton, elder brother of William Tindall.

and soe well approved of that it was signed by all the gentlemen of the county whos occasions led them to Yorke that assizes, carried up by four gentlemen then named to my Lord Halifax to introduce to the King.

My Lord Burlinton had promessed to sign with us such an addresse as the gentlemen of the country should agree to upon that occasion, but an accident hapned to prevent it, which was that being invited to dine with the high sheriff upon the 25 I gott togather as many as I knew were my Lord Marquis of Halifax friends to dine ther also, and as soon as dinner was done I mooved for a ressolution which way, and to whom to be presented to the King, this addresse ought to be convayed (haveing found the sheriff inclineing the day before that all that matter should be left to the Earl of Burlinton, and then I knew that my Lord Rochester, his son-in-law, would be the person appointed to present it to the King). I would not appear very pressing in it myselfe that it should be sent up to my Lord Halifax, haveing a mind to keep fair with my Lord Burlinton, but had soe laid the thinge that it being after a long debate putt to the question, it was carried that it ought to be sent up to my Lord Halifax. This being agreed, I sent away my servant that night to my Lord Burlinton to acquaint him how the gentlemen had ressolved, and that in case he thought not fitt to joine with them under thos circumstances I would prevent the sending of the addresse to him at all, and take it upon myselfe that soe it might not be ill taken that he did not signe it as he had promessed. This he well approoved of, and thanked me for it, by this means he avoiding this or any construction for his refuseing to sign.

Most of the gentlemen of the county came and dined with me this assizes. My Lord Maior came incognito (for he could not carry the mace out of the citty gate wher the Mannour stands), and persons of very contrary persuasions were very civil to me, as appeared by the visits of the two Lords Fairfax to me the same day, one being

* 17/28: The Yorkshire Address to the king as drawn up by Reresby 1683.

a great leader of the popish party,[1] and the other of the Presbuterian.[2]   And the thruth is I did endeavour to doe the duty of my place with as much softnesse as I honestly could, and found it was for the Kings service not to refuse a fair correspondence with every man (however his principles stood) that would give faithfull assurances to be true and constant to the Goverment; and by this method, though it displeased some, the citty of Yorke was much changed to the better in a short time.

I had this while severall informations given me of dangerous designs and expressions against the King used   *
by some persons in Yorke, which I endeavoured to sift out to the bottom, but found them to proceed from artifice or malice.   However, I represented the whole matter as I heard it above or could discover it, and left the construction to them.   Upon thes occasions I writt to my   *Aug.* 4
Lord Privy Seale, his Royall Highness and the Secretary.[3]

---

[1] Charles, fifth Viscount Fairfax of Emley in the peerage of Ireland. His principal Yorkshire seat was Gilling Castle.

[2] Henry, fourth Baron Fairfax of Cameron in the peerage of Scotland.

[3] Reresby's letters to Secretary Jenkins show that the chief persons implicated were John Wilkison, the county clerk, and Symond Scott, the under-sheriff.   The original document on which the charges against them were based has not been found, but their answers at their examination are preserved in S.P. Dom., Charles II, 430, along with the following covering note from Sir John :

Yorke, August the 8th, 1683.—Sir, The inclosed is a copie of a letter which was brought to me last night at nine of the clock by three persons, who deposed upon oath that they found it upon the ground in the Minster yard of this citty ; and the persons whom it concerns, viz., Mr. Wilkison (the county clerk) and Mr. Scott (the under-sheriff), being in town, I immediately sent for them and examined them, and have bound them with their suretys in 800 *l.* a man to answer what shall be objected against them at the next assizes or before the Privy Councill.   Sir, you will find by their inclosed examinations that they will not confesse anything of the matter. The first (Wilkyson) hath a better reputation both as to his principles and conformity to the Church ; the other hath been (and is yet) esteemd a favourer of phenaticks, as appears by his last return of jurours for this county.   As I can learn further, I shall not faile to give you an account and to obay such commandes as in the mean time I shall recieve from you, that

---

* 23/54: copy by Reresby of the examination of Wilkinson, 7 July 1683.

Aug. 12   I returned to Thriberge August the 12th.   Before
I left Yorke I went to wait on the Earl of Burlinton at
Lawnsbrough, who tould me that I had been soe industrious in the King's service that he must have the greater
esteem for me whilst he lived, and that he had given my
Lord Rochester an account that I had a great load of
business upon me.

12   At this time Christendome was in great apprehensions
to be overrun by the Turke, who had besieged Vienna for
some time and reduced it to great extremity, soe that
15,000 men were reduced before the siege was raised to
5,000 fighting men, a pound of beef was sould for 20
stivers, an egg for 5 stivers.   On the 12th of September
the King of Poland[1] came with a considerable army, and
joined that of the Emperor under the command of the
Duke of Lorrain[2] as generall not farr from Vienna, which
togather with some assistance from the Electors of
Saxony and Bavaria,[3] who were ther in person with some
other princes of the Empire, made up a body of 80,000
fighting men, and attacking the Turkish army consisting
of 150,000 men close by their trenches, gave them a
totall overthrow, slew and cut in pieces many thousands
of the ennemy, took their camp, cannon, ammunition and
treasure, the hors of the Grand Visier,[4] that commanded
the Turkish army, himselfe narrowly escapeing, to the
great joy of all Christendome.   The governor of Vienna
was Count Sterenberg,[5] a person that shewed great conduct

am, Sir, Your most humble and most faithfull servant, J. Reresby.   I have
since thought fit to send up the originall.

[1] John Sobieski.

[2] Charles IV, whose duchy remained in French hands from before his
accession in 1675 until after his death in 1690.

[3] John George III and Maximilian II.

[4] Kara Mustapha, who succeeded his brother-in-law, Ahmed Kiuprili,
as Grand Vizier in 1676 and was executed by order of the Sultan at
Belgrade a few months after his failure at Vienna.

[5] Count Ernest Rüdiger von Starhemberg, to whom the Duke of
Lorraine had entrusted the defence of the capital.

and courage in the soe long and desperate defence of that place.

The Maior and aldermen of the corporation of Don- *Sept.* 11 caster, with severall other members of it, made me a present of two runletts of white and claret, a kagg sturgian, and sent word that they would dine with me the next day, which they did, and recieved such entertainment as gave them satisfaction.

I mustered my troop at Doncaster, wher I entertained 18 the Maior, some aldermen and severall other gentlemen, to the nomber of eighteen, at dinner at my charge.

The Maior of that corporation sent to invite me to 27 dinner, it being his feast at the going out of his maioralty, which I accepted, sent him a buck, and was very well entertained. My Lord Castleton dined ther the same day, whome I had not seen to convers with him of some years. He surprized in calling for wine and drinkeing to me as soon as he came into the room.

I about this time recieved a confirmation of the bad news that my sister (notwithstanding all my endeavours to prevent it, and her ofton repeated vows never to doe it) had marryed one Burt before mentioned, a fellow that had raised himselfe from a common souldier in France to be a lieutenant of foot, but a person neither of parts, person, fortune nor extraction, and at that time out of all imploy-ment, which was a great trouble to me.

I went to a meeting of the deputy lieutenants at *Oct.* 4 Doncaster.

Ther was another day appointed for the same service 8 at Barnsley, where I was likewise. The day after began the sessions at that place, wher I assisted, and my wife comming to meet me we passed some days to visit some friends and relations on that side, and had stayed longer if some company, viz., Sir John Kay, &c., had not come 12 to pass some time at my hous, with his wife and family.

I recieved news by letter from my Lord Halifax that 13 I had the Kings leave to goe to London, which I desired to have that I might be near the King at a time that I thought he would take new measures as to the scheam of affairs, officers and other publique concerns, for his own and the nations security after the late hellish conspiracie.

Oct. 16   I went with my wife to wait on the Duke and Duchesse of Newcastle at Welbeck, wher I stayed two days. The Duke gave me the copie of the letter he writt to my Lord Rochester upon my account for the continuance of Yorke as a guarison, wherin he writt (after severall publique reasons) very obligeingly of me in perticular. He promessed me to give me his picture, and (acquainting me with the contents of severall of his letters from the Secretary and other statesmen, and his answers) assured me that he had tould me all things of moment that he remembred had passed either relateing to the goverment or his private affairs since he see me last. I found he took some things ill from my Lord Privy Seale, which I was sorry for. He commanded me freely to make use of him in all things, for (to use his own obligeing expression) he would serve me by writeing or speakeing here or above wher it was in his power upon all occasions; and the thruth was I found this good lord allways as ready to doe for me as to professe it.

18   I was followed with a letter of kindness from his Grace, in which was this expression: I am sure ther is nothing of friendship and service a friend ought to doe but I will pay it.

21   My Lord Darcy of Aston and severall others came and dined with me. By the post of this day came an account of a secound victory obteaned by the King of Poland and the Imperialists against the Turkes,[1] to the joy of Christendome.

23   I went to my command at Yorke, wher thes accidents did happen—that one Mr. Rogers,[2] enseign to Major Sterlings company, haveing had some dispute with my portor, that gave him some ill language, he had complained

---

[1] At Parkány on September 29/October 9.   [2] Francis Rogers.

to me of him by letter, but in a straine or phrase not soe respectfull as I expected, which I returned an answer of with some sharpness. At our meeting he began to expostulate the matter, till I tould him he was insolent. He replyed that he was a gentleman, and could take that language from the governor, but from noebody else. I tould him I would take noe protection from that character, and if he thought himselfe injured I devested myselfe of it from that minuit to give him what satisfaction he desired. After this the gentleman was more moderate, and I made him soe sensible of the provocation he had first given by his letter to me that he was very submissive, and willing to sitt down with my answer and reply.

The Sunday following, being in the Minster, I found the cussin which used to be in my seat remooved into the next, wher Sir John Brook[1] was to sitt (a person that I had thought fitt, with other deputy lieutenants, to disarm in our late search for arms). This gentleman riseing at the psalmes, I took up the cussin and replaced it in my seat. Service being ended, Sir John asked me if I had the same commission to take his cussin that I had to take his arms. I said I took it as my own, as I should always doe when I see it misplaced; and if he took his being disarmed ill from me he made choice of an ill place to quarrell in, and that hee durst not say thos things in any other.

The next day I expected to hear from him, he seeming very much disturbed with this treatment; but not sending to me for reparation, the next morning I sent the captain that then commanded a company in Yorke to tell him that I had stayed some time at home, thinkeing to hear from him, and believed the reason why I did not to be the character I bore in that citty, and did therfore now send to him to tell him that if he had any ressentment either for my takeing his cussin or arms, I was ready to give him satisfaction as a private person. He returned me this answer, that he was most concerned at my takeing away

[1] Sir John Brookes of York, created a baronet in 1676.

the cussin, bycaus it did prevent his giveing it to me, which he intended; but that for satisfaction he thought what had passed between us did not oblige him to aske it in his circumstances, and was willing to be quiett. Soe that the substance of this matter was this, that he foolishly owned himselfe under such circumstances as to own himselfe affronted, but not to see himselfe righted. I could have been very well content that noe occasion of such disputes had offered themselves, but when they doe I have found that the best way to prevent them for the future is not to seem too backward in seeking reparation.

I waited one day on Doctor Dolbin, late Bishop of Winchester, and now lately translated to the diocesse of Yorke,[1] who recieved me with great kindness and respect; and afterwards of my Lord Maior, with whom I dealt something freely in matters which he had lately done relateing to the Kings service; but we parted very fair.

Oct. 30 I returned to Thriberge the 30th.

After the setling of my affairs ther, though much interupted by the visits of many nighbours to take their leave *Nov.* 14 of me, I set forward for London, November the 14, with my wife and family, wher I arrived without any accident on Saturday the 19th.

By visit to my Lord Privy Seale I found him still in the King's good esteem; that the Duke was not soe gratefull to him as the services done by him deserved; that the differences between him and my Lord Rochester lasted still, and with more animosity then before. Waiting upon the Secretary of State, Sir Lionell Jenkins, he tould me the King ressented my carriage in respect to his service in the country very well; that the Lord Maior of Yorke was sent for up by order of Council for some words he had spoaken,[2] and asked my opinion of him, in

---

[1] John Dolben, enthroned at York on August 23, 1683, had previously occupied the see, not of Winchester, but of Rochester.

[2] In his reply to Jenkins, dated November 21, 1683, Edward Thompson declares the accusation against him to be the result purely of personal

which I spoake according to my judgement.　The King recieved me gratiously, and the Duke seemed kind to me, and my Lord Rochester the same, to whom I paid a visit.

Mr. Sydney,[1] one of the conspirators, was tryed for his *Nov.* 21 life, and found guilty of high treason.

I found the hopes of a Parlament a great way off, tho Flanders laid under the danger of being won the following spring by the French, and the nation to be dissatisfyed for the want of it, viz., such as were against the French interest.　The Grand Prior of France being com'd over, and observed to be very kind to the Duchesse of Portsmouth and she to him, gave soe great jealousie to the King that he sent him away, and twas suspected the Duchess would not stay long behind, which few people seemd sorry for.

I had heard from a great man that something would shortly happen which would proove a mortification to the Duke of Yorke and that party.　And it seemed to be explained on the 24th, that the Duke of Monmouth, 24 suspected to be fled into Flanders or some other part of the world beyond sea for the conspiracie, surrendered himselfe to Mr. Secretary Jenkyns at Whitehall, wher (the thing before concerted) the King and the Duke went to him, and after an hours discours allowed him to goe to his lodgeings at the Cockpit, attended by his own servants, and under noe other restraint then that of one sergiant-at-arms.　But what was said or done might be conjectured, but not known.　This was a great surprize to all people.

spite, and protests against the charge of using seditious words as " a thing far contrary to my nature as well as principles, as I abiminate the very thoughtes of it, and shall beg noe greater favour from his Majesty then that he out of his accustomed clemency would be graciously pleased to appoynt some persons of quality to have the matter examined here, where I am confident the whole bench except myne accuser will vindicate my loyelty as well as innocency in that particuler " (S.P. Dom., Charles II, 434, where are also the articles exhibited against Thompson).

[1] Algernon, elder brother of Henry Sidney.

Nov. 25   Waiting of my Lord Privy Seale, he tould me that he
doubted not but the Duke of Monmoths admittance to
the King and the Duke (for that day he had kissed the
Kings hand, the Duke's, and the Queens) would have
various interpretations and guesses by whos intercession
chiefly it came to pass.   I tould him the report of the
world was that the Duchesse of Portsmouth and my Lord
Sunderland had done it, and that it was publiquely known
that the King had said in Councill the day before that it was
at the request of the Duke of Yorke, to whom he had made
submission and disclaime of all competition to the Crown.
My Lord said that was a mistake, for the Duke of Yorke
and that interest of his had opposed it to the last, and did
own that himselfe had chiefly laboured in it and brought
it to effect.   He gave severall reasons as well publique
as private for his soe doing, not soe fitt here to be mentioned.   By this it appeared that notwithstanding the
great interest against this lord he reserved a great power
with the King.   I found by his lordship the Duke of
Monmoth had confessed the thruth of the late plott to
the King and Duke, but would not give any publique
evidence against the conspiratours.   But tis certain,
whatever interest it was that effected this matter, the King
himselfe had a great hand in it, who had a paternall
kindness for the Duke of Monmouth, and could not
contean himselfe from giveing opon and publique expressions of it wherever he mett the Duke; and the Duke
on the other hand showed all the respect and diligence
imaginable in attending upon and following the King.

28   The whole Court began now to discover that though
the Duke of Yorke seemed consenting to the Duke of
Monmouth's readmittance into the King's favour, it was
not freely but from nescessity, the King declareing he
would have it soe; for the Duke was not made privy to it
not above two days before it came to pass.

29   The King then, as he came from my Lady Portsmouth,
asked me (leaneing upon my arm) if I knew sufficient

matter for bringeing a *quo warranto* against the charter
of Yorke. I answered noe, but would endeavour to
inform myselfe. I said I feared I could not doe it soe
well at this distance as if I were upon the place. The
King replyed, I only recommend it to you. My Lord
Maior of that citty had denyed leave to a mountebanke,
that had the King's own recommendation, to erect his
stage in that place, which he haveing complained of, his
Majesty gave me order that night [to] suffer without my
Lord Maior.

My Lord Maior of Yorke, being comd up, came to *Dec.* 4
see me, and desired leave, when he came before the King
for his justification, to make use of my name soe farr as to
say that the governor knew how ready he was in the time
of the plott to give all the assistance he could to the discovery of it and of the persons suspected of it in the country, which I gave him leave to doe. I knew the Duke of
Yorke, who thought him accessary to his once ill reception
at Yorke, wished his punishment. However, I did the
man right to justifie him in what I might, and to carry
him to my Lord Privy Seale, who promessed to assist him
at the Councill; for I knew ther was some private
animosity in the complaint against him, and I hoped it
might be a means to make him a thorow convert to the
Goverment if he was but mercifully handled in this
matter.

Being at my Lady Portsmouths, the King tould me 5
ther was a new complaint against my Lord Maior of
Yorke, and that he feared he was but a bad man. I said
that I was obliged to acquaint his Majesty with this
thruth, that he was very ready to give me his assistance
in York at the time of the plott, but that I had nothing
to say in his defence for any new matter laid to his
charge, and which might be committed since I came from
thence.

The Duke of Monmouth, haveing obteaned his pardon, 6
refused to sign a publique declaration of his knowlege

of the late conspiracie, for which the King sent to discharge him from comming into Whitehall. My Lord Privy Seale said to me that the manner of doing it was something hard (as it was required), but he ought to have submitted entirely to the King in it; and I found his lordship was concerned (as he had reason to be, being looked upon as his friend in the matter of his admittance) that he was soe obstinate. The same day[1] Mr. Sydney was executed on Tower Hill as one of the conspirators, but said nothing before he suffered, only left a paper with the sheriff, which I heard the King say was very treasonable and evasive, but not absolutely negative as to the fact of which he was accused. It was not thought fitt to be allowed to be printed.

I found the Duke of Yorke was much displeased with my Lord Privy Seale (though he showed it not oponly) that he was not consulted in the affair of bringing in the Duke of Monmouth; and it was my Lord Privy Seale his expression that the Duke would never forgive him it. But the King being the chiefe instrument of it, it did [not] appear that his lordship lost any interest with him, though the Duke of Monmouth performed not what was expected from him.

The confederates in Spain, Holland, Sweden, &c., that were now prepareing to resist the French and to preserve Flanders, were very angry with us that we still continued in our nutrality, and, as the Spaniard said, contrary to our league with them. But our King said his own affairs were in soe ill a posture at home that he was not in condition to come into the warr. This confirmed the jealousie of our adhering to the French interest, and of a private commerce with them, and by the means of the Duchesse of Portsmouth, &c.

Dec. 11   It was much reported in town that my Lord Privy Seale was not well with the King upon the late affair of the Duke of Monmouth, and that he had mett with discouragements

[1] Really on December 7.

at Court to soe great a degree as to make him leave businesse.　My Lord tould me, upon my acquainting [him]
with this, that he had mett with discouragements from
some, but not from the King, for he was as well ther as
ever; and that ther would be a further production of
affairs in a little time then was expected, and soe pointed
at the thing as I guessed what he meant.

I was at the sessions at Hicks his Hall, wher a non- *Dec.* 12
conformist minister was prossecuted upon the statute of
the 35 Eliz., cap. 1 [1] in order to abjuration, which was the
first president of that kind in my time.

I dined with my Lord Privy Seal, and desired him to 16
take the first opportunity to speake to the King for me
in two things.　One was that the Mannour of Yorke
might not be sould (which had long been in suspence),
and the other was that one of the companys that were
now comming from Tangers (that guarison being
demolished)[2] might be assigned to Yorke of addition to
that ther before.　His lordship tould me the same night
at Whitehall that the King, upon his speaking to him,
had answered to the first, that he would not sell the
Mannour, and he found him well disposed as to the
second.

The same day, being with the Duke of Albymarle, he
tould me he was sorry to find that my Lord Privy Seale,
only out of design to outdoe his adversary my Lord
Rochester, should have soe great a hand in bringing in the
Duke of Monmouth, wherby he had lost much of the

---

[1] A statute applying to those who obstinately refused to come to church,
and also attacked the ecclesiastical power of the Crown, persuaded others
to abstain from attendance at church, or joined unlawful conventicles.
Such offenders were to be imprisoned, and on failure to conform within
three months were to abjure the realm.

[2] The decision to evacuate Tangier, which had been brought into the
possession of England by the marriage of Charles II with Catherine of
Braganza, had been taken early in the year.　Money was lacking to maintain its harbour and fortifications, and it was felt that the garrison of 3,000
men might be useful at home.

Duke of Yorks friendship and a great nomber of the loyall party that were all his friends before; that the Duke of Yorke had tould him not many hours since that if my Lord Privy Seale had noe friendship for him, yet, as being the Kings brother, he might have tould him of the design, and not have brought in Monmouth without acquainting him with it in the least; that he could never forget the former services done him by my Lord Privy Seale, but he took a method to bring it to pass were it possible, for to his knowlege he was yet labouring to reunite the King and the Duke of Monmouth. The Duke of Albymarle said his Highness knew his relation to my Lord Privy Seale, but his loyaltie and respect to his Highness was more valuable to him then all that, and he hoped my Lord designed noe disservice to him in that affair, with much more to the same effect, his Grace seeming to lament my Lord Privy Seal's actings in this concern.

I tould his lordship thes perticulars, to which he made this answer, that this complaint from the Duke looked as if hee had a mind to be upon better measures with him, but that he had not seen the Duke of Monmouth since he last went from Court, and that he only acting in that affair by the King's command could not acquaint the Duke with it when his Majesty would not allowe him to doe it; but said on Wedensday after he was to dine with the Duke of Albimarle, and should then be better able to demean himselfe in this matter, if he spoake to him in it, by knowing of it before, for which he thanked me. His Grace tould me further that if the Lord Privy Seale would trust him he could tell him a way to be too hard for Rochester without useing such means as this to effect it.

His Grace desired me to be with him the next day at ten in the morning, to advise with all the officers in town, that were to meet to consider of a proposition sent them by the King relating to the standing forces throughout the kingdome, wher I attended with the rest. The matter related to a new way of paying the souldiers, not by the captains, who had been complained of to cheat the souldiers of part of their pay; but it being represented to the King from the officers that it would in a great measure cut of that respect and dependencie from the officer that was due to him from the souldier, his Majesty was willing to continue it as formerly, the collonels undertakeing to take care that the respective captains should doe right to the souldiers.

Dineing in the Citty with six gentlemen of quality, *Dec.* 18 comming away with two of them after dinner, they quarrelled in a coffy hous, wher we stayed to drinke coffeè, and though I did what I could to reconcile them went presently out and drew in the street, and made a pass one at [the other], but missing one another, closed. By this time I gott into them and broake one of their swords, and soe they were parted. The one of them, which was Major Orbe, eldest son of Sir Thomas Orbe of Lincolnshire[1] (the other's name was Bellengeambe, of the north, the chiefe of that familie),[2] not thinkeing this full satisfaction, notwithstanding all my endeavours to make them friends, challenged Bellengeambe a second time; and takeing coach, and I with them, bought new swords by the way, and came towards Hide Parke to fight. As we came by the way I offered to be secound, since they would fight, to either of them, and the other should look out for another to be his. Mr. Orbe chose me, and bid Bellengeamb seek his friend. Bellengeamb said he never would make use of any secound, but would decide it presently by moonshine, for it was nine a clock at night and very light, and said he would confide in my honour to see fair play done between them; which at the last I accepted

[1] Charles Orby, who was to succeed his father Sir Thomas as second baronet, was at this time Guidon and Major of the Queen's troop of guards (Dalton, *English Army Lists*, i. 188, 253).

[2] Allan Bellingham of Levens, near Kendal, who had represented Westmorland in the four Parliaments of Charles II.

at both their entreatys, and by the mercy of heaven missing one anothers bodys as they passed one against another the secound time, and closeing togather, I came in to part them, and Mr. Orbe's footman doeing the same with me, we held their swords soe as noe mischiefe was done, only Mr. Orbe had a slight prick in the thigh, and Mr. Bellengeamb had a race on the forehead, and myselfe a slight hurt as I came in to part them. After this we went all to supper, and parted good friends.

The same day I recieved news that Sir Roger Stricland[1] had a design to stand for Parlament man at Audbrough, and that some gentlemen of the nighbourhood, formerly my friends, upon the rumour that I intended to stand at Yorke, had recomended him to that bourough; but the design was, I knew, privately to oppose me, Sir Thomas Slingsby and Sir Thomas Mauliverer being privately angry that I still continued governor of Yorke, and had an interest in Yorke, wher they were hated and reputed papists.

Jan. 2 [1683/4] But I learnt from a great man that noe Parlament was near, and that some near the King were designing other measures then thos of Parlaments, and lamented at the same time that now that the phenatick party had nothing to say or argue against the Goverment [they] must have some colour of complaint given them by this and some other things in agitation.

I spoake to the Duke to befriend me near the King for the obteaning some additionall forces to Yorke. He tould me, with couldnesse (as I thought), thos troops would not be setled till the spring, but then he would see what could be done. My Lord Burlinton at my request desired the same favour for me of my Lord Rochester,

---

[1] Although coming of a Lancashire family, Sir Roger Strickland had estates near Catterick and at Thornton Bridge near Aldborough, on the latter of which he generally resided. He had served with distinction in the navy, and in the autumn of 1688 was to be entrusted with the command of the English fleet until superseded by Lord Dartmouth.

* 24/17: Edmund Jennings, 21 December 1683; 24/29: E. Morris, 3 January 1683/4; 25/9: E. Morris, 25 December 1683; 25/26: E. Morris, 30 December 1683. These letters indicate the seriousness with which people considered the possibility of a new parliament.

who answered he never did concern himselfe in military
matters, but he would not oppose it. My Lord Privy
Seale desired Sir Stiphen Fox[1] for me in the same matter
to assist me, which he promessed.

My Lord Privy Seale tould me he had been very *Jan.* 1c
earnest with the King for a Parlament, but to noe purpas;
that he had used for arguments that though he had slipped
his opportunity of calling one soon after the last plott
(when he could not have missed of one according to his
own desire), that if he feared not to have a good one now,
the longer it was deferred the wors it would be, till at the
last it might be made an argument never to call one at all;
that nothing ought to be soe dear to him as to keep his
word with his people; that the law required a Parlament
to be called every three years, his Majesty had promessed
upon the last dissolution to observe the lawes, by a proclamation setting forth the reasons at the same time why
he had dismissed that Parlament; that the generall use
of that was that he intended to call another within the
three years, and that he feared an ill construction might
be made of his not doing accordingly; that though the
anti-monarkicall party was very low and discouraged,
yet this might raise a discontent in another party, thos
which were for the service of the Crown, but for his
Majesty observeing the lawes at the same time, especially
wher they had his royall word for it ; however, if his
Majesty thought not fit to doe it, he would not relinquish his service, but if he could find out any reasons as
an excuse for his not doing it, would study to doe it; soe
that ther seemed noe possibility of a Parlament, except
we were compelled to it by a forraign caus, for if the
warr went on between France and Spain we continued
in danger that Spain and Holland would declare warr
against us.

[1] Sir Stephen Fox was then one of the Commissioners of the Treasury,
a position which he held almost without interruption from the fall of Danby
to the accession of Queen Anne.

Jan. 15   The sessions for Middlesex being at Hicks his Hall and the Ould Bailiff, my Lord Chiefe Justice Jefferys [1] had reflected upon the whole bench of justices of the peace for that county, by useing generall words as he found fault with one of them, who indeed had acted not according to law for bailing a person that had committed murther, saying the justices of the peace of Middlesex did what they ought not to doe, that they took noe care of acting according to the law or their dutys, &c. Notice of this being brought to us sitting at Hicks his Hall, and that his lordship had said this and more to the same effect in opon court at the Ould Bailiff, I mooved that some gentlemen might be sent to his lordship to require reparation, it being hard the whole bench should suffer in the esteem of the world for one man's fault. This was agreed unto, and I, being one of the four sent, soe laid the matter before him that his lordship gave us that satisfaction as to declare in court that he ment to reflect upon noe person but only the person that did the fault, not upon soe many worthy and eminent as well as knowing gentlemen.

17   The King and Duke both commanded me to take care at this sessions that Scotch pedlers might be punished within the county of Middlesex, in which matter a very strict order was made, of which his Majesty had an account from me that night, as also concerning some commandes he had given me before relateing to the charter of Yorke.

28   At this time there was soe great a frost (which began about the middle of December) that Thamise was frozen over belowe the Bridge. Ther were bull-baitings and hors-races upon the Thamse; coaches went and passed

---

[1] Sir George Jeffreys, the judge who was later to earn an evil reputation by his treatment of those engaged in Monmouth's rebellion, had himself been Chairman of the Middlesex Sessions before his appointment to the post of Lord Chief Justice in September 1683. He was created Baron Jeffreys of Wem in May 1685 and promoted to the post of Lord Chancellor in September of the same year.

ther as in the streets.[1]   The sault water was frozen upon
all the coasts above a league into the sea, soe that we could
have noe commerce from any part of the world, noe shipps
or boats being able either to goe out or come in.

I was desired by the Duke of Albemarle to acquaint *Jan.* 30
my Lord Privy Seale with his continued project to farme
all the King's revenue (with others engaged with him in
it) at 1,575,000 l. per annum, and to desire his lordship's
assistance in it.   My Lord Privy Seale tould me it would
intrench too much on my Lord Rochester to suffer that
to be done, but that he wished the Duke good luck in it,
and would assist him what he could.

The Duke of Yorke did now chiefly manage affairs,
but with great hautynesse; yet my Lord of Danby was
likely to gett out of the Tower against the Dukes will.
But my Lord Privy Seal tould me it would be done, that
he was that lords friend in the thing, and that the King
had made both the Duke and my Lord Rochester content
with it.

For all this it was strongly opposed underhand by [*Feb.*]8
Rochester and my Lord Sunderland, soe that by their
devises, though both the King and Duke were hearty in it,
the judges delayed my Lord his being bailed to the last
day of the terme.   The reason was that thos two lords
feared Danby might joine with Halifax to weaken their
interest.

I haveing caused two Scotch pedlers to be punished
as vagrants, one of them caused me and the constable to
be arrested, of which I went and complained to the King
in Councill.

Sir Thomas Slingsby, Sir Thomas Mauliverer, and *Feb.* 10
some other gentlemen of Yorkshire, to show their

---

[1] A printing-press was even set up on the Thames, where it became
fashionable to have one's name printed with the place and the date ; and
the train-bands were exercised upon the ice.   The frost lasted about eight
weeks.   A full account is given in Newdigate-Newdegate, *Cavalier and
Puritan*, pp. 233-40.

diligence for the King's service exceeded mine, sent up an agent with some matter wheron to ground a forfiture of the charter of the citty of Yorke; of which haveing early notice from a friend, I first went and informed the Duke of York and the Secretary with it, and used means to introduce their messenger myselfe to the Secretary, wherby I did prevent any jealousie at Court of my being to much a friend to that citty, and them of the credit they pretended to have by it.   And now it was resolved a *quo warranto* should be brought against that citty if the matter to ground one upon was sufficient.

Feb. 12   My Lord of Danby was bailed from his long confine- ment of five years, and all the popish lords that had laid ther since the first plott, excepting the two that were dead.[1]

The same day my Lord of Danby came to kiss his Majesty's hand in the bedchamber, wher I chanced to be present.   The King recieved him very civilly, and when the earle complained of his long imprisonment, tould him that he knew it was against his consent, which my Lord owned with thankefulness; but ther was noe discours between them in private.   My Lord Privy Seale came into the presence soon after, and the two lords saluted each other, but slightly.

The next day, going from my Lord Privy Seale to wait on the earl, my Lord bid me give him his service, and tell him that he should have taken a more perticular sort of notice of him but that he thought it might not proove soe well for his service.   The earle said that it was for that reason he took also soe little notice of his lordship, the jealousie being great of a friendship between them.   My Lord of Danby said to me then he would goe to his hous out of town, and not meddle with publique business; that he could noe doubt arrive to it, if he would, but not upon that nationall foundation wher he would only

[1] Stafford, who had been executed in 1679, and William, fourth Baron Petre, whose death on January 5, 1683/4, had roused public compassion and helped in some measure to secure the release of his fellow-sufferers.

engage, declareing his aversion to a French or a popish interest.   He tould me further what had passed between the Duke of Yorke and him at his late visit to him after he had been with the King, wherby I found him disgusted with that prince; and that upon his telling the earl that he had heard of something of slight he should say concerning him, the earle should reply that it was true he had ofton been soe unfortunate as to differ with him in opinion, and had not yet found reason to repent of it, but that he never sayd anything against his person, and if anybody had tould him that, they were but whispers and lies, and should be glad to know who were his informers (but the Duke evaded that).

My Lord Privy Seale, at my instance, obteaned leave *Feb.* 16 of the King for me to buy an independent company, and to have it remooved from Portsmouth to Yorke.   The same day I thanked the King for it, had a long discours with him of the temper and condition of the citty of Yorke, his Majesty thankeing me for my care of that place, but concludeing it nescessary that a *quo warranto* should issue out against their charter.   I desired of him at the same time a lease of the Mannour, which he bid me petition him for, and he would advise with the Lords of the Treasury concerning it.   I bought the said independent company of Captain Rowe for nine hundred pounds,[1] but 18 was not allowed to remoove it for the present.

I found by my Lord Privy Seale that he and my Lord 20 Danby understood one another.

I waited on my Lady Portsmouth (her son, the Duke of 22 Richmond, being Master of the Hors to the King, and under whom the pages of honour were admitted) to desire she would putt the King in mind of a former promess he had made to accept my second son Tamworth in that quality when a vacancy should happen.   She answered

---

[1] Reresby's commission as captain of the company is dated February 26. His predecessor, Thomas Rowe, had been appointed in 1680, when the company was in the Tower (Dalton, *English Army Lists*, pp. 272, 324).

the King had already promessed many, but she would speake to him concerning my son.   The boy, being then some twelve years old, was hansome, had good parts, and, I thanke God, every way hopefull; and though he was fitt in his nature and disposition for a court, yet I long disputed with myselfe whether or noe to put him into that way of education, which was more wicked and debauched at that time then in former ages.   But I considered it would proove a better provision for him then I was otherwise able to make, and that if he inclined to be ill he might find opportunities for it in all conditions, and soe resolved to place him ther if I could.

Feb. 25   I drew a petition, which, without amendments by my Lord Privy Seale, my Lord Burlinton, or others to whom I showed it, I presented to the King, which he recieved, and sent himselfe for the Secretary to give it him with his own handes, ordering him to referr it to the Lords of the Treasury to report their opinions of it to him.

27   My Lord Mougrave tould me that he believed the business of my son's being a page of honour would succeed, for that he had accidentally heard of my pretention in that kind accidentally, and had secounded me in it to the Duchesse, who was serious in it, telling her severall kind things of me and the antiquity of my family.

March 1   The King went to Newmarkit, and I followed the 14th.

14   I went by Cambrige to see my brother Yarburgh Reresby, then fellow of St. John's, and arrived at Newmarket the 17th.

17   That night, waiting on his Royall Highness, amongst other discours he was speakeing of the Duke of Buckingham's consumption of his great estate, and of some other of his qualities (for he did not love him), and as to his courage that noebody was better able to give an account of it then Sir John Reresby (meaning the business when hee and my Lord Falconbrige should have fought at Yorke).

18   The weather was very unseasonable and durty, soe

that walkeing the town with his Majesty, who observed I had but thin shoos, advised me to gett a stronger pair to prevent getting could, which I hear mention as an exemple of that prince his great goodness and care of all persons that came near him, however inconsiderable.

Hearing soon after my arrivall that the Duchesse of Portsmouth had spoaken again to the King to accept my son as his page of honour, I thanked her for it, who tould me she would present him herselfe at her return to London to his Majesty. She invited me the day after to dinner, wher his Majesty, haveing dined before, sate by us all the while. The next day[1]

I dined with the Duke of Albemarle; the day after with *March* 20 the French embassader by invitation. The same day that Duke tould me that he had recieved a letter from the Duke of Newcastle to be kind to me, and bid me when I writt to him to assure him that he had commanded him a thing that he had as much a disposition to doe as his Grace to direct him to it.

Being mounted on a good hors of my own breed, both 22 the King and the Duchess commended him; but I had the ill fortune to lame him as he came to London. That day the Court returned for London, and I went to Berry to see my Ant Monson, whom I found in good health, though of great years. The next day I returned for Newmarket, and then to London.

The diversions the King followed this time at Newmarket were thes—Walking in the morning till ten a clock; then he went to the cockpitt till dinner time; about three he went to the hors-races, at six to the cockpitt for an hour, then to the play (though the comedians were very indifferent), soe to supper, next to the Duchess of Portsmouth's till bed time, and then to his own apartment to bed. Ther were seven dukes at once.[2]

---

[1] Written thus in the original. There is no sign of any omission or excision and the sentence appears to be continued in the next paragraph.

[2] The unusually large number of dukes in existence at this time was

March 24   I had an account from Yorke that (some of that corporation being for surrendring, others for defending their
*   charter, and that the consent must be generall to doe either)
it would proove of consequence that it would fall into the
King's hands by default of defence, which I acquainted
the King and the Duke with.

[1684]

March 25   The warr in Europe seemed now again to be likely to
goe on between the French [and] the Spaniards with their
confederates, though the French King offered either a
trucc or a pcacc for scven ycars upon such hard tcrms
(for they would keep whatever they had taken from the
Spanniards or the Empire) that it could not be agreed to.
The King of England secounded the French Kings proposals, and recommended them both to Spain and the
United Provinces as resonable, and offered to be guarantie
of the said peace or truce.

April 2   My Lord Rochester's friends were advanced, and Mr.
Godolphin,[1] one of the Commissioners of the Treasury,
was made Secretary of State in the place of Sir Lionel
Jenkyns (who had leave to retire by reason of his great
age); but this gentleman had the assistance of the
Duchesse of Portsmouth also in that promotion.   My
Lord Privy Seale tould me the same day that though all
thes interests continued avers to him, the King was as
kind to him as ever.   However, it was visible he was less
in business then before.

3   I waited on my Lord Rochester at his hous (who was
very civill to me) to desire he would come to some
resolution in the business of my petition for a lease of the

due to the ennobling of the King's illegitimate sons, several of whom were
probably among the seven at Newmarket.

[1] Sidney Godolphin, created Baron Godolphin of Rialton in the following September and Earl of Godolphin in 1706.   He was sworn Secretary
of State on April 17.

* 25/16: Thos. Fairfax, 22 March 1683/4. The disagreement over what to do
about the charter was so heated that Fairfax compared the mayor and citizens
to fisherwomen of Billingsgate scolding one another.

Mannor of Yorke as soon as could be with his conveniency, who promessed me he would, but could not dispatch it as yet. That day the Duchess of Portsmouth presented my second son Tamworth to the King for page of honour, who gave him his hand to kiss, and commended the child for hansome and well-behaved.

The King and Queen went to Windser for the summer. *April* 5 I spoake to his Royall Highness concerning the intended saile of York Manner, and gave him some reasons why it should not be sould, which soe farr convinced the Duke that he tould me he was of that opinion that twas the Kings interest to keep it.

My Lord Dartsmouth, Master of the Ordinance, being 15 now returned from demolishing Tangers, and being better recieved by the King and Duke then was expected by his adversarys, each faction was ready to gain him to their side; but he tould the King and Duke that he would joine with noebody but himselfe for their service, and stand upon his own leggs. When I tould this to my Lord Privy Seale he said everybody had not witt and strength to stand alone; that it was true he had done soe, which he attributed to the Kings kindness to him and his good fortune, and to some measures (especially that of not seekeing his own gain or profit) which his lordship in his circumstances was not soe well qualifyed to followe, and that he had at the last this advantage by it, that he hoped ere long to find his greatest opponants court him for their friend (meaning Lord Rochester and Sunderland), for at this time it was given out that they began to disagree.

Sir Henry Gooderick, brother to my Lord Dartsmouth, 19 tould me that the said lord was under some intention to make himselfe the head of a third faction, in opposition to thos of Halifax on one side, Rochester, Sunderland and Portsmouth on the other, as the only way to bring things to a nationall bothum, which was the thing he contrived, being avers to fenaticisme on one hand and to popery and a French interest on the other; and that himselfe had tould my Lord of Danby of this, who approoved it extreamly, which would make him very great or very little.   My Lord Dartsmouth touching at Cadiz in his return, my brother Jarvase Reresby waited on him and gave him a horse worth 200 l.; but I found his lordship, however, not kind towards me in the business of my concern of the guarrison of Yorke.

April 24   I had some heats with Captain Burke, that marryed my unfortunate sister, and with Colonel Oglethorp at this time, but it came not to a quarrel with either.

24   My Lord Rochester gave charge to the sollicitor that managed my suit against the Scotch pedlers, or rather defended it, that whatever the account of the expence were it should be brought to him, for the King would pay it himselfe.   Waiting on my Lord Chiefe Justice Jefferys, he tould me I had proceeded legally in that affair, and that should appear when the caus came to be tryed before him, and that he had given the same laws against Scotch pedlers as well as other vagrants in his late circuit, and by the Kings order.   The Atturney-general was also of the same opinion.   At the same time the partys that had brought ther action found little encouragement from the law or others to proceed, and sent me word they intended to lett it fall.

I tooke the sacrament the 20th and the oaths the 24 in the Kings Bench for my company of foot.

25   The charter of Yorke being now likely to fall into the Kings hand by default, Sir Thomas Slingsby and Sir Henry Marwood, myselfe, &c., mett to agree upon persons for bearing office in that citty that were of best ability and loyalty, and made a list, which we presented to Secretary Godolphin, as the Duke had directed me, to which were added six gentlemen of the country for justices of the peace (though not freemen of the citty), to be joined with them for the administration of justice within the same.

26   I recieved the unwelcome newes by an express from York that on St. George his Day, on which seven gunns

had been fired, the Tower was sett on fire and all the inside
of it burnt;[1] only the powder and some part of the arms   *
were saved.   This hapned in the worst conjuncture that
could be (my Lord Dartsmouth, Master of the Ordinance,
being returned, and was noe friend to the guarrison) to
have it reduced.

I went to Windser to acquaint the King with it, who *April* 27
was soe kind as to promess me it should continue, or, if
not, he would not reduce it till he had provided for me
in some kind as beneficiall.   He promessed the same on
my behalfe some days after to my Lord Privy Seale; but
I continued, however, doubtfull of the issue.

My Lord Dartsmouth tould me that if I would accept *May* 1
of lieutenant-governership of Hull, with the same sallary
the King gives me as governor of Yorke, he would obtean
it for me, the present lieutenant-governor[2] being likely to
be remooved; but I tould him I could [not] in honour
descend from governor to lieutenant-governor.   He
reply'd it was as honourable to be the King's lieutenant
in soe great a guarison as to be governor of a less.   However, I resolved to continue the command I had if it was
possible.

I went to Windser, and ther meeting my Lord Privy 10
Seale, he had a confirmation from the King that Yorke
should continue a guarrison, and that my company should
be remooved from Portsmouth thether.   And the King
was soe just to his promess in this perticular that of himselfe he gave order that night at his coucheè to the Secretary of Warr[3] that an order should be drawn up against

---

[1] The fire began about 10 p.m. on April 23, and reduced Clifford's
Tower to a mere shell.   There was a general belief at the time that it was
not accidental in origin.

[2] Lionel Copley, of Wadworth, Yorkshire, appointed lieutenant-
governor of Hull at the close of 1681.

[3] William Blathwayt, who had been secretary-at-war, or chief clerk for
military affairs, since August 1683.   In this capacity he received many
letters from Reresby, some of which are printed below.

* 26/20: Fr. Sterling, 26 April 1684.

the next Councill day for his signing for the company to march.

May 11 This day the Duke of Yorke was declared Lord High Admirall of England, or at least to have the power, the name and patent not being given him bycaus of the Act of Parlament for takeing the oaths and the sacrament. However, this did dissatisfie some people.

This day, the Queen being at dinner, the Duchesse of Portsmouth, as a lady of the bedchamber, came to wait on her (which was not usuall), which putt the Queen into that disorder that tears came into her eyes, whilst the other laughed and turned [it] into jeast.

20 My company of foot marched from Portsmouth for York, haveing 26 days assigned them for their march. I went and see them at Acton.

Ther being a design to make eleven of the independent
25 companys regimentall, my Lord Dartsmouth tould me at Windser, wher I then was, that if I would be of his regiment I should be his first captain, though by the date of my commission I ought to be the last. I answered I would leave it to the King to dispose of me as he pleased, but at the same time made it my request privately to his Majesty that I might continue independent, but that he would pleas to take it upon himselfe, that I might give that lord noe occasion of distast by my refusall, which the King promessed me.

Then came the news of the takeing of Luxenbourg by the French King,[1] which our Court seemed well pleased with, but others (and some of the Kings best friends) were dissatisfyed at, bycaus it was looked upon as the key of Germany and Holland, as well as of Flanders, and might probably proove too great a setting up of the French.

29 I went to Windser, it being the Kings birthday, to wish him happiness and long life. Ther was a great croud attending upon the same occasion, but not much gallantry of cloaths. The Duke of Yorke was declared then at

[1] May 25/June 4.

Councill to be of the great councill, commonly called the Privy Councill, wher he had been excluded ever since the makeing of the statute for takeing the oaths; nor did he now take the othes notwithstanding his readmission, which gave some occasion of discours as if it was breakeing through one of the most strickt Acts of Parlament.

I returned to Windser with my wife to take leave of the *June* 12 Court. The same day I recieved an account by expresse from Doncaster of a quarrell that had hapned ther between the Maior of that corporation and my company of foot quartering ther in their march to Yorke, upon the occasion of the beating of a drum by the leave or licence of the Maior, and without the leave of the officer commanding in chiefe, or indeed without his knowlege (who went upon the presumption that noe drum ought to beat wher the King's drum is without the officers knowlege). However, the Maior to justifie his power tooke the part of the drummer, licenced by himselfe, and the officer sending a sergiant and three souldiers to take away the drum, was encountred by the rabble headed by the Maior, and being overpowred in nomber they were seized and their arms taken away, and afterwards the rest of the souldiers were faln upon in their quarters, and some of them haveing wounded a justice of the peace in the fray were committed to prison.

I recieved the same night a letter from the Maior complaining of the insolencie of the officer and souldiers, but in fyne I laid the whole matter before the King and the Duke, who ressented it from the Maior, and ressolved in Councill upon the 14 that my Lord Sunderland should 14 write to the Maior by his Majestys order commanding him to release the men and their arms, and to acquaint him with his resolution that my Lord Chiefe Justice should enquire into the further merit of the matter very speedily. I was at some losse how to behave myselfe between the company being mine and the corporation being my nighbours, the Maior haveing appealed or written to nobody in this matter but myselfe. However I resolved to stand by my officer and souldiers as farr as I legally might.

June 15   I took my leave of the King, who said to me that thos that served him soe carefully and soe well as I had done should be in his thoughts, and that I should find it. I tould him that I feared that some in my absence might possibly persuade his Majesty that York was not soe nescessary to be continued a guarrison, and I gave him severall reasons of its usefulness. He tould me he did apprehend it a place fitt to be continued, and that he would not reduce it till he took care of me in some other capacity, and that he was thinkeing of me. I asked his Majesty if any resolution was taken as to my company's continuing independent or being regimented. He said the thoughts of that regiment was laid aside.

I waited then on his Highness the Duke, desireing his commandes for Yorke. He tould me that he doubted not but I would doe what became me in order to his Majestys service, and that as to his own perticular he depended on me. I assured him I should never faile him in that trust; only desired him not to believe stories of me to my prejudice, for all countys had competitions, and that I could not hope to live without ennemies, that had the honour to serve the King before others of equall quality to myselfe or of better, which did certainly create envie to me.

16   Carrying my wife to see the Duchesse of Portsmouth, she invited her and my daughter to dinner, said very kind things to them, and desired me, whenever I came afterwards to Windser, to make her table my own. That day I returned for London.

20   Sir Thomas Armstrong, one of thos that were outlawed upon the late plott, and the debaucher of the Duke of Monmoth, being taken in Holland, was brought over and executed at Tyburn.

22   I visited my Lord of Danby, who tould me my Lord

Rochester was makeing an interest with thos they call the moderate party, not, I soppose, soe much from inclination as art, to rivall my Lord Privy Seale, who was suspected to have a better interest, and consequently better able to bear the shock of a Parlament, in case one should be called, then himselfe. But Parlaments seemed things very remote, for it was that lord's opinion that we were in a very strait conjunction with France (that had taken Luxenbourg, and was likely to be successfull according to its own wishes). He tould me many other things very perticular to that purpas, and relateing to my Lord Privy Seale, who continued well with him, not soe fitt for this narrative.

I sett forward with my family for Yorkeshire, arriveing happily at Thriberge the first of July. *June* 26

I went for Yorke, the assizes ther being appointed to be held on the 14th, and my Lord Chiefe Justice Jefferys haveing chosen that circuit. This gentleman, first known by the name Lawyer Jefferys, then knighted by the King by the name of Sir George, made Justice of Chester, then Recordor of London, and last Lord Chiefe Justice of England (for his quick parts and bouldnesse and zeale for the King's service more then any perfect knowlege of the lawe), had been soe obnoxious to all the late Parlaments, especially that of the year 1680, which sate at Westminster, that they did addresse against him to the King that he might be laid aside from his chiefe-justiceship of Chester, and from all other his publique offices and employments; but his Majesty would not consent to it. *July* 8

This gentleman, in whome the King and the Duke both much relyed, I resolved to recieve with all the respect I could, and the rather becaus I had been formerly his clyent, and he had ever been kind to me. The night therfore that he came to Yorke I caused my officers to recieve him with a guard at the town gate, went to wait on him myselfe soe soon as he lighted at his lodgeing, 12 offered to recieve orders from him (but he would not give them), sett him two sentirys at his door, invited him to

July 13 dinner the next day, which he accepted, with his fellow judge, Mr. Sergeant Holoway,[1] and severall of the chiefe gentlemen of the country to wait upon him. Another night several men of quality, that took that occasion of comming down with his lordship to see the north, came and took a collation with me; and my Lord himselfe came to me incognito one evening, and being a jolly, merry companion when his businesse was over, stayed with me over a bottle till one a clock in the morning.

The matter before mentioned of the quarrell between the corporation of Doncaster and my company (which was left to him to hear and determin) was found upon enquiry to be as much occasioned by the fault of the souldiers as the Maior and his bretheren. We thought it therfore the best way (my Lord himselfe approoveing of it) to take the submissions of the Maior (which partly out of fear, and partly out of respect to me, he was willing to make), and not to rip into the miscarriages of either. Soe both the Maior and the officers (especially the first) were reprooved by his lordship, and soe dismissed.

The seizeing the liberty of the citty of Yorke was also suspended by order of the King till his lordship arrived, who informing himselfe of the temper of that place, which he found not soe bad as it had been represented, and the Lord Maior[2] and aldermen subtilly submitting to his lordship and offering to give up their charter into his hands for the Kings use, his lordship was content to continue their privileges till his return to the King, and, upon their invitation, to dine with the citty. This was disgusting as much as it was disappointing to the Slingsby party (as it was then called), severall of the new named aldermen and officers haveing bought their gowns to

[1] Sir Richard Holloway, King's Serjeant, Puisne Justice of the King's Bench from 1683 to 1688.

[2] Robert Waller.

enter presently into office, which vexed them the more.

In this matter I intermedled the least I could, not busying myselfe to inform his lordship either as to matters or persons, knowing that to appear for or against the town was equally dangerous, as his lordship might take or represent it, either at Court or upon the place; and the thruth was the great prossecution against that place was more for private revenge then publique reasons. This manner of carriage contributed to make people of both factions very civill to me, soe that I had more visits and respects paid me then I ever had before for the time I stayed, which was near one month. I see my company here compleat, and it was a very good one; and haveing two companys in town we made a guard of twenty every night.

The archbishop, first sending his wife[1] to see mine, made me a visit at the Mannour afterwards himselfe.

My Lord Chiefe Justice assured me at his going away that he would acquaint the King and the Duke how good service I did them in that place.

I returned to Thriberge.   *Aug.* 2

The generall sessions for the West Riding was held 5 at Rotherham by adjurnment.

Came the newes that Buda in Hungary was taken by the 24 Duke of Lorrain for the Emperor,[2] after a long siege and much harm recieved by the Christians, which made them give noe quarter upon the takeing of the town; as also that the truce was signed between the Emperor and the King of France,[3] which looked as if a generall peace would succeed between all the Christian princes, for the better carrying on the warr against the Turke.

---

[1] Catherine, daughter of Ralph Sheldon of Stanton, Derbyshire, and niece of Archbishop Gilbert Sheldon.

[2] The attack on Buda at this time was only partially successful and the siege had eventually to be raised.

[3] The Truce of Ratisbon, concluded on August 5/15.

Aug. 27   I went to see my Lord of Danby, returned to Kiveton after his long absence and imprisonment. At this time some alterations had been made amongst the great men at Court, of which my Lord Rochester was one, remooved from First Commissioner of the Treasury to be President of the Councill,[1] a place though of greater precedencie then the other, yet nothing soe considerable either in point of profit or dependence, power always attending the purs. By this it was easy to guesse it was not a thing of his seekeing, but that his opponant the Lord Halifax had brought it to pass, which showed his interest was still good with the King. This was my Lord of Danby's conjecture, which was soon after confirmed to me by a letter from my Lord Marquisse, wher he writ litterally in thes words: You may believe I am not displeased to see such an adversary remooved from the only place that could give him power and advantage; and he beareth it with soe little philosophy that if I had ill nature enough for it ther is occasion given me to triumph. You see I cannot hinder myselfe from imparting my satisfaction to soe good a friend. But the wonder was how the finger of my Lord Privy Seale was able to effect this against the shoulder of the Duke of Yorke, who continued constant Rochesters friend.

Sept. 4   I went to the Duke of Newcastle at his castle of Nottingham, who lodged me ther, though all visiters except near relations laid in the town. He entertained me with the storys of his daughter's marriage to the Earl of Thanet,[2] which was privately done some days before, I haveing been the first that had proposed it to the Earle. The Duke of Buckingham had been ther not long before, that had given him a long scheme of affairs above, wherby it

---

[1] Rochester was succeeded by Godolphin, whose place as Secretary was in turn conferred upon Charles, second Earl of Middleton, a Scottish peer who played a considerable part in England during the reign of James II.

[2] Thomas Tufton, the sixth earl, married Catherine, fourth daughter of the Duke of Newcastle.

should seem that the French interest prevailed still at Court. He tould me Buckingham was angry with the Marquis of Halifax for refuseing to admitt of private communication with the French embassador when he offered to bring him to his lordship, and said his power would never be considerable bycaus he was averse to that interest. In fyne I belive ther was little which the Duke knew of this kind that he concealed from me. All the nobility and gentry of that and the nighbouring countys had met ther at this time upon occasion of a hors-race, most of which his Grace entertained one night at supper and a ball.

I returned to Thriberge. *Sept.* 7

I mustered my troop at Pontefract, wher Sir Thomas 16 Yarburgh mustered his, and Colonell Darcy [1] his regiment of foot at the same time. Severall gentlemen, officers of that regiment, thinkeing themselves neglected by their field officers (the collonel being most commonly at London, and the lieutenant-collonell, Sir Ralph Knight, not well, and consequently seldome at the musters), would needs have thrown up their commissions and surrendered them into my hands had not I pacified them. Severall gentlemen of the country came and dined with me whilst I stayed, and the Maior and aldermen of that corporation came and made me a present of wine. I made some visits on that side, and returned home the 20th. 20

I recieved a kind letter about this time from my Lord Marquis of Halifax, and some others from other persons, by which I understood a probability of some further changes at Court, and that his lordship stood very firm in his Majestys good opinion. This made us believe that the French interest did something abate.

I went again to visit my Lord Danby, who was very 25 ill of a quartan ague, and of his usuall stoppage in his

[1] John Darcy, eldest son of Conyers, Lord Darcy and Conyers, third son of the first Earl of Holderness.

throat when he dranke or eat anything. I found him in bed extream weake, but he tould me that if ever he lived to come into businesse he would doe me all the service that laid in his power. Two days after he sent his sons my Lord Latimor and my Lord Dunblain[1] to dine with me at Thriberge, and recovering much better went soon after for London.

Oct. 14   The sessions for the West Riding of Yorkshire were held at Barnsley, wher I assisted. The Teusday after,

21   the deputy lieutenants mett at Doncaster, wher I also was present.

Nov. 17   I went with my family to Yorke. Upon the 19th the two new shcrifs for that citty did ride and treat their friends severall days according to custome. They both sent to invite me and my wife to dinner the same day that the magistrates were entertained, wher I went; and my Lord Maior being at London, solliciting the business of the new charter, the deputy maior would not take place of me, but made me sit in my Lords chair, and with the rest of the magistrates ther used me with all the respect and kindness imaginable. Besides the magistrates ther dined severall of the chiefe cittizens and many gentlemen, to the nomber of above 300. One of the sherifs entertained much better then the other in the marchants hall, wher ther was severall long tables well served, especially that wher I sate, with all veriety the season would afford, and not inferiour to some entertainments in London upon the like occasion.

I had some difference at this time with Mr. Butler my lieutenant, who had exchanged his partizan with Lieutenant Oglethorp (who belonged to that company when I bought it),[2] one that I had not as yet seen, for listing some men into the company without leave from me, and suffer-

---

[1] His second surviving son, Peregrine, Viscount Osborne of Dumblane in the peerage of Scotland, who eventually became second Duke of Leeds.

[2] George Butler had been commissioned in place of William Oglethorpe in June (Dalton, *English Army Lists*, i. 328).

ing others to be absent upon furlong, &c. But when we had discoursed togather, he understood me soe well to be one that would not be imposed upon, or suffer the company to be managed by or depend upon any officer but myselfe, that he owned himselfe in the wrong, and promessed another carriage for the time to come.

I entertained the said two sherifs, with severall magis- *Nov. 30* trates and gentlemen, at dinner at the Mannour.

Mr. Christofer Tankard being appointed high sheriff for the county of Yorke, the like difference was started by him as formerly by Mr. Louther, concerning the doors or gates of the Castle. However, I prevented (after some * discours of the thing with him) its comming to an opon dispute, till I acquainted my Lord Privy Seale with it, who sent word it was not a fit season to stirr in it, and advised me to compose it if it were possible.

One of the leading and most intelligent magistrates, *Dec. 10* one Alderman Ramsden, tould me that at a late meeting of the most eminent cittizens ther hapned a discours concerning me which ended in this, that the citty was soe sensible of my respects to them, that in case a Parlament should be called I might certainly be chosen to represent them ther, provided I would declare that I would accept of it. I answered that if I had done that citty any service, they should not say that I had any such end or design in it, and therfore (as I had formerly declared) I would never aske them to choose me; but if, when such an occasion should offer, they thought me worthy of that favour, I should not only accept of it, but doe the citty the best service I could in that capacity.

I stayed ther till near Christmas, in which time I was visited by the archbishop, Dalbyn, and most of the best company in the town. Many of them came to dine with me, and I gave the ladys a ball.

I see both the companys exercize, and visited the guards, wher finding some souldiers absent I caused them to be severly punished.

* 29/9: Jo. Greatheed, 25 November 1684.

Dec. 27   I returned to Thriberge, by Gods mercy, in safety, to keep Christmas amongst my nighbours and tenents.

Jan. 6
[1684/5]   I had more company this Christmas then heretofore. The four first days all my tenents of Thriberge, Brinsford, Deneby, Mexbrough, Hoton Roberts and Rotherham dined with me. The rest of the time some four scoor gentlemen and yeomen, with their wives, were invited, besides some that came from Yorke, soe that all the beds in the hous, and most in the town, were taken up. Ther were seldom less then four scoor (counting all sorts of people) that dined in the hous every day, and some days many more. On New Years Day chiefly ther dined above three hundred, soe that whole sheep were roasted and served soe up to feed them. For musick I had five violins, besides bagpipes, drumms and trumpet.

15   An order being issued out from the Lords of the Treasury for the collecting of the duty of hearth-mony upon the smiths forges in Sheffield and Hallamshire, after haveing made me but bad returns for the favoures I had done them before in that case (I mean the cutlers and corporation ther), they came to me to desire my assistance that they might be excused from that duty (if possible) by my means or intercession. I tould them it was much fitter they should apply themselves to that interest wher they had done it soe lately, for I should not concern myself any more in that affair; that as to favour, I doubted not but they thought themselves able to find it by others, or else their application would have been more constant to me; and as for hopes of reliefe by justice, the law was now much changed since this matter was first in question, by reason of the opinions of the judges given in the case, and of severall verdicts both in the Courts of the Kings Bench and of the Exchequer concerning it.

20   The generall quarter-sessions for the West Rideing were held at Doncaster, wher ther appeared as justices

Sir Michael Wentworth, Sir George Cook[1] (whom I had gott putt into commission and was ther to be sworn), my oncle Yarburgh, Mr. Blythman and Mr. Ramsden, wher I gave the charge.

A *quo warranto* being at this time served upon that corporation, they resolved to send up their charter, and not to make any defence against the King. I was suspected to have had some hand in this prossecution, but had not, the true reason being a difference amongst the aldermen, who accused one another. Thos that informed designed some change in the constitution of that body, the other party hoped to gett both men and things to be continued as they had been before, and both partys desired my direction and assistance in it; but I denyd to be concerned oponly on either side, only gave my Lord Privy Seale and my Lord Burlinton some intimation how things stood, they being the persons to whom both sides intended to address above in this affair. The justices desired me to write to the first of thes lords, and to inclose to him a printed paper conteaning libellous matter against the magistrates (composed by one of thos dissenters called Quakers), to the end the King in Councill might be acquainted with it; which I did, and all the rest of the justices subscribed to it.

I went to make a visit to my uncle Yarburgh of Camp- *Feb.* 2 sall, and to my cozen Tindall of Brotherton.

It was here wher I recieved the sad newes from the 4 Earle of Burlinton that his Majesty had been taken upon the 2nd, about eight in the morning, with a fitt of an apoplexy (though they called it an epelepsie), and had continued dead near three hours; that at last he was returned to life by blooding, cupping, vomiting, and severall other applications and medicins; and that his lordship had order from the Secretary to write to me to take care, and

---

[1] Sir George Cooke of Wheateley, Yorkshire, the first baronet, died on October 16, 1683. Reresby probably means his brother Sir Henry, who succeeded him by special remainder.

* 27/17: Thos. Yarburgh, 14 January 1684/5.

to caus a meeting of the deputy lieutenants and justices of the peace to doe the same, that noe meetings or seditious assemblies should be made by reason of such a rumour.   My Lord Burlinton had sent his secretary with this letter, who came soe fast that I recieved it upon the 4th of February about two in the afternoon.   That instant I began to write and dispers letters by severall messengers to soe many gentlemen that we had a meeting of the greater part of the deputy lieutenants and justices of the peace the next day at Doncaster before noon, wher, recieveing an account by the post that his Majesty recovered, we only granted out orders and warrants for the militia to be ready to appear under arms upon an hours warning, and that strict watch and ward should be kept in every town for the stopping and apprehending of such as did appear dangerous.

I writt before to Yorke, to my officers to double the guards, and to my Lord Maior [1] to be carefull to keep the peace of that citty.

Feb. 6   I went to Yorke, wher the newes being arrived that the King continued better ther was nothing but bonefires and signs of joye from one end of the town to the other.[2]

[1] John Thompson.

[2] On the following day Reresby sent an account of the situation to Lord Burlington :

February 7th, [16]84[/5].—My Lord, As I gave you an account in my last, we mett at Doncaster on Thursday at noon, viz., Mr. Wortley, Sir John Bointon, Sir Michael Wentworth, and severall other justices of the peace, wher upon the news of his Majestys better health (which God continue) all we thought necessary to doe was to cause strict watch and ward to be kept, and to issue out orders for the militia to be ready to be called togather upon an hours warning ; which (by sending the copies of what wee did to other gentlemen) was observed in other divisions, and was the last night also done here, wher I mett with the high sheriff, my Lord Fairfax, Sir Thomas Slingsby, Sir Thomas Mauleverer, and Mr. Moyser.   They stay expecting this post.

As to this place, the Lord Maior (now one Thomson) hath been very ready to doe his duty for the peace of the place, and our souldiers are upon every other nights duty.   I found not that ther was the least contrivance to disturbe it.   All were dismally sad at the first news, and as glad of the

* 31/28: Burlington, 2 February 1684/5.

The high sheriff of the county, with many of the chiefe of the gentry, came to Yorke to consider which way to take to secure the peace of the county in case of ill newes. That night we sate up togather till one in the morning expecting the comming in of the post, which acquainted us at the last with the Kings relapse, and the fears of his phisitions that he might not recover. Upon this the sheriff, myselfe, and all the deputy lieutenants ther present, resolved to doe our utmost, should the King die, to obviate all things to the best of our power that should anyways obstruct the Duke of Yorkes just claime to the crown; and considering that the safety of the county did most depend upon that of this citty (for this they unanimously agreed to), they issued out orders that night for four companys of Sir Thomas Slingsby's regiment to be raised, and to relieve one another, by way of additionall guard to the guarrison under my command as governour.

Being Sunday, meeting the archbishop at the Minster, 8 he tould me he had an account that the King had been ill again, had an intermitting feavour and some fitts of convulsions, but that it was hoped he was out of danger, though my letters spoake in a different stile.

I ordered the male to be brought unoponed to my hous, 9 soe that noe letters could be dispersed till I knew the true state of the Kings condition. The letters came not in till four in the morning, and then they gave me an account of my gracious and great master's departure out of this   * world upon the 7th at night.[1] I was up expecting the

second ; ther was scarce a hous here without a bonefire. I have given my Lord Sunderland an account of our proceedings and of your Lordships great care and diligence that directed them. I am, My Lord, Your Lordships most humble and most faithfull servant, J. Reresby. Since I writt this I hear some few would have raised a rumour as if the King had been murdered by the papists. We are seeking out the authours to have them punished. My Lord Maior hath sent some townsmen to the goale for affronting one of my souldiers going last night to mount the guard. (S.P. Dom., James II, 1, f. 143.)

[1] Charles actually died on February 6 about noon.

* 29/28: Edmund Reresby, 7 February 1684/5; 29/32: Thomas Yarburgh, 7 February 1684/5; 31/32: Burlington, 7 February 1684/5.

post when it arrived, and suffered noe letters to goe out till I had been with the Lord Maior and the high sheriff, and delivered their only letters to themselves, by which they had order, and myselfe also, from the Privy Councill and the Secretary of State, to proceed immediately to proclaime the King, James the Second. Soe soon as we had prepared all things nescessary for this ceremony, which was done before day, I gave leave for the disperseing of the severall letters according to their directions, and by seven a clock in the morning the high sheriff, mett by the archbishop and most of the gentlemen in town, went towards the castle yeard to proclaime the King ther, whilst I caused all the guarrison to be drawn togather (except the nescessary guards) into Thursday markit, viz., our two companys of the Kings foot and two companys of the militia then under arms, to oppose any tumult or insurrection that might happen on this occasion.

Feb. 10 The King was proclamed by nine in the morning by my Lord Maior, myselfe and the high sheriff. The first did it in the usuall places of that citty for that ceremony; I did it to the guarrison, drawn togather in Thursday markit; and the high sheriff did it in the castle yard for the county. Afterwards I caused all the great guns to be twice discharged, and severall vollys of small shott, according to the orders recieved from my Lord Sunderland, all this being done with all the signs of peace and satisfaction that could be, not only in Yorke, but afterwards throughout the county, and indeed the whole kingdome.

It was a strange effect of power from above that soe strong a party as had not long before appeard in Parlament to exclude the Duke of Yorke from the Crowne of his anchesters should submitt to his now comming to it with soe great defference and submission. But they knew well the difference that ther was between the spirits of the late and the present King, and thought the first would sooner be induced for peace sake to relinquish his brother,

* 31/25: Sunderland, 7 February 1684/5.

then that the latter would tamely renounce his just possession of three kingdomes out of fear of a warr. That which in a great measure did quiet the minds and apprehensions of people was the declaration made by King James to the Privy Councill immediately after the breath was out of the body of his brother, that he would defend the goverment of England both in Church and State as by law established; that he would follow the steps of the late King in kindness and lenity towards his people; and that as he would defend the just rights and prerogative of the Crown, soe [he] would invade noe mans property.

I stayed at Yorke, to take care that noe uproars or disorders should arise ther, till February the 15th, in *Feb.* 15 which time I recieved letters from my Lord Burlinton, wher he tould me that he had acquented the King with the constant accounts I gave him of the state of that citty and of the West Rideing, and of my diligence in preserveing the peace of both, with which his Majesty declared himselfe well satisfyed; from the Secretary of Warr, Mr. Blathwait, to the same effect, who said he writt to me by the King's especiall order; from my Lord Privy Seale likewise, who said the King had tould him that he took perticular notice of my care and diligence for his service in this conjuncture, and that his Majesty had granted me leave to come up when I pleased (which indeed I had desired his lordship to obtean for me).

At the same time I had notice from the Secretary of State that I was continued in my command, as indeed all officers were whatsoever for the present. However, ther began to be great changes at Court. My Lord Rochester was made Lord High Treasurer of England; my Lord Privy Seale, Lord President of the Councill; but whether this preferment (though a degree higher as to place) was desired or not by his lordship was a doubt, the trust and profit of Privy Seale being thought to be greater.

At this time came the newes that his Majesty intended

---

* 31/26: Burlington, 10 February 1684/5; 31/29: Blathwayt, 14 February 1684/5; 31/30: Burlington, 14 February 1684/5.

to call a Parlament, to assemble in May next. After I recieved my letters I went to advise with some aldermen if they thought it probable for me to be chosen in Yorke, which they tould me they did.

Feb. 16   I came home to settle my affairs at Thriberge.

23   I returned to Yorke, wher ther was a great meeting of most of the gentlemen of the whole county, to sign an addresse to the King to condole the death of his late Majesty and congratulate the present's happy comming to the Crown, which was accordingly done, and sent up within few days after.

The same day I sent to my Lord Maior to desire him to assemble all his bretheren and the two sherifs, for I had something to impart to them. Being met at my Lord Maiors, I made a discours to them of about halfe an hour, setting fourth the King's intentions to call a Parlament, and of mine to represent them as one of their burgesses therin; of my constant practice in my command since I had it in that citty to serve the King in the first place and them in the next, and that I should doe the same in Parlament as I had done ther; that I had an estate of my own to venter in that service as well as theirs; that I had had some experience in Parlament to enable me the better to performe it, with severall reasons to the same purpas. Haveing done, my Lord Maior desired me to withdraw whilst he and they took what I had said into consideration; and then, calling me in again in lesse then one quarter of an hour, his lordship tould me that by an unanimous consent they had ressolved upon me for one of their representatives for that antient and loyall citty; that I did them an honour to accept of it, though they looked upon it as the greatest trust they could repose in me. I assured them I would never betray that trust, and returned them my hearty thanks.

24   I was invited to dine with my Lord Maior and Sir Medcalfe Robison,[1] one that had been member for that

[1] Sir Metcalfe Robinson of Newby, Yorkshire; created a baronet in 1660.

* 29/15: copies of the York and West Riding addresses; 30/4: copy in Reresby's hand of the address to the king from the lord lieutenant, deputy lieutenants, justices of the peace and other gentlemen of the county of York; 31/22: Burlington, 28 February 1684/5, notifies Reresby that he has presented the West Riding address to the king.

citty in the Long Parlament,[1] and whom they had accepted
for the other burgesse in this; and the same day my Lord
Maior granted me the freedome of the corporation, and
obliged Sir Medcalfe Robison and me to joine our two
interests togather, which he then promessed.   Haveing
some days before acquainted my Lord Burlinton, who
was now the Recorder of this citty, and my Lord President
with my intentions to stand ther, I had both their encour-
agements in severall letters, which they allowed me to   *
show to the magistrates to confirme them in their good
intentions towards me.

I heard that one Colonel Jenkyns[2] and Mr. Moyser, *Feb.* 25
my father-in-law, intended likewise to stand ther, persuaded to it by a party that was ever ready to oppose the
choice of the magistrates or anything they did, for which
reason ther had been great feuds and differences between
them.   Thes were some of the most eminent of the
Common Councill of the citty.

Mr. Moyser came to me, tould me he was very sorry 26
that we two were likely to be in competition; that it was
not what he desired or sought, but was putt upon it by
some people.   I answered noebody could compell him in
a thing of that nature; that it looked very unkind towards
me; that he could not but be sensible that thos that
engaged him did it neither out of friendship to him nor
aversion to me soe much as out of crossness to the Maior
and aldermen, to caus a disturbance and heats in the citty,
when union and agreement were soe desireable ther as
well as in the whole kingdome, &c., with much more to the
same effect.   At last he said if he knew but how to
disengage himselfe without too rudely breakeing with his
party he would study to doe it.   But hearing that he still
persued what had been begun (or his friends for him), I
engaged my Lord Maior to deny the granting of freedome

[1] Of the reign of Charles II. He had also represented York in the
Convention.

[2] Toby Jenkins of Grimston, Yorkshire.

* 31/27: Newcastle, 17 February 1684/5.

either to him or Colonel Jenkins, and without it t'was concieved they could not be chosen; wherupon they endeavoured to procure a *mandamus* to be made free. The writts for elections being expected speedily, I continued to strengthen my friends and to encrease them every day.

March 2   It being in a mans power in point of law to be chosen in severall bouroughs, and haveing been invited by my friends at Audbrough, I went thither, wher calling the bourough men togather, after I had spoaken to them setting fourth the obligations they had to me and the promesses they had made me to choose me for the next Parlament, with such arguments as I was able to use to persuade them to it, they unanimously (one only excepted) promessed under their hands to give me their voats, to the nomber of thirty-nine, all the electours for that bourough being sixty-four.   But being men of low ranke, subject to change and much importuned by others for that service, how they will acquitt themselves is the question.

It was now out of doubt that the King was a papist, for he went publiquly to mass, but ordered the chappell at Whitehall to be kept in the same order as formerly, wher the Princesse of Denmark went daily.   The King repaired to the Queens private chappell.   I recieved the news of this from Mr. Peebles,[1] my good and faithfull friend (one that had been some time in the commission of the peace for the West Rideing, and by my means) then at London, by letter dated the 19 February.   The next account I had of him was that he was dead not many days after, which showes the uncertainty of this life.

5   Haveing some occasions at home, I came for Thriberge, left my Lord Maior in the firm resolution to deny freedome to Mr. Moyser and Colonel Jenkyns.

9   I returned again to Yorke, and took my wife with me, but was surprized at my arrival ther to hear my Lord Maior, contrary to his word, had been wrought upon to

[1] John Peebles of Dewsbury, Yorkshire.

† 30/6: Reresby to Alderman Waller, 25 February 1684/5 (copy).

give thos gentlemen their freedomes or enfranchisments. That night I went to his lordship, who tould me that it was looked upon as a partiality in him to bestowe it on one and to deny it to others; that the judges (who were then arrived, it being the time of assizes at Yorke)[1] had advised him to it, as well as some letters from above; and that he could not avoid the doing it in case a House (consisting of himselfe, the twelve aldermen, the sherifs, and the twenty-four comoners) advised him to it. This putt me into some heats, taxing his lordship with breach of promesse, and urgeing the ill consequences that might happen, not only in disobligeing me by it but the most of his bretheren, who were still positively bent to deny their freedome; but all my arguments could not bring him back to his first resolution.

I went to the judges, tould them that the reason why *March* 10 my Lord Maior had taken this measure of denying to make thos gentlemen free was only to prevent contention in the citty, and opposition to the magistrates by a sort of people who only endeavoured to sett up thos persons for burgesses bycaus the magistrates had approoved of others; that should thos gentlemen be now admitted into a capacity of being elected, what heats might be occasioned by it was very doubtfull, or what breach of the peace; and if such things should happen it might reflect upon their lordships, since my Lord Maior seemed now inclined to doe it, and, as he pretended, by their advice. They answered indeed my Lord did say something to them in common discours, but not by way of askeing their advice; that his lordship ought, in the first place, to preserve the peace of the citty; and that they denyed that they gave their opinion in a concern of this weight, desireing me to goe and tell his lordship soe much from them.

[1] The judges were Sir Edward Atkyns and Sir Robert Wright, Barons of the Exchequer. Atkyns became Lord Chief Baron in 1686 and Wright was created Lord Chief Justice, first of the Common Pleas and then of the King's Bench, in the following year.

I did soe immediately; but he, haveing sommoned a Hous, was not to be altered, and the issue at last was that it was carryed by one voat only that they should be made *March* 12 free.   They haveing gained this point, I found I was to use all diligence and to spare noe charge if I expected successe, and therfore went about the streets from hous to hous (the aldermen attending upon me) to aske the voats of the cittizens.   And the 13th I made a generall entertainment throughout the town, viz., in three or four houses in every street, for thos to entertain themselves with good liquor that had promessed to be for me, though my competitours had begun that custome long before to gain friends.

14   I had used means above by my Lord President to gett the writt to be sent to me.   It arrived that day, and was

*   to be executed the 16, it being the next county court day in that citty.

16   All the candadates went into the streets to gather their party to them, wher it was presently seen I had a greater nomber of followers then any of the rest.   At eight of the clock the poule began at the common hall, and lasted till six at night, when the bookes being cast up, their appeared that Sir Medcalfe Robison had pouled 781, Mr. Moyser 770, Colonel Jenkins 502, and Sir John Reresby had pouled 937; soe that the sherifs published me and Sir Medcalfe Robison duely elected for burgesses to serve in the next Parlament for that citty.[1]   The charge I was at in this election came to 350 l., though it cost them more that lost it.   It was believed in the town that my interest was the least, insoemuch that Sir Medcalfe, that had promessed to joine his with mine, receded from it, and Mr. Moyser durst not doe it neither, believeing his own interest the better; and Sir Thomas Slingsby's friends (that were against me) had written letters above before

[1] Moyser, however, petitioned the House of Commons against the return of Robinson, and Jenkins against Reresby's own return (*Journals of the House of Commons*, ix. 716, 723).

* 28/9: J. Greatheed, 12 March 1684/5.

† The original reads:

The charge I was at in this Election
came to 25011–00–00
Though it cost them more
that lost it: 35011–00–00.
British Library Additional MSS 29441, fol. 11. This folio is damaged, and Professor Browning observed that where the manuscript had become worn he

the day of election that I must certainly loos it, which made
the victory the greater, and very seasonable to me upon
severall accounts.

My Lord Clifford came from London to be chosen *March* 20
knight of the shire with Sir John Kay. There was
none stood but them two. I paid my Lord all the respect
I could (knowing how welcome it would be to my Lord
Burlinton), by entertaining his lordship at dinner at the
Mannour, makeing him a guard at his comming into the
town and at his going out, and giveing him the great guns
on the day of election for the county, which was upon the
23rd. That day I recieved the Kings orders for Captain 23
Sterlings company to march from Yorke to the guarrison
of Scarbrough, commanded by Sir Thomas Slingsby,
which looked like an ill presage to what was then dis-   *
coursed, that the King intended to disguarrison the citty
of Yorke.

Anno Domini 1685

The yong men and apprentices of the citty of Yorke *March* 25
came and petitioned me in writing that, wheras ther had
been formerly a custome ther for the youth to exercise
themselves in arms some days in every year (especially
that of the coronation), which had, however, discontinued
for some years, that I would please to allowe them to use
the same libertie again, that they might therby showe
their loyaltie and gain experience to serve the King,
desireing of me at the same time to be their collonell, and
to appoint them such officers and captains as I thought
fitt. I tould them that I would acquaint the King with it,
and give them notice of his Majestys plesure therin, which
I endeavored to doe by writing in it to my Lord President
by the next post. I was not, I confess, sorry for this
application of theirs, it being still a further confirmation
of my interest in that place.

The bourough men at Audbrough, viz., the greater
nomber of them, stood very firm to me all this time, and

---

had relied on previous versions for guidance; in this case he presumably used
the edition by J. J. Cartwright (1875), p. 320. The first figure was apparently
initially rendered 350 and then corrected by Reresby who simply overwrote it,
making it hard to read.

* 35/8: D. Crauford, 28 March 1685, proves that Slingsby was involved.

sent me word that they would choose me one of their burgesses if I would come over, or any person that I would recommend to them.   But being chosen already I gave them leave to make their own choice, which was cast on Sir Michael Wentworth and Sir Roger Stricland.

March 26   I returned to Thriberge.

April 1   A servant going into the lofts of Thriberge Hall discovered that a fire had been not long before begun ther, occasioned by an end of a principal's being fixed in a chimney, which took fire from the heat, was burnt down and all the ends of the sparrs which rested upon it, and yet by the mercy and providence of Almighty God, for all the said wood fell down burning amongst other wood and latts (which made the roofe of the rooms), it extinguished of it's selfe and went noe further, noebody knowing either when it began or when it ceased, a good omen; I hope that it is God's will that Thriberge hous shall yet stand.

2   I had a letter from my Lord President that he had spoaken to the King, and found noe reason to thinke that ther was any designe to disguarrison Yorke.

3   I recieved an addresse from Yorke, signed by 440 yong tradesmen and others ther, which they desired me to present to the King as ther congratulation for his happy accession to the Crown.

13   I sett forward for London, leaveing my wife and family at Thriberge.

18   I learnt from my Lord Marquiss of Halifax that he and my Lord Rochester, Lord Tresurer, continued kind, that he used his constant endeavours to serve the King, and would continue them, hopeing his Majesty would put noe discouragement upon them by imposeing the popish religion, though the greatest imployments in the army of Ireland were now putt in papists hands.   He tould me severall passages of the late King's kindnes to him, and certainly noe man was in greater favour with him, when he unfortunately dyed, then the marquiss.   As to my

* 29/1: Reresby at York to the boroughmen of Aldborough, 20 March 1684/5 (copy).

† Reresby has here erased an entry recording that he travelled on his own horse.

concern, he tould me the King had assured him he had noe intention to disguarrison York, but it was soe much pressed by some that noe certain measures could be taken till the sitting and ending of the Parlament, wher everybody's carriage would be strictly observed.   As to the petition of the yong men of Yorke to exercize and appear in arms upon the coronation day, my Lord said his Majesty did thanke them for their offer and me for acquainting him first with it, but he did not thinke it fitt to allowe of it, least the exemple of it ther might be followed in other places, and soe the thing might become too generall.

I waited on the King and kissed his hand, and pre- *April 22* sented him at the same time with an addresse from the yong men of Yorke, which his Majesty recieved kindly.

That day I waited on my Lord Burlinton, who after some discours tould me he thought I had used him very ill in not writing to him, being Lord Lieutenant of the citty of Yorke, to speake to the King about the yong mens desires to form themselves into a regiment, rather then to the Marquiss of Halifax.   I answered that being governor of the place I thought I needed not to write soe much as to the King, but might claim the privilege to lett drums beat and men exercize once a year for their diversion or oftner from my own power, and that I had been soe ready to serve him that he expected more then I was obliged to pay him, or to that effect, which brought us to some heats and distance for the present.

I understood from my Lord Hallifax that he had, in two *23* perticular and private audiences with the King, tould him his mind with that planeness in relation to his service in point of goverment that he wondered the King (considering his temper) took it with that calmness.   He said some bils might possibly be insisted upon to be repealed in the next Parlament, which would deserve to be first well considered of, and some other things not soe fitt for this time and place.

---

* 35/7: Edward Baldock, 25 April 1685.

April 23 The King was crowned, with the Queen, in the Abbay of Westminster by the Bishop[1]   with all the pompe and splendour immaginable; only ther was noe cavalcade thorow the citty as heretofore. The King and Queen went privately to the Palace in Westminster, wher they, the nobility, and all the officers of the Crown putt on their robes, and soe went thorow the Palace Yeard (railed in and prepared on purpass) in procession to the Abbay, wher the ceremony being ended, they all returned to Westminster Hall to a most somptious dinner.

Now began the consideration amongst gentlemen of the Hous what would be asked by the Court and what would be granted in the ensuing Parlament, which consisted of a great many loyall gentlemen, and the generality, however, good patriots and Protestants. Some things to be asked were such as (report said) gave more countenance to popery then the laws then in force did permitt; secondly, the settlement of a constant revenue upon the Crown, suitable to that of the late King, and ready mony besides for the Kings present occasions. In the first classis the repeale of the lawe of habias corpus was one which I found the great men opposed in their private discours, as well as some of us. For a toleration or libertie of concience (which the papists seemd to apprehend), if it were generall, some seemed willing to grant, but resolved at the same time not in any alteration to give a capacity to the papists to come into any place or imployment in the goverment. In the affair of mony men seemed content to settle a hansome revenue on the King and to give mony; but whether this was to be a constant revenue, or only temporary, and to be renewed from time to time that Parlaments might be consulted the oftner, was the question. In all this concern I ressolved to doe my duty to the Crown, but yet with a good concience to my religion and country.

[1] A space is left in the original at this point. The coronation was performed by William Sancroft, Archbishop of Canterbury.

Our sessions began for Westminster, wher I was *April* 24 sworn of that commission, which was lately renewed by that King.

The sessions for the county of Middlesex were held at 27 Hicks Hall and at the Old Bailiff the 29. The 27 I was 29 sworn of the commission for the county at Hicks his Hall.

I dined with my Lord Maior and the judges at the 30 Old Bailiff, wher my Lord Maior led me by the hand (being Sir James Smith at that time, my old acquentance), and my Lord Chiefe Justice dranke to me publiquely at the table the healths of our friends at Yorke, which made me believe that he was not privy to a secret design which   * was carrying on by Sir Thomas Slingsby and his party to putt five aldermen of the greatest note in Yorke[1] out of imployment, the charter not being yet passed, and intended as said by his interest.

I took my sons from the school at Kinsinton, and putt *May* 4 them to another in the same town.   †

Thes things were tould me in discours by Mr. Hilliard,[2] Sir Roger Martin and others, at this time gentlemen of interest amongst their party, the papists: that the King would expect the takeing away of the sanginary lawes, and the allowance of the practice of the Roman religion in private for the papists, from the next Parlament; and that they, or at least such as had served the royall family in the warrs or otherways, might be made capable of imployment under him; that his Majesty would give satisfaction to the nation in Parlament as to the preserving their religion and properties, but if reason would not serve, he knew what he had to doe; that the King would never divide

---

[1] The five aldermen were Ramsden, Elcock, Herbert, Edward Thompson, and Waller. Their real crime was that they had supported Reresby's election to Parliament; but they were accused of disaffection to the Government, and during Monmouth's rebellion all except Herbert were sent prisoners to Hull.

[2] Probably Christopher Hildyard of Beverley, Yorkshire.

---

* 38/23: E. Thompson and W. Ramsden, 15 July 1685. This letter from the dismissed aldermen shows that it was their support of Reresby which cost them their positions.

† Reresby here erased an entry about his sons.

his regall power by admitting that of the Pope here; he loved power too well himselfe, and therfore his adhearing to the defence of the Church of England was but a good reason to the Pope not to pretend to urge him to admitt of his supremacy; that it was reasonable to the King to insist upon the recalling of the most severe penall laws against the papists, else if he should die, he should leave them in as ill a condition as he found them. Such arguments were not wisely urged at this time.

May 3   My Lord Clifford, haveing been twice at my hous, tould me his father my Lord Burlinton would be gladd to see me. I waited then upon him, and he recieved me civilly, without any mention of the late differance between us.

4   I had an opportunity of speakeing to the King at his couchee, and tould him that I desired to pay him my humble thankes for the hopes he had given me by my Lord President to be continued in the imployments I had under his Majesty. He answered I needed noebody to recommend me to him; he knew me very well, and I might be assured he would take nothing from me. I replyed that I had served the King my late master with all diligence and fidelity, and thought I could not serve him without serveing at the same time his present Majesty, and if I did what I could to serve him then he might be confident I should not omitt my endeavours to doe it now.

6   The Secretary of Warr tould me the King had ressolved to make an addition to my company of granadeers by adding one drum and one sergiant more, and makeing my ensign a 2nd lieutenant; but this resolution was afterwards changed.

7   I dined with the archbishop, who was very free with me in some things he had discoursed with the King, and in others he had said to my Lord Burlinton, relateing to his not being soe active as it became him to be in preventing the turning out of some of the magistrates of Yorke. He then said for all my Lord Chiefe Justice was to be a baron,

he was not in that favour with the King as formerly; but it prooved otherways.

Waiting on the King in his barge from Whitehall to *May* 8 Sommersit Hous to see the Queen Dowagere the day that Doctor Oates, the great evidence in the Popish Plott, was convicted of perjurie (it being prooved that he was at St. Omers the 24 of April, 1678, when he swore he was at the White Hors Tavern in the Strand, when Pickering, Groves, Ireland, &c. Jesuists signed the death of King Charles the Second), the King said indeed ther was a meeting of the Jesuists on that day, which all the schollars of St. Omers knew was to be, but it was well Doctor Oats knew noe better wher it was, for it was then held in St. James his, wher the said King then dwelt; for, said the King, if that had been understood by Oats, he would have made ill worke for me. The King said upon it that now Oats was thus convicted the Popish Plott was dead. I answered it was long since dead, and now it would be buried; which he approoved soe well of that goeing with him afterwards to the Princesse of Denmarke, I heard him repeat to her the same thing.

Going to the Secretary of State for my commissions 10 of governor of Yorke, he tould me my Lord Burlinton had put in a caviat to the grant of them in the same forms as formerly, as entrenching upon his power as Lord Lieutenant of the citty of Yorke.

Came news that severall arms had been bought up and 12 convayed from Holand for Scotland, and that my Lord Arguile, Lord Gray, and some said the Duke of Monmoth with 400 men, were gone either with them or after them.

The Archbishop of Yorke tould me he had spoake to the King for the aldermen of Yorke to be continued in office; that the King seemd much possessed against them by Sir Thomas Slingsby and his friends; that his lordship answered that he thought ther might be some sparring one against another by some gentlemen that were truly lovall in and about that citty, meaning Sir Thomas and myselfe, for whos sakes they might be wors represented; but that his Majesty might find it for his service to make as little change ther as it was possible.

May 19 The Parlament mett at the usuall places in Westminster. We did nothing that day but take the oaths, and chose Sir John Trever Speaker,[1] whom the King accepted. The two next days were also spent in swearing the Commons and takeing the test.

22 The King spoake to both Houses, giveing them assurances to support and defend the Church of England, whos members had shewed themselves soe loyall in the worst of times in the defence of his father and the support of his brother; and to support the goverment both in Church and State as by law established; and that as he would never depart from the just rights and prerogatives of the Crown, soe he would never invade any mans property; desireing suitable returns from them in the settling of his revenue for his life, as it was in the time of the late King. He closed with an account his Majesty had recieved that day from Scotland, that Arguile was landed with men and arms in the western islands of Scotland, and that he had published two declarations,[2] in both which the King was charged with tyranny and usurpation.

The Commons, returning to the Hous, voated his Majestys speech to be speedily taken into consideration, and were soe well pleased with the solomn security the King gave them as to their religion and propertys that they voted him the same revenue for his life that the late King had for his life. Then they voted that the King should be thanked for his speech by the whole Hous in a body, in which the Lords joined, and it was accordingly done the next day.[3]

---

[1] Sir John Trevor, M.P. for Denbigh Borough, a cousin of Sir George Jeffreys, to whose recommendation he probably owed his appointment.

[2] " One in the name of those in arms there, the other in his own."

[3] The afternoon of the same day (*Journals of the House of Commons*, ix. 715).

They voated an address to his Majesty to stand by him *May* 23 with their lives and fortunes against Arguile, his assistants, and all other traiters whatsoever. This was presented to the King the same day in the bankiting hous, who returned this answer, that he expected as much from a Parlament soe well composed as this was of monarchicall and Church of England men, and that he feared noe ennemys that he either had or might have, being thus assisted. As the King went out, comeing near me, he tould me that I had contributed to this good worke (for I had spoaken in the Hous for the settlement of his revenue), and he hoped I would persevere.

My commission for governor of Yorke was allowed me by the Earle of Burlinton, with very little alteration of * words and with none as to power.[1]

Going with the Duke of Newcastle in my coach to visit 24 my Lord Keeper, I acquainted him that I heard Colonel Jenkins (who was much his friend) would petition to † vacant my election in the Hous. He writt the next day to the Colonel to lay thos thoughts aside, I being his perticular friend.

All things seemed now to look very auspicious, the King not giveing the least token to change the religion, but much the contrary.

A subscription was obteaned by the industry of Sir Thomas Slingsby, the high sheriff, and others to the nomber of eighteen gentlemen of the county, certifying notorious crimes of the five aldermen of Yorke, and presented to the King in order to their turning out. The archbishop seemed now could in the case, my Lord Burlinton the same, when my Lord Halifax (hearing the King speake of it and knowing my obligations to them) interposed and desired that since gentlemen did sometimes sign such papers upon credit, and that since neither the archbishop his hand, the lord lieutenants, nor the gover-

---

[1] The commission was signed on June 23 (Dalton, *English Army Lists*, ii. 46).

* 36/31: George Butler, 23 May 1685. At this late date, there were rumours that Slingsby was to be made Governor of York.

† 34/2: Newcastle, 24 May 1685. There is some confusion as to whether Reresby was with Newcastle on this date. As the letter states, Newcastle was to visit Col. Jenkins. Possibly, Reresby saw the duke briefly when they shared the ride.

nours was ther, it was fit the matter should be made known to them and the thing heard before they should be displaced. Further, that good lord was soe much concerned for me that, finding Sir Henry Gooderick his hand to the subscription, he fell into soe great passion with him for doing it, without acquainting me with it (pretending soe strict a friend and correspondencie with me at the same time), that it had like to have made a difference between Sir Henry and me. But Sir Henry protesting to me that he intended noe prejudice to me by it, and fearing to be under my Lord's jealousie of betraying his friendship with any man (least he might thinke him capable to doe the same thing to himselfe), he prevailed with me to sett him right in my Lord's good opinion in that perticular. My Lord was very warm in telling me of this affair. He said Sir Henry had done ill to me in it; this was to make a cyfre of the governor; and reflected on Sir Henry Goodericks understanding in generall, and of his foolish carriage in Spain when embassador ther. The prossecution against the aldermen haveing mett with this rub, I stirred in it the more confidently, but all to noe purpas, for thes gentlemen pressed their complaint soe home and with that earnestness that the King declared in Councill the 29 of May that they should be turned out without being heard.

May 25   A motion was made in the Hous that something ought to be done that would please the people, as well as giveing of mony, meaning to secure the Protestant religion; upon which a debate ariseing, it was referred to the committè of religion.[1]

26   It was voted in that committè that the Hous be mooved from the committè to pass a voat to stand by the King with their lives and fortunes for the defence of the religion of the Church of England as by law establist; secondly, that an addresse be presented to the King from that Hous to issue out his royall proclamation that the lawes be putt

[1] The date for this should be May 26 (*Journals of the House of Commons,* ix. 719).

in execution against all dissenters whatsoever. Thes voats passed the committee (which was very full) *nemine contradicente*.

Thes voats being reported to the Hous, a great debate *May 27* began whether the House should agree with the committè or not.   The arguments against agreeing were: that this was to putt the King in mind of a neglect of his duty; that the fault was in the justices of the peace that the lawes were not executed; that thes voats would alarm the king-dome, and expresse a jealousie of the King, when he had positively declared to defend our religion; that the King had tould us the way to keep a good understanding between him and his Parlament was to use him well, but he could not ressent this well from us; that this might encourage the rebels already in arms in Scotland, &c. On the other hand it was argued that it would look ill to the nation that we, being Church of England men, after haveing begun to take care of our religion and made such voats in order therunto, should lett the matter fall and doe nothing in it.   At last the previous question was putt, whether the question to agree with the committè should be putt or not, and was carryed in the negative.   Then the whole matter ended in this voat, that an address should be made to the King by that Hous, that it did entirely rely and rest wholly satisfyed in the Kings declaration to them to defend and secure the reformed religion of the Church of England as by lawe established, which was dearer and nearer to them then their lives.

A motion being made to call Colonel Whitley, Colonel Burch, Sir Gilbert Gerrald (commissioners of the dis-banding the late army) to an account how the mony given for that service was disbursed,[1] and another about

---

[1] The commissioners appointed in 1679 for disbanding the army raised by Charles II in the previous year were four—John Birch, Sir Gilbert Gerrard, Sir Thomas Player, and Roger Whitley. They were now summoned to attend with their accounts on May 30 (*Journals of the House of Commons*, ix. 720).

the altering the method by the new charters for chooseing
Parlament men, they were both referred to be considered
of the 30th instant.

May 29   Came the news that Arguile was gott into his own
territorys in the north of Scotland with 3,000 men, and
was fortifying himself ther.

30   The 28 and the 29 were holydays. The 30th the
King came in his roabes to the Hous of Lords, and passed
the bill for the continuance of the revenue of excize and
customes for his life.

When he had passed the bill his Majesty spoake to
both Houses, thanked them for their chearfulness and
readiness in passing the same, said that the dispatch of it
was as acceptable to him as the bill itselfe, but at the same
time desired an extraordinary supply for the stoors of the
navie and ordinance, and for paying the late Kings debts to
his servants and family, and for defraying the charge the
rebellion in Scotland was likely to putt him to. He
further recommended to them the care of the navie, which
was the strength and glory of the nation, assuring them
that he had a true English heart and was jealous of the
honour of the nation, pleasing himselfe with the thoughts,
by Gods blessing and their assistance, to carry the reputation of it yet higher in the world then ever it yet was in the
time of his anchestors. Upon the consideration of which
speech it was voted in the committè of the whole Hous that
a supply should be granted to his Majesty for the uses
expressed in his speech. It was then mooved that part
of it should be laid upon wines and vinagre by way of
additionall duty upon thos comodities, which I did speake
to promote, being desirous it should be laid upon anything
rather then land.

Colonel Jenkyns, one of my competitors in my election
at Yorke, had attended from the begining of the Parlament
to find some member of that county to preferr his petition
to the Hous against the election of me ther, and could not
find one to charge himselfe with it all this time, till at the

last Sir Hugh Chomley[1] presented it. I being then in *May* 31 the Hous opposed its reception, and was secounded by Sir Henry Gooderick, that it should be thrown out for some reasons then offered. But it was admitted and referred to the committè of elections.[2]

Ther was further given towards the extraordinary *June* 1 supply an imposition upon sugars and tobacco. This was much opposed by severall members of the Hous, who had either themselves or their friends an interest in the plantations; and they argued that the French now endeavouring to encourage the planting of thos comodities in their plantations, this imposition might put a discouragement upon ours, and caus our servants and slaves, that would not be soe well paid by us, run over to them. To this I answered that if the rates imposed should be soe great as to raise the rate of thos comodities here soe high that they should be less sould, what they seemed to urge was reasonable; but if they sould as much as formerly, it could neither prejudice our plantations nor navigation; besides the Act was to be only temporary, and if it was found prejudiciall, it might be repealed and something else given the King in lieu of it.   Severall spoake to the same purpas, and it passed that 6d. per lb. should be imposed upon Spanish tobacco, and 3d. upon that of Virginia and of other places; that 1d. should be laid upon white pouder sugar, ½d. on Muscovado, and soe proportionably on other sorts that should be consumed at home, and to be paid by the buyer.   I spoake three times in this concern, and was tould by my Lord Preston[3] and others that I had

[1] Sir Hugh Cholmley had been resident-engineer at Tangier from 1663 to 1674, and had been largely responsible for the construction of the mole there.   At this time he was M.P. for Thirsk.

[2] June 1.

[3] Richard Graham, Viscount Preston in the peerage of Scotland, M.P. for Cumberland, and one of the managers of the House of Commons in the interests of the Court.   At the close of October 1688 he succeeded Sunderland as Secretary, and endeavoured to avert the Revolution by urging a policy of moderation upon James.

considerably assisted to this work, which I had severall reasons to promote at this time.

June 2   I dined with my Lord Tresurer, who meeting me as I came from the Hous carryed me home with him, wher I gave him an account of the perfecting of the bill of imposition on wines and vinigre that morning, and the Common's haveing given it the King for eight years. I took that opportunity to tell his lordship of the dispute (not yet perfectly ended) between my Lord Burlinton and me as to my commission of governor of Yorke, and offered to referr it to his lordship, who promessed to speake to my Lord Burlinton in it, and said as it was fitt his lordship should preserve the dignity of lord lieutenant, soe he would take care that I should keep the fitt powers belonging to me as governor.

The merit of the return from the bourough of Thetford being this day heard at the barr, it was voated the return to be void (the Maior of the town haveing returnd himselfe), and further that noe Maior, bailiff, or other officer to whom the writt was directed, had power to return themselves, which last words I mooved to be added to the question.

3   A bill was read the first time for the pressing of carriages for the King in his progresses.[1]   What passed more this day was of little moment, and therfore I mention it not. The committè of privileges sate in the afternoon, wher I mooved for a longer day then the 13 June (the day set before for the hearing the caus of the election between Sir Medcalfe Robison and Mr. Moyser), but it would not be granted.

4   I found that a soreness that I had felt in my toe, first in the extreame joint (though I had before found a tenderness underneath the joint in treading), encreased soe much upon me that I began to keep my bed, hopeing that rest

---

[1] The Bill was read a second time, and Reresby was appointed a member of thé committee to whom it was referred (*Journals of the House of Commons*, ix. 726).

might cure it. The next day it encreased and sweld, and changed from joint to joint, at the least seven times in both feet, till I visibly saw it was a rumatisme rather then the gout, bycaus it gave me little pain. But it left a weakeness behind after it had continued a week, for in that time I was able to rise, by keeping strictly to the milke dyet, but not to goe out of doors in four days after. In this time I was visited by my Lord Hallifax, my Lord Burlinton, and many more lords and gentlemen of my acquentance; but I was altogather ignorant of the perticular proceedings of the Hous of Commons, not being able to attend the Hous. It was then Whitsontide, when my two sons were with me from Kensinton schoole, and that I began to hope that my son William would succeed better in his studys then I expected. Tamworth continued his usuall improovement.

Came an expresse from Lyme in Dorsetshire (and *June* 11 another was soon followed from the Maior ther) to the King, that brought newes of the Duke of Monmoth's being arrived ther (being landed not farr off)[1] with one boat of 32 gunns and two less boats bringing arms for 20,000 men, severall officers and souldiers to the nomber of about 200; and that severall ordinary people flocked in to him from that factious country; that he declared himselfe the protector of the Protestant religion, and against popery. The King sent down the Duke of Albemarle with all speed, being Lord Lieutenant of the county of Dorcester,[2] to raise the militia, and after him some companys of the standing foot and six troops of hors and dragoons. Lyme is naturally strong, soe that not above three abreast can enter the town at once. The Duke of Monmoth stayed ther (the town being at his

[1] Monmouth landed on June 11. News of his invasion reached the King early on the morning of June 13 and was communicated by him to Parliament that day.

[2] Devon. Albemarle was at Exeter when Monmouth landed, having been sent down in expectation of his attempt.

disposall), and before the 14th came notice that he was 3,000 strong, but that the Duke of Albemarle had raised the militia and was marching towards him with some 8,000 men.

June 12   The King sent to the Commons the news he had recieved of the Duke of Monmoth.   Upon the reciet of it they voated his Majesty their thankes, and to goe to him to offer themselves in a body of the whole Hous to carry their own address, wherin they promessed to stand by him with their lives and fortunes against that ingratefull rebell, James, Duke of Monmoth, and all others whomsoever, &c.

13   I had orders to fill up my company from 50 to 100 men, haveing first written to the Marquis of Halifax that I heard the King had given such orders to some, and that I desired him to tell the King that being as willing to venter my life for him as others I desired to be in the same condition to doe it.

14   The King had an expresse that Arguile was com'd into his own country, out of the island, wher they intended to block him up.[1]

The same day[2] the Duke of Monmoth's declaration (which arrived the day before) was sent by the King to both Houses, which passed the bill of attainder against his Grace that very day, and voted 5,000 l. reward to any that should apprehend the Duke, and bring him to the King, dead or alive.   This declaration charged James, Duke of Yorke (for soe it called the King), with the burning of the citty, the death of Sir Edmondbury Godfrey, the murder of Colonel Sidney, my Lord Russell, with poysoning the late King, tearing his crown from his head, with being led by popish councils, with packing the present Parlament (it not one freely chosen);   that he

---

[1] Argyll had landed in Bute, and was now aiming at an advance on Inveraray to drive out the clans which had invaded his territory in the name of the Government.

[2] Really June 15.

came to revenge thes things upon the King, and would
never come to any terms or accommodation till it was
done; that he would give noe quarter to thos that opposed
him, and therfore desired all good people to come in and
assist him.   He further declared that he had a just title
to the crown, but he would [not] claime that till he had
called a free Parlament, which he would fully satisfie in
that matter, promessing that Parlaments should sitt every
year, and not be dismissed till all grievences were
redressed; that he would give libertie of concience to all
persons, even to papists themselves, with much more to
this or the like purpass.

An expresse brought word that the Duke of Monmoth *June* 14
had marched out of the town with 200 foot and 100 hors,
had light of some forerunners of the Dorsetshire militia
and killed some persons of note, as Collonell Strangways
brother[1] and some others, and taken some prisners; but
that advanceing to the main body they were repelled,
putt to flight, threw away their arms and lost some
prisners.[2]

I went to the Hous, but stayed a short time.   16

An additionall supply was voted to the King towards 17
the defraying of the warr against the Duke of Monmoth
and the rebels, and the Hous resolved into a committe
of the whole Hous to consider of the manner; and ther it
was voted: 1st, that it should be laid upon such new
foundations as had been built upon within the compas of
the bils of mortality since the year 1660, excepting of the
late generall fires within the citty of London and the
bourough of Southerick; 2ndly, that it be laid only upon
the rents of such houses for one year; 3rdly, upon such
foundations as are now laid; 4thly, that a clause be

---

[1] Wadham Strangways, brother of Colonel Thomas, who commanded
the Red Regiment in the militia of Dorset.

[2] This engagement took place on June 14 as a result of an attempt made
by the insurgents to seize Bridport.   Lord Grey was in command, not
Monmouth.

brought in to prohibit any more buildings within the said limits; 5thly, that the House be mooved to order that a bill be brought in to the said intent.   In all which the Hous agreed with the committè.

I spoake thrice in this debate, first in answer to a gentleman that said this was laying a tax for a publique use upon one piece of a county and upon private persons; to which I replyed that this one county drayned all England of its people, especially the north, our tenents all coming hyther, finding by experience that they could live here better in a seller or a garret then they could live in the country of a farm of 30 l. rent; that hereby this little piece of England had laid a tax in a manner upon all the rest of England, and was a nusance to all the rest; and therfore it was not soe improper that it should be taxed seperately, and the rather bycaus it was never taxed before, or but once very little.   Some mooved it should be laid for one year and a halfe; but that I opposed, for I said ther were some few foundations taxed in Oliver's time, and that tax was laid but for one year in the worst of times, and therfore we ought not now to lay it for a longer time in good times.   It was mooved that more mony might be laid upon brandys towards this supply to the King; but this I spoake against, saying it was fitt this should be computed how much it would arise to before another fond was encombered or more mony voted to be raised.

June 18   The King sent to desire the Commons that they would voat him credit upon some fond for such a sum as they should thinke fitt to give him towards the suppression of this rebellion in the west, and that they should soe prepare their business as to be in a condition to adjurn for some time within few days.   They resolved, upon this, into a committè of the whole Hous, and voted the sum which was to be given to the King (as it had been debated the day before) to be 400,000 l., appointing a committè at the same time to inquire and to bring in an estimate what was one years value of the rents of new buildings upon new foundations.

Severall bils were read the second time, and many of them committed.

The Hous of Commons did little but read severall bils.   *June* 19

Now the Court seemed more concerned at the encrease of the Duke of Monmoth's forces (which were reported to be 4,000 foot and four troops of hors), with the which he had marched towards Taunton, a populous and factious town, and made himselfe master of it, two militia regiments that were in the town running away when they heard he came near the place.[1]   The Duke of Albemarle had orders all this while not to fight him till the standing troops came up to him, which were expected to joine him the 20th.

Some 2,500 men of the guards, hors and foot, marched 20 to reenforce the troops sent before to the Duke of Albemarle, commanded by my Lord Feathersham.   Severall new troopes were ordered to be raised at the same time, three regiments to be commanded by the Earl of Peterbourough,[2] my Lord Ferrers[3] and my Lord Dartsmoth, with four independent troops of hors commanded by Sir Thomas Mauliverer, Mr. Fairfax, son to my Lord Fairfax,[4] and others.

The same day the Commons (finding that the fund of the new foundations would proove tedious to raise the tax upon, the committè appointed to bring in the estimate

[1] The reference appears to be to the skirmish which took place at Axminster on June 15.

[2] Henry Mordaunt, the second earl, who had been Groom of the Stole to James while Duke of York and had acted as his proxy in his marriage with Mary of Modena.   He was received into the Roman Church in March 1687, and on that ground was impeached after the Revolution.

[3] Robert, Lord Ferrers of Chartley, youngest son of Sir Robert Shirley, fourth baronet, of Staunton Harrold, Leicestershire.   He was created Earl Ferrers in 1711.

[4] Thomas, eldest son of Henry, fourth Baron Fairfax of Cameron, whom he succeeded in 1688.

of the yearly rents reporting to the Hous that it would require a long time to perfect) laid the tax upon French linnin, brandys, and East India callicoes, lining, and wrought silkes, according to severall rates from all parts, and ordered a bill to be brought in to that purpas.

My Lord Halifax took ill from me that I had been active in the Hous in the debate of taxing new buildings, he haveing a deep concern therin; but I tould him it was my judgement, and that if my father's interest were in it I should have done the same thing. However, it was my great trouble that he of all men should disapproove of anything I did; but we presently understood one another, and he said he was sorry he had said anything to disturb me. This was the only time that we seemed to differ, and it was soon over, for at the same time he asked me, now that severall persons were desireing commissions to raise troops, if he should aske one of the King for me. The King being then in the Hous of Lords (I consenting to it), he went straight to the King, and returned with promess from his Majesty to give me the next day a commission. That night as the King came from Council he called me to him and tould me that he had considered of it, that t'was true he had promessed me a troop and I should have one, but must tell me that he was not sure to continue both the troop and company long under the command of one person, besides it might be of exemple to other governors to expect the same thing; that he had a kindness for me, and would doe as far as it was he conveniently doe to oblige me;[1] but I must either stick to the troop or company, and he would give me which I pleased.

I replyed I was ready to serve his Majesty in as many imployments as he pleased, or in which he pleased to appoint, but I feared when the warr was over the new raised troops would be disbanded. He said that was not impossible, and therfore rather seemed to advise me to

---

[1] Some slip has obviously been made here, but the meaning seems plain.

keep my company. The King was very gracious to me in this, for besides the charge of 1,000 l. which it would have cost to have raised the troop (his Majesty advanceing noe mony towards it), if the troop had been commanded upon service I must have been at the head of it, and this might have given opportunity to another to have slipt into my goverment of Yorke, at a time when it was nescessary that he that commanded a place of that importance should be personally ther.

Severall other troops and companys were ordered to *June* 22 be raised by men of estates, and some regiments.

The Hous of Commons did little this day but read and prepare bills in order to their passing.

The same day his Majesty recieved this news from Scotland: that the Earl of Dunbarton,[1] Commander in Chiefe of his Majestys forces in Scotland, haveing notice that the rebels had passed the river Levin above Dunbarton, marched from Glascow to Sterling and overtook them near Killern, wher they intended to fall upon them, but that night prevented, and gave the rebels opportunity to steale away and to gett into Renfrew. The Earl of Dunbarton persued them with his hors and dragoons, and in his way understood that they were running away in great confusion. The same day, which was the 18th June, three servants belonging to some gentlemen of Renfrew found the Earl of Arguile runing away in the habit of a countryman, with a blew bonit on his head. They asked him who he was, but he refused to tell his name or to render himselfe, till, being wounded in severall places of the head and fearing to be killed, he confessed he was the Earl of Arguile. Whereupon they took him prisner and carryed him to Glascowe, wher he was committed. The King sent to give an account of this to the Commons, who returned their thankes to his Majesty for it by the members of the Hous that were privy councillors. The King returned this answer to the Commons, that he was every

[1] Lord George Douglas, created Earl of Dumbarton in 1675.

day more and more satisfyed of their loyalties, for which he returned them his thankes.

June 23 The bill for the 400,000 l. was read for the first time, and severall other bills in order to their passing.

The same day the King recieved notice that the Duke of Monmoth had writt to the Duke of Albemarle by the name of his trusty and well-beloved cozen and councillor, Christopher, Duke of Albemarle, chargeing him upon his allegiance to come in to his aid, soe that now he took upon him the title of King; that he was marched from Tauntan towards Bristow with about 5,000 men and boys, and that the Duke was following after him.

The same day the Lord President tould me that Yorke would be made a considerable guarrison, and that some other place in the west would be fortifyed (as he guessed).

24 I dined with Sir James Smyth, Lord Maior of London, whom I had formerly known very intimately. He was of the clubb with some other loyall aldermen of the Citty, wher I used to goe when the phenatique plott was in contrivance. He tould me that he had the tytle of Lord Maior, but my Lord Chiefe Justice Jeffereys usurped the power; that they had noe accesse to the King, nor noe message or directions from him as to any businesse but by that lord; that whatever was well done in the Citty was attributed to his influence and contrivance, and that him-selfe and the aldermen were but looked upon at Court as his instruments; and that upon all occasions his lordship used them contemptably, and not according to the dignity of the Citty. In fyne, he said my Lord Chief Justice was to be pittyed, for his haughtiness would undo him, and that he intended to acquaint the King with thes things, but this was not a fitt time for it, bycaus it might look like muteny. I tould him the King knew his services and integrity too well for that, and in my opinion it was the fittest time to expose a man in that credit at Court, bycaus it would be most reguarded now.

I was sorry to se soe good men dissatisfyed in any

perticular; but I was not soe to see this proud man soe understood, for he had used the citty of Yorke as scurvily as that of London, in contributing underhand to the putting out of the five aldermen, when he had engaged at Yorke to keep them in and had assured them of it afterwards, and that too without allowing of them to be heard as to the crimes of which they stood accused. My Lord Maior said he had done the same thing severall times in London, and that many were laid aside from imployments, not being suffered to make their defence.

I was informed also by one of the lieuetenancy of the Citty that should the Duke of Monmoth give a blow to the Kings forces, he much feared ther might be a riseing in London by the factious party.

I understood the King had given a commission for the *June* 25 raiseing a troop of hors to my Lord Plimoth, governor of Hull, a regiment of foot to the Earl of Bath, governor of Plimoth, both which had independent companys of foot as well as myselfe. By this I found the King had broaken the rule he said he intended to goe by, in not giveing additinall commands to such persons, and therfore desired my Lord Halifax to aske his Majesty that he would please to give me also a commission for a troop of hors. I had thes reasons to doe it: if any considerable action did happen I thought it was fitt to be in it as well as others, which I had a better occasion for haveing an independent troop then by haveing only a company of foot in a guarrison; I heard the charge of raiseing a troop would be much less then was reported, and if the troop should continue it was both an honourable and profitable command. The King did very readily grant me a commission, and (which was a greater kindness and favour) another for my son Tamworth, a child of fourteen years of age, to be my cornet. The King named my lieutenant, one Mr. Arther,[1] an Irishman and a papist,

[1] Nicholas Arthur. All the commissions are dated June 25 (Dalton, *English Army Lists*, ii. 15).

the King thinkeing fitt to give commissions to severall of
that persuasion in thes new troops.

July 1   I mustered twenty-three men of my troop.

I recieved the same day an account from my brother
Edmond, that commanded a company of the guards, from
the army then at Bradford, that the severall partys that
had been sent down against the rebels were now joind,
that the Duke of Monmoth had been near the Bath with
the army, and had sent to sommons the town, my Lord
Fitzhardin[1] being governor, but that being refused
entrance, and the army belonging to the King to the
nomber of 7,000 being drawn out of the town, he drew off
his men and marched back toward Croom,[2] and that the
King's forces intended the next day to follow him.   This
letter was dated the 28 of June.   He further said that
Monmoth's army was betwixt seven and eight thousand
men, of which 500 were hors.   I tould the King of this at
supper, who said his account was much to the same
purpas, and that he had since recieved another from my
Lord Feathersham, that said the ordinance and the
carriages with their tents were now gott up to them, soe
that they hoped to lie near the rebels and to be in a condition to give a good account of them speedily.

A bill for naturalizeing all French Protestants and
strangers held a long debate in the Hous of Commons,
whether it should be committed or not.   I spoake for
the committing it, provided they would conforme to the
lithurgie of the Church of England, and that thos that
did not should loos the benefit of their naturalization.
The Court was not for the bill; however, it was at the last
committed.[3]

I had a letter then from my wife, whos fear that a man

---

[1] Maurice Berkeley, third Viscount Fitzhardinge of Berehaven.

[2] ? " Frome."

[3] Sir John was a member of the committee, which was instructed by the
House to prepare a clause giving effect to the provision regarding the
liturgy which he had supported (*Journals of the House of Commons*, ix. 755).

* 36/17: Edmund Reresby, 28 June 1685.

was less safe for haveing severall commands made her not satisfyed with the last the King had done me the honour to bestowe upon me, a woemans kindness being sometimes soe mistaken as to wish a husbands safety before his honour and preferment.   The thruth is few things are persued in the world without hazard, and Providence suffers sometimes thos men to fall into it the soonest that avoid it the most.

Both Houses attended the King in the Hous of Lords, *July* 2 wher his Majesty passed five bils, and then ordered the Houses to adjourn till the 4th of August, which was done accordingly.[1]

The fears of all thos that loved the Goverment improoved as the hopes of the discontented by the encrease of the Duke of Monmoths party, who was now swelled to an army of 12,000 men and near 1,500 hors,[2] mooved place to place in the west, in the hilly and enclosed country, wher, though the Kings army kept pritty close to him, yet could not fight him.   That army of the Kings nearest to him, commanded by my Lord Feathersham, did not consist of above 3,000 foot and 500 hors, but thes were of the guards (or the most of them).

The King had notice that the Duke was gott into 4 Bridgewater, intending to fortifie himselfe ther whilst he refreshed his army, and that my Lord Feathersham was following of him very close.

The Duke, being informed that my Lord Feathersham 6 laid encamped at three miles from Bridgwater,[3] that his army was small, and that three English regiments and three Scotch regiments from Holland, as also more hors from London, were upon their march to reenforce his lordship,

---

[1] This short adjournment was with the object of making an early meeting possible in case of emergency.   It was not intended that Parliament should actually reassemble until the winter.

[2] These figures represent the exaggeration of rumour, especially that given for the horse.

[3] On Sedgemoor, with his head-quarters at Weston Zoyland.

steales out about one a clock in the morning with his whole army towards the camp, but with that silence that the Kings forces knew nothing of their approach till they came to the centry, whos fire gave them the first notice. The Duke of Monmoth marched in the head of the foot, my Lord Gray led up the hors and brought their canon within pistoll shott.   Our men gott into order as soon as they could, and recieved them as well as they could, but were soe outpowred in nombers that, till my Lord Gray ran away with the hors, being frightened with our cannon, we were in great danger to loose the day.   The Duke of Monmoth stood, however, till a great part of his foot was cutt in peeces, and then made his escape, but soe narrowly that his coat, papers, and secretary were taken.   Farguison, that arch Presbuterien priest and rebell, was killed, and my Lord Gray taken three days after in a disguise.[1]

July 7   I recieved a letter from my brother (that was a captain in the Duke of Graftons regiment of guards, that was in the action), who sent me the perticulars of it by the expresse that came to the King, and writt more fully as to some things then my Lord Feathersham had writt to his Majesty in that disorder.   I showed the King my brothers letter, who said that the foot fought very well, as indeed they did, my brother saying that they were either killed or wounded on both sides of him, though he happily escaped.   I showed his letter the same day to my Lord Tresurer, to the Prince, and to my Lord President.

The Duke of Monmoth, from the begining of this his desperate attempt, had showed the conduct of a great captain, insoemuch as the King said himselfe he had not made one false stepp.   And thus this great storme, which began from a little cloud (for the nomber of men which he brought ashoar were not above 150), was thus fortunately dispersed; for had he gott the day, it was to be

[1] Grey was taken early in the morning of July 7.   Robert Ferguson, the " Plotter," escaped altogether and returned in 1688 with William of Orange.

* 38/18, 19: Edmund Reresby, 6 July 1685.

feared that the disaffected were soe numerous that they
would have risen in other parts of England, to the very
hazard of the Crown. The nomber of the slain of the
ennemys side were computed about 12,000;[1] on our side
near 300 kild and wounded. We took about 600
prisners.

To compleat the Kings good fortune came the newes *July* 9
of the Duke of Monmoth being taken in a wood disguised,
by a company of country fellowes hunting after him, with
one Count Horn,[2] who was first light upon in a bush and
said that the Duke was not farr off. The same day the
Duches of Monmoth and her two sons were sent to the
Tower. When the Duke was taken he was almost
spent, haveing not been in bed of three weeks. He had
noe arms, nor made any defence, only he carryed a watch
in his pockit and 300 l. in gould, which was the only mony
he had left. His Majesty, as he had reason, was very
well pleasd with the newes, though he was of a temper
soe equall as not to appear transported upon any occasion;
for he could not have a greater then this, to see this
rebellion thus pulled up by the roots, and himselfe
the faster in the throne by this endeavour to cast him
out.

When he came to town the King see him at his request
at Whitehall, wher he expressed some detestation of what
he had attempted to doe, and laid the fault on my Lord
Arguile and Mr. Farguison for adviseing him to it,
disclaimed any title to the Crown, and said he was putt
upon takeing the name of King, believe[ing] it might
make men of quality repair the more to him. This I
heard the King say, but [what] he further confessed was
not then known. He ended all with desireing pardon
and his life of the King upon his knees, and soe continued

---

[1] Obviously a mistake for 1,200.

[2] Presumably the reference is to Anthony Buyse, a German who had
been in the service of the Elector of Brandenburg and was eventually sent
back to his own country.

to doe by letters to the two Queens till he was executed by his head being cutt from his body (at five blowes) upon Tower Hill.[1]

When he came to die he submitted to it inconcerned, disowned all pretence to the Crown, and impiously desowned his Duchess, that brought him, haveing nothing, 10,000 l. per annum, saying she was given him for wife in his minority, but the wife of his own choice was the Lady Henrietta Wentworth (the only daughter and heiresse of the Earl of Cleveland,[2] whome he debeauched), with whom he owned he had lived according to the rules of his concience, though not according to thos of the lawes of the land, for two years last past.   He further said he was sorry for the effusion of blood of which he had been the cause, but would not name it a rebellion in his whole discours. Ther was taken in his pockit, bookes of his own hand-writing, wherin were charms or spels, to opon the door in case he should be in prison, not to [be] wounded in battle, &c., songs and prayers.

July 17   It was ordered that the late raised troops should be reduced from 100 in a company to 60, the hors from 60 in a troop to 50, and that some whole troops should be reduced or disbanded; but what troops thes were was not yet known.   Everyone feared it would fall to their share, and myselfe in perticular, who had other commands; only I made what friends I could to be continued.

18   Some believed thos that had the last commissions were to be reduced, others such whos troopes were least com-

[1] July 15. " The executioner had five blowes at him.   After the first he lookt up, and after the third he put his leggs across, and the hangman flung away his axe, but being chidd tooke it againe and gave him tother two strokes, and severed not his head from his body till he cut it off with his knife " (*Memoirs of the Verney Family*, iv. 358).   The executioner was the notorious Jack Ketch.

[2] She was the only child of Sir Thomas Wentworth, eldest son of Sir Thomas, fourth Baron Wentworth and first Earl of Cleveland.   Her father died in 1665, two years before her grandfather.

pleat. For this reason I made the King acquainted that
mine was full (as it truly was), and prevailed with my
Lord President to speake to the King that it might stand.
The King tould him that must be resolved on in Councill.
I also applyed myselfe to my Lord Tresurer, who *July* 20
promessed to assist me in it, and not content with this gave
his Majesty a paper, telling him at the same time that it
was soe hard by reason of his great business to have access
to him, that I desired he would please to cast his eye upon
that paper, in which were some reasons for the continuance
of my troop. The King recieved it smileing. The
Earles of Thanet and of Plimoth (who were both to command two regiments made of thes new raised troops)
desired the King, and without my privitie, to have my
troop of their regiment. The King tould them he could
give them noe answer till he considered his list.

The Earle of Feathersham, who had commanded the 20
forces against the rebels in the quality of lieutenant
generall, was much consulted by the King as to the
captains of troops to be continued or broaken. His
lordship, upon my enquiry if my troop was likely to
stand, tould me in confidence that he heard the King say
that he would not continue both troops and companys to
any one person, noe not soe much as to Sir John Reresby,
for whom he had as much reguard as to another; and that
he heard his Majesty further say that I had besides the
best sallary of any governour of England. But, said he,
noe ressolution is yet absolutely taken. From this time I
much feared the loss of my troop, but ressolved the endeavour to keep it if I could, and rather to quitt my company
of granadeers of the two for many reasons, especially if I
could be assured that it would always stand, when once
fixed.

Ther was a generall order to reduce the troops to 40, 27
the companys to 50 men. I heard it was believed the
troops that should now be admitted to stand would many
of them be disbanded soe soon as the fleet was putt into a

better condition for the guard of the seas.   This and some
other reasons made me change my mind of quitting my
company rather then my troop, which I was confirmed in
by the advice of my Lord President.

July 28   I learnt from the Secretary of Warr that ther was some
regiments of foot, severall independent companys of foot
of the old establishment, and eighteen of the new raised
troops, were ordered to be disbanded, of which nomber
mine was one.

The same day my Lord Halifax tould me he had spoak
to his Majesty for the continuing of my troop; that his
answer was that he would allowe of noe mans haveing
severall commands; that however he spoak kindly of me,
and gave some assurances of continuing me in thos other
imployments which I had before.   The same day I
waited of the King to recieve his commands for Yorke.
He said that if he had continued a troop to any man in
England in my circumstances, he had done it to me.
I answered he might always dispose of me as his Majesty
pleased, that I was only concerned for my yong cornet.
He said he would take some care of him, and bid me goe
to my Lord Tresurer to doe that for me which he had
ordered him to doe.   I went to my Lord and tould him
the message, who said it was to give me a consideration
for the charges I had been at in raiseing my troop, but
I must first give him a perticular of them.   I made one
the same day and sent it to his lordship.

29   I sett forward for Yorkshire.   I gott to Thriberge in
my own coach the first of August, wher by Gods mercy
I found my wife, children and family very well.

August 2   I recieved the ill newes that the ship called the *Tryall* of
Yorke, aboard on which I had sent cloaths and provisions
for my troop and company at Yorke, with other goods
to the value of about 300 l., was cast away, the men all
saved, but few of thos goods.

5   I went for Yorke, wher the assizes were then held, and
paid off the troop that was before disbanded.   My ant

---

* 38/16: Edward Baldock, 20 July 1685; 38/10: G. Butler, 3 July 1685. As
early as 3 July, Reresby was finding it difficult to raise a troop because of a
shortage of men, equipment, and horses; 38/20: F. Reresby, 3 July 1685,
informs him that there are no men to be got unless Reresby advances 10 or 15
pounds.

† 38/25: W. Blathwayt, 25 July 1685, about disbanding Reresby's troop;
38/22: G. Butler, 30 July 1685.

‡ 37/24: E. Reresby, 5 September 1685; 39/46: John Thackary, 29 August
1685. Attempts were made to recover the items on the beach where they were

Monson haveing ther a tryall with Mr. Foljambe[1] of 6,000 l. concern, she desired me to be assisting to her husband Mr. Felton in the management of it; but the caus being to come on upon the 8th, that very morning they both came to me, both Felton and Foljambe, and desired me to make an end of it. I was unwilling to take a referrence upon me of soe great a value, but being pressed to doe it I did determin it to both their satisfactions.

That day came down the charter of Yorke renewed,[2] *Aug. 8* and the five aldermen changed as was before mentioned, which the friends to my opponants did much rejoice at, and did cast about a discours as if their standing soe firmly by me in my election was the reason of their being put out of commission. This was some trouble to me, but ther was noe remedie at that time. I returnd to Thriberge the same day.

Came the news that the Serasquier Bassa, generall of 20 the Ottaman army in Hungary, was routed near Gran, all his ammunition, baggage and artilary taken by the Dukes of Lorrain and Bavaria, generals for the Emperour, in which battle 6,000 were killed upon the place, 4,000 of them being Janizarys. At the same time Newheusal was taken by another part of the Emperors army after a long siege, and the guarrison, consisting of 1200, all putt to the sword.[3]

I went to Loudham in Nottinghamshire, wher I had *Sept. 4* some pretention to about 80 l. per annum, which was the estate of the Tamworths (my granmother being heiress

---

[1] Presumably Francis Foljambe of Aldwark, a distant relative of her first husband, who now held the Foljambe estates.

[2] The official account of the reception of the charter can be found in the *London Gazette*, August 13-17, 1685.

[3] The Turkish attack on Gran was intended to draw off the besieging army from Neuhäusel. The rout of the Turks by the Duke of Lorraine on August 6/16 practically ensured the fall of the latter fortress, which was stormed by Aeneas Caprara three days later.

---

washed up; 37/10: George Butler, 19 August 1685, relates that some of Reresby's things were distributed among the country people.

* 40/1, 2, 10, 15, 20, 21, 30: letters from his aunt Monson which show that Reresby was very much involved in the affair as a trustee of the jointure.

† 37/10: George Butler, 19 August 1685: 'ye whole towne [were] ahorseback to meete itt at least 3,000 horse that night ye charter was read, two h[ogs]hds of claritt sett out in ye street for ye mobbily and a fine collation in ye guildhall where the kings health etc and yours [were] drunk and bell ringing and burnt fires all ye night'.

to it). I endeavoured to try if the tenents would atturn [1] to me, but they refused.

Sept. 5   I called at Bolsover in my return to Thriberg to dine with the Duke of Newcastle. The Duke of Albemarle not long before [2] had quitted all his imployments at Court. He commanded the Kings first troop of guards, was lord lieutenant of two counties, Chancellor of the University of Cambrige, with other imployments. The reason was the Lord Feathersham had power to command him by his commission in the late rebellion in the west, and at their return his lordship and my Lord Churchil were made major-generals, when his Grace thought that by his quality and his families services to the Crown he deserved it as well as they. This, with the Duke of Newcastle's believeing himselfe neglected when last at London by the King, made him free of his discours in relation to affairs at Court, and declare positively that he would not repair thether any more, and should be glad to be out of all manner of publique imployment.

8   The tenents of Loudham lands in Nottinghamshire came over to Thriberge, and haveing considered of it atturned tenents to me, which giveing me the possession of thos lands prevented my going to Nottingham, wher I should have had a tryall for them the 11th of the same month. The rents of the said landes were about 60 l. per annum, besides two woods, one of 80 acres, the other of 60, for the felling of both which I had liberty granted by the Duke of Newcastle, who was Justice in Ouir of the Kings forrests on the north side Trent, thes woods being within that precinct.

The newes of the continued success of the Christians against the Turkes, as well by the Venitians as the Imperialists, was very gratefull to Christendome, of which we had frequent newes.

22   I had the account of the breakeing of a gouldsmith in London, who had 700 l. of mine in his hands.

---

[1] *i.e.* agree formally to accept as landlord.   [2] July 31.

I remooved with my family to the Mannour at Yorke. *Sept.* 28
I found ther that the deputy governor, my lieutenant of
granadeers, had done severall things by colour of the   *
authority that he recieved from me which had dissatisfyed
the citty and the high sheriff of the county, which had like
to have revived the old dispute as to the gates of the Castle
and the garden ther; all which I prevented with some
trouble, and putt things into pritty good order.   I gott
new cloaths at that time for the company, paid the officers
and souldiers all their arrears till the first of September last.

The Archbishop of Yorke, his lady, son and his wife [1] *Oct.* 5
did me the honour to come and dine with me at the Mannour, wher I diverted his Grace (haveing been a souldier) [2]
by showing him my company, and makeing them exercize
before him, and with fireing their granado shels.

I found then that Collonel Jenkins intended to persist
in persuing his petition against me concerning my election
in Parlament at the next session, which was to be the 9th
of November next, being the day to which it was adjourned.

All things being well setled I returned for Thriberge. 12
I went to the generall quarter-sessions at Barnsley.   13
I went to the muster of my militia troop at Wakefild, 14
wher severall gentlemen of the town and country came and
dined with me at my quarters.

I returned home and mett the newes that I should 16
recover 500 l. of the 700 l. which I feared to loos by the
breakeing of the goldsmith.

As I rid late between Barnsley and Wakefield I lost my
sword out of my belt, and not discovering it till I came to
my journey's end I was troubled at it, bycaus it is reputed

---

[1] Gilbert Dolben, elder son of the Archbishop, who was to be active
in Parliament and on the judicial bench in the reigns of William and Anne,
had married Anne, eldest daughter of Tanfield Mulso of Finedon, North-
amptonshire.

[2] While still a student of Christ Church Dolben had joined the army
of Charles I, been wounded at Marston Moor and again in the siege of
York, and promoted to the rank of major.

---

* 39/28: Edmund Reresby, 6 October 1685. Reresby's brother Edmund, apparently responding to a request for advice on the duties of the deputy governor,
advised that it was not in that official's power to command officers unless he
had the king's commission.

unlucky for a souldier to loos his sword.   But it soe
hapned that as I returned to Thriberge two days after my
man found it close to the road side, though many persons
travelling that way past very near it, yet did not find it.

Oct. 22   The Duchesse Dowager of Norfolke and my Lord
George Howard [1] came to pay us a visit at Thriberge.   She
had been a woeman of ordinary extraction, and of a
wors cours of life.   My Lord Chesterfield tould me that
he kept her sister as his wench for some years, at which
time this woeman being a child lived with her and made
her fires.   When she came to years she followed her sisters
trade, and was common about the town.   At the last she
fell to the share of my Lord Henry Howard (afterwards
Duke of Norfolk).   He had some children by her whilst
he owned her as his whoor, and many more when she was
his wife.

Ther seemed to be a strange fatality to attend that
family at this time in relation to their wifes.   The yong
Duke of Norfolk,[2] eldest son of the said Lord Henry by a
former wife,[3] Lord Martiall of England, marryed the only
daughter and child of the Earl of Peterborough,[4] and had
lived with her in very good understanding for six or seven
years, when, being tould that she was in league with one
St. Germain, a Duch gentleman,[5] he was not willing to
believe it till, pretending to goe from Windser to Winchester with the King this very sommer, he returned the
same evening and surprized them soe near that St.

---

[1] Henry Howard, sixth Duke of Norfolk, who died in 1684, had married
as his second wife Jane, daughter of Robert Bickerton, gentleman of the
wine cellar to Charles II.   Lord George Howard was the eldest son of
this marriage.

[2] Henry, the seventh duke.

[3] Lady Anne Somerset, daughter of Edward, second Marquis of Worcester.

[4] Lady Mary Mordaunt, daughter of Henry, the second earl.

[5] John Germain, who was reputed to be the son of a private in the
guards of William II of Orange but advanced claims to a more exalted
parentage.

Germain, being in bed with the Duchess when the Duke came to the chamber door, was forced to leap out of the window to save himselfe, and the Duchess was found in all the confusion that soe black a guilt could occasion. However, the Duke had the temper not to hurt her, but sent her some days after into a monastery in France.[1]

I had the ill newes of the death[2] of my good lord and *Oct. 24* friend the Earl of Ailsbury, Lord Chamberlain of the Houshould; but that which was much more afflicting was the account that my Lord Marquis of Halifax, Lord President of the Council, was in disfavour with the King, and dismissed the Privy Council,[3] who had been ever a true and kind patron to me, a man of extraordinary parts, which made me the more concerned, fearing that the publique might suffer as well as his friends for want of soe able a person in all business. But it being the Kings plesure it became all good men to submitt to it.

I went to meet my Lord Archbishop of Yorke and Sir 28 Henry Gooderick at Doncaster in their journey up to the ＊ Parlament which was to sitt the 9th of November next. They tould me it was true the Kings haveing laid aside the Marquis of Halifax from all business, but that he had assigned noe caus for it. I found also they were very jealous that the King might offer something in Parlament this session in favour of popery.

This terme severall had been convicted and suffered death for haveing been in the last rebellion and in the plott to have taken away the life of the late King. My Lord Gray made a considerable discovery in both, and some lords were clapt into the Tower, and bills were found for high treason against others for high treason.

I sett forward for London with my familie. I arrived *Nov.* 9 ther the 13th without accidents. I found ther the Hous of Commons had adjourned the takeing into consideration

[1] He divorced her in 1700 and she married Germain in the following year.

[2] October 20.　　　　　　　　　　[3] October 21.

＊ 39/29: Sir Henry Goodricke, 'Tuesday' [26 October] 1685.

the Kings speech, which he had made to them the day of their meeting, viz., the 9th, till Fryday the 13.[1] The Hous of Lords had voted his Majesty thanks for it, but being mooved to be done also in the Hous of Commons it did not pass.

The King in this speech tould the Houses that he was glad to meet them in better times then when he parted with them last; that the rebellion was now perfectly quashed; that the goverment was liable to such attempts by reason that the militia of the kingdom was useless, and that the standing force was soe small that he had now raised it to a greater nomber, which would be a double charge upon him to maintain, and therfore desired a proportionable aid to sopport it and pay his forces; that twas true ther were some popish officers in this army, but he hoped that would caus noe misunderstanding between him and his Parlament, for although they were not quali-fyed by law, yet they were such as had showed their principles by their loyalty; and that he had had experience of it, and would not expose them to shame by parting with them (or to this effect), and would venture his life for the true interest of this nation.

Nov. 13   The 13 [2] the Commons voted a supply to be granted to the King for his extraordinary occasions; but would neither consent to name the *quantum* nor the use to which it was to be given, viz., to the support of the army. It was a long debate, and ended in a question, on which the Hous devided. The noes were 250, the ays were but 125 for that use.[3] It came afterwards the same day to another devision, upon the question whether that Hous should first proceed upon the supply to the King, or upon the second paragraph of his Majestys speech, concerning

---

[1] Thursday the 12th.   [2] Really the 12th.

[3] The division was taken on a motion made by Sir Thomas Clarges that the words " towards the support of the additional forces " should be added to the resolution concerning supply. The voting was 225 to 156 against (Grey's *Debates*, viii. 360).

the popish officers in the army; and it was carryed for postponeing the supply by one voice only.[1]   In this devision it was tould the King that severall of his servants and officers of the army that were of the Hous devided against him.

I waited upon the King to kiss his hand, who asked *Nov.* 14 me when I came to town.   I tould him the night before. He said he was sorry for that, for if I had been ther sooner he had not lost the vote the day before for one voat, which he said was hard, and the more soe bycaus he lost it by his own officers (which I thought was offered by way of admonition to me).   That day the second part of the Kings speech was debated, and the result was that an address should be made to the King to represent to him that the recieveing of popish recusants into the army was contrary to law, and to desire that they might be remooved from the same.[2]   A comitteè was appointed to drawe up this address, and to frame a bill at the same time for the endemnifying of the said officers for the time they had served, they haveing entered into that service in soe eminent a time of danger.

My Lord Halifax tould me this day, waiting upon him, the perticulars of his being dismissed from the President-ship of the Councill.   He said he might have continued with greater advantages then ever, if he would have joined in some things which he sawe was contriveing to be carryed on, which he could not agree to; that the King parted with him with kind expressions, did assign noe caus for his dis-mission, nor would putt any person in his place.   This lord was soe generally looked upon as a wise man and a good subject that the remoove of him (especially at the begining of a Parlament) astonished a great many, and made

---

[1] The division was taken on the question whether the motion for pro-ceeding with supply should be put, and the voting was 183 to 182 against (*Journals of the House of Commons*, ix. 757).

[2] This is substantially the resolution adopted in Grand Committee.   It was somewhat modified before being accepted by the House (*ibid.*).

them fear that ther was a change of councils as well as councellers.

Nov. 16   The debate of the aid to be given to the King came on. 200,000 l. was first mooved to be given, then 400,000 l. by the country gentlemen.   The courtiers insisted upon 1,200,000 l. for paying the new raised forces for five years.   The Hous would not hear of that use for the mony, though it was asked for it, least it might proove an establishment of a standing army; but would give it the King to be employed as he thought fitt.   At the last 700,000 l. was named, and granted to the King.   In this debate the usefulness of a standing army till the rebellion (or rather the ferment of it) was perfectly quieted was much insisted upon on one side, the danger of it and the inconveniences (especially considering the unruliness and insolency of souldiers, their ill exemple in the countrys, and the burden of free quarter) on the other.   But all this was comprimised in the declared intention of the House to make the militia more usefull, untill which time it was agreed as a thing nescessary the army ought to be kept up.

The address for the Kings dismissing of popish officers from the army being prepared was this day read and agreed to.   A long debate hapned upon this, whether the concurrance of the Lords should be desired or not in this matter.   The Court party was against it, that the King might have a better excuse not to grant it when it came but from one of the two Houses; the country gentlemen thought it nescessary to enforce it the more. In this vote I devided (for it came to a devision upon the question) for joining with the Lords, or rather in askeing their concurrance with us in this address; but we lost it by some forty voats.[1]

---

[1] The voting was 212 to 138.   While Reresby voted for the affirmative his " brother " Sir Henry Goodricke was one of the tellers for the negative. This is only typical of the confusion of parties which seems to have taken place in a division of which it is impossible to determine the real significance (*Journals of the House of Commons,* ix. 758).

The Commons considered of fonds for the raiseing the
700,000 l. before given, and after proposeing the new
foundations in the citty of London, forraign salt, iron,
and French lining, and severall other commodities, it was
voted to be laid upon the same sort of trade, viz., silkes
and stuffs from France, East India comodities, &c., on
which the former tax was laid the last session, to be
continued for five years longer; that is 400,000 l. of the
700,000 l. was to be laid ther, and the 300,000 l. was laid
upon French wines at 4 l. per tun more then was imposed
before, for soe long as that sum was run up.

The same day the Commons went in a body to present
the address to the King, he haveing appointed that time
to recieve it.   His answer was this, that he did not expect
such an addresse from such a Hous of Commons, haveing
soe lately recommended to their consideration the great
advantages a good understanding between us had produced in a very short time, and gave them warning of fears
and jealousies amongst ourselves.   I had reason to hope
the reputation that God had blessed me with in the world
would have created and confirmed a greater confidence
in you of me, and of all I say to you; but however you
proceed on your part, I will be steaddy in all the promesses
I have made, and be very just to my word in every one of
my speeches.   The King spoak this with great warmth.

Was appointed to consider of a bill to make the militia 18
more usefull.   Accordingly the Hous resolved itselfe
that day into a committeè of the whole Hous to consider
of it accordingly, in which I spoake three times; but that
matter seeming of some difficulty the debate was adjourned, or rather the whole matter, till the 21 day.

The same day it was mooved by Mr. Wharton, eldest
son to the Lord Wharton,[1] that a day might be named to

[1] Thomas Wharton, the eldest surviving son of Philip, fourth Baron
Wharton, had been returned to Parliament by Buckinghamshire in spite of
the most strenuous efforts of the Court to exclude him.   He was an ardent
supporter of the Revolution and is best remembered as the author of

take the Kings answer to our address into consideration. It was secounded by Mr. Cook of Darbyshire,[1] a gentleman of 3,000 l. per annum, who used thes words, that we were all Englishmen, and he hoped we should not be frighted from our dutys by a few high words. This was looked upon as soe undecent an expression to the King (tho the Hous generally liked the motion), and put it into such a flame, that they sent that member to the Tower, and left that business *sine die*. That day I dined with my Lord Tresurer, who was civill to me.

Nov. 19   We took into consideration the time for raiseing the tax voted to the King upon the respective comodities on which it was laid, which was accordingly perfected and prepared for a committeè to draw the bill with a clause for credit. A bill was also ordered to be brought in to prevent the soe frequent cheats by the pretending breakeing of bankeers and gouldsmiths.

The same day the Lords began to consider of his Majestys speech wher it relates to popish commanders, and the debate was very warm, but was at last adjourned till the 23. The King was present (as he was usually constant in the Hous of Lords), and was much concerned at the planeness which they said was used in this debate. The thruth is it gave great dissatisfaction to see the lawes invaded in that perticular; and the Kings best friends, with his domestick as well as military officers (except some few that were popishly affected), were much alarmed at it, and were very free in their discourses concerning it.

20   The King, comming in his robes, acquainted both Houses by my Lord Chancellor that for some weighty reasons his Majesty thought fitt to proroague this Parlament untill the 10th of February next, and that accordingly it was proroagued.

"Lilli Burlero, Bullen-a-la," by which he later claimed, with some justice, that he had sung a king out of three kingdoms.

[1] John Coke, M.P. for Derby Borough, captain of a company in the Princess Anne's regiment of foot (Dalton, *English Army Lists*, ii. 29).

Many were the conjectures concerning this prorogation. Some said the King had soe good a revenue and
was soe good a manager that he would be able to subsist,
and maintain both his fleet and army, without more mony,
and therfore would scarce have occasion for more Parlaments; and the rather bycaus he had refused 700,000 l.
by this dismission, which the Commons were prepareing
to give him. Others were of opinion that the Houses
would meet again at the time, and that the King would
find out some expedient before then to give them satisfaction in the only point of difference between them,
which was that of the popish officers. In the meantime
some of thos gentlemen that had most remarkably voted
for the address to the King for laying them aside from
their imployments were forbidden the Kings presence,
as Mr. Fox, paymaster of the army,[1] Lieutenant-Colonel
Darcy, Major Webb,[2] &c.

My Lord Brandon[3] was tryed for being in the late *Nov. 26*
plott with the Duke of Monmoth. My Lord Gray,
Colonell Rumsey[4] and others were evidence against him,
and the matter appeared soe plane that he was found
guilty, and had sentence passed upon him as a trayter.

Some had reported that my company was to be reduced,
and the goverment of Yorke with it; but attending on the
King at Whitehall at supper this evening, I had some
reason to hope that the report was groundless, for the
King called me to him, and tould me that he had now
made all the governours companys in England granadeers, which his saying of it to me I thought looked like
a confirmation of both.

The popish party at this time behaved themselves

[1] Charles Fox, eldest son of Sir Stephen, had succeeded his father as paymaster in 1680.

[2] Probably Edmund Webb, who was M.P. for Cricklade.

[3] Charles Gerard, eldest son of Charles, first Earl of Macclesfield.

[4] John Rumsey, who had been one of the witnesses against Lord Russell
and others implicated in the Rye House conspiracy.

with an insolency which did them a prejudice. The King of France continued to practice all the crueltys immaginable towards the Protestants in France to make them turn papists, commanding that all extremities should be used but death, as seizeing their lands, razeing their temples and houses, takeing all their goods, putting them into prisons, quartering dragoons with them to eat up their estates and to watch them that they should not sleep till they changed their religion. Many of them fledd into all parts as they could escape, poor and naked, for their estates were stopt and themselves condemned to the gallies if they were taken attempting to flie.

This campayne ended in Hungary and Greece to the great advantage of the Christians and prejudice of the Turkes; and Count Teckely,[1] that first began the rebellion in Hungary and called in the Turke to his assistance against the Emperour, had now that just reward as to be taken by his accomplices the Turkes and to be carryed prisner to Constantinople as the sacrafice of their joint ill success. The Great Turke sued for peace with the Emperor, but he seemed as yet more desirous to persue his good fortune.

Dec. 2   Being near the King as he supped, I asked leave to stay in town. He tould me he left it to my own choice to stay or to goe down to my command at Yorke.

His Majesty this day declared that he had reprived my Lord Brandon, who had his day sett to be executed three days after. This was a great act of clemencie in his Majesty, he haveing been pardoned before by the late King for breakeing a boys neck when he was drunke, which he had been condemned for as guilty of murther.

A party of the late rebels to the nomber of 200, haveing hid themselves for fear of being taken and hanged, gott togather in the west, robbing and doing great mischiefe.

Mr. Tankard, being continued high sheriff of Yorkshire for another year by the interest of my Lord Jefferies, late

---

[1] Count Emeric Tökölyi.

Lord Chiefe Justice, now Lord Chancellor of England, sent again to me by letter to aske the garden belonging to Clifford Tower.   I writt him word I would not part with it except the King did soe order it, but was willing to referr it to my Lord Chancellor.   When I spoake of it to my Lord Chancellor he tould me he would doe anything to preserve a good understanding betwixt me and the sheriff of a private concern, but wher it related to the King it was fitt he should be acquainted with it.   He desired me to come and dine with him.

The favourits of the Court began to differ amongst themselves.   Lord Sunderland was made President of the Councill, and continued Secretary of State.   The Queen was artificially possessed by this lord (who was faln out with the Lord Tresurer) that the relations and friends of the King's first wife were in greatest favour and had the best places, as Rochester, Clarendon, Dartmoth, &c., whilst her friends, that was Queen Regent, had none soe considerable, of which nomber were reckned Lord Sunderland, Lord Chancellor, Lord Churchill, &c.; upon which they began to worke secretly one against the other.

I had seen soe many changes, and soe many great and little men remooved in my time, that I confess it began to cool my ambition, and to thinke ther was a time when every thinkeing man would choose to retire and to be content with his own rather then venter that and his concience for the getting of more, and a little left to his family that way was better then more gotten by other means; not that I found the King less kind, or dispaired of makeing or preserveing my interest, tho my great friend was remooved, for could I have persuaded myselfe to have com'd up to the point that some did, I had a fairer opportunity of raiseing myselfe now then ever; but I was convinced that safety was better [then] greatness, and a good foundation in all conditions the greatest happiness.

Mr. Fox, paymaster of the army, whos imployment *Dec.* 16 was valued at 10,000 l. per annum, Colonel John Darcy, granchild and heir to the Earl of Holderness, haveing not pleased the King in their voats as members of the Lower Hous (haveing been suspended the Kings presence since the prorogation), were now laid aside from their employments; and twas said that it was agreed in Council that all persons that should hereafter offend soe should be likewise suspended, which startled many. It was observed that my Lord Tresurer was more humble and obligeing then formerly, which made most believe that the game went ill on his side, and soe it was confessed by Sir Henry Gooderick, brother-in-law to my Lord Dartmoth, another of that party. Thes pretended to stand upon a Protestant interest, the Queen and hers upon the popish.

Mr. Tankred, high sherif of Yorkshire for the ensuing year, writt me word that except I would deliver up the garden to him belonging to Cliffords Tower he would possess himselfe of it. I answered as before that I held it in right of the King, and would give it up to noe man but by his order.

Dec. 19   My lieutenant gave me the newes that the high sherif had com'd in person and made an entry to it. Upon this I acquainted my Lord Chancellor with it, who advised me to inform my Lord Dartmoth of it, which I did, and his lordship tould me it should be represented to the King. In the meantime he gave me leave to speake to Sir Henry
*   Gooderick to write to him from his lordship to leave the possession with me, and not to disturbe it, which both Sir Henry and myselfe performed.

Severall other gentlemen, members of Parlament that had imployments, were laid aside for not voating as was expected by the King, as my Lord Willoughby, eldest son to my Lord High Chamberlain, with two Mr. Bertues, his relations, who had all troops of hors;[1] Mr.

[1] " My nephew Willoughby, my brother Dick and brother Harry (the three battering ramms of our family) are all turned out of their employ-ments as captains " (Charles Bertie to the Countess of Rutland, December

* 39/29: H. Gooderick, 26 October 1685.

Fizwilliam, another captain of hors, brother to my Lord Fizwilliam;[1] Mr. Cook, before committed to the Tower by the Hous of Commons, captain of a company of foot; Mr. Kendall, brigadeer in the hors guards,[2] and others. This made it the more wondered at, bycaus these were some of them eminent men as to their families and services to the Crown.

The Archbishop of Yorke came to see me, but not finding me tould my wife that he heard my Lord Marquis of Halifax was comming again into business; but upon discours with the Marquis the day following I found it was a mistake. *Dec.* 22

The Duke of Albemarle tould me some things in relation to the present affairs of that time which surprized me extreamly, &c. Some gentlemen had been lately attempted upon in the streets. One had a pouder thrown in his eys, that made him loos his sight; another had his throat cutt by two men (neither of thes giveing the least provocation); and the Duke of Albemarle was mett by a gentleman and threatned as he passed in a chair. 23

The high sherif of Yorkshire returned answer to Sir Henry Gooderick that he conceaved himselfe under an obligation of office to mentain the right of the county, which was invaded by me by keeping possession of the garden, and therfore he could not desist (as my Lord Dartmoth designed he should) till the matter was decided above. 26

I tould my Lord Chancellor the sherifs answer, who said he would not concern himselfe in it. 28

The same day it was whispered that the King would proroague the Parlament till May; and twas certainly

17, 1685, in *Rutland MSS.*, ii. 97). Robert Bertie, Lord Willoughby de Eresby, was the eldest son of Robert, third Earl of Lindsey. Three battering-rams are shown on the first and fourth quarters of the family arms.

[1] Charles Fitzwilliam, M.P. for Peterborough, brother of William, third Baron Fitzwilliam in the peerage of Ireland.

[2] James Kendall, M.P. for West Looe, captain in the Coldstream regiment of foot guards.

better soe to doe then to let it meet at the time, except his Majesty had resolved to comply in some expedient for satisfying both Houses in the matter of popish officers, which was soe far from being done that some others were lately recieved into military imployments.

The Byshop of London, brother to the late Earl of Northhamton, and of the Privy Council, a sober and learned prelate, was putt out of the said Council[1] for a speech he made in the Lords Hous the last session concerning the popish officers, though I was tould by the Archbishop of Yorke that he spoake it with all the respect imaginable to the King.

Dec. 29 I tould the King the whole matter of the dispute between the sheriff of Yorkshire and me concerning the garden, who said my Lord Dartmoth might acquaint him with it (for I said his lordship understood it and had a draught of it), and he would give orders in it. In the mean he commanded me to keep possession. The same day I see my Lord Dartmoth, who advised me as a friend not to make too much bustle in this matter, least if it came to be heard at Council, the whole scheme of the guarrison of Yorke comming before the King, he might not think it a place of that use or benefit to him to be kept up as a guarrison, and soe occasion its being disguarrisoned. However, haveing now entered into it, let the consequence be what it would, I said I would not desist without the King's order in it, and offered some expedients to conclude this contraversie, which my Lord promessed to offer to the King.

His Majesty, after I had discoursed him as aforesaid about the garden, and putt him in mind of his promess to consider the charge I was at in raiseing my troop of hors lately disbanded, laid his hand upon my shoulder and said, You may be sure you are one of thos that I will consider.

I recieved notice that the sheriff had made an entry

[1] December 23.

upon the garden by the bailifs, and my lieutenant had made up the fence, and thus they stood at bay one against the other.

I dined with my Lord Chancellor, wher I compli- *Dec.* 30 mented him upon some civilities I tould him I hoped I had recievd from him, and perticularly for the Kings kindness to me, which I attributed to his character of me in some measure (though I was not very much persuaded he was my friend to that degree, but the way to make friends at Court is to pretend you thinke them soe already).   He took it very kindly, said he had rather doe me a curtesie then tell me he had done it, that he always esteemed me since he knew me, had always heard well of me, especially as to the Kings service, and had not done me right if he had otherwise represented me to him.   I replyed I always had been firme to the Crown, and soe should continue, and he might assure the King of it. He promessed me he would, and desired me to come to see him sometimes.   At this time some were very cautious in declareing themselves too fully, doubting what kind of measures would be taken at Court; but my principle as well as my duty (being actually in the Kings service) induceing me to serve him with life and fortune, I knew noe reason why I should not as well say it as doe it.

I tould the King I thought the best way both to defend 31 his right and prevent a further dispute between me and the sheriff about the garden would be to throw down the enclosure about it.   He bid me only be carefull that what I did was according to lawe.

The Bishop of London, brother to the Earle of North- Jan. 3 amton, a learned and discreet prelate, was turned out of [1685/6] the Councill for freely speakeing in the Hous of Lords in that debate concerning his Majestys entertaining popish officers; others said for his being industrious to preserve the Princess Ann of Denmarke in the Protestant religion, whom ther were some endeavours to gain to the Church of Rome.

Jan. 7 The generall quarter-sessions were held for the citty of Westminster at Westminster Hall, wher I attended.

9 Came out the proclamation to proroague the Parlament till the 10th of May.

Not being very desirous that my daughter Frances, who was now near twenty years of age, should appear ofton at Court, she had not been at that of the Queen Dowagers till about this time since she came to town, that being presented with her mother to kiss the Queens hand, she tould her, calling her by her name, that she was grown very tall and very pritty since she see her; and without partiality she was then as hansome as most woemen of that time, had a great deale of witt, and vertue and goodness with it. I began now to hope, to, my eldest son William would proove a schollar, haveing hytherto noe other reason of dispute with him, he and the rest of my children being, by God's great mercy, very hopefull and dutifull.

14 Was my Lord Delamere[1] tryed by a perticular commission directed to a Lord High Steward[2] and thirty other peers in Westminster Hall for high treason, viz., for conspiring to raise rebellion and to subvert the goverment with the Duke of Monmoth and other false trayters, &c. I was near the King during the whole tryall, and the only chiefe evidence against him was one Saxton,[3] an obscure fellow, who swore that about the time of the Duke of Monmoth's landing he, being recommended by the Lord Brandon to the said Lord Delamere, discoursed with him at his hous in Cheshire upon the 4th of June, Sir Robert Cotton[4] and Mr. Ofley[5] being present, concerning a riseing ther to aid the said Duke; and that his lordship said he was engaged to raise 10,000 men for that service, but

[1] Henry Booth, who succeeded his father as second Baron Delamere in 1684. He was one of the first to rise in the north at the Revolution, and as a reward for his services was created Earl of Warrington in 1690.

[2] Jeffreys.   [3] Thomas Saxon.

[4] Of Combermere, Cheshire ; created a baronet in 1677.

[5] Crew Offley.

could not doe it soe soon as was promessed, the mony being not yet ready, &c. The evidence of all the other witnesses was but circumstantiall and by hearsay; they were six or eight. Some said that the Duke of Monmoth had tould them that he depended on the assistance of my Lord Macclesfield, my Lord Brandon, and my Lord Delamere, and that they would rise in Cheshire as soon as he landed. Others swore that the said Duke had written and sent messages to his friends at London, to give notice to the said lords to be ready, for that he was prepareing to come for England.

In this tryall a new piece of law was insisted upon by the Lord High Steward and the Sollicitor-General,[1] not practiced before, viz., that if there was but one positive evidence to any one fact of high treason which was clear, that other evidence, though it were but circumstantial, concurring with that was sufficient to find the prisner guilty. As for exemple, if ther was one positive witness that a man heard another say that he did intend to kill the King such a day, and another swears that he see the said party lie in wait to persue that intent, this is sufficient evidence. However the law is in the case, it was not applicable in this lords perticular, for he clearly disproovd the main witness, which was Saxton, produceing very clear testimony that neither Sir Robert Cotton, Mr. Ofley, nor himselfe were ther the said 4th of June, but two of them in London and the other sixteen miles off. Besides, the prisner urged that had this Saxton spoak true he was not a legall witness, being then himselfe a prisner and taken in actuall rebellion in the defeat of the Duke of Monmoth, and might swear to save his own life.

Upon the whole matter my Lord was acquitted, every one of the peers declareing him not guilty. Some persons

---

[1] Heneage Finch, second son of the first Earl of Nottingham. Shortly after this trial he was deprived of his position, and in 1688 was leading counsel for the seven bishops. He was created Earl of Aylesford by George I.

condem'd the lawyers for adviseing the King to bring a
peer to tryall upon soe slender evidence. Others said that
the King haveing putt him in prison, it was fitt he should
have his publique tryall, least it should be thought he had
been deteaned without any matter against him. When
the tryall was ended I saw the King was very angry with
Saxton, and he declared the next day that he should be
first endicted for perjury and then hanged for high treason.

Jan. 16   I was tould that the King had at his coucheè declared
to my Lord Sunderland that understanding ther was some
difference arisen between me and the high sheriff, two
gentlemen that both served him well in our respective
stations, he would have an end put to it, and therfore
ordered him to command the high sheriff to withdraw
his officers, and me also to remoove my souldiers from the
garden in contraversie between us. Accordingly I
recieved my order the 20th of January, and another was
sent to the sheriff the same day from his lordship; by
which means I prevented the sheriff from getting the
possession of the garden, and gott a great part of my
point by laying it opon to the Castle, of which I had the
command.

18   I dined with my Lord Chancellor, wher my Lord
Maior of London [1] was invited and some other gentlemen.
After dinner the Chancellor, haveing drunke smartly at
dinner (which was his custome), called for one Monfort,[2]
a gentleman of his that had been a comedian, an excellent
mimick, and to divert the company, as he called it, made
him give us a caus, that is plead before him in a feigned
action, wher he acted all the principal lawyers of the age,
in their tone of voice, and action or gesture of body, and
thus ridiculed not only the lawyers but the law itselfe.
This I confess was very diverting, but not soe prudent
as I thought for soe eminent a man in soe great a station
of the lawe, since nothing could gett a man more

[1] Sir Robert Geffrey.

[2] William Mountfort, the actor and dramatist.

ennemies then to deride thos whom they ought most to sopport.

I recieved notice from my lieutenant at Yorke that the *Jan.* 21 day the Countesse of Straffords[1] body came ther to be ✱ buryed (being attended with severall gentlemen of the country and a guard out of my company), the rabble, to tear off the escutions from the hearse, had made an assault upon them; that the souldiers endeavering to beat them off were driven and persued into the Minster, wher the quire being hung with black cloath and escutions was plundered of them, severall of the souldiers hurt as well as thos of the rabble, soe that a greater ryot hath not been known in that place; that he (meaning my lieutenant) had complained to my Lord Maior of some of the leaders of this fray, and that he refused to punish them as he ought. At the same time I had a letter from my Lord Maior, who complained of the lieutenant and the souldiers, and denyed but that he was ready and active to inflict such punishment upon the offenders as the law allowed in that case.

I acquainted his Majesty with the whole matter, who 22 gave present order to my Lord Sunderland to inform himselfe from me perticularly of it.

Being sent for by my Lord Sunderland I gave him an 23 account in writing of the riott at Yorke, who bid me attend † the King in Council the next day, for then it would be taken into consideration.

It was now certain that Mrs. Sidley, who had been formerly the Kings mistris and brought him children when Duke of Yorke (but deserted for a while after he came to the Crown), was soe much again in his favour that he created her Countesse of Dorchester, and did visit her

[1] Henrietta Maria, daughter of James Stanley, seventh Earl of Derby, and wife of the second Earl of Strafford. She died on December 27, 1685. Evidence concerning the riot at York Minster, which took place on January 13, is printed in *Depositions from the Castle of York* (Surtees Society), pp. 278-81.

✱ 43/29, 42/27, 64: George Butler, 15 January, 1 & 27 February 1685/6; 44/26: Henry Watkinson, 30 January 1685/6. Although the first letter is the one referred to on this page, the following letters provide the details of subsequent events pertaining to the riot.

† 42/78: William Bridgeman, 22 January 1685/6, summoning Reresby on behalf of Lord Sunderland.

frequently.[1] This gave great discontent to the Queen, but ther was noe remedie for the present.

Jan. 24   It was ordered by the King in Counci that my Lord President should write two letters, one to the Atturney-General to take care that evidence should be prepared against the rioters in Yorke for the next assizes, and that the judges should be instructed to enquire strictly of it, and that I should also attend the Atturney in this matter (which I did accordingly the 26 of January). The other letter was to my Lord Maior and the magistrates of Yorke, to tell them that the King expected that they would have had more care of the goverment of the place as to civils, and more respect to his guarrison, then to have suffered such disorders to be committed, and that he expected that due punishment should be inflicted on the offenders, &c.

25   I recieved the unwelcome newes from Spain that my brother Jarvase Reresby was marryed ther to a Spanniard of noe great extraction nor estate, and, which was the worst, that he was likely to fix himselfe ther. I had a letter from him soon after to the same effect.

*

26   The Queens party and the priests did soe importune the King (setting before him the sin, and the discouragement his amour with the new Countess of Dorchester would give to the gaining of converts to their Church) that it was said he would abandon his mistris, and had sent her word either to goe into France or he would withdraw the pention he gave her of 4,000 l. per annum.

Feb. 2   The lieutenent that commanded in my absence at York sent me severall affidavits of the riot ther, of which I gave the King himselfe an abstract, and the originals to the Atturney-General by his order, and copies at large to my Lord President at the same time. I tould the King that

†

---

[1] Catharine Sedley, only child of Sir Charles Sedley, the dramatic author, was more famous for her wit than for her beauty and enjoyed a very real political importance owing to the fact that she was a Protestant. The title granted to her is a measure of James's infatuation, for she herself had too much commonsense to desire it.

* 42/35, 43/41: Gervase Reresby, 24 December 1685 & 29 April 1686.

† 42/27, 47, 54: George Butler, 1 February 1685/6, 28 March 1686, & 26 January 1685/6.

the souldiers were soe followed since that disorder by some angry people against them, who sought to find them alone or at advantage, that they did their duty in some danger, and that if some severe punishment was not inflicted upon the offenders it would encourage the same abuse to souldiers in other guarrisons. The King said it should be done, and that he would make Yorke a stronger guarrison.

Was the annuall feast of Yorkshiremen at Marchant *Feb.* 9 Tailers Hall, wher the archbishop dined, and most of the principall gentlemen of that county then in town, and wher my Lord Latimor, Sir John Kay and myselfe were chosen three of the stewards for the ensuing year.

My Lord Chancellor had like to have dyed at this time of a fitt of the stone, which he brought upon himselfe by a great debeauch of wine at Alderman Duncombs,[1] wher he and my Lord Treasurer, with others, dranke to that height as twas whispered that they stripped into their shirts, and had not an accident prevented had gott upon a sign-post to drinke the King's health, which gave occasion of derision, not to say more of the matter.

Being the day to which the Parlament was proroagued, 10 thos members of the Hous of Commons, as well as the Lords, did meet in their respective places. The Commons that appeared were to the nomber of about 150. Being summond by the Black Rod to attend in the Hous of Lords, the commission directed to my Lord Chancellor, Lord Treasurer, &c., was read, commanding them (or any one of them) to proroague the Parlament till the 10th of May next, which my Lord Chancelor did accordingly.

I heard some aldermen of Yorke were comming up to 11 excuse the disorder of that place and themselves to the   * King. I went the same day to the Lord President, tould him this matter, that I was not against the Kings mercy to that citty, but desired I might be owned in the

---

[1] Charles Duncombe, then Alderman of Broad Street Ward, one of the leaders of the Tory party in the city.

* 42/18: Edward Baldock, 11 February 1685/6.

thing, and that they might not however be excused without makeing some application to me, least it might in some measure prejudice the Kings service and make them slight me that commanded the place. My Lord bid me not fear, for the King would support me and my authority in that concern.

The same day I waited upon my Lord Tresurer, desired his assistance for some consideration for the charge I was at in raiseing my troop that was disbanded. He replyed that I must first obtean the Kings order in it, and that he would not oppose it; but said that I had a very good imployment already, and that it had never been continued with that great salary for any man whatever but for me. I tould him I owned the favour of it to his lordship. Noe, says he, doe not say that. Yes, said I, to your lordship and my Lord Halifax, for he could not have obteaned it but by your lordship his consent. He replyed that at that time they were friends good enough for my Lord Halifax to consult him in it, and he was not against it, though he had heard the King resolve before my Lord Fretwell dyed that that goverment should die with him. But I knew in thruth it was intended by his lordship for his father-in-law my Lord Burlinton.

Feb. 15

*

Haveing had notice from Lieutenant Butler that the two aldermen from Yorke had drawn up some information against him as to his carriage in that guarrison when he commanded in my absence, and would present it to the King, and desireing me to assist him therin, I went to his Majesty, acquainted him with that matter, telling him that I could not excuse my lieutenant in all perticulars of his carriage; that he had been arbitrary in some things; but if his Majesty should putt any disgrace upon him at their complaint it would seem to give a victory to the town, and prejudice his service. He said I was in the right, and he would be carefull in the doing of it. The best argument to be used with the King in thes cases was from point of honour.

* 44/49: George Butler, 12 February 1685/6;

Being Shrove Teusday, was the day for licenceing of *Feb.* 16
ale-houses for Holborn devision of the county of Middlesex.

I went to tell my Lord Sunderland (Lord President and   17
Secretary of State) that the aldermen were comd up with
the intention and to the same effect as I had before tould
the King, who answered me very surlely, and said the
King was the best judge when and in what manner to
punish his officers; that my lieutenant was not to escape
noe more then others in case he deserved it; which did
something surprize me, his manner of speakeing it being
angry and haughty.

Dineing then with my Lord Chancellor I interceded   19
to him, and the next day to my Lord Dartmoth, on the   20
behalfe of my lieutenent; who both agreed that whatever
he deserved it was for the Kings service he should be
stood by this time.

Dineing with the Marquis of Halifax, we had much   21
discours concerning affairs as they then stood.   He
advised me to accept of an embassy, if it could be exchanged for the goverment of Yorke, and tould me which
way it might be obtaned; but we did not agree in the
proposall.

Being at the Kings couchè I tould him one of my   22
sergiants was suddenly dead.   He asked me if it was of   *
the bruises he gott in the ryot.   I said he imputed his
ilness to that caus.   The King tould me two of thos
aldermen were come to town, but that he had not then
seen them.   I tould him they came not to me.

The King went into Hide Parke to see his two regiments   23
of guards mustered.   He had seen some part of them
some days before, and found fault with their being not
full.   He excepted my brother his company, and both
tould him in the field and the next day at Whitehall that
it was the best company ther, and bid the Duke of
Grafton take notice of it that the rest should be as good.
And for that reason he saw them again, to know the reason

---

* 39/6: George Butler, 15 February 1685/6. The deceased was Sergeant
Fowler. Butler attributed his death directly to 'being bruised by the mobbily';
42/44: John Thackeray, 17 February 1685/6.

of their being soe defective, for he was exact in thes things.

About this time the Duke of Gourdon, a papist, was made governor of Edenbrough Castle,[1] and the Duke of Queensborough, who was adversary to my Lord Pirth (Lord Chancellor of Scotland, and had lately professed himselfe a papist), was laid aside from his office of Lord Tresurer.[2] This declared favour to persons of that religion gave great disgust in that kingdome.

Feb. 28   I understood that the two aldermen of York, after long solliciting to be admitted to speake to the King, were to be brought to him the next day by my Lord High Tresurer, by means of my Lord Burlinton. I waited that night on the King at his going to bed, and tould him that the aldermen were as I heard to attend him the next day, but were soe angry with me for telling his Majesty what had lately hapned at Yorke that they had not been to see me since they came to town; that I was not against his clemencie to them, only desired he would please to own me soe farr in this matter, that they findeing I had the honour of his countenance might obay me the more in the station wher I was. His Majesty bid me not apprehend otherwise, for he did warrant me he would stand by me, and they should see it, or to that effect. A gentleman tould me the same day, whom they had persuaded to intercede to the King for them, that he said in reply to the gentleman that Yorke was a very bad town.

[1] George Gordon, fourth Marquis of Huntly, created first Duke of Gordon in 1684. After the Revolution he continued to hold Edinburgh Castle in the name of King James, but surrendered in June 1689.

[2] William Douglas, third Earl and first Duke of Queensberry, occupied somewhat the same position in Scotland as Rochester did in England. His supersession by Gordon as governor of Edinburgh Castle and removal from the post of Lord Treasurer to that of President of the Council gave warning of the changed policy which the King was soon to adopt in both kingdoms. James Drummond, fourth Earl of Perth, was to be the chief agent of the Government's Catholic policy in Scotland.

The sessions for the county of Middlesex held at Hicks his Hall ended the same day.

The two aldermen were brought to the King by my *March* 1 Lord Preston. They endeavoured to excuse themselves and the rest of the magistrates as to the blame laid upon them for the late ryot. The King replyed that their town laid under an ill repute; that they had not behaved themselves well to suffer such a disorder: that as he would not have his souldiers misbehave themselves, soe he would not have them abused; that he expected more respect should be paid to his officers and guarrison, and that they that were magistrates should perform their parts. His Majesty gave order, however, that the rioters should be prossecuted at the assizes.

One of the aldermen of the citty of Yorke came to me 5 to excuse their not comming to me sooner, occasioned, as he said, bycaus they had noe order to doe it from their corperation. I replyed I did not deserve soe ill either from him or them as to be soe neglected; it was true I did complain to the King of the ryot according to the duty of my trust, but had I been soe strict in that representation as I might have been it would have appeared a worse matter; but that I should not proceed to perticulars that would look too like an apologie, which I was not to make to them for doing my duty to the King; that it was enough that I had always been kind to that citty wher the caus would allowe it, and that they ought to consider it was in the power of a governor to be less or more strict in his office as they endeavoured to deserve it. He said my officers and souldiers had been to blame in wrong representing this matter. I answered I laid nothing before the King but what was sworn to by the souldiers. He said he had severall affidavits which he brought up with him quite contrary to what the souldiers had sworn, and one from my Lord Maior himselfe, which he gave me; but that they had not made use of them, nor made any complaint of the lieutenant, though he had deserved it in many perticulars. As to my officers or souldiers, I tould him I would never protect them in anything that was bad, if they made their complaints in the manner they ought, which was first to myselfe; but to pass over me, and to goe with complaints to great men or the King, was endeavoring to make me a party to their crime; and that they should never either punish or displace my officers by that method, if I could helpe it; but for the time to come if they did anything amiss they knew how to inform against them.

I heard afterwards that they came up intending to
*   excuse the corporation by this argument amongst others, that I, being a friend to the old aldermen tourned out, complained of the present magistrates to cast a reflexion upon them, bycaus they had opposed me in my election, especially the two that came up. But they found I had soe shutt the door upon them at Court, both as to that argument and the other of ill representing the lieutenant and souldiers (that were the complainants), that they durst oponly make use of neither.

The briefe for a collection in all parishes of England for some thousands of French Protestants that had refuged themselves here from the barbarous prossecution against them at home after a long stop did pass the great seal at last.

Though it could not be said that their was as yet any remarkable invasion upon the rights of the Church of England, yet the King gave all the encouragement he could to the encrease of his own, by putting more papists into office here (but especially in Ireland); by causeing or allowing popish books to be printed and sould and cryed publiquely; by publishing some popish papers found in the late Kings closet, and the declaration of his dying a papist and the manner of it, with that of the conversion of the late Duchess of York and her reasons for it, as written by herselfe; by a letter or order to the Archbishop of Canterbury to direct the ministers of his diocese

* 42/60, 64: George Butler, 10 March & 27 February 1685/6.

to preach a good life, but not to meddle with contraversies in their sermons; by sending my Lord Castlemain upon a solemn embassy to the Pope, and many other such things; which made all men expect that more would followe of a greater concern.

The King of France began to recover after a sickness *March* 8 not much lamented either at home or abroad.

Great preparations were makeing in Germany, Poland, state of Venice, against the Turke for the ensueing year.

I had a little fitt of the gout, which lasted but five days 9 or six.

I was tould by the Secretary of Warr that by reason the 20 town of Yorke sett soe little esteem by one company of foot as to offer to use it soe ill, the King did thinke it of noe use ther, and therfore had ordered that it should march to Hull, and continue ther till the encampment was over (for his Majesty had ordered the greatest part of his army to encampe this next summer at Hownsley Heath), that he could spare a more considerable force to send thether. This I confess did much trouble me for many reasons.

I found an opportunity to speake to the King, and desired 22 to know if he had such an intention. He tould me, Yes. I asked his Majesty what he then intended to doe with the keys of the citty; that the only thing that gave it the face of a guarrison was the small force that was ther, and the keeping the keys, the shutting and oponing the gates by the souldiers; soe if that force was remooved, either his Majesty must pull down the walls, or deliver up the keys to the magistrates; and that with submission I concieved it better to keep the keys whilst he had them then to ask them again when he should stand in need of them. He replyed that ther seemd to be some weight in what I said; soe that I found thos that had advised the King to this had not thought of the keys or how they should be lodged. I desired his Majesty to consider that ther had been lately a difference between the citty and the guarrison; that in case the force should be remooved (but for the present), and the keys restoored to the town, the citty would seem to gain their point extreamly in this matter, and I to suffer for asserting the right of the guarrison, for this would seem an absolute disguarrisoning of the place for soe long; but that which was my greatest trouble was that this might be construed as if I had not the honour of his Majestys favour, as if I had done amiss in the management of that contraversie (or other concerns of that place), and that the takeing away the keys from me to give them to the magis-trates might be thought a decision of such matters in favour of them. The King replyed that he had noe thoughts to disguarrison the place, but to send a greater force thether towards winter; and as to his good opinion of me, I might be confident it was not lessened in the least towards me, for I had carryed myselfe soe well that I deserved its continuance, and had it; therfore he would consider further of it.

By this I was satisfied in two materiall things. One was the state of the Kings present opinion of me; the other was a likelyhood of the guarrisons longer con-tinuance. I went afterwards and acquainted the Secretary and my Lord Dartmoth with what the King had said, who both promessed to assist that either mine or some other company of foot should quarter ther, till more force could be sent. The same day my Lord Halifax retired to Rufford.

1686

March 28   I was robbed at Yorke by some souldiers of my Lord Ferrers regement, in their march to Barwick, of some wine, some straglers getting into the Mannor yeard and breakeing opon my sellar; but my servants took them and committed them to the guard.

29   I was robbed at London, whether by servants or others was not discovered, of about 30 l. worth of plate. Such

*

---

* 43/1: Edward Baldock, 5 April 1686; 42/29: George Butler, 14 April 1686; 42/33: John Beaumont, 29 March 1686.

accidents, I thanke God, had scarce ever before befaln me in my whole life.

The French King was now near recovered of his ulcer.

The King adjourned his Parlament in Scotland, which should have mett the begining of Aprill, till the latter end of that month, suspecting that things would not goe soe clever as was first believed, the discontents seeming to encrease that the Chancellor and other great men that were turned papists continued in office, and had soe great countenance at Court. The head of the other faction was the Duke of Queensbrough, a great man of interest in that kingdome, and the Chancelors great ennemy.

I heard the King had ordered my company to march to *April 2* Hull, but had appointed another of Sir William Clifton's regiment to relieve it at Yorke as I had desired.[1]

The quarter-sessions of the peace were held for the 10 liberty of Westminster in the Kings Bench, and thos for the county began the 13. 13

I was fifty-two years of age, and thanked God for his 14 great mercys to me during my whole life.

I recieved news of the death of Doctor Dalbin, Arch- 16 bishop of Yorke, a man of excellent parts and piety, and much to be lamented for the loss the Church had by him as well as his friends. I acquainted the King the same day with that newes.

I waited upon his Majesty to Hounsley Heath, who 16 went to choos the ground wher his army was to encamp that summer. He was afterwards entertained at dinner by Mr. Shales, the providor,[2] in a little hous built near ther for the conveniency of his business, wher his Majesty was

---

[1] The change is referred to in a letter from Reresby to Halifax, dated April 6, 1686, preserved among the Spencer MSS. : " The King confirms his order of my company's going to Hull, but hath been pleased to grant my request that it may be relieved by another (one of Sir William Cliftons regiment) that comes from Tinmouth."

[2] Henry Shales, the Commissary General, who earned an unsavoury reputation by his complete failure to provide proper supplies for the English army in Ireland in 1689.

* 42/30: George Butler, 3 April 1686.

† 44/16: George Butler, 12 April 1686; 43/3, 4: Edward Baldock, 10 & 12 April 1686. The archbishop died of smallpox.

more pleasant and entertaining to all the company then he used to be. I rid of a hors of my own breed that I was offered fifty ginnies for that day. I asked seventy ginnes for him.

I discovered the party that had stoln my plate, by a gilt cup that was pawned for 10s., and clapped him in the goale.

April 21 I dined with my Lord Chancellor. I tould him I understood the high sherif of Yorkshire was not content with the late determination his Majesty had made concerning the garden belonging to the Castle of Yorke (lately contraverted between the sheriff and me); that the judges the last assizes and the grand jury had vewed it at the sherifs request, brought up a report of it to the King as if it belonged to the county. He tould me it was all true, that the King was satisfyed it was soe, and had ordered it should be possessed and enclosed by the sherifs. He desired me to acquiesce in it, for that it was of noe value, and should not the King gratifie the county in this the gentlemen would be dissatisfyed. I tould his lordship this proceeding had been all *ex parte*; that I had noe notice here, nor my officers at Yorke, of this revewe; that I had severall affidavits to proove it belongd to the King and the guarrison; that I neither contended for benefit nor victory by it, for the King might dispose of his own as he pleased, but only for his own advantage, for the county might as well dispute the soile of the Castle with him as the garden; and soe I took my leave of him to goe into the country.

22 Being the first of the terme, ther was a great change in Westminster Hall of the judges. Ther was a new Lord Chiefe Justice of the Common Pleas and another new judge ther, a new Lord Chiefe Baron, in fine, four new judges of all courts.[1] This made the greater noise bycaus

---

[1] Sir Henry Bedingfield, who had already been appointed a Puisne Justice of the Common Pleas, took the place of Sir Thomas Jones as Lord Chief Justice ; two new Puisne Justices, Sir Edward Lutwyche and Sir

severall of thos turnd out were knowing and loyall gentlemen, and their crime was only this, that they would not give their opinions (as most of the rest had done) that the King by his prorogative might dispence with the taking of the test to Roman Catholicks.

The same day I acquainted the King to the same purpas with what I had said the day before to my Lord Chancellor. The King tould me it was of soe little value the garden, as neither to deserve a dispute or a denyall; that my Lord Chancellor and the judges of the circuit had soe represented it to him, and he had now setled the matter. I tould him it was nothing to me, what I had done was in relation to his service, and was ever content with what his Majesty pleased. After this I putt him in mind of the compensation he promessed me for disbanding my troop, desired some consideration for my son Tamworth, and did enumerate to him how ready I had been from time to time to serve himselfe and his late brother. The King did own to me that I had served him very well, but said, It is for your sake only that I keep up Yorke as a guarrison; however, I shall take care that you have the same consideration that others have. To which I answered that whatever his Majesty was pleased to give me I would be thankefull for it, and if he gave me nothing I should not repine; that I was much obliged to him for the kindness he expressed to me as to the keeping Yorke a guarrison for my sake, but did not doubt but to convince his Majesty it deserved to be kept soe for its own when he would allowe me the honour to discours him in that perticular. He assured me that he would doe something for Tamworth. Though it was a great compliment the King made me, I was sorry to hear it, for

---

John Powell, were appointed to succeed Bedingfield and Sir Job Charlton ; Sir Edward Atkyns became Chief Baron of the Exchequer instead of Sir William Montagu, and the places which he and Sir Edward Nevill had filled were given to two new barons, Sir Richard Heath and Sir Christopher Milton, brother of the poet.

thos things seldome continue that consist for one man's sake.

The King went from thence to see the Queen Dowagere at Sommersit Hous. I went with him to the water side, and he called me along with him into his barge.

April 23 I was informed by Mr. Jones, son to the late Chiefe Justice,[1] late turnd out, that his father tould the King at his dismission that he was not sorry for himselfe to be laid aside, being old and worn out in his service, but that his Majesty should expect such a construction of the lawc from him as he could not honestly give; and that none but indegent, ignorant, or ambitious people would give their judgements as he expected; that his Majesty replyed it was nescessary that all his judges should be of one mind. He tould me further that Sir Robert Sawyer, the Atturney-General, had been directed by the King to drawe a warrant by vertue of his prorogative for a priest of the Church of Rome being put into a benefice, and for one Walker, a master of a college in Oxford,[2] and some more fellowes of the same college, turned papists, to be confirmed master and fellowes by *non obstante*; the Atturney said that would be against not only one statute but all the lawes since the time of Queen Elizabeth, that he durst not doe it, and desired the King would consider of it, since this struck at the root of the Protestant Church, which was contrary to his Majestys late gracious promess; that the Atturney said further that as soon as one could be found that would doe it he expected to loose his place.[3] Such power had the council of priests over his Majesty.

[1] Probably Thomas Jones, the second son, who had been made a king's counsel in 1683.

[2] Obadiah Walker, Master of University College, whose inclination to the Roman religion had been suspected even in the reign of Charles II.

[3] A similar account, with some additional particulars, is given in a letter from Reresby to Halifax, dated " Aprill 27," preserved among the Spencer MSS. :

I had it from thos to whom the Atturney General tould it, that he

Being with the King at his couchè, I tould him that *April* 23 when I last spoake to his Majesty concerning some reparation for the raising of my troop he seemed to doubt if it or the recruits of my company were compleat; that I had a certificate from the commissary ther, which would satisfie him in that; and presented it to him, which he recieved. I had notice that day that my company was marched to Hull the 20th, and that one Captain Barns[1] commanded the company at Yorke which had relieved mine.

I went to Newhall in Essex, the Duke of Albemarls *May* 2 house, the King having promessed that Duke to come and stay two days ther to hunt, which he, comming the day after, performed accordingly. Thes two days the King killed two stags. He was indefatigable at that sport, loveing to ride soe hard that he usually lost his company. The entertainment which the Duke gave the King was very noble. The Prince was ther, and a great part of the Court.

The King returned, as we all did, to London.   5

The Parlament of Scotland mett near this time,[2] wher the King omitted noe endeaver by the Lord Commissioner[3] and others to gett some indulgence to Roman Catholicks in that kingdome.

Mr. Finch, Sollicitor-Generall, was turned out, and expected to be turned out five days before it hapned, he haveing denyed his Majestys commands to make a warrant with an *obstante* to admitt a parson new turned papist, and soe declared, into a benefice, and for confirming Doctor Walker and his fraternity in the mastership and fellowships of that college in Oxford. Tis said ther is, or speedily will be, some publication that whosoever being now beneficed shall become Roman Catholiques shall not for that reason forfeit their preferments or liveings. Mr. Powis is Sollicitor, Mr. Williams, late Speaker of the House of Commons, Atturney Generall. . . .

[1] William Barnes, captain in Sir William Clifton's regiment of foot (Dalton, *English Army Lists*, ii. 36).

[2] April 29.

[3] Alexander Stewart, fifth Earl of Moray.

one Mr. Powis[1] put in his stead, who did what the other refused, viz., to draw a warrant for the confirming Walker Master of University College in Oxford, and three fellowes and the parson of Putney[2] in their respective benefices and places, which after passed the Great Seale notwithstanding their being papists.

At the same time most of thos officers that were Protestants in the army in Ireland were turned out, and papists putt in their rooms.

May 10   The Parlament mett, and was proroagued by commission till the 22nd of November following. The King said that morning in his bedchamber that many of the polititions of the Hous of Commons were com'd up, fearing he should surprize them by letting the Houses sitt to doe business; but he would not doe with them as they used to doe with the Crown.[3]

---

[1] Sir Thomas Powys, knighted at the time of his appointment. He was later promoted to be Attorney-General, and conducted the prosecution of the seven bishops.

[2] Edward Sclater, curate of St. Mary's, the parish church at Putney. Having become a Catholic on the accession of James II, he publicly recanted and was received back into the Church of England after the coronation of William and Mary.

[3] In a letter preserved among the Spencer MSS., dated May 11, 1686, Reresby informs Halifax of this and other developments :

... Mr. Powis, the new atturney generall, hath complyed with what the atturney generall refused, and it hath passed the seales. My Lord President hath relapsed, but is now better, and my Lord Spencer not well by the ill usage he and the rest of his company recieved from the constables and watch three nights agoe, being upon a high ramble. Some, they say, complaining of it to my Lord President, he said it was pitty it was not wors. Mr. Bucley was wounded in the head with a halbard, and hath lost a piece of his lip in the service. Sir Jervase Clifton's regiment is given to Admirall Herbert. It is rumoured that the currier that arrived here lately from Rome brings news that the Pope will not recieve our embassador ther in the forms expected till some hopes or assurance of further obedience. The French King continues much as he was. The Parlament was yesterday prorougued till the 22 November next. The Hous of Commons was thin, though some had tould the King it would be very full, many being com'd out of the country for fear of being surprized by their sitting to doe business.

I presented the King with six medals or old Roman *May* 11
coins found at Audbrough in Yorkshire,[1] which he accepted
very kindly.

Takeing my leave of my Lord of Dover (late Henry 13
Jermin, Esquire, a papist and great favourite),[2] he tould
me that the Parlament would certainly meet at the time
limited, and if they did not comply with the King they
might expect the issue. He tould me further that the
King confided in my loyaltie, and that if he could serve
me in anything I should write to him.

This terme licence was given to one Hill to print and
sell severall popish bookes, which had been prohibited
by law.

The Earle of Feathersham, one of our lieutenant-
generals, haveing promessed me to speake to the King to   *
put him in mind of his promess to give me some consideration for raiseing my troop, was the more ready and earnest
in doeing it by reason it was, he thought, in my power to
doe him a kindness, which was to speake for him to the
Duke of Newcastle, to whos daughter, my Lady Margaret
Cavendish,[3] he was a pretender. The Duchess of Albemarle,[4] her sister, was very averse to this marriage, being
engaged for another, my Lord Chomley,[5] and came to
visit my wife, and desired her to recommend him rather
to my Lord Duke in that concern; but my interest as

I heard the King say he would not use that method. The King and Court
goe on Fryday to Windser. I mett yesterday my Lord Thanet, who is
jealous of a designd marriage of the Lord Feathersham with my Lady
Margaret Cavendish. . . . I intend the next week but one for the north,
and hope soon after to kiss your lordships hands at Rufford.

[1] The site of the Roman town of Isurium.

[2] Henry Jermyn, nephew of the first Earl of St. Albans, by whom he
was adopted. He was created Baron Dover in May 1685.

[3] Third daughter of the Duke of Newcastle.

[4] Elizabeth, the eldest of the five sisters, who had married the second
Duke of Albemarle in 1669.

[5] Hugh Cholmondeley, who had succeeded his father in 1681 as second
Viscount Cholmondeley of Kells.

* Bundle 52 contains the correspondence between Reresby and Feversham
concerning the negotiations for the hand of Newcastle's daughter.

well as my obligations obliged me more to serve my Lord Feathersham.

May 18   The sessions began at Hicks Hall, wher the bill was found against one Spencer that rob'd me of my plate, and the 19 he was found guilty at the Old Bailiff and burnt in the hand.

The King haveing lately gott a Jesuist for his confesser [1] went on faster then formerly in promoting the Roman Catholique religion.

After a long expectation of the success of the Scotch Parlament, we had many reports suitable to the severall interests that either desired its complyance or refusall; but the business of religion in England much depending upon it, it was some satisfaction to Protestants to find the newes that came from time to time did not answer the expectation of papists.

22   I had a fitt of the gout in my finger, wher I had not been seized before; but my milke, which I took every morning, did soe correct its acidity that I had little pain. The swelling continuing longer then ordinary, I went to Epsome with my family, wher the Earl of Barkley [2] sent me a present of wine, and invited us to dinner. From thence I carryed my wife and daughter Frances to see the camp at Hounsley.[3]

---

[1] Edward Petre, who had come into favour immediately after James's accession. It is just possible that Reresby is induced to mention him here by the fact that he originally entered the Society of Jesus under the name of Spencer.

[2] George, ninth Baron Berkeley, who had been created first Earl of Berkeley in 1679.

[3] Difficulties with the army at Hounslow, as well as more general matters, are the subject of comment by Reresby in a letter to Halifax, dated May 22, 1686, preserved among the Spencer MSS. :

... The King is com'd this day to town, but hath left the Queen not well at Windser. A discours is here very common of some judges more to be remoovd and some of thos last putt in. The Recorder of London is not yet persuaded to believe it for lawe that departing from a mans colours without licence is felony without benefit of clergie, though severall did suffer for it in the time of Sir Thomas Genner. My Lord Chiefe Justice

My Lord Feathersham (then one of the two lieutenant- *June* 2 generals of the army) haveing tould me that he had spoake to the King, who tould his lordship he would consider of my request, being to goe to Windser, I went thether that day.   That night I was with the King at his coucheè, who spoake kindly to me of generall things.

I attended his Majesty to the camp, which consisted 5 of twelve batallions of foot, each batallion of 500 besides officers (the hors was not yet encamped, which was to be near as many).   The King see them exercize and marched them himselfe out of the line, and everything was in exact order.   That night I had drawn up my case in writing, and prevailed with my Lord Feathersham to give it the King at Windser.   He promessed to aske his plesure concerning it the next day; but being with 6 the King in his bedchamber, and haveing an opportunity, I desired to recieve his commandes for Yorke, who tould me my Lord Feathersham had given him my paper, and he would know of my Lord Tresurer what had been given to others towards their charge of raiseing their troops.   I said I was content with whatever he should please to give me, though the loss of my equipage at sea made mine greater, and the charge of raiseing my troop, then other mens.

After this I entertained him long upon the subject how usefull and nescessary Yorke was for a guarrison, of its scituation, capacity for quarters, and the influence it had upon the whole county and others adjacent to it.   The King approved the reasons I gave, and said he would

Herbert and my Lord Chancellor differ. The first reflected the last day of the term upon soe many haveing suffered for the plott in the west, saying the poor and the miserable were hanged, but the more substantiall escaped, or to that effect.

It is said Mr. Eveling, one of the Commissioners of the Privy Seale, consents not to the passing the dispensations by *non obstante* at that office. Severall have passed by immediate warrant.

The King lately healing at Windser made use of his other chaplyns and another form of devotion framed for that occasion in Latin, haveing dismissed his Protestant ones.

send a good force to it at the riseing of the camp. I concluded with nameing my son to him, and assuring him of
my faithfull duty and service. He answered that he did
confide in me, and would be kind both to me and my son,
and soe I kissed his hand.

The same night as his Majesty came from Council I
asked him if he had spoake to my Lord Tresurer. He
said noe, but would doe it, and was as good as his promess,
for soe soon as my Lord Tresurer came into the presence
the King took him aside, and said something to him.
My Lord came to me afterwards, tould me he had order
to speake to me, which he would doe the next day if I
came to him. When I attended him, he said he had the
Kings commands to aske me what I expected for raiseing
my troop, or losses at sea. I said it was very chargeable to
me, and I hoped his lordship would thinke 500 l. a reasonable demand. He replyed that I should have it, and he
would give order when he came to London accordingly.
I followed his lordship to town, who did give directions to
the Secretary as he promessed; but I found severall rubbs
in the matter afterwards.

June 10   I remooved my two sons from Kensinton to Eaton
School, wher ther was at least 300 schollers, and some of

*   them men; as well to improove their conversation by
degrees (their schoolfellowes at Kensinton being little
boys) . . . [1]

14   I returned with my family from Epsome Waters by the
way of the camp, as I observed before, with better health
then I carryed with me.

17   I attended my Lord Tresurer at the Treasury Chamber.
He sent for me in, tould me he had acquainted the King
with my request, who thought my demandes too great,
and had ordered him to give me three hundred pounds.
I said though it was less then I expected I was always
content with what his Majesty pleased, only desired I
might not stay for it. He said it should be ordered for me

[1] The remainder of the sentence has been deleted.

---

* 43/10: A. Lloyd, 7 September 1686. Reresby's oldest son, William, the cause
of his greatest concern, ended up as a tapster in Newgate prison, having
squandered his father's wealth.

before I went out of the room, which was done accordingly, and the next day I recieved it in the Exchequer.   I had not much reason to complain of this abatement, considering that when all officers of the army (very few excepted) were at the double expence of their pay by rouleing and encampment, I gott this mony, and was excused from that charge.

Then came the newes of the adjournment or prorogation of the Scotch Parlament [1] without doing what the King expected.   As soon [as] it was proroagued (which was to the 17 of August next) my Lord Murry, Lord Commissioner, and my Lord Chancellor of that kingdome hasted up to London to impeach one another to the King of being the caus of the ill success (as some called it) of things in that Parlament.

I sett out for Thriberge with my family, and arrived *June* 21 ther safe the 25 by the way of Stamford.

This terme an action being brought against Sir Edward Hales,[2] a professed papist to whom the King had given a regiment of foot, upon the statute for 500 l. for haveing that imployment, not haveing taken the oaths and the test as that lawe requires, it was agreed by all the judges (Baron Street only excepted) [3] that the King had power by his prorogative to dispence with all penall statutes, and that he was the only judge of the nescessity of dispenceing with the penall statutes; soe Sir Edward pleading the Kings pardon had the better of the caus.   This judgement was very surprizeing, and occasioned much discours in the kingdome.

I went to the Duke of Newcastle, wher (as I had pro- 26   *

[1] On June 15.

[2] By his coachman, Arthur Godden.   The case was a collusive one, designed to secure the decision the King desired.   Judgement was given on June 21.

[3] Sir Thomas Street had been removed from the Court of Exchequer to the Common Pleas some time before this.   His dissent was generally believed to have been inspired by the Court with the idea of giving an air of independence to the Bench.

*   34/10: Newcastle, 30 June 1686.

messed my Lord Feathersham) I took what pains I could to serve him with that Duke, and gett his good opinion soe as to thinke him a fitt person to marry my Lady Margaret his daughter; and I found the only objection that remained was that his estate in land (though in places and land togather he had 8,000 l. per annum) was not soe much as was desired. I gave his lordship a perticular account of his Grace his sentiments, and put him into the best way I could to suremount that difficulty.

July 5   I went for Yorke. When I came ther I found the discours was noe less ther then it was elsewher that my Lord
*   Plimoth was putt out from being governor of Hull and myselfe of Yorke, and that two popish lords were placed in thos commands; but I did not believe it at that time for the favours, &c., I soe lately recieved from the King. At my comming to town the citizens were generally glad of my return, thos that were not my best friends not being desirous a papist should be made governor ther in my stead; and this they expressed by causeing the bels to be rung, as well as by their expressions and visits. I found the garrison in good order, and the officers that commanded the company ther a very discreet man. I stayed ther five days, and then returned to my hous at Thriberge.

16   I was at Doncaster to meet the judges in the way to Yorke, wher the assizes were to be held the 19.

18   I recieved the newes that the King had sworn four
†   papist lords of his Privy Councill (three of which had been in the Tower for the Popish Plott),[1] and had appointed a commission[2] for my Lord Chancellor, Lord Tresurer and some others (of which three were bishops) to inspect and enquire of ecclesiastical affairs and persons.

The success of the Christians against the Turkes had been considerable, both on the Emperours behalfe in Hungary and on the Venetians in Morea, wher the

[1] The Earl of Powis, Lord Arundell of Wardour, and Lord Belasyse. Along with Lord Dover these three were sworn of the Council on July 17.

[2] The Ecclesiastical Commission, which was abolished at the Revolution.

* 43/5: Edward Baldock, 30 June 1686. There were also rumours that Reresby had been replaced as Governor by Lord Fairfax of Gilling.

† 43/2: Edmund Reresby, 20 July 1686; 43/9: Charles Johnston, [?] July 1686.

Turkes lost severall skermishes and towns, but noe formed battles as yet, the Turkes haveing brought this year noe great armys into the field, but rather being upon the defensive. The Duke of Lorrain, generall for the Emperour, and the Duke of Bavaria had laid seige to that important place in Hungary some time before called Buda or Offen,[1] wher by the desperate defence of the beseiged the Cristians had lost a great many officers and souldiers by their sallys and mines. It was believed that it cost the Christians near 50,000 mens lives. At last it was taken by assault, and all the Turkes within it (who from 15,000 fighting men besides the inhabitants were reduced to 4,000) were put to the sword, excepting some hundreds that fled to a redout, and putting out a white flag obteaned quarter. This hapned on the 2nd of September,[2] to the great joy of Christendome.

I went to Welbeck with my wife, wher the Duke and *August 4* Duches recieved us with great civility and entertained us three days.[3] I found by him that he was sensible of the Kings going on very fast in the promoting his own religion, but did resolve to be very loyall, and yet firm to his religion. He oponed his heart to me in many perticulars.

I had had a tryall at Nottingham some days before for some lands of my granmothers estate in Loudham, but was cast, more by the ignorance of a new judge then the defect of my caus. My Lord Duke offered himselfe to *   assist me by his influence or interest if I would bring it over again. At the request of the Duchesse I left my daughter at Welbeck.

[1] The capital of Turkish Hungary for the previous century and a half.

[2] August 23/September 2. There is a long account in the *London Gazette* for September 16-20.

[3] Apparently Reresby left Welbeck on Saturday, August 7, called on the Marchioness of Halifax at Rufford the same day, and reached home on August 8. On August 9 he wrote to Halifax from Thrybergh, " I came yesterday from Welbeck, wher I had not gone soe soon (with my wife) if it had not been to pay our duty to my Lady Marquise, whom we had the honour to wait upon on Saturday last at Rufford " (Spencer MSS.).

* 34/11: Newcastle, 8 August 1686.

August 10   Were the quarter-sessions held at Rotherham, wher I gave a short charge. The business was more then ordinary. I caused ther Mrs. Savile of Mexbrough[1] to be endicted for encloseing some part of Mexbrough field; and some suits of lawe ariseing between us for her claimeing pasterall tyths in Deneby lordship (for which ther had been noe custome), I forbad her to come over at any of my fords to fetch her tyth either of corn or hay from Deneby, which I had formerly allowed from curtesie.

The Marquiss came not down from London as was expected,[2] soe that some reported he was to be in business at Court; but I thought it impossible according to the measures then taken.

18   I recieved the Kings orders signed by himselfe to recieve four companys of Colonel Oglethorps regiment

*   of foot[3] and five of the Earl of Huntintons[4] into Yorke guarrison, as also my own company from Hull, wher they were to continue for the security of that place.

21   I had an invitation from the Duke of Newcastle to meet the Earle of Thanet, his son-in-lawe, at Welbeck, wher I

†   went and stayed till the next day. This earle whilst he was a yonger brother was groom of the bedchamber to the King whilst Duke of Yorke. He complained, however, of the Kings proceedings in point of religion, and appeared dissatisfyed as to his own usage.

27   I went to Yorke. The 29 ther marched into that guarrison four companys of Colonel Oglethorps regiment,

Sept. 2   and the 2nd of September five of the Earle of Huntindons regiment. My own company was comd from Hull some

---

[1] Martha, daughter of Richard Cudworth of Eastfield, whose husband, Samuel Savile of Mexborough, had died at the close of the previous year.

[2] Chiefly owing to anxiety for his youngest son, George, who had been wounded at the siege of Buda (Foxcroft, *Halifax*, i. 470-1).

[3] The Holland regiment, of which Sir Theophilus Oglethorpe had been appointed colonel in the previous October.

[4] A regiment raised in July 1685 to deal with Monmouth's rebellion. Huntingdon was its first colonel.

* 41/5: Thos. Mosley (Lord Mayor), 22 August 1686; 41/13: Leo Wilkerson, 31 August 1686. As these letters show, there was concern about the billeting of soldiers.

† 34/3: Newcastle, 27 August 1686.

days before, soe that ther was ten compleat companys well officerd. The officers by commission were some fifteen, amongst which were my Lord Hunsden,[1] lieutenant-colonel to Colonel Oglethorpe; Captain Cornwallis, brother to the Lord Cornwallis;[2] Major Morgan, major to my Lord Huntindon,[3] with severall others of good quality. All thes gentlemen understood their duty and the discipline of warr soe well that they paid me all fitt obedience and respect as governor; and I was carefull not to be unreasonable or too imposeing, but I demeaned myselfe with civility, and was soe carefull in giveing of orders suitable to the directions recieved from above, or consisting with the rules of warr, that we agreed very well. This good understanding was not only amongst ourselves, but also between the citty and the guarrison. My Lord Maior[4] and his bretheren (two aldermen only excepted, whos companys I did not much desire, haveing been my greatest opponants at my election, and since that made aldermen) came to the Mannor to make me a visit, and ther thanked me for my care and kindness to the citty in keepeing the souldiers in soe good order, and invited me and all the officers to dinner at the charge of the corporation.

The guarrison I formed at that time into this method. The ten companys consisted of 500 (besides officers) and the dayly guards of 80 men (by detachment of eight out of every company), of four sergiants, six corporals, and one commissioned officer. Thes met at the place of

---

[1] Robert Carey, sixth Baron Hunsdon. Writing to Halifax on September 6 about the garrison at York, Reresby remarks concerning him, " That lord tould me he had sitten formerly in Parlament as a peer, and hoped to doe it again this winter " (Spencer MSS.).

[2] Thomas Cornwallis, brother of Charles, third Baron Cornwallis, was captain of a company of grenadiers in the Holland regiment (Dalton, *English Army Lists*, ii. 47).

[3] Charles Morgan, recently promoted from captain in the Earl of Bath's regiment of foot (*ibid.* 31, 34).

[4] Leonard Wilberfoss.

parade in the Minster yeard between nine and ten every
morning.   At ten a clock they marched off to relieve the
severall guards, which guards were in all six, viz., the
main guard, consisting of thirty-two private sentinals, one
drummer, one commissioned officer, one sergeant, one
corporall; the other guards were kept at the severall gates,
which were five.   At Boldome Barr [1] ther was eight souldiers, one sergeant, one corporall, one drummer.   That
being next to the Mannour, the two sentrys at my door
relieved from thence.   At Micklegate Bar [2] ther was
twelve souldiers, one sergeant and one corporall (the
sentrys at the two posterns on that side of the water [3]
relieveing from thence, for the posterns of the citty had
only a sentry in the daytime, but had noe guard in the
night).   The rest were accordingly distributed to Walme-
gate, Castlegate, and Monke Barr.[4]   The taptoo was
beaten every night by five drums at ten a clock, at which
hour every souldier was to goe to his quarters, or be
punished if found after that hour in the streets by the
patroulle that went the round of the streets to see that good
order was kept.

Noe souldier was suffered (nor indeed citizen) to goe
out of the gates in the daytime with firearms, dogs, or
engins for the distruction of game, except gentlemen or
officers, or such as had leave in writing from myselfe.
I did not suffer any quarters to be given without my
allowance, and wher I found the magistrates did oppress
I relieved as I thought fitt, and was impartiall in that and
all other matters; which surprised a great many, who

[1] Bootham Bar, on the north-west, commanding the road to Edinburgh.

[2] On the south-west, across the Ouse, commanding the road to London.

[3] Northstreet and Skeldergate Posterns.

[4] Walmgate Bar on the south-east, commanding the road to Hull, and
Monk Bar on the north-east, commanding the road to Scarborough, were
two of the four principal gates or bars. Castlegate was one of the five
posterns or lesser entrances, but had a certain added importance owing to
its vicinity to Clifford's Tower.

expected that haveing it now in my power to oppress my opponants and to ease my friends, I would have done it; and gott me the good opinion of thos that had been against me, insoemuch as severall of them sent to me to desire I would not leave the citty, but stay ther for their protection, and a gentleman, one Mr. Fairfax, that had been my greatest enemy at my election, and upon other accounts, desired me to forgive him and to recieve him into friendship upon his knees, a submission which I noe way desired.

I see both batallions exercize two severall days, and my own company ofton. I punished such souldiers very severely against whom any complaint was made out to be just, which being done at the first prevented many disorders. Ther was one that was accused of a felony. I presently turned him over to be punished by the civil magistrate. I called but one council of war whilst I stay'd ther, and returned the 27 of September to Thriberge, leaveing Major Morgan comander-in-chiefe in my absence, he being the then first officer upon the place. All the time I lived ther I kept a good table for the officers, some of which dined with me dayly, and when I came away most of them got horses and attended me two miles out of the town. I left orders in writing of such things as I thought most materiall to be observed in my absence.

Ther hapned a dispute between me and my own lieutenant, one Mr. Butler, who (being as I have formerly remarked not very easy in his fortune, and extravagant in his expences) had sould some of my souldiers whilst he was at Hull with the company, that is he had taken mony to sett them at large, and entertained others in their roome without my knowlege or consent. When I tould him of this he justifyed himselfe in it, said that other lieutenants had done the same thing. I tould him that was noe rule to me, that it was me only that was to answer to the King for my company, which was impossible

Sept. 27

* 43/8: order by Reresby for punishment of Robert Dunkin, 21 September 1686.

if he modelled it at his plesure, and enlarged old disciplined men for mony and tooke novices and unexperienced in their stead, and therfore expected that he beg'd my pardon and owned his errour. This he denyed to doe, soe that I sent to confine him and resolved to suspend him the next day, and the rather bycaus he pretended to have some letters from me by which he was able to make out something to my prejudice. *But the next morning he came and offered me to submitt himselfe, which I would not accept till he brought me thos letters and gave them into my hands, with great promesses of repentance and of better carriage.

Oct. 12 The sessions were held at Barnsley, wher I assisted. I gott ther an order for 10 l. to be raised upon the weapontack of Strafford and Tickil, for the repair of Saddle Brige or New Brige, being that which parts the lordships of Rotherham and Brinsford or Ickles in the way from Rotherham to Sheffield. This brige was built about 100 years before by the family for their own conveniency, and was a publique brige and a highway only since Sir George Reresby's time, that suffered it to be lost, for till then the highway to Sheffield was by Knouck Brige. And though the use of it was now publique, yet the charge of repairs was still the families bycaus we built it, till by this 10 l. being given or raised upon the weapontack it will now be entitled to be soe repaired for the future. I gott also ten pounds to make Dern Brige passable for coach and carriage, which was only before used for horses.

Ther passed little this sessions but the usuall business of the court; only I caused some endictments to be preferred (which were found) against Mr. Savile[1] and others for fishing on that side the river Dun towards Mexbrough (my father, though he sould the mannor of Mexbrough, reserveing the stream), and for incloseing within Mexbrough fields, contrary to custome and the consent of the freehoulders.

[1] Probably William, second son of Samuel Savile.

Came forth the proclamation for proroagueing the *Oct.* 15
Parlament from the 22nd of November next to the 14 of
February.[1]

The great success of the Imperialists in Hungary,
and of the Venetians in Candia, and of the King of Poland
against the Turkes, continued, to the great joy of all
Christendome.

I went to see the Duke of Newcastle at Welbeck, but *Nov.* 4
was extreamly surprized to find a great disorder in the
family by reason of soe great a falling out between the
Duke and Duchesse that they were parted from bed and   *
board.   The occasion of it was my Lady's desire to have
her daughter Margaret marryed to my Lord Shrewsbury [2]
with a greater portion then his Grace was willing to give
her, and her unwillingness to marry her yongest daughter [3]
to Fitzroy, the King's naturall son,[4] which the Duke
desired, saying she should never marry a papist and a
bastard.   The yong ladys took the part of the mother,
and joined with her against their father, which infinitely
troubled my Lord Duke.   He desired me to goe and
speake to the Duchess and his daughters to make them
friends, which I endeavoured all I could, but to noe purpass.
I found them very foolishly obstinate, for the Duchesse
had had soe great a share of goverment in that family that
she expected that everything should goe as she pleased.
In this humour he burnt his will, and made another
settlement, not at all to the advantage of thos daughters.

This campayne ended in Hungary and in other parts

[1] The proclamation came out on October 9, and was for proroguing
Parliament to February 15.

[2] Charles Talbot, twelfth Earl and later first Duke of Shrewsbury.

[3] Arabella, who married Charles Spencer, third Earl of Sunderland, in
1695.

[4] James Fitzjames, son of the King by Arabella Churchill, who was later
to show, as Duke of Berwick, that he possessed much of the military ability
of his uncle Marlborough.   At this moment he had just returned from the
siege of Buda, where, although only sixteen years of age, he had greatly
distinguished himself.

* 34/15: Newcastle 24 November 1686, vowing never to sleep with the
duchess again unless he can dispose of his daughters as he wishes.

against the Turkes with the continued success of the Christians, to the great consternation of thos infidels.

Nov. 12   I went to Yorke, wher I found some disorders since I left that guarrison. I had severall complaints from the citizens against officers and souldiers for takeing mony for quarters and giveing ease to such as feed them the best. For this crime a Scotchman of my Lord Huntindons regiment was punished at a councill of warr, to lie at the Martials for three days, to ride the wooden hors every day at the reliefe of the guard with a paper upon his breast expressing his crime.

I confined two comissioned officers, one for lying out of the guarrison without acquainting me with it, the other for quarrelling with and misuseing a citizen, and afterwards committing him by his own authority to the guard with a file of muskiteers. I committed another to the dungion for beating a constable, and punished severall for leaveing the guard without leave and neglect of their duty.

24   I was invited to the feast of the sherifs of the citty, and none but Major Morgan, the field officer, with me; but I carryed severall others, who were well recieved, only we sate devided from my Lord Maior in a perticular room, which was not soe well taken, however it was meant. Every day some disorder or other was committed, though none passed unpunished either by judgement of a councill of warr or my own appointment, to the satisfaction of the citty.

30   I recieved a letter from the Duke of Newcastle, who
*   writt word that himselfe and his Duchess were at the same distance as when I left Welbeck, and another from
†   my Lord Feathersham that he now thought himselfe in his single condition more happy then marryed into that family as things stood, or to that purpas; soe fatall to families are thos differences occasioned by the folie of husband or wife, or both; and if of the latter, though the man hath sperit (if he hath sence with it), he will suffer in

* 34/15: Newcastle 24 November 1686; 34/16: same, 5 November 1686.

† 33/14: Feversham, 27 November 1686.

some degree the insolencie of a woeman rather then make it publique to the prejudice of his children, especially daughters, who are seldome desired out of such families.

I had an account from my Lord President's secretary *Dec.* 1 that his lordship had mooved the King (as I had desired) for a liveing for my brother, lately faln void in his Majestys guift; that the King was very favourably inclined to doe it, but was engaged six months before to another.   *

I gave a ball and supper to the ladys of the town and 2 the officers of the guarrison.

I had a great trouble upon me from a near relation.   4   †

I committed three souldiers to the guard, and then 5 sent them to my Lord Maior, two of them for suspicion of robbing a man of a gun and a pair of stockins in the highway, another for cutting cloth out of some tenters.[1] Two more were concerned in the last felony, but they ran away before they could be catched, and soe committed one felony by deserting to escape the punishment of another.   I caused a hue and cry to be sent after them.   ‡

Mr. Prickit,[2] deputy-recorder of the citty of Yorke, 9 invited me, my wife and family, with such officers and others as I should bring with me, to dinner at his hous, wher he gave us an extraordinary intertainment.

Sir Stiphen Thomson, marchant and alderman of 10 Yorke, gave me and my familie a supper and ball.   All the ladys of the town appeared ther, and but few gentlemen besides such as I invited to come.

Mr. Chancellor of the province of Yorke, Doctor 11 Watkison,[3] came and invited me and my familie to dinner, desireing that I would appoint the time; but I was not very well and feard the gout, soe that I gave noe answer to it at that time.   I was desired by others to entertainments at their houses, but was hindered for the same reason.

---

[1] Wooden frames on which cloth was stretched after being milled.

[2] George Prickett.

[3] Henry Watkinson, LL.D., was Chancellor of York from 1673 to 1712.

---

* 45/24: Jo. Mounsteven, 30 November 1686.

† 45/23: Tamworth Reresby, 9 December 1686, asking Reresby to lend him £20 to help towards costs incurred by proceedings in chancery.

‡ 45/13: [?] December 1686 petition of Thomas Woodhouse on behalf of himself and other sergeants to punish soldiers who had helped another soldier to escape arrest.

I had the trouble of the gout soe much that I was confined to my bed for five days. I had it in my right foot and knee, and the middle finger of the right hand, but without any matter of pain. It swelled very little, and in two days after I could walke without trouble. My finger was not restoored of a week.

Dec. 22   I went for Thriberge, leaveing the care of the town to Major Sterling, major to Colonel Oglethorp. On Christmas Day I entertained the poorer sort of tenents of Thriberge and Mexbrough; on St. Stiphens Day thos of Deneby and Hoton; on St. Johns Day the richer sort of tenents of Thriberge, Brinsford and Rotherham; on Innocents Day thos of Mexbrough, Deneby and Hoton. Five other days were sett as days of invitation to gentlemen round about us and the chiefe tradesmen of Doncaster and Rotherham, who generally came as invited, besides severall that came further off and laid at my hous.

This Christmas ended without any disaster, save that some gentlemen returning home late got some falls, but without much harm.

*   I had recieved a letter from my Lord Burlinton, with another directed to me and the rest of the deputy lieutenants, purporting an order his lordship had recieved from the King, to caus his lieutenants to make diligent search for all guns and muskits kept by persons not qualified soe to doe by law within his lieutenancy. Ther hapned to be a mistake in law in the order as to the method of makeing this search, it not being proper to doe it as deputy lieutenants, except the persons to be disarmed had been looked upon as dangerous to the goverment, as
Jan. 4 by justices of the peace. I represented this mistake to his
[1686/7] lordship, but he not darring to offer it to the Court insisted by a second letter to have it done, which I imediately putt in execution with the assistance of Sir Ralph Knight, another deputy lieutenant, within this devision, but as justices of the peace.

†   6   I had an account that severall gentlemen in this Rideing

* 33/3: Sunderland, 6 December 1686; 33/6: Burlington, 11 December 1686.

† 47/5: Sir Henry Goodricke, 4 January 1686/7.

were putt out of commission of the peace to the nomber of nineteen, and ten papists putt in their room; that my Lord Rochester, Lord High Tresurer, was laid aside from that office,[1] and that it was putt into the hands of five commissioners, of which two of them were papists.[2]

The sessions of the peace were held at Doncaster, where *Jan.* 18 Sir John Bointon, sergeant-at-law, gave the charge. Ther was noe alteration then in the commission, nor did anything happen but according to the usuall method and business of sessions. The Maior of Doncaster presented me with some wine and oisters, and my Lord Darcy sent me a doe.

I returned home the 21, haveing first taken the return of the constables at Doncaster of the precept issued out by Sir Ralph Knight and myselfe for searching for arms; and the whole nomber of muskits and fouling pieces brought in for Strafford and Tickil and Staincross were forty-four.

I ther recieved ten pounds for the repair of the brige leading from Rotherham to Sheffield near Ickles (according to an order obteaned at the last sessions at Barnsley for that purpass), which 10 l. was raised upon the weapon-tack of Strafford and Tickil.

I recieved the newes that Mr. Morgan, major to my 22 Lord Huntindon (that had quartered some time at Yorke, and removed by his Collonel's order to Carlisle, wher he went very unwillingly), was unfortunately stabd by a lieutenant of the same regiment drinking togather, of which he presently died. He was a fine gentleman, and one that had concieved a perticular friendship for me.[3]   *

I recieved a letter from my Lord Maior elect of Yorke,[4] 24

---

[1] On his refusal to change his religion. His dismissal, determined upon in December, took effect on January 4.

[2] Belasyse and Dover, the former of whom was First Lord.

[3] " He was a fine gentleman, had a good plantation in Verginia, and hath ofton owned the obligations he had to your Lordship " (Reresby to Halifax, January 26, 1686/7, in Spencer MSS.).

[4] Thomas Mosely, an apothecary, elected according to custom on January 15 to take office on February 3.

---

* 40/22: Tho. Mosley, 25 January 1686/7.

who sent by advice and consent of his bretheren a gentleman on purpas to invite me and all the officers of the
guarrison to dine with them upon the 3rd of February at
the publique charge of the citty.

Jan. 30   I went for Yorke from Thriberge, leaveing my wife
ther.

Feb. 2   I went to dine with all the officers of Colonel Oglethorp's batallion at a relation's hous of that colonels, wher
wee were invited to a great dinner.

3   I was accompanyed with all the officers of the guarrison
to Marchant Tailers Hall, wher the two Lord Maiors,
all the aldermen and common councill recieved us with
the waits of the citty at our entrance into the Hall, and
treated us at dinner very splendedly, wher wee debeauched
a little too freely.   I called a councill of warr that morning.

I found the report very currant in Yorke that the King
intended to build a chappell at the Mannour for use of
the mass, and that some papist lord was to be appointed
governor in my place; and that which seemed to give
more ground for that rumour was the King's takeing
away at that time the commissions of the Lord Shrewsbury and Lord Lumley of two regiments of hors they
commanded, for noe other reason that appeared but for
being firm to the Protestant religion, to which they had been
converted from the Roman Catholique some five years
before.

5   I committed two prisners to the main guard, ther to
remain till the next day, that one was to ride the woodden
hors, and the other to be tyed neck and heels at the reliefe
of the guard.   The captain of the guard, one Lieutenant
Fry,[1] took upon him without any order from me to change
my order, and sent them both to the Martials.   I sent
for the captain, and enquireing of him by what authority
he had done this, he justified himselfe, which putt me
into that heat that I presently confined him for thirty hours,

[1] John Fry, lieutenant in the Earl of Huntingdon's regiment (Dalton,
English Army Lists, ii. 34).

and had represented that and some other misdemeaners by him formerly committed to the King and his colonel, had he not presently submitted himselfe, both by words and in writing, and obteaned of all the officers of the guarrison to come and to intercede for him, he being very sensible that had I complained it would probably have cost him his commission.

I was treated at dinner by the Chancellor of the diocese, *Feb.* 7 with such officers as I thought fitt to bring with me. That afternoon as I was going to visit the main guard, seing a great croud and disorder in the streets, I found it was occasioned by six souldiers, three of each regiment, who had quarrelled and fought, two of them being fresh killed upon the place, and a third desperately wounded. I took all the speedy care to gett the last man dressed by a chirurgien, and to persue the murderers that had escaped. One of them we soon took.   For the other two I doubled the guards, and caused search to be made for them that night, but ineffectually.

Being Shrove Teusday (a day that the youth and 8 apprenticies of Yorke doe claim to themselves a more then usuall liberty, haveing some years committed great disorders on that day), I continued the guards doubled. At night I had some notice that Doningfield, the person that wounded him that was not yet dead, was in such a hous.   I sent a file of muskiteers to take him, but he being locked in a chamber denyed to render himselfe, soe that I was forced to send more men, and was going myselfe as I had newes he was taken.   I sent him to my Lord Maior, who took his examination and committed him. He denyed that he had wounded the party, or that he had a sword, but it was prooved that he got his comrades sword and made use of it in that fray.

As I was going for Thriberge I had letters from the 11 Secretary that I should recieve orders (as it hapned the next post) for Colonel Oglethorps batallion to march to ⁎ Caerlile and other guarrisons northwards, and my Lord

⁎ 47/27: Theo. Oglethorp, 8 February 1686/7. Three companies went to Tynemouth and one to Scarborough.

Huntintons to Chester the week following, and my company only to remain at Yorke.   I presently called the officers, and gave such nescessary orders herein as the shortness of time and the care of the souldiers paying their quarters and parting well with the town required.   Afterwards I went to my Lord Maior to give him soe timly notice that he might see right to be done to the town, and soe recommending it to the officers that all things might be done at their departure that might conduce to the Kings service and their own credits (of which I said I should give the King a suitable account) I persued my journey.[1]

Feb. 13   I had an account from Yorke that the third souldier of my Lord Huntinton's batallion that lay wounded was that
*   day departed.

18   I recieved his Majestys orders dated the 15 by the hand of the Secretary of Warr concerning the matter of place or precedency amongst officers, and concerning the tryalls of thos that had lately killed the men at Yorke, and some in prison for deserting the Kings service.   By the same letter the Secretary hinted to me that he did find that no company was yet named to succeed mine at Yorke, when mine was to march to the camp, which gave me good opportunity to putt the King in mind of the need ther would be of it.

Every post brought fresh newes of gentlemen's looseing their imployments, both military and civill.

---

[1] The uncertain relations of soldiers and citizens are brought out in Reresby's letter to Halifax, dated " Thriberge, February 19, 1686[/7]," preserved among the Spencer MSS. :

I had orders on Saturday last for both the batallions here to march, Colonell Oglethorps northwards, my Lord Huntintons for Chester ; soe that noe force remains ther but my company. We have all agreed very well since their being in that quarter, and they have paid their quarters at their departure excepting some little, for I refused to certifie for them in that perticular till I had my Lord Maior's his testimoniall that all was cleared. His lordship gave me and the officers a very great entertainment or dinner at the publique charge before we recievd thes orders, and yet I presume the citty is not sorry to be quitt of their guests.

* 40/25: William Blathwayt, 15 February 1686/7, refers to the killing of the soldier.

Some gave up their commissions and places, but most had them taken away, and papists for the most part put in their rooms. The Lord Clarendon, Lord Lieutenant of Ireland, was recalled, and Mr. Talbot, a strict Irish papist (made a little before Earl of Treconell),[1] sent over to succeed him, which made a great many people that were Protestants leave or sell their estates and come over for England. Mr. Savile, vice-chamballan to the King, brother to the Marquis of Halifax, who had been of the bedchamber to the King whilst Duke of Yorke, and since that embassador in France, was put out of his imployment.[2] Sir Michael Wentworth and Mr. Bierley,[3] who had both troops when I had mine in the Duke of Monmoths rebellion, now lost their commissions.

I recieved the King's warrant or commission from the *Feb.* 22 Secretary, my Lord Sunderland, to preserve the game for the King for ten miles about Yorke, and five miles about Thriberge, with power to take away guns, dogs, netts, or other engins for the distruction of hares, phesants, partrige, &c., and to return the names of such to the King and Council as did not conform in this perticular. This commission, though soe late recieved, was dated in November. It was under the Kings own hand and the privy signet.

I remooved with my family to Yorke, the assizes *March* 7 haveing begun ther upon the 5t, attended but by one judge, Sergiant Powell.[4] The two souldiers that had been of the nomber which had killed the three of my Lord Huntintons company were tryed; but noe malice

---

[1] Richard Talbot, whose elder brother Peter was Roman Catholic Archbishop of Dublin. He had been created Earl of Tyrconnel in June 1685, and had been gradually encroaching on Clarendon for more than a year.

[2] Henry Savile was dismissed early in March (Foxcroft, *Halifax*, i. 479).

[3] Robert Beverley or Byerley (Dalton, *English Army Lists*, ii. 15, 18).

[4] Sir John Powell had been appointed to the northern circuit along with Sir Robert Wright (*London Gazette* for January 31-February 3).

---

* 47/35: R. Byerly, [February 1686/7].

appearing the jury brought it in manslaughter, and they were burnt in the hand.   The jury would not find it felony against the souldier that desserted, soe he was acquitted.   Four felons recieved sentence of death, of which a poor old woeman had the hard fate to be condemd for a witch.   Some, that were more apt to believe thos things then me, thought the evidence strong against her, the boy that said he was bewitched falling into fits before the bench when he see her, and then on a sudden comming to himselfe and relating very distinctly the severall injurys she had done him.   But in all this it was obscrved that the boy had noe distortion, noe foaming at the mouth, nor did his fitts leave him gradually, but all of a sudden; soe that the judge thought fitt to reprieve her.

However, it is just to relate this odd story.   One of my souldiers, being upon the guard at eleven a clock at night at Clifford Tower Gate the night the witch was arraigned, hearing a great noise at the Castle, came to the pourch, and being ther see a scroule of paper creep from under the door, which, as he imagined by moonshine, turned first into the shape of a monkey, then of a turky cock, which mooved to and fro by him; wherupon he went to the goale and called the under-goyler, who came and see the scroule dance up and down and creep under the door, wher ther was scarce the room of the thickness of half a crown.   This I had from the mouth both of the souldier and goaler.

I had this assizes a tryall with Mrs. Savile of Mexbrough, tenent to the tyth of that town and Deneby from the archdeacon, upon this account.   She had been suffered (and her husband) to goe over the foard at Deneby town end to bring over her tyth from thence to Mexbrough, that she now pretended to doe it of right; and yet foreseeing some danger of this kind whilst her husband lived, I had ofton caused his draught to be stopped, and had obliged him to pay an acknowlegement.   In short the evidence was soe clear for us that the judge directed the jury to find it for the plaintiff, but by a confederacy (which we after found out between their atturney and the foreman of the jury) they found it against me; but she gott little by it, for the judge thought it soe ill a verdict that he certified for me and stopt the record, soe it was to be tryed over again.

I recieved a letter from the Earl of Huntinton, whom I *March 9* had desired amongst others to represent the ill consequence it might be of to the King to leave York without soe much as one company, and to deliver up the keys to the magistrates of walled towns in a county wher they had once shown the trick of shutting their gates against their King (for soe did Hull against King Charles the First in the begining of the late warrs). My Lords answer was   * this: that he had offered to the King as my opinion what I had mentioned in mine concerning the withdrawing all the force from Yorke, and the consequence of it; that his Majesty spoake of me as haveing a very good esteem of me, but in case he should be advised to disguarrison that place (it being inland, and Cliffords Tower burnt down) his kindness should not be less to me, soe that I might depend upon it that my sallary would however be continued to me. About the same time I had an account from Mr. Blaithwait, Secretary of Warr, that haveing laid my reasons before the King for the need of another company's comming to Yorke to relieve mine, his Majesty had given order that one of the Holland regiment from Beaverley should be appointed for it, as I soon after recieved orders to recieve them. By this I could not thinke that his Majesty designed to reduce this guarrison soe speedily. And yet every day produced soe great a change in officers, both military and civil, that would not comply with what the King desired of them, that ther was noe assurance of anything.

The only tryall of men, especially members of both Houses of Parlament that had places and came near him,

* 47/21: copy of the letter sent to Huntingdon, to which 33/20 is the reply. Huntington Library, Hastings MSS. HA 10466, acknowledges the receipt of 33/20: 'Letters on the Administration of James II', ed. G. Davies, *Journal for Army Historical Research* (1951), no. 12.

was this. He took them aside, tould them that the Test Act was made in the height of faction, not only to prejudice the Roman Catholicks, and chiefly himselfe, and to prevent his comming to the Crown; but that soe long as that and the penall lawes against them continued, noebody was safe of that persuasion; that it was against all municipal lawes for subjects to be denyed, being free born, to serve their prince, or for a prince to make use of whom he pleasd for his service; and therfore he hoped they were soe loyall as not to refuse to give voats for the takeing away of soe unreasonable lawes. Every man that resisted the King in this were discharged of their imployments.

The time for the sitting of the Parlament now drawing near, and severall Parlament men not goeing to London, the King ordered the judges in their severall circuits to feel their puls in this matter; and perticularly I was surprized when the judge [1] tould me privately at York that he had order to speake to me on that subject. I asked him if he had it from his Majesty, and namely to me. He replyed he recieved it in generall from the King to sound all members of Parlament, and from my Lord Chancellor me in perticular. I then desired some time to consider of it, and the next morning returned him this answer: that since the denyall of what the King asked was interpreted as an act of disloyalty, and I had soe lately waited upon the King personally and given him such assurances of my loyalty (when he was pleasd to speak to me in his bedchamber), that I could not believe this message was directed to me, and the rather bycaus he did not name me; and I did not concieve that I was obliged to declare myselfe to anybody else; but if his Majesty did thinke fitt to say anything further to me when I waited upon him (which I intended speedily), I should consult both my loyalty and concience to give him what satisfaction I could.

[1] Powell. This is made quite clear in Reresby's undated letter to Halifax printed *infra*, p. 581.

* 48/20: Edmund Reresby, 31 March 1687 advising him to delay his journey to London.

The judge tould me he would return what I said, seemed not forward to advise complyance, but was meerly passive. This was the best reply I thought at that time, for had it been affermative, it was not safe, as the bent of the nation stood, to declare one's mind to a third person; had it been negative, it had disobliged the King perfectly, when, if the Parlament should not meet (as it was not likely by the generall opposition this found), the matter might probably never come in question. However, it is most safe to deliver one's own mind in such cases to a prince, and to avoid if possible either the treachery, prejudice, or ignorance of such as report.

We now heard that Captain Fairfax, eldest son to my Lord Fairfax, had his commission taken from him; Colonel Herbert the same, Vice-Admiral of England and Master of the Robes (he enjoyed in places at that time 3,000 l. per annum).[1] My Lord Preston had the wardroabe taken away, refuseing, as the rest did, to comply.[2]

I prepared my company to be ready to march, against *March* 18 the Princess An's regiment came from Barwick to Yorke, now commanded by Mr. Fizjames, lately created Duke of Barwick, my orders being to send my company with that regiment to the camp. That night my Lord Maior, the Chancellor, and severall friends came to sup with me, and the next day I returned towards Thriberge.

Ther were this assizes sworn and served on the grand † jury severall papists, as Sir John Lawson,[3] Sir Walter Vavasour,[4] &c., and most of them being in comission of

[1] Arthur Herbert, who was to carry over the invitation of the English nobles to William of Orange, command William's fleet during his expedition, and in return for his services receive the title of Earl of Torrington.

[2] Reresby is guilty of some confusion regarding Lord Preston, whom he refers to elsewhere (*infra*, p. 461) as Master of the Robes. Preston was Master of the Great Wardrobe, and was not deprived of that post. Herbert's successor as Master of the Robes was Lord Thomas Howard, brother of the seventh Duke of Norfolk.

[3] Of Brough, Yorkshire; created a baronet in July 1665.

[4] Of Haslewood, the third baronet.

* 48/1: Edmund Reresby, 10 March, 1686/7.

the peace sent for *dedimus* to be sworn, a sight not seen in England for many years before.

The King, haveing used all the means, both of threats and persuasions, to bring the Parlament men to comply in takeing away the Test Act and the penall laws, and all to noe purpas, thought it not safe to call the Parlament as it was appointed, and therfore declared in Council upon *March* 18 the 18 of March that for weighty considerations the Parlament should be proroagued till the 22nd of November following. His Majesty declared at the same time that uniformity of religion not haveing been able to be effected by the endeavours of four of his predicessors succeeding one another, assisted by their Parlaments, but that it had rather prooved prejudiciall to the kingdome (as was lately experienced by the late rebellion in his father's time), he was now ressolved to issue out a declaration for toleration or liberty of concience to all dissenters, hopeing it would contribute to the peace and quiet of this kingdome, and to the increase of people as well as of trade. The King had done the same thing not many weeks before in Scotland,[1] the Parlament ther not complying noe more then in England to abrogate the penall lawes. Whatever reasons were alleged, the true reason appeared to most men to be a design therby to weaken the Church of England; and its professors feared it would feel more blowes then this in a short time, though many were of opinion that such a toloration was not of prejudice upon a politique account.

A justice of the peace, whos office it is to punish (and it being naturall to thos that suffer to complain of the blow, how justly soever it be deserved), must very ofton have ennemys, lett him behave himselfe never soe uprightly. I found the experiance of this oftner then once. However, it was my method to persue a right cours, and to undervalue their reflexions, which at the last did ofton

[1] The first grant of toleration in Scotland was made on February 12, 1687.

vanish into smoake.   But wher I found the insolency
too great, I took all legall means to justifie myselfe, and
to retort it upon them.   The sessions at Pontefract being
to begin the 5t of Aprill, I had two yong fellowes, one
Savil and one Horn of Mexbrough,[1] to persue in some
matters of this kind, wher I caused severall traverses to be
persued against them, and some new indictments to be
preferred to their noe little charge and mortification.
One of the said indictments against Mr. Savile was for
fishing on Mexbrough side in the river Dun, and therby
committing a trespass, it being within my royalty.   He
pleaded that I had noe royalty ther, and that he had a
grant from the archdeacon with his lease of the rectory of
Mexbrough to fish ther.   To the first I answered that
though my father sould the mannour of Mexbrough, yet
he excepted the stream or water-cours, and produced the
counterpart of the deed;   to the secound that the archdeacon, haveing noe manour nor royalty belonging to the
rectory, could not grant a liberty to a tenent which he
wanted himselfe, soe that Savile

1687

was found guilty of the trespas and fyned by the Court.
    Ther was much business this sessions, and the second
day ther appeared twenty-three justices of the peace   *April* 6
(without the Roman Catholicks lately added to the commission, who came not, the *dedimus* to swear them not
being sent down as yet).[2]   That day I went to Doncaster
to meet my company, which haveing joined the Duke of
Barwicks regiment was soe far on their march towards
the camp.   That night I entertained all the officers of

[1] Possibly Thomas Horne of Mexborough, who, however, was about
forty-five years of age at this time.

[2] " Our late Pontefract sessions was attended by twenty-three justices.
Some of thos lately added to the commission came to be sworn, but noe
dedimus being comed at that time (though it is since to swear five) they
did not act " (Reresby to Halifax, April 15, 1687, in Spencer MSS.).

the regiment, being above twenty, at supper at my own charge, amongst which was the lieutenant-collonell[1] and the major.[2]   But I found their companys very inferiour to mine, both in nomber and quality of the men, which I was not sorry to see.

April 7

*   Ther came down the declaration for liberty of concience, guilded over with tenderness to his Majestys subjects in generall: invitation to strangers of differing opinions, improovement of trade, promesses all this time to protect the bishops and ministers of the Church of England in their functions, rights and propertys, and free exercize of their religion in their churches.   But the design was well understood, viz., to devide the Protestant churches, that the popish might find less opposition. (Devide et impera.)   The Presbuterians or Calvanists, who most of them had begun to conforme, continued to come to our churches.   The Anababtists, Quakers, Independents made addresses of thankes to the King for this indulgence.

Severall gentlemen of addition to thos before named had lost their imployments for refuseing to give their voats for takeing away the penall and test laws, being all members of Parlament; after which, and the Parlament's being proroagued, the question how men inclined as to that matter was not soe frequently putt, nor did any nomber of prosselites, considerable either as to estates or quality, goe over to the Roman Church, as yet neither invited by great preferments that waited on them, nor frighted with the King's frowns and the loss of their imployments.   Soe far did honour helpe religion that gentlemen were the more firm, least the world might thinke that they changed their opinions for reward.

---

[1] John Beaumont, second son of Sapcote, second Viscount Beaumont of Swords, and brother of Thomas, the third Viscount.   He was shortly to gain fame by his resistance to the introduction of Irish Catholics into his regiment.

[2] John Innes.

---

* 48/35: Nathaniel Johnston, 9 April, 1687: 'many begin to see. . .it [The Test] had much better have been yielded generously at first than have suffered the consequences of standing so stiffly upon it.'

Great preparations were now makeing for the war of the ensueing campagnia betwixt the Christians and the Turkes. The Czars of Muscovie[1] joined with the Emperour, and Persia gave some hopes to come into the war against the Grand Senior on that side. The Poles were not less active to prepare on theirs, nor the Venetians in Candia and Morea.

The great man once in estate, severall times soe in *April* 12 favour with the late King Charles the Second (but never with his brother), the Duke of Buckingham, died about this time.[2] He was certainly the most witty man of his time, and the hansomest, as well as the best bred, but wholly addicted to his plesures, and unsteady.

I had a letter from my brother Edmond (captain in the 29 guards) that informed, the King tould him that I had sent   * up a very good company of granadeers, for ther was not a man in it but he was taller then the captain. He spoake this as a jeast, bycaus I was little, but my souldiers all very tall.

By this time the church was near finished at Thriberg, wher I had been at some charge to repair and beautifie it and the windows, and had given a new bell to the steeple. I built a great deale this year at Ickles, the dwelling as well as the outhouses being much out of repair. I sould about sixty acres of Deneby Wood, for which I was to recieve 7 l. per acre.

I recieved newes from my brother that the Duke of *May* 15 Barwicks regiment had appeared and exercized before the   † King, that the King seeing my company should say over and over that it was a very good company, and that it exercized very well.

---

[1] Ivan V and his younger half-brother, known to history as Peter the Great. At this time they were both minors and occupied a double throne.

[2] At Kirkby Moorside on April 16, in circumstances which accorded little with his life as a whole, but yet fell far short of those suggested by Pope's famous lines. Some account of his last moments is contained in Reresby's undated letter to Halifax printed *infra*, p. 581.

* 49/1: Edmund Reresby, 28 April, 1687.

† 48/37: Edmund Reresby, 14 May 1687.

May 16   Being Whitson Monday and Rotherham fair day, I went in the afternoon to the Sign of the Swan to recieve my rent of one penny, a rent reserved upon a sale of my predicessours of that hous some 400 years since, with the best room and stable to the use of the heir of the family upon Rotherham fair day.[1]

17   Being Whitson Teusday, the Maior of Doncaster with the chiefe of that corporation came to dine with me at Thriberge, and were entertained to their satisfaction.

23   I went to Yorke. The only company (commanded by Captain Cornwallis of Colonel Oglethorps regiment) ther behaved itselfe very well; I heard very few complaints of it. After nescessary orders given I returned to Thri-

28   berge the 28. That day I had a letter from an officer of my own company, purporting that the day my company exercized before his Majesty he ordered the officer the next time he writt to me to thanke me for sending him

*   up soe good a company. I thought myselfe obliged to write to the King to thanke him for this condescention, which I did in thes terms verbatim (or very near it):

To the King.

May it please your Majesty,

I have recieved the welcome newes that your Majesty was pleased to approove of my company of granadeers, which had lately the honour to appear before your Majesty. And as nothing can be soe great a happiness to me in this world as to have my endeavours for your Majestys service accepted, soe I can never be sufficiently thankfull for the honour and favour I have

---

[1] " I finde a deed wher Richard de Gotham and Cecilie his wife give to Joane their daughter that land which Mr. Alexander, vicar of the moyetie of Rotherham, held of them ther, reserving the rent to them and their heirs of one penny per annum (dated Anno 1280), which penny is yearly paid to me from the owner of the Swann Inn in Rotherham; and the best roome in the house and the best stable is by custome reserved for the heir of this familie upon the fair day " (*Family History*, i. f. 18).

* 47/44: Bartme. Colyer, 17 May 1687.

recieved by it. Great Sir, I should not have presumed
to have given your Majesty this trouble on this occasion
had I not hoped that the same condescention and goodness
which your Majesty did practice in takeing notice of the
one will forgive the other. I have nothing further, Sir,
to trouble your Majesty with from this citty or county,
but that I find men generally conformable to the duty
which they owe to your Majestys royall person and
goverment, and well satisfyed with the privileges and
libertys they enjoy under it, which that it may long continue happy and prosperous is the constant prayer of,

> May it please your Majesty,
> > Your Majesty's most obedient and most
> > faithfull subject and servant,
> > > JOHN RERESBY.

My wife was godmother in one week to two children,
one the son of my oncle Yarburgh of Campsal,[1] the other
son to Sir Jervase Cutler of Stainbrough, and his one-and-
twentyth child.

My brother John Moyser, the only child surviveing of _June_ 8
James Moyser, Esquire, by my mother in second marriage,
being marryed to one of the daughters of Mr. Aire of
Rainton of Nottinghamshire,[2] came with his bride and
relations to dine with me at Thriberge.

The same day I recieved an answer to mine from the   *
Earle of Huntinton, in thes words verbatim, as may be
seen by my letters from noblemen of this year sowed up
togather:

[1] Thomas, the eldest son, baptised May 23, 1687.

[2] Anthony Eyre of Rampton, who died in 1671. By his second wife,
Elizabeth, daughter of Sir John Packington of Westwood, he had three
daughters, of whom either Mary or Margaret is here referred to. From
Reresby's letters among the Spencer MSS. it is clear that the marriage had
taken place only a short time before. On April 15, [16]87, he wrote to
Halifax, " I presume it will be a marriage between Mrs. Eyr her daughter
and my brother Moyser."

* The bundle sewn together is number 33. The letter referred to is 33/16
Huntingdon, 4 June 1687.

Sir,

I am always glad of any oppertunity to expresse my
respects to you, and wish you had imployed me in something more considerable then your last commands.
Yesterday being at Windser to take my leave of the King
before I goe for Lecestershire, I delivered his Majesty
your letter, who upon the reading it tould me it was nothing
of business, and that I should tell you that the King was
very well satisfyed as wel with your person as with your
company, which he heard and found to be very good.
And upon the whole I find his Majesty reteans a very good
opinion of you, the fruits of which I make noe question
but you will find whenever ther is an occasion. I cannot
sufficiently return you my thankes for your kindness to
my regiment when it was at Yorke, but shall always retean
your favours as very valuable to me, who am with much
respect,

Your affectionate cozen and humble servant,

HUNTINGDON.

Gerard Street,
June 4, 1687.

Addresses were dayly presented to the King from all
manner of dissenters for his late indulgence for liberty of
concience, and in some places from the Church of England
party upon that claus in his Majestys indulgence wher he
declared that he would, however, defend that Church in
its rights and possessions, &c., or to that effect.[1]

June 22 I had notice from the Secretary that the King had
*   incorporated all the governours company's of England
into some regiments, which were before independent,
and that mine was joined to the Duke of Barwicks. I
was sorry for it, but the thing being generall we could not
complain.

[1] The operation of the indulgence in Yorkshire is described in Reresby's
undated letter to Halifax printed *infra*, p. 581.

* 48/27: Edmund Reresby, 21 June 1687.

After severall rumours that the papists had been very *June* 24 pressing with the King for the Manour of Yorke, to make it a seminary or school for the instructing of youth in that religion, I was informed that it was granted accordingly for thirty years to one Mr. Lawson, a priest.[1]   I writt   *
upon it to my Lord Belasise, principal commissioner of the Treasury, setting forth that I had it granted by my commission of governor of Yorke from the late King, and confirmed by this; that it was of 60 l. per annum advantage to me; that it had cost me near 200 l. in repairs since my abode ther, and had noe allowance for it from the King; and therfore desired that it might either be continued to me, or that his Majesty would grant me such a compensation for the want of it and the repairs as in his Majestys justice and wisedome I might be thought to deserve.[2]

Sir Theophilus Oglethorp, Collonel of the Holand 26 regiment (who had contributed considerably to the defeat of the rebels in Scotland when the Duke of Monmoth marched against them, and to the defeat of that rebel Duke lately in the west), came to Thriberge, and brought me a letter from the Earle of Feathersham, to request my   †
endeavours with the Duke of Newcastle that the treaty for his marrying the Lady Margaret Cavendish might be renewed.   With that letter came one from the King to the Duke, recomending his lordship, with orders to me to deliver it and to improove the contents.   In that letter

---

[1] Francis Lawson, " one of his Majesty's chaplains." The lease of the manor was for thirty-one years, and was made on his petition and for his use ; but the name in which it was ultimately carried through in November was that of his nephew, Captain Henry Lawson, second son of Sir John Lawson of Brough, who succeeded his father as second baronet in 1698 (*Calendar of Treasury Books*, viii. 1308, 1602, ix. 711 ; Hist. MSS. Com., *Leeds MSS.*, p. 30).

[2] " I hear the King hath granted the Manour to one Lawson, a priest, for a schoole or seminary. I have writt to my Lord Belasis and desired a compensation for the repairs and loss of it, but I fear to noe purpas " (Reresby to Halifax, " Thriberge, June the 26, 1687," in Spencer MSS.).

* 50/6: Edward Baldock, 18 April 1687; 48/25: Nathaniel Johnston, 23 June 1687.

* 50/6: Edward Baldock, 18 April 1687; 48/25: Nathaniel Johnston, 23 June 1687.

was this expression, that what favour the Duke showd his lordship he should consider it as done to himselfe.[1]

June 28 I went to Welbeck, and found the Duchesse of Newcastle returned, who had been parted some months from the Duke, but yet not perfectly reconciled. I used all the means I could to promote the thing with them both, and partly by this and by an after visit brought it soe far on that the Duke said if his wife would consent, and give it under her hand that she desired his Grace to accept of my Lord Feathersham to marry his daughter, he would doe it. She said that she was consenting to it, but would not give it under her hand that she desired it. I used all the persuasions I could to show the unreasonableness of such a punctilio, but was not able to overcome it, but got leave that my Lord Feathersham might make a visit in person and try if he could prevaile with the Duchess to doe that. I further obteaned his promess to give my Lady Margaret 15,000 l. down, besides expectations. To repeat all the arguments I used in this concern would be tedious to bring it to this, both the Duke and Duchess being very

*

[1] Halifax was also interested in the match and Reresby's letters to him, preserved among the Spencer MSS., contain many references to the negotiations. In the letter of June 26 already referred to, Sir John writes :

My Lord, Noe man is more desirous then myselfe to performe the service last recommended to me from your Lordship and the lord concerned, and noe man shall more truly use the little interest he hath for that end. But the man and woeman I have to deale with in this matter are soe uncertain that it is very discourageing to goe about it. My wife was lately to visit the lady thirty miles off, and found her noething discouraged by the late difference as to the disposall of her daughters. The thing in question came in discours amongst others by accident, and the mother said she thought this proposal when made the most suitable as to the person ; but as to the fortune it was like marrying a daughter to a parson, and her daughters were not yet soe desperate to be disposed of soe. She had recieved the day before a message from Welbeck to knowe why she did not return home, but tould her visiter she would not goe till he writt to her and assured her that way that ther should be noe further occasion given of dispute between them concerning the disposall of their children. Since that I hear she is returnd, and if upon thos terms ther is little hopes of success. . . .

* 33/19: Halifax, 7 July 1687. Feversham 'is resolved to storme the inchanted castle.'

positive in their opinions, and not inclineing to accept this gentleman, being a Frenchman and of very little certain estate, though he had 3,000 l. per annum of his first wife's estate for his life, and 5,000 l. more in imployments, being captain of the Kings guards, lieutenant-general of the army, Master of the Hors to the Queen Dowager, and of his Majestys bedchamber, and Knight of the Guarter.

His lordship writt me word that he intended to be at *July 6* my hous the 8th, in order to his going to Welbek to try what could be done. Colonel Oglethorpe stayed with me all that time, during which the Duke of Norfolke, comming to Sheffield, came and dined with me at Thriberge with severall other gentlemen.

Came the proclamation to hand wherby the King dis- 7 solved the Parlament, bearing date the 2nd, which startled many.

The Popes nontio[1] being to make his publique entry 8 at Windser with great solemnity, and the Duke of Sommer-sit (one of the lords of the bedchamber) being in waiting, he refused to attend in that ceremony, for which he was forbid comming to Court, and lost all his places. Five of the six gentlemen of the privy chamber in waiting were put out of their imployments for the same caus.

My Lord Feathersham came to my hous with my Lord 9 Preston (the Kings last embassadour in France) with a great retenue, and the next day being Sunday, we went to dine at Welbeck on Monday. My Lord Feathersham 11 was of the family of the Duke de Boullion, lately soverain prince of Sedan, and nephew to the Marischal de Turenne,[2] the great general in France, a fyne gentleman of his person and a good souldier. It was he that comanded in chiefe at the defeat of the Duke of Monmoth. The Duke of

[1] Ferdinand, Count of Adda, who had shortly before been consecrated Archbishop of Amasia in St. James's Palace. The date in the margin is correct, and is that of his public reception.

[2] His mother, Elizabeth, was daughter of Henry and sister of Frederick Maurice, successive Dukes of Bouillon. Turenne was her brother.

* 52/2 Feversham, 3 July 1687; 52/3: Same, 4 July 1687.

Newcastle recieved us very kindly, tould my Lord
Feathersham how far I had engaged him as to his consent
to marry his daughter to his lordship; but the obstacle
still remaind on his side that his wife must request his
consent in writing before he would give it (which seems
a strange fancy, but they being but halfe reconciled ther
was some reasons for it).   Ther was another remora[1] on
our side.   My Lord Feathersham thought the 15,000 l.
too little, except the Duke would settle some part of his
land in reversion upon him, his daughter and their heirs.
The Duke was not to be brought to this, saying if they
had issue he might expect that of cours, or without it,
if he did not live to have sons of his own; but he would
reserve that in his own power.

My Lord Feathersham desired the Duke that I might
goe and intercede for him to the Duchesse to give her
consent in the forme he desired it, which he allowed of,
and I went.   I found her Grace and my Lady Margaret
well enough content with the man, and not averse to come
up to what was desired, if the Duke would make any
settlement of his estate after his death to descend to them.
I asked her if she believed it was practicable to persuade
the Duke to it.   She said she feared not.   Then, said I,
it comes to this short question, whether such an opportunity ought to be lost as of this marriage for a thing that
was impossible to be obteaned at present, when it is very
likely to happen hereafter.   When I found they began to
incline to the thinge I tould them I concieved it best not
to declare themselves at the present; that the Earl of
Feathersham desired the settlement as well as they, and
since the Duke was averse to make it he thought first to
return to the King, to try if he could persuade him to
give him something (for the late King had given him
20,000 l. when he marryed his first wife, who was Sir
George Sands his daughter), and to make that the foundation for the Duke of Newcastle to make some addition to

_____
[1] Obstacle or hindrance.

it; in the meantime he desired her Grace and my Lady Margaret to take him into their good opinions. And soe I returnd, and tould the Duke the Duchesse would not consent in that manner. He said it was bycaus she expected to make him settle his estate in present, but she should be decieved; but turning to my Lord Feathersham bid him not dispair but she would doe it at last, for he knew their mindes, that the woemen approoved of him very well.

Thus we took our leaves, and returned to Thriberge, wher the lords stayed with me the next day. The Duke sent his compliment in the morning to desire their lordships to make use of his castle at Nottingham in their return to London, wher they went on Wedensday, and *July* 13 were greatly entertained at the Duke's charge. The thing was left as my Lord Feathersham desired, either to take it up again if he pleased (if noe better terms were to be had), or to leave it off. He was very well satisfyed with my proceeding, and with his entertainment at my hous. He gave ten guinnies to my servants at his going away, my Lord Preston (who was Master of the Robes to the King) six, and Colonel Oglethorp gave five.

I went to the assizes at Yorke. Of the two judges that 15 came down this circuit one was a papist, his name Alabon,[1] the first that ever sate as judge of that persuasion. He was strict and rigid in his opinion, but indifferent equall in gieving his judgement and in the tryalls that came before him, for he sate of the *nisi prius*. An address was endeavoured by the sheriff[2] from the gentlemen of the county to be presented to the King to thanke him for some words which he used in his late proclamation for liberty of concience, wherby he still promessed to mentain and protect the Church of England. This indeed had been done by severall dissenters, but by very few of the Church

[1] Sir Richard Allibone, appointed a Puisne Justice of the King's Bench in April 1687.

[2] Thomas Rokeby.

* 47/41: Thomas Rokeby, 4 July 1687. Rokeby wrote to Reresby at this early date asking him to join in the intended address. It appears then that Reresby's late arrival was intentional.

of England, they concieveing the very indulgence a contradiction to that security. The appearance of gentlemen at the assizes being little, and thos not inclined to comply with the high sherif, he attempted to gett an address to the same effect from the grand jurys, but they, being composed of some papists and some Protestants, who had different matter to thanke the King for, could not agree of frameing an addresse, and one that was offered to them by the high sheriff was stolne away and never seen after. This disappointment and aversion to the thinge putt the judge into some heats, which was also increased by but one Protestant justice of the peace attending the sheriff when he came to meet the judges, soe that he tould me (I mean Judge Alabone) that he would complain to the King, for that this looked more like a disrespect to him then to them. My late comming to the assizes kept me out of this business, soe that I was not blaimed on either side.[1]

I had my second tryall this assizes with Mrs. Savile of Mexbrough about comming over the ford at the lower end of Deneby, to fetch over her tyth from Deneby to Mexbrough that way. She cast me (as I have said) the assizes before, but the verdict was soe unjust and soe contrary to evidence that the judge had certified of it above, and granted a new tryall by a jury of gentlemen, which coming on this assizes I had a verdict against her.

*

Whilst I was at Yorke I had a letter of thankes from my Lord Feathersham, and in it this account, that he had spoaken to the King (for soe he promessed to doe for me)

---

[1] Reresby appears to have been at some pains to avoid declaring himself too soon. On July 6 he wrote from Thrybergh to Halifax :

I yesterday recieved a letter from the high sheriff to assist him in frameing and presenting an address from the Church of England gentlemen of this county for his Majestys (to use his words) gracious repeating by his last declaration to protect and preserve the Church of England. I have returned answer that I am deteaned here by the Kings commands in a private concern of his for the present, but if I come soon enough I shall concurr with the rest of the gentlemen and him in it. (Spencer MSS.)

* 52/5: Feversham, 20 July 1687.

about the Manour of Yorke, but found that he had promessed it to Father Lawson to the uses before mentioned; that his Majesty said that he did not know that I lived in it, and if I had been at any charge in repairs, &c., I should be considered for it. His lordship further added in that letter (to use his own words) that the King said that if I were not soe good a man as I were he had not kept a governor ther soe long as he had done, and that he spoake of me with all the expressions of kindnesse and esteem I could desire. Severall citizens enquired if I intended to stand for the next Parlament when one should be called. I said first I heard of none to be sommoned as yet; when that was I should declare what I was to doe.

I had the ill newes that my hous was broaken opon by *July* 28 thieves at London, and that I had lost severall sorts of goods and furniture. I returnd to Thriberge two days before, viz., the 26 of July.

I recieved a letter from my Lord Belasyse, First Lord 29 Commissioner of the Treasury, to whom I had written and sent up a state or case of the Manour of Yorke (as I said before), to this effect, that the Commissioners of the Treasury were resolved to lay my pretentions before the King concerning the Manour of Yorke, with such favour (to use the very terms) towards me as my services had merited, to which he in person would contribute more effectually for the respect he had for me did his health permitt to attend his Majesty at Windser when the Board wated upon him, &c.

The generall sessions by adjurnment were held at *August* 2 Rotherham, wher I carryed in seventeen recognisances. It was the first time that Roman Catholique justices of the peace acted ther in that commission. Ther were two that appeared, Mr. Hansby, Esquire, and Mr. Ann of Frickly,[1] men altogather unversed in business, now in years, and educated another way. Ther were four indict-

[1] Ralph Hansby of Tickhill Castle and Michael Anne of Frickley and Burghwallis.

* 49/25: A. Lloyd, 26 July 1687.

† 40/6: Belasyse, 27 July 1687.

ments against Mr. Horn of Mexbrough this sessions to which he was to travers, of which fearing the issue he sent to me to desire the prossecution might cease, and he would sell me a close called Kirke Holme in Deneby, and referr the price of it to myselfe. I was indeed before in possession of that close upon a mortgage, but upon this offer I gave him the full value, and took off the prossecution as he desired at the sessions.

August 8   I had something further to say to the Duke of Newcastle in the matter of my Lord Feathershams marriage with his daughter, the Lady Margaret; and not willing to goe on purpass, I took the occasion of an offer his Grace had made me to hunt in his parke at Clipston, soe called at Welbeck in passant (wher I left my daughter Frances with my Lady Margarite Cavendish to facilitate the thing ther), and went on that night to Clipston to meet four or five gentlemen out of Yorkeshire, who met me to pertake of that diversion. My Lord Duke pressed me to stay with him at Welbeck, and to hunt at Clipston, the accommodation not being ther very good; but I excused the giveing his Grace that trouble by reason of my company that I was to meet, and soe went to lie at Rufford, wher ther was a good inn. I setled the matter of my Lord Feathersham soe well in some minuits with the Duke and Duchesse that I remooved some mistakes between them upon the last conversation they had togather at Welbeck, and gott his Grace to confirme the portion and his consent for the marriage, provided the Duchesse would observe the forms of desireing the Duke to consent in writing. And I prevailed with her (by the force of some reasons which I gave her) to doe it, but at the same time desired her not to declare she was content soe to doe, that the difficulty of it in his Grace his opinion might make him the more earnest.

9   I killed only a brace of bukes at Clipston. I ran them down in three hours. We were about thirty hors in the parke, and afterwards I entertained most of the company at dinner, and that evening returned to Thriberge.

I had the newes that the Duchesse of Modena, mother *Aug.* 11 to the Queen, being dead, the Court was gone into morning for six months,[1] that her Majesty would goe to the Bath for her health, that the King would goe a progress during her stay ther to Glocester, Worchester, Ludlow, Shrewsbury, Chester, Leitchfield, Coventry, Banbury, Oxford, soe to the Bath to bring home the Queen; and that he had given orders for my company, though regimented, to return to their winter quarters in Yorke, as also that it was assigned for the quarter of Colonel Cornwels[2] regiment this winter.

I had a letter from my Lord Feathersham that he had **16** spoaken to my Lords Commissioners of the Treasury at   * Windser, and that they had represented to the King that they did concieve that he ought not to take away the Manour of Yorke from the governour, and that the Majesty therupon had taken noe ressolution for the present.

I had notice from my first lieutenant that my company **19** was on their march towards Yorke as far as Doncaster,   †

[1] The Duchess Laura Martinozzi died at Rome on July 9/19, and the Court went into mourning on July 31.

[2] Henry Cornwall, appointed in June 1685 to the command of a regiment of foot raised to deal with Monmouth's rebellion (Dalton, *English Army Lists,* ii. 30). The news that his regiment was coming to York caused Reresby to write the earliest that has survived among his letters on military matters to William Blathwayt :

From Thriberge, near Doncaster, Yorkshire. August the 16, [16]87.— Sir, Hearing that Colonell Cornwels regiment and my company have Yorke for their quarters, I should be glad to recieve your directions concerning it as soon as possible, as also such other orders, if ther be any new, or what change ther is in the old, that I may [be] instructed to settle the guarrison as soon as they arrive ; and perticularly if that of the 21 day of June, 2nd of the Kings reign, or the printed one for the attendance of officers in their guarrisons is to take place ; how far that for payment of quarters of the 30 October [16]85, that for wearing bionets only upon duty, and that of the ranke of granadeers (being now regimented) continue in force. Thes, what other commands you have for me, I shall be glad to recieve by the first opportunity, that am, Sir, Your faithfull humble servant, J. Reresby. (B.M. Add. MSS. 9735, f. 18.)

* 52/6: Feversham, 13 August 1687.

† 50/35: Bartme. Colyer, 17 August 1687.

all the men returning safe but three since the time they went from thence.   One was discharged, another deserted, and the third, quarelling upon the road with some reapers of corn, was cutt into brains with a scith or reaping hook by one of them after he had killed one and wounded severall of them, soe that he dyed upon the place before the rest of the company overtook him.

Aug. 21   Judge Alabone designing me a visit two days after, and haveing other business to keep me at home, I went to meet Colonel Cornwels regiment in their march to Yorke at Doncaster, wher I gave nescessary orders against they came to Yorke as to their deportment ther, and writt to my Lord Maior to accommodate them with quarters and other conveniencys in the mean time.

22   I had two letters from his lordship, the one of thankes for being kind to the citty in some thinges I had recomended to the officers concerning that place, the other to desire my comming over as soon as I could, fearing that things could not be setled as they ought to be till I came.

25   The happy newes of a great victory obteaned by the Duke of Lorrain and the Duke of Bavaria against the Turkes was confirmed.   The battle was fought not farr from Mohacz and Darda,[1] the Turkes being 80,000 men strong, the Christians not much above 40,000.   Ther were killed of the Turkes about 8,000 men, and near as many driven into the Drave, that were drowned in that river.   The Christians lost not 1,000 men, took all their canon, baggage, and attirals of warr, and found in their camp about 200,000 l. of mony besides other rich prize.

28   Sir Theophilus Oglethorp came to Thriberge in his return from Scotland.   The next day we went to see the Marquis of Winchester [2] at Rufford, he haveing borrowed

---

[1] This battle of Mohacz, fought on August 2/12, completely reversed the decision given by Solyman's great victory over the Hungarians at the same place in 1526.

[2] Charles Paulet, who succeeded his father as sixth marquis in 1675 and was created Duke of Bolton in 1689.

that hous in his journey to London, wher he rested ten days. This lord had a vast estate, and his extravagancie was as great in his way of liveing as his plenty. He travelled this time with four coaches, and a hundred hors in his retenue. His custome was to dine at six or seven at night, and his meale lasted till seven or eight in the morning. Sometimes he dranke, sometimes heard his musique, sometimes discoursed, sometimes took tobacco, and sometimes eat, whilst the company did what they pleased. They might doe the same, or rise, goe and come, sitt down, sleep, the meat and bottles continuing all the night before them. In the morning he would hunt or hawke, if the weather was seasonable; if not, he would dance, goe to bed about eleven, and sleep till the evening.[1] The man all this time was not mad, but had good sence, and most thought he counterfitted this that he might be free and inconcerned from affairs of that age, not careing to be under censure that his estate might be safe, which he studied and managed exactly in all this seeming disorder. I went from Rufford to Welbec about the concern in hand, with good success.

I went to Yorke to settle the guarrison.   *Aug.* 29

I found my own company in good condition and as 30 compleat of the same indevidual men as when it marched to the camp; only one had deserted, and another was delivered to justice for quarelling upon the road.

---

[1] Rufford was the seat of the Marquis of Halifax, to whom Reresby wrote from York on August 31 describing the effect of Winchester's visit:
My Lord, I went with Colonel Oglethorp on Saturday last to see the sight of the Marquis of Winchester at Rufford, but saw only the markes of his haveing been ther (for he was gone the day before), and he had dirtyed the hous more in that short time he stayed then your Lordships family would doe in a year. I confess, my Lord, I thought it impossible to ad to the disorder of it much, and therfore (as well as to obay your comands) the colonel and I laid ther that night. We dined the next day at Welbeck. The Duke had been drinkeing the night before with one Irail Fielding, then with him, and was both out of order and humour. . . . (Spencer MSS.)

The same day Lieutenant-Colonel Purcel [1] and the rest of the officers of Colonel Cornwels regiment came to visit me, being sixteen in nomber.

Aug. 31   I called a councel of warr, wherin I acquainted them with the customes and orders to be observed in that guarrison, and what I expected as to their demeaner ther both from souldiers and officers. I had fair assurances, but a few days after ther hapned a drunken quarrell between a gentleman of quality of the town and a captain of that regiment, which I had much adoe to reconcile, blowes haveing passed. But at last I did it effectually, and with much entreaty from all the officers did not complain of the captain to the King, fearing it might cost him his commission, he haveing killed a gentleman not long before in a like fray.

Sept. 1   They dined with me at the Manour, excepting some few that came and dined with me the next day.

4   I heard that some souldiers had exacted mony from their landlords. I called a council of warr, wherin I found the officers not inclineing to punish them, pretending they had done it in other guarrisons. I tould them that they were not to teach us ther the rules of other guarrisons, but to learn thos of this, which I knew to be grounded upon the Kings orders, and with much adoe a severe sentence did pass the councel to be inflicted upon the offenders or some of them.

The rest of the time (which was seven days in all) was passed in regulating quarters and hearing complaints, to all which I gave such remedy as was well taken both by the citty and guarrison.

6   I returned for Thriberge, and ther I met this account, that one Mr. Maddox, postmaster of Doncaster and my quarter-master to my militia troop, that was run in debt to the post office 240 l., and had petitioned the King in

[1] James Purcell, who had been promoted from major to lieutenant-colonel of the regiment in the previous May. He adhered to James II after the Revolution.

* 50/33: Brian Fairfax, 2 September 1687 the man of quality was one Mr. Banks, a servant of the writer's brother.

his then progress at Leckfield by my recomendation, his Majesty had graciously pleased to forgive him the debt. I had obteaned at the same time that another friend was to succeed him in the office of postmaster (the other haveing quitted), and that he was to recieve 20 l. per annum additional sallary to the former given to Maddox.

The little bell which I gave the parish, being the first *Sept.* 12 of five, was put up and tuned.　It cost me 18 l.

The President of Maudlin College in Oxford being dead, the King sent a *mandamus* to them to choose the Bishop of Oxford to succeed him; but their answer was, *locus plenus est.*[1]　The King in his progresse comeing to Oxford, the master and fellowes of that colege comeing to wait on him,[2] he tould them that the Church of England men did not use him wel, that they had not behaved themselves neither like gentlemen nor good subjects, and bid them goe presently back to their election and choos the said bishop, or they should feel how heavy a hand a King had.　They went, but returned his Majesty this answer, that they were sorry to fall under his displesure, but they could not make a new choice without committing wilfull perjury, and therfore desired to be excused.

It was generally observed in this progress that the King courted the dissenters and discouraged thos of the Church of England; for the papists not being numerous enough by much to contest with the Church of England, he thought to make that party the stronger by gaining to it the dis-

---

[1] Reresby gives a curiously abbreviated account of the origin of this important affair.　On a vacancy arising owing to the death of the former President of the college, Dr. Henry Clerke, on March 24, 1687, the King had recommended as his successor Anthony Farmer, a recent convert to Catholicism, who was in every way so unfit for the post that the Fellows of the college on April 15 had elected instead John Hough, later to be Bishop of Worcester.　Only after an investigation by the Ecclesiastical Commission in June had revealed the complete unsuitability of Farmer was Samuel Parker, Bishop of Oxford, put forward by the King, and by that time the Fellows had gone too far to retrace their steps.

[2] September 4.

senters, whome he bated with liberty of concience, and
with telling them that the desire he had that the test and
the penall lawes should be taken away was for their ease
and security as well as the papists.   However, this looked
very strange, that thos people that soe lately were the most
busy in all Parlaments to take away his right to the crown,
nay, his life too (for it was attempted in one Parlament to
impeach him of high treason, upon the statute of reconcileing himselfe to the Church of Rome), should now find
preference to thos of a Church that had preserved him
against them, not only in Parlament, but in the field.
But all things vale to the true zeale of the Roman Church,
and nothing is longer esteemed or remembred then it is
pro bono ecclesie.

Sept. 20   I recieved his Majestys orders that Colonel Cornwels
regiment quartered at Yorke should march to Hul, to

*   worke at the fortifications of the citadel which was makeing
ther; [1] soe that noe force remained ther but my own company, which made me delay going thether.

[1] Notice of the departure of the regiment was sent by Reresby to Blathwayt in two letters which illustrate the lack of proper discipline prevalent
in the army at this time :

September 23, [16]87.—Sir, Yours and his Majesty's orders for the
march of Colonell Cornwels regiment to Hull were recieved by me, and
they are observed accordingly.   Ther hapned lately an accident which it
is fit to acquaint you with, least it may be misrepresented to you by the
general rumors.   A gentleman (in appearance) calling himselfe a lieutenant
of fusilliers, but not known either by his name or person for such by any
officer or person in this guarrison, being refused some kindness which he
desired from the servant of the inn wher he laid, he endeavoured to obtean
it from her by force ; but she prooveing the stronger made her escape.
The gentleman persues, and meeting another woeman enquired which
way the other was fled.   She denyed to tell him, at which he was soe
angry that he drew his sword and run her into the belly below the navle,
of which if not dead (for I am at present a few miles out of town) it is
believd she can scarce recover.   I am, Sir, Your most humble servant,
J. Reresby.   He afterwards made his escape, notwithstanding all the care
imaginable used to apprehend him.   (B.M. Add. MSS. 9735, f. 20.)

September 30, [16]87.—Sir, The regiment (being hindered for some
days) marched for Hull from Yorke but on Munday last.   They parted
very fair with the town, and paid their quarters.   Since their going, by

* 50/41: William Blathwayt, 13 September 1687.

Was held a private sessions at Doncaster, and on *Sept.* 24
Monday after at Rotherham, by my appointment, wher
an account was taken of such matters as are usuall in such
cases.

My Lord Feathershams page came down post to bring *October* 6
me a letter from his lord, another from my Lord Halifax,   *
both to intimate to me that the King had promessed to doe
something for my Lord Feathersham if he proceeded in
the match proposed at Welbeck, but the quantum was
not named by his Majesty; that his lordship therfore
designed to proceed, provided he might be accepted,
setling his estate at Holnby only in jointure to the lady,
and resserve the 15,000 l. portion to buy land with, but
not to be part of the jointure.

The 7th I went to Welbeck, assured the Duke and 7
Duchesse that this delay in writing by my Lord Feathersham was from noe disrespect, but by reason of his waiting
the Kings answer, which was at last as aforesaid.   But
when I tould the Duchess the other part (for the Duke
left all the terms of treaty to his wife) she would not hear
of it, and positively insisted that the portion should buy
land to be added to the jointure.   That night I made a
little debauch with the Duke.   The next day I returned
and writt letters of answer,[1] which the page carryed back,
in which I tould my Lord plainly it did look more like
interest then love to barter in a case of that nature, and

reason of one of my lieutenants being lame and keeping the hous, and the
other, viz., Lieutenant Flud's, being at London (wher he hath continued
ever since he left the camp without either leave or notice from or to me),
ther is noe commissioned officer in a manner (but myselfe) with the
company. I therfore desire, if Mr. Flud have not the Kings leave for soe
long an absence (especially he never soe much as desireing mine, and haveing writt to him to return, which he doth not answer), that he may be
respited by Mr. Crawford upon the last muster. He may be heard of at
the Naked Boy in Fleet Street. I desire, Sir, also to know if you believe
the regiment or any other force will come to Yorke this winter. I am,
Sir, Your most humble servant, J. Reresby. (*Ibid.* f. 22.)

[1] The letter to Halifax, dated October 8, [16]87, is among the Spencer
MSS.

* 52/8: Feversham, 3 October 1687.

used what reasons I could not to stand upon that if he liked all the rest.

Oct. **11**   The general quarter-sessions for the West Rideing held at Barnsley, wher I assisted. I carryed in nineteen recognisances, gave the charge, and had great civilitys paid me from the justices and other gentlemen of the nighbourhood that came and mett ther. The business lasted near three days.

16   I had an answer of mine from the Earl of Feathersham, wherin he declared the 15,000 l. should be laid out in land and added to Holnby for a jointure to my Lady Margaret. The next day I went to Welbeck and acquainted the Duchesse therwith, who was satisfyed with it, and immediatly writt to my Lord Duke that she thought my Lord Feathersham a fitt match for her daughter, and therfore desired his Grace to concurr with her in it, and to give his consent. I carryed this paper to him, who when he saw it flew into passion, saying he never thought his wife such a fool as to doe it; that this was to begger his daughter; that she was lost for ever; and yet he would subscribe his consent, bycaus he had promessed it, but he would not give her in marriage, nor any more of his estate; and that he would leave the hous when my Lord came to marry his daughter. I was much amazed at this transport. I knew he cared not for the match, haveing a desire to marry her rather to the Duke of Barwick, and being of an unsteady, fickle humour. But when the thing came to him in the very manner that he had prescribd himselfe I could never believe that he would give his consent with his hand, and deny it with his tong. I used all the arguments I could to reconcile him to himselfe and to the match, but to noe purpass. At the last I was something rough, and took my leave in some discontent and returned to Thriberge that night.

†   The next day I writt him a letter wherin I used this expression, that his carriage was certainly not prudent the day before, bid him consider who this lord was, one

* 52/12: Feversham, 13 October 1687.

† 52/13: [Reresby to Newcastle] [ ] October 1687.

of the first men of England for quality, alliance, preferments, vertue, &c., one recommended to him by the
King and with this expression, that what the Duke did to
him he should consider as done to himselfe; that he had
promessed to give his consent if the Duchesse desired it
under her hand, without any such reserve; he had writt
the King word to the same effect, and promessed it to my
Lord Feathersham when he was in the country; that some
ill construction would be made of this proceeding; that it
must look very strange to recieve and make much of my Lord
when he came to aske his daughter in marriage, and to putt
either himselfe or my Lord out of doors when he comes
to marry her, and by his consent under his own hand, that
he should use his hand to subscribe his consent, and deny
it to give her in persuance of it; how would this sound
to the wise part of the world, that he should thus interfere
with himselfe; either he was indiscreet to promiss it, or
not wise to deny to performe it; to be firm and what we
appear is the best character of a great man, and the best
security to their friends and dependents; but if the
trumpet give an uncertain sound, who can prepare themselves to the battle.   In short, for thes and many other
reasons I desired him only to withdrawe thos hasty
expressions of not giveing his daughter in the ceremony
(when he had given her in act), and of going from Welbeck
if my Lord Feathersham came.

He returned me thankes for my letter, recieved it *
patiently, but was not to be mooved. The Duchesse †
writt me word that after I was comd from Welbeck the
Duke came to her and her daughter and used them very
roughly in discours; tould her she was led by her daughter,
and woemen must now be glad of husbands at any rate,
&c., which soe galled the yong lady that she declared
since her father was soe avers to this marriage she would
live single til both father and mother agreed on a husband
for her.

I gave my Lord Feathersham an account of all this *Oct.* 20

* 52/11: Duke of Newcastle, 18 October 1687.

† 52/10: Duchess of Newcastle, 18 October 1687.

proceeding, and tould him if he thought it worth solliciting any more ther was noe way to gain my Lord Duke but to gett the King to continue his titles (in case he died without sons of his own) to my Lord Feathersham and his heirs by the Lady Margaret, and to change his name for Cavendish; for he had, I found, a desire to preserve the names and tytles of his family. But how far too this might operate after such a ferment was very hard to tell.[1]

Great was the successe of the Christians against the Turkes this campania, which ended in the takeing some very considerable towns, Esseck[2] perticularly by the Imperialists, and Castelnovo in Candia[3] by the Venetians.

Oct. 22
*
I had letters from the Duchesse of Newcastle, wherin she complained of the continuance of my Lord Duke's severitys to herselfe and daughters; that she asked leave to goe to London, that he had granted it for herselfe (for upon some warm discourses that passed between them he bad her begon out of doors), but that she would not leave her daughters behind her. She gave me an account of severall other unhappy circumstances of that family, and owned very perticularly the obligations she had to me.

[1] The bitterness which Reresby naturally felt at so ridiculous a result of his efforts is shown in a letter which he wrote to Halifax from Thrybergh on October 19. The afflictions to which he refers are the almost simultaneous deaths of Halifax's brother Henry and his eldest son Lord Eland :

... I am very sorry to hear of the afflictions of your family, and pray God to restoor you to satisfaction in your own which you have soe charitably procured to others. The Duke hath behaved himselfe after soe brutal a manner in the last issue of that matter that I know not how to retaile it to your Lordship without too much trouble to your Lordship at this time, and without some to myselfe. I have drawn his true portrature this post to my Lord Feathersham, wher you may see enough of him ; and noe signpost painter can endure to draw such a figure often over . . . (Spencer MSS.).

[2] On the Drave, commanding the principal bridge across that river. It was abandoned by its garrison and occupied by the Imperialists towards the close of September.

[3] September 20/30.

* 52/14: Duchess of Newcastle, 21 October 1687: The Duke is unmoved by Reresby's intercession. She would rather have him a tiger than a crocodile.

I had one from the Lord of Feathersham in answer to   *
mine, to this purpas (dated October the 22), that the surprize was as great to him as me of my Lord Duke's
proceeding; that he was ever suspicious that he was not
heartily for the match, but that which I had writt to him
was beyond immagination, and soe extraordinary it was
the best for him to say nothing, but to thanke me for all
my trouble.   The thruth is he gave me more expressions
of kindness then it is fitt for me to own for this abortive
work.   He said that the Duke for the future should be
very quiet for him; but he was extreamly concerned for
the Duchesse and my Lady Margaret, but he hoped they
would have more peace when he desisted.   He sent alsoe
a letter inclosed to me for the Duchesse, wherin he
acknowleged the obligations he had to her Grace, &c.

His lordship ended his letter with this, that finding in
a letter of mine to Colonel Oglethorp (which it seems he
showed him) a request to the collonell to speake for a
liveing sopposed to be faln void (called Etton near
Beaverley) for my brother, his lordship had volontorarily
spoaken to the King himselfe in it; the King's answer was
that he was pre-engaged; that soon after he recollected
himselfe, and tould my Lord that he did not know it was
for my brother, that he should be glad to show me any
kindness, for (to use the Kings own words) I was a very
good man, and he would try to find out some other thing
for the other and give this to my brother, with severall
other kind things his Majesty was pleasd to expresse
of me upon this occasion.   But the incombent recovered
for the present, soe that we had little warmth by this sun-
shine at that time.

I had a letter from the Marquis of Halifax by the same   †
post upon the same subject of Welbeck (as he had assisted
to it underhand all along).   One expression of it was this,
that my behaviour had been so clear and free from the
possibility of haveing any part of this ill successe imputed
to me, that it had increased the esteem of thos for me on

* 52/16: Feversham, 22 October 1687.

† 52/50: Halifax, 22 October 1687.

whos behalfe I was willing to undertake the troublesome negotiation.

Oct. 28　I sent my Lord Feathershams letter to Nottingham to the Duchesse, to which place, with much adoe, the Duke had released her with both her daughters from Welbeck in order to their going to London.　The Duchesse writt back to me thus, that she did acknowlege the great civilities and compassion of my Lord Feathersham, but she would give him noe trouble of a letter of thankes, being to be in London the next week, but desired me to perform it for her; that by an unexpected providence the Duke had given her leave to goe, and to take her two daughters with her, but the perticulars of it was too long to write; till she see me in town she would therfore deferr that histery.　She ended her letter with this assurance, that as long as she lived she would esteem me one of thos whom she was most obliged to, and that she would ever be with respect, &c.

The King now putt out severall aldermen that had ever been reputed faithfull and loyall men to the Crown, and had stuck by his interest in the worst of times in the citty of London.　They were Church of England men that were displaced, and thos nonconformists that were putt in their places.　Doctor Hough, President of Maudlyn College in Oxford, was putt out by certain visitors appointed by the King for that purpas, for being elected, though according to the statutes of the college, yet contrary to the Kings *mandamus*, which had recommended the Bishop of Oxford to that office.　The doctor refused to quitt til he was forced out of the college,[1] and appealed from the visiters to the King in Westminster Hall.

Mr. Bankes, parson of Hoton Roberts[2] (who had been my chaplyn for some time), desired me to write to a friend for him to speake to a King for a prebandary likely

---

[1] October 25.

[2] Robert Banks, appointed rector of Hooton Roberts in 1678.　He was a prebendary of York from 1695 to his death in 1715.

* 52/18: Duchess of Newcastle, 29 October 1687.

† sic. The word 'king' has been written over another.

to fall void at Yorke. I made it my request to the Duke
of Norfolk to that purpas, who spoake to his Majesty
and obteaned his promess against it fell void.

The corporation of Doncaster sent over their solicitor *Nov.2*
with a letter from their Maior, declareing that they had   *
consented to an address to his Majesty, and desired me
to recommend the bearer of it to some person of interest
above to present it to the King.[1] I returnd Mr. Maior
and the corporation thankes for their application to me
rather then to others of greater quality and interest then
I was, and recomended them to the Earl of Feathersham.
I writ his lordship word the same day that the Duchess
of Newcastle and his mistresse the Lady Margaret were
upon their journey to London (and that when the mountain would not come to Mehomet, Mehomet went to the
mountain).

I came to Yorke with my family. I stayed ther till 5
December the 2nd, in which time severall things hapned.
One was that I had a letter from one Lawson, a priest,   †
wherin he gave me notice that the King haveing given
him his hous, the Manor of St. Marys in Yorke, for the
honour of God and the good of his people, he hoped that
the same civility would be practiced towards him which I
used to others, in giveing him a free and easy possession
of it. I answered that it was part of my commission
wherby I was governor of the place; that he did not thinke
that I would devest myselfe of it by my own authority;
I esteemed the Kings bounty, and was too proud of his
service to doe that, but if his Majesty did command it I
had nothing to say but to obay; only I hoped that his
Majesty, if he gave it away (and it was but just in him to
endeaver it), would give me some equivalent for it.

Severall letters passed between us. At last I heard
from the Earl of Feathersham that it was absolutely   ‡
granted. Lawson putt me in hopes that the King would   ‡

---

[1] The Doncaster address is printed in the *London Gazette* for November
21-24.

* 50/60: Richard Fagram Mayor of Doncaster, 2 November 1687; 50/47: T.
Martine, 19 November 1687; 50/49: T. Martine, 12 November 1687.

† 51/25: Nathaniel Johnston, 18 December 1687; 50/54: Same, 22 November
1687.

‡ 33/15: Feversham, 26 November 1687.

consider it to me one way or other, and writt word of severall kind things the King said of me. December the 17th he comes down to Yorke and claims the possession, which it being to noe purpas to contest I ordered my houskeeper to give him, but he left it again for the present till I could send order to remoove my goods. The clear profits, besides the use of the hous for myselfe and friends, grass and hay for my horses whilst I stayed in town, was about forty pounds per annum.

After this I did not expect that the rest would continue long after, for the King caused the lord lieutenents of most if not of all countys of England to call togather all their deputy lieutenents and the justices of the peace, and to aske them thes three questions:

1. In case the King should call a Parlament and they should be chosen of it, would they give their voats to take away the test and the penal laws?

2. Would they give their voats for the chooseing of such members as they believed would be for the takeing them away?

3. Would they live peaceably with such as dissented from them in religion, as good Christians ought to doe?

Severall lord lieutenents that refused to execute this order were turned out, and papists putt in their places; and the deputy lieutenants and justices of the peace that did not give a satisfactory answer were generally displaced. This was indeed putting the thing too farr, and the wonder of all men to what purpas it was done. For what answer could a man give that was to be a member of Parlament, till he heard the reasons and debates of the Hous? And who could tell the temper or intention of him that was voted for, til he came into the Hous? And if men had a mind to decieve the King, how easy (nay, how likely) was it for them to pretend to be of one judgement now and of another when they were of the Hous? Besides, it struck at the very foundation of Parlaments to pre-engage men before they came ther, wher they were to be allowed the

freedome both of their speech and judgements. The
most generall answer that was given by Protestants of the
Church of England was this, that they would give their
voats soe, if of the Hous, as the reasons of the debate
directed them; that they would voat for such as they
thought would doe so; and that they would live quietly
with all men as good Christians and loyall subjects.

Ther was about this time great remooves of officers,
military and civil, and most corporations were purged of
their Church of England aldermen, and papists or dissenters putt in their places.

The Christians continued their success against the
Turkes both in Greece and Hungary. Agria and severall
other towns were surrendered to the Emperor, Athens
and others to the Venetians.[1] The Turkish army
mutinyed, strangled the Grand Visier,[2] and marched
towards Constantinople, threatning to lay aside the Grand
Senior and to set up his brother.[3]

Whilst I stayed at Yorke I had all the civility which
I could desire from that citty. They gave me severall
entertainments; I dined twice at the Lord Maiors, once
at the sherifs at his feast, which was very extraordinary,
besides severall private invitations. I had word sent
from the citizens of all quarters of the town that if I would
stand they would choos me one of their citizens in Parlament, whenever it should please the King to call one. I
thanked them, but gave noe answer whether I would
stand or not.

Some souldiers in my company committed a robbery,
and three others mutinyd upon the guard and broake
the leg of the sergiant that comanded. I gave the King
an account of it. This was after I left the town, for my

---

[1] Athens was taken on September 19/29, Agria on November 18/28.

[2] Solyman Pasha.

[3] Mohammed IV, whose long reign had begun in 1648, was deposed
on October 29/November 8 and his brother Solyman II put in his
place.

first lieutenant was but a bad officer and infirm, my second was absent from the guarrison.[1]

Dec. 3 I sett forward for Thriberge, laid at Campsal by the way, wher my wife fell il of the gout. However she travelled the next day, but continued some time il of it after she came home.

Lying seperate from my wife the night I came home (she not being wel), by the carelesness of servants I laid in a wett bed, occasioned by the dropping of a gutter into the room, which gave me a gripeing of the gutts, and afterwards the gout in my knees and feet, which held me three weeks before I came down.[2] But then it pleased

---

[1] News of what had happened was sent to Reresby by his second lieutenant in a letter from which it is apparent that that officer had returned to the company :

Yorke, December the 19th, 1687.—Sir, This morning Mr. Butler and the rest of his family set forward for London. I am sorry my first letter to you in his absence must informe you of a mutiny that happin'd in the guard room, wherein Serjant Baldock was like to be barborusly murther'd by Gascoine, Blunt, and Frank. Serjant Baldocks leg is broke ; Serjant Doleman was knocked downe ; they likewise threatn'd us commission officers. I referr you to Serjant Colliers letter, wherein are the particulars more at large. I pray, Sir, lett me receave a letter from you by the next, that I may know what your pleasure is shall bee don in this matter. This is all at present from, Sir, Your most obedient servant, Ralph Fludd. Mr. Baldock is just now at the Manner House with Father Lawson. (B.M. Add. MSS. 9735, f. 26.)

[2] This illness came at an inopportune moment, as it prevented Reresby from dealing personally with the mutiny in his company. It is referred to in his report to Blathwayt, enclosing apparently the accounts both of Lieutenant Flood and of Sergeant Collier, in which he asks for instructions in dealing with the mutineers :

December 20, [16]87. Thriberg.—Sir, Hospitality being much laid aside of late in thes parts of this time of the year, which dissatisfyeth the common sort of people and makes them apt to dispond, I left Yorke very lately to observe my constant custome of keeping an opon Christmas here, but fell soe very ill the next day of the gripeing of the gutts (which hath since turned to a rhumatisme) that I have kept my bed ever since, and am forced to writ this to you by another hand.

It is to desire you would pleas to know his Majesties pleasure concerning the contents of the inclosed, and till I receive it I have committed the three mutanears into the county geole as a justice of peace, haveing noe other

God to restoor me to health and to enable [me] to keep a
Christmas amongst my tenents and nighbours, though
something later then ordinary.   I pray God I may be
sensible of this and other deliverences of the same kind
for the time I have yet to live here.

I had the Kings order that the souldiers that mutiny'd *Dec.* 30
of my company should be tryed by a councel of warr soe
soon as Colonel Cornwels regiment returned to York,
which was ordered then to return from Hul to that
guarrison.   *

The regiment returned to their quarters in Yorke the
29 of January.   I sent orders in writing to Colonel
Pursel, lieutenant-colonel of the regiment, that the guards
should be the same and all other things in the same manner
as when they left that guarrison, which the lieutenant-
collonel writ back word should be complyed with in every
perticular.

A court martial sitting at Yorke upon the three mutineers according to his Majestys order, the sentence was
soe very severe[1] that I acquainted the King with it, not

safe place for that purpass.   The thruth is the sergant had noe right to
demaind the coales of the main guard to make himselfe a fire in another
roome.   The King allowes but one fire to the guard wher ther is noe
comissioned officer ; and though thes men stood upon their right after a
very ill manner, yet they are very good souldierlike men.   If they must
be tryed by a court martiall, either officers must come from Hull or they
must be sent thether ; and how safe it may be to trust them under the
guard of their fellow souldiers may be doubtfull.

Wee have five more of my company now in the citty goale, three for
robbing a man in the night of three pounds, and two for breaking a hous
and stealing corn out of a hous, which they have confessed, soe that some
punishment must be inflicted to prevent further disorders.   It might be
convenient (if you thinke it soe) to moove his Majestie that wee may have
a company of addition from Hull till thes matters be a litle setled, and
till such orders be observed as I shall receive from you, that am, Sir, Your
most humble servant, J. Reresby.   (B.M. Add. MSS. 9735, f. 24.)

[1] The decision of the court was reported by Purcell in an undated letter
addressed to Reresby at Thrybergh :

Sir, According to your orders wee held a court marshall upon these
three soldiers that mutinyed upon the guard.   I shewed the officers your

* 50/63: William Blathwayt, 24 December 1687; 50/71: Same, 19 January
1687/8.

presumeing to mitigate it without his leave, the court haveing sate by his own appointment.[1] But the King would not have it moderated in the least.

Jan. 8
[1687/8] The Maior of Doncaster sent a present of a cagg of sturgion and four dozen of bottles of wine with this message, that he and his bretheren intended to dine with me the next day, to thanke me for my kindnes to their corporation. Ther was at that time a great difference amongst them about choice of their town clerke. The recorder, Sergiant Bointon, and some of the body were for one, the Maior and the rest for another. And besides they were in fear of being many of them put out, to the end that such men might be put into power as would themselves, and influence others to, voat for the takeing away the test and the penal lawes.

The next day, when I should have recieved them, I fel ill again of the gout, and was forced to keep my bed, not

letter that you would not have them cashierd ; but every one of them will have it in that theire opinion is that the said soldiers should never beare armes in his Majesties service. Theire sentence is eache of them to have forty lashes att the maine garde the first day and to run the gantlet through Collonel Cornewal regiment the same day, and to have twenty lashes three tymes a week for three weekes and to run the gantlet once every week dureing that tyme. This punishment is next doore to hanging, which they deserved ; but you know you have the power when you come heither to abate what you thinke fitt of it, though it be verey heard to doe it considering theire offence. I am heartily sorry for your indisposition, and soe are all the officers heare, and in particular, Sir, Your most humble faithful servant, J. A. Purcell. (B.M. Add. MSS. 9735, f. 44.)

[1] The reference presumably is to Reresby's letter to Blathwayt enclosing Purcell's report :

Thriberge, January the 14, [16]87.—Sir, Being again confined to my chamber by a relaps, I sent the Kings commands concerning the tryall of the three mutineers to Lieutenant Colonell Purcell. You wil find the performance of them by the inclosed, and the severe sentence, if any can be soe upon thos that deserve it soe notoriously. I shall not therfore undertake to mitigate it, or to recieve them again into pay, without his Majestys leave, though they are the choicest men in the company, and almost dead before their punishment through the sence of their fault. I desire I may recieve your answer to this by the first opportunity, that am, Sir, Your very humble servant, J. Reresby. (B.M. Add. MSS. 9735, f. 14.)

only that day but eight days after, and came not down stairs of twenty days. It took me in my right ankle, went into three places of my foot, changed afterwards into as many in the other, from thence into both knees, and performed this cours in less then ten days and without much pain. I kept the milke dyet for three weekes, and recovered pritty well, but continued weake in my knees especially some time after.

The Maior coming according to promess, and being with his company (which were above twenty in nomber) wel entertained, desired me to take them into my protection, and to helpe the corporation (by appearing for them both at home and above) from ruine, which was designed by the malice of some il men amongst them. I tould him that as to their body in general I should be glad to serve them, either here or at Court, with the little interest I had, but to take any party I should not doe that, but advised them to agree their differences amongst themselves.

The King began to abate his being soe pressing for the takeing of the test and the penall lawes, but yet the lords lieutenents continued to know the opinions of the justices of the peace and deputy lieutenants in most countys, but with little success.

The French King's difference with the Pope [1] grew very high at this time about the matter of takeing away the antient privileges of embassadors quarters in Rome, which though all other Christian princes submitted to, the King of France would not, for the which the French embassador [2] sent to demand his masters right in that perticular of the Pope, was refused audience, and being after something pressing, was declared excommunicated. The Cardinals were forbidden to visit him as an embassador, and the church of St. Lewis at Rome (the reputed parochial church of all the French ther), wher the said

[1] Innocent XI.

[2] Henri-Charles de Beaumanoir, Marquis de Lavardin.

embassador and his attendants went to midnight mass on Christmas Day, was also interdicted for admitting them to partake of their devotions. Upon notice of this to the French King the Parlament of Paris was assembled, wher the atturney-general[1] drew up an appeale from thes proceedings at Rome to the next generall council, the supream and infallible tribunal of the Church, setting forth that the Pope is not infallible; that he hath noe power to excomunicate princes or to use his priestly authority in temporal matters; that the power of the keyes was abused when it was imployed to serve secular ends; that the Pope had not only acted otherwais then became the vicar of St. Peter in this perticular, but also in refuse-ing his buls to such as his Majesty had named and recom-mended to his Holiness to fil vacant bishopricks in that kingdome, only bycaus they did not own the Pope to be infallible, or as the Italian doctors call him universal monarke, wherby ther were noe fewer then thirty-five vacant and unsupplyed at that day; that this refusal ought to be remedyed by such means as had formerly been used in the Church on like occasions, which was by calling national or provinciall councils.

After this and much more said to the same effect by the atturney-general, he withdrew and was admitted an appellant as of the abuse of the said bul and ordinance by the Parlament, which declared the same to be void, and forbad the disperseing of them within that kingdome, and ordered that the King should be humbly intreated to use his authority to maintain the immunities of his embassadors quarters at Rome, as also to call provinciall councils, or nationall ones, or an assembly of the great men, to remedy the disorders which the long vacancies of archbishopricks and bishopricks had produced, and lastly that his Majesty would prohibit al commerce with the Court of Rome and the sending mony thither. This looked very strange to England, that when it was sopposed

[1] Denis Talon.

that Italy and France were soe nearly linked togather, the one was endeavouring to submit its selfe to the Popes authority, whilst the other was withdrawing itselfe from it.

About this time my Lord Langdale [1] was made governor of Hull in the stead of my Lord Plimoth, lately dead, and my Lord Fairfax of Gilling lord lieutenant of the North Rideing, both papists; my Lord Mougrave was lord lieutenant of the East.[2]

Jan. 20 I heard of great disorders committed in Yorke by the souldiers ther; but my lameness would not allowe me to goe to give order in it, which troubled the citty.

29 Was a day appointed by proclamation of thanksgiveing for the Queen's finding herselfe with quick child.

I recieved the Kings leave to goe to London as soon as my health would allowe.

Feb. 3 My Lord Maior of Yorke chose that day, being that of his Majestys accession to the Crown, to invite all the officers of the guarrison to dinner.[3] The person com'd in some few days before for the ensuing year was one Rains,[4] an atturney, who was keeper of the county court by my appointment when I was high sherif of Yorkshire, a place of considerable advantage; and yet he was my greatest opposer when I stood for citizen of Yorke in the last Parlament. However now findeing himselfe in a manner perticular in that citty as to want of respect towards me, he performed this respect to the officers in a great measure upon my account, and sent a messenger on purpass with a very civil letter to invite me to this intertainment; but not being perfectly recovered I excused myselfe from going.

---

[1] Marmaduke Langdale, the second Baron, whose father had been prominent among the Royalist commanders in the north during the Civil War.

[2] He had taken the place of the Duke of Somerset in October.

[3] February 6, the day of the King's accession, was actually the day of the feast. The date in the margin refers to the Mayor's admission to office.

[4] Thomas Raynes.

* 33/18: Halifax 7 February 1687/8.

That day one of the gunners dischargeing one of the great gunns on Clifford Tower Hill (the cartrige takeing fire as he was putting it into the canon) was blown into the ditch, and soe hurt that both his arms were directed by the chirurgien to be cutt of the next day, of which he soon after dyed.[1]

I was pritty wel recovered, soe as to be able to goe with a staff, and was gott down stairs some ten days, though I found myselfe weake in the parts wher I had had this running gout or rhumatisme, but especially in my knees; when about the 13 day of February, ventring too soon, I relapsed a second time. It began in my right knee, then fell to my foot on the same side, then to my left knee, wher I only suffered pain for one night, but a weakeness long after, that left knee being disjointed. It returned after again to my right foot, and soe went of in eight days. I kept to the milke dyet during that time, and one week longer, by which time I was able to goe with the helpe of a cane or stick, for which God be praised.

I recieved orders for my company to march from Yorke to Portsmouth, ther to joine the rest of the Duke of Barwicks regiment, wher it laid in quarters all winter, in order to their marching togather to the next camp,

Feb. 13 (margin)

28 (margin)

---

[1] Little is added to this by the account which Reresby sent to Blathwayt :

Thriberge, near Doncaster, February 12, 1687[/8].—Sir, I yet continue soe weake that I have not been able to goe to Yorke ; but I had an account that the three mutineers had their full punishment, and were whipt out of the guarrison on Saturday last. On Monday last, being the day of his Majestys accession to the Crown, it was ther solomnly observed. My Lord Maior invited all the officers to dinner ; the regiment and my company were drawn out in the afternoon, and gave severall vollies of small shott. But after that, Lieutenant Colonel Purcell haveing it seems a mind to have three or four great gunns discharged that remain stil since the burning of Clifford's Tower, the gunner fired the cartrige by chance as he was putting it into the canon, which blew him down into the Tower dich, and soe broake his arms that they were forced to cutt them off, soe that it is feared he cannot recover. I am, Sir, Your most faithfull humble servant, J. Reresby. (B.M. Add. MSS. 9735, f. 16.)

* 50/66: Edward Baldock, 21 January 1687/8.

† 50/79: Wm. Blathwayt, 21 February 1687/8.

which the King had appointed to be formd at Hownsley Heath as he had down the year before.

My Lord of Oxford, first earl of the realm (but low in his fortune), being commanded by the King to use his interest in his lieutenancy for the takeing off the penall laws and the test, tould the King plainly he could not persuade that to others which he was avers to in his own concience, for which the King took from him his regiment of hors, and gave it to the Duke of Barwick.

At this time dyed Sir Thomas Slingsby, who had a troop in that regiment which he bought for 2,000 l., which the King denyed to his son, though cornet in it, but gave that also to the Duke of Barwick.[1]

I had notice by the deputy recorder of Yorke by an expresse that the lieutenant-colonel comanding in my absence had dealt very severely and illegally with the cittizens, and that the occasion of it was a little tumult raised on Shrove Teusday in this manner. That day being one of great liberty for boys and apprentices to play and throw at cocks, some of them playing near a hous in the Minster Yeard disturbed the company in it. The master comes out, strikes one of the boys, and knocks down another. They, getting some of their companions togather, throw stones at the man, and accidentally breake the window of a popish chapell that was in his hous. He being a Roman Catholick presently makes his religion the caus of the quarrell, sends to the lieutenant-colonel for two files of musketeers, who presently sends them, being of his own persuasion, and very ready to espous the dispute upon that foot. At the comming of the

March 1

*

---

[1] This paragraph is scarcely fair to James. The Duke of Berwick, although colonel of the regiment, had not, as was customary at that time, a troop of his own in it. On the death of Sir Thomas Slingsby, therefore, it was only natural that he should be appointed to command the vacant troop. Henry Slingsby, eldest son and successor of Sir Thomas, who had previously been cornet in the troop commanded by David Lloyd, was compensated by being appointed captain-lieutenant under Berwick (Dalton, *English Army Lists*, ii. 120, 149).

* 53/4: George Prickett, 1 March 1687/8.

souldiers the boys disperse, some of them are taken, and some citizens (being by as spectators but not concernd in the matter) to the nomber of fiveteen.   The souldiers carry them to the main guard, ty them neck and heels and make them ride the wooden hors, not carrying them at all to the Lord Maior (which ought to have been done, being citizens) to be punished according to lawe.   And an ensign, one Oard,[1] struck a cittizen in the presence of my Lord Maior.   The lieutenant-collonel's account was little different as to the fact, but altered as to the occasion, for he said that some priests had informed him the night before that they heard the rabble intended to pull down that hous and the chappell, which made him act more severely; but I truly believe the uproar was merely accidentall.

I gave the King a perticular account of the thing as it appeared most likely from the recorder; the lieutenant-colonel gave another himselfe.   But at the same time I excused the souldiers in this, that if they did transgresse something in the method of punishing, the citizens deserved it a little for their former offences in this kind, for they rose in the same place and on the same day in my Lord Fretwels time, and had near killed Doctor Lake (since Bishop of Peterbrough)[2] bycaus he checked them for makeing a noise in the time of devine service, and they endeavered to pull down his hous that stood in the Minster Yeard.   Another time they fell upon my company ther at the funerall of my Lady Strafford, as I have before taken notice in the proper place.

March 7
*   My company quartered at Doncaster in their march to Portsmouth.   I was not able to meet them, soe the officers came to Thriberge to recieve mony and orders.

[1] George Ord, ensign in Colonel Cornwall's regiment of foot (Dalton, *English Army Lists*, ii. 104).

[2] John Lake, who had come into collision with the citizens of York while Archdeacon of Cleveland, never held the see of Peterborough, but was at this time Bishop of Chichester.   He was later one of the seven bishops who opposed James's ecclesiastical policy, and was committed to the Tower.

* 53/6: Edward Baldock, 29 February 1687/8; 54/2: William Blathwayt, 6 March 1687/8; 54/3: James Purcell, 11 March 1687/8; 54/5: George Prickett, 12 March 1687/8.

The judges appointed for the northeren circuit went the same day from thence towards Yorke to begin the assizes.

I then recieved notice from Colonel Oglethorp that this unruly regiment of Colonel Cornwels would be sent to Barwick, and five companys of his regiment would come to relieve them at York very speedily.   I call it unruly bycaus I had great complaints of their disorders.   This piece of a letter was sent me by a friend: We have had sad worke with the souldiers; they are soe insolent that they neither spare age nor sex, insomuch that a man cannot be safe in his own hous, and if abroad after nine a clock he cannot without a fee avoid haveing the guard room for his lodgeing, with severall other insupportable injuries.

I had notice by another letter from Colonel Oglethorp *March* 8 that the King tould him ther had been a ryot at Yorke, that he had some account of it from Lieutenant-Colonel Purcel, but had yet recieved none from me, which he wondered at, bycaus I used to be extream punctuall and exact.   The lieutenant-colonel, being upon the place, had writ a post before me of this matter, but the King suspended his judgement till he heard also from me, which he did the post after.

The Secretary of Warr writ to me thus, that the King 9 utterly disapprooved of the military punishment inflicted upon the cittizens, for when they comitted faults they ought to be turned over to the civil magistrate to be dealt with according to law; and as for the officer that struck the citizen, the King comanded me to inquire more perticularly into the fact, and to return his name that he might have his due punishment.   Soe little was the King pleased with this insolent proceeding.

The same day I had his Majestys commands by the hand of my Lord Sunderland (Lord President)[1] to examin a stationer in Yorke, wher he had some pamflets reflecting upon the goverment which he had vented and sould;

[1] The words within the brackets are added in the margin.

* 53/1: Stephen Thompson, 10 March 1687/8; 54/6: William Blathwayt, 7 March 1687/8.

but not being then able to goe to Yorke I sent the letter to one of the judges then ther, desireing him to perform that service, and to give the King an account of it, as I did wher I had lodged the thing and the reason of it.

I had a souldier of my company that played very wel of the bagpipes, who by the practice of my own lieutenant and the lieutenant-colonel, Purcel, was persuaded to goe into Colonel Cornwels regiment in exchange for another. I could not suffer such tricks, and therfore though the company was as far as Warsup upon their march without him, I writt a severe letter to the lieutenant-colonel to deliver my man by my servant, who brought him away, and I restoored him to the company. The lieutenant-colonel writ a very submissive letter disowning the thing to have been managed by him, but by another captain in the regiment and my own lieutenant, who being but a man of weake parts was not improbable.

March 12   It pleased God that I fell down again of the goutish humour of which I was soe lately recovered. It seized me in the most sensible part, my weake knee. I had pain of it that day and the night following, but not soe much as before. I kept to milke five days, rose the fourth day from bed, and gott down stairs that day sevenight.

Haveing had a return, both from the magistrates and the lieutenant-colonel, of the officers (one Ensign Ord's) carriage in strikeing a citizen before my Lord Maior, I thought it the most equall way to send both up togather to the Secretary to be laid before the King. But before it was recieved, upon the Lord Maior's and the aldermen's own representation of it to my Lord President, I had order from his Majesty to direct Mr. Ord to be confined and suspended til the Kings pleasure was further known, which I imediately sent orders to the lieutenant-colonel to see executed.[1]

---

[1] Trouble with the soldiers continued, however, as Reresby informed Blathwayt :

Thriberge, March the 22, 1687/8.—Sir, I have sent orders for the

* 54/8: Richard Lambert, 10 March 1687/8.

† 54/2: William Blathwayt, 6 March 1687/8; 54/4: Reresby to Mrs Blathwayt, 14 March 1687/8 (copy); 54/5: George Prickett, 12 March 1687/8. The citizen concerned was Lewis Wood, a barber.

I had an account that it was done.   *March* 14

Five companys of Colonel Oglethorps regiment 24
marched into Yorke, and the eight remaining companys
of Colonel Cornwels regiment marched out the Monday 26
following.

About this time the Earl of Burlinton gave up his
commission of Lord Lieutenant of the West Rideing
into his Majestys hands, and he gave it to my Lord
Thomas Howard, only brother to the Duke of Norfock,
a zealous papist, which method of placeing successors
of that persuasion the King had followed in most lieuten-
ancies in England as they became vacant.

1688

I recieved a letter from Mr. Beaumont, brother and *April* 2
heir to my Lord Beaumont, querry to the King, and
lieutenant-colonel to the Duke of Barwicks regiment of
foot, part of which was verbatim in thes words: About
a week since, being a hunting with the King, I heard Sir
Theophilus Oglethorp talkeing to the King of you, which
made me the more intent; and that you may know your
friends at Court and take notice of it, I heard him speake
much for your service and with great respect for you,
insoemuch that the King concluded the discours saying
you was a very good man, of great courage and good
sence; I was not remiss in giveing you my voat.   As this

confineing and suspending of Ensign Oard.   Lieutenant Collonel Purcelle
I presume made you acquainted that two souldiers of that regiment about
twelve a clock on Saturday night last had killed a citizen in the street.   The
souldiers being apprehended were tryed by the judges the day they went
out of town.   They denyed the fact, till, the evidence being very clear, the
jury brought them in guilty, and then one of them confessed he had
committed the murder and would have excused his partner.   The judge
gave judgement of death upon both.   I am, Sir, Your most humble
servant, J. Reresby.   The Lieutenant Collonel I percieve is comming up,
for he sent me word he would be here in his way on Fryday next.   (B.M.
Add. MSS. 9735, f. 28.)

was a very generous and worthy act in thes gentlemen to speake soe kindely of a distant friend, and of one soe little deserveing it either in itselfe or from them, soe it was an everlasting obligation upon me from his Majesty to honour me with such a character, which with that little that I am I shall ever own to soe good a master with my best and just services.

April 2   As this gave me some comfort I was mortified the same day by a fift return of the same gout or humour into my left knee. That night I had some pain, and soe the next day but with more moderation then formerly. I kept my bed two days, and the fourth day I came down stairs, though thes ofton returns made me very lame. I continued, however, to take the Jesuists barke or pouder,[1] which I began to take a fortnight before.

5   I had letters from my Lord Hunsden, lieutenant-colonel to Sir Theophilus Oglethorp at Yorke, of the now quiet condition of the guarrison. He was then com'd down from London to comand the five companys of that regiment then ther. Five companies of my Lord Mongummeries[2] regiment marched the 4th into that guarrison.

15   I by Gods mercy continued soe wel (takeing still the cortix) that I ventured to goe to Yorke in two days in my coach. The same day[3] five companys that were comd of my Lord Mongommeries regiment into Yorke the 4th instant marched out, and the eight remaining companies of Colonel Oglethorps marched in, soe that the whole guarrison then consisted of that entire regiment, being thirteen companies. The officers were all civil gentlemen, but the souldiers had committed some disorders. One had wounded his landlord, another had beaten a citizen and causd a great disturbance in the street, another had

[1] Quinine, the use of which had only recently become common.

[2] William Herbert, Viscount Montgomery, son and heir of the first Marquis of Powis.

[3] Presumably April 17, Reresby having taken two days on the road.

been very insolent to his officer. I called a council of warr, wher their respective punishments were appointed.

My Lord Hunsden desired leave to goe to Durham, *April* 18 and went. We had some contraversie about the method which I ordered to be observed for the paying of quarters in that guarrison, which had very much suffered by the neglect of officers formerly quartered ther in that perticular, but we parted good friends, for my Lord found that I was not worded out of anything, or to be persuaded to depart from that I once resolved to have done in persuance of my duty according to right.[1]

[1] That this question of the payment of quarters was causing serious trouble is shown by another of Reresby's letters to Blathwayt :

April 18, Yorke, [16]88.—Sir, Soe soon as I was able to moove I came to this place, wher I found things in good order, and consequently few complaints of the men now in guarrison, which is only Collonel Oglethorps regiment, his eight companys marching in yesterday, and the five of my Lord Montgomeries going out at the same time. I shall carefully observe his Majestys orders last recieved except in the perticular of Ensign Oard, who had taken off his own suspension before I came to town, and went norwards to the regiment on Monday was fortnight.

Sir, findeing the matter of paying the quarters of late more then usually contraverted in this guarrison, and the clamour greater, it being soe great a pass, and few going this way that leave not some debts, I desire to know his Majestys plesure if governors be to take the same care formerly ordered for paying of quarters and certifying accordingly in case the souldiers recieve duely subsistance from their officers, and that notice be given by beat of drum and by the civil magistrate to give noe credit to souldiers. I confess I always tooke the said publique notice to be a sufficient warning for not trusting at large (or out of quarters), but thought it was the duty of officers not only to pay the souldiers, but to see it applyed to the satisfying of quarters as far as the 3s. would extend, to which purpass it hath been customary here to send an officer or sergiant to the quarters of their respective men every week before the pay day to see the mony imployed to that use, and I have found a very good effect by it.

Now I am tould his Majesty hath declared himselfe that he dispenseth with this caution, and that ther is noe stoppage of pay in the office whether officers obtean certificates or not from the gouvernors or magistrates, which I the rather believe bycaus certificates are very seldome desired. But, Sir, I am not to trust reports til I hear from you, and I desire you would inform me by the first opportunity, that am, Sir, Your most humble servant, J. Reresby. (B.M. Add. MSS. 9735, f. 30.)

April 22   Being St. George his day,[1] I drew out the whole regiment to exercize. By message I and my Lord Maior had some dispute about quarters and other things, soe as I did not visit him whilst I stayd. I putt the town into as good order as I could in that time, and had the thankes and visits of the most considerable men and citizens and clergie, who were desirous to know if I intended to stand for the next Parlament that they might serve me, but I neither answered affermatively nor negatively.

After I had performed what I had recieved in command from the King (except takeing off the suspension and confinement of Ensign Oard, who had left the guarrison contrary to his duty before he was restoord, of which I gave the King an account), and haveing a second time recieved leave from his Majesty to goe to London, I went

24 from Yorke the 24th to Pontefract, wher the generall quarter-sessions began that day for the West Rideing of Yorkeshire. Ther were four-and-twenty justices of the peace of the principall gentlemen of the country togather, the West Rideing haveing not been yet examined as to their disposition of takeing away the test and the penal laws as the East and North Rideings had been before, wher the prime of the gentry in both had been put out of commission of justice of peace and deputy lieutenants for declareing themselves in the negative, and ordinary persons both as to quality and estates (most of them dissenters) had been putt in their room.[2]

25   I returned to Thriberge, continuing still to gett more strenth, wher I began to prepare for my journey to London.

The day I came home the popish justices, in nomber six, and Sir John Bointon, the King's sergiant (who aspired, I presume, to be made a judge), mooved an address to be signd and presented to his Majesty of thankes for

[1] St. George's day is April 23.

[2] The answers given by the magistrates of the three ridings to James's inquisition are printed in *Yorkshire Archæological Journal*, vol. v.

his late indulgence for liberty of concience,[1] not only from the justices ther, but the two grand jurys. But neither any of the justices but thos I named (and one Mr. Bull), nor any of the grand jurys would joine in signing the address. However the Roman Catholicks and thos two gentlemen sent it up, subscribed by themselves, as the act of the whole sessions. By such acts as thes the King was much deceaved as to the opinion of his subjects concerning the indulgence, three or four men in divers places pretending to represent the thoughts of a whole corporation or county.

The first battallion consisting of five companies of my Lord Dunbartons regiment[2] marched into Yorke, and six companys of Colonel Oglethorps marched out.[3]   *May* 1

[1] The second Declaration of Indulgence, dated April 27, was issued at this time.

[2] More commonly known by this time as the Royal Regiment ; later the Royal Scots.

[3] As May 1 was a Tuesday, the following letter, in which Reresby continues his correspondence with Blathwayt regarding the payment of quarters for the troops in his garrison, must be dated a day too late:

May 2, [16]88, Thriberge.—Sir, As to the first part of yours recieved lately, I shall leave it to you whether you thinke it convenient the King should know Mr. Oards manner of leaveing the guarrison (when under a confinement and suspension by his Majestys own order) or not. For Lieutenant Collonel Purcel, he gave me notice that he intended for London.

The copies of the orders you sent me give me answer to some part of my doubts, but not all, for if that order of the 30 [October, 16]85 be yet in force, wherin the payment of quarters, as wel as the payment of private souldiers to that purpas, is soe strictly enjoined, and all governors, &c., be to take perticular care in it, I concieve it implys that governors have liberty to use such means as they thinke most expedient to effect it ; and if that of sending an officer weekly to know how the account stands between the souldier and his quarters be one, they may order it to be observed. But, Sir, this or some such method seems nescessary to me, not from choice, but that the Kings intention of the souldiers applying their pay to the purpas to which it [is] given may be observed ; for if you make a distinction betwixt a volontary trusting in quarters and a compulsary, the first of which you say is at the landlords peril and the second is not to be suffered, how must the governor make the difference ? If by complaint of landlords,

May 3   The second batallion of Lord Dunbartons entered into that guarrison, and the second of Colonel Oglethorps marched out. The officers (several of them) visited me at Thriberge in their march.

7   Was the petit sessions for licences of alehouses at Rotherham, wher Mr. Hansby (a Roman Catholick justice) tould me that the King was now convinced that he had been il advised in putting the question soe far concerning mens inclinations to take away the test and the penall lawes; that he did intend to putt some justices out and to admitt others, but not by that method, but by informing himselfe from such as he knew were true to his service how they stood affected as to liberty of concience; and that he had perticular order from my Lord Thomas Howard, who had it from the King, to advise first with me in that matter. I tould him it was certainly of disadvantage to his Majestys service the method lately taken, most of the principal gentlemen for estates and interest in their countrys being therby thrust out of imployment; but this would proove a worke of as much difficulty and falacy, noe man being able to give an account of another mans heart; nay, it was very hard in that perticular for a man to give one

many we find are afraid to doe [it] at the first comming of souldiers, and all doe it at the last, when they are going to march.

When this comes to be examined, the souldier confesseth he owes mony to his landlord, but the trust was volontary. The landlord pleads that it was forced, or he was cheated into it by promesses. Which way soever it be, the pay is all gone ; the quarters are thus left unpaid. The officer expects the governor should certifie that they are satisfyed, or thinkes he is hardly used if it be refused. If he doe, the town thinkes him not just, and a great clamour follows upon it. All which might be easily prevented by such inspection by some person weekly appointed by the commandant of each company to see the subsistance imployed to its proper and intended use. For thes reasons I would know whether it may be thought reasonable that I still persue the usuall method in our guarrison.

Ther are six of Sir Theophilus Oglethorps companys march out of Yorke on Teusday (this present day), and the other seven on Thursday next. Thos of the Royall Regiment are expected in thos very dʒvs. I am, Sir, Your most humble servant, J. Reresby. (B.M. Add. MSS. 9735, f. 32.)

of his own; for either he was to be a Parlament man, or he was not; if he was, noe man could honestly say how he would voat til he came ther; and if he was not, noebody could tell what they would be for till the meeting of their representatives in Parlament, on whos result they were to rely and to be concluded; not but I believed most men were now convinced that liberty of concience was a thing of advantage to the nation, as it might be setled with due reguard to the rights and privileges of the Church of England.   As to that he said the King declared oponly that the Church of England should have any reasonable equivalent it could desire for its security, provided that an Act of Parlament might pass for liberty of concience.[1]   He tould me we should meet and talke further of this matter. However, I then evaded as much as I could comming close to the thing, haveing noe mind to declare myselfe too much or to caracterize others.

I had a letter about the same time from Sir Theophilus Oglethorp that this was the best time to come up, for the business of the question at Court was much laid aside.

I began my journey with my wife and family for *May* 22 London by the way of Cambrige, wher I arrived the 26t, to inform myselfe in what college and under whos care to place . . .[2]

I got to London the 26[3] day without accidents, and 29 performed my journey with better health then (I thanke God) I could reasonably expect.   I found things much in the posture ther which I expected, the popish party extreamly pressing the King to persue the takeing of the test and the penal laws, and the other party unwilling to

---

[1] The whole difficulty was that James wanted, not merely liberty of conscience, but the repeal of the Test Act, and the consequent admission of Catholics and Dissenters to offices of state.   In his *Anatomy of an Equivalent*, published in September of this year, Halifax showed the hollowness of James's suggestions.

[2] The remainder of this sentence is deleted.

[3] Presumably a mistake for " 29."

comply with it. That which made it the more warm was a late thing that had hapned, which was this. The King had lately renewed his proclamation for libertie of concience, with an order to the bishops to have it read in all the churches of their respective diocesses.[1] The Archbishop of Canterbury and all the rest of that order (five only excepted) petition the King,[2] and sett forth therby that they could not obay his Majesty therin; that noe bishop or minister of the Church of England could give their consent for the declaration of liberty of concience, and the reading of it by them or their order must imply an interpretive consent; that the like declaration had twice before been condemd in Parlament in the late Kings time, and they might be accountable for it hereafter for a thing that was adjudged contrary to law; though the King could doe noe wrong, yet his agents or ministers were accountable for what they did by his command that was not legall; that the King though he thought fit to declare libertie of concience, the ministers of the Church of England ought to persuade men as much as they could to adhear to their Church; but this publication of it in that manner was to tell men that they needed not to come to church except they pleased, and it was noe less then declareing that lawfull to others which was against their own conciences; that by the same rule, if the King command the bishops to read mass in their churches, they are obliged to obay. Thes and many other arguments were used by the bishops. The King upon their refusall gave a very angry answer, and they were commanded to appear before the King and Council on the 8 of June.

June 1   I kissed the Kings hand, who recieved me very graciously. The next day I attended the King on horseback into Hide Park to see a regiment exercize, wher he called

---

[1] The Order in Council to that effect was dated May 4.

[2] The petition to the King, presented on May 18, was signed only by seven bishops.

to me twice, and discoursed with me upon severall
subjects.

My Lord Marquis of Halifax came to see me, whom *June 2*
I found willing to consent to libertie of concience, but
not to take away the test; and not all the penall laws
togather, but gradually, and upon good considerations.

Seven of the bishops appeared before the King in 8
Councell, wher they were commanded to enter into
recognisance of 500 l. a man, to answer to an information
against them in the Kings Bench the next term for disobedience to his Majestys order concerning reading the
declaration for liberty of concience.[1]   This the bishops refused to doe, saying they ought not to enter into any security
of that kind till the information or indictment was found,
and that if they did otherways it would be not only contrary to law but a betraying the liberty of the peerage;
upon which the Archbishop of Canterbury and six more
(being all that appeared) were committed to the Tower.
This was very deeply ressented by thos of the Church of
England.   I saw the bishops, being then at Whitehall,
come by me, going to take water for the Tower.   They
all looked very chearfully, and the Bishop of Chichester
called to me, askeing me how I did.   The next day my
Lord Huntinton (one of the Privy Council) tould me that
if the King had known how farr this matter would have
gone, he would not have enjoined the reading of the
declaration in churches.

Being Trenity Sunday, about four minuits before ten 10
in the morning, was born the Prince of Wales,[2] to the great
joy of the Court.

All the time that the bishops continued in the Tower,
which was til the first day of the term, the nombers of
thos that came to the Tower were soe great to aske the
blessing of the bishops and to lament their confinement,

[1] The information was one of seditious libel in petitioning against the
order.

[2] James Francis Edward, best known as the Old Pretender.

that remarkes were made both of the persons and carriage.

June 15   Being the first day of the term, the Archbishop of Canterbury and the rest of the bishops mooved for their habias corpus, twenty-one of the prime nobility (both for quality and estates) appeared at the Kings Bench to give baile for them, and they were set at liberty upon baile. The hall and palace yards at Westminster were crouded with thousands of people begging their blessing as they passed, and the Bishop of Canterbury giveing it and adviseing them at the same time to be constant to their religion.

Ten nonconformist ministers went to visit the bishops in the Tower, which the King took il, and sent for four of them to repremand them. They answered that they could not but adhear to them as men constant to the Protestant faith (or to that effect). The souldiers that kept guard at the Tower dranke very ofton the bishops good health, which being tould to Sir Edward Hales, Lieutenant of the Tower, he sent word to the captain of the guard to doe it noe more. He returnd answer that it was doing at that time, and that they would drinke it and noe other health whilst the bishops stayd ther.

16   I found some little return of the gout in my knee, which made me enter into the milke dyet and kept it strictly sixteen days, which restoored me to a greater strength then before.

18   Being at the commissarys office I mett my lieutenant, Flud, who not haveing behaved himselfe with due respect towards me behind my back, as I had been informd, though always very civil when I was present, I threatned to bring him before a council of warr, and to breake him if I could; but he made soe many submissions afterwards that though I had acquainted the colonel, the Duke of Barwick, with it yet I forgave him.

Being now regemented, and the pay being recieved by the agent of the regement for my company as for the rest, and distributed by him both to the officers and soldiers, I found a great disadvantage by it, and showed such reasons for it that I obteaned of the Duke of Barwick that I should recieve my own pay for my company, and cloath it myselfe as when it was independent, which was allowed as a great favour.

The information against the bishops being tryed in the *June* 29 Kings Bench for frameing and publishing a seditious libel (meaning the paper which they presented to the King conteaning the reasons why they could not order his Majestys declaration for liberty of concience to be read in churches), the jury would not find them guilty, and the council for the bishops (which were the ablest in England) used such arguments on their behalfes that the judges were devided, two of them declaring that the proofs did not extend to make it a libell,[1] and two that it did;[2] which cost the first two their places after the term, and two new judges[3] were put in their steads.   In this great argument the Kings power to dispence with the lawes was extreamly arrained, and the Kings council soe much outdone that it was wisht at Court that the thing had never been begun. Westminster Hall and the palace yeard, with the streets near them, was soe full of people, and their huzzas and shouts for joy of their lordships delivery soe great, that it looked like a little rebellion in noise though not in fact; and bonefires were made not only in the citty but in most towns of England, when the news of it came, though order was given to the magistrates in the citty and elsewher to prevent it.   The parsons now began also to preach more loud and opon against popery then ever.

I waited on the King to Hounsley Heath, wher the 30 camp was then mett.   Everybody observed he was disturbed; but he spoake very kindly to me as I rode with him upon severall occasions.

[1] Holloway and Sir John Powell.

[2] Wright and Allibone.

[3] Sir Robert Baldock and Sir Thomas Powell.

July 9   The Queen appeared in publique the first time after
her delivery. I carryed my wife and daughter to kiss
her hand and to give her joy of the Prince of Wales.
She was kind to France[s], and both the King and she
tooke notice of her for hansome.

10   I went to the camp with the King. I ther acquainted
him with a disorder which had hapned at Yorke upon
occasion of some bonefires made by the rabble upon the
news of the bishops being found not guilty. It should
seem the magistrates not suppressing them nor extin-
guishing the fires, Captain Monroe,[1] comander-in-chiefe,
caused the souldiers to putt them out, and to breake the
windows of such citizens as he concieved were concerned
in the contributing to them, and in that zeale a great many
innocent suffered with the guilty, especially the Chancellor, Doctor Watkison, who complained of his usage to
me. I knew the matter very nice to meddle in. However, I represented it, and obteaned of his Majesty that
the officer should aske his pardon; but this was all, soe
angry was the King with fires upon that occasion.

12   I was at the generall sessions held for the liberty of
Westminster, and some days after at that for the county
of Middlesex held at Hicks his Hall, wher I found such
a change of justices of the peace, and soe many papists
and fenaticks put into commission, that I did not seek
business, and mix with them as little as I could. The
justices at Hicks his Hall caused severall to be indicted
for makeing bonefires and for contributing to them as
rioters. The proof was very plane against them, but the
grand jury would not find the bill, though the justices
sent them out three times; such kindness men generally
had for the bishops and the Protestant religion. My
Lord Halifax advised me, as things now inclined at Court,
to consider if it were safe to continue my imployments.
I answered that I had great obligations to the King, and

---

[1] Andrew Monro, then in command of a company in the Royal
Regiment.

would serve him as wel as I could, whilst he allowed it
without prejudiceing my religion.

My Lord Sunderland, long suspected to be a papist, *July* 13
declared himselfe oponly in the King's chapell of that
religion with the usuall ceremonys.

I went to the camp with the King, wher the Duke of 16
Barwick gave me the assurance that I should recieve and
dispose of my own and my companys pay. He asked me
what I had done with my lieutenant. I said he had made
a very humble submission under his hand, which inclined
me to forgive him. His Grace said that himselfe shared
with me in the injury, whatever was done to me from an
inferiour officer was a breach of respect to him, and he
would not forgive it but at my intercession, which I
desired him to doe.

I ther recieved the Kings orders about a souldier that
had deserted in my company, and how he should be punished. He was to be sent to Portsmoth to be tryed
ther.

[1] I see the finest fireworks made at the Kings charge on 17
occasion of the Prince of Wales that ever was seen in
England.

The King went down to the mouth of the Thams to 24
see the fleet, but the true caus was to appease the seamen,
who were ready to mutiny upon occasion of some sea
captins useing mass oponly aboard their ships. The King
flattered the seamen all he could, went from ship to ship
and called the seamen his children, said that he had nothing
to say as to their religion, that he granted liberty of
concience to all, but expected that they should behave
themselves like men of honour and courage when ther was
occasion for their service; but all the popish priests were
ordered to be brought on shoar. Admiral Herbert, an
able seaman that the King had putt out of great imployments bycaus he would not promess to take off the test,
went privately into Holand and was made reer-admiral

[1] The words " Being St. James Day " are struck out.

ther, which made the King very angry, a great many seamen going after him.

The King and Queen went the same day to stay at Windser by the way of the camp, wher I carryed my wife and daughter to see the camp. The King, seeing the coach, rid up to it, and laying his hand upon it spoake to the company in the coach a good while.

July 28   I went to Windser, stayed ther all night, left my second son Tamworth at Eton, and returnd the next day. I desired the King that my company might return to Yorke in winter, but he said it could not, but might continue with the regiment.

August 1   I and my family went to Epsome to drinke the waters.

4   I went to the camp from thence to gett the place of the Queen Douägers reciever in Yorkshire, lately vacant by the death of one Lockwood. I spoake to my Lord Feathersham in it that night at Hamersmith, wher the Queen had a hous, but it was disposed of some days before.

The Prince of Wales, then at Richmond, fell very ill, to the great trouble of the King and Queen. It was believed he was dead in the morning; but that night the Queen Douägere, who had been to see him, said that he was better. He recovered perfectly soon after by haveing the brest, being nursed before by the spoon.

5   I returned to Epsome. As I was going into the boat at Lambeth ferry I was stayed by the constable ther to grant a hue and cry after some robbers who had committed a murder lately before, and were persued to a hous hard by. I went into the hous, but they were escaped, and whilst the constable went after them, one of them, thinkeing the coast was clear, returned into the hous, wher I took him with my own hands. The constables seized of the rest soon after, and I committed them, being three, to Newgate.

8   I findeing advantage by drinkeing the waters stayd till the 8th, and returned to London that day. When I came to London I found my Lord Feathersham and my Lord

Preston [1] had done all they could to gett me the recievers place, but it was promessed before I knew of it.

I mett the Duke of Norfock at Epsome, and he came to see me in London, wher, discourseing of him, I found him firm to the Protestant religion, to the which he had been converted in the late Kings time, and not satisfyed with the Court.

I went to Windser, wher I asked the King the arch- *Aug.* 11 deaconry of Yorke for my brother, lately faln void by the death of the incombent.[2]   He tould me he was sorry I asked it not sooner, for he had promessed it before.   I desired the King that he would please to recieve my son William into his service by makeing him my lieutenant, one of my lieutenants being very infirm and incapable to doe duty, and that he would give that lieutenant some pention when a vacancy fell.   The King said he would consider of it, and give me his answer some other time.[3] I did severall other things ther relateing to business, and returnd the 13th with good success.

Mr. Thyn,[4] treasurer to the Queen Dowagere, tould me 23 that he was free again from the ingagement he had made to dispose of the recievers place, and if I desired it I might have it upon the same terms, which was to give him 300 l. The reciet was 1,300 l. per annum of the Queens rents within Pontefract, Tickil and some other places, for the which the Queen allowed 5 l. per cent for recieveing and returning her mony, which made it 65 l. per annum, and gave moreover a sallary of 55 l. per annum, which in all was 120 l. per annum.   In fyne I consented to give him 260 l., and had the place.

---

[1] Feversham and Preston were two of the Queen Dowager's trustees.

[2] Edmund Diggle, who had died on August 1.   He was succeeded by Knightley Chetwood, installed on November 10.

[3] Reresby was still pressing for the appointment of his son three months later (*Hist. MSS. Com.*, vii. 413).   The lieutenant, of course, was Butler.

[4] Henry Frederick Thynne, cousin of Lord Halifax and younger brother of Thomas Thynne, Viscount Weymouth.

I carried my wife and daughter to Windser to wait on the Queen. The Court was in some trouble and the King out of humour (though he was always of soe even a temper that it was hard to discover it) at the news of the Dutch haveing sett out a great fleet as designed against us, that the French and the Dutch were to fall out, and that we were pressed on both sides to declare speedily which to take. This, considering our affairs at home (viz., the jealousies about religion, discontents about the army, and the ill time to call a Parlament to gett mony), did reasonably enough disturb our councils.

The King the first thing he did was to declare that he would call a Parlament to meet the 27 of November following, and gave severall reasons for it in Council, relateing to the good and satisfaction of the nation more then the apprehension that he seemd to have of the Dutch. However, he comanded all officers whatsoever to repair to their comands, and drew the forces out of other guarrisons and places to man the seaports, and perticularly that the force then at Yorke should be drawn from thence to Hul, soe that not soe much as one company was to remain behind. Soe soon as I heard it, I represented the inconvenience of it to the Kings service as soe great upon severall accounts to his Majesty by my Lord Feathersham, that the King ordered an express to be sent to Yorke to countermand his first order, and that at the first one company, and afterwards that three companys should remain at Yorke.

26 The King mett me as he went to see the Prince of Wales, who was then nursed in a hous by the parke. As soon as he see me he laughed and said, We had like to have made you noe governor. Or, Sir, said I, a governor without a guarrison.

28 I tooke my leave of the King, but with apprehensions that he would have put the questions to me which he had to others, if I would consent or endeavour to the takeing off the test and penal laws in Parlament; but he said

nothing of that to me, only enjoined me to stand for the next Parlament at Yorke, which I would have excused myselfe from but could not, and wished me a good journey. At the same time I had news that the question had been put the week before to all our justices of the West Rideing, who had given their negative to it.[1]

I returned to London, and attended the sessions at *Aug.* 29 Hicks his Hall, which began the same day.

The news then came that Belgrade was taken by the Christians in Hungary,[2] that the Seraskier [3] was fled with his army, and that the rest of Hungary must now needs fall into the Emperor's hands. The Venetians continued the like successe against the Turkes on their side, and had taken Candie.[4]

I writt severall letters to the Lord Maior of Yorke, Mr. *Sept.* 1 Rains, to the aldermen and severall cittizens, declareing my intention to stand for cittizen ther in the next Parlament, and to desire their voats. The next post after I recieved for answer from his lordship that a court of aldermen had been called the day before he recieved my letter, and that they had ressolved, as most of the twentyfour and of the commons had done, to choos two of the bench for their members, viz., Mr. Prickit, their deputy recorder, and Sir Stiphen Thomson. The Maior, as he had ever been my adversary, had done this purpasly to prevent my admission. I had encouragement, however, from other cittizens that I might succeed. The thruth was I was at some loss how to act in this matter. I was

[1] The reference is to the answers given at Pontefract on August 20, printed in *Yorkshire Archæological Journal*, v. 459-61. Reresby is noted as absent.

[2] August 27/September 6.

[3] The Turkish commander-in-chief, Yeghen Pasha. He was put to death early in the following year.

[4] The rumour that Candia had been, or was about to be, surrendered to the Christians was without foundation. The chief feature of the campaign conducted by the Venetians at this time was the failure of their attempt to conquer Negropont.

not very desirous to be of this Parlament, for severall reasons. I was more infirm, and less able to travell and to attend the duty it required. I believed the King would expect that from me ther which my concience would not permitt, and as I was resolved not to violate the one, soe I was unwilling to offend soe good a master on the other side.

Sept. 6 I went to Windser, and acquainted the King with my letters and their answers, desireing three things of him. One was, if, since the contest was like to be both chargeable and difficult, and the success doubtfull, it were yet his plesure I should stand, to which he said positively I should. Secondly, that in case I miscarryed he would not (the opposition being soe strong against me) impute it to my fault, which he promessed me he would not. Thirdly, that he would assist me all he could not to be bafled in the contest, by such means as I should propose, to which he complyed, and gave orders to the lords for the purgeing of corporations (as my Lord Marquis of Powis tould me, and Mr. Brent)[1] that whatever change or alteration I desired in that citty it should be complyed with, and that they should putt in or out amongst the magistrates and officers as I pleased (which the King, it seems, had reserved power to doe by the last charters).

I was very carefull to act in this matter, considering, if I putt out none, it would showe I had noe power, and they would dispise me; if too many, it might exasperate, and make the citty jealous that I was too deep in the Court interest, which might prevent my successe. I therfore only desired that the Lord Maior might be laid aside and Sir Stiphen Thomson be made Maior (which would prevent his being a member of Parlament),[2] and that two, viz., Mr. Edward Thomson and Mr. Ramsden, who had been my principal friends in the former election

[1] Robert Brent, agent of the committee for regulating corporations. Powis was a member of the committee.

[2] The mayor being the returning officer.

of me for Yorke, and were turned out afterwards partly upon my account, might be putt into their places.

Takeing my leave of the King, and giveing him some *Sept.* 8 Roman medals (which he accepted kindly), he charged [me] again to doe what I could to be chosen.

I after desired of Mr. Brent (the agent in matters of corporations) that, if they had power, I might, with some I could name, be added to the bench of justices in the citty by a writt of assistance, which he promessed me should be done.

At this time fifty Irishmen and papists had been sent for from Ireland by the Duke of Barwick to be putt into his regiment, and every captain was to have some. The lieutenant-colonel, Mr. Beaumont, and five captains, being all that were upon the place in quarters at Ports-moth, refused to take a man, saying their companys were compleat, and that they were not to part with good men and Englishmen to take wors men and forraigners, and desired they might either choos their own souldiers or give up their commissions. The Duke was angry, and sent an account of it to the King. The King sent twenty hors to bring them up to Windser in custody, wher they were to be tryed by a council of warr. I spoke to them that day at Windser, wher they were just arrived, and they all were ressolved to stand it out. They tould me that the Duke had not offered one man of them to my company, which was kind.[1]

The Prince of Orange and the Dutch embassador[2] had lately given the King assurances that their preparations were not against us; but the French caused his troops to march that way, and the Dutch marched towards the country of Liege to meet them. The King of England made great preparations for a fleet against the spring.

[1] The explanation probably is that Reresby's was the grenadier company, which it was generally considered should be composed of the finest men in the regiment.

[2] Arnold van Citters.

I was well assured by one that our King had twenty-five hundred thousand pounds in his coffers. I asked my Lord Dartmoth if anything was to be done at Burlinton if we fell out with the Dutch, it being the best port to secure our coale trade. He enquired of the condition of the place. I tould him the plattform and carriages of the guns were much decayed. He bid me send him an estimate what it would cost to repair it, for something should be done ther.

Sept. 10 The council of warr sat upon Colonel Beaumont and the captains, and they were all casshered, but with unwillingness from the King for the consequence. They had offers of forgiveness if they would have accepted the men, which they all denyed. This spred a great discontent and jealousie throughout the army, and most of that regiment soon after quitted.

The same day Sir Walter Vavasour and Mr. Middleton of Stockill[1] came up to give an account to the King of the answers of the Yorkshire West Rideing gentlemen and thos of the corporations to the quœries, in which the Lord Maior and aldermen of Yorke were soe faulty[2] that I found my greatest opposers ther would be turned out without my helpe. And soe I left them to their accusation, only insisted upon the commission of assistance for justices of the peace, wherin I named two persons to be joined with me. Every post brought new fears that I should not be chosen at York. Severall alterations and restrictions from popular elections to a Maior and twelve aldermen, which the King appointed as he pleased, was now made by new charters for the better chooseing such Parlament men as he liked.

16 My Lord Halifax, whom I took leave of the 16, advised me not to be too earnest to be chosen, or at the

[1] John Middleton of Stockeld, who had been among those accused by Bolron and Mowbray at the time of the Popish Plot.

[2] Their answers are printed in *Yorkshire Archæological Journal,* v. 452-4.

least not to take the Court assistance too much, for many reasons then offered.

I went for Yorkshire by the way of Bury. I stayed *Sept.* 20 ther two days with my ant Monson, who gave gould to four of my children then with me. I arrived at home on Miclemas even. I ther recieved news that my interest for being chosen a member of Parlament was much lessened for want of my presence ther; but what most discomposed me was what I recieved by an expresse, that my Lord Mongomeries company,[1] then at Yorke, was ordered to march for Hul, soe that if I came not speedily his lordship should be forced to give up the keys of the citty to my Lord Maior. I imediately went for Yorke, wher I recieved the keys, and the company marched. I represented to the King the inconvenience of ther wanting a company of foot at the least in this guarrison, and if it could not be spared, desired orders what to doe with the keys. As to the first his Majesty answered he had re-called the company upon mature deliberation, and as to the second, I might dispose of them as I pleased.

I desired my Lord Maior to call a hall (viz., the alder- *Oct.* 1 men, the common council and the twenty-four) that I might say something to them. A hall was called, but the Lord Maior (a great ennemy to my election), not haveing patience to stay til I came, dismissed the assembly almost as soon as it met. Hee feared that what I had to say might make too many converts for my election. A day or two after comes down a proclamation setting forth a certain intention of the Prince of Orange to invade this nation, assisted by the States General, with a great fleet and a strong army, commanding all lord lieutenants, deputy lieutenants and other his Majestys officers to be in readinesse for the defence of the King and kingdome. At this time my Lord Thomas Howard was lord lieutenant

---

[1] William Herbert, Viscount Montgomery, eldest son of the first Marquis of Powis, commanded a company in the regiment of foot of which he was colonel (Dalton, *English Army Lists*, ii. 141).

of the West Rideing, a papist who was gone embassador to Rome, and he had left but three deputy lieutenants behind him, two of which were Roman Catholiques also, and but two of them in the country.

Ther was at the same time most of the gentry of Yorkeshire in that citty, com'd upon expectation to meet writs for the choice of Parlament men. I therfore pressed the high sheriff, one Mr. Rokesby, to give notice to some gentlemen, and I convened others, to meet the next day; wher Sir Henry Goodrick began a discours, and I secounded, setting forth reasons of our incapacity to serve the King with the militia without another lord lieutenant and under whom we might lawfully serve, meaning as being a Protestant, and at the same time subscribed a representation of our condition to the same effect to his Majesty. I knew how ungrateful this would be to the King, and therfore both gave him private notice of the intention of it, to prepare him for it, and beg'd my own excuse for complying in it, assureing him that now it was also for his service.

Oct. 4   Comes a messenger to purge the corporation to put out the former Maior and aldermen, and to put in others, almost all papists; but it was soe lame by mistakes in the execution of it that it could not be done.[1]

---

[1] The difficulties raised were explained by the magistrates in the following letter to Sunderland :

Yorke, October the 6th, 1688.—May it please your Honour, Yesterday wee received his Majesties order for the displaceing and turning out our Lord Major, five of our aldermen, eight of those that are called the four-and-twenty, and ten of the comon councellmen ; which order being read, all of them submitted with much willingnesse to his Majesties pleasure in turning them out.

Wee also at the same tyme received his Majesties mandate, dated the 12th of September last, for electing Mr. Charles Fairfax to bee Lord Major, and for the electing others therein named into the places of those that are turned out. But none of them that are soe named for Lord Major, aldermen, and four-and-twenty, are free citizens of this citty ; nor can wee (our Major being now turned out) make them free, for noe man was ever made free of this citty but by the Major in the presence of one

My Lord Maior before his being thus superseded had complained at the meeting before mentioned to the gentlemen of the condition of this citty by the gates not being locked, and would have fixed it upon me, as keeping the keys now that ther was noe souldiers in town to lock the gates, contrary to order. I answered his lordship at this meeting as effectually as I could, setting forth his injustice to me upon severall accounts and perticulary in this, produceing my authority to keep the keys altogather if I pleased, which made him much asshamed.

of the chamberlains. And besydes, wee have noe power to elect but by our charter, and it directs our elections to bee made in this manner— When a comon councellman is to bee elected, the comons must upon their oaths present the names of three of the most fit, able, and discreet citizens unto the Major, aldermen, and sherriffes, to the end that they out of these three citizens soe presented may upon their oaths elect one to bee a comon councellman. And when an alderman is to bee elected, the comons must upon their oaths present three of the most discreet, fit, and able citizens to the Major, aldermen, and sherriffes, to the intent that they out of those three citizens soe presented may elect one to bee alderman. And when a Major is to bee elected, the comons must upon their oaths present three of the most discreet, fitt, and able aldermen unto the aldermen and sherriffes, to the intent that they out of these three aldermen soe presented may upon their oaths chuse one to bee Major. Soe that wee whoe are now aldermen and sherriffes cannot elect any persons into the offices of Major, aldermen, or comon councellmen, untill they bee presented to us as our charter directs.

Wee this day called the comons togither, who after consultation among themselves told us they could not present Mr. Fairfax to us in regard hee was neither alderman nor citizen; nor could they present the rest of the gentlemen nominated to bee elected into the vacant places of aldermen without violateing their oaths, which their conscience would not suffer them to doe and they humbly conceived his Majestie did not expect from them. This is the difficulty wee now labour under, how to elect those gentlemen nominated in his Majesties mandate and yet to keep our oaths, which two things wee cannot reconcile. And therefore wee doe humbly beseech your Honour to represent the state of our case unto his gratious Majesty, for whose prosperous and happy reign over us wee doe heartily pray, and shall ever remain his Majesties most dutifull and loyall subjects, and Your Lordshipps most obedient and humble servants, Leonard Wilberfoss, Roger Shackleto[n], William Tomlinson, Samuel Dawson, Joshua Earnshaw, Matthew Bayocke, vicecomes. (S.P. Dom., James II, 4. f. 93.)

The next day I prevailed with him to call a hall, wher I spoake to the assembly hafe an hour, and soe far convinced them of the base practices that had been used against me, and of the injustice of them, that they all seemd to be for me; at which time I also gave them the keys, but made them own it as a curtesie, with condition that they should restoor them whenever I desired them for his Majestys service.[1]

My Lord Fairfax of Gillin, a Roman Catholique, tould me, comming to Yorke (he was then lord lieutenant of the North Rideing), that ther was some caus to suspect my Lord of Devonshires comming at this time into Yorkshire and my Lord of Danbys. The one came pretending to see his estate, the other to drinke the sulfer

---

[1] The dates of the various meetings to which Reresby refers are neither clear nor, perhaps, accurate. The following letter from Reresby to Blathwayt seems to prove that the keys were handed over on October 2 :

October 3, [16]88.—Sir, It is not possible for me to keep the keyes of this citty if his Majesty thinke it not convenient to spare a company to attend the oponing and shutting of the gates, for they lie soe distant one from another that it requires six or eight men to perform it every morning and night ; soe that I did yesterday, according to his Majestys permission and the nescessity of the thinge, deliver them to the magistrates, upon condition that they would restoor them whenever I had occasion for them for his Majestys service.

Since the King may have such use for his standing forces in other places and guarrisons, I desire you would putt his Majesty in mind that this citty is a distinct county of itselfe, and though it hath usually gone along with the lieutenancy of the West Rideing yet it may have a lord lieutenant of its own ; and if it please his Majesty to grant that commission to me (which is most proper, being governor), I could give commissions to such loyall gentlemen to be officers in the militia regiment which belongs to this citty that I hope we might with that regiment be able to defend ourselves and this guarrison. If his Majesty thinke fitt to continue the lieutenancy as it was before, I desire, however, to be collonel of this regiment, which hath none at present, it being formerly commanded by Sir Thomas Slingsby, now dead.

I had yesterday some discours with the magistrates and most considerable citizens of this place, who all seem ressolved to venter their all in defence of the King and this citty against all invaders. I pray you, Sir, to lay this humbly before his Majesty, and to be assured that I am, Sir, Your most humble servant, J. Reresby. (B.M. Add. MSS. 9735, f. 34.)

* York City Archives, York Corporation House Book 38, f. 254.

water at Knaisbrough. They both met at Sir Henry Goodricks and other places, wher they conversed ofton, and the first came to Yorke, wher I paid him civilities and recieved others from him. The other I went to see at Sir Henries, not believeing that men of that qualitie and estate could design anything prejudiciall to the goverment or dangerous to themselves; and their carriage appeared very innocent.

I had letters by expresse from my Lord Preston, the new Secretary of State (my Lord Sunderland being laid aside,[1] who was turnd papist and had done great harm since he was near the King), that the King had recieved our representation of the county very kindly, and had complyed with it in nameing the Duke of Newcastle lord lieutenant of the whole county,[2] who came to town soon

Oct. 6

---

[1] Sunderland was not superseded by Preston until some three weeks later, and the change is noted by Reresby in its proper place (*infra*, p. 523). There was, however, at this time a rumour of Sunderland's disgrace (*Ellis Correspondence*, ii. 237).

[2] What appears to be Reresby's reply to the official intimation of this change is as follows :

Yorke, October 8, 1688.—My Lord, I recieved the honour of your Lordships on Saturday about two in the afternoon, which I presently communicated to the high sherif, and both of us to this citty and the gentry of the county with what hast we could possible. The messenger persued his journey straight to Newcastle, and we expect his Grace here tomorrow.

My Lord, I presume to acquaint your Lordship that there was a former regulation of this citty by their new charter granted three years since upon a *quo warranto* brought against it, by which five aldermen or six were turned out, who are thought better disposed men to his Majestys service, and more beloved in the town (being men of greater substance and parts) then thos that succeeded them, and who at this time deny to pay obedience to the Kings *mandamus*. If his Majesty should not thinke fitt to enforce the execution of it at this time, it is the opinion of most here that to restoor the ould charter and the old aldermen togather would be the best expedient to settle the present difference and to disappoint thos who by their disobedience hope at this time to continue themselves in power. But this is offered with all submission to your Lordship by, My Lord, Your Lordships most obedient and most faithfull servant, J. Reresby. (S.P. Dom., James II, 4. f. 102.)

after, and calling togather the gentry, appointed his deputy lieutenants and militia officers, both hors and foot. I had not seen the Duke never since the difference we had upon account of my Lord Feathersham. But that grudge soon blew over at our meeting, and I had that credit with him[1] that he scarce appointed an officer without my consent, and whoever I recommended was accepted; and if my interest had not contributed his Grace would have been unprovided in some stations.

Most of the places of profit were given to my friends, as the muster-masters of the three Rideings, the two treasurers of the East and West Rideings, the martial's place of the West, besides others. The Duke had a regiment of foot given him to raise at this time, to the which I had letters from above the King designed me his lieutenant-colonel; but the commissions being all promessed before the Duke came to Yorke or that he had that notice, I was disappointed of it. I had then a militia troop in the West Rideing, which I gave up, telling my Lord my desire rather to serve in the foot, wherupon he gave me a commission for colonel of the citty and ansty regiment. But I tould him it would be a greater honour to Yorke to have him colonel of their regiment, and soe gave up my commission and took another as lieutenant-colonel of it to the Duke.

The King began now to find his errour, but too late, in carrying things soe high upon popish councils and foundations. He now restoored several justices of the peace in countys, and the old charters all over England. He restoored the Bishop of London, Maudlin Colege, and begins again to court the Church of England.

Oct. 10   The news of the Prince of Orange encreaseth dayly as to his great fleet ready to saile.

A company of foot of Colonel Cornwel's regiment

---

[1] " Sir John Reresby is here most reddy to serve his Majeste " (Newcastle to Sunderland, York, October 10, 1688, in S.P. Dom., James II, 4. f. 113).

comes from Scarbrough to Yorke by the Kings order.[1]
The Earl of Danby arrives to make a visit to the Duke,
who was not pleasd at it, saying he came to govern him
and to have the reputation of being his adviser and coun-
celler. The question was now whether Roman Catholiques should have commissions. The Duke inclined to
it, but it being debated the deputy lieutenants convinced
the Duke against it. My Lord of Danby made very merry
with the Duke upon several steps of his proceedings, but
the perticulars are not worth mentioning. The Duke
would not disoblige the papists by leaveing them out of
commission til he writ to the King,[2] who writ order they
should not be put in till he directed it.

[1] The following letter from Reresby to Blathwayt makes it clear that
the company sent to York was that commanded by Thomas Williams,
but its chief interest lies in its account of the condition of the garrison :

October 13, 1688, Yorke.—Sir, Captain Williams company marched
in here on Wedensday night last, and are upon duty, the keyes with some
reluctency being restoored me by the magistrats. We hear of 3,000 foot
and dragoons from Scotland intended for this guarrison. If it be soe, I
desire some care may be taken to provide some pouder and ammunition,
for we have none, only some few balls, and some match, which is most
of it decay'd. I have ofton represented our wants of that kind to my Lord
Dartsmoth, and have lately written to the Board, but to noe purpas.

We have six piece of canon ready mounted upon the Tower hill, which
a little breast-worke might make usefull, if ther were occasion. The
raiseing of it would cost about 20 l. The gunner had two shillings a day
allowed him, for which he also served as stoor-keeper ; but that being
lately withdrawn, he refuseth to worke longer without wages.

The Duke of Newcastle hath been here since Teusday ordering the
militia, but I doe not find that he intends to raise it without the danger
come nearer thes parts. I am, Sir, Your very humble servant, J. Reresby.
(B.M. Add. MSS. 9735, f. 38.)

[2] In this letter, the longest and most interesting of those which he wrote
at this time, Newcastle laid before the Government a full account of the
position in the north, and enclosed also a letter from the deputy recorder
of York requesting him, in the name of the aldermen, " to mediate on their
behalfes with his Majesty that he would be gratiously pleased of his bounty
to restore unto them their old charter without any provisoe for the dis-
placing of those that heerafter shall beare office in this citty " :

Yorke, October the 11th, [16]88.—My Lord, I humbly writ to your
Lordship last post ; and since that I have ordered very loyall persons to

Oct. 13   I had orders from the King that some 700 Scotch hors and dragoons being on their march from Scotland I should recieve them into this guarrison, that Major-General Graham that comanded them [1] and my Lord see what horses there are kept neere the cost with secresey, and what account I have from them I shall present to your Lordship. I have by this post noe letter from your Lordship, nor commissions for the officers in my regement. I have by this post an order from his Majeste to present an account how the corporations are in this county, which I will inquier into.

As to Newcastle, I humbly assure your Lordship I thinke the present Mayor a very loyall man, though he is a nonconformist ; and I doe beleeve there is of the Church of England, and of the Presbeterians that will be called of the Church, forty for one to the nonconformist. And truly I conceve it is for his Majestes service Sir William Blackett and Mr. Devison may be aldermen againe, and what more is to be don I assure your Lordship my cosen Edward Widdrington and Sir William Creagh are most able to informe your Lordship.

The gentlemen of the three rideings are here, and I give noe deputations but to such as I speak with and are willing to serve his Majeste. I humbly intreat your Lordship to present my suit to his Majeste I may have his leave to goe to Wellbeck when I am of noe use here. That place is within three miles of Yorkshire, and I can be here in a day.

I humbly begg his Majestes order wheather I should give deputations to Catholicks. Thay are most reddy to serve his Majeste with great affection and loyallty, and what his Majeste would have me doe in that matter I will obay ; but it is my duty to acquante your Lordship the gentlemen that did petition his Majeste are most violent against them. My Lord Farfax of Gilling is most industreus in his Majestes service, and truly but for his advice I could not have don halfe of what I have don. By the next I shall send your Lordship a list of what deputy lieutennants I have made.

Truly, my Lord, I dare not presume to give my opinion what is best for his Majestes service to be don concerning this corporation. In the morning I had discourse with them. Thay would make bargaines with his Majeste. I told them I would not speak for them if thay thaught of that, and this night the recorder braught me the inclosed. I told him I wold not promis him to speak for them, but I sayd I would present it to your Lordship. I am with all respect, My Lord, Your Lordships most humble and obedient servant, H. Newcastle. (S.P. Dom., James II, 4. f. 114.)

[1] John Graham of Claverhouse commanded the horse in the Scottish army which James was bringing south to his assistance. Immediately after his junction with the royal forces he was created Viscount Dundee.

Leviston[1] had direction to pay me all due respects as governor, but out of regard to the Duke of Newcastles quality that I should recieve the word from him whilst he stayed in Yorke, and they from me.[2]

Being the Kings birthday, I gave the great guns at *Oct.* 14 Cliffords Tower, and entertained the high sheriff and severall gentlemen with several sorts of wine at the grand jury hous in the Castle, wher the company gave severall vollies also of small shott.

The Scotch troops arrived,[3] and I was in great hopes 15

---

[1] George, Lord Livingstone, who succeeded his father in 1690 as fourth Earl of Linlithgow.   At this time he was in command of the Scottish troop of life guards (Dalton, *Scots Army*, ii. 8, 141).

[2] Reresby acknowledged these instructions in the following letter, directed to Blathwayt :

Yorke, October 15, 1688.—Sir, I had his Majestys comands to admitt the Scotch troops into this guarrison by the last post, as also concerning my behaviour towards the Duke of Newcastle during his stay here.   The first shall be exactly obayed, and the secound was observed before I knew his Majestys pleasure, though his Grace made some difficulty to give the word at the first, which he now accepts to perform.

The Scotch forces you mention march into this guarrison this day, comanded by Major Generall Graham.   Some officers are com'd before with that notice.   We are absolutely unprovided of ammunition, which I have ofton represented ineffectually.   Sir, I desire you would please to lay it before his Majesty, that if any more independent companies be to be raised ther is noe place certainly that seems more to require one then this.   That which was lately granted to Captain Witham, the men come in very slowly.   If his Majesty please to grant me his commission I doubt not but to raise a good company in few days, that am, Sir, Your very humble servant, J. Reresby.   (B.M. Add. MSS. 9735, f. 40.)

[3] Their presence raised some additional problems, which Reresby hastened to lay before Blathwayt :

October 17, [16]88, Yorke.—Sir, I recieved the Scotch forces here on Monday last.   They are arrived in very good condition, considering their long march.   The officers insist upon haveing fires in their respective lodgeings or chambers, at the charge of their landlords, a thing never practiced in this guarrison, all fewel here being very dear ; but this being a case wher I never had occasion to consult you, I desire to know by the first how the generall order or practice is in it.

Not haveing been acquainted with hors or dragoons in this guarrison, I would be informed at the same time of the rate of the establishment for

they would have continued at Yorke for the security of it and the country; but the danger encreaseing hourly above from the apprehension of the Prince his landing, and the King haveing a desire to encrease his army by that addition, they had orders to march southwards after three days stay in that guarrison.[1]

The Duke of Newcastle, who kept nothing from me,[2]

hay, oats, ordinarys, and ale. The dragoons, by reason we have soe little infantry, are ordered to doe duty of foot, and are posted at severall guards at the gates of this citty. The Duke is yet here forming the militia. We hear noe news of the Dutch on this side. I am, Sir, Your very humble servant, J. Reresby. We hear just now that great shooting was lately heard to Hull and places therabouts. (B.M. Add. MSS. 9735, f. 42.)

[1] The last surviving letter from Reresby to Blathwayt makes it clear that their departure took place on October 19 :

October 20, [16]88, Yorke.—Sir, The Scotch forces marched yesterday out of this guarrison southwards, and discharged their quarters. However, I desire an answer to the contents of my last, that I may be provided what orders to give in the like cases.

We have had noe newes of the Dutch since the Duke's last account sent up from hence. His Grace continues stil here. I am, Sir, Your most humble servant, J. Reresby. (B.M. Add. MSS. 9735, f. 36.)

[2] The intimate relations of Reresby and Newcastle are illustrated by the following letter from Newcastle to Sunderland, the main interest of which, however, lies in the lists of deputy lieutenants which it encloses :

York, October the 14th, [16]88.—My Lord, I receved yesterday your Lordships letter of the 11th, and most humbly thanke his Majeste for the great honnor his Majeste has don me in ordering I shall give the word here. Sir John Reresby is very kind and frendly to me, and dus everything with great prudence ; and I perceve his indevors are wholly to serve his Majeste, and I assure your Lordship he has great intrest in this city. I present to your Lordship the names of such persons as I have made at present deputy lieutennants in the three rideings, but it will be necessary, as I humby conceve, there should be more made. But these are sufficient to putt the melitia in order to be reddy at an hours warning, as I have given them order. I am with great respect, My Lord, Your Lordships most humble obedient servant, H. Newcastle. (S.P. Dom., James II, 4. f. 139.)

Deputy lieutenants for the West Rydeing of Yorkeshire : The Lord Lattimer ; Thomas, Lord Fairfax ; Sidney Wortley, Esquire ; Sir Henry Goodricke ; Sir John Reresby ; Tobias Jenkins, Esquire ; James Moyser, Esquire ; Christopher Tankard, Esquire.

Deputy lieutenants for the North Rydeing of Yorkeshire : Thomas Rookby, Esquire, high sheriffe ; John Darcy, Esquire ; Sir David Fowles ;

advised me that he heard my Lord of Danby had a great deale of mony in the Banke of Holand; that he had been invited up to London by my Lord Belasis and the Kings order; that he had made some offers of his service to his Majesty, but that he did not intend to goe up. I knew the thruth of the latter part of this from other hands.

Upon some discours with the said earl at the deans hous the 15th October, he used thes expressions: We are in an il condition now in this nation all wayes, for [if] the King beat the Prince, poperie will return upon us with more violence then before; if the Prince beat the King, the Crown and the nation may be in some danger. All which was not altogather untrue.

I recieved the Queens rents by my servants upon the *Oct.* 17 17th at Pontefract, the 19 at Naisbrough, the 23 at Pickering.

The citizens of Yorke, being now brought over, were generally kind to me, and promessed to be for me in my election. Being lieutenant-colonel to that regiment, the Duke left the findeing of officers for it entirely to me, which I did in two days time, and denyed some that would have served in of the principal citizens. The late Lord Maior being superseded, and the new one [1] not sworn by reason of some mistakes about the new charter, the citty, wanting their head in civil matters, made their application to me ofton in that capacity also. Ther was about that time three extraordinary things which might properly be said of Yorke, that it was an archbishoprick without a bishop, a citty without a Lord Maior, and a guarrison without a souldier. But thes were soon after all supplyed. The old charter of all was restoored to the citty and the old

Sir Thomas Pennyman; Thomas Worsley, Esquire; John Gibson, Esquire.

Deputy lieutenants for the East Rydeing of Yorkeshire: Sir Thomas Rudstone, baronet; Sir Ralph Warton, knight; Sir James Bradshaw, knight; Tobias Jenkins, Esquire; James Moyser, Esquire; Thomas Hesketh, Esquire. (S.P. Dom., James II, 4. f. 120.)

[1] Robert Waller.

Lord Maior, as it stood upon the delivery of the first and the antient charter, without one papist in it; the Bishop of Exeter,[1] who fled from thence upon the landing of the Prince of Orange, was made Archbishop of Yorke; and I had one company of foot sent to continue, as I said before.

It was very strange, and a certain forerunner of the mischiefs that ensued upon this invasion, that neither the gentry nor common people seemed much afeard or concerned at it, saying, The Prince comes only to mentain the Protestant religion; he wil doe England noe harm. On the other hand it was suggested from Court that he aimed at the Crown, and the Dutch, who assisted him, at the trade of England. And the thruth is his own declaration when it came, which was a little before he landed himselfe,[2] seemed suspitious enough, for it sett forth all the grievences of the nation with great aggravations, as the Kings intention to subvert both the goverment in Church and State; that he intended to make himselfe absolute, to rout out the Protestant religion, to which purpas he had sett up the dispenceing power with the laws; had moulded all the charters to his own mind, to the end he might have such members of Parlament chosen as he desired; had examined and pre-engaged such as he intended for members in the matter of takeing of the test and the penal lawes; and had chiefly put a feigned or soppositious Prince of Wales upon the nation, only to promote poperie and to defeat the Prince and Princesse of Orange of their right of succession.

A little before the invasion the King, hearing that the Prince his being born of the Queen made soe much noise, called an extraordinary council,[3] wher all the nobility,

---

[1] Thomas Lamplugh, who had refused to sign the petition against the Declaration of Indulgence and had caused it to be read throughout his diocese. His election at York took place on November 28 and his official translation on December 8.

[2] It was circulated in London on November 1.

[3] October 22.

bishops, foraign ministers, &c., were sommoned that were in London, and appeared; wher the Queen Douagere, severall lords, ladys, and the Kings and Queens servants, to above the nomber of forty, both papists and Protestants, give pregnant evidence of the true birth of the Prince, all which was re-examined in Chancery upon oath, and ther recorded.

Haveing ofton dined with the Duke, who kept a great *Oct.* 18 table, and spent whilst he stayed at Yorke as he said above 100 l. per week, I invited him to dinner. He brought his own company with him, my Lord Fairfax, Sir Henry Goodrick, Sir Michael Wentworth, and Mr. Moyser. I had the musick to improove the entertainment, and wine that the Duke tasted of soe plentifully that he grew soe kind as to kiss me and to call me his mistrisse.

The same day I persuaded him [to unite] all the eight troops of the county into a regiment, he being lord lieutenant of the three rideings, which he accepted, and offered me to be lieutenant-colonel to it; but I declined it, and he gave it to my Lord Fairfax.[1]

All the troops are called to Yorke, regimented and 26 officerd. The Duke draws them up in a common near Yorke, and marcheth them into town.

Came the report as if the Dutch fleet had been much 29 shattered by the storm; that my Lord Sunderland was certainly out, and my Lord Preston Secretary of State.[2]

The citty regiment was called togather. His Grace 30

---

[1] Sir Henry Goodricke, writing to the Earl of Danby from York on October 20, 1688, gives a somewhat different account of this transaction : " My Lord Duke has been prevailed upon to forme the horse of the three ridings into one regiment, which is appointed to be here in quarter on the 29th instant, to be commanded as colonell by his Grace ; lieutenant colonell, my Lord Fairfax of Denton ; major, Mr. Moyser. Our governor was desirous of the second command, but was opposed." (Leeds MSS.)

[2] In this capacity Preston received a number of letters from Reresby, which are printed in *Hist. MSS. Com.*, vii. 412-20.

went the same day for Welbeck, and left the care and comand of that regiment to me. I kept it up fourteen days, and the deputy lieutenants called up my Lord Fairfax his regiment of foot to relieve it, thinking this citty ought not to be without a regiment at least for its guard besides the standing company at such a time.

The King all this time was makeing great preparations and levys for his army, and had brought it by computation to 6,000 hors and dragoons, and 38,000 foot. The fleet was also out at sea, commanded by my Lord Dartsmoth, but much inferiour to the Dutch, and did nothing to the purpas.

Nov. 1   I caused the companies of the citty regiment to exercize
2 by companys.   The 2nd I drew them out and exercized them regimentally to the same place wher the hors exercized before, and then marched them myselfe into the citty, attended by a troop of volontiers of citizens that offered to march with me, my son William being in the head of them.   I gave the regiment, when I dismissed
3 them, 5 l. to drinke.   The 3rd I entertained all the captains at dinner, the next day the lieutenants, and the day after that all the ensigns.

That day the Prince of Orange his declaration, sent by an unknown hand to a citizen, was brought to me, which I sent up to the Secretary of State.   Orders were sent at the same time to secure my Lord Lomley, then in the North Rideing; but he that was comanded in that service, Colonel John Darcy, pretended he could not find him, though it appeared afterwards that he was not far off, and might have seized him if he pleased.

4   I recieved by an express from the Secretary of War that the Dutch fleet was seen off Dover sailing westward, which gave us hopes, however, that they would not land in the north.

7   I had another expresse that the Prince was certainly landed at Torbay in the west the 5th of November, and marcheth strait to Exeter, attended by the Mareschal de

Shomberg (an experienced officer),[1] my Lord Macclefield, my Lord Wiltshire,[2] Sir John Hothom,[3] Doctor Burnet,[4] Sir William Waller,[5] and a great land army.

I sent the Duke word of this invasion, though he had notice of it from above; but he writes back that they being landed at that distance his being at Yorke was less nescessary, which I much disapprooved of, the danger not being only from the invaders but their confederates at home, it being impossible that the Prince durst attack England with an army of under 20,000 men if he expected not very good helpe in England.　The deputy lieutenants then at Yorke, to the nomber of ten, seemed much concernd for securing the peace of this county with me, and at a meeting held the 15[6] of November did all agree that *Nov.* **15** it was fitt, besides the regiment of foot to be always relieved by another of the militia whilst the danger continued, that two troops of hors of the militia should continue at Yorke to supresse any sudden riseing if it should happen; and at the same time that the gentry and freehoulders of the county should be desired from that

---

[1] Frederick Herman, created Duke of Schomberg immediately after the Revolution, whose mother was an English lady and whose father was a trusted official of the Winter King, Frederick V of the Palatinate.　He served with great distinction in the armies of nearly every power of western Europe, was given a marshal's truncheon by Louis XIV, but as a Protestant found it advisable to quit the French service and was appointed second-in-command by William of Orange because he was well known and highly esteemed in England.　He was killed at the battle of the Boyne.

[2] Charles Paulet, eldest son of the sixth Marquis of Winchester, who succeeded his father as second Duke of Bolton in 1699.

[3] The second baronet, whose wife Elizabeth was a sister of John Beaumont, cashiered from Berwick's regiment.

[4] Gilbert Burnet, later Bishop of Salisbury, author of the *History of My Own Time*.

[5] Son of the parliamentary general.　He had been in exile for some years and was one of the leaders of the more extreme section among William's adherents.

[6] Altered from " 13," which is the correct date (*Hist. MSS. Com.*, vii. 415, 417).

meeting to attend here on Thursday the 19,[1] to draw up some instrument or declaration of our loyalty to the King in this time of danger, and to consult of such things as might tend to the honour of God and our own safetys. This being mooved by Sir Henry Goodrick, I said I thought a thing of that nature, declareing our adherence to the King according to the laws of the land and the obligation of our religion, might be soe good for the goverment and soe discourageing to its ennemies that I did heartily concurr in it; and accordingly a paper of sommons was writt, and dispersed to give notice thorow the county to meet. At the same time I writt to my Lord Preston, Secretary of State, of this sopposed loyall intention of the gentlemen of this county, and to my Lord Duke of Newcastle, desireing he would be here at that time.[2]

Nov 15   Being that day[3] at dinner with my Lord Fairfax, Sir Henry Goodrick, &c., at one Squires, wher we were invited, the clerke of the peace for the West Rideing comes to give notice of a new commission, wherby some thirty principal gentlemen of the West Rideing were left out, and Sir Henry Goodrick amongst others, which put him into a passion, and made him declare that he was sorry for promoting soe good a thing as the said meeting for the Kings service. This same day I heard ther was something more then appeared intended to be done at the time of it. Some said a petition for a speedy and free Parlament, &c.; others said more things would be represented and insisted upon. But Sir Henry and others absolutely denyed it, to which (he being an opon man) I confess I gave credit more then I ought to have done; but friendship decieves many.

---

[1] Really Thursday the 22nd.

[2] The letter to Preston, dated November 13, is printed in *Hist. MSS. Com.*, vii. 415-6. A copy of the summons to the gentry, originally enclosed in the letter, is calendared along with it. The letter to Newcastle, dated November 14, is printed *infra*, p. 583.

[3] Still November 13.

* A copy of the 'paper of sommons' dated 13 November 1688 and signed by Reresby and eight others is in B.L. Add MSS 63780 (Preston papers) fol. 67.

I went to Thriberge to see my family, and returned the *Nov.* 16
19th.   My Lord Duke came to Yorke the same day.
At his coming he said he heard ther was a design to
petition for a free Parlament and he thought it not fitt
soe much of the militia should be togather, the deputy
lieutenants haveing ordered all the regiment of hors to
return to Yorke at or before the 19th of November, under 19
pretence to secure the citty and to exercize them that they
might be more usefull upon occasion.   We sate that night
togather til twelve at night, and ressolved that except the
petition or the intended addresse were very loyall we
should not joine in it.

He calls togather all his deputy lieutenants then in 20
Yorke, viz., my Lord Fairfax, Sir Thomas Gower,[1] Sir
Henry Goodrick, Mr. Robinson, Mr. Danby,[2] Mr.
Jenkyns and others to the nomber of ten, and desired to
know if ther was any other design by this assembly on
Thursday then to make a declaration of loyalty to his
Majesty.   Sir Henry said plainly he did intend to petition for a free Parlament, and he hoped the rest that would
meet would concur in it, after the exemple of a late
petition from some bishops and some temporal lords.[3]
The Duke then said he would not stay to be affronted or
overuled by his deputies, but would return the next day.
I opposed this extreamly, saying that nothing could be
absolutely resolved of til all the gentlemen appeared;
that if any other thing besides a declaration of loyaltie
should be thought nescessary, it might be soe penned,
and with that modesty, that it might satisfie here and not
displease above; however, it was fit his Grace should be
here at a time of such difficulty.

He went away, declareing that noebody had stood by 21
him at this debate (for I had said many things against this

---

[1] The third baronet.

[2] Apparently William Robinson and Christopher Danby.

[3] Presumably the petition presented to the King on November 17, news
of which would have reached York by this time.

way of petitioning) but myselfe.   I pressed him to dismiss the hors, but he did not.

The day being comd (and the fatall one, viz., the 22), I would not goe to the common hall, wher the meeting was appointed (nor indeed was I very able, being il bruised by my hors falling upon me as I came from home); but I heard that amongst about 100 gentlemen that mett Sir Henry Goodrick spoake to this purpas, that ther haveing been a great endeaver by the goverment to bring in popery into this kingdome of late years, and to invade the lawes many ways, that ther was noe way to redresse grievences of this and other natures but by a free Parlament; and therfore this was the only time to petition the King for it, and a better pattern could not be followed then what the lords spirituall and temporal (or some of them) had done before, which he read ther before them. Some differed from him in this matter, as Sir Thomas Yarburgh, Sir Lionel Pilkinton,[1] and one Mr. Stockdale, who said it ought to be moderated in some expressions, and that at the same time that we petitioned we ought to assure the King to stand by him in thes dangers which threatned both him and his kingdomes, with our lives and fortunes; but it was opposed.

When such a draught was finished as Sir Henry and his party approoved of (though many that disliked it went away), they began to sign; and as Mr. Wortley Mountegue[2] and Sir Henry had done, before a third man could sign, Mr. Tankard runs into the hall and crys that the papists were risen and had fired at the militia troops.   At this all the gentlemen run out, and thos that were privy to the design gett their horses, which were laid ready for them, as Sir Henry Goodrick, Mr. Mountegue Wortley, Mr.

---

[1] Sir Lyon Pilkington of Stanley and Nether Bradley, Yorkshire, the third baronet.

[2] Sidney Montagu, second son of the first Earl of Sandwich, who had added the name of Wortley to his own on his marriage with Anne, daughter and heiress of Sir Francis Wortley, baronet, of Wortley, Yorkshire.

Tankard, my Lord Danby, that was ready in his lodgeing expecting this feigned alarme, my Lord Dunblain his son, my Lord Wiloughby, two Mr. Bertue that were comd to him,[1] my Lord Lomley, my Lord Horton [2] and severall others, which made a party with their servants of 100 hors, wel armed and well mounted, and rode up to the four militia troops drawn out for another purpas,[3] and cryed for a free Parlament and the Protestant religion and noe poperie. The captains of thes four troops were Lord Fairfax, Sir Thomas Gower, Mr. Robinson and Captain Tankard,[4] who, being made privy to the design but the night before, but men ready enough in their tempers for such an action, complyed, and led all their men to joine with them.

The first step they made was to the place wher the guard of the standing company was kept, consisting of about twenty men, which they surprized before I had the least notice or jealousie of such an attempt, not believeing it possible that men of such quality and estates (however dissatisfyed) would engage in a design soe desperate, and soe contrary to the laws of the land and the religion which they professed. As soon as I heard of it I sent for the officers and the guard, but found it was surprized. I then sent to every captain of the troops to bring their troops to me as the Kings governor, as also to the other guard of foot of the militia regiment, who all denyed to march or to obay orders. I then sent for my horses, and as I was prepareing to goe to the troops, hopeing to regain

[1] Peregrine and Philip Bertie, brothers of Lord Willoughby and nephews of Lady Danby, were certainly in the north at this time (Hist. MSS. Com., *Lindsey MSS.*, p. 453).

[2] John Holles, Lord Haughton, eldest son of Gilbert, third Earl of Clare, whom he succeeded in January 1689. In February 1690 he married Lady Margaret Cavendish, concerning whom Reresby had conducted so many negotiations, and after the death of his father-in-law was created Duke of Newcastle.

[3] " Pretendedly to go to Doncaster by the Duke's order " (*Hist. MSS. Com.*, vii. 420).

[4] Charles Tancred.

them to the Kings service if I appeared, Sir Henry
Belasis (who had commanded a regiment in Holland under
the Prince,[1] and lurked long here in Yorkeshire for his
service) drew up a party of thirty hors before my door,
and ther prevented my going out, til my Lord of Danby
with his chiefe companions came up to me.

My Lord tould me that to resist was to noe purpas;
that he and thos gentlemen were in arms for a free
Parlament, and for the preservation of the Protestant
religion and the goverment as by law established, which the
King had very near distroyed, and which the Prince of
Orang was com'd to assist them to defend, and he hoped
I would joine with them in soe good a design. I tould
him I was for a Parlament and the Protestant religion as
well as they, but I was also for the King. He replyed
that he was soe too, and therfore he hoped that as we
agreed in principles soe we should agree in action. I
tould his lordship that though we agreed in the matter
I could not agree with them in the manner; I did not
concieve anything out to be exerted from the King by any
manner of force, and that perticularly, haveing his
Majestys commission of governor and for his service, I
could not joine with thos that acted against his authority
and commission, let the consequence be what it would.
He then said he must emprison me. I tould him I was
naked, my friends had relinquished the King's service
and me, and I was in his power. After they had considered togather he tould me he knew me to be a man of
honour, that my engagement not to stirr nor write was
as good a restraint upon me as a guard or a prison, soe I
was only confined upon honour to my room, recomending,
however, to me to consider of his offer.[2]

---

[1] Sir Henry, son of Sir Richard Belasyse of Ludworth and Owton in
the county of Durham, had commanded one of the three English regiments
in the Dutch service (Dalton, *English Army Lists*, ii. 228).

[2] Further details are to be found in Reresby's letter of December 9 to
Halifax, printed *infra*, p. 585.

After this the same day they secured all the gates, sett strong guards upon them, suffered none to goe in nor out, secured such persons as they thought approoved not of their proceedins, especially the officers of the standing company, which the next day revolted all to them except the officers. The militia, both hors and foot, entirely joined with them except one Mr. Colins, lieutenant to my company of the citty regiment. They next entered to the magazin and the stoors, which, God knows, were very inconsiderable,[1] notwithstanding my frequent representations of it to the King both before and of late, soe that a defence with but one company of about fifty men, and but twenty of them on the guard, without amunition or stoors, against 500 hors and two militia regiments of foot (who treacherously joined with them), nay, the whole citty almost, which either for fear or inclination declared for them, was a mockerie, and what could never be expected in our unfortunate case had ther been noe surprize.

The militia troops and some of the gentlemen that were *Nov.* 23 volontiers (which were not sixty men besides gentlemen's servants) ransacked severall houses which belonged to papists (or wher they laid) for priests, arms and horses, and took them wher they found them. They tooke a company of foot just raised by Captain Witham,[2] not yet armed, quartered at Tadcaster, and another of granadeers, comanded by Captain Villars,[3] in their rout for London as they came to Yorke; but as yet they did not touch any property but the Kings and the papists, and mine by takeing coales and some other provisions which I had laid in for the use of the guarrison, &c.

[1] " Three barrels of powder and some old rusty arms " (*Hist. MSS. Com.*, vii. 420).

[2] Thomas Witham. The company under his command, at first independent, had just been incorporated in Colonel Bevil Skelton's regiment of foot (Dalton, *English Army Lists*, ii. 189).

[3] Henry Villiers commanded the grenadier company in Colonel Cornwall's regiment of foot (*ibid.* ii. 139).

Nov. 24   The earl caused my Lord Maior to call a hall, wher the said Earl of Danby made a speech setting forth the caus of their riseing and of their declaration, desireing that the citty would concurr with them in the latter, which they ther did agree to sign, as also severall gentlemen. The declaration being the next day printed, ther were of hands of lords, six; of lords' sons (yonger ones), three; of baronets, five; of knights, six; of squires and gentlemen, sixty-six; citizens of Yorke, fifty-six. The news from Nottingham was then that the Earl of Devonshire, the Lord Delamer, with many more lords and gentlemen, were risen ther upon the same account, and that great nombers flocked to them. The King was this while marching to Salisbury, wher he had appointed the rendezvous of his whole army, and had sent the yong Prince of Wales to Portsmoth, some said to France.

26   Haveing made it my request to the Earl of Danby that I might have leave to be a prisner at my hous in the country, wher I would engage not to act, but to acquiesce and abide as a true prisner, he sent for me to come and dine with him. At my comming he tould me, that I might eat my dinner the better upon the said terms, I should have leave to go when I pleased. At dinner he tould me that the Dukes going away had given room for their design, that I [1] feared I knew or suspected something of it. I answered I did believe they would goe high in their petition, but never suspected soe many gentlemen of that ranke and quality would venter to engage in soe dangerous a matter; and if I had known it, I should certainly have resisted, though to little purpas, or have escaped out of the town.

Upon discours with severall of the gentlemen I found they began to consider of the thing as more dangerous then they thought at the first, and were troubled that men came not faster into them. My Lord Willoughby said it was the first time that any Bertie was ever engaged against

[1] Presumably a mistake for " he " or " they."

the Crown, and it was his trouble; but ther was a nescessity either to part with our religion and properties or doe it. I gave him reasons why all thos invasions upon either might have been prevented without a force, as by a thorow representation of the whole kingdome concerning them, and desire of a redresse in Parlament, which his Majesty must have nescesserily complyed with in a short time, the want of mony, the distraction and discontent of the nation, and a plane discovery that poperie could never now be setled in England obligeing the King to it for his own safety and interest as wel as theirs.

Sir Henry Goodrick would have persuaded me the same day to have signed the declaration; but I tould him I could not doe it, for though I should agree to the matter of it, yet since they were now in arms to assert it, the signing of the declaration and petition was noe less, in my judgement, then joineing in the force. Mr. Tankard pressed me to be of their party the same day, setting forth the great advantage it would be to them, which I stil persisted to deny.

That day the clerke of the peace gave me notice that a new commission was brought down, and all thos gentlemen added of the West Rideing formerly put out, as I mentioned before; but that myselfe and two more were now left out. My Lord of Danby took hould of this, and said at dinner that this showed a ressentment against me, and that I should find I should be wors used by that party then by them; but did not affect me.

The Duke of Newcastle sent orders to his captains of *Nov. 27* hors to dismiss their militia troops, but they refus'd to obay him, and laughed at him for his message. One of his gentlemen that came from him with an expresse was persuaded not to return, but to ride one of the Earl of Danby's horses in this expedition. My Lord Lomley tould me the same day that for all he was sorry I did not joine with them, yet I had performed a wise and a generous part in my circumstances to refuse it.

I obteaned a pass of their generalships to goe home to Thriberge, upon engagement to be confined to that place or five miles from it, to live peaceably, and not to act in any hostile manner. The news came then as if the army had voated for a free Parlament, but declared at the same time that they would defend the Kings person against all men, which was the very thing I desired to be the subject of our Yorkeshire petition or declaration, and the denyall of which made me refuse to subscribe or agree to it.

Soon after we heard that severall great men, officers of the army and perticular confidents of the King, had revolted from him and were gone to the Prince of Orange; and that perticularly the 19 of November, the King being got to Salisbury, wher his army then rendevoued, the Lord Churchil, one of his major-generals, under pretence of showing his Majesty the outguards of his army, had led him into a traine, wher he had certainly been betrayed into the hands of a party of the Prince his army, but that an immoderate bleeding at the nose prevented his going. My Lord Churchil, finding that he missed of his design, went immediately over to the Prince,[1] accompanied by the Duke of Grafton, Colonel Berkley[2] and others. This ungratefull Lord Churchill was raised from page to the King to the degree of a vicount of England, and had gott a great estate with it by the Kings bounty.

But what was the most surprizeing was that the King, seeing that it was hard to know whom to trust and returning to Andever the 24th, ther supped with him Prince George of Denmarke (his son) and the Duke of Ormond,[3] both which left him and went over that night

[1] On the night of November 24-25.

[2] John Berkeley, who succeeded his eldest brother Maurice as fourth Viscount Fitzhardinge in 1690. At this time he was colonel of the Princess Anne's regiment of dragoons.

[3] James Butler, who had succeeded his grandfather as second duke in the previous summer.

to the Prince, with my Lord Drumlenrick (son to the Duke of Queenborow)[1] and Mr. Boyle, heir to the Earl of Burlinton.[2]   The 25 the Princess of Denmarke withdrew herselfe privately from Whitehal with my Lady Churchil,[3] and came to Nottingham.   The nomber of thos that revolted were not 1,000 in all as yet, but everyone was soe jealous one of another that they knew not who to trust; soe the army and artilery marched back towards London, and the King came ther on the 26.   The out-quarters of his army was at Windser, Reding, &c.

On the 27 the King called all the lords spirituall and temporall then in town, about fifty in nomber, whos advice he took to order writs to be issued out for calling of a free Parlament, for putting all Roman Catholiques out of his councils and imployments, for issuing out a general pardon to all thos that were assisting to the Prince, and for sending commissioners to treat with him.   The proclamation came out accordingly for a Parlament to be called to meet the 15 of January next, and my Lord Halifax, my Lord Nottingham,[4] and my Lord Godolphin were named commissioners to goe to the Prince.

I gott to Thriberge with my horses and arms without *Dec.* 1 any disturbance, and I thanke God I left Yorke without any clamer or reflection upon me in the least in the matter of my command.

Kingston-upon-Hul, that considerable guarrison, and 3 looked upon as one of the strongest in England both for

[1] James Douglas, Earl of Drumlanrig, was the eldest son of the first Duke of Queensberry, whom he succeeded in 1695.

[2] A mistake on Reresby's part.   Henry Boyle, who went over to the Prince at this time, was the youngest son of Charles, Lord Clifford, who was Burlington's heir.   In 1714 Henry was raised to the peerage as Baron Carleton of Carleton, Yorkshire.

[3] Sarah Jennings, whose influence over Anne began when she was still a member of the household of Mary of Modena and continued when she was Duchess of Marlborough.

[4] Daniel Finch, who had succeeded his father, Heneage, as second Earl of Nottingham in 1682.

the citadel, its scituation and nomber of men, was surprized by Mr. Copley, lieutenant-governor, who, getting
a party with him, seized the governor, my Lord Langdale,
in the night, and a great many Roman Catholiques then
in town who had fled thether for safety; and the souldiers
joining in the treachery, they declared for the King and
the Protestant religion, giveing immediately notice to the
gentlemen at York what was done. If such places as
this revolted, it was no wonder if Yorke could not be kept.

About the same time a party was sent from Yorke to
Welbeck to take the Duke of Newcastles horses and arms,
which they effected, but did not meddle with his person.

Plimoth, also a strong guarrison, was taken; but that
was by the treachery of its governor (the Earl of Bath,
who had been raised from baronet to that degree and to a
great estate by the Court), who revolted to the Prince.
Bristow and severall other less places followed the same
fate. In that part of Yorkeshire wher I lived very few
gentlemen continued firm to the King, nor indeed in any
part of the north of England.

Dec. 8　The Prince of Wales, poor infant, was brought from
Portsmoth to London, when everybody believed he had
9 been sent into France; and on Sunday night, being the
9th, the Queen with the Prince went down the river about
twelve a clock to a barge secretly prepared, and the wind
being fair wafted over to Dunkirk.

10　A regiment of Scotch hors deserted and went over to
the Prince of Orange from the Kings army, and ther was
scarce an hour but his Majesty recieved, like Job, some
message of some revolt or misfortune or other; soe that
the King himselfe upon the 11th[1] (by ill advice) did also
withdraw himselfe privately with only two or three persons
along with him, as most thought to follow the Queen.
This absenting himselfe was the more wondred at bycaus
the commissioners sent to the Prince of Orange had sent
him word that day that they thought that things might

[1] During the night of December 10-11.

be accomodated with his Highness to his Majestys satisfaction; wherupon he ordered the Cabinet Council to
meet the next day at nine in the morning, but intended
nothing less then to be ther, but went away that very
night without leaveing behind him any orders or directions
in the least.   My Lord Chancellor withdrew himselfe at
the same time, and took the great seale along with him;
soe that all things seemd to be left in confusion, and the
generall consternation was suitable to it.   Upon this the
lords spirituall and temporall and the generall officers
writt to the Prince to let him know that the King had left
them, and that they would endeaver to keep all things in
order till they recieved his Highness his directions,
inviteing him to town at the same time.[1]

The rabble, being sufficiently animated against the
papists before, and more especially now (thinkeing, and
reasonably, that the council given the King to withdraw
himselfe came from them), rose in prodigious nombers,
and divideing themselves pulled down the chappells of
that worship and many houses of such as did profess it,
takeing and spoiling their goods, imprisoning such as they
suspected to be priests.   Nor did they forebear the very
chappels and houses of embassadors and other publique
ministers, and perticularly that of the Spanish embassador,[2]
who had, as it was believed, of his own and other persons,
who sent their plate to him for protection, goods and plate
taken from him to the value of a hundred thousand pounds.
What was of less value relateing to that superstition was
publiquely burnt in the streets.

The same day my Lord Chancellor, who had stayed *Dec.* 12
too long at London for the tide, though he was disguised
like a seaman and had cutt off his eyebrows, was stopt
for want of the tide at Wapping, and ther taken and committed to the Tower by order of the Lords.   He was

[1] The peers did not actually invite William to town but the city of
London did.

[2] Don Pedro Ronquillo.   His chief personal loss was his library.

first brought before the Lord Maior [1] upon suspicion, but as soon as known they were forced to give him a strong guard, or else he had been torn in pieces by the rabble. Soon after, Mr. Pen [2] (the great Quaker, who had joined with the papists in all their late councils at Court, a very witty man, and one the King trusted in very much for his advice in promoting the dispenceing power for liberty of concience) was taken, and Father Peters, [3] the Kings confessor, who was the greatest incendiary in that transaction, and one of the Privy Council, the first Jesuit that had sate ther for many years.

The King at his going away writt to the general officers of the army to this effect, that things being com'd to extremity, and being forced to send away the Queen and Prince, he was forced to followe himselfe, hopeing it may at some time please God to touch the hearts of this nation with true loyalty and honour; that if he could have trusted in his troops he would in the least have had one blow for it; but though ther [were] some loyall and brave men amongst them, both officers and souldiers, yet it was their own advice to him not to venter himselfe in their head or to fight the Prince of Orange with them. He thanked thos that had stuck to him for their fidelity, and though he did not expect they should expose themselves by resisting a forraign army and a poysoned nation, yet he hoped they would preserve themselves free from associations and pernicious things. Postscript: that as he had ever found them loyall, soe they ever had and ever shold find him a kind master.

My Lord Feathersham, commanding as general, sent this letter to the Prince, and tould him that it bearing directions or orders not to make opposition against anybody, he had given notice of it in the army to prevent the

[1] Sir John Chapman, who was so much upset by the events of this day that he did not long survive it.

[2] William Penn, the founder of Pennsylvania.

[3] A mistake. Petre escaped to France.

effusion of Christian blood ; and upon it a great part of the army disbanded.

About the 11 or 12th day[1] his Majesty, being in a hoye with very few with him (amongst others Sir Edward Hales), and passing from an island in Kent, was boarded by a boat that [had] thirty-six armed men on board her, which was going (as they called it) a priest codding or catching.   They used the King (especially thos that were with him) very uncivilly, tooke from his Majesty 300 ginnies, all he was worth at that time, and his sword. When they knew it was the King they offered to restoor both.   The King recieved the latter, but not the first. Being brought to shoar, he went to my Lord Winchelseys,[2] wher he was taken with another fitt of bleeding at the nose, which made him very weake and sick.   Information being given to the lords above at Whitehall, they ordered four lords, Ailsbury,[3] Middleton, Yarmouth,[4] &c., with some of his servants, to attend him and to carry him nescessarys.   Some of his guards also and my Lord Feathersham waited upon him; but their orders were to leave it to his Majesty's choice to goe or return, which he pleased, it not being thought fit to put any restraint upon his person.   The Lord Peterborough, the Earl of Salisbury[5] (two new converts), and Father Walker, Master of University Colege in Oxford, were also taken.

The Prince of Orange, being invited to London by the lords that sate at Whitehall and the Citty, was comd as far as Windser before the news came that his Majesty was intercepted.   *Dec.* 13

---

[1] Actually on December 12.

[2] Heneage Finch, second Earl of Winchilsea, who had been Lord Lieutenant of Kent until dismissed by James in the previous year.

[3] Thomas Bruce, who had succeeded his father as second Earl of Ailesbury in 1685.

[4] William Paston, who had succeeded his father as second Earl of Yarmouth in 1683.

[5] James Cecil, fourth Earl of Salisbury.

The same day I hearing the writts were comd to Yorke for chooseing members of Parlament, I writt to my Lord Maior and some other friends that whatever change I suffered my principles were the same, to secure the Protestant religion and to preserve his Majestys person, and if they thought fit to choos me I was ready to serve them upon that foundation. It was not that I either expected to be chosen or desired it. I foresaw severall things would be attempted or done in this Parlament which were very dangerous, and wher honesty and true principles could neither consent or be able to oppose. I writt to my Lord of Danby at the same time, letting him know my pretention and asserting my principle. He writt me a very civil letter, in which he tould me that he neither questioned my principles as a gentleman nor as a Protestant, and could therfore wish I was a member of the ensuing Parlament; but the citty of Yorke haveing offered his son, my Lord Dunblain, the cittizenship for one, and Mr. Alderman Thomson pretending to the other, he thought I should find it a difficulty to succeed ther; however I had liberty to goe wher I pleased, and that for the future I was noe longer under restraint, and that if he could serve me in anything he should be very ready.

Dec. 17   The Lord Dunblain and Alderman Thomson were elected without competition citizens for that Parlament.

19   My Lord of Danby and his son went towards London, being Wedensday. The Sunday before, the King returned to London and the people made great acclamations of joy as he passed in the streets, but it was observed that very few lords attended on him at his arrival.

Upon the 18th the Prince, before he came to London, sent in his own forces, possest himselfe of the Tower, quartered them in and near the town, placed them at Whitehall, and sent the King this message at two a clock in the morning, that his Majesty must remove from thence that day to some place ten or twelve miles from London, and to be attended by the Prince his guards. His Majesty accordingly went to Rochester, accompinyed by my Lord Dunbarton, my Lord Ailsbury and my Lord Arran.[1] Then the Prince came to St. James his, wher he was complimented and attended by a great many of the nobility, and the night was spent in ringing of bels, bonefires, and other expressions of joy by the rabble; but thinkeing men of the Citty seemd displeasd at the King's being forced to withdraw himselfe a second time.

At this first comming the Prince seem'd to countenance Presbutery more then thos of the Church of England, which startled the clergy. He ordered as many of the Kings forces to be called togather again as could be gott, and confined my Lord Featthersham in Windser Castle for haveing disbanded them and some other things laid to his charge. He took soe much upon him that he made the Duke of Beauford wait four hours before he gave him admittance to him.

The King from this proceeding began to apprehend he was in danger, and sent to [the] lords that he desired to withdraw himselfe out of the kingdome. They took some time to consider what answer to give his Majesty. In the meantime he went away privately a second time.[2] Thos that were of the Kings guards or other his troops in London, the Prince sent them twenty miles from thence to make room for his own men.

The lords haveing sate in the Lords Hous for some time, *Dec. 20* finding his Majesty refused to appoint another Chancellor or Lord Keeper or to produce the great seale, they being about sixty in nomber, spirituall and temporal, and my Lord Marquis of Halifax chairman, they made an order for the banishing of all papists, but such as had been househoulders for four years last past, ten miles out of London.[3]

[1] James Douglas, Earl of Arran, who became fourth Duke of Hamilton in 1698.

[2] During the night of December 22-23.

[3] This order was made on December 22, the first day on which the Lords met in their own House.

Dec. 25   Being Christmas Day, the lords did not cease to sit on that day, and amongst other things fram'd an address to the Prince to take the goverment upon him til things were setled.

26   Such a nomber of the lords were appointed to carry it to the Prince,[1] to which he returnd this answer, that he could give noe answer to it til he had the opinion of the Comons.   Two days before, the Prince had ordered my Lord Maior and fifty of the aldermen and common council,[2] with all such as had been members of the Hous of Commons in town in the Parlaments of King Charles the Second, to meet in the Hous of Comons, and to sit ther as a comitteè of that Hous, as the lords fram'd one of theirs.   Ther mett to the nomber of about 300, who voted to agree with the lords in most things, perticularly in their address to take the goverment upon him until the 22nd of January that a convention was to be agreed upon to be called, thos writts (it should seem) that were issued out for calling a Parlament, and the elections that were made upon them, being void.[3]

29   I recieved a letter from Colonel Beaumont, late lieutenant-colonel to the Duke of Barwick, that the Prince had given him that regiment, and that he desired me (my company being squandred) to gather as many of them togather as I could, and to raise new men to recruit them.

It was very much that in thes confusions noe more mischeifs had been comitted.   In the West Rideing ther was few or noe justices of the peace sworn but papists,

---

[1] The address was resolved upon by the lords on the 24th and presented to the Prince on the 25th.

[2] The Lord Mayor, the aldermen, and fifty representatives of the common council.

[3] It had been suggested as a possible method of settling the Government that those who had been elected in accordance with the writs issued by James II should meet at the time specified in these writs and provide for elections in constituencies which had not returned members ; " but this was slighted " (*Clarendon Correspondence*, ii. 235).

who all absconded, nor any almost that acted as deputy lieutenants; and yet very few roberies, felonies, and not one murder, and scarce a battery had been committed; only some arms and horses had been seized of Roman Catholiques, and that under colour of authority.

The Prince, upon the address made to him from the Lords and the representative of Commons, as is before mentioned, to take the goverment upon him until the 22nd of January next, made this answer to it, as also to *Dec.* 28 other perticulars relating to the revenue, the Protestant religion and the kingdome of Ireland, that he would endeavour according to their advice to secure the peace of the nation til the meeting of the convention, for the meeting wherof in January next he would issue out letters to the countys and buroughs; that he would apply the revenue to the most proper uses that the present affairs requird, and endeavour to put Ireland into such a condition as that the Protestant religion and the English interest might be mentained in that kingdome; and that he would hazard himselfe for the laws and liberties and the preservation of the Protestant religion at all times in thes kingdomes, it being the end for which he came.

At this time the news came that the King was safely arrived in France, and was gone to the Queen, who was at Paris, the French King haveing prepared the castle of Vincennes for their Majestys reception and entertainment; but afterwards they remooved to St. Germain.

I found by the letter I had from Colonel Beaumont that the officers who were Protestants were to be continued, and by the Kings commission, till some change of goverment was to be setled, at which time if it were such as a man could not honestly serve under, I considered it would be in a mans power to lay down his commission, and possibly have leave to sell the company or to dispose of it to a friend, and therfore did order the getting togather as many of my men as I could. But indeed ther appeard some nescessity for it besides, ther comming out a publique advertisment or proclamation in the *Gazet*,[1] that thos of the Princesse Ann of Denmarkes regiment that did not repair to their quarters before the 26 of January should be proceeded against, if taken, as deserters. Besides, that which made the thing to appear more warrantable was that the King seemd at his second going away, as well as the first time, to give some encouragement to it, telling his officers that they might doe the best they could for themselves, only that they should not enter into associations.

My Lord Treconell, Lord Lieutenant of Ireland, all this while continued firm to the Kings interest, with a great army of papists; and my Lord Insequine[2] raised another of Protestants and declared for the Prince and the Protestant religion, haveing taken London Derry and some other strong towns in that kingdome.

Cercular letters were written by the Prince to the peers, desireing them to give their attendence at the Lords Hous *Jan.* 22 upon 22, that being the time appointed for the meeting [1688/9] of the convention both for Lords and Commons; and accordingly both knights, citizens and burgesses were elected, by virtue of such letters to the severall countys and burroughs.

Finding but very few of the ould souldiers of my company in Yorkshire, I sent to Sheffield and Rotherham to make new recruits, and in three days time, only by sending my servants, I raised near sixty yong men without beat of drum, and choosing the most likely sent them with an officer to the quarter at Southampton the 16th of January.

I went to see the Duke of Newcastle at Welbeck, whom I found very loyall and firm to his master the King, and consequently as angry against the Earls of Danby and Devonshire, and such others as had been the actors in thos parts for the Prince of Orange. He said he would

---

[1] The *London Gazette* for December 27-31, 1688.

[2] William O'Brien, second Earl of Inchiquin.

always be loyall to the King, firm to his religion, and act always according to lawe. He showed me a copie of a letter he writt to the King some few days before the Kings first withdrawing himselfe, wherin he expressed very kind things of me to his Majesty. He tould me he had recieved a letter of sommons to be at the convention, but that he would not goe nor act in that assembly; that he had offered to surrender the commission of his lieutenancys into the Kings hands before he went, but the King would not recieve them; and that he would act soe long as he might doe it by them, but would not take any commissions from the Prince, or any such authority.

The 17th I recieved a letter from the Duke of Newcastle, incloseing others which he had recieved from my Lord Danby, Sir Henry Goodrick, my Lord Devonshire (all flattery, lies, and pretentions of loyalty) whilst the rebellion was hatching.

I went to Mansfield, and the next day went thence for London in the hacney coach. When I arrived I found London much changed. The guards and other parts of the army, which both in their persons and gallantry were an ornament to the town, being sent to quarter ten miles of, the streets were filled with ill lookeing and ill habited Dutch and other strangers of the Princes army. And yet the Citty was soe pleased with their diliverers that they did not or would not perceave their deformity, nor the oppression they laid under, which was much greater then what they felt from the English army. *Jan.* 22

Though the convention had mett the 22, yet nothing was done considerable till the 28th, that the settlement of the nation being taken into consideration by the Commons, they passed this voat, that King James the Second, haveing endeavoured to pervert the goverment of this kingdome by breaking the original contract between the King and his people, and by the advice of Jesuists and other wicked persons haveing subverted the fondementall lawes, and haveing withdrawn himselfe 28 out of the kingdome, had abdicated the goverment, and that the throne is therby vacant.

Jan. 29   The Lords entered into consideration of the same matter, wher severall motions were made to the same purpas as ther was the day before in the Hous of Commons. Some were for recalling the King upon conditions (but thos very few); others for the goverment to be continued in the Kings name, and the Prince to have the executive power of it by the name of regent or protectour; others for haveing the King forfeit the crown and the Prince of Orange elected into it; others for haveing the said Prince and Princess crowned, as it was in the case of Philip and Mary, and to hould it by descent in right of his wife, without takeing notice of the Prince of Wales, who was to be made incapable to succeed, bycaus a papist, being

30 christined in that Church. At last the Lords voated to agree with the Commons in the maine as to the vacancy of the crown, only differing in some words, and adjurned the debate till the next day. That voat was only carried by three.

The same day [1] the Commons did pass thes voats: that it was found by experience inconsistant for a Protestant kingdome to be governed by a popish prince; secondly, that a committè be appointed to bring in generall heads of such things as are absolutely nescessary to be considered of for the better secureing our religion, laws and libertys. The reason of this last voat was that before any person was named to fill the throne they would frame conditions upon which only he should be accepted as King, and tie him up more strictly to the observance of them then other princes had been before.

The Prince all this while seemd not much to concern himselfe, only desired that, the case of Holand and of Ireland requireing it, they would dispatch and come to an early resolution.

31   That being the day for a thankesgiveing for the Prince

----

[1] January 29.

of Orange his arrivall, &c., and, as it was worded, for the
delivery of this nation from poperie and slavery, or to
that effect, it was observed that the rejoiceing was not soe
great either by ringing of bels or makeing of bonefires as
was expected in the citty of London, soe mutable are the
minds of Englishmen that they are never long very fond
of anything.

That day the Lords, sitting in the afternoon, resumed
the debate, and could not agree with the Commons in the
word *abdicated*, as being too high a word, and changed it
into *deserted*.   Nor did they concurr with them that the
throne was absolutely vacant, soe that by the voat of the
Lords ther yet remaind room for a regent or protectour,
or the King to be recalled himselfe upon terms.

I see my Lord Halifax.   Ther was with him Mr. *Feb.* 1
Seamure, quondam Speaker of the Commons, a man of
great parts, and much for power to continue in the Kings
name, nay, in his person, if we could but be secured against
poperie, &c.   Doctor Burnett was ther also (the great
creature of the Prince of Orange), who argued violently
for the crowning of the Prince.   Burnet mentained that
England could never be happily setled till the Prince was
placed in the head of the gouverment and was in strict
conjunction with Holand.   Seamure said it was not
practicable, for if the Prince was King he must mentain
it by an army, and that was not to be trusted against their
natural prince, for as the late English army would not
fight for poperie, soe neither would they fight against
their King, as was apparent by their dayly deserting and
quitting their commands; nor was it possible for Holand
and England to be heartily united, they both courting
the same mistriss, trade.

My Lord Halifax tould me that night that he was not
privy to this design of the Prince his comming at the
first; but now that he was here, and upon soe good an
occasion, we were obliged to defend him.   I acquainted
him with what I heard, that my Lord Danby expected

preference before him in the Prince his favour.   He gave me some reasons that satisfyed me of the contrary, and that his lordship began to lagg in his zeale for the Prince his interest in the Hous of Lords.   One was that he was never to hope to be Lord Treasurer, the Prince haveing declared he would manage it by commissioners.   My Lord Halifax spoake further that himselfe should be imployed, and used some arguments to me to proove the legality of acccpting to be soe.   One was that the King haveing relinquished the goverment, it was not for that to be lett fall, and it could not be supported if men did not act under thos on whom it was conferred, and that as things stood now *salus populi* was *suprema lex*.   His lordship said further that ther were soe many declined to serve, and ther was soe few fitt for it, that if I would doe it ther would noe question be room for it; and that after things were setled he thought it adviseable for me to goe embassador to some prince or state, by which means I might be out of the way till the clouds that appeard were dispersed, being soe fitt for that sort of imployment.   He said other kind things to me, and offered to carry me the next morning to the Prince, whom I had not yet seen, and gave me some advice to be careful of my company, and how to manage myselfe at such a time as this was.

Feb. 2   I went to meet the marquis, who was with the Prince in his bedchamber. But comming out to me, he said the Prince could not be publiquely seen of two hours, and therfore advised me to deferr waiting upon him til the next day.

This day the lords that were for conferring the crown immediately upon the Prince, fearing the contrary interest of makeing him only regent, or crowning him in right of his wife, might prevaile, sent some instruments to stirr up the mobile,[1] who came in a tumultuous manner with a petition, offering it both to the Lords and Commons, to this purpas: to crown both the Prince and Princess of Orang, to take speedy care of religion and property, and

[1] The early form of the word " mob."

for the defence of Ireland. The Lords rejected it bycaus it was not signed, and the Commons did the same, saying they would not be awed into their voats nor directed, for they ought to be free.

The same day the King sent two letters, one to the Lords, the other to the Commons; but the person that brought them not being ther present to testifie that they came from the King, they were not read but laid by, and the messenger ordered to attend the Lords Hous on Monday morning.

I was then tould by a Court lady [1] that it was much wondered that my friend the Marquis of Halifax was soe much for the King's haveing abdicated the goverment, when he knew he had not gone if he had not been frighted into it. She tould me that his lordship had treated with the King to come again into business some weeks before the certainty of the Prince his invasion was certainly known; that she was the very person sent by him to the King, that the King mett him in her hous, and that they agreed upon terms, nay, that his lordship treated with some priests concerning his return to Court; that for this reason the King depended most on him, and nam'd him one of the three lords to be sent to the Prince of Orange to treat for him; that the marquis sent the King a private letter, after he had spoake to the Prince, threatning some ill design against his person, which was the true reason of his Majestys flight and of sending away the Queen; and after the King was brought back, that my Lord Halifax was one of the lords that came and advertised the King on the behalfe of the Prince to goe from Whitehall to Rochester or Ham in two hours; and that the reason his lordship gave for bringing the King soe ungratefull a message was that he was assured that the Prince his party had ressolved in council to seize and imprison him; soe that it was obvious to my Lords own knowlege that

[1] Possibly Eleanor, daughter of Richard Wall of Tipperary and wife of Sir Theophilus Oglethorpe (Foxcroft, *Halifax*, ii. 2).

it was neither the Kings inclination to fly either the first or the second time, but selfe-preservation.

She tould me further that the King was soe fully possest of his danger, and afflicted after the Princesse Anne went away, that it disordered his understanding the first time, but after he returnd was very well restoored. She said further that the second time he went away he soe little designd it that he knew not wher to goe; sometimes he ressolved to goe into the north to the Earl of Danby; once he ressolved to goe to the Bishops of Canterbury or Winchester,[1] and that she was sent by the King to them to know if they would recieve and secure him, and that the two bishops neither accepted nor rejected the offer. She tould me, moreover, that the lords intended to make use of the marquis for the Prince his service, but not for any advantage to his lordship; and that he haveing been the first adviser of takeing away the charters of corporations, when the goverment was once setled he was in danger to be called to account for that and other things, haveing great ennemys of that party to which he adhered. At last she desired me to contrive it soe, if possible, that she might speake to his lordship, to the end she might soe far moderate him if possible as, however, to be for a regency, and not a forfiture or abdication of the Crown. I tould her I would endeavour it, but I found his lordship too far engaged with the party to recede.

The same lady tould me that a great lord of Scotland had tould her some few days before that in case the two Houses agreed to make the goverment vacant, that Scotland would choos for itselfe, and be noe longer a province to England, or dance attendence at the door of an English court.

[1] Peter Mews, appointed in November 1684. He took part in the suppression of Monmouth's rebellion and was wounded at Sedgemoor, but as visitor of Magdalen College supported Hough there and approved of the petition of the seven bishops.

All that the Lords voated or did more that day was to order the 6 day of February, usually kept as an anniversary for the Kings comming to the Crown, not to be observed, and to send down their voat to the Commons concerning the abdication, with its alterations.

The Commons, haveing considered of it, voated to *Feb.* 2 adhere to their own voat *totidem verbis*.

I see the Duke of Sommerset, the Earl of Burlinton, 3 the Earle of Scarsdale and some other lords who had all been active to bring in the Prince speak in another strain. Some said the thing was gone further then they expected, others that they never believed the Prince would contend for the crown; and all were of opinion the crown ought to be sett upon the Princesse head, and soe to descend in its right cours. The Earle of Scarsdale tould me the Princess of Denmarke was very sensible what a mistake she had committed to leave her father to come into the Prince, who was now endeavouring to invade her right and to gett priority of succession before her.

The reasons being sent down from the Lords to the 4 Commons for adhearing to their word *deserting*, and that ther was noe vacancy, it came to a devision of the Hous, 183 for agreeing with the Lords, 251 against it.[1] I had some private discours with Lord Halifax that day.

A free conference was held between the two Houses, 5 the issue of which was the next day, upon considering the reasons of the Commons, that it being put to the voat in the Hous of Lords, whether or noe they should 6 agree with the Commons, it was carryd in the affirmative. The vacancy being thus agreed to, the Lords proceeded to consider how the throne ought to be filled, and voted that the Prince and Princess of Orange should be crowned 7 King and Queen of England by the names of King William and Queen Mary. The Commons went further, and

---

[1] This division took place on February 5 and the voting was 282 to 151 against the Lords' amendments (*Journals of the House of Commons*, x. 20).

voated not only that, but that all sanction of the lawes,
or the negative voice, should be in the King singly and
not in the Queen, it being improper to have two negatives,
in case of disagreement in their opinions; that the succession of the crown should be to them and the longer liver
of them, then to their issue, and for want therof to Princess
Ann and her issue, and next to the issue of the Prince of
Orange in case he had any by another venter, and soe to
the right line, papists excepted.

Feb. 8   The Commons finished certain grievences or usurpa-
tions upon the rights of the people by the Crown (as they
called them), which they sent up to the Lords for their
concurrance, and which they intended to lay before the
Prince and to desire remedie in, at the same time that they
offered him the crown of England with its dependencies.

9   The Marquis of Halifax desired me to bring the lady
to my hous, wher he gave her a meeting and had a
conversation with her for two hours, in which, she tould
me afterwards, she delt soe freely with him as to tell him
that she wondered he of all men could consent to the
Kings abdicating the goverment, when he knew it was
from the notice himselfe gave him that, by what was
ressolved in council by the Prince, &c., at Windser, if he
stayed he was in danger of his life; that for this notice
the King had own'd his life to him now as he had his
escapeing being excluded before.   My Lord replyed that
the King dealt il with him in sending him a message to
the Prince, and going away before he returnd.   She said
he should not say soe to her, that knew that his lordship
sent him away, and then was angry that he went.   The
lord complained to her that the King never sent for him
til the Prince was landed.   She said his lordship knew
that herselfe was privy to his being ofton invited to Court,
and that he might have had his own terms long before,
but held off; but though he had now embarked soe deep
in another interest it became him to be aware, for the
Earl of Danby would certainly gett before him and play

the same part with him in this Court that Lord Sunderland
had acted in the other; that all that was doeing was upon
sandy foundations; that Scotland would now choos a
king of their own; Ireland was probably lost (the Lord
Deputy Treconel haveing an army of 40,000 men), and
England was much devided; and said a great deale more
to the same effect. His lordship confessed that ther was
noe great hopes of a lasting peace from this settlement;
however, it was the best that could be made at this time
of the day; that he knew what interest she had with the
King, and in case anything hapned desired she would be
his friend, as he would be hers in another place. The
thruth is she dealt more bouldly then any other could
venter to doe with soe great a man; but his lordship knew
her and was prepared for it before, for he tould me it was
not amiss to hear what everybody had to say.

Ther was truly great discontents at this day, and the
causes of them were thes: The Prince declared that he
had noe design for the crown, and yet sought it all he
could. He came to settle the Protestant religion, and
yet brought over 4,000 papists in his army, which were
near as many as the King had English of that religion in
his. It was published that the false or supositious birth
of the Prince of Wales, a private treaty with France to
invade and enslave England, the murders of the late King
and of the Earl of Essex, would all be made out; and yet
nothing appeared, only some little matter as to that of the
Earl of Essex. The Prince kept his Dutch forces in
London, and sent the English army to remote quarters,
declared that he would keep his own men here and send
the English into Holand and Ireland. The Princess
Ann of Denmarke was postponed in the succession,
severall noblemen disappointed of expected preferments
for comming into him, bycaus they voated not for his
Highness soe readily as he expected. The letters his
Majesty writt to both Houses were not soe much as
oponed or read, and trade (the Dutch being a frugal

people) much abated in London to what it was in the Kings time.

Feb. 11 Both Houses having agreed at severall conferences on their grivences, or invasions, as they called them, upon the liberties of the people by former kings, now expected to be redressed, and the Princess of Orange being safe arrived from Holand, the day after, which 12 hapned to be upon Shrove Teusday, both Houses in a body went to attend their Highnesses, sate in two chairs of state in the Banketting Hous at Whitehall;[1] wher the Lords Speaker,[2] after haveing read their said grievences and desired redress of them, desired them also to accept of the crowns of England, France and Ireland, with the dependencies and dominions therto belonging. The Prince, after a short speech wherin he tould them that he did accept of the same, and would do what he could to preserve their libertys, went away with the Princess; and the heralds with severall of the nobility proceeded to proclaim them King and Queen through the Citty according to the usuall forms, the rest of the day being spent in ringing of bels, bonefires at night, and other expressions of joy, though a great many looked very sadly upon it.

Some of the chiefe things which the conventioners declared illegal and desired redress of for the future at this time were as follow: suspention of laws or their execution by the King without consent of Parlament; dispenseing with laws or the execution of laws as aforesaid; the court of commissioners for ecclesiastical causes; the raiseing of mony by prerogative without Parlaments; the keeping a standing army in time of peace without consent of Parlament; obstructing the free choice of members for Parlament, or freedome of speech in Parlament; imposeing

[1] The Declaration of Right was completed on Tuesday the 12th, Mary arrived at Whitehall on the evening of the same day, and the ceremony in the Banqueting House took place on the 13th.

[2] Halifax.

excessive baile or fynes upon the subjects; the illegall choice of jurors.

The oaths of allegiance and supremacy were then desired by the two Houses to be supprest, and thes two were framed to be taken in their stead. In the room of the first was this:

I, A.B., doe sincerely promess and swear that I wil be faithful and bear true allegiance to their Majestys King William and Queen Mary. Soe helpe me God.

For the second thus:

I, A.B., doe swear that I doe from my heart abhor, detest and abjure as impious and heretical that damnable doctrin and position that princes excomunicated or deprived by the Pope or any authority of the sea of Rome may be deposed or murdered by their subjects or any other whatsoever, and I doe declare that noe forraign prince, person, prelate, state, hath or ought to have any jurisdiction, power, superiority, preheminence or authority, ecclesiastical or speritual, within this relm. Soe helpe me God.

The days following were spent (the two Houses adjurning for some days) in the new Kings recieveing the congratulations of his subjets, which came in such croudes as are unspeakeable, and nameing and swearing a new Privy Council consisting of thirty-two persons, twenty-four lords and eight comoners. The King with the advice of *Feb.* 15 his Council proceeded to name first the great officers of the Court and kingdome. The great expectation was who would have the preference, Halifax or Danby. The latter expected to be Lord Treasurer; but as Lord Halifax tould me, he was disappointed, and was forced to take up with President of the Council, a place of credit and place but of small profit. My Lord Halifax was Lord Privy Seale of his own choice, and wher he had been before, of great trust and worth 3,000 l. per annum. My Lord Halifax tould me before this was published that Danby was down in the mouth, and would now lett his nighbours be quiet about him; and for his own part, as they yet stood seemingly fair, he would give him noe just occasion of difference.

The King being thus made, the next business was how to gett a Parlament, especially such an one as would confirm what the convention had done. And bycaus a new choice of members for a Parlament might proove hazardous in that respect, or (as it was pretended) might loos time, when the settlement of the nation requird hast, they agreed, after great disputes as to the legallity of it amongst the lawyers, and long debates in both Houses, to convert this convention into a Parlament, which they did by frameing a bill to that purpas in the Hous of Lords, first passing it ther, then in the Hous of Commons, and at the last getting the royall assent to it, which was easily compassed upon

Feb. 23 the 23 of February.

A Parlament being thus obteaned, though after a very extraordinary manner, they first proceeded to prepare severall bills, one for comprehension, another for toleration of Protestant discenters (this was first moved by my Lord Nottingham in the Hous of Lords, and secounded by some of the bishops, but more out of fear then love), another for raiseing 420,000 l. by a tax upon land.

28   My Lord of Arran, who had been sett upon in Lecester Fields a little before by eight ruffians (son to the Duke of Hambleton), and who had mooved, in a meeting of the Scotch nobility in London a little before, to call back King James, was committed to the Tower, and many of that nobility that were going to the convention in Scotland (appointed to meet the 24 of March)[1] were stopped.

The same day I dined with the Earl of Danby, who treated me with more intimacy and freedome then I expected. He tould me that he had given a very fair character of me to the King when he made him the relation of takeing Yorke. But I found him extreamly altered in his warmth for the affairs as then managed. He said

[1] Really March 14.

that being concerned for his all he was sorry to see things managed noe better, and with noe more expedition; Ireland was in a manner becomed invincible, by neglect of not sending forces thether before now, which he had pressed the King to soe much (as well as to other things which were slighted) that he was uncivil in pressing it; that he had tould his present Majesty that he saw he did all things to encourage Presbutery and to dishearten the Church of England, and that he would absolutely prejudice himselfe and goverment by it; but that at present he medled very little in councils, neither his desires nor health disposeing him to it.   And indeed he looked soe ill, and the stoppage in swallowing wherwith he was troubled was soe great upon him, that he seemed to me not able to continue long.   He tould me he was made President of the Councell against his will (after the King had acquainted him that he could not give him the staff of Lord Treasurer, being ressolved to putt that office into commission); that he was offered to be Secretary of State and President both, but he had declined the first; that all he had asked of the King for himselfe was a patent to which he had a right by a former grant,[1] and that he would gratifie some gentlemen that had served him in this revolution in the north; and that the King tould him it would not be for his own service that his lordship should decline imployment himselfe, and in a manner forced the presidentship upon him.

He spoake very doubtfully of the continuance of the present state of affairs; tould me King James sent down to him in the north to offer to put himselfe into his hands before he went away; that his answer was (by Mr. Charles Berty,[2] that came from the King) that his own force, which he depended upon in the north, was not

---

[1] The patent for the title of marquis granted him by Charles II in 1679.

[2] Charles Bertie, the most intimate of Danby's associates among his numerous brothers-in-law. He had been Secretary to the Treasury when Danby was Lord Treasurer.

sufficient to trust to, but if his Majesty would bring a
considerable party with him, and come without the papists,
he would sooner loos his life then his Majesty should be
injured; but that the King, that had noe mind to devide
himselfe from the papists, would not come.   One thing
my Lord President said further, that if the King would
quitt his papists it might possibly not be too late yet for
him.[1] He tould me the Duke of Gordon, a papist and
governour of Edenbrough Castle, the only magazin of
Scotland, who was willing lately to surrender it to anybody,
kept it now resolutely for King James, and the discontents
of England grew dayly greater and greater.   He said
Lord Halifax, the King and all his councils were strangly
conceited for all this of their security, tould me some things
of my Lord Halifax and his interferings in their debates
in the Hous of Lords, especially in that wherin, upon
declareing the Prince of Orange King, my Lord Halifax
insisted violently that he might be entitled legall and
rightfull King of this realm (the intent of which was, I
presume, that the ould oaths of allegiance and supremacy
might be continued, to avoid scruples about the takeing
of the new ones); but that it was nonsence, for had the
Prince of Wales been made king, he could not have been
our lawfull king whilst his father lived, bycaus in here-
ditary monarchys *non est heres viventis*.   He seemd,
however, very earnest for the legallity of takeing the new
oaths of allegiance and supremacy, and condemd the
bishops that now scrupled at it, when their actings in
some things and their indifferency in others had soe far
contributed to this change of goverment.   He quoted
my Lord of Nottingham's speech in the Hous of Lords,
wher he said that he had not consented in the least to this
change, but had opposed the Prince his accession to the
crown, not believeing it legall, but that since he was ther,
and that he must now owe and expect his protection from

[1] This whole sentence has been written by Reresby in the margin,
probably at a later date than the rest of the text.

him as king *de facto*, he thought it just and lawfull to
swear allegiance to him.

I have been the more perticular in this entertainment,
to show how the opinion of the greatest men stood as to
matters at that time.   I wondred he durst trust me soe
farr as to be soe opon before me, but he knew I would not
betray him, not soe much as to my Lord Halifax.

The same day after many attempts my Lord Halifax,
or Lord Privy Seale, presented me to the King.   He had
mooved him before that a yong son of mine[1] might have
my company, and that he might be excused from duty a
year or two for his education; but the King thought that
an ill president, and would not grant it.   Haveing kissed
his hand, I tould him that I had a trust upon me from the
late King to the last, not being made privy to his Majestys
designs til I saw them in execution, and that I could not
then, in honour or justice, comply with them; but that I
was a firm Protestant, and had suffered in my estate for
being of that religion; and that I should be faithfull to my
duty wherever I served.   My Lord desired him that I
might continue my company without any attendance,
which I secounded, saying, Sir, if you have resolved to take
away my two goverments of Yorke and Burlinton, I hope
you wil not expect I should wait on a single company.
He said, Noe, he did not expect any attendence from me.

The thruth is I had made noe endeaver to keep the
goverment of Yorke.   I did then not thinke it safe or
honest.   But for the company, I thought it both to keep
it, not being obliged to act personally with it, and haveing
a good excuse to lay down at any time if it should be
enjoined.   Besides it entitled me to the recovery of some
arears which I feared to loos, had I given up my commission at that time.   Besides, tho' they began to be very
scrupulous in keeping in any but thos that had either good
principles or good friends, I found most wise men willing

---

[1] Presumably William, who, however, was by this time more than
twenty years of age.

to stay in, and as much to prevent others comming in their steads as for any other reason.

I was tould from a lady that was entrusted by King James with some seales and jewils, that the King had writt to her to put them into the hands of a person that he sent for them; and showing me his letter, I found it was dated the 17 of February *stilo novo*, as also that he therin expressed his setting forwards for Ireland the day following, and that he depended upon his ould friends to stand by him. She tould me further that the King of France had furnished him with a great treasure and 6,000 Swisters Protestants; that he intended to goe thorow Ireland for Scotland, to call a Parlament ther instead of the intended convention, and to march for England and to put himselfe entirely into the hands of a Protestant interest; that she had a friendship for my Lord Privy Seale, and had a mind to opon herselfe to him if she might doe it safely. I promessed to speak to his lordship that night, and to tell her more afterwards.

Haveing an opportunity, I was as good as my word. I confess I was cautious of speakeing too broad, but I said enough to let him understand that the chiefe motive the lady had to speake to him was to inform him of something that might be for his own as well as the publique service. Upon this he began to be freer with me then usuall upon that chapter; and when I tould him in general that great designs were on foot, he said he believed it; and that though men were in the present interest, it was not discretion to venter too far; and if things were as I said, it was safe to carry fair to thos of that party, and to let some know that he spoake always very respectfully of King James, for it might come to blowes; and he should be glad to meet the lady at my hous when she pleased. He said, however, all the care that could be would be taken to prevent it; an army would presently be raised of 20,000 men; all suspicious persons would be secured, for the Parlament would give the King power to imprison whom he pleased, and to keep them secured til they could come to tryall, and that they would plentifully furnish him for the warr.

At this time severall gentlemen and lords of both Houses withdrew themselves into their severall countries, and some that appeared great friends to the present goverment were said to be treating on the other side, all which I made known to his lordship, nameing some that he little suspected. He said further that if King James was about such a design he believed the papists would assassinate or kill King William, knowing what a tax they should have upon their hands to defend the crown upon a woeman's head, &c.

I waited upon my Lord Belasise, chiefe commissioner *March 3* of the Treasury under the late King James. He tould me that he had been very averse (though a papist) to the measures used in that reign for promoteing that religion, as the putting of papists into office in countys and corporations, the high commission court, the laying aside Protestants for refuseing to take away the test and the penall lawes, &c.; but his counsel was suspected as comming from a man that the hott party informed the King was ould and timerous, and that haveing a good estate was in fear to hazard it. He tould me as to myselfe that he understood from all hands that I had acquitted myselfe of my trust as governor of Yorke like a man of honour, and that my Lord of Danby himselfe, though my adversary, had confessed as much to him, and that I had not in this perticular deceaved the late Kings opinion of me, who ever spoake kindly and respectfully of me, and used to say that he recieved always the most faithfull and best informations of affairs in thos parts by my letters.

He said that ther being soe many great men concerned in this revolt, it was almost impossible to be thought that the King (especially being a Roman Catholique) should be restoored, but if he were a Protestant it would certainly happen in a very short time, with much more relateing to the then present conjuncture. I asked him if it would be ill taken that I endeavored to obtcan to be houskeeper of the Maner (the Kings hous at Yorke), Father Lawson haveing obteaned a grant of it from King James (though possibly in some other name). He advised me to gett it by all means if I could. I did this to prevent any ressentment, should I succeed, from that interest, in which I knew he governed most eminently. He was one of the wisest men of that party.

Mar. 4   Five bishops more took the oaths of allegiance and supremacy to the three that had taken them upon the 2nd of March, being the day appointed for swearing the members of both Houses. Most if not all the Commons did swear, but some of the Lords refused, and the greater nomber of the bishops, from the principle that they thought it unlawfull, haveing before taken the oaths to King James; and thos that swore looked upon it as a locall and temporary oath, and only owing to the present protection they recievd under King William and Queen Mary.

This day my Lord Halifax mett the lady before namd, who had a letter from King James. She dealt very franckly with his lordship, but durst not say all she knew. However he desired her, in case of any alteration, to stand his friend.

The two Houses had voated some days before to stand by King William and Queen Mary with their lives and fortunes; and now the Commons finished their bill of laying a land tax, and consulted of other ways to raise mony for the Crown, both for raiseing of men and supplying the loss of that branch of the revenue called hearthmony, which they were takeing quite away by Act of Parlament, as troublesome to collect and oppressive.[1]

It was now more and more feared that King James was actually in Ireland,[2] that Scotland would take his part. Commissions were given out for the raiseing 10,000 foot,

---

[1] William himself had proposed to Parliament that this tax should be abolished.

[2] He landed at Kinsale on March 12.

and 20s. for every man as levy mony. The colonels were most men of quality and interest, and yet it was much feared whether men could be raised. The French King had assisted King James for his Irish expedition with fourteen men-of-warr and six less frigats and three fire-ships well mand and provided, 200,000 l. in ready money and 50,000 pistols as a present for his pockit, with plate, tents, and a very royall, splendid equipage. He furnisht him with eight experienced field officers, 100 other officers, a guard of 100 Swisters, severall knowing pioneers, 15,000 of his own subjects, 40,000 arms, canon and ammunition, and offered him 15,000 more French souldiers; but the King refused them, saying he would succeed by his own subjects or perish in the attempt.

I did Colonel Beaumont a kindness by my interest with *Mar.* 7 my Lord Halifax. That lord tould me the same day that the Commons ressolved stil to persue him and my Lord Danby, and that some of them had declared they would give noe mony to the King til he had laid them and some other of his present officers aside; but he said the King would not be wrought upon as they thought of, and that he was very able to defend himselfe. The crimes of which he was accused was adviseing King Charles Second to take away the charter of London, and opposing the bil of exclusion. I tould my Lord it looked very foolish for men that were about building a new fabrick at the same time to pull down the main piller that supported it. His lordship said he did not value it though they succeeded, he should not be sorry to surrender his place. He prayed me then to reconcile him to the lady that I had formerly brought to him about some business in which she thought herselfe not well used, for she had a good interest with King James.

Colonel Reresby [1] leading the battallion of the guards 10

[1] In June 1687 Edmund Reresby, along with other captains in the guards, had been given rank as lieutenant-colonel of foot (Dalton, *English Army Lists*, ii. 114).

from Oxford in order to their imbarkeing for Holand, most of them (being 400 and odd) deserted, and it was tould the King that it was done by the colonels advice, soe that the general sent to confine him to his hous. The thruth is my brother had been twenty years in the regiment, had been in four sea engagements in the last Dutch warr and one year against the French in Flanders and upon the hardest dutys of any captains in the regiment, and had a mind to lay down rather then be now sent into Holand, haveing the gout and stone very much; but he never encouraged the men to desert. I acquainted the Lord Privy Seale with the thruth of the thing, and my Lord promessed to speake to the King on his behalfe; but soe many left the Kings service dayly that it seemd a hard thing to gett his pardon.

Mar. 12   My Lord Marquis tould me that my Lord Mordent and others were violent against him, being disappointed of their expectations at Court, caused as they suspected by my Lord Marquis his means, in that he had brought in my Lord Nottingham to Court, made him Secretary of State, and some others whom indeed the King as wel as himselfe had a mind should be in business, being eminent in parts. My Lord Godolphyn was another he named, &c.; and it was thes chiefly that followed and persuaded his impeachment. But he said the King was soe much his friend that he was too eager on his lordships behalfe, insoemuch that he was forced to desire him to be more moderate.

12   I had news from Thriberge that my yongest son Leonard[1] was recovered of the small-pox, for which I praised God.

13   I heard my Lord Privy Seale say that as the nation now stood, if the King was a Protestant (viz., King James), he could not be kept out four months; but my Lord Danby went further, for he said that if he would give the

[1] " Born September the 22nd between eight and nine in the morning, Anno Domini 1679 " (*Family History,* ii. f. 17).

satisfactions in point of religion which he might, it would be hard to ressist him as he was.   I thought thes things looked strangely, falling from soe great men, of the times.

A violent could that had troubled me six weeks with a *Mar.* 14 cough turned to the gout in the great toe of the left foot, notwithstanding the precautions I had used of blooding, sweating, &c.; but blooding did not agree with me at any time.   It changed from foot to foot, and upon 16 it began to goe to the most tender part, my weake knee, but this without much pain, and upon the 17th both the could 17 and my gout began to abate by keeping myselfe to the milke diet.

I heard the 17th that my Lord Dunbarton's regiment, which he had long since brought out of France, quartering now at Ipsick, being all Scotch and consisting of 1,300 men, chose rather to march in a body with their arms and four pieces of canon towards Scotland then to obay orders, which was to goe on board and saile for Holand.

My Lord Privy Seale did me the honour to visit me 17 for an hour that day.   He tould me the King had sent after them two regiments of Dutch hors and one of dragoons; that if thes men did this of themselves without confederacy, they were lost; if it was laid soe as other forces were to stirr in other places, ther might be danger in it.   I found he was jealous that my Lord of Danby did, under pretence of ilness, more absent himselfe from business then reason required, and that he was discontented, and was wondring that some had gott into places by his means that were soe little qualifyed for them, perticularly my Lord Willoughby, a very yong man, unused to business, made Chancellor of the Exchequer.[1] I tould him it was noe less wonder that my Lord Mordent, that never saw 100 l. togather of his own mony, should pretend to be the First Commissioner of the Tresury.

[1] Lord Willoughby had been appointed Chancellor, not of the Exchequer, but of the Duchy of Lancaster (*Cal. S.P. Dom.*, 1689-90, p. 12).

I then dealt very freely with my Lord as to the uncertainty of the times, desired him to act with caution, and assured him that I wished his safety and his family's as much as my own.

His lordship said he had named my brothers concern to the King; but Prince George being present, who tooke part against him, hindered the good success at that time; since that he had recieved a state of the matter from my brother (which I had drawn up for him), and had given it to the Secretary, the Earl of Nottingham, to lay before the King. He said he wished that it did me noe prejudice in the Kings good opinion. I said that would be hard that I should answer for the actions of a brother, but he said he should be able to clear that. I was glad to hear that the Duke of Grafton and the slender part of his regiment that remained was disbanded.[1] I heard also that noe less then seventy officers had laid down their commissions in four days time.

My Lord Privy Seale, amongst other things, said that this King used noe arts. I reply'd some arts were nescessary in our English goverment in my opinion. He said he was of the same, and that we acted a little too plainly. I acquainted my Lord with some grounds of discontents much murmered at in the town and some in the country. My Lord said, Come, Sir John, we have wives and children, and we must consider them and not venter too far. He spoake further as if, whenever a change hapned, ther would be a generall pardon, though he said he heard ther was one from King James that crept up on down in the world, and that he was excepted in it. But, said his lordship, as you know, I gave you some little hints of this change before you went down last (which were soe obscure that I did not observe them), soe you must tell me what you hear on the other side. And indeed I loved him soe well that I was ready enough

[1] On March 16 Henry Sidney was appointed in Grafton's place, but the regiment was reconstituted.

to informe him of what related to the publique for his private service, provided it was said in generall, and not to the prejudice of any perticular person or of a confidence reposed in me.

I still continued to mend of my indisposition.　God be *Mar.* 19 praised.

I went abroad, free'd from my could and gout, only a 22 little weake.　The same day my Lord Privy Seale tould me that the rebels (meaning the Scotch regiment) had yielded themselves to the Kings mercy; the officers would have had them to have fought, though the Dutch hors and dragoons was four times their nomber; but the common souldiers laid down their arms.　His lordship further added that ther was a confederacy in that revolt, but the partys durst not venter to appear.　He tould me more that they had now great hopes in Scotland, and it did after appear that the kirke party (which was for King William) was the more prevalent.　The thruth is, King James lost his business by not appearing sooner in Ireland (or rather in Scotland); but the winds were soe contrary he could not sett out sooner from Brest.

The Church of England was much laid at by some members of both Houses of Parlament at this time, King William seeming to favour Calvanisme.　For in the Lords Hous it was strongly debated (and perticularly by the 23 Lord Privy Seale, which lost him some credit) that the takeing of the sacrament should be noe part of the test according to the statute of King Charles the Second; and in the Hous of Commons it was as stiffly argued, in the debate of forming the coronation oath, that that part of it which bindes the King to mentain the Church of England as by law established should be omitted.　But in both thes it was carried in the affirmative in favour of the Church of England.　This showed the strength of that interest in Parlament, and would, as t'was believed, oblige his Majesty to be more favourable to the Church of England.

Mar. 23   I attended my Lord Nottingham (haveing first prevailed with the Lord Privy Seale to get him to assist me
therin), and desired him to speake to the King that I
might continue houskeeper to his Majesty of his hous
called the Maner of Yorke; but it seems my Lord of
Danby had spoaken before for another. However that
Lord tould the Lord Secretary and me the day after waiting
upon him that I had free liberty to continue my pretention
to it by what interest or reasons I pleased, and that he
would be modest in his persuit of it for his friend.

All the affairs of Europe seemed now to be at some
stand, though all nations were also prepareing for warr.
The whole Empire was calling their respective quotas
togather to be imployed against France and the Turkes,
in case the treaty then on foot between the Emperour
and the Turkes should breake off, which was not unlikely,
he and the confederates, viz., the Venetians and the Poles,
insisting upon very severe conditions. Spain was likely
to joine with the Emperor against France, as also Sweden,
Holand and England; and Denmarke to stand neuter.
The Pope continued angry with France at the same time,
though France endeavered to mollifie him, pretending to
make it a warr of religion; but his Holiness, thinkeing
the French King grown too big for his nighbours, had
some reguard to his temporal estate as well as to the Church
of which he was the head, and considered interest as wel as
concience, a known principle in the Church of Rome.

1689

March 26   I attended the Queens council in order to that part of
her revenue of which I was collector. My Lord Halifax
was then her Majestys Chancellor, my Lord Preston being
laid aside.

That day the Bishop of St. Davids,[1] meeting me, asked

[1] Thomas Watson, a zealous promoter of the Declaration of Indulgence.
He was deprived for simony towards the close of the reign of William III.

my opinion if he should take the oaths of allegiance and
supremacy, he being one of the bishops that had refused
them all this time, and being now cited to appear before
the Lords.　I tould him it was fitter for his lordship to
advise me in such a case, and certainly his concience was
the best guide in the matter; but I found he had ressolved
before what to doe, and the next day he went and swore
in the Hous of Lords.　My Lord Archbishop of Canterbury all this while refused to swear or to come at all to the
Hous [of] Lords, not soe much as owning the authority
either of King or the Parlament.　The Lords sent his
Grace a letter to come to the Hous, and he returnd his
answer excuseing his attendance, directed not to the Lord
Privy Seale or Speaker of the Lords, but only to the Lord
Marquis of Halifax.　The Hous voated his answer not
satisfactory.　However they thought it not adviseable to
persue him too far, knowing what ill blood the imprisonment of the bishops had lately made in the body of the
nation.

　The Church of England party carried a second voat in　*March* 28
favour of that Church; and it was high time to show
themselves, the dissenters not only haveing prevailed that
the oaths in some respect made for the security of that
Church, some prayers in the liturgie and the ceremonys
should be altered or dispenced with, but it was moved in
the Hous of Commons that ther might be some alteration
in the very creed.

　The same day my Lord Halifax and my Lord Nottingham mooved the King in Council that I might have the
keeping of the Maner of Yorke.　But by the underhand
dealing of my Lord Danby, who had certainly pressed
him in it for Alderman Waller, late Lord Maior of Yorke,
I recieved a flatt denyall, and with this reason of unkindness, as my Lord Privy Seale tould me, that the alderman
had done something for the service of the present goverment, but Sir John Reresby had done nothing.

　Being Good Fryday, I recieved the sacrament with my　29

second son Tamworth, who was then of years to be therby confirmd in the Church, at the new church of St. James in Germain Street. I recieved the same day the news of George my third son's[1] being sick of the small-pox, which gave me great apprehensions, he being fatter then the rest of my children.

Some days following ther were very warm debates in both Houses of Parlament between the dissenters and thos of the Church of England, the first endeavering to carry their act of comprehension and toleration further then the Church of England was willing to agree to, and the partys seemd soe equall in nomber that sometimes one side carryed a voat in both Houses, and sometimes the other.

April 1   It was ordered that seventeen regiments (and many of them unarm'd, uncloathed and without sufficient pay to clear their quarters) should march northwards, it being now certainly confirmd that King James was in Ireland, and intended for Scotland, though the kirke party in the Scotch convention seemd to oppose his comming into that kingdome. And for all mony was very scarce at Court, yet great preparations were dayly makeing for the coronation of King William and Queen Mary, though ther wanted nescessarys for the army, the Court and support of the goverment; not but the Parlament was ready to give, but it could not be raised soon enough for the uses to which it was given, and the Citty refused to give credit or to advance mony upon the mony acts that were passed. Great discontents still continued, or rather dayly improoved.

5   I recieved the unfortunate news of the death of my son George by the small-pox, a very beautiful, apt, understanding child. It was a great affliction to me; but God gives, and God takes, and blessed be the name of the Lord (and especially for thos that are left).

7   My Lord Privy Seale tould me if the Church of

---

[1] Fourth son.

England suffered, it was by their pretending to have too much; that the Commons acted very slowly, and as if the whole world was noe more then Westminster; that the King was very delatory too in his resolutions, which was a great prejudice to business at a time when it soe much required dispatch: said ther was a nescessity of acting with soe many fooles that they were only wise that had nothing to doe; and further that he heard some Irish were landed in Scotland, but that nation would recieve them very coolely; and that nothing was to be apprehended here for King James but the army, which would be soe disposed of abroad, and others raised at home and sent for from Holand, that if he came not soon he would be disappointed of that hope. He further concurred with me in one thing, which was that the Earl of Danby had gott the goverment of Hull as a place of retreat, and wherby to make his terms, should ther be any change of times. He tould me besides that he feared more the danger of King Williams cough (which increased upon him) then any other. I confess I did a little temporize in thes things, it not being convenient to be too opon with a privy councillor and soe great a minister, especially haveing used a freedome of that kind before with his lordship to noe purpas, and haveing a little pretention at that time in which I wanted his lordships assistance. However, wherever he asked me my opinion, I dealt truly with him.

Was the day of the coronation of King William and *April* 11 Queen Mary, performed with great splendour according to the usuall ceremonys. The procession to the Abbaye of Westminster was very regular, but not attended by soe many of the nobility as when the two last kings were crowned. The Hous of Commons were taken great care of at this solemnity, had a side of Westminster Hall prepared for them to see it, another place in the Abbaye to see their Majestys crowned, and severall tables prepared and covered with all sorts of meat, wher they dined by themselves. Only some friends were admitted amongst them, and I amongst others, which gave me a good opportunity to see and observe all. The Bishop of London crowned the King and Queen, assisted by the Bishops of Salesbury (the late Doctor Bournet, who preached the coronation sermon) and by two others.[1]

April 14 Which was my birthday, I humbly thanked God for preserveing me thorow soe many dangers til the 55th year of my age, and beg'd of Him to lead the remainder of my life better then I had hytherto done.

That day I was with the Lord Privy Seale, wher the Bishop of Salisbury comming in arraigned the slowness of the Hous of Commons in their proceedings, and said the Dutch would agree with France if they did not mend their pace. He laid the fault chiefly on the Church of England party, and spoake as if they designd the advantage of King James and his service by it. My Lord Privy Seale agreed with him therin, said they hated the Dutch, and had rather turn papists then take in the Presbuterians amongst them; that the Presbuterians hated the Church of England men as much, and spoiled their own business by the ill prepareing of their bil of comprehension, and the untimely offering of other bils and matters in both Houses to disoblige thos from whom they expected this indulgence. They were both angry at the address made to the King by the Commons the day before, that he would support and defend the Church of England according to his former declaration, and that he would please to call a convocation of the clergie, which latter they said would ruin the design of comprehension. In fyne, the marquis said that this goverment would be very short-lived at this rate.

I had news that day that the King of France had declared warr against Spain, and that the treaty between the Emperour and the Turke was broaken off. A prisner

---

[1] William Lloyd, Bishop of St. Asaph, and Thomas Sprat, Bishop of Rochester.

was brought before me for committing a burglary, that finding the evidence very clear against him attempted whilst he was under examination to cut his own throat in my hous.

King James continued all this while in Ireland, the kerke party in Scotland continuing to oppose him in the convention, they haveing declared the throne vacant of that kingdome.   And soon after came the newes that they had voted King William and Queen Mary King and Queen of Scotland, that they turned the name of convention into that of a Parlament, had invited the English forces that were upon the boarders into that kingdome, to be ready to assist them against any attempt of King James or his friends, but had prepared severall conditions or grievences for the King to pas, one of which was that episcopacy should be noe longer established in Scotland, and that the Kings therof should be of the Presbuterian religion, with many others.   The Castle of Edenbrough, comanded by the Duke of Gourdon, held out still.

At home the Parlament voated a poule and other mony to be raised.   The Comons made an address to the King to declare warr against France, promessing to stand by him in a parlamentary way.   Great heats hapned between the two Houses concerning the bill for takeing the oaths of alegiance and supremacy, the Lords being willing to excuse the bishops, bycaus they knew that severall of them would loos their bishopricks rather then take them, and the Commons urgeing that all persons should take them without distinction.   There passed both Houses the bill *April* 20 of toleration for all Protestant dissenters.[1]

The King gave a favourable answer to the address for 21 sopporting the Church of England and for calling a convocation.[2]

The King gave an answer to the Commons their address 25

[1] The toleration bill, which had already passed the Lords, only received a first reading from the Commons at this time.

[2] April 20.

to him for makeing war with France,[1] wherin he tould them that he complyed with their request, since the King of France had begun the warr in a manner himselfe, and that whatever mony they gave should certainly be laid out to that end.

April 26   Desireing my Lord Halifax to doe a kindness for me to the King, he tould me that he was informed that I had discouraged my lieutenant to serve King William, and that I was therfore looked upon as disaffected.   It is true, said he, you and I speake our thoughts freely one to another, but I know you are too wise to opon yourselfe (should you have such thoughts) to such people.   I replyed that though I was guilty of follies, yet his lordship had seldome found me in soe gross ones as that; and it would be very unfit doctrin for me to preach to another, that acted contrary to it myselfe and kept my imployment. But, said I, if your lordship have a mind to believe it, that you may thinke me unfit for that which I aske of you to doe for me, I have noe more to doe but to acquiesce.   He tould me, noe, I knew how willing he was to serve me, and he had only tould me this in friendship; that he would find out whence it came; and gave some hintes as if he suspected that it came from the Lord of Danby (lately made Marquis of Glamorthen,[2] amongst many others then promoted to new honours).   I said, whoever said it, that it was false.   But, said I, if your lordship pleas, you may give a speedy remedy to such aspersions as thes; if your lordship would tell the King that it is not possible for men that have had soe considerable a post as I had under the late goverment to live without some back friends, but that your lordship knew me soe well that you would undertake for me and my behaviour, I am sure it would wipe away all jealousies.   In fyne, he tould me he was very willing to doe it, and to see if he could gett the Kings promess in what I desired.

[1] This address was adopted on the 24th, presented to the King on the 25th, and answered on the 26th.

[2] Carmarthen.

The thruth is I found it was hard for one that did not heartily and early come into the present goverment to live either in town or country without censure, and found it adviseable to accept of what my Lord Privy Seale had offered to me at my first comming to town (if it could be obteaned), which was to be sent envoye to some forrain prince, and this was that which I had desired his lordship to effect for me. He promessed to gett me a generall promess, if possible, to goe to some place; but the goverment was as yet soe little owned abroad that ther was not much room for that kind of service for the present. This delay pleased me more (provided I had but a promess) then a more speedy dispatch. I had time by it to see how things fram'd before I imbarked in any sort of business (though this was the most innocent), and the expectation of it gave me a protection from being looked upon as an ennemy to the goverment. His lordship dissuaded me also then from going down as yet, it being dangerous til the King was satisfyed concerning me, especially now when the north was looked upon as the nest of the malecontents, and gave me some other reasons to stay a little longer. I said whatever hapned I could not stay long from my family and business, and therfore desired him to speake for me as soon as he could. He bad me come and dine with him the next day, which I did. We then talked this matter over again, and much to the same effect.

A sad accident hapned at this time, which gave great occasion of discours. One Temple (only son to Sir William Temple), a gentleman of 2,000 l. a year, the son haveing married a French lady with 20,000 pistols, a very accomplisht, sober yong man, and lately made Secretary of War (which was a great place) by King William, tooke a pair of owers, and when he came near the bridge upon the Thams leaped into the river and drownd himselfe, leaveing a note in the boat to this pur- pas: My folly in undertakeing what I could not perform, wherby some disadvantages have accrewed to the King, is the caus of this; I wish him success in his undertakings, and that he may have a better servant.[1]   It is a dangerous thing for some constitutions to give themselves over too much to melancholy or discontents.   God keep us from the sad effects of it.

April 27   I dined with the Earl of Alesbury, who was a true subject to King James, and when at his request I had given him an account of the manner how Yorke was surprized, he told me that he was present a little before the King went away, when one tould him (but who it was he had forgot) that it was believed that I was acquainted with the conspiracy, and suffered myselfe willingly to be confined, but that the King did not seem to give ear to it.   I tould his lordship if that had been soe I had been restoored to my goverment before now, and as that knave could not know me that said it, soe the King knew me too well to believe it.

The Parlament went on in raiseing of mony, and upon terms and persons that very much disobliged.   Ther was a very strict poule, wherby almost noebody escaped paying more or less save such as recieved almes, and the computation consented to in the Hous was noe less then four millions for one year: the pay of the army for that time 1,700,000 l., the fleet 1,300,000 l., for the charge of the Court or houshould 600,000 l., the debt to Holand 6,000 l.,[2] in all four millions and 200,000 l.

May 5   The Marquis of Halifax tould me that the Marquis of Caermarthen's going into the country, pretending to be sick, and seldome comming to Council, gave new jealousies of him; that he heard he had said that things could

---

[1] John Temple had undertaken to facilitate a settlement between William and Tyrconnel, and the discovery that Tyrconnel had only been using him as a tool to secure a breathing-space for Ireland preyed on his mind.

[2] The figure intended is obviously 600,000 l.   That sum had been voted to repay to the Dutch the expenses of the expedition to England.

not continue thus; that his relations and friends spoake dangerously and himselfe very oponly; that he found that new marquis would not be inward with him or his friend, for all he had endeavered it on his side; that he stil looked upon him as the caus that he had not the Lord Treasurers staff, though he did not altogather deserve it, for of all men the King would never have put him into that office, nor indeed into any other very considerable at this time, as he would find if things continued fair til September. I heard some things, which I tould my Lord Privy Seale, which gave ground to suspect my Lord President was discontented.

As to himselfe, his lordship tould me he found the King very fair towards him personally, and he had it from third hands that his expressions were kind of him behind his back; for he gave him few troubles upon his own or other peoples account, and the Lord President was constantly importuneing him. I tooke upon that the confidence to say that I did not know what that lord lost with the King by it, but he gained much upon others; for it was generally said that noe lord made it their business to doe good offices for their contrimen but my Lord President (for indeed I had found my Lord Privy Seale, though thus very free with me, something slowe in interesting himselfe soe far for me as I expected).

His lordship tould me further that the Kings inaccessibleness and liveing soe at Hamton Court altogather, and at soe active a time, ruined all business; that he had desired him but to lie sometimes in town, and his answer was that it was not to be done except he desired to see him dead, which, said my Lord, was a very short answer. But this entertainment ended in this, that it was his lordship's opinion that if the King overlived this sommer (which he thought he might, notwithstanding his consumptive distemper, if he were not kild by the papists) the goverment would scarce be shaken, though it should devolve upon the Queen singly. He said, however, the concern

of his family should make him act with as much moderation as was possible, and therfore he took noe great nor
additional places, noe honours or blew rubans, as others
had done.

The next day I was to goe to Hamton Court to meet
his lordship, to present me to the King before I went
into the country; and he repeated his promess of doing
for me what he could, but said that it was discretion to
lett two or three months pass before I pressed the thing
too much, to see what became of things.

APPENDIX

THE following letters and documents have appeared either too long to be included in the notes or too general in their interest to be attached to any one part of Reresby's narrative:

ACCOUNT OF YORK FROM SIR JOHN RERESBY [1]

The loyall party in York is much inferiour in nomber to the factious. The first consists of the gentry, clergie, officers and dependents of the Church, militia officers and souldiers, and about a fourth part (as is computed) of the cittyzens; the secound of the Maior and whole magistracy (two aldermen only excepted), the sheriffs and most of the common council, with the rest of that citty. Not that this nomber soe much exceeds the former by reason of principle as influence, ther ever being a great many in such a body that either from fear or interest joine with the strongest, and severall ther have confessed that they darr not act according to their judgements (viz., for the goverment) for fear of being undone in their trade. It is now come to that, that ther is not only a separation of interests, but few doe buy of, or have any commerce but with thos of their own principle.

And this nice difference hath been contrived, and is yet industriously mentained, by eight or ten persons of that citty and this county, viz., Sir Henry Tomson [2] and Sir

[1] Memorandum in Reresby's handwriting thus endorsed by Halifax and preserved among the Spencer MSS. From internal evidence its composition may be assigned to the latter part of 1682.

[2] Sir Henry Thompson of Escrick, Yorkshire, who had represented York in every Parliament since 1673.

John Hewley, the late burgesses of York; Edward Tompson, alderman (a close, sensible fellow); Alderman Waller, a rich atturney, very spitefull but opon, that putt up the inscription in the church (the memoriall against the papists), and which the Chancellor tels me he hath now order to take down, and to call him to an account for some extravagances in its substance, the matter of form being liable to ecclesiasticall censure, as well as his haveing placed any inscription ther without leave from the ordinary; one Rooksby, a lawyer rich and well versed in his calling, that stears them in their proceedings as to point of law ; Sir John Brooks, who marryed Sir William Waller's daughter,[1] hath been twice burgesse for Bouroughbrig, one of little judgment and lesse courage, but the only Churchman amongst them (which I am sorry for); Mr. Stockdale and Mr. Paulins, who are only called to advise as emergencie requires; with some few others more inferiour. I fear ther is little to be hoped for from thes leaders. The only way to gain others will be to possesse them that whilst they that are the magistrates suffer themselves to be soe gouverned by men for their perticular advantage, and that can never essentially serve them, they expose themselves to severall hazards and (which is the greatest both as to interest and reputation) his Majestys displeasure.

I tould my Lord Maior when I showed him my commission (amongst other discours) that if they had made any false steps in matter of respect or service to the goverment (meaning amongst other things their ill reception of the Duke), they ought to repair them by expressing their sorrow for what was past and by better performance for the time to come, which they seemed to take well and to thanke me for. The thruth is thes gentlemen haveing been noe more cautious then others in the due execution of the power given them by their charter, and not without apprehension that that enquiry may be made ther as well

---

[1] This is a mistake. Sir John Brookes married Mary, daughter of Sir Hardress Waller.

as in other places, and the news of his Majestys committing the Middlesex sherifs to the Tower,[1] was observed to cast a damp upon some of the principall mutineers of that citty; and it is not to be doubted but by some means or other the place may be reduced to a better temper in a short time, in which I shall ever be ready to employ my utmost endeavours. Only I beg your Lordships advice how far tis fitt to meet any offers or submissions from them, since thos of the other party ther seem much against any complyance, which I fear hath been much the occasion of the breach being soe wide at this day. My Lord Fairfax, tis thought, will not stand for knight of the shire, nor Sir John Hewley for burgesse of Yorke.

[To the Marquis of Halifax] [2]

[May or June 1687]

MY LORD,

Haveing this perticular opportunity, I could not but make use of it to assure your Lordship of the continuance of my most faithfull service, though the quiet and reserve people are under in thes parts afford little matter of a letter. At Yorke the old magistrates repent not their fate, and the new ones (chiefly governed by Alderman Rains, an atturnay, who married a papist) behave themselves with great loyalty, but are not willing (though pressed to it by some), nor the Dean [3] and Chapter (though advised to it by the Bishop of Chester [4] and others from above), to make an addresse.

Mass and preaching are publique in some five severall rooms taken for that purpass, but it is computed the whole

[1] June 26.

[2] Autograph letter, undated and unaddressed, preserved among the Spencer MSS.

[3] Thomas Wickham, Dean of York from 1677 to 1697.

[4] Thomas Cartwright, who made himself very unpopular by his activity in trying to secure addresses in favour of the King's ecclesiastical policy.

nomber of that persuasion wil not reach sixty of the whole citty, in which nomber ther are but three known converts. Yet some are soe earnest to gain them that one Doctor Vavasour, who had the best practice in phisique, hath now the worst, by offering to put a priest upon a dying patient, the parson of the parish being sent for before and then present. The generality in thes parts seem very firm and very quiet of the Church of England, and the only dissenters that seem pleased with their toleration are the Quakers and Independents, the nomber of either not very considerable, for notwithstanding they have meeting houses the churches are observed not to be less full in Yorke, Leeds, Sheffield, in all which places I have been very lately.

Sir Thomas Slingsby, Sir Thomas Mauliverer, both went up with intentions not to be shaken, and ther is none suspected to leave the Church of England (imployed from thes parts) but Sir Roger Stricland. I have been attacked by side winds, but my answer was that I could give noe opinions till I was in the Hous, or that the King comanded me to deliver it. This was Powel, the last judge of assize for this circuit. He then asked me what I thought of the generality of the representatives for the county. I answered that I did not beleeve that ther were two of the whole nomber would doe what was desired. He tould me that he would not then trouble himselfe with speakeing to any more, though he had order from my Lord Chancellor to aske thos he met with. The judge appeared modest and defensive in the matter.

The Duke my nighbour makes bould with him in his common discours that would have had the yonger for his son when he designed him the elder, but he says he writt him word he never intended it, and that when my Lord Arran was lately ther to have his consent for Lady M[argaret] he would not give it, it being a trick only for him to marry the elder, that they might worke upon the yonger to accept the other.

I was tould by one present when the Duke of Buckingham dyed, that he fell into great disorder at the newes of dying, would not admit of a priest, my Lord Fairfax of Gillin, Troutback (who tould me the story),[1] and some other papists offering one to him. He recieved after the Church of England; but my author said my Lord Arran tould him that he had it from the King that the Duke had communicated with him after the Roman before he left London.

The guarrison and citty agree well togather. My company lately appearing in Hide Parke had the Kings approbation. I hope near winter to assure your Lordship at London that I am

Your Lordships most obliged and most
obedient servant,
J. Reresby.

[To the Duke of Newcastle] [2]

November the 14, [16]88, Yorke.

May it please your Grace,
At our generall meeting yesterday for the three rideings it was agreed that the whole nomber of hors should be called up, and that intimation should be given to the gentlemen and chiefe of the three rideings to give a meeting here upon Thursday senit to advise for the safety

[1] John Troutbeck, M.D., second husband of Frances, daughter of Sir Francis Foljambe of Aldwark by his first marriage, and therefore a distant connection of Reresby himself.

[2] Autograph letter in B.M. Add. MSS. 28053, f. 353. Although it is without address there cannot be any reasonable doubt that the letter was intended for the Duke of Newcastle, but it must in some fashion have fallen into the hands of the Earl of Danby, for it is preserved among the Leeds MSS., and is endorsed, in the handwriting which the Duke of Leeds developed late in life, " From the governor of York, 14 November 1688, by which I timed my going to surprize York, which I did on the Thursday mentioned for the gentlemens meeting there."

and defence of thes parts for his Majestys service; and the declared intention of it was that we might assure the King of our intention to adhere to him faithfully in this conjuncture. Colonell Darcy was dispatched at the same time to your Grace (intending, I presume, too, to wait upon you on some other account) to have your approbation herein, and to desire your Grace his appearance here about the time limited for that meeting, off all which the papers which he brings wil give you full satisfaction.

But in the afternoon we was all surprized by the clerke of the peace comming to supersede Sir Henry Goodrick, Mr. Tankard, Sir John Kaye, Sir Michael Wentworth, Sir Thomas Yarburgh, and above twenty more principall gentlemen of this rideing (the most eminent for quality and estates) from being justices of the peace, bringing at the same time another commission wherin severall new ones are put in, and amongst others John Eyre of Sheffield Parke, Mr. Ratcliff, &c. The first can neither write nor read, the second is a bailiff to the Duchesse Dowagere of Norfolk's rents, and neither of them have one foot off freehould land in England. My Lord, I fear this matter being unseasonably notified at such a time may change the good measures we were upon and divide the country, though the gentlemen here appear not much concerned at it. However, I have given my Lord Preston an account of both thes affairs, and tould him that as I presume this was the effect of former councils (for the new commission bears date September the 22nd), soe if ther be any mistake in its publication at this time, the sooner it is rectified the better it will be for his Majestys service in this rideing. And I wish your Grace would likewise thinke fitt to recommend this to his Lordship.

Upon the whole matter, the case being thus, it is essentially nescessary your Grace doe us the honour of your company as soon as your conveniency permits, least the Kings service suffer by this il contrived accident (at this

time of the day), when everything rather of union then
devision is expected from above. I am,

> May it please your Grace,
>> Your Grace his most humble and most
>>> faithful servant,
>>>> J. Reresby.

[To the Marquis of Halifax] [1]

> Thriberge, December 9, 1688.

My Lord,

Although I have attempted by other hands to
give your Lordship some relation of the surprize of York,
my restraint would not suffer me to write sooner myselfe,
and letters continuing to be oponed I thought it the safest
way to send this by the currier.

After my Lord Danby, Lomley, Dunblain, Willoughby,
Fairfax, Sir Henry Goodrick, Mr. Tankard, Sir Henry
Belasis, &c., had drawn on the innocent country gentlemen, that met to sign a loyall address to the King, and
the four militia troops of hors to rise with them after
the manner you have heard; after they had surprized the
guard, which consisted but of eighteen men, that the
rabble joined with them, that my hous was besett by a
party of forty hors, and myselfe was taken (haveing noe
assistance) by my Lord of Danby, his lordship urged me
by severall arguments to joine with them. I declared that
I was as much for the Protestant religion and for a free
Parlament as himselfe, but my principles and the circumstances I laid then under to the King would not allowe
me to doe it. Upon this I was confined twelve days in
Yorke, though more favourably then I expected, it being
confessed I had a more reasonable plea for refuseing then
others, and at last I am permitted to be at my own house,
wher I continue under promess of good behaviour.

Sir John Kaye, Sir Michael Wentworth, Sir Jervase
Cutler and all that nighbourhood being gone home return

[1] Autograph letter among the Spencer MSS.

noe more; few gentlemen of the North or East Rideings mix with them. They raise foot and hors, but slowly; the citty of Yorke engage with them. His Grace his conduct is something censured in the management of this affair. After he had approoved of this convening of the gentlemen togather, and found at his comming to Yorke upon the 19 of November that they did prevaricate with him and intended to petition for a free Parlament (which he was against), he left them in town to doe what they pleased, would not dismiss the militia hors, which he himselfe suspected, and after a great quarrel with Sir Henry Goodrick in the debate of this matter gave him a commission for colonel of a militia regiment that morning he went away.

I denyed to sign their declaration or petition for thes reasons : They had made me write up to my Lord Preston that nothing was intended by this meeting of the gentlemen but to testifie their adhearance to the King, and my signing or subscribeing this, which was clear of another nature, must perfectly contradict what I had written; 2ndly, I did not find your Lordships hand to the petition of the Lords Spirituall and Temporal; 3rdly, they refused to admit of any expression of duty or of standing by the King in it.

My Lord, we are all surprized with this great and generall revolution. I could not be satisfyed till I had opened myselfe thus far to your Lordship. I have noebody to advise with in your absence but my own thoughts, and should believe myselfe happy in this (as in all other things) that they were not very different from your Lordship. I should be glad to recieve some light in this obscure matter, and what shines from your Lordship is ever clearer to me then what I recieve from others.

Some here are not soe kind to your Lordship in their expressions as I expected. The great earl is their only idol, but this may be artifice. I am bold to averr that I have left Yorke, wher I have been seven years (and principally by your Lordships assistance), without any reflection as to religion or miscarriage as governor, insomuch as if I was allowed to stand I believe I could yet be chosen for the ensuing Parlament. They take noe notice of the King in their actings or discours; only the Earl of Danby declared they did not intend him the least harm. They have had some quarrels amongst themselves, especially the Lords Lomley and Willouby, which went high; but this wil be a slow messenger of news.

I doubt not but you have heard from Welbeck that the Duke was disarmd and lost some of his horses, and that he is angry with the Duchess as being, he thinkes, in the plott. Princess Anne was invited to Yorke, but refuseth to come from Nottingham til she hear from the Prince.

I am, My Lord,
Your ever most obedient and most
humble servant,
J[OHN] R[ERESBY].

My Lord, I presume to desire of you that your servant may acquaint Mr. Thyn, her Majestys Treasurer, that I have recieved some of her rents, but know not yet how to return them, or own that I have them, least if it were known here they should bring them within the compas of the Crowns mony, which they seize with all persons. For this reason I dar not write directly to him.

INDEX